BCL - 3rd ed.

The Commonwealth Caribbean

A World Bank Country Economic Report

The Commonwealth Caribbean

THE INTEGRATION EXPERIENCE

Report of a mission sent to the Commonwealth Caribbean by the World Bank

Sidney E. Chernick
Chief of Mission and Coordinating Author

Published for the World Bank
The Johns Hopkins University Press
Baltimore and London

The views and interpretations in this book are the author's and should not be attributed to the World Bank, to its affiliated organizations, or to any individual acting in their behalf. The map on pages 26–27 has been prepared by the staff of the World Bank exclusively for the convenience of readers of this book. The denominations used and the boundaries shown do not imply, on the part of the World Bank and its affiliates, any judgment on the legal status of any territory or any endorsement or acceptance of such boundaries.

Library of Congress Cataloging in Publication Data

Chernick, S. E.
The Commonwealth Caribbean.
(A World Bank country economic report)
Includes index.
1. Caribbean Community. 2. Caribbean area—Economic integration. 3. Caribbean area—Economic conditions.
I. International Bank for Reconstruction and Development.
II. Title. III. Series: World Bank country economic report.
HC155.C53 330.9'729 77-17246
ISBN 0-8018-2089-8
ISBN 0-8018-2090-1 pbk.

Foreword

THIS IS THE SIXTEENTH IN THE CURRENT SERIES OF WORLD BANK COUNTRY economic reports, all of which are listed on the following page. They are published, in response to a desire expressed by scholars and practitioners in the field of economic and social development, to aid and encourage research and the interchange of knowledge. In contrast to other books in this series, which each focus on the economic position of a single developing country, *The Commonwealth Caribbean* uses an areawide approach to analyze the prospects and problems of twelve territories and their experience with regional integration.

Economic reports on borrowing countries are prepared regularly by the Bank in support of its own operations. These surveys provide a basis for discussions with the governments and for decisions on Bank policy and operations. Many of these reports are also used by the governments themselves as an aid to their economic planning and by consortia and consultative groups of governments and institutions providing assistance in development. All Bank country reports are subject to the agreement of—and several have been published by—the governments concerned.

HOLLIS CHENERY
Vice President for Development Policy
The World Bank

Washington, D.C.
August 1978

World Bank Country Economic Reports

Published for the Bank by The Johns Hopkins University Press

The Commonwealth Caribbean: The Integration Experience
Ivory Coast: The Challenge of Success
Korea: Problems and Issues in a Rapidly Growing Economy
Kenya: Into the Second Decade
Yugoslavia: Development with Decentralization
Nigeria: Options for Long-Term Development
Economic Growth of Colombia

Published by the World Bank

Papua New Guinea: Its Economic Situation and Prospects for Development
The Philippines: Priorities and Prospects for Development
Lesotho: A Development Challenge
Turkey: Prospects and Problems of an Expanding Economy
Senegal: Tradition, Diversification, and Economic Development (also published in French)
Chad: Development Potential and Constraints (also published in French as *Le Développement du Tchad: Possibilités et Limites*)
Current Economic Position and Prospects of Peru
Current Economic Position and Prospects of Ecuador
Employment in Trinidad and Tobago

Contents

Tables

Acronyms

ACP	African, Caribbean, and Pacific States
AMCS	Agricultural Marketing Corporations
AMP	Agricultural Marketing Protocol
BCCB	British Caribbean Currency Board
BOAC	British Overseas Airways Corporation
BWIA	British West Indies Airways
CAB	Civil Aeronautics Board (U.S.)
CANAC	Canadian Airlines Consultants
CARDI	Caribbean Agricultural Research and Development Institute
CARICOM	Caribbean Community and Common Market
CARIFTA	Caribbean Free Trade Association
CBEA	Caribbean Banana Exporters Association
CCRS	Commonwealth Caribbean Regional Secretariat
CDB	Caribbean Development Bank
CDC	Commonwealth Development Corporation
CET	Common External Tariff
CFC	Caribbean Food Corporation
CGED	Caribbean Group for Cooperation in Economic Development
CHIC	Commonwealth Holiday Inns of Canada
CIB	Comité Interprofessionel Bananier
CIC	Caribbean Investment Corporation
CIDA	Canadian International Development Agency
CPP	Common Protective Policy
CRIB	Comité Restraint Interprofessionel Bananier
CSA	Commonwealth Sugar Agreement
CTA	Caribbean Tourism Association
CTRC	Caribbean Tourism Research Centre

ECCA	Eastern Caribbean Currency Authority
ECCM	Eastern Caribbean Common Market
ECTA	Eastern Caribbean Tourism Association
EEC	European Economic Community
GDP	Gross Domestic Product
GIEB	Groupment d'Investissement Economique Bananier
GMS	Guaranteed Market Scheme
GNP	Gross National Product
GRR	Gross Reproduction Rate
ICA	International Caribbean Airways
IDB	Inter-American Development Bank
ILO	International Labour Organization
IMF	International Monetary Fund
ISA	International Sugar Agreement
LDCS	Less Developed Countries
LIAT	Leeward Islands Air Transport
MDCS	More Developed Countries
OAS	Organization of American States
ODA	Overseas Development Administration (U.K.)
OFA	Oils and Fats Agreement
OTC	One-Stop Tour Charter
PAHO	Pan-American Health Organization
PREALC	Programa Regional del Empleo para America Latina y el Caribe
QRS	Quantitative Restrictions
RFC	Regional Food Corporation
RFP	Regional Food Plan
RRC	Regional Research Center
RSC	Regional Shipping Council
SCMT	Standing Committee of Ministers Responsible for Transport
SDRS	Special Drawing Rights
SITC	Standard International Trade Classification
SNA	System of National Accounts (UN)
UNDP	United Nations Development Programme
UNIDO	United Nations Development Organization
UWI	University of the West Indies
WINBAN	Windward Islands Banana Growers Association
WISA	West Indies Sugar Association
WISCO	West Indies Shipping Corporation
WITASS	West Indies Transatlantic Steamship Lines

Preface

THIS BOOK IS CONCERNED WITH THE PROBLEMS AND PROSPECTS OF ECONOMIC integration among small developing countries. It focuses on a group of twelve (British) Commonwealth Caribbean territories that are in the process of forging an integrated community. The group comprises five independent countries —Jamaica, Trinidad and Tobago, Guyana, Barbados, and Grenada; five Associated States—St. Vincent, St. Lucia, Dominica, Antigua, and St. Kitts-Nevis;[1] and two Crown Colonies—Belize and Montserrat. Some affinity is evident throughout the region because of a common British colonial heritage of language, traditions, customs, and tastes, and also because of common economic and social problems. After an abortive experience in federation between 1958 and 1962, the twelve territories formed the Caribbean Free Trade Association (CARIFTA) in 1968 and subsequently moved into a higher stage of integration with the establishment of the Caribbean Community (CARICOM), a major element of which is the Caribbean Common Market.[2] In evaluating this integration experience, the intention of this book is, first, to provide a regional economic framework for the World Bank and other development assistance agencies[3] and, second, to identify potentially valuable

1. Anguilla, an island of about 7,000 people, was formerly an integral part of the state of St. Kitts-Nevis-Anguilla. Following an uprising in 1967, Anguilla was placed under direct British administration after July 1971 and now is a separate entity with its own constitution.

2. The Bahamas, although not a member of CARIFTA or CARICOM, participates in the Heads of Government Conference and in other areas of functional cooperation, and contributes to the budget of the Secretariat.

3. The study concentrated on the broader issues of regional integration rather than on a review of development problems from the perspective of each of the region's constituent members. Issues that may be important at the national level have not been included unless they impinge directly upon the integration movement.

lessons for those other small developing countries that might seek economic viability through coordinated development and economic integration.

With the assistance of the Commonwealth Caribbean Regional Secretariat (CCRS), of other regional agencies, and of researchers in the region, a special effort was made to compile a basic set of regional statistics. A substantial volume of statistical information was indeed collected and appears in the Statistical Appendix to this book. Nevertheless, some remaining serious data deficiencies—especially in the areas of national accounts, production cost, price and wage structures in industry and agriculture, income distribution, and private and public financial flows—have handicapped the analysis. Even where reliable data are available for some of the territories, they are usually not comparable because of differences in definition and coverage. This experience suggests that a major and urgent effort is required to design and implement a regional statistical system. A proposal for such a system is contained in Appendix B, "A Statistical System for Caribbean Integration." In the absence of a much improved information system for planning and monitoring integration programs and policies, the Community's capacity for rational decisionmaking is severely limited.[4] Appendix A presents "A Note on the Distribution of Benefits from Integration," an important issue for both the more and less developed countries of the Community.

A large number of persons contributed to this book. An original version of the text was based on the findings of a field mission that visited all twelve members of CARIFA/CARICOM in late 1973. The field mission comprised Sidney E. Chernick, chief of mission; Francesco Abbate, deputy chief of mission; Shankar N. Acharya, monetary and fiscal affairs; Geoffrey Shepherd, industry; Nizar Jetha, fiscal affairs; Manmohan L. Agarwal, quantitative analysis; Ricardo Moran, manpower and employment; Bernard Braithwaite, consultant on education; Doreen Calvo, tourism; Olivier Lafourcade, agriculture; George Hunt, consultant on livestock (sponsored by the Canadian International Development Agency); Howard Sprague, consultant on agricultural research and training (sponsored by the U.S. Agency for International Development); George Bacs, consultant on sugar industry; Surendra K. Agarwal, transportation; Peter Wickenden, consultant on transportation (sponsored by the Canadian International Development Agency); and Beatrice Lubsey, secretary.

Other contributors to the original report include Kunniparampil C. Zachariah, Michael Sharpston, Vijay Joshi, David J. Turnham, Carl A. B. Jayarajah, George Buckmire, Narendra P. Sharma, E. Baccus, G. Roberts, I. Marshall, G. Boucher, D. Rose, D. Mahabir, Dolores Velasco, Murray Ross, Alfredo Gutierrez, and D. Goldsbrough. Appendix B was prepared by Alan R. Roe and Jeffrey I. Round.

4. In so crucial an area as intraregional trade, it proved impossible to balance goods exports and imports among the member countries, leaving sizable unallocated residuals. Data on employment are also deficient in many countries. Fundamentally contradictory pictures emerge from census data on the one hand and household budget surveys on the other.

In mid-1976, a follow-up mission comprising Eric Cruikshank, Josefina G. Valeriano, and Sidney E. Chernick visited the various regional agencies and a few selected countries to update some of the statistical series and review the status of the integration process. Byron Blake, formerly of the CARICOM Secretariat, helped to update the material further in late 1977; the CARICOM Secretariat also reviewed a draft of the book and made some valuable suggestions for revision.

Throughout the preparation of the original report and this book, the staffs of the CARICOM Secretariat and the Caribbean Development Bank were willing sources of encouragement and advice. In particular, I wish to thank Sir Arthur Lewis, Alister McIntyre, Joseph Tyndall, Edwin Carrington, and—most of all—William Demas. Peter Bocock edited the text for publication, Richard R. Herbert copyedited the manuscript, Florence Robinson prepared the index, and Brian J. Svikhart directed design and production of the book. None of these, however, is in any way to be held responsible for the views expressed in this book. That responsibility is mine alone.

SIDNEY E. CHERNICK
Chief of Mission
and Coordinating Author

Washington, D.C.

The Commonwealth Caribbean

Chapter 1

Introduction

THE MANY VEXING PROBLEMS FACED BY THE TWELVE COMMONWEALTH Caribbean states derive partly from their small size, partly from economic fragmentation, and partly from the fact that they have not had coordinated strategies for their economic development. In common with most small developing nations, moreover, the countries of the region have found it hard to reconcile their aspirations towards economic and political independence with their marginally viable economies. Variously described as "micro-states" or "mini-states"—their populations range from about 12,000 in Montserrat to 2 million in Jamaica—they are all highly vulnerable to external economic events.[1] This vulnerability is enhanced by the basic facts of geography. Ten of the twelve states under study are tiny islands, the largest of which is Jamaica (11,424 square kilometers).

Whatever the cause—the fact of geography, the design of colonial history, or both—the English-speaking Caribbean territories evolved as separate, social, economic, and political entities. In the heyday of the colonial plantation, the size of a territory was not a significant variable; the economies of all of the territories were based on imported slave or indentured labor, and secure metropolitan markets, and were large enough to sustain at least one plantation at an efficient level of output under the prevailing technology. The decline of the slave plantation system, technological change calling for larger

1. Comparative studies of development patterns suggest that in the absence of special resources, the smaller the country, the greater the handicap in attaining self-sustaining economic growth. See, for example, Hollis B. Chenery and Moises Syrquin, *Patterns of Development 1950–1970* (Oxford University Press, 1975). For the Commonwealth Caribbean region as a whole, natural resources such as bauxite, petroleum, cement, arable land, the potential for tourism, and geographic location, are relatively abundant in relation to the size of population.

units of production, and increased competition from Asian and African producers of agricultural goods combined to make the small size of these countries a severe impediment to their economic and political modernization. In subsequent years, their diminutive domestic markets have forced them to forego many of the economic advantages of scale; and even the few successful import-substituting or import-replacing activities have been prone to monopolistic practices. Modern technology requires productive and administrative units which are simply too large for the domestic markets of most of the Caribbean Commonwealth states. Since the capacity to adapt this technology is limited, the choice has usually been confined to the costly extremes of either doing without or creating excess capacity.

Some Background Features

Some basic structural information about the twelve states of the Caribbean Community (CARICOM) is presented in Table 1.1. With some exceptions, it shows a group of extremely open economies. The less developed countries (LDCS)[2] and Barbados depend very heavily upon agricultural exports and tourism for their foreign exchange earnings, while raw or processed minerals—bauxite, alumina, and petroleum—are important export items in the three remaining more developed countries (MDCS).[3] Governments of CARICOM countries are relatively active—in terms of their investment and tax efforts—in the functioning of their individual economies. Population densities vary greatly, and, in all the territories except Guyana and Belize, the ratio of arable land to labor is very low, a legacy of the plantation economy with its reliance on slaves and indentured labor. Finally, job opportunities are far below available manpower resources; as a consequence, average rates of unemployment are high.

The data in Table 1.1 reveal the deep-seated imbalance in the region's economic organization. The pattern of regional demand is strongly influenced by external tastes and standards, communicated directly by tourists and expatriate professional and managerial workers, and indirectly by the media; it is less well matched with locally available resources than in most of the developing world. Consequently, the import bill for food and other consumer goods remains high while the capacity for the local production of many of these goods remains low.

The small size and high production costs of the LDCs and Barbados make them particularly dependent on countries outside the region; the latter have

2. The eight less developed countries (LDCS) are the seven Eastern Caribbean islands—Grenada, Dominica, St. Lucia, St. Vincent, Antigua, Montserrat, and St. Kitts-Nevis-Anguilla—together with Belize. The four more developed countries (MDCS) are Barbados, Guyana, Jamaica, and Trinidad and Tobago.

3. In 1971, four products—bananas, sugar, bauxite/alumina, and petroleum—accounted for 75 percent of the value of commodity exports from CARIFTA countries. Tourism accounted for 20 percent of export earnings from commodities plus tourism.

provided guaranteed markets for Caribbean agricultural exports, have supplied a large volume of technical and financial assistance on highly concessionary terms, and have in turn owned or controlled major productive assets in these nine CARICOM members. The three larger countries—Jamaica, Guyana, and Trinidad and Tobago—have achieved a greater degree of independent decisionmaking because they have more diversified natural resources. Until very recently, their principal resources and industrial enterprises were nevertheless also largely owned and controlled by foreigners. In broad terms, therefore, each of the twelve territories has found economic and political viability an elusive goal.

From this perspective, the integration movement among the Commonwealth Caribbean states can be viewed as an attempt to overcome the handicaps of small size, economic fragmentation, and extensive dependence on extraregional markets and suppliers of resources of all kinds. The principal idea behind integration is that a pooling of local resources and markets will yield a higher level of economic and social benefits than could be attained by "going it alone." On the expectation that mechanisms can be designed which will lead to this end, or will at least give them a stronger bargaining position in relation to the outside world, most of the Commonwealth Caribbean states consider the integration option worthwhile. Since each of the alternatives available to them involves some degree of dependence, it is understandable that they would want to choose that course which provides the best combination of economic viability and political autonomy. The integration movement represents the closest approximation to that ideal.

The idea of integration or federation predates World War II. It arose out of frustration with the slow progress of democracy under colonialism. Federalism was initially fostered by contacts among trade unionists and was seen as a vehicle for developing more democratic institutions. A parallel and reinforcing movement was that of local independence, which became feasible once India and Ghana had provided the precedents. During the 1950s, the movement towards local autonomy advanced faster than that of federalism among the larger British possessions in the Caribbean. By the time of its establishment in 1958, therefore, the West Indies Federation was no longer viewed as a necessary instrument of reform. Indeed, the Federation had built-in "self-destruct" features, the most important of which was its lack of power to tax. When Jamaica withdrew in 1962, following a negative referendum vote, the Federation fell apart.[4] Independence was achieved in 1962 by Jamaica and by Trinidad and Tobago, and in 1966 by Guyana and Barbados. With the break up of the Federation, the renowned West Indian economist, Sir Arthur Lewis, attempted to organize a smaller Federation among the Eastern Caribbean islands, but his efforts proved unsuccessful. Instead, the islands, except for Montserrat, became Associated [British]

4. One lasting legacy of the federation movement is the University of the West Indies. It has campuses at Mona, Jamaica; St. Augustine in Trinidad; and Cave Hill in Barbados. It also maintains close working relations with the University of Guyana. Another regional institution which survived is the regional shipping service.

TABLE 1.1. BASIC INDICATORS FOR CARIBBEAN COMMUNITY (CARICOM) COUNTRIES (latest year available)

	Less developed countries (LDCS)					
Year and item	*Antigua*	*Dominica*	*Grenada*	*Montserrat*[a]	*St. Kitts*	*St. Lucia*
1977						
Rate of unemployment (percent estimated)	20.0	23.0	15.0–20.0	4.7	13.5	18.0
1974						
Population (thousands)	69.8	76.2	107.6	11.6	46.8	108.0
GDP at factor cost (millions of U.S. dollars)	55.9	27.9	36.0	6.3	26.4	54.2
GDP per capita (U.S. dollars)	801.0	366.0	335.0	537.5	564.0	502.0
Agriculture as percent of GDP	6.9	37.8	24.9	16.0	30.4	20.6
Exports as percent of GDP[f]	45.7	32.0	23.8	19.3	31.2	25.3
Imports as percent of GDP[f]	85.7	61.8	50.8	60.2	57.0	74.6
Agricultural exports (percent of total goods exports)	1.5	93.0	98.6	80.1	48.0	83.4
Tourism (percent of total exports)[g]	21.6	14.3	10.1[h]	89.3	28.6	34.3
Tax revenue (percent of GDP)	15.8	23.7	15.6	17.2	21.6	18.5
Area (square kilometers)	441.6	787.4	344.5	102.3	352.2	616.4
Population density (persons per square kilometer)	158.1	96.8	312.3	113.4	132.9	175.2
Arable land (square kilometers)	267.9	219.5	240.2	23.7	217.9	480.9
Arable land per capita (hectares)	0.38	0.29	0.22	0.20	0.47	0.45
1971						
Investment as percent of GDP	19.3	29.2	26.4	28.7	46.9	48.1
Public investment (as percent of total investment)[i]	21.0	60.8	74.8	60.2	57.7	15.6

. . . Not available.

Note. Except for calculations of GDP at factor cost, GDP per capita, and agriculture as a percent of GDP, the ratios are calculated from data at current market prices.

a. Except for the data on agricultural exports, the latest available data for Montserrat are for 1971.

b. The data are for 1971, except the data on population and agricultural exports, which are for 1974. The 1971 population figure was, however, used to estimate the 1971 GDP per capita.

c. For 1971.

d. For 1972.

e. The 1972 population figure was used to estimate the 1972 GDP per capita.

f. Export and import data for the LDCS exclude nonfactor services.

g. Total exports comprises exports of goods and tourism.

h. Includes hotels only.

i. For the LDCS, it is the ratio of public capital expenditure to gross capital formation, so that the ratio may be somewhat higher than the actual share of public investment in total investment.

Source: Statistical Appendix and World Bank country reports.

St. Vincent	*Belize*[b]	*Barbados*	*Guyana*	*Jamaica*	*Trinidad and Tobago*	*Year and item*
		More developed countries (MDCS)				
						1977
18.0	4.7	7.7[c]	12.8[c]	11.3[c]	22.0[c]	Rate of unemployment (percent estimated)
						1974
91.0	136.0	241.0	791.0	2,008.0	1,070.0	Population (thousands)
34.1	68.9	185.8[d]	403.2	2,271.6	953.2[d]	GDP at factor cost (millions of U.S. dollars)
375.0	550.0	777.0[de]	510.0	1,131.0	910.0[de]	GDP per capita (U.S. dollars)
21.4	15.3	12.4[d]	30.5	7.8	4.7[d]	Agriculture as percent of GDP
13.2	20.0	67.5[d]	40.6	36.8	38.3[d]	Exports as percent of GDP[f]
65.9	48.0	91.0[d]	55.3	45.7	46.8[d]	Imports as percent of GDP[f]
98.2	82.5	61.7	62.1	19.5	4.2	Agricultural exports (percent of total goods exports)
51.5	. . .	61.5[c]	. . .	19.4[c]	14.1[c]	Tourism (percent of total exports)[g]
26.6	12.3	22.3[c]	29.0	22.5[c]	14.9[c]	Tax revenue (percent of GDP)
384.0	22,966.0	429.9	215,000.0	11,424.0	5,128.0	Area (square kilometers)
237.0	5.9	560.6	3.7	175.8	208.7	Population density (persons per square kilometer)
158.4	8,740.0	300.0	31,500.0	4,880.0	1,688.5	Arable land (square kilometers)
0.17	6.43	0.12	3.98	0.24	0.16	Arable land per capita (hectares)
						1971
38.8	30.1	24.6	19.4	26.1	29.0	Investment as percent of GDP
63.1	11.1	17.4	35.5	26.0	19.2	Public investment (as percent of total investment)[i]

States—a half-way house towards independence. In ambitiously tackling the difficult aspects of regional association first, the West Indies Federation had ignored the lessons of history, which suggest that the chances of successful integration are enhanced when a community of economic interests is established beforehand.

The idea of a regional economic association was revived in the mid-1960s. At the initiative of Guyana (which had remained outside the West Indies Federation), articles of a Caribbean Free Trade Association (CARIFTA) were drawn up in 1965, and were accepted by Barbados and Antigua. The provisions of the Agreement were largely modeled on those of the European Free Trade Association (EFTA). All twelve Commonwealth Caribbean countries were able to agree on the formation of a free trade area, based largely on the text of the 1965 Agreement, and CARIFTA came into existence in May 1968. At the same time, the Eastern Caribbean islands were developing closer forms of cooperation which culminated in the formation of the Eastern Caribbean Common Market (ECCM) in June 1968.

Another important regional institution established during this period was the Caribbean Development Bank (CDB). Under the firm guidance of Sir Arthur Lewis as president, the Bank began operations in 1970 with fourteen founding regional members, and two nonregional members—Canada and the United Kingdom; the United States also provided financial assistance, and Venezuela and Colombia joined later. The main purpose of the CDB, according to its Charter is to ". . . contribute to the harmonious economic growth and development of the member countries in the Caribbean . . . and promote economic cooperation and integration among them, having special and urgent regard to the needs of the less developed members of the region."

In October 1972, some of the CARIFTA member countries decided to form a Caribbean Community and Common Market (CARICOM). The Community, which came into being on 1 August, 1973, represents a deepening of regional integration and has achieved such objectives as the establishment of a common external tariff, a harmonized system of fiscal incentives for industry, double-taxation and tax-sparing agreements, and the formation of a Caribbean Investment Corporation (CIC), designed to channel equity funds to the less developed member countries.[5] It initially comprised the four MDCs—Jamaica, Trinidad and Tobago, Guyana, and Barbados; by the end of July 1974, all the other CARIFTA members had acceded to the Community Agreement.

Recent Developments Affecting Regional Economic Integration within CARICOM

Since 1974, when all twelve Commonwealth Caribbean countries became members of CARICOM, there have been a number of developments with an

5. The Community also provides for cooperation in "noneconomic" areas—health, education, culture, meteorology, sea and air transport—and for consultations to harmonize the foreign policy of the independent member states.

important bearing on the course of the Caribbean integration movement. Some have helped to strengthen it; others have had a severely adverse impact on its evolution. The most important changes in institutional arrangements within CARICOM are:

a. On 1 January, 1976, a single-column structure of the Common External Tariff (CET) was adopted. It provided for the streamlining of the administration of the tariff system, and for restructuring it, to make it more protective in the light of recent experience.
b. In May 1976 the CARICOM Market Standards Council began operations. This represented an important step towards harmonizing standards of regional products. It should help to encourage exports outside of the region.
c. Also in May 1976 the regional ministers of finance agreed to proposals for the establishment of the CARICOM Enterprise Regime to provide a new business structure which could be a vehicle for regional ventures. As a legal regional entity, the most significant feature of the CARICOM Enterprise is its right to transfer currency, purchase land, and move labor specifically connected with its business.
d. In June 1976 the four MDCs agreed to harmonize their air transport policy. In May 1977, regional governments agreed to guarantee a CDB loan and, if necessary, to provide a subvention to Leeward Islands Air Transport (1974) Ltd. (LIAT)—a small intergovernmentally owned airline linking the LDCs of the Eastern Caribbean. They also decided that LIAT should continue to maintain full service to the islands it now serves.
e. In September 1976 the Caribbean Food Corporation (CFC) was set up with broad powers and objectives as the principal executing agency of the Regional Food Plan (RFP).
f. Since the rise in oil prices in 1973, Trinidad and Tobago has made available about US$150 million to its CARICOM partners largely by way of medium-term loans for balance of payments support to the other MDCs, and to a lesser extent, by way of longer-term development loans (both bilaterally and through the CDB) to the LDCs.
g. In 1976 a regional financial "safety net" was established to provide interim support for intraregional balance of payments deficits. A permanent arrangement (either a support facility or a stabilization fund) has been agreed in principle by the ministers of finance. Progress in activating the permanent mechanism has been slow, however, largely because of the serious economic difficulties which all CARICOM members (except Trinidad and Tobago) have experienced in the last few years.
h. In 1976 a reorganized West Indies Shipping Corporation (WISCO) came into being. Financial support was obtained for the company's five-year investment program, including the purchase of four new ships. The first ship, financed by the CDB, has gone into service, and a loan for the acquisition of a second ship has been approved by the CDB.
i. In June 1977 the CARICOM Multilateral Clearing Facility came into effect, as the result of an agreement signed by the Central Banks of Barbados,

Guyana, Jamaica, Trinidad and Tobago, the Monetary Authority of Belize, and the East Caribbean Currency Authority. It replaces the previous bilateral clearing arrangements between Central Banks or Monetary Authorities. The new Facility provides for the settlement of payments between participating countries up to a maximum of US$40 million. Under the Facility, agreed lines of credit will be accepted from, and extended to, each participant, and transactions will be calculated in United States currency.

j. In January 1978 a new Process List providing a "substantial transformation criterion" to the rules of origin for intraregional trade was introduced. The new criterion alters in a major way the criteria for Common Market treatment since it encourages greater utilization of regional raw materials and productive factors while dispensing with the Basic Materials List,[6] and reduces the scope for manipulation under the value-added criterion. A contentious issue still to be resolved is the treatment to be accorded to the LDCs under the new system.

Taken together, these measures represent substantial progress in strengthening the institutions and mechanisms of regional economic integration. At the same time, however, the movement towards a coordinated regional development strategy has recently suffered such a serious loss of momentum that the very survival of CARICOM is in danger. This situation has come about mainly as a consequence of the severe economic difficulties faced by most of the CARICOM member countries during the past three or four years. By and large, these adversities originated outside the region. The dramatic increase in the world price of petroleum and in the prices of other essential regional imports in 1973 and 1974 came at a time when CARICOM members had already begun to experience acute economic difficulties in the form of unprecedented inflationary pressures, and deteriorating balance of payments and government finances. To some extent the shock of external price increases was mitigated for Trinidad and Tobago as a result of its indigenous petroleum and natural gas resources; in the case of the sugar-producing states, the unusually high price of sugar in 1974–75 helped to cushion the initial impact.

For a time it appeared that a heightened sense of regional communality and cooperation would save the day. An early response to the international economic events was to launch a regionally coordinated import substitution program,[7] and Trinidad and Tobago stood ready to contribute a significant volume of financial assistance. The long subsequent period of stagflation in the developed countries, however, combined with ineffective domestic economic management, aggravated the economic dislocation in most of the

6. The Basic Materials List sets out a large number of intermediate products which, even though imported from outside the region, are deemed to be of regional origin for the purpose of computing value added in the region.

7. See "Report of Committees on Coordinated Emergency National Agricultural and Additional Development Programmes in the Region" (Georgetown, Guyana: CARICOM Secretariat, 1974).

Figure 1. INSTITUTIONAL ORGANIZATION OF THE CARIBBEAN COMMUNITY

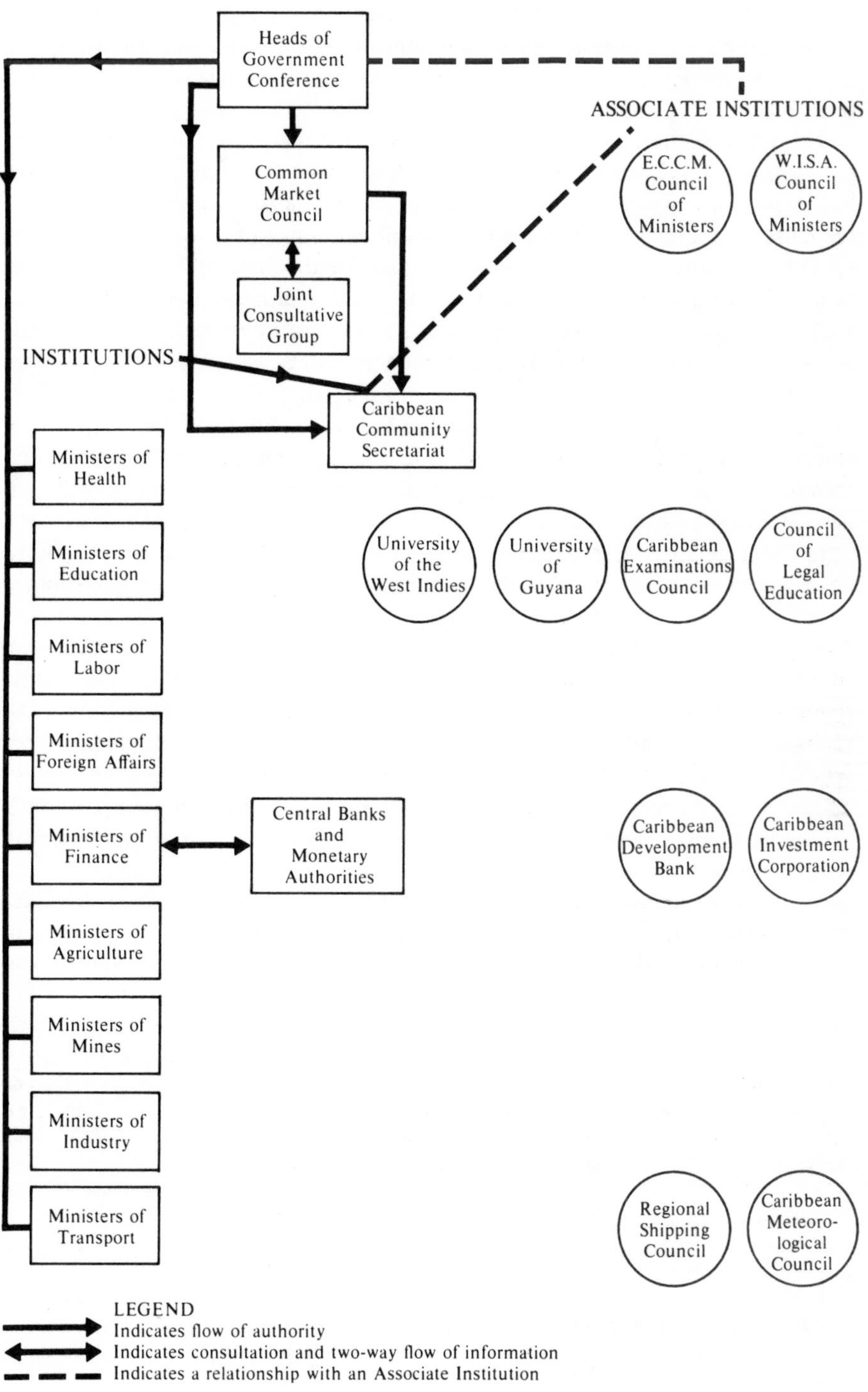

CARICOM states. Economic conditions in Guyana, Jamaica, and the ECCM countries reached alarming proportions in 1977, and by early 1978, these countries were in, or approaching a state of financial and fiscal emergency.[8] Jamaica, for example, was impelled to introduce a stabilization program involving some very austere fiscal and financial measures. The International Monetary Fund (IMF) and the World Bank provided financial support for this stabilization program.

The LDCs of the Eastern Caribbean have experienced an actual decline in consumption levels and living standards during the past few years, and have had great difficulty in maintaining minimum standards of public services. In response to the especially severe economic situation of the LDCs, a Special Emergency Fund was established in the CDB for the year 1976 on an interim basis. With contributions from the MDCs and from the United Kingdom, EC$10 million[9] was disbursed in 1976 for certain community and national economic services; the Fund also helped to cover the cost of ECCM and CARICOM common services. A Five-Year Emergency Fund was to come into effect early in 1977. Its establishment has been delayed, however, until a task force studying the establishment of common services in administrative and technical areas of government activities in the smaller Eastern Caribbean islands, has submitted an acceptable plan.

In the face of severe external economic pressures, Guyana and Jamaica have sought to adjust their economies through restrictive import licensing, a practice inimical to regional integration. In taking this step, Jamaica and Guyana invoked the terms of Article 28 of the Annex to the Common Market Treaty.[10] The adoption of national protectionist policies by these CARICOM members has provoked considerable antagonism throughout the region; Trinidad and Tobago, for one, has gone so far as to threaten taking retaliatory measures. Unless the economies of the region recover rapidly and/or governments begin once more to cooperate in attacking the economic problems which have beset some CARICOM members, the future of Caribbean regional integration will remain precarious.

Recent events have clearly demonstrated the vulnerability of the economies of CARICOM countries to external economic adversities, and the consequent fragility of integration arrangements. The consequences of these shocks can

8. These economic misfortunes were responsible, in part, for the convening of a conference on economic development in the Caribbean, in Washington, D.C., on December 14–15, 1977, chaired by the World Bank. The conference invited the World Bank, with the direct participation of the CDB, the IMF and the Inter-American Development Bank to organize a Caribbean Group for Cooperation in Economic Development (CGCED). The Group would aim to mobilize additional external assistance for the Caribbean (including, apart from the CARICOM countries, Haiti, the Dominican Republic, and other Caribbean islands) and to improve aid coordination among donors and recipients.

9. For exchange rates for the Eastern Caribbean dollar (EC$) and other related currencies, see Statistical Appendix, Table SA11.2.

10. The intention of Article 28 was to provide for import licensing as a monitoring rather than as a restrictive device.

already be traced in the latest estimates of intraregional trade shares—the best available single indicator of the degree of regional economic interaction.[11] In 1967, the share of intraregional trade in total trade was estimated at 8 percent. The share peaked at about 11 percent in 1973 and, then dropped to 8 percent in 1975 and 7 percent in 1976. The precipitous increase in the price of petroleum towards the end of 1973 probably contributed to the decline in the intraregional trade percentages, since the value of Trinidad and Tobago's exports of oil to extraregional markets rose proportionately more than the value of its exports to regional markets. Trade in manufactures—largely nonessential consumer goods—has also been subject to the intraregional trade squeeze, and Trinidad and Tobago, the major exporter of manufactured products to CARICOM, has had to contend with increased unemployment in its manufacturing sector.

Despite their costs, the economic adversities of the past few years have had the positive effect of making clear a number of weaknesses in integration mechanisms, to which CARICOM must address itself urgently. In particular, new or improved mechanisms are needed in the areas of: (a) licensing and restriction of intraregional imports; (b) state trading and public sector procurement codes; (c) monitoring and surveillance of intraregional trade practices; (d) financing of intraregional trade; (e) production and trade in agricultural products; (f) regional industrial programming designed to enhance industrial complementarity; and (g) the more effective coordination of external economic policies and actions of member states.

In tackling the general trade issues, consideration should be given to the annual preparation of an agreed minimum intraregional import program so as to improve balance of payments management, and to encourage the orderly financing of intraregional trade. An agreed import program would also help prevent discriminatory treatment associated with state trading, and make it easier to finance intraregional trade through clearing arrangements. In the case of arrangements for agriculture, major steps have already been taken in the form of the Regional Food Plan and the establishment of the Caribbean Food Corporation. As for the intraregional marketing of fruits and vegetables under the Agricultural Marketing Protocol (AMP), it seems that nothing short of providing guaranteed markets for certain quantities of these agricultural products (especially those exported from the LDCs) will yield a rational system of production and intraregional trade in these items.

Finally, it can be noted that a major area of regional integration that has remained untouched is that of industrial programming. A coordinated planning effort is needed to exploit the region's industrial potential; this should lead to regional agreements covering the timing, location and output capacity of new investment which needs all or part of the regional market to be economic. A regional program of industrial complementarity is a technically

11. The local or regional value-added in production of goods entering into intraregional trade would be a better measure. In the absence of data on this aspect of trade, the much cruder measure using the gross value of traded goods has to be used.

complex matter; it also requires sustained political support if it is to be effective. Consideration should be given to establishment of a regional industrial corporation to foster industrial programming. To the extent that the region can establish a significant degree of industrial coordination, it will reduce its vulnerability to external shocks.

Overview of Progress and Problems

The Caribbean regional movement has two main long-term goals: to foster general economic development, with a strong accent on the creation of employment, and to reduce the region's external dependence. This book deals principally with the efforts which the CARICOM countries have made to achieve the first of these goals; the achievement of the second requires actions outside the range of economic policy.

More specifically, the region's economic goals are: (a) to improve efficiency through greater competition and specialization in an extended market; (b) to make this market sufficiently large to support viable new industries; (c) to achieve greater national or regional linkages between sectors (and in particular to increase the use of regional natural resources); (d) to develop a common position towards nonmember countries on relevant policy matters (such as foreign investment, trade preferences, and shipping); and (e) to provide for the equitable sharing of the fruits of development. The creation of CARIFTA in the late 1960s was central to the realization of these goals; they are currently being pursued further by the gradual move towards a customs union within the framework of CARICOM.

Trade and monetary arrangements

The process of harmonizing trade and monetary arrangements has been at the heart of Caribbean integration efforts over the past decade. Under the CARIFTA Agreement in 1968, tariff and nontariff barriers between member countries were reduced or removed, and some tentative steps were taken towards fiscal harmonization. The CARICOM Treaty of 1973 significantly extended the scope of integration: it proposed the establishment of a single regional market with a common external tariff for imports from nonmember countries, together with common policies for the economic development of the region, including cooperation in monetary policy, harmonization of industrial incentives and fiscal policies in general, and regional planning for agricultural and industrial development. Two agreements, one establishing the Common External Tariff (CET) and the other setting out harmonized fiscal incentives to industry, were signed in 1973; in the same year, a unified system of tax concessions on exports was set up. More recently, a double taxation agreement has been negotiated between the MDCs and the LDCs, with provisions designed to be of special benefit to the latter. As previously noted, the CET was restructured and streamlined in 1976; further modifications to it—involving a rationalization of the rules determining whether goods are treated as being of CARICOM origin—were introduced early in 1978.

For the region as a whole, the consequences of the trading arrangements made over the decade have been positive. Intraregional trade has risen sharply, quadrupling in money terms between 1967 and 1974, and the share of intraregional trade in the total trade of member countries has also risen. In real terms, however, the bulk of this improvement has been accounted for by export increases achieved by the MDCs, notably in manufactured goods; the LDCs have done less well. This situation reflects the general resource imbalance between the two groups, a fundamental problem for the Community which recurs throughout the analyses in this book.

The fact that relatively greater benefits have accrued to the MDCs than to the LDCs has led the latter group to complain recently that the special concessions to the LDCs built into the trade arrangements made under the CARICOM Treaty have been ineffective. This hypothesis, together with a number of anomalies which have emerged as the arrangements have been put into effect, will need careful examination by the Community.[12]

On the monetary front, the past decade has seen modest progress. Lines of credit have been arranged between member countries so as to simplify intra-CARICOM transfers of funds and a financial safety net facility has been established by the four MDCs (Barbados, Guyana, Jamaica, and Trinidad) which gives them a degree of mutual balance of payments support. Little progress has been made as yet on liberalization of capital flows within the region, largely because it is feared that relaxation of the existing controls would lead to a flow of funds away from the LDCs to the MDCs. Exchange rate policy remains based on the concept of separate currencies and fixed parities, which are to be adjusted only in the case of a "fundamental" disequilibrium in a country's balance of payments.

An important development under CARICOM has been the Community's commitment to the provision of assistance to its less developed member countries. The institutional consequences of this commitment have already been noted: the Caribbean Development Bank (CDB) was established in 1969, and the Caribbean Investment Corporation (CIC) in 1973. By the end of 1977 the CDB, whose membership include Canada, Colombia, the United Kingdom, and Venezuela, as well as the members of the Community and three other territories in the region, had approved loans of roughly US$140 million, of which nearly two-thirds had been lent for national or regional development projects in the CARICOM LDCs. The Corporation supplements the CDB's activities by promoting private sector ventures in the manufacturing or agro-industrial sectors of member countries through equity subscriptions or loans. Its role is inevitably small by comparison with the CDBS, and it got off to a slow start; nevertheless, by the end of 1977, cumulative approvals of loans and equity investments amounted to US$1 million, mainly to enterprises in the manufacturing sector.

Both trade and monetary arrangements in the Community have been put to a severe test by the consequences of the oil price increases of 1973. As

12. See Appendix A, for a discussion of the distribution of benefits from integration.

already noted, Trinidad has provided generous financial assistance to other CARICOM countries to offset the problems they have faced, but both Jamaica and Guyana (despite increased foreign exchange earnings from sugar and bauxite exports) have recently had to impose stringent economic controls, including import restrictions. The LDCs, meanwhile, have suffered even more badly; because the Monetary Authority for the seven Leeward and Windward Islands (the Eastern Caribbean Currency Authority [ECCA]) regulates the amount of currency in circulation according to the foreign exchange available to back it, the recent outflows of foreign exchange, entailed by increasingly heavy import bills, have severely reduced domestic money supply and the availability of credit, leading to falls in consumption and real incomes.

Thus, CARIFTA and CARICOM monetary and trade arrangements may be said to have had a generally useful effect, taking the region as a whole; at the same time, however, they have not dealt adequately with the problem of polarity between the region (the divergence between the LDCs and the MDCs), and—perhaps not surprisingly, given the extremely open nature of the economies of CARICOM countries—they have been unable to cope with the trade and balance of payments consequences of recent international dislocations. Even without these dislocations, however, it would be wrong to draw any firm conclusions from the experience of the Commonwealth Caribbean countries thus far in operating cooperative trade and monetary arrangements. They have had to struggle against major economic, social, and political constraints to achieve even what has been achieved, and they are still evolving a common approach to meet their problems.

Important as unified tariff structures, harmonized fiscal systems, and cooperative monetary arrangements are for the progress of integration, it can be argued that the integration of markets has taken up a disproportionate amount of CARICOM's time and that more intensive efforts are needed to develop and integrate the directly productive sectors of the economies of member countries. The results of these efforts thus far, and the medium-term prospects for integrated development in a number of key sectors, are summarized in the rest of this chapter, and described in some detail in other chapters of this book; before examining specific sector integration issues, however, it is necessary to discuss a problem which underlies any analysis of CARICOM's recent past and any prognosis for the community's medium-term future—that of the demographic trends which have been developing since the beginning of the present decade, and which, together with their consequences for employment, threaten to worsen appreciably in the 1980s.

Population, manpower, and employment

The outlook for population, manpower, and employment in the Commonwealth Caribbean is complex and potentially alarming. During the 1960s, the natural population growth rate in the region (2.8 percent a year) was halved to 1.4 percent a year by emigration. Because those who emigrated tended to be young adults, they left behind a population disproportionately biased towards extremes of youth and age. As the children of the 1960s (who represented over 60 percent of total population growth in that decade) grow up, they will become the working age adolescents and young adults of the late 1970s and early 1980s.

Thus, despite a general decline in crude birth rates, the proportion of the population represented by the young of working age is expected to grow very rapidly during the years up to 1985. The gross rate of increase, moreover, is no longer likely to be offset by large scale emigration as was the case in the 1950s and 1960s, because of the generally restrictive attitude towards immigration which has developed in traditional recipient countries. If the downward trend of the past two decades in the proportion of those of working age who are actually in employment persists, it will compound the problem of population growth among those of working age in terms of their employment and income prospects.

Finally, gross figures underestimate the seriousness of the problem, because they mask both the fact that a very large proportion of those counted as employed are in reality earning very little, notably in the agricultural sector, and the disproportionate extent to which unemployment affects young adults in urban areas. In the cities, there is an evident gulf between workers in the organized labor markets, with their relatively high wages and good conditions of employment, and those in the unorganized markets where rewards are low. The existence of this two-market system may itself be contributing to open unemployment.

The consequences of these various factors have already become apparent. Increased social unrest, urban squalor, and rural-urban polarization have become more marked in a number of countries during the last few years. Until now, the structure of the agricultural and industrial sectors has been such that they have been able to absorb only a portion of new entrants on the labor market into productive employment. As the supply of labor increases, this mismatch between people and jobs, exacerbated by problems of underemployment and poor wages in the unorganized sector, will become more acute.

The integration process seems to have had only a minor effect on the employment and manpower picture thus far. Opportunities exist, however, for developing improved manpower information and training services as part of the integration process, and for matching the output of those services to the requirements of rationally planned regional agricultural and industrial sectors. Deliberate policies in these sectors for investment programs which greatly increase the level of productive employment will be essential, if the existing and potentially more extreme imbalance between labor supply and demand is to be righted.

Transport

This book examines four key sectors of CARICOM's economy—transport, agriculture, tourism, and industry. The balanced, integrated development of the last three of these sectors depends significantly on the efficient operation of the first; it is therefore appropriate to begin any discussion of the past progress and future possibilities of sectoral integration, with an outline of the state of affairs in transport.

The CARICOM comprises a group of territories scattered around the Caribbean basin. With the exception of Guyana and Belize, they are all small islands (as already noted, Jamaica, the largest of them, has an area of just under 11,500 square kilometers). Adequate transport links between member countries represent a crucial element in the growth of intraregional trade, and in the process of sectoral integration. Because the individual territories originally developed separate lines of communication directly with external suppliers and purchasers, however, the region does not have a long-standing intraregional transport network; the slow and sometimes difficult process of developing such a network preceded the foundation of CARIFTA, but has become a matter of increasing importance and concern during the past decade.

Surface transport links involve four types of carrier: the West Indies Shipping Corporation (WISCO), which handles about a quarter of intraregional cargo; regionally based shippers of bauxite and bauxite products from Guyana and Jamaica, in which the governments of the two countries have substantial equity interests; foreign-owned ships, which carry about a third of intraregional cargo and all of the products (other than bauxite and alumina) traded between countries of the region and the rest of the world; and the small vessels serving the Eastern Caribbean islands, which carry about half of total intraregional cargo, but on a basis which is considered to be generally unreliable.

The principal regionally based carrier, WISCO, which is owned by CARICOM member governments, has been in difficulties virtually since its establishment in 1960, mainly because it has not been permitted to act as a commercial entity charging economic rates. Instead it has been operating on a deficit-and-subsidy basis (on the dubious grounds that the low subsidized shipping rates which it could charge would by themselves encourage intraregional trade). This state of affairs has recently been remedied with the conclusion of an agreement among CARICOM governments that WISCO should restructure its tariffs and routes on a broadly commercial basis. There has also been agreement on a new investment program which will modernize the line's obsolescent fleet.

Extraregional carriers, which handle a significant proportion of intraregional trade, and virtually all traffic to and from countries outside the region, present CARICOM transport planners with a fundamental problem. Because they are almost exclusively under foreign control, their charges are set without reference to regional economic needs, and their routes tend increasingly to ignore the smaller islands, because it is only marginally economic to serve them. The controlling body for shipping matters in the region, the Standing Committee of Ministers Responsible for Transportation (SCMT) has authority to negotiate rates with these carriers, but, in the final analysis, the region is dependent on them and, therefore, is in a weak negotiating position. Apart from the two regionally based carriers which were recently set up to break the monopoly of the overseas lines in moving bauxite and alumina, the large scale diversion of freight to regional carriers is unlikely in the near future.

Communications with the smaller islands are in need of urgent improvement. This will require development of these islands' ports to make them suitable for deepwater ships and a program to provide minimum standards and some financial support for the small vessels service so that it can carry goods from smaller to larger islands more efficiently than hitherto.

Air services in the region are provided both by regional and foreign carriers with varying degree of efficiency. British West Indies Airways (BWIA), the principal regionally based carrier to external destinations, has had a chronic debt problem, and Leeward Islands Air Transport (LIAT), the main intraregional airline, went into receivership in 1974—although, as already noted, a new company was incorporated in the same year to take over its operations. Links between the MDCs are generally good; as with shipping, the LDCs tend to be less well served.

Policy relating to airports and seaports is currently handled on a national rather than a regional basis. This has led, in the case of airports, to a certain amount of overinvestment. Regionwide coordination is needed to establish optimum locations.

In general, the transport sector badly needs a regionally integrated strategy for service, routes, and investments in fixed plant and operating equipment. Such a strategy would take into account the transport needs of other sectors (especially agriculture and tourism), and plan services accordingly. It must be recognized, however, that in practice the decisions to be made on the basis of any integrated strategy will be liable to benefit one island's economy at the expense of another's, and arrangements to compensate those who suffer may have to be devised. If the directly productive sectors are to be served by an efficient transport network (a matter of particular importance in the case of air service for tourism development), and if wasteful investment is to be avoided, a policy based on the needs of the region as a whole rather than on the national aspirations of individual countries is nevertheless essential.

Agriculture

Agriculture remains the most important of the directly productive sectors in most of the CARICOM countries, accounting for about 20 percent of the region's output and 30 percent of its employment. The dominant export crop is sugar, followed by bananas. Both have declined substantially in the volume of their output in recent years. This fall has been masked, however, by sharp increases in prices, especially for sugar, so that the value of agricultural exports has in fact risen; nevertheless, the value of agricultural imports has risen even more rapidly, turning a sizable net credit balance of trade on the agricultural account in the late 1960s into a large and widening deficit by the mid–1970s.

Agricultural policy for the region needs to concentrate on two broad objectives: the revival of the principal agricultural export crops in which the region continues to have a comparative advantage, and the development of sources of supply within the region for currently imported foods. Subsidiary objectives include the framing and implementation of a master plan for regionwide agricultural development, to encourage national specialization in crops for which particular countries are better suited than others; the upgrading of the quality of output and the timeliness of its delivery (much of the food supplied to the tourist industry has to be imported because domestic supplies are of too low a standard and unreliable in delivery); the reform and rationalization of land holdings which are often inefficiently small; and the development of institutions to encourage better agricultural practices, notably in the areas of marketing, extension services, research, and education.

The integration process has not yet impinged significantly on the agricultural sector. The two major instruments for the harmonization of agricultural production and trade under CARICOM are the Agricultural Marketing Protocol (AMP) and the Oils and Fats Agreement (OFA). Both instruments regulate prices for specified products and allocate markets for them between member countries on the basis of the declared surpluses and deficits of members. Neither has had the effect of increasing intraregional trade at the expense of imports to a marked degree. Recently, however, a Regional Food Plan (RFP) has been approved; this covers a wide range of schemes but its main component is an ambitious program for regional livestock development, designed to achieve an important degree of self-sufficiency by 1985. The Plan covers meat, poultry, and dairy products, and its component projects have been tentatively allocated between different countries (for example, Belize and Guyana, with their large reserves of unused land, would specialize in dairy farming). Although the program faces a number of severe problems—notably the inadequacy of existing livestock for breeding purposes and the small number of skilled livestock managers in the region—it represents an important new departure in regionwide planning for agricultural development.

Institution-building is another area where an integrated approach would pay dividends. The Caribbean Agricultural Research and Development Institute (CARDI) is the only regional institution established thus far; other regionwide initiatives should include better education and training facilities, improved extension services, new efforts to improve facilities for the marketing and distribution of agricultural products, and regional quality control standards.

Equally important for the future prosperity of the region is the rehabilitation of the two main export crops, sugar and bananas. In both cases the priorities are twofold: to strengthen the bargaining position of Caribbean producers in their negotiations with overseas purchasers, and to increase production, which has fallen in recent years to levels well below those achieved in the latter part of the 1960s. Both land and labor resources are available, and the potential benefits would be appreciable; moreover, from the point of view of general economic welfare in the region, an increase in productive agricultural employment based on export crops would have positive repercussions far beyond the agricultural sector.

Tourism

Tourism has been an increasingly important industry for the CARICOM countries since the 1960s, providing valuable foreign exchange earnings and employment opportunities. The past decade has seen some slackening in tourism demand, a trend which has become more serious in the recent past as a consequence of rising air transport costs, economic difficulties in the countries from which tourists have traditionally come, and social and political unrest in a number of Caribbean countries. Prospects are now expected to improve somewhat, however, and the region's natural advantages are likely to ensure that the demand for Caribbean tourism remains high over the long term.

It is nevertheless important to remember that tourism is by no means regarded as an unmixed blessing by the people of the region. Tourists are blamed for social tensions, the disruption of traditional lifestyles, the destruction of natural amenities, the overloading of infrastructure facilities, rising prices, and the drift of workers away from the land. In economic terms, opponents of the industry point out that a significant proportion of tourists' expenditure does not remain in the region but returns to the developed countries (directly in the form of repatriation of profits by foreign-owned hotels or other tourist operations, or indirectly as a result of the high import content of the goods and services on which tourists spend money).

The tourist industry urgently needs to plan for its future, both in order to build a tourism sector which will be able to respond fully to medium-term demand and also in order to meet valid social and economic objections. It is especially well-suited to an integrated strategy of development involving regionwide action in different sectors (transport, public services, agriculture and industry, for example), because the tourist buys a package of goods and services which eventually involves, in one way or another, virtually all major areas of productive activity. Hotel fittings and food could be supplied from within the region rather than from overseas; better air transport links could markedly improve the region's attractiveness to visitors (notably in the Eastern Caribbean islands); and a carefully coordinated physical planning policy could ensure that the amenities which originally drew tourists to the region are not spoiled by insensitive overdevelopment.

All policies for tourism, however, must depend on adequate forecasts of demand. These are difficult to make because of the complicated variables involved (many of which—general economic conditions in developed countries, or the structure of international air fares, for example—are wholly outside the control of the CARICOM countries). The present situation of oversupply in accommodation, with its attendant direct and indirect costs, is an example of the penalties which poor forecasting can impose.

Thus far, both general demand forecasting and specific policy actions in the tourism and tourist-related sectors have been undertaken at the national level by the members of the Community. Some countries (Barbados and Jamaica, for example) have generally efficient organization for the promotion of tourism and the coordination of policy to meet demand; nevertheless, a regionwide approach could pay important dividends, especially in promoting local agricultural and industrial production which could substitute for imports, and in developing an efficient transport network to tourist destinations.

Although tourism demand is ultimately a function of factors outside local control, the ways in which it is met are not. The Community needs to plan explicitly for much more extensive linkages between tourism and other sectors of the regional economy to meet the various needs of tourists, and to work for the integrated development of the sector itself. As in the agricultural sector, research, education, marketing, and coordinated planning are urgently required. At present, the Windward and Leeward islands benefit much less from tourist expenditures than do the MDCs; integrated planning could be of disproportionate benefit to the smaller islands, and could thereby help to reduce the tendency towards polarization between them and their wealthier, more developed, fellow members of the Community.

Industry

Industry in the CARICOM region is overwhelmingly concentrated in the MDCs. Even in these countries, moreover, it is relatively underdeveloped, consisting mainly of the small- and medium-scale production of consumer goods which generally depend on imports for a major proportion of their basic components. Small national and regional markets have impeded the development of intermediate goods manufacturing.

Industrial development in the region has been given official encouragement by investment incentives and tariff policies for many years. Since the establishment of CARIFTA, trade in manufactured goods has increased in the region, but has been disproportionately concentrated among the MDCs. Consumer goods have been the most rapidly growing category of manufactured exports.

The manufacturing sector exhibits a number of unsatisfactory features. Exports to markets outside the region are very small; even industries producing goods to substitute for imports are in reality heavily dependent on imported components; inefficient local production is encouraged by tariff and incentive policies. Above all, the sector has largely failed to take advantage of the opportunities to link its activities to those of other sectors (notably agriculture, through processing of agricultural products, or tourism, through the supply of furniture, fittings, textiles, and other requirements of hotels). Still another characteristic is the dominance of final, rather than intermediate, production in industrial output.

The main effect of the integration process on the industrial sector thus far has been through CARIFTA and CARICOM tariff arrangements. As has been noted, this has led to increases in intraregional trade, but the effect has been biased in favor of the MDCs and has resulted mainly in an increase in trade (and output) of items which are already produced in the region, rather than a diversion of trade away from overseas imports and towards new regional output. A new approach is needed in the direction of explicit regionwide programming of industrial development, which would involve the planning on a cooperative basis of the location of new industrial plants in the region, and of how much they might economically produce. This is not going to be an easy task, but it might help to avert the present dangers of duplicative industrial investment and the concentration of industry in the relatively more advanced countries of the Community. Industrial programming could also encourage the growth of enterprises which would match the product structure of the industrial sector more closely to the output of agriculture or the needs of tourism.

The position of manufacturing in the LDCs is especially difficult. They have very little in the way of raw materials, very few skilled workers, and are penalized by the costs of transporting whatever goods they may produce to markets in the MDCs or outside the region. As a consequence, their share of CARICOM industrial output is tiny, and the concessions to the LDCs in the CARIFTA and CARICOM arrangements seem to have been more apparent than real in their effects. In order to offset all the disadvantages which the LDCs face, it will be necessary to devise specific policies to encourage enterprises to develop in these countries. These might include an industrial development corporation for the Eastern Caribbean countries, and closer subregional integration among them to encourage internal trade.

In adhering to CARICOM, members have made far-reaching commitments to integrate their economies so as to respond more to regional, and less to national, interests. Although the implementation of these commitments is under way, it is important to note four serious obstacles which the integration movement needs to overcome. In the first place, the total population of the twelve states amounts to barely 4.8 million and their total GDP is only about $4 billion;[13] and while the average per capita income for the region, $860 a year, is high by developing country standards, this has to be set against the fact that the member countries are scattered around the Caribbean basin, with consequently high communications costs. Spatial dispersion thus limits their ability to capitalize on the benefits of economies of scale. In the second place, the Community's objective of reducing intraregional income disparities has to contend with the existing extreme variation in its members' capacity for economic growth. In relative terms, Jamaica and Trinidad and Tobago are the giants of the region; they account for more than three-quarters of total GDP and nearly three-quarters of intraregional trade. Under these circumstances, it will be extremely difficult to attain the goal of equity unless special interventionist policies are adopted. In the third place, there are some difficult political issues. Integration means yielding some degree of sovereignty. Given the jealousy with which newly acquired independence is guarded in the region, the balance between loss of sovereignty and economic gain as the integration process deepens must be maintained in such a way as to retain the interest of CARICOM member countries. In the fourth place, the integration movement will have to tackle the vexing social problems of poverty, unemployment, and racial and ethnic tensions. These raise complex problems of regional identity and culture, which are intertwined with education and communication.

Finally, the CARICOM countries face, to a greater degree than most groups

13. This is more or less the population of such countries as Finland, Malawi, Zambia, and Haiti, while the region's aggregated GNP is equivalent to that of Ghana, Burma, or Uruguay. The total GDP of the next smallest integration grouping in Latin America—the Central American Common Market—is $8.9 billion.

of integrating economies, the dilemma of balancing progress towards integration on the one hand with retention of a broadly outward-looking posture towards the rest of the world on the other. The Community cannot afford the luxury of economic introversion; its prosperity depends critically on the demand in external markets for regional products, and on supplies from those markets of goods which cannot be produced on an economic basis by national or even regional enterprises. The need for a coordinated outward-looking policy, even while pursuing integrationist strategies, has been and will remain, a fundamental challenge to CARICOM policymakers.

All in all, bearing in mind the many problems they face, the Commonwealth Caribbean countries have made some real progress in their efforts towards balanced integration over the past ten years. This progress has shown itself in the growth both of regional institutions and of economic welfare in member countries, although the very recent past has seen a number of serious setbacks. Despite these shocks to its structure, however, it is a measure of the Community's success that it remains intact at the end of an eventful decade. This is no small achievement for a group of small countries trying to reconcile national and regional aspirations against the backdrop of the turbulent world economy of the 1970s.

The chapters which follow present an economic evaluation of the integration experience over the past decade, the national and sectoral policy issues which it has raised, and an assessment of CARICOM's medium-term prospects. Where the supporting evidence has appeared to be strong enough, policies and programs have been suggested to strengthen integration mechanisms and institutions in line with CARICOM's objectives.[14]

14. This book builds on a lengthy bibliography of Caribbean studies. In the late 1950s and throughout most of the 1960s, Caribbean economists and other social scientists at the University of the West Indies and elsewhere, focused much of their research and writing on integration and the development problems of the region. Some excellent studies were produced; they have remained relevant for an understanding of the social and political dynamics of the region.

Chapter 2

Cornerstones of Integration: Trade and Monetary Arrangements

ARRANGEMENTS FOR COOPERATION IN TRADE AND MONETARY AFFAIRS ARE THE basic building blocks of economic integration. This chapter examines the progress which has been made, first in intraregional trade development, and second in monetary and fiscal cooperation. It investigates the various mechanisms developed and agreements reached by the CARICOM countries; assesses their effectiveness; and discusses the prospects for their modification or further evolution in the light of regional needs.

Developments in Intraregional Trade

The 1968 CARIFTA Agreement[1] laid the foundation for subsequent progress in intraregional trade. The following discussion begins by focusing on the liberalizing mechanism embodied in the Agreement, and then moves on to examine the later CARIFTA experience and the instruments chosen to deepen the regional integration process.

The CARIFTA *trade liberalization mechanism*

The 1968 CARIFTA Agreement immediately freed trade between member countries from import and export duties and from nontariff restrictions, although with certain exceptions which are discussed below. National tariff and quota regulations relating to third countries remained untouched. To

1. The 1968 agreement came into effect on May 1, for Antigua, Barbados, Guyana, and Trinidad; on July 1, for Dominica, Grenada, St. Lucia, St. Vincent, and St. Kitts; on August 1, for Jamaica and Montserrat.

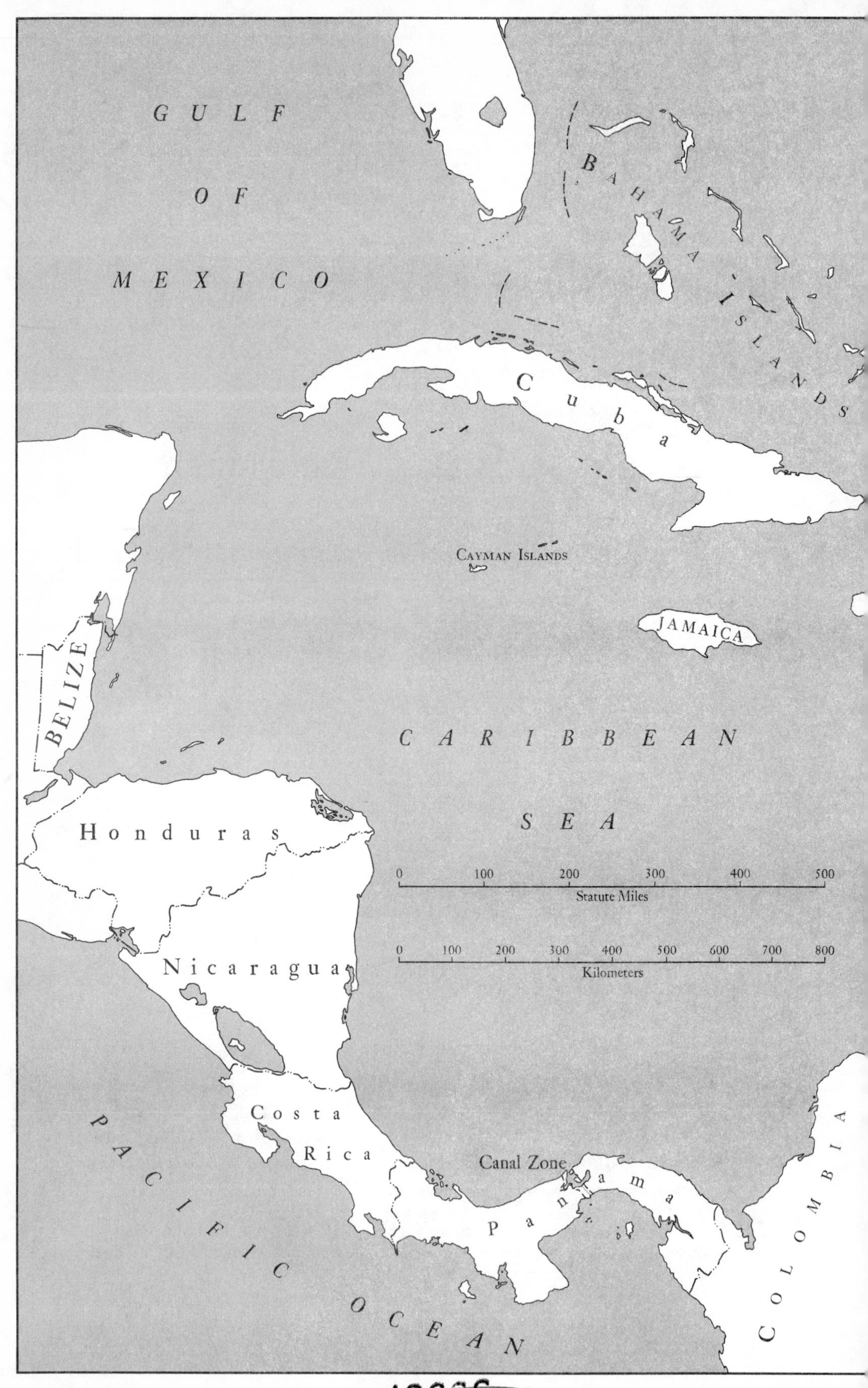
GULF OF MEXICO
BAHAMA ISLANDS
Cuba
Cayman Islands
JAMAICA
BELIZE
CARIBBEAN SEA
Honduras
Nicaragua
Costa Rica
Canal Zone
Panama
COLOMBIA
PACIFIC OCEAN
0 100 200 300 400 500
Statute Miles
0 100 200 300 400 500 600 700 800
Kilometers

THE COMMONWEALTH CARIBBEAN

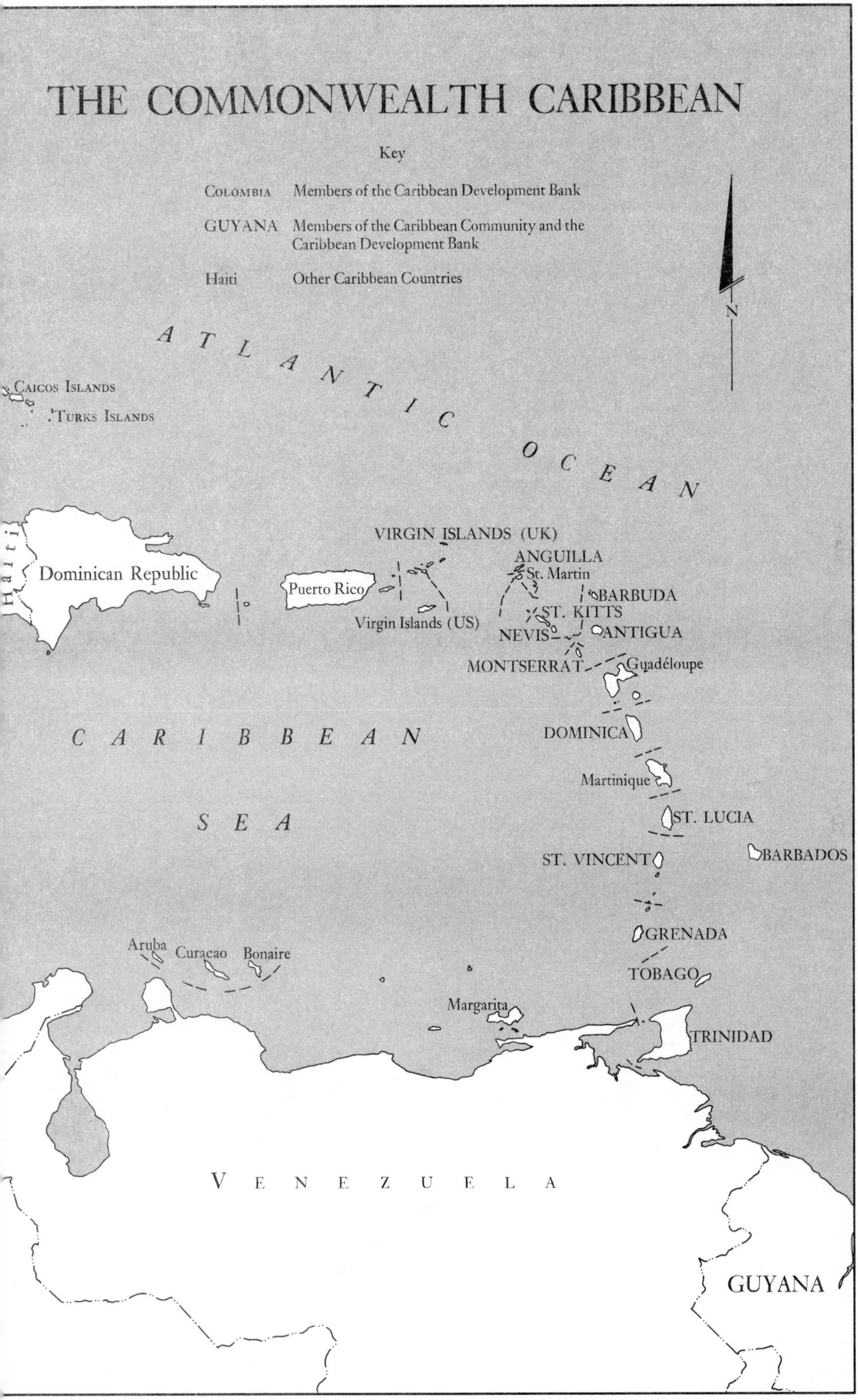

Key

Colombia	Members of the Caribbean Development Bank
GUYANA	Members of the Caribbean Community and the Caribbean Development Bank
Haiti	Other Caribbean Countries

N

ATLANTIC OCEAN

Caicos Islands
Turks Islands
Haiti
Dominican Republic
Puerto Rico
VIRGIN ISLANDS (UK)
Virgin Islands (US)
ANGUILLA
St. Martin
BARBUDA
ST. KITTS
NEVIS
ANTIGUA
MONTSERRAT
Guadéloupe
DOMINICA
Martinique
ST. LUCIA
BARBADOS
ST. VINCENT
GRENADA
TOBAGO
TRINIDAD

CARIBBEAN SEA

Aruba
Curacao
Bonaire
Margarita
VENEZUELA
GUYANA

qualify for duty-free treatment, 50 percent of the value added of products exported from one member country to another had to originate in the CARIFTA area. Because many raw materials and intermediate inputs were not produced in the region, some 200 imported items were incorporated in a Basic Materials List, and treated as though they were of regional origin when used in the manufacture of products exported to other countries within the region.[2]

The first group of exceptions to the general removal of tariff and nontariff restrictions consisted of a small number of products which individual member countries had given contractual undertakings to produce. Most of these exceptions were produced in what were characterized as the four more developed countries (MDCs), and Antigua and Belize.[3] The second group of exceptions was made up of a Reserve List of "sensitive" items for which a phased elimination of tariffs on intraregional trade was stipulated. The List included some fifteen important products which were made locally, ranging from processed fruits through paints, radio and television sets to shoes and clothing; the MDCs were given five years and the LDCs ten years to eliminate tariffs on these items.[4] Member countries were obliged to phase out the protective element in revenue duties on alcoholic beverages and petroleum products according to a similar timetable. The imposition of quotas against member countries was allowed in the case of balance of payments problems, or substantial disruption of domestic production. Products falling under the Agricultural Marketing Protocol (AMP) and the Oils and Fats Agreement (OFA) were subject to trade regulations in addition to those stipulated in the trade liberalization clauses of the CARIFTA Agreement.

The Agreement also included some steps towards fiscal harmony. Newly introduced incentives were not to be more generous than those existing in member countries. Intraregional exports were not allowed to benefit from direct tax concessions or subsidies, duty drawbacks on inputs, or discrimination in internal indirect taxation.[5]

Apart from the Reserve List provisions, there were several other concessional elements for the LDCs. On the one hand, the Reserve List was not applicable to intra-LDC trade; on the other, the LDCs could, with the agreement of the majority of member countries, impose infant industry tariffs

2. Provision was made to remove items from this List as local supplies became available. The List thus allowed some products, such as canned apple products, clothing, shoes, prints and metal products, to qualify for regional preferences. On the other hand, items such as animal feeds and cigarettes did not qualify. The value added for goods from the LDCs was later reduced to 40 percent.

3. The only item of this kind which was excluded in the MDCs and Belize was wheat (and wheat flour). Evaporated and condensed milk were excluded in the MDCs except Guyana. Other exclusions include tires in Jamaica and Trinidad; certain stock feeds in Barbados, St. Lucia, and St. Vincent; and coconut products in St. Vincent. In all about twenty items were affected.

4. The period for phasing out tariffs has now been extended for an extra five years.

5. While drawbacks were prohibited, tariff exemptions on inputs for the production of goods for local and CARIFTA export markets were not affected.

against imports from MDCs. These concessions were necessary to permit the formation of the Eastern Caribbean Common Market (ECCM), a month later than that of CARIFTA. The establishment of the ECCM meant complete free trade among the seven Windward and Leeward islands, committed them to an eventual common external tariff (which came into force in 1972) and made provision for the ultimate free movement of capital and labor within the common market. This latter feature was notably absent in the CARIFTA Agreement.

The CARIFTA *experience*

Within the general context of regional integration efforts, CARIFTA is essentially an instrument for stimulating production in its member countries by accelerating trade among them. An adequate assessment of its performance in this respect is hampered by a number of analytical difficulties and data deficiencies. Apart from the inadequacy of the data—notably the absence of series of trade figures expressed in constant prices—some special features of CARIFTA trade complicate any quantitative analysis.[6] The exports of CARIFTA countries are generally dominated by a single commodity; export receipts and import propensities are therefore highly dependent on changing conditions of world demand, and relationships such as the income elasticity of demand for imports cannot be confidently measured and extrapolated. Another difficulty is that the share of intra-CARIFTA trade in the total trade of the region, and the ratio of intra-CARIFTA trade to gross domestic product (GDP) are relatively small; even substantial changes in intra-CARIFTA trade will have only minor effects on the larger magnitudes, which themselves are subject to many other influences. Finally, the MDCs are undergoing major structural changes as a result of import substitution policies, and any data time series will consequently be highly unstable over time.

After the establishment of CARIFTA in 1968, intraregional trade increased significantly (Table 2.1). Between 1967 and 1974, the value of intraregional exports of all CARIFTA countries more than quintupled from an admittedly low base of EC$86 million to EC$451 million,[7] while the share of intra-CARIFTA exports in total regional exports rose from 6.0 percent to 7.2 percent over the period. This represents an annual average increase of close to 27 percent as compared to less than 5 percent before the establishment of CARIFTA. These increases, it should be noted, are measured in current prices

6. An attempt was made to apply a comparatively sophisticated methodology to isolate the impact of CARIFTA on the various member countries. The methodology was adopted from Norman D. Aitken, "The Effect of the EEC and EFTA on European Trade: A Temporal Cross-Section Analysis," *American Economic Review*, vol. LXIII, no. 5 (December, 1973) pp. 881–92. The results, however, were statistically insignificant so that a quantitative balance sheet of the benefits and costs of integration could not be drawn up.

7. For exchange rates for the Eastern Caribbean dollar (EC$) and other related currencies, see Statistical Appendix, Table SA11.20.

TABLE 2.1. INTRA-CARIFTA TRADE BY CATEGORY, 1967–74
(thousands of Eastern Caribbean dollars)

Category	1967 Amount	1967 Percent	1972 Amount	1972 Percent	1973 Amount	1973 Percent	1974 Amount	1974 Percent
Domestic exports (f.o.b.)								
MDCS								
Barbados	5,593	6.5	17,709	8.0	21,847	8.2	30,141	6.7
Guyana	19,903	23.0	34,722	15.6	39,128	14.7	60,909	13.5
Jamaica	10,598	12.3	41,179	18.6	47,241	17.7	64,002	14.2
Trinidad and Tobago	44,631	51.6	114,356	51.5	143,384	53.8	279,147	61.9
Subtotal	80,725	93.4	207,966	93.7	251,600	94.5	434,199	96.3
LDCS	5,755	6.6	14,022[a]	6.3	14,691[a]	5.5	16,608[a]	3.7
Total	86,480	100.0	221,988	100.0	266,291	100.0	450,807	100.0
Imports (c.i.f.)								
MDCS								
Barbados	13,414	14.0	36,501	15.1	42,863	15.0	72,292	15.6
Guyana	25,741	26.9	47,337	19.6	75,987	26.5	138,013	29.7
Jamaica	8,895	9.3	63,864	26.4	68,943	24.1	145,861	31.4
Trinidad and Tobago	15,982	16.7	41,167	17.0	41,153	14.4	61,261	13.2
Subtotal	64,032	66.9	188,869	78.1	228,946	80.0	417,427	89.9
LDCS	31,652	33.1	52,953	21.9	57,457	20.0	46,863	10.1
Total	95,684	100.0	241,822	100.0	286,403	100.0	464,290	100.0
Trade balance								
MDCS								
Barbados	−7,821	—	−18,792	—	−21,016	—	−42,151	—
Guyana	−5,838	—	−12,615	—	−36,859	—	−77,104	—
Jamaica	1,703	—	−22,685	—	−21,700	—	−81,859	—
Trinidad and Tobago	28,649	—	73,189	—	102,231	—	217,886	—
Subtotal	16,693	—	19,097	—	22,654	—	16,772	—
LDCS	−25,897	—	−38,931	—	−42,766	—	−30,255	—
Total	−9,204	—	−19,834	—	−29,112	—	−13,483	—

— Not applicable.
a. Including re-export data for Belize.
Source: Caribbean Community Secretariat.

and reflect a higher rate of inflation towards the end of the period, especially the effect of the precipitous rise in oil prices at the end of 1973. (The increase in the percentage share, however, is not influenced by inflation.) Another marked feature of the trade pattern is the dominance of the MDCS, which accounted for 96 percent of exports and 90 percent of imports in 1974.

As Table 2.1 shows, nearly all CARIFTA countries have experienced increases in their intraregional trade since 1967. On the export side, Jamaica has shown the fastest growth rate, while Trinidad and Tobago has experienced the largest absolute increase and by 1974, accounted for almost 62 percent of intra-CARIFTA exports. As might be expected, the MDCS' exports increased disproportionately rapidly in the initial years, because their industries were relatively well developed and they had a certain amount of excess capacity. The LDCs were not able to increase their exports to the MDCs to any appreciable extent, despite the Agricultural Marketing Protocol which allocates regional surplus production to deficit areas at guaranteed minimum prices. On the import side, Jamaica and Guyana registered the largest absolute increases.

An analysis of the intraregional trade balance in 1967 and 1974 (Table 2.1) shows that: (a) while in 1967, Trinidad and Tobago and, to a much lesser extent, Jamaica recorded an intraregional trade surplus, only Trinidad and Tobago was a net exporter by 1974; (b) between 1967 and 1974, all the CARIFTA countries, except Trinidad and Tobago, experienced a deterioration in their trade balance. The largest absolute decline was experienced by Jamaica.

Table 2.2 shows the trade matrices for the CARIFTA countries for 1967, 1971, and 1973. Comparative analysis of the matrices for 1967 and 1973 demonstrates that although the trade between Trinidad and Tobago and Guyana still represents the single largest flow (close to 23 percent of total CARIFTA trade in 1973), the major development since the inception of CARIFTA has been the expansion of trade between Trinidad and Tobago and Jamaica, especially of exports from Trinidad and Tobago. The declining share of MDC exports going to the LDCs is also worth noting.

A comparison of the product composition of the MDCs' intra-CARIFTA exports in 1967 and in 1971 indicates that major structural changes have occurred during that period (Table 2.3). In 1967, exports were almost equally divided between three groups: food and beverages, raw materials and manufactures. By 1971, the share of manufactures had grown to 45 percent of the total, with the remaining 55 percent divided almost equally between the other two groups. Among manufactured products, the most dynamic categories were clothing and footwear and, to a lesser extent, chemicals, pharmaceutical products, and cosmetics.

Although intraregional trade in manufactures has risen dramatically since CARIFTA's establishment in 1968, it is important to note that the trend was already rising in earlier years (Table 2.4). This trend corresponds, moreover, with an acceleration in the ratio of CARIFTA trade in manufactures to regional manufacturing output (Table 2.5).

Two factors have inhibited even faster growth in intraregional trade. In the first place, there is a built-in time lag before entrepreneurs adjust to new trading arrangements and distances which dampens the initial impact of the establishment of any free trade area. (This was particularly true in the case of Jamaica.) In the second place, the CARIFTA countries all produce basically similar goods; free trade cannot therefore be expected to foster the development of many products based on new combinations of factors of production.[8]

8. The combination of Trinidadian gas with Guyanese or Jamaican minerals is an example, but since the processed product is for extraregional markets, the free trade area is largely incidental to cooperation possibilities.

TABLE 2.2. CARIBBEAN FREE TRADE ASSOCIATION (CARIFTA), MATRIX OF TRADE BY IMPORTERS AND EXPORTERS, 1967–73
(f.o.b. values; percentages)

	Exporters						
	MDCS						
Importers	*Barbados*	*Guyana*	*Jamaica*	*Trinidad and Tobago*	*Sub-total*	LDCS	*Total*
1967							
MDCS							
Barbados	—	0.6	...	1.5	2.1	4.4	6.5
Guyana	5.8	—	4.4	9.7	19.9	3.1	23.0
Jamaica	1.3	2.6	—	3.5	7.4	4.9	12.3
Trinidad and Tobago	8.4	21.3	3.0	—	32.7	18.9	51.6
Subtotal	15.5	24.5	7.4	14.7	62.1	31.3	93.4
LDCS	1.6	0.7	0.9	2.2	5.4	1.2	6.6
Total	17.1	25.2	8.3	16.9	67.5	32.5	100.0
1971							
MDCS							
Barbados	—	0.5	0.5	2.0	3.0	4.1	7.1
Guyana	4.3	—	3.5	6.6	14.4	2.8	17.2
Jamaica	2.3	2.3	—	6.9	11.5	5.3	16.8
Trinidad and Tobago	9.7	17.5	10.4	—	37.6	16.5	54.1
Subtotal	16.3	20.3	14.4	15.5	66.5	28.7	95.2
LDCS	1.3	0.5	1.3	1.1	4.2	0.6	4.8
Total	17.6	20.8	15.7	16.6	70.7	29.3	100.0
1973							
MDCS							
Barbados	—	0.7	1.4	2.8	4.9	3.4	8.3
Guyana	2.3	—	5.8	4.7	12.8	2.1	14.9
Jamaica	2.8	4.2	—	7.1	14.1	3.9	18.0
Trinidad and Tobago	8.8	17.8	15.3	—	41.9	12.8	54.7
Subtotal	13.9	22.7	22.5	14.6	73.7	22.2	95.9
LDCS	0.6	0.5	0.6	0.9	2.5	1.5	4.1
Total	14.5	23.2	23.1	15.5	76.2	23.7	100.0

... Zero or negligible.
— Not applicable.
Source: Trade publications; East Caribbean Common Market (ECCM) *Annual Digest of Statistics.*

TABLE 2.3. COMPOSITION OF INTRA-CARIFTA EXPORTS OF THE MDCS BY COMMODITY GROUP, 1967–73
(percent)

SITC[a]	Commodity group	Year 1967	Year 1971	Year 1973	1967–73 Average annual growth rate
0	Food	30.8	25.4	22.9	15.0
1	Beverages and tobacco	2.8	2.9	3.4	25.4
	Subtotal	33.6	28.3	26.3	16.0
2	Crude materials	1.7	2.9	0.8	7.5
3	Fuels	28.2	23.1	24.7	18.2
4	Oils and fats	0.4	0.2	0.2	11.0
	Subtotal	30.3	26.2	25.7	17.6
5	Chemicals	17.2	14.7	15.3	18.5
6	Wood, textile, metals	12.1	13.5	13.1	22.5
7	Machinery and transportation equipment	0.3	1.2	2.7	74.4
8	Clothing, footwear, and similar items	6.4	16.0	16.8	42.0
	Subtotal	36.0	45.4	47.9	26.8
9	Miscellaneous	0.1	0.1	0.1	7.9
	Total	100.0	100.0	100.0	20.9

a. Standard International Trade Classification.
Source: Statistical Appendix, Tables SA3.17, SA3.18, SA3.19, and SA3.20.

TABLE 2.4. SHARE OF MANUFACTURES (SITC 5–8) IN TOTAL TRADE OF CARIFTA, 1963–71
(percent)

SITC[a] Category	1963	1967	1971
Share of manufactures in total imports	50	54	55
Share of manufactures in imports from CARIFTA sources	25	33	46
Share of manufactures in total exports	4	10	9
Share of manufactures in exports to CARIFTA destinations	26	34	44

a. Standard International Trade Classification.
Source: Statistical Appendix, Tables SA3.1–3.12, SA3.17–3.20.

TABLE 2.5. RATIOS OF TRADE TO MANUFACTURING OUTPUT, 1963–71
(percent)

Category	1963	1967	1971
CARIFTA imports	8	9	15
Non-CARIFTA imports	269	255	285

Source: Statistical Appendix, Table SA10.11.

The change in the regional structure of protection brought about by CARIFTA has nevertheless probably enhanced the already accelerating intraregional trade in manufactures by eliminating intraregional barriers to trade in manufactured products. A corollary of the new situation is that the growth of intraregional trade is more likely to involve trade creation than trade diversion.

This suggestion merits some explanation. Historically, the CARIFTA countries have imposed high barriers (for protective purposes) on trade in items which they produce and lower barriers (for revenue-raising purposes) on trade in items they import. In such a situation, if barriers are abolished for intraregional trade, but retained for extraregional imports, intraregional trade will be likely to grow most rapidly in products for which barriers were formerly highest, because these are the ones where the new arrangements give the greatest advantages. Thus, those countries already producing a given item (where protection against extraregional imports was, and remains, prohibitive) will enter into competition (trade creation). On the other hand, countries formerly importing a given item will offer a relatively mild extra margin of preference to regional partners as a result of the removal of intraregional barriers, and trade diversion from extraregional to intraregional sources will consequently be minimized. Thus, where the level of national protection against extraregional imports is directly related to the existence of local production (the case with a free trade area rather than a customs union), there appears to be a built-in mechanism to limit the effects of trade diversion away from extraregional imports, and, instead, to create competitive intraregional trade in items which are already produced locally.

This hypothesis finds some limited statistical support in the case of CARIFTA. The countries which already produced manufactured goods (and therefore had imposed the highest protective tariffs against manufactured imports) were the ones which experienced the most rapid rate of market penetration from CARIFTA imports under the new arrangements. Imports from other CARIFTA countries, for example, thus tripled their share of the heavily protected Jamaican and Trinidadian markets for manufactures in the period 1967–71, while they hardly increased their share at all on the ECCM and Barbadian markets.

The growth of the industrial sector in the region is examined in detail in Chapter 7. As far as trade-related growth is concerned, the rate of increase has been most marked in consumer goods already produced in all the MDCs. While positive, if limited, benefits can be expected to flow from this increased competition, the products traded were largely import-dependent and lacking in local linkages.

Since the most obvious benefits from CARIFTA in the first few years have been limited to increasing competition in a small range of manufactured goods, a number of the Association's objectives remain unfulfilled at this stage. In particular, the larger market has not led to new, regionally based industries, to greater sectoral linkages or to a clearly more equitable sharing of benefits. Not surprisingly, the most rapid progress has been made in integrating the manufacturing sector, rather than in the development of agriculture or new basic industries. This is not merely the result of relying on the price mechanism inherent in the trade liberalization effort; it is dictated by the fact that trade liberalization has its most important effects on the previously more highly protected sectors.

Although the achievements of CARIFTA have been small, they have nevertheless been positive. The absence of complementarity (a state of affairs in which one country produces a given item which can be combined, following trade liberalization, with a different item produced by another country to make a new, third, product) has impeded the emergence of new factor combinations at this stage; nevertheless, the integration of economies with similar industrial production structures and demand patterns has helped to strengthen competition among them, reducing the danger of dominance by one or a few firms. The modest achievements of CARIFTA in trade liberalization contrast favorably with the experience of other regional groupings of developing countries; moreover, they must be judged in the light of the comparatively large shifts which are needed to bring about even small changes in the share of intraregional trade in CARIFTA's total trade. Finally, entrepreneurial behavior in the first four or five years of CARIFTA's operation have inevitably been affected by time lags, and although the initial effect of trade liberalization has mainly been felt in the manufacturing sector, the experience has provided a valuable demonstration effect for other sectors.

Deepening the regional integration process

The objective of the Caribbean Community is to deepen the integration process initiated by CARIFTA. Three specific instruments for this purpose have been agreed between member countries since 1973; these will now be considered in turn.

With the signing of the "Treaty Establishing the Caribbean Community" by the four MDCs on 1 August, 1973, CARICOM came into being. The concept of the Community covers functional cooperation,[9] foreign policy coordination, and economic integration, the last named being spelled out in a separate Annex to the Treaty. The components of integration laid down in this annex can be summarized as follows:

a. The creation of an integrated regional market for goods through the adoption of a Common External Tariff (CET) and a Common Protective Policy (CPP).
b. The adoption of joint actions and common policies among member countries in order to promote coordinated regional development. This would include (i) the coordination of national development planning, regional industrial programming, and the rationalization of regional agriculture; (ii) the joint development of regional natural resources and regional cooperation and consultation in monetary, balance of payments

9. Functional cooperation refers to cooperation among the members in the provision of public services such as education, transportation, and meteorological services.

and exchange rate policies; (iii) the harmonization of fiscal incentives to industry; (iv) intraregional tax harmonization and double taxation agreements; (v) the harmonization of commercial legislation including company laws; and (vi) the formulation of a process list as a criterion for the establishment of the origin of goods.

c. Provision for the negotiation of external trade agreements on a joint basis.

d. The formulation of a special regime for the less developed countries, including the creation of the Caribbean Investment Corporation (CIC).

While progress has clearly been made in many of these areas, the critical element of economic policy coordination has yet to be tackled. As yet, only a few preliminary steps have been taken; conferences of regional planners have been held, and a study on regional income and price policy has been commissioned.

The establishment of an agreed Common External Tariff (CET) is a major accomplishment of the Common Market Treaty. By and large, the other trading provisions of the Treaty conform to the CARIFTA Agreement; the major exceptions are a number of new concessions given the LDCs. Thus, rules of origin remain the same, national quota regimes remain intact for the interim period up to at least 1981 (and are only applicable against third countries), and contractual exclusions to the Agreement remain the same (although the transitional period for Reserve List restrictions has been extended five years).[10]

The "Agreement Establishing the Common External Tariff for the Caribbean Common Market" was signed in July 1973, and the CET came into effect for the MDCs in August 1973. A phasing-in period was allowed, however, for sensitive products in certain countries lasting until 1978 or to 1982, as in the case of Barbados.[11] The widespread, but differing, national practices of exempting certain industrial inputs from import duties represent a special problem for the operation of the CET. To overcome this difficulty, the CET Agreement established an Exemptions List of those industries where member countries would continue to allow, on a discretionary basis, duty exemptions for imported inputs. This List is, in fact, a consolidated list of all the nationally exempted industries and covers, therefore, almost every existing industrial activity in the Commonwealth Caribbean.

The basic principle underlying the structure of the CET has been to charge very low rates of duty (from 6 to 8 percent) on the capital goods and raw materials which CARICOM needs for its industries, slightly higher rates on

10. A new origin system was accepted in 1976. This was due to be implemented among the MDCs in January 1978. Regional quantitative restrictions were placed on five products in 1975.

11. As of October 1977, almost all the CET rates had been implemented among the MDCs. Permission has been granted by the CARICOM council to Jamaica to impose higher rates on certain imports (mainly alcoholic beverages) and to Barbados to impose lower rates on certain items (mainly agricultural and fishing inputs).

semimanufactured articles, and the highest rates on final products.[12] Compared with tariffs in developing countries generally, the CET rates are relatively low (about 25 percent on textile fabrics, for example),[13] and are to some extent based on the CET of the ECCM which went into effect in October 1972. Although it is rather more protective than the ECCM tariff, the CARICOM CET nevertheless remains relatively moderate and is designed to protect local industries, with rates which usually represent the average of the individual national MDC tariffs that preceded them. In fact, some 60 percent of the tariff headings remain the same as in the ECCM schedule; the two differ mainly with regard to the more important items in CARICOM trade. The higher rates in the CARICOM CET largely apply to these items (notably canned goods, alcohol and cigarettes,[14] fabrics and garments, furniture, paper articles, bottles, cement, and tires). In addition, some high CARICOM rates have been set on items which do not feature significantly in regional trade; bricks, motorcars, cycles, and television sets are examples. Weighted by the current pattern of LDC imports (the trade of St. Kitts is taken as the example), the CARICOM tariff averages some 19 percent ad valorem as against 14 percent for the ECCM tariff.[15]

The Common Market Treaty includes no immediate, concrete requirements for the harmonization of national quantitative restrictions. Under Article 33 of the Treaty, member countries undertake to administer their quota regulations and to consult on harmonization with a view to attaining common regional quantitative restriction as soon as possible after 1981. The undertaking is, thus, neither very strong nor binding. This is entirely to be expected because of the very large differences in national quota regulations. These differences, combined with those of the Exemptions List provisions, make for a regional trade regime which is not very rigorous: discretionary national exemptions on inputs on the one hand, and different degrees of quantitative protection on output on the other, clearly mean that there is common protection neither of inputs nor of output.

An important consequence of this situation has been the need for rules-of-origin, or agreed-process lists. These are not required in a bona fide common market where, once a product has entered any part of the Common

12. For representative rates, see Statistical Appendix, Table SA10.5.

13. In restructuring the CET in 1975 (implemented January 1976), an attempt was made to make the tariff more protective. Chapter 7 examines whether the CET grants enough protection for promising local products, and whether low rates on capital goods constitute a bias in favor of capital-intensive techniques.

14. Alcohol and cigarettes are among the principal items facing specific tariffs. The ad valorem equivalent of CARICOM's specific tariffs is a good deal higher than most of the ad valorem tariffs.

15. This comparison, which includes the effect of duty-free CARIFTA imports, excludes Standard International Trade Classification (SITC) 1 (beverages and tobacco products) because of the very high specific CARICOM rate associated with this section. If SITC 1 is included, the averages become 15 percent for the ECCM tariff and 22 percent for the CARICOM tariff.

Market and paid the Common External Tariff, it is allowed to circulate freely.

Article 14 of the Annex to the CARICOM Treaty established rules of origin for the region in its first paragraph. They stipulate that for goods to be treated as of Common Market origin they must:

"(a) have been wholly produced within the Common Market;
"(b) fall within a description of goods listed in a Process List to be established by the decision of Council and have been produced within the Common Market by the appropriate qualifying process described in that List; or
"(c) have been produced within the Common Market and the value of any materials imported from outside the Common Market are of undetermined origin which have been used at any stage of the production of the goods does not exceed
 "(i) in a Less Developed Member Country 60 percent of the export price of the goods;
 "(ii) in any other Member State 50 percent of the export price of the goods."

In order that Article 14 be applied, the following complementary rules were provided:

"(i) Materials listed in the Basic Materials List, which forms the Appendix to Schedule II to the Annex, which have been used in the state described in that List in process of production within the Common Market, shall be deemed to contain no element from outside the Common Market;
"(ii) The terms 'produced' and 'process of production' include the application of any operation or process, with the exception of any operation or process which consists only of one or more of the following:
 "(a) packing, wherever the packing materials may have been produced;
 "(b) splitting up into lots;
 "(c) sorting and grading;
 "(d) marking;
 "(e) putting up into sets.
"(iii) 'Materials' includes products, parts and components used in the production of the goods;
"(iv) The values generally to be used for the calculation of the percentages laid down in the Article are c.i.f. value accepted by Customs authorities for the imported materials and the f.o.b. price for the exported goods."

Until January 1978 only the criteria in subparagraphs (a) and (c) of paragraph 1 of Article 14 were applied. The Process List referred to in subparagraph (b) was not introduced until that date. The concept has changed and the Treaty had to be amended to accommodate the new criterion. Under this new origin system the process criterion replaces the other qualifying criteria although within the process criterion and pending further studies, some products still qualify on the basis of value added (the percentage value added has been lowered on some items and the Basic Materials List eliminated). It is expected that the introduction of the new origin rules, based largely on the process criterion, will do more than merely streamline the application of the change-in-classification rule. Under the new system, it should be easier than it had previously been to achieve other objectives, such as inducing producers to use only certain regional materials and specific manufacturing processes.

A regional value-added requirement of 50 percent, the level laid down in Article 14 (c) (ii), is high by the standards of average levels of national and regional value added in MDC industries. Largely because of the Basic Materials List, it is estimated that the actual local value-added component has been about 25 to 35 percent of final output value. It is possible, of course, that some industries adding less than 50 percent of value have been adding this value efficiently, while many of those adding 50 percent or more have only been able to do so because of high levels of effective protection (that is, protection allowing domestic value added to exceed world value added).[16] Thus, the manner in which the percentage value-added rule has been designed and applied may have been conducive to inefficient production; it is hoped that the addition of the Process List as the origin criterion will partially alleviate this problem.

The "Agreement on the Harmonization of Fiscal Incentives to Industry" was signed in July 1973 by all the MDCs and now covers all twelve CARICOM countries. The signatories undertook to offer fiscal concessions to industrial investment and exporting under the conditions laid out in the Agreement. The Agreement allows a standard package of investment incentives similar to the various national programs of incentives it replaces (which emphasize tax holidays and duty-free imports of capital goods). A major feature of the new package, however, is a variation in the length of tax holidays offered according to (a) the level of industrialization of the country, and (b) the degree of local or regional value added in the activity qualifying for incentives. The national share of local value added in total sales is increased according to a weighting formula which takes into account the contribution of local labor.[17] Table 2.6 spells out differences in the maximum length of tax holidays according to country and the degree of local value added. Exporting industries of the enclave type (that is, industries producing exclusively for sale in foreign markets, exporting 100 percent of their output)

16. The new harmonized fiscal incentive system, which offers differential incentives according to the degree of local value added, creates parallel problems. The numerical example illustrating these in note 20 to this chapter is equally applicable to the present problem. In this example product A would qualify for area tariff treatment purely by virtue of the greater protection it receives than product B. Hence, although product B saved foreign exchange more efficiently, it would not be able to compete with extra-regional imports in the markets of other countries of the region while product A would.

17. The actual value-added share is multiplied by the ratio of the wage bill for nationals to total sales.

are treated specially; they receive the longest tax holidays. In cases where, as Table 2.6 indicates, activities fall within Groups I, II, or III, but where 100 percent of output is not exported, the MDCs can only offer investment incentives to "pioneer" industries (that is, to those industries where local production accounts for no more than 40 percent of the market in Guyana, Jamaica, and Trinidad, and 10 percent in Barbados). The LDCs do not face this constraint.

The Agreement is to be supplemented by the conclusion of a series of CARICOM double-taxation agreements, which will encourage intraregional investment by ensuring that investments by CARICOM nationals in other CARICOM countries will not be discouraged by unfavorable treatment of repatriated income.[18]

The fiscal incentives agreement represents a hard-fought compromise, and is a real achievement in removing arbitrary distortions. It systematizes differentials between countries and industries, and introduces a formula which provides a modest bias in favor of labor-intensive processes. Some fundamental problems nevertheless remain. There are three areas of special difficulty where current arrangements may actually discourage the most efficient and appropriate forms of industrialization. In the first of these, the whole question of investment incentives is open to objection. This is the case of an industry intended for import substitution, where quantitative restrictions continue to assure investors of viability, but which is also eligible for incentives under present rules. In such a situation, financial incentives to investment represent a source of excess profits or of marginal reductions in the price of output which are not necessarily justifiable in view of the public revenue foregone.

TABLE 2.6 TAX HOLIDAYS PERMITTED UNDER CARICOM REGULATIONS BY COUNTRY AND PERCENTAGE OF LOCAL VALUE ADDED
(maximum number of years)

Percentage of local value added[a]	*Guyana, Jamaica, Trinidad and Tobago*	*Barbados*	ECCM *member state Belize*
Group I (50 and over)	9	10	15
Group II (25 to 50)	7	8	12
Group III (10 to 25)	5	6	10
Enclave industry[b]	10	10	15

a. Percentage of the amount realized from the sales of an approved product.
b. Industry producing exclusively for export to countries outside the common market, and drawing all their material inputs from outside the common market.
Source: "Agreement on the Harmonization of Fiscal Incentives to Industry," (Georgetown, Guyana: CARICOM Secretariat, 1973).

18. From this point of view, a stronger inducement to invest in the LDCs might have been provided by tax concession periods of equal length in all CARICOM countries which ranged, however, from full tax holidays in the LDCs to only partial tax concessions in the most advanced industrial countries (tax concessions on, say, only 20 to 40 percent of income).

The second problem area is that of an industry awarded the maximum tax holiday by an LDC. When this occurs, the government concerned will be foregoing tax revenues for a period of ten to fifteen years; this may be longer than the total lives of some projects. The very idea that longer tax holiday periods give LDCs an advantage in attracting investment may, moreover, be somewhat illusory: entrepreneurs in developing countries tend to operate with short-term horizons (that is, with high discount rates on future earnings); consequently the impact of the extra years of tax holiday on entrepreneurial decisionmaking is significantly lessened.[19]

The third area of difficulty is the provision of differential tax holidays according to the level of local or regional value added. This arrangement is intended both to promote industries with substantial proportions of value added and to encourage local or regional sectoral linkages. As in the case of the rules-of-origin criteria, however, there has been a notable absence of emphasis on efficiency. Thus, the effect of high levels of protection may be to inflate the level of local value added to a point where the maximum tax holiday becomes justified, though very little value is in fact being added at world prices.[20]

The 1973 Agreement represents a first attempt at harmonization. In the longer term, CARICOM may review it with a view to introducing efficiency criteria by relating local value added to world value-added levels. Meanwhile, the sanction on efficiency is still, as it has been in the past, the judgment of the individual governments; they can set the levels of incentives on the basis of various criteria, one of which is efficiency (however defined). The removal of the distorting consequences of different levels of effective protection requires governments to give less than the maximum incentive to overprotected industries.

19. To date only the inter-MDC/LDC agreement (1973) has been completed. Work on the intra-MDC and intra-LDC agreements has been proceeding very slowly.

20. A hypothetical numerical example can illustrate this effect. In terms of world prices, the two products A and B below have identical cost structures in which value added is only 37.5 percent of the final value of output ("world price"). The protection on product A permits local production at 25 percent above world prices and local value added at 67 percent above world value added (assuming no duty on imported inputs). The "excess" value added, in turn, makes product A eligible to receive the maximum rate of tax holiday since, in local prices, value added constitutes 50 percent of output value (Group I in Table 2.6). Product B, with only 12 percent of protection is only allowed 33 percent "excess" value added; this, in turn, only qualifies it for Table 2.6's Group II tax holiday treatment, as value added in local prices is only 44 percent of output. Thus product B gets less favorable treatment because it saves foreign exchange more efficiently than A (that is, the rate of effective protection for B is half that for A).

		Product A	*Product B*
World price:	inputs	50	50
	value added (dollars)	30	30
	world price (dollars)	80	80
	tariff (percent)	25	12.5
	landed price (dollars)	100	90

The above points are intended only to qualify, not to deny, the effectiveness with which the new incentives system can be expected to encourage linkages. At the same time, some aspects of the overall system, notably the concessions on imported inputs in the Agreement, together with the Exemptions List, will continue to encourage the use of imported inputs.

In addition to the three instruments discussed above, tax concessions on exports were introduced in 1973. This common approach to export incentives is a significant new departure for the Commonwealth Caribbean countries, replacing specific export incentive laws in the case of Barbados and Jamaica, and minor concessions in the case of Trinidad. The new export concession is the same for all CARICOM member countries and consists of a partial rebate of tax paid on income from exports. The rebate is proportionate to the share of export profits in total profits. That is, when export profits are, respectively, 10–20 percent, 21–40 percent, 41–60 percent, or over 60 percent of total profits the corresponding rebates of income tax are, respectively, 25 percent, 35 percent, 45 percent, and 50 percent of the tax on export profits.

The new incentives, like the investment incentives, present several potential problems. They do not apply to firms already enjoying tax holidays with investment incentives. Unless certain export performance conditions are attached to the granting of investment incentives therefore, newly investing "pioneer" firms do not have an incentive to export. (Such conditions could be imposed under existing regulations.) In addition, the maximum value of the tax credit to exporters may not, in many cases, represent a very substantial rate of subsidy. According to the formula for the calculation of the tax credit, a firm deriving more than 60 percent of its profits from exports would, with a pretax return on sales of 20 percent, and a corporation tax rate of 50 percent, receive a tax credit equivalent to 5 percent of the value of export sales. On labor-intensive products—and for "infant" exporting activities in general—20 percent is usually considered a very high rate of return on export sales. The effective overall subsidy rate is likely to be even lower. For a firm deriving only 10–20 percent of its sales from exports, a 20 percent return on sales would yield the equivalent of only 2.5 percent of the value of export sales. Other developing countries which are beginning to promote industrial exports have distinctly higher rates of subsidy. The CARICOM formula, of course, encourages those firms which export the largest proportion of their total output; by the same token, it does not encourage firms to engage in marginal exporting, especially exporting on the basis of spare capacity. Apart from the special case of the 100 percent exporting firms of the enclave type, this is

---

Local price:	inputs (tariff free, all imported)	50	50
	value added (dollars)	50	40
	local price (dollars)	100	90
Effective protection (excess of local over world value added, percent)		67	33

precisely the basis on which a great number of firms in developing countries might be expected to begin to export.

The experience of the CARICOM countries to date, in expanding and extending their trade relations, and the regulations governing those relations, shows that real progress has been made, if at a relatively modest pace, and with certain anomalies in the specific provisions of the various regulations. Another important area in which the countries of the region are currently making progress towards integration through institutional arrangements is that of monetary affairs. Developments in this area are discussed in the next section.

Monetary and Fiscal Cooperation

The members of CARICOM engage in a modest but nevertheless valuable degree of monetary cooperation. The Windward and Leeward islands participate jointly in the Eastern Caribbean Currency Authority (ECCA),[21] which issues the Eastern Caribbean dollar (EC$) used in the small islands. Guyana, Jamaica, Trinidad and Tobago, and Barbados all have separate currency-issuing central banks. Belize has its own Currency Authority. The ECCA, the central banks and the Belizean Currency Authority operate a series of bilateral arrangements for intraregional financial transactions, and have agreed to establish mutual balance of payments support facilities to enable individual countries to economize on their holdings of foreign exchange reserves. The trend towards greater financial cooperation has also been strengthened by the MDCs' decision to provide additional medium-term loans for Jamaica, which has been facing serious economic difficulties.

There are two main issues to be decided upon in the field of monetary and fiscal cooperation. These are the degree of capital mobility to be allowed within the Community, and the amount of exchange rate stability which should be sought between member countries. This second question became a major issue in the post–1973 period of economic turbulence, but later virtually corrected itself as the various countries of the Community untied their currencies' links to sterling and began pegging them to the U.S. dollar. The Eastern Caribbean dollar and the Belize dollar, switched from a sterling to a U.S. dollar peg in mid-1976. The source of the problem—the ability of national governments to change their intervention currency—nevertheless remained.

A survey of Caribbean monetary and fiscal cooperation must also examine the special efforts which are being made to channel extra financial resources to the less developed small islands. The two institutions chiefly involved in these efforts are the Caribbean Development Bank (CDB), founded in 1969, and the established Caribbean Investment Corporation (CIC), established in 1973. The region has also established a special emergency fund to help finance a number of common services for the small islands.

21. Barbados withdrew from ECCA to establish its own central bank, and issued its own currency towards the end of 1973.

Fiscal harmonization in the region has mainly consisted of the conclusion of agreements to avoid double taxation of individuals and firms operating in more than one country of the Community. Discussions are now under way to find means of removing the other fiscal and legal barriers which currently hinder the operation of regional companies. In addition, some agreement has been reached on the harmonization of incentives to industry.

Monetary cooperation: existing and alternative arrangements

A number of agreements have already been reached to reduce the cost of the financial transactions which CARICOM members undertake with one another, and to economize on countries' holdings of international reserves. The central banks, ECCA, and the Belizean Currency Authority have agreed to exchange the notes and coins of other member states at par without exchange commissions[22] and, since 1969, special arrangements have been in force for payments between member countries. These have taken the form of a series of bilateral agreements between member countries, whereby each monetary authority grants a line of credit to other members, which can be drawn on to make day-to-day payments needed for intraregional trade. Initially, the lines of credit were uniform for all countries regardless of the volume of trade between any two members of the agreements. Each credit limit consisted of a noninterest-bearing portion of £ sterling 100,000 (US$180,620) and an additional £400,000 (US$722,480) on which interest was charged. Settlements of the credits were usually made quarterly in sterling or U.S. dollars.

The arrangements reduced transaction costs in a modest but useful way; they also permitted some small reduction in members' reserve holdings, by minimizing the use of international currencies in intraregional payments.

The arrangement was modified in 1976 by relating credits to intraregional trade flows, and by increasing the volume of credit to £20 million (roughly US$36 million), which was equivalent to about 20 percent of intraregional imports for 1974. In 1977, it was agreed to merge the network of bilateral credits into a multilateral clearing arrangement (intraregional clearing house). One effect of the new arrangement is to significantly increase the net credit provided by Trinidad and Tobago, which is a large net exporter to the rest of the region. A second effect is the additional advantage that a given country's net surplus with one partner could be used to offset its net deficit with another. Only the overall regional deficits would have to be settled in sterling or U.S. dollars, thereby economizing on scarce foreign exchange. The potential savings from such a proposal should not be exaggerated, however, since intraregional exports only account for around 7 percent of total CARICOM trade.

A more significant reduction in reserve holdings is likely to be achieved by the "safety net" arrangements agreed in 1976 between Barbados, Guyana,

22. Jamaica and Guyana no longer permit the encashment of their notes and coin in other countries; Trinidad and Tobago restricts such encashment to TT$50 (US$25) for each individual. (For exchange rates see Statistical Appendix, Table SA11.20.)

Jamaica, and Trinidad and Tobago. These arrangements are temporary in nature, intended to last for five years, or until the introduction of a more permanent agreement, and are designed to provide mutual balance of payments support for members. The "safety net" facility consists of a series of commitments to provide finance to any member in balance of payments difficulties; unlike a stabilization fund—such as the International Monetary Fund (IMF)—which involves an initial contribution of capital by its members, no finance is provided under the "safety net" until a borrowing request is received. The basis for determining a member's share in the financing of loans and the amount it may borrow under the facility is provided by its quota. Expressed in Special Drawing Rights million,[23] these are as follows: Barbados, 4.0; Guyana, 6.0; Jamaica, 22.0; Trinidad and Tobago, 28.0; for a total of 60.0

The limit of a member's borrowing is 200 percent of its quota, and the maximum duration of loans is five years. All loans made under the facility are to be financed either by direct transfers from other members (up to a maximum of 50 percent of their quotas), or by raising loans to be guaranteed collectively by members up to the value of their quotas.

It has not yet been decided whether any permanent arrangement will take the form of an extension of the above scheme, or whether it will involve a fully fledged stabilization fund with initial equity contributions by the members and a full-time staff charged with ensuring that borrowers pursue appropriate economic polices to regain balance of payments equilibrium. One of the main advantages of such a fund would be that its equity base and well-defined legal position would permit it to borrow relatively easily on international capital markets. This would be a significant improvement on the existing arrangement, which provides for the "collective guarantee" of loans raised by the facility. Such a guarantee contains an element of vagueness as to who is ultimately responsible for repayment of the loan, which could inhibit potential lenders. (It would, of course, be possible to correct this problem without establishing a separate fund if the various central banks were each to assume sole responsibility for different parts of any proposed loan—a modification which has already been proposed within the region.)

The basic principle of the existing "swap" arrangements, or of any alternative to them involving a stabilization fund, is to reduce aggregate holdings of reserves, relying on the assumption that not all member countries will need to draw on reserves at the same time. While this assumption is acceptable as an underlying principle, there are problems associated with the calculation of its benefits in practice; reserves may be held for purely psychological reasons such as to generate confidence in local monetary authorities. A rough attempt can nevertheless be made to measure the likely economies based on the historical pattern of reserve use in the community.

Table 2.7 presents, by quarters, details on seasonal reserve fluctuations for Guyana, Jamaica, and Trinidad. The final column in Table 2.7 depicts

23. As of June 1977 1 SDR = US$1.17.

TABLE 2.7. QUARTERLY RESERVE VARIATIONS BY COUNTRY, 1969–73
(millions of U.S. dollars)

	Quarter				
Country	*I*	*II*	*III*	*IV*	*Range*
Guyana	−2.4	−2.8	−2.0	+5.4	8.2
Jamaica	+27.4	−5.9	−13.8	−6.2	41.2
Trinidad	−2.5	+4.8	−1.7	−0.7	7.3
Pooled	+22.5	−3.9	−17.6	−1.6	40.1
Unpooled					56.7

Note: See text discussion.
Source: International Financial Statistics, International Monetary Fund.

the range of fluctuation over the year for each country and for nationally pooled reserves. A simple addition of the individual country ranges gives the range of fluctuations corresponding to all countries with reserves unpooled. The lower the ratio of pooled to unpooled ranges, the higher the potential for finding economies in the use of reserves by exploiting different patterns of seasonal variations in country reserve movements. In this case the ratio is 0.71, which suggests that if reserves had been pooled the range of fluctuation experienced by a joint fund would have been 29 percent less than the sum of that experienced by individual countries. This, in turn, means that pooling permits some saving in the use of reserves to deal with seasonal variations in foreign exchange receipts and expenditures.[24]

This saving is relatively modest. Even if we regarded the new "swap" arrangements as equivalent to a complete pooling of reserves, the reserve saving would amount to only US$17 million which represents 7 percent of the average reserve holding of US$233 million during these years. This calculation depends crucially on the expected pattern of country seasonal variations, however, and the 1969–73 experience may present a more conservative picture than can be expected in the future.[25]

The potential savings in reserves due to longer term complementarities in payments positions are analyzed, for Guyana, Jamaica, and Trinidad and Tobago, in Table 2.8. This sets out, for each country, the average reserves held each year, and the year-to-year changes in them. The reserve gains and losses are then accumulated. To the extent that gains balance losses, there is scope for economizing on the use of reserves by institutionalizing intercountry reserve credits, such as "swaps." These overlaps between reserve gains and

24. The methodology is admittedly crude. Ideally, the quarterly variations should first be corrected for the trend component. This was not possible, given the lack of data.

25. For example, if the 1969–71 data were used as a basis for projection, the estimated saving would have been twice as great, because the ratio of pooled to unpooled reserves was only 0.46.

losses are shown in Table 2.8 as "mutually compensable payments." Inspection of Table 2.8 reveals that between 1969 and 1974 the scope for mutually compensable payments was rather small because the annual reserve changes experienced by the three countries tended to move in phase. Available 1975 data for Jamaica and Trinidad indicate, however, that the "swap" arrangements might help the economies of the oil-importing countries to make a more orderly adjustment to the new oil prices.

If the experience gained between 1969 and 1975 is used as a basis for prediction, then the potential economies to be achieved by a "swap" arrangement based on offsetting country reserve movements (whether quarterly or annually), would appear to be a modest US$20 to 30 million. This estimate is, however, based on historic data and should therefore be treated cautiously. The emphasis so far, moreover, has been on the transactions motive for holding reserves. The new arrangements may also lead to economies in the precautionary requirements.

The "safety net" facility was used when Barbados, Guyana, and Trinidad extended short-term balance of payments support of approximately US$25 million to Jamaica as part of the "Port-of-Spain Agreement" of 1976. At the same time, Jamaica was also to be provided with approximately US$55 million of longer term budgetary support. Trinidad was the major lender under both parts of the agreement.

TABLE 2.8. ANNUAL RESERVE GAINS AND LOSSES AND MUTUALLY COMPENSABLE PAYMENTS, BY COUNTRY, 1968–75
(millions of U.S. dollars)

Country	*1968*	*1969*	*1970*	*1971*	*1972*	*1973*	*1974*	*1975*
Guyana								
Average reserve	19.49	20.28	17.89	18.73	30.26	21.58	47.50	n.a.
Change	—	−0.79	−2.39	+0.84	+11.53	−8.68	+26.08	n.a.
Jamaica								
Average reserve	135.20	126.80	150.40	171.20	179.70	160.60	187.00	154.8
Change	—	−8.40	+23.60	+20.80	+8.50	−19.10	+26.40	−32.2
Trinidad and Tobago								
Average reserve	44.70	47.00	42.30	60.40	72.90	47.10	200.50	511.0
Change	—	+2.30	−4.70	+18.10	+12.50	−25.80	+153.40	+310.5
All countries								
Reserve gains	—	+2.30	+23.60	+39.70	+32.50	0.00	+205.90	+310.5
Reserve losses	—	−9.20	−7.10	0.00	0.00	−53.60	0.00	−32.2
Net change	—	−6.90	+16.50	+39.70	+32.50	−53.60	+205.90	+178.3
Mutually compensable payments	—	+2.30	+7.10	0.00	0.00	0.00	0.00	+32.2

n.a. Not available.
— Not applicable.
Source: International Financial Statistics, International Monetary Fund.

The Eastern Caribbean Currency Authority (ECCA)

The ECCA[26] was established in 1965 following the decision of the two major participants, Trinidad and Tobago, and Guyana, to establish their own central banks and the consequent dissolution of the British Caribbean Currency Board (BCCB). The BCCB had exemplified a typical colonial currency board operating as a passive money changer, issuing or redeeming BCCB currency for sterling on demand. By contrast, ECCA was established with fairly wide powers. Under its regulations it can engage in a fiduciary issue of up to 30 percent of its demand obligations; purchase, sell, and discount a wide range of bills; purchase and sell long-term bonds of eastern Caribbean governments and government-approved enterprises; and grant ninety-day advances to commercial banks.

The ECCA still falls well short of being a full-fledged central bank, however, largely because of the dependent economic status of the small islands, but partly also because it has not made much use of the powers at its disposal. On the other hand, the Authority does face the problem that it can exert very little direct control over monetary and credit conditions. It cannot impose reserve requirements or quantitative credit controls on the commercial banks. Further, although it has the necessary prerequisites for an open market policy (in that it can buy and sell government securities), the thinness of the securities market and the strong borrowing and lending links between the local banks and their head offices have thoroughly inhibited the development of any such policy. On the other hand, ECCA could influence the money supply through increased use of its fiduciary issue powers, especially since currency constitutes roughly one half of the money supply in the islands. In practice, however, it has made virtually no use of the fiduciary issue and, since its establishment, has maintained external asset backing for more than 95 percent of its outstanding currency obligations. In the absence of deliberate action by ECCA, the level of the money supply in the islands has thus been determined by the net result of the balance of payments on current and capital account and autonomous credit activity by the commercial banks.

The Authority's impact on the mobilization and allocation of financial resources in the region has also been limited. Its main role in the mobilization of resources had been the purely passive one of assuring convertibility between the E.C. dollar and the pound sterling (until July 1976), and the U.S. dollar (since that time). Convertibility has undoubtedly helped to encourage private foreign investment, but it has also permitted the free movement of domestic financial savings; until recently, this led to an outflow of domestic savings from the region. The asset portfolio decisions of local branch banks have reflected the creditworthiness criteria of the Anglo-Saxon banking tradition, which stress collateral requirements more than the potential profitability of a project. Given these criteria, the local banks have found eligible local investment opportunities severely limited and have historically tended

26. Membership consists of the Windward and Leeward islands and, until 1973, Barbados.

to send abroad a proportion of their local net deposits. Recently, however, these exports of capital have stopped; a significant amount of excess funds has been placed with ECCA, and issues of government securities have both increased sharply and have been purchased by the banks as suitable vehicles for investment. In case the tendency toward net capital exports should reappear in the future, ECCA could nevertheless usefully be granted explicit authority to impose local asset ratio requirements on commercial banks and other financial institutions.

Although it has the legal authority to rediscount private loans, ECCA has not as yet used this power to affect the distribution of commercial bank credit between sectors of the economy because, until recently, the commercial banks' local deposits were much larger than were the opportunities for local investment permitted by their lending criteria. In such a lax monetary situation, the offer of favorable rediscounts from ECCA would have been unlikely to have generated a significant response, especially since branch banks had easy access to loans from their head offices. Recent changes in the financial environment suggest, however, that the rediscount instrument should be seriously considered by ECCA for future operations. Net balances held abroad by the local banks have fallen sharply since 1971 and the high nominal interest rates prevailing in the overseas financial centers now make local rediscount facilities much more attractive to the banks.

The power to make fiduciary issues could be used to free some resources for a selective rediscount facility. In 1974 ECCA held approximately EC$55 million (US$27.5 million) of external assets; if the full 30 percent fiduciary issue were used, the resources available for domestic use would be EC$16 million (US$8 million). This once and for all increase is small compared with, say, the annual flow of investment expenditure of EC$120 million (US$60 million) in 1971, but it would permit ECCA to begin exerting a more positive influence on domestic credit allocation. Channeling the new resources selectively through the commercial banks, rather than using them to purchase government securities, would help to make the banks aware of the sectoral priorities of member governments. It would also help to forge links between ECCA and the commercial banks, a necessary precondition for any future evolution of the Authority into a central banking institution.

If ECCA is to make greater use of fiduciary issues it will have to establish guidelines for the interterritorial allocation of its new resources. Perhaps the best solution would be to allocate resources so as to achieve the greatest expansion in output and employment. Because such an allocation may favor some islands over others, it is unlikely to be politically acceptable. The next best method of allocation would be to advance resources in proportion to the net total of currency issued in each island. The Authority could then set down the broad range of terms and maturities under which these advances could be offered, but a financial authority in each island would have to have the specific power to determine which sectors or classes of bank loans would be eligible for rediscount. Such an arrangement would devolve selective authority to the governments of the islands, each of which may have different sectoral priorities. Since ECCA is not in a position to take a serious part in financial resource planning (a prerogative of island governments), it would be inappropriate for it arbitrarily to select sectors eligible for rediscount.

Intraregional capital mobility

CARICOM differs sharply from the European Economic Community model in that unregulated intraregional flows of capital are implicitly discouraged. Instead, the emphasis is on exploring and expanding regulated flows of capital within the region. This emphasis is based on the fear that free intraregional capital flows would entail a movement of capital away from the poorer territories to the more developed ones. Economic theory might suggest that the capital flow would work the other way, towards the lower-wage countries, but practical considerations such as government policies, size of market, and quality of infrastructure, frequently outweigh the considerations of relative prices of factors of production enshrined in classical static economics.

At present, the three largest MDCs and Barbados all operate global exchange controls against capital movements to other Community members, as well as against countries outside the Community. Even without the intra-Community restrictions, free capital flows would not be possible unless all CARICOM members were to impose uniform exchange controls against extraregional countries. The ECCM territories have legislative authority to operate exchange control regulations, but differing practices among the member states render such controls ineffective. Until the region has a uniform and effective exchange control system, the most probable result of free intraregional capital flows would be a movement of capital out of the region altogether.

Attempts are being made, however, to liberalize intraregional capital flows, within the framework of existing national exchange controls, especially in the case of flows from the MDCs to the LDCs. Thus, double taxation agreements have been worked out between MDCs and LDCs as groups, and intragroup arrangements are in the process of being agreed. These provide for arrangements to protect regional companies from double taxation. There is also a move to reform the various "alien laws," which inhibit the flow of funds between member countries, so that nationals of other CARICOM countries would be on an equal footing with nationals of any given member country with regard to the purchase of assets within that country. In this connection, the creation of a new legal framework for companies which operate throughout the region has been agreed within CARICOM. One of the main advantages of such a framework would be the recognition of the legal personality of CARICOM enterprises across borders. This would enable such companies to avoid both the duplication of fees and the restrictions involved by alien landholding legislation. These restrictions usually apply not only to land but also to both direct and portfolio investment. National legislation on local asset ratios of financial institutions such as insurance companies is also being amended (for example, in Trinidad) to permit the inclusion of extranational investments in the CARICOM region within the definition of "local." Jamaica has permitted companies incorporated elsewhere in CARICOM, but with subsidiaries in Jamaica, to borrow and transfer funds from Jamaica, even though this exposes the island to the risk of some capital lending abroad to the sterling area via the LDCs. A number of institutions, such as the Caribbean Development Bank (CDB) and the Caribbean Investment Corporation (CIC), have also been established to channel funds from the MDCs to the LDCs. These are discussed in more detail below.

Exchange rate policy

The role of the exchange rate and the degree of intraregional exchange rate stability have been the subject of lively discussion in the Caribbean in recent years. The predominant view seems to favor fixed exchange rates between member countries. Thus, the Community Treaty states that "exchange rate stability between the Member States is necessary to promote the smooth functioning of the Common Market." Individual parity changes by a member country are basically seen as disturbances of the agreed ground rules of a common protective policy.

Before the issue of intraregional parities is examined, however, certain features of the CARICOM economies need to be remembered:

a. the share of intraregional trade in the total trade of member countries is comparatively small, varying from 5 to 9 percent;
b. intraregional labor mobility is quite low, and is unlikely to improve dramatically, since free movement of labor is not part of the CARICOM Treaty;
c. the Treaty's desire for stable intraregional exchange disparities is best described as a "pseudo-exchange-rate union." Member states will retain autonomous control over monetary policy and over the use of their international reserves for the foreseeable future.

Given these factors, it is likely that differing rates of change in internal wages and prices, external shifts in product demand, changes in the production decisions of multinational corporations and a host of other factors are likely to affect member countries differently. There is no guarantee that—in the case of economies as open as those of the CARICOM countries, where extraregional transactions dominate the national balance of payments—any particular "regional exchange rate" would simultaneously satisfy the requirements of different countries.

At present, the Treaty envisages recourse to nationally imposed quantitative restrictions for the purpose of safeguarding the balance of payments during temporary exchange rate fluctuations. In case of more fundamental balance of payments disequilibria, CARICOM countries will probably still have to rely on explicit changes in national exchange rates undertaken after appropriate consultation with other CARICOM members. The adjustment of exchange rates should be considered as a potentially powerful measure in support of structural change. In countries with large petroleum or mineral exports, an effective downward adjustment of the exchange rate may be necessary to restore the competitiveness of the nonmineral or nonpetroleum sectors in relation to external markets. Although the distortions in the structures of wages, prices, and costs are not so sharp in countries without large petroleum or mineral exports, these countries would also secure long run benefits from an adjustment in their exchange rates. Both the continued upward pressures on the cost of living throughout the region and the powerful forces pushing wages and prices upwards in most CARICOM member countries mean that any adjustment in the exchange rate of a given country must be properly timed, gradual, and carried out within an appropriate framework of incomes policy.

Finance for the LDCs

It is an objective of CARICOM policy to provide special assistance to the less developed members of the Community. To this end, a number of institutions have been established to channel financial resources to the LDCs. The most important of these is the Caribbean Development Bank (CDB), established in 1969 in order to "contribute to the harmonious economic development of the Caribbean countries, and to promote economic cooperation and integration among them, paying special and urgent attention to the region's less developed members."[27] The CDB's operations are classified into two main groups: the ordinary (loans bearing an interest rate of 8 to 10 percent and with a term of ten to fifteen years) and the special (loans bearing an interest rate of 4 percent, for fourteen to twenty years). Loans to the MDCs and to the private sector in the LDCs fall into the first category, while loans to LDC governments belong to the second.

The CDB's main sources of funds are the initial equity contributions by its regional members, together with financing from Canada and the United Kingdom (which are extraregional members), and from the United States and West Germany. Venezuela and Colombia have also recently become members. Trinidad, in addition to its equity contributions, has also made a loan of roughly US$5 million, in turn to be loaned to the LDCs at a low interest rate. This loan is designed to help finance the local costs of CDB projects which are not normally covered by external aid. During 1976, the CDB's ordinary resources were increased, funds having been obtained from the Japan Export-Import Bank ($6.7 million), the World Bank ($20 million) and two-year bond issues to regional central banks ($10 million).

Total approved loans by the CDB, as of June 1977, amounted to US$123 million, of which US$70 million (57 percent) had been allocated for national or regional projects in the CARICOM LDCs (the ECCM countries and Belize). By the end of June 1977, disbursements had attained a satisfactory level; almost 50 percent of cumulative loan approvals had been disbursed. Over the years, funds have been provided for projects in a wide range of

27. In addition to Belize and the ECCM countries, these include the British Virgin Islands, the Cayman Islands, and the Turks and Caicos Islands, which are outside CARICOM.

sectors. Somewhat less than one-half of total lending has been for infrastructure; an increasing share of lending has recently been allocated to projects in the directly productive sectors of agriculture, tourism, and manufacturing. Loan approvals for regional (as opposed to national) projects reached US$14 million or 11 percent of this cumulative total in mid-1977, with the approval of two new regional projects—a second "trunk route" ship for the West Indies Shipping Corporation (WISCO) and a loan for the Caribbean Investment Corporation (CIC).

The Caribbean Investment Corporation was established in 1973 with the aim of promoting manufacturing and agro-industrial enterprises in the LDCs, thereby complementing CDB assistance to the LDCs by encouraging the flow of private investment. The Corporation provides medium- and long-term development finance for suitable projects, primarily by subscribing to the equity of the firm concerned, but also through long-term loans or by providing guarantees for suppliers' credits. It was originally intended to have a capital value of EC$15 million (US$7.5 million) with shares to be issued over the first five years, of which 60 percent was to be subscribed by governments of the region and 40 percent by the private sector. Only about half of the projected private sector subscriptions were raised, however, and the Corporation has now borrowed EC$3 million (US$1.5 million) from CDB to supplement its resources.

By December 1975, CIC had approved approximately EC$1.29 million (US$645,000) of investments whose average size was just under EC$100,000 (US$50,000). Most investments have been in the manufacturing sector, covering an extensive selection of products including footwear, garments, printing, brewing and bottling. It is significant that the output of nearly all the enterprises supported is geared to supplying not only their respective local markets, but also the larger CARICOM market. Thus, although the Corporation's activities are still on a very small scale, it can nevertheless help the LDCs to secure benefits from the expanded CARICOM market.

International economic trends over the last few years have adversely affected the LDCs. Rapid increases in the prices of many traded goods have led to very high rates of imported inflation in these countries and a very sharp deterioration in their terms of trade, with a consequent reduction of real income and real purchasing power. If the LDCs had independent monetary systems, they would now be experiencing severe balance of payments crises, but the nature of their monetary arrangements has led the crisis to manifest itself in the form of severe government liquidity constraints. At the suggestion of the Secretary General of CARICOM, the MDCs and the United Kingdom helped establish the "Fund for Emergency Programme Assistance and for Common Services" for the Leeward and Windward islands to help alleviate these liquidity difficulties. As an interim measure for 1976, approximately EC$10 million were contributed to the fund; a study is under way to establish it on a five-year basis. Although the current critical financial situation is the direct result of specific recent events, the crisis has exposed more general, long-term weaknesses in the fiscal, economic, and administrative structures of the small islands. Consequently, the emergency financial aid which the region has mobilized for the LDCs is designed to help the small islands attack some of their underlying problems by making fundamental improvements in their fiscal and development planning systems, rather than simply to help them finance a temporarily higher level of imports.

The governments of the region have proposed the creation of a special fund which would be used to finance the establishment and operations of common services for the Leeward and Windward islands. This would provide the specialized expertise required in the region while economizing on scarce supplies of money and skilled manpower. The particular group of common services to be financed has not yet been finally agreed, but will probably include such activities of common importance to the islands as tax administration, development planning, public administration, and specialized engineering services. During its first year, the proposed fund will be financed through loans on concessional terms from the MDCs totaling EC$5 million (US$2.5 million), matched by an equal amount in grants from the United Kingdom.

Fiscal harmonization

Fiscal harmonization within the Community so far has covered double taxation agreements and arrangements for fiscal incentives to manufacturing industry (discussed earlier in this chapter); harmonization of incentives to agriculture and tourism are also under discussion.[28]

The recent double taxation agreement negotiated between the MDCs and the LDCs should be of special benefit to the latter. Under this agreement, the LDCs can impose their full rates of income tax on interest payments made to MDCs, while concessional rates of tax are levied on dividend and interest payments made by the MDCs to the LDCs. To ensure that the tax inducements granted by the LDCs are not nullified by the policies of the MDCs, the agreement provides that when a company resident in an LDC distributes profits to residents of MDCs from profits exempt from tax in the former under an incentive scheme, this distribution will also be exempt in the receiving country.[29] The agreement to ensure that the flow of capital from MDCs to LDCs is thus not impeded by tax considerations, and also improves the small islands' revenue prospects.

The possibility of achieving greater uniformity in income tax regulations for both individuals and companies is also under study. This is a complex area of policy in which the objective of uniformity needs to be pursued in

28. See also Nizar Jetha and Norali Peera, "Tax Structure and Policy in the Windward and Leeward Islands of the Caribbean Community," Bulletin of International Fiscal Documentation, vol. XXI (May 1977), pp. 209–18, for further details on the tax structures of the small islands.

29. See "Agreement for the Avoidance of Double Taxation and the Prevention of Fiscal Evasion with respect to Taxes and Income and for the Encouragement of International Trade and Investment," (Georgetown, Guyana: CARICOM Secretariat, 1976) for further details.

the light of the higher objective of efficiency. For example, it is desirable to eliminate unnecessary differences in regulations in order to avoid the wasteful use of resources, but because national revenue requirements differ widely, every country should retain a number of independent tax sources whose rates can be altered by each member country in line with its own revenue needs.

The process of harmonization, moreover, should not be confused with standardization of rates of tax. There is a great deal to be said for standardizing income tax legislation, but uniform personal income tax rates, and allowances throughout the region would not be desirable. Given the substantial disparities between countries in levels of per capita income, distribution of incomes and structures of production, tax rates and personal allowances appropriate for one country are unlikely to reflect the needs of another. If a country with relatively low per capita income adopts personal allowances prevailing in a country with relatively high per capita income, then the former's ratio of income tax collections to gross domestic product (GDP) would thus be much lower than the latter's. Further, uniform rates of personal taxation have little or no positive economic effect, since only very substantial discrepancies in personal income tax rates will significantly affect the allocation of resources.

The adoption of a uniform system of taxation for companies would certainly help to attract foreign investment and encourage intraregional mobility of capital. There is now a bewildering diversity of company tax systems in the region, ranging from a company income tax at one end of the spectrum to a full corporation (profits) tax at the other.[30] As with personal taxation, there is clearly room for work on harmonizing national systems and regulations, but a continuation of moderate differences in tax rates should not be ruled out.

Finally, the imposition of consumption taxes on intermediate goods needs to be examined very carefully, since indirect taxes on such goods will affect the level of effective protection received by processes and industries utilizing them as inputs. Consumption taxes paid on imports used in the manufacturing sector are generally refunded, but this is not the case in other sectors, including agriculture. It is thus important to pursue policies to coordinate the taxation of intermediate goods in the context of the goal of a common protective policy.

30. The crucial difference between a company income tax and a corporation tax is that the shareholders receiving dividends can claim credit against their income tax liability under the former, but not under the latter.

Chapter 3

Population, Manpower, and Employment

IT HAS BEEN SAID THAT PEOPLE REPRESENT THE GREATEST NATURAL RE-source of the countries of the Commonwealth Caribbean. At the same time, however, people—in the form of a population which is growing rather moderately in overall terms but at unprecedentedly rapid rates among particular age groups—present the twelve Caribbean Community (CARICOM) countries with what is perhaps the most fundamental challenge to their prospects for accelerated economic growth and balanced increases in per capita income during the coming years.

This chapter first examines the demographic data for the region, and then analyzes information on manpower availability and utilization. It surveys employment by sectors and the problems and prospects in organized and unorganized labor markets. The discussion concludes with an overview of the population and employment situation from the point of view of regionally integrated policies to meet the problems identified in the analysis.

Population of the Region: Structure and Change

The total population of the twelve territories which make up the Commonwealth Caribbean was less than 5 million in 1974. The territories vary greatly in size: Jamaica, with a population of just over 2 million, has nearly 44 percent of the regional total; Montserrat has only about 12,000 inhabitants. Table 3.1 sets out the basic data.

Size, density, and age composition

The total area of the region, a little under 100,000 square miles, and its total 1974 population, somewhat over 4.6 million people, suggest an average

TABLE 3.1. POPULATION, LAND AREA, AND POPULATION DENSITY, BY TERRITORY, 1974

Territory	1974 population	Distribution (percent)	Land area (square miles)	Distribution (percent)	Density (persons per square mile)
MDCS					
Jamaica	2,017,191	43.5	4,410	4.4	457
Trinidad and Tobago	985,828	21.2	1,980	2.0	498
Guyana	768,242	16.6	83,000	83.3	9
Barbados	237,193	5.1	166	0.2	1,429
Subtotal	4,008,454	86.4	89,556	90.0	45
LDCS					
Windward Islands	370,853	8.0	821	0.8	452
St. Lucia	106,362	2.3	233	0.2	456
Grenada	97,393	2.1	133	0.1	732
St. Vincent	91,796	2.0	150	0.2	612
Dominica	75,302	1.6	305	0.3	247
Leeward Islands	137,180	2.8	303	0.4	379
Antigua	70,000	1.5	170	0.2	412
St. Kitts-Nevis	44,311	1.0	101	0.1	439
Montserrat	12,057	0.3	32	0.0	377
Belize	132,456	2.9	8,866	8.9	15
Subtotal	629,677	13.6	9,900	10.0	63
All countries	4,638,131	100.0	99,546	100.0	47

Source: Estimates based on Commonwealth Caribbean Census, 1970.

density of forty-seven persons per square mile that year. This average is, however, highly artificial, a point which is well illustrated by the fact that ten of the countries of the region have densities at least five times the average. The only sensible interpretation to be given to this overall regional average is that the physical potential exists to redistribute the region's population in such a way that the ratio of people to land for any one territory could be held below fifty. This is not merely to state a didactic point about descriptive statistics; this interpretation has important implications for regional employment and population policies.[1]

The age structure of the populations of CARICOM members is heavily biased toward the young: on average, 46 percent are under the age of 15, and only 4 percent are over 65.[2]

Age structure is a function of fertility rates, mortality rates, and the extent

1. The best single statistic giving some idea of the demographic density of a "typical" Caribbean Community territory is the (unweighted) mean of the densities in each of them. This mean density turns out to be 474 persons per square mile, which is extremely high by international standards.

2. See Statistical Appendix, Table SA1.1.

and nature of emigration. These rates are discussed in detail in the next section. To summarize the trends briefly, mortality rates have continued to decline over the period from 1960 to 1970, but fertility rates have also fallen. Given this decline in fertility, the proportion of children in the population is surprisingly high: the explanation lies in the fact that the fertility decline was offset by large-scale emigration of adults.[3] The territories differ with respect to age composition: in Belize, Guyana, Jamaica, and the Windward Islands, children under fifteen years account for almost half the total increase in population, while in Barbados and Montserrat they are less than 40 percent of the total. These differences are caused by differing emigration and fertility patterns.

Population growth

Emigration has had a major effect on net population growth in the region. Substantial throughout much of the twentieth century, emigration grew to exceptional proportions in the 1960s and 1970s. Table 3.2 presents selected demographic indicators for recent decades. As Table 3.2 indicates, more than half of the natural increase in the region's population between 1960 and 1970 was lost to net emigration; consequently, the rapid rate of natural population increase (2.8 percent a year) was translated into an atypically slow rate of actual growth of 1.4 percent a year.[4] Owing to the highly selective nature of emigration from the CARICOM territories, its impact on the composition of their populations has also been substantial.[5]

Looking forward over the decade of the 1970s and beyond, both natural

TABLE 3.2. SELECTED DEMOGRAPHIC INDICATORS FOR THE CARIBBEAN COMMUNITY, 1946–70
(all territories)

Year	*Crude birth rate (per thousand)*	*Crude death rate (per thousand)*	*Total growth (annual percent)*	*Natural increase (annual percent)*	*Net migration (annual percent)*
1946	34.5	n.a.			
1960	41.1	9.3	+2.2 (1946–60)	+2.7 (1946–60)	−0.6 (1946–60)
1965	38.2	n.a.	+1.4 (1960–70)	+2.8 (1960–70)	−1.5 (1960–70)
1970	31.8	7.6			

n.a. Not available.
Source: Statistical Appendix, Tables SA1.5; SA1.6; SA1.7.

3. The uneven age structure provided by emigration can be seen clearly in Statistical Appendix Table SA1.11, which shows the growth of population between 1960 and 1970 by age and by sex.

4. See Statistical Appendix, Table SA1.5.

5. According to George W. Roberts, "Working Force of the Commonwealth Caribbean at 1970—A Provisional Assessment," (University of the West Indies, Nona, Jamaica, 1974) (processed) fertility levels before the 1940s were somewhat lower due to the highly male-selective emigration prior to 1921, consequently, an unusually large fraction

growth rates and net migration are expected to slow significantly within the region. Since these changes have opposing effects on actual population growth, the current actual rate of approximately 1.7 percent a year is not likely to change drastically in the near future; it will probably rise gradually to around 2 percent a year by the end of the 1970s or early 1980s.[6]

HISTORICAL BACKGROUND. Extraregional migration has a long history in the Commonwealth Caribbean countries. They were originally colonized in the sixteenth and seventeenth centuries by European immigrants who imported African slaves to provide cheap plantation labor. By the end of the nineteenth century, the world market for Caribbean sugar and other tropical products weakened considerably; with the ensuing retrenchment, inflows of migrants dwindled substantially and the region became a net exporter of unskilled labor, primarily to other areas of the Caribbean. From the late 1880s to the second decade of the present century, developments such as the construction of the Panama Canal, the establishment of the banana industry in Central America and the resurgence of the sugar industry in Cuba attracted considerable flows of migrants from the CARICOM region, particularly from Jamaica and Barbados.

Opportunities for extraregional employment elsewhere in the Caribbean gradually diminished; a migratory flow to the United States began to develop between 1910 and 1920 but was severely cut back by the Quota Acts of 1921 and 1924. This situation lasted until the end of World War II, when avenues for extraregional emigration reappeared. Census data, beginning with the 1911 enumeration, partially reflect these events. Total population in the region grew hardly at all between the census of 1911 and that of 1921. The overall increase was from about 1,953,000 to about 2,003,000—a gain of less than 3 percent over the whole decade—while Barbados experienced a net population decline of 15,600 persons.[7]

Until the early 1920s the population of the CARICOM region was relatively stable. Both birth and death rates were quite high, probably fluctuating between 30 and 40 per thousand. Consequently, natural population growth tended to be negligible and extraregional migration levels accounted for the bulk of population change. The decade of the 1920s saw the onset of secular mortality decline in the region—particularly among infants and children—and hence the stage of demographic transition. This is characterized by an accelerated rate of natural increase with the excess of births over deaths growing wider over subsequent years.

During the period between 1921 and 1946, there was minimal extra-

---

of females could not find partners in procreation. The gradual redress of this imbalance in the sex ratio, together with reductions during the 1940s in the incidence of pathological conditions (such as venereal infection and malaria) leading to sterility, accounts for the increase in fertility as of that period.

6. See Statistical Appendix, Table SA1.8.
7. See Statistical Appendix, Table SA1.2.

regional migration. Emigration was reduced by markedly lower incentives and opportunities to move abroad; immigration was discouraged by persistent labor surpluses in the area. Population growth during this period, almost entirely governed by the excess of births over deaths within the region, was at an average annual rate of 1.3 percent a year. Jamaica and Trinidad and Tobago grew most in both absolute and relative terms; they together accounted for three quarters of the regionwide intercensal population gain.

Extraregional migration—especially to the United Kingdom and, to a lesser extent, Canada—began again in the period between the census of 1946 and that of 1960. Total net emigration throughout this period amounted to approximately 250,000 persons, or roughly a fifth of the natural increase experienced during the same period. New medical and public health measures raised the rate of natural increase to an average of 2.7 percent a year over the period, combined with a net emigration rate of 0.6 percent a year.[8] Intraregional differentials in actual growth rates were dominated by differences in net migration rates rather than rates of natural increase.[9]

FERTILITY. The region has experienced a general decline in both the crude birth rate and in fertility rates in recent years. The crude birth rate appears to have fallen from 41 to 32 per thousand between 1960 and 1970, with most of the decline in the second half of the decade. Birth rates are now extremely low in some countries in the region—notably in Barbados, Trinidad and Tobago, and St. Kitts. Declines during the 1960s were large even in areas where rates had been high early in the decade. The gross reproduction rate (GRR)[10] is estimated to have fallen from about 2.8 in 1960 to about 2.4 in 1970.[11]

MORTALITY. The region as a whole has extremely low mortality rates. The crude death rate[12] fell by about 2 points to 7.6 per thousand during the period from 1960 to 1970. This rate is a poor indicator, however, in an area whose populations have irregular age compositions. A more appropriate measure is life expectancy. The expectation of life at birth is over 60 years throughout the region; the average figure is 67, which compares favorably with an average of 71 in the developed nations. During the intercensal period between 1960 and 1970, life expectancy rose by four years.[13]

8. See Statistical Appendix, Table SA1.5.

9. The variance of net migration rates is over 65 percent greater than the variance in the rates of natural increase.

10. The crude birth rate refers to births with respect to a thousand population; the fertility rate refers to births with respect to women in the 15–54 age group; the gross reproduction rate (GRR) refers to births of daughters with respect to a woman's lifetime. Since the crude birth rate is affected by the age distribution of the population, changes in the rate could diverge from more refined indexes of fertility, such as the fertility rate or the GRR.

11. See Statistical Appendix, Table SA1.6.

12. The crude death rate refers to deaths with respect to a thousand population.

13. See Statistical Appendix, Table SA1.7.

MIGRATION. Emigration is a very important determinant of the low rates of population growth in the region as a whole, and of the variations in rates between its constituent countries. They have all experienced net emigration in recent years,[14] amounting in total to about half of the natural increase of 1,180,000 during the same period. Although statistics are less reliable for previous intercensal periods, it appears that the effect of migration on population growth was less pronounced between 1946 and 1960. In this period, population grew naturally by about 1,256,000, but was reduced by emigration to an actual increase of 1,005,000. Thus, for the region as a whole, the influence of migration on population growth appears to have more than doubled in recent years. The relative influence of emigration and natural increase varies substantially, however, between territories. For example, the influence of migration was relatively great in Barbados, Grenada, St. Vincent, and Jamaica, and small in Guyana, Belize, and the Leeward Islands. Both the large overall amount of emigration and the age and sex composition of the emigrants have affected fertility rates. The young of working age were most affected by migration.[15]

A comparison of the rate of natural increase over the period from 1946 to 1960 with that over the period from 1960 to 1970 shows a substantially broader variation between territories in the later period; since actual population growth rates did not change significantly, this suggests that natural increase and net emigration were positively correlated.

Looking ahead, George W. Roberts, of the University of the West Indies and one of the region's leading demographers, envisages the possibility that "emigration outlets to the industrialized societies which so strongly dominated growth rates in the post-war period are now about to be entirely closed.[16] This will have an enormous impact on the growth of population and potential labor supply during the next ten years unless new avenues of migration into other countries are found.[17]

POPULATION CHANGE BY AGE GROUPS. Rates of population growth vary considerably from one age group to another in most countries. In general, in the period between 1960 and 1970 the population aged less than 15 and more than 55 years grew much faster than the population aged between 15 and 54 (see Table 3.3 for net population changes). In most territories the population in the prime working ages 24 to 54 actually declined. Of course, patterns of population growth vary considerably among countries,[18] but the sharp differences between age groups—absence of growth or decline in many adult ages, together with rapid growth in both the very

14. See Statistical Appendix, Table SA1.5.

15. See Statistical Appendix, Table SA1.11, which gives the growth of the population of the CARICOM territories by age and by sex between 1960 and 1970.

16. Roberts, "Working Force of the Commonwealth Caribbean at 1970," p. 3.

17. The population projection in Statistical Appendix, Table SA1.15, quantifies the impact on the regional labor force.

18. See Statistical Appendix, Table SA1.11.

TABLE 3.3. NET CHANGES IN POPULATION, BY AGE CATEGORY, ALL CARIBBEAN TERRITORIES, 1960–70

Category	*Net change*
Under 15	+346,373
15–24	+133,410
25–54	−25,773
Over 55	+105,726

Source: Statistical Appendix, Table SA1.11, and World Bank estimates for Antigua.

young and the relatively old age groups—seem to be peculiar characteristics of overall population growth in this region.

URBANIZATION. Urban lifestyles are more common in the Caribbean region than in most of the developing world, and urban living has been increasing relatively rapidly. The accepted census definition of urbanization does not present a clear picture, however. In the census definition, individuals are classified as urban if their dwelling lies within the fixed political boundary of a city. As a result of a marked shift in the location of dwelling units from the center of cities to the suburbs over the past couple of decades, this definition leads to the remarkable result that the number of persons classified as urban in Trinidad and Tobago, for example, was almost 20 percent smaller in 1970 than in 1960, and that only 12 percent of the country's total 1970 population was urban. To a person familiar with Trinidad and Tobago such figures are nonsense.

A more accurate assessment of the degree of urbanization must take account of the special social and economic conditions of the Caribbean region. In the first place, simply because of the relatively small size of these territories and their reasonably good networks of main roads, most of their population are within about two hours by bus from a major urban center. Thus from a sociological point of view, even households located outside a city's boundaries and having agricultural activities as their main sources of income are a lot more urbanized on the average than their comparisons in most developing countries. In the second place, the proportion of total employment in the region accounted for by agriculture is both relatively small and falling. The share of agriculture in total employment is a reasonable quantitative index of the degree and evolution of urbanization. Data on the composition of employment presented later in this chapter confirm the decline in the agricultural labor force.

POPULATION GROWTH PROSPECTS. The mortality trend is the least important of the three components of population growth for future population growth in the Caribbean region. Death rates are now very low, and although health conditions may improve in the future, such improvements could have only a minimal effect on crude death rates.

Fertility rates, on the other hand, are critical. Current levels are expected to decline as they have in the recent past. Between 1960 and 1970, the GRR fell on average by 1.5 percent per year and a similar decline is projected to 1985. Adjustments should be made for some country projections, however, to take account of past and current rates of decline and family planning programs. (It may be noted that assumptions about fertility changes have no effect on the size or age distribution of the labor force until 1984.)

Migration is the most uncertain element affecting future population growth. If past trends are any guide, it could be the most important factor of the three for most territories; except in Guyana and Belize, natural increase was more than halved by external migration in the 1960s. There are few ways of forecasting migration trends, however, since they depend on social, economic, and political conditions in both sender and recipient countries. One factor which could promote continued migration is past migration itself. It is generally observed that migration begets migration. The large numbers of Caribbean migrants to countries outside the region (notably the United Kingdom, the United States and Canada) could help to generate fresh migrations in the coming years. On the other hand, greater entry restrictions are being imposed in traditional destinations of Caribbean migrants. Thus, while continued net emigration from most of the territories may be expected in the 1970s, the numbers could be much smaller than hitherto. Because of these uncertainties, and because of the importance of migration as a determinant of labor supply, the implications for population growth of three different assumptions about rates of migration have been calculated. The assumptions are (a) no migration during 1970–80; (b) net emigration at a reduced rate compared with 1960–70; and (c) net emigration at more or less the same level as during 1960–70.[19]

If migration were to dry up altogether after 1970, the population of the region as a whole would increase from 4,310,000 in 1970 to 4,880,000 in 1975 (a rise of 2.6 percent per year), to 5,564,000 in 1980 and to 6,354,000 in 1985. On the other hand, if future migration were to take place at the same level as in the 1960s, the total population in 1985 would be about 5,279,000 (1 million fewer persons) and the average growth rate would be only half as high. An intermediate trend, as in assumption (b) above is more plausible. Under this assumption, the increase of population would be about 1,401,000 during the fifteen-year period from 1970 to 1985, representing an average annual growth rate of 1.9 percent.

Compared with many other developing regions, population growth rates in the CARICOM countries thus have been and will probably remain relatively low. A possible reduction in emigration and the existence of a relatively

19. The population totals in 1975, 1980, and 1985, based on these three assumptions about migration, are given in Statistical Appendix, Table SA1.8. Detailed projections by age and sex are shown in Table SA1.10.

high proportion of women in the young reproductive ages may, however, raise the growth rate in the 1970s above that of the 1960s. A rate slightly below 2 percent per year is the most likely estimate in the light of available data. Differential rates of growth in different age groups are more significant than the total rate.[20] Table 3.4 summarizes the regional situation.

Between 1970 and 1980, the population of the region is expected to increase (under this assumption of reduced emigration levels) by 831,000, of which 461,000 would be in the adolescent and young adult age groups (15–24 years). Nearly 80 percent of the increase would be in the age span from 15 to 34. There would be hardly any growth in the 35–64 age groups, but the elderly (those over 65) would increase substantially, representing about 6.5 percent of all population growth.

The contrast between the situation for the 1960s and that of the 1970s is sharp. Between 1960 and 1970, nearly 62 percent of total population growth was in the under fifteen age group. In the 1970s, children in this group would contribute less than 13 percent to total growth. Working age adolescents and young adults are projected to make up by far the largest share of the overall increase. The demographic problems of the CARICOM region seem likely, therefore, to include unbalanced population growth by age groups as well as a projected overall increase. This state of affairs will make the employment problems of the 1970s very different from those of earlier periods.

Current population policies

The view that lower fertility rates would be desirable is widespread in the Caribbean. Official attitudes towards family planning, however, differ

TABLE 3.4. POPULATION GROWTH BY AGE GROUPS, CARIBBEAN COMMUNITY, 1960–80

	1960–70 Actual		*1970–80 Projected*	
Age group	*Number (amount)*	*Percent distribution*	*Number (amount)*	*Percent distribution*
Under 15	+346,373	+61.9	+102,106	+12.3
15–19	+92,379	+16.5	+242,125	+29.1
20–24	+41,031	+7.3	+218,868	+26.3
25–34	−14,363	−2.6	+205,628	+24.7
35–54	−11,410	−2.0	−11,457	−1.4
55–64	−49,225	+8.8	+20,525	+2.5
Over 65	+56,501	+10.1	+53,299	+6.4
All ages	+559,736	100.0	+831,094	100.0

Source: Statistical Appendix, Tables SA1.11 and SA1.12, and World Bank estimates for Antigua.

20. The pattern under assumption (b) is given in Statistical Appendix, Table SA1.12.

sharply from country to country. None of them follows policies which could be described very strongly pro-natalist by international standards (such as making the sale of contraceptives illegal, or paying bonuses for very large families); they all, however, have anti-abortion laws, and dependency allowances for children are the rule for government workers.

Trinidad and Tobago, Jamaica, and Barbados have officially adopted a reduction of the birth rate as a matter of national policy. The official stance in the other CARICOM countries is one of neutrality toward nongovernment family planning efforts, which are neither supported nor opposed to any significant degree.[21] This stance may need to be reconsidered in the light of currently pessimistic population and unemployment projections.

Guyana and Belize are special cases. Efforts to curb fertility suffer from official disapproval—apparently because of low population densities and the availability of virgin land for settlement. The central issue here, however, is whether high fertility actually promotes new land settlements, and, even if it does, whether it justifies the social cost entailed.

Three considerations need to be taken into account in judging this issue. In the first place, the manpower required to implement any settlement scheme involves adults, not children; current and future births could contribute to a program's manpower needs only after a lag of around fifteen years. In the second place, capital is the limiting factor to rapid and successful settlements. The flow of savings required for this purpose might be increased if fewer resources had to be diverted to provide food, shelter, clothing, health and educational services for additional children. Finally, patterns of internal migration, rather than a high or rising fertility rate, are the key to achieving the objective of settling virgin land. This means that the recent pattern of flows of migrants away from the countryside into the cities must be reversed. Without such a change, the only result of current population policies would be larger cities.

Guyana and Belize are not alone within the CARICOM region in their concern about relatively massive population movements during the past few years out of rural areas. The intensification of urban problems—especially the increasing pressure on infrastructure and social services, and the growing social and political tensions consequent upon high and rising unemployment among young adults—is a phenomenon affecting the region as a whole. The decline of the agricultural sector in most of the region and the geographical pattern of public investment, particularly in the social services have exacerbated the virtually universal trend toward urban concentration. The problems of agricultural decline and the skewed composition of public expenditure, together with possible policies for dealing with them, are discussed in detail in Chapter 5.

21. In St. Lucia, for example, the government has occasionally allowed the family planning association a few minutes of free radio time to inform the public of its existence and location.

Manpower Availability and Utilization

The combined labor force of the countries making up the Caribbean region was estimated to be about 1,323,000 in 1970, or about 30 percent of the total population. Thus, for every 100 persons in the labor force, there were more than 230 others who were dependent upon them.

Labor force participation rates

The average participation rate[22] in 1970 of the population aged 14 years and over was about 53 percent for men and 31 percent for women.[23] The male rates are fairly close to the average in most of the individual countries; at least three-quarters of the working age population are in the labor force. Variations between countries are much greater among females.

Where country differences in participation rates exist, they are only partially due to differences in the age and sex composition of the populations. The differences narrow down in the case of males when the rates are standardized for differences in age distribution, but actually increase in the case of females. Thus, the relatively low male participation rates in Grenada and St. Kitts are related to differences in the age and sex composition of the population, but the relatively high female rates of Barbados cannot be attributed primarily to the island's particular age structure. Although, as would be expected, the chief differences in age- and sex-specific participation rates are found among the relatively younger and older ages, they are also plainly present among workers in the intermediate age groups.

22. The following definitions will be used in this discussion. *Labor force* (L): includes (a) persons who worked during most of the year preceding the census, (b) those who had never worked but were actively engaged in trying to get work, and (c) those who for most of the 12-month period before the census were not working and were actively trying to get work but who had been employed at some time prior to this period of looking for work; *working age population* (P): population aged 14 years and over; *employment* (E): employed members of the labor force. Four measures of labor utilization are used. *Work rate*: proportion of the working age population actually employed ($= E \div P$); *unemployment rate*: proportion of the labor force unable to find jobs ($= U \div L$); *employment rate*: proportion of the labor force who are employed ($+ E \div L$); *participation rate*: proportion of the working age population who declare themselves to be members of the labor force as defined above ($= L \div P$). Unless otherwise stated, activity categories (such as "worked") are defined on the basis of responses to the question: "What did . . . do most during the *twelve-month* period preceding Census day, that is, up to April 7, 1970—worked? looked for work? kept house? went to school? or something else?" (Commonwealth Caribbean Census, 1970.) Thus, the period of reference is the twelve months between April 7, 1969 and April 7, 1970.

23. See Statistical Appendix, Tables SA1.13 and 1.14, for labor force size and participation rates by CARICOM countries. The averages given for participation rates do not include Antigua or St. Kitts. Detailed age and sex specific participation rates are given in Statistical Appendix, Table SA1.16.

Trends in labor supply

The labor force of the region[24] appears to have fallen somewhat during the 1960s, from about 1,335,000 in 1960 to about 1,289,000 in 1970—an overall decline of about 46,000[25]—despite increases in some countries (Trinidad and Tobago, Guyana, Grenada, and Belize). Analysis by sex shows that the decline was mainly among females; even where there was a net increase in the labor force, the female labor force fell. Despite the natural increase in the population of 365,000, the labor force was reduced by 272,000 through migration, and there was a further loss of 138,000 because of decreases in participation rates. These effects combined to produce a net decrease in the labor force of 46,000.[26] In general, changes in participation rates show that the decline among females is slightly greater than that among males.[27] Among males, the sharpest falls—of more than 10 percent—were in Jamaica and Guyana; these two countries account for 60 percent of the male labor force of the region. Among females, Dominica and Jamaica show the largest losses.

The deterioration in manpower utilization can be clearly illustrated (Table 3.5) by figures showing the ratio of those actually employed to those of working age (the work rate). As Table 3.5 indicates, although the population 14 years of age and over grew by about 11 percent between 1960 and

24. Because of a lack of comparable data, Antigua and St. Kitts are not included in the analysis.

25. It is possible that both the total population and labor force are underenumerated in the 1970 census. It would be inappropriate to continue analysis of the decline in the labor force without discussion of the questionable accuracy of the data. Sample surveys of the labor force are taken at periodic intervals in both Jamaica and Trinidad and Tobago. These surveys estimated an "employed labor force" larger than the "working population" enumerated in the census. Definitional discrepancy is ruled out by the comparability of questions asked; seasonal differences are unlikely because the census was taken in the same month as some of the surveys had been. A further possible source of variation lies in the selection of the samples for the surveys which were made on the basis of the 1960 census: substantial migration from rural to urban centers occurred in the decade, with people moving from rural areas where employment rates were higher to urban areas where they were lower, which could have caused the sample surveys to overestimate employment. In any case, two assertions seem warranted in this connection: (a) the magnitude of the observed divergences between census and survey employment estimates in Jamaica and Trinidad poses a major problem with regard to the reliability of basic labor market data and hence should be investigated as a matter of high priority; and (b) regardless of which set of estimates one relies on, the most favorable conclusion that can be reached is that employment did not grow appreciably in either of the two countries during the period from 1960 to 1970. The two other MDCs, Guyana and Barbados, both show small declines in total employment during the decade; the LDCs as a group show less of a decline in manpower utilization over the decade as their work rate fell only by 7 percent compared with 22 percent for the MDCs. In the light of the discrepancies in the data, it is probably more appropriate to focus on trends and magnitudes than exact numbers.

26. See Statistical Appendix, Table SA1.17.

27. See Statistical Appendix, Table SA1.14, for changes in participation rates.

TABLE 3.5. CHANGES IN WORKING AGE POPULATION, EMPLOYMENT, AND WORK RATES, CARIBBEAN COMMUNITY, 1960–70
(percent)

	Population 14 years and older[a]	*Employment*[b]	*Work rate*[c]
MDC total	+11.7	−13.4	−22.5
LDC total	+7.5	−0.4	−7.3
CARICOM total	+11.1	−11.8	−20.7

a. (P).
b. (E).
c. (E/P): in this case (100 − E)/(100 + P).
Source: Statistical Appendix, Table SA1.27.

1970, those actually employed fell by approximately 12 percent during the same period, and the work rate dropped by 21 percent.

In 1970, 44 percent of the 2.2 million individuals 14 years of age and older living in the CARICOM states were employed. This work rate is virtually identical to the average rate for a group of five Latin American countries for whom a roughly comparable index can be constructed, although it is considerably lower than 68 percent average of a sample of highly industrialized nations, as shown in Table 3.6.

TABLE 3.6. WORK RATES IN SELECTED COUNTRIES
(percent)

Country	*Year*	*Work rate*
Latin American		
Brazil	1970	45
Chile	1970	44
Guatemala	1964	41
Panama	1970	53
Venezuela	1970	42
Average		44
Industrialized		
Belgium	1961	59
Czechoslovakia	1961	70
Finland	1960	76
Hungary	1960	72
Norway	1960	62
Average		68
Caribbean Community	1970	44

Source: Statistical Appendix, Table SA1.27. *Labour Statistics.* Geneva, 1972.

Unemployment rates in the region vary widely between countries, ranging from 5 percent in Montserrat, St. Kitts, and Belize to 22 percent in Trinidad and Tobago. The unweighted average unemployment rate is 13 percent for the MDCs and 7 percent for the LDCs. The most notable features emerging from a breakdown of intercensal percentage changes in labor supply variables—working age population, employment, and work rates—by sex[28] are: (a) For the region as a whole, the supply of males of working age grew by rather more than that of females (by 13 percent, compared with 10 percent). This difference was more marked on average in the LDCs where the mean percentage increase for males was more than twice that for females. This state of affairs may be the result of high differential female migration. (b) Employment for females fell proportionately about three times as fast as that for males over the region during the decade. Female employment fell by 11 percent in the LDCs and 23 percent in the MDCs while male employment showed an actual gain of 6 percent in the LDCs.

To summarize, the decade of the 1960s witnessed a severe erosion in manpower utilization in the CARICOM region. This erosion showed itself in two ways: (a) the population of working age rose, but the size of the labor force fell; and (b) the employment rate of even this reduced labor force declined. The effects were greatest among MDC women and least among LDC men.

Analysis of the combined effects of all three manpower utilization indexes discussed above (work rate, participation rate, unemployment rate) by country showed, in overall terms, that (a) five territories fared better than the average (Barbados, Dominica, Montserrat, Grenada, and St. Lucia) and (b) four states fared more badly than the average (Trinidad and Tobago, Guyana, St. Vincent, and Jamaica).

Adjusted indexes of manpower utilization

The information on manpower utilization discussed above needs some modification to account for a number of factors which affect labor supply, but which are not easy to measure directly.

HIDDEN UNEMPLOYMENT. Empirical evidence supports the logical supposition that the participation rate is systematically related to labor market conditions. If the market is depressed, individuals who would have otherwise claimed to have been in the labor force fail to do so, thus biasing downward the labor force participation rate. These individuals are sometimes referred to as discouraged workers or hidden unemployed. Because it is felt that these individuals should be included among the unemployed (rather than excluded from the labor force altogether), the census attempts to identify them on the basis of a positive reply to a question asking whether they

28. For unemployment rates, see Statistical Appendix, Table SA1.25. For intercensal changes in labor supply variables, see Statistical Appendix, Table SA1.27.

wanted work and were available for work during the greater part of the year. Table 3.7 shows the effect of adding hidden unemployment to open unemployment for each of the CARICOM countries.

UNDEREMPLOYMENT. The unemployment rate may also understate the magnitude of excess labor supply by including among the employed individuals who are underemployed in the sense that they work less time than they would like to (or that the time they claim actually to work is below some predetermined standard of full-time work). While available information does not permit a direct assessment of underemployment in this sense, it does make it possible to distinguish between individuals who claimed to have worked at least ten out of the twelve months preceding the census (or, for brevity, full-time workers) and all other workers. Table 3.8 presents the ratio of full-time workers to total employment as a rough index of the degree of underemployment in the CARIFTA states. The LDCs have relatively low rates, averaging 66 percent compared to 73 percent in the MDCs.

STUDENTS OF WORKING AGE. The proportion of the population aged fourteen years and over claiming to be full-time students during the twelve-

TABLE 3.7. HIDDEN AND OPEN UNEMPLOYMENT RATES, CARIFTA REGION AND MEMBER STATES, 1970
(percent)

	Unemployment rate	
Territory	*Open*	*Hidden and open*
Total CARIFTA	13	17
MDCS		
Jamaica	11	18
Trinidad and Tobago	22	23
Guyana	13	16
Barbados	8	9
LDCS		
Windward Islands	9	10
St. Lucia	11	12
Grenada	7	7
St. Vincent	9	9
Dominica		
Leeward Islands		
Antigua	8	11
St. Kitts	5	6
Montserrat	5	7
Belize	5	5
Mean	9	12

Source: Commonwealth Caribbean Census, 1970.

TABLE 3.8. RATIO OF FULL-TIME WORKERS TO TOTAL EMPLOYMENT, 1970
(percent)

Territory	*Ratio*
Total CARIFTA	70
MDCS	
Jamaica	66
Trinidad and Tobago	78
Guyana	72
Barbados	75
LDCS	
Windward Islands	
St. Lucia	72
Grenada	65
St. Vincent	58
Dominica	70
Leeward Islands	
Antigua	66
St. Kitts	62
Montserrat	65
Belize	72
Average	68

Source: Commonwealth Caribbean Census, 1970.

month period preceding the census varied from less than 7 percent (Montserrat) to over 15 percent (Grenada). This range is sufficiently wide to make it reasonable to adjust the working age population of each territory to take into account full-time students of working age when calculating both the work and labor force participation rates. Since education is an economically significant activity, because it enhances the stock of human capital, and since most countries want to distinguish between school age and working age population, the adjustment seems justifiable. The result is shown in Table 3.9. While the MDCs were clearly better off with respect to underemployment than the LDCs, their worse than average unadjusted work rates (with the exception of Barbados) keep the rates adjusted for part-time employment below those of the LDCs.

Future size of the labor force

If the substantial decline of participation rates in most of the countries of the region continues during the 1970s, the average rates at the end of the decade would be 73 percent among males and 24 percent among females. The decline may not be as large in the 1970s, however, as it was in the previous decade. A comparison[29] of the 1970 male participation rates of the

29. See Statistical Appendix, Table SA1.18.

TABLE 3.9. WORK RATES ADJUSTED FOR STUDENTS OF WORKING AGE AND PART-TIME EMPLOYMENT, 1970
(percent)

		Adjusted excludes		
	Unadjusted[a]	*Students of working age*[b]	*Part-time employment*[c]	*Both*[d]
Total CARIFTA	44	49	31	34
MDCS				
Jamaica	46	52	30	34
Trinidad and Tobago	40	44	30	34
Guyana	40	44	29	32
Barbados	54	59	41	44
LDCS				
Windward Islands				
St. Lucia	50	53	36	38
Grenada	50	58	33	38
St. Vincent	47	52	27	30
Dominica	53	58	37	41
Leeward Islands				
Antigua	47	54	31	36
St. Kitts	50	58	31	36
Montserrat	52	55	34	36
Belize	48	53	35	38
Mean	48	53	33	36

a. The originally defined (unadjusted) work rate, that is, the ratio of total employment to working age population.

b. Work rate adjusted for students of working age by removing them from the population aged 14 years and older.

c. Adjusts the work rates in the first column for part-time employment, using the ratios in Table 3.8.

d. Shows the level of full-time employment of the nonstudent population of working age, by applying the ratios in Table 3.8 to the figures in the second column.

Source: Commonwealth Caribbean Census, 1970.

CARIFTA countries with the averages for industrialized, semi-industrialized, and agricultural countries in four critical age groups—15–19 years, 20–24 years, 55–64 years and 65 years or more—shows that only in the 20–24 age group are the rates in some of the Caribbean countries higher than the averages for any of the three other groups of countries. Comparisons are more difficult in the case of females because cultural factors carry more weight in their case: consequently, they have not been included.

In estimating the future size of the labor force, two alternative assumptions about the probable trend of participation rates are used. These are (a) age- and sex-specific participation rates of 1970 remain constant through the entire decade; (b) the percentage change in the overall participation rates in the 1970s will be the same as that of the 1960s. It is expected that the actual rates would lie in between these two sets. On these assumptions, which represent a medium projection, the figures[30] suggest that, in sharp contrast to the decline of 52,410 in the labor force during the 1960s, a dramatic increase of 415,310 can be expected in the 1970s.[31] The breakdown of the increase by age groups for the region is shown in Table 3.10. Clearly the projected change in the labor force will be different if migration and participation rates were to alter from those assumed in the above calculations.

The expected differential increases in the various age groups are even more important than the total. These differences affect labor supply in the various age groups. Over one-fourth of the total increase would be accounted for by workers under 20 years of age, 65 percent would be under 25 and nearly all of the additional labor force (97 percent) would be under 35. The net growth in the groups aged between 35 and 64 would be negative.

It is vital to note that these projections are based on the assumption that the 1970 age- and sex-specific participation rates remain constant throughout the decade. The period between 1960 and 1970 showed an average decline in the participation rate of 6 percent and the employment rate fell by 12 percent. (The participation rate is standardized for age; the employment rate is not.) The problem of expanding employment opportunities to maintain stable labor force participation rates with a rising population of working age is discussed further below.

TABLE 3.10. ESTIMATED LABOR FORCE GROWTH BY AGE GROUPS, CARIBBEAN REGION, 1970–80

Age group	*Growth 1970–80*	*Distribution (percent)*
14–19	+110,678	26.6
20–24	+160,590	38.7
25–34	+131,367	31.6
35–54	−8,005	−1.9
55–64	+6,653	+1.6
Over 65	+14,027	+3.4
All ages	+415,310	100.0

Source: Statistical Appendix, Tables SA1.19a, SA1.19b and SA1.19c.

30. Statistical Appendix, Table SA1.20 gives estimates for the total labor force in 1980 under three assumptions about future emigration and two assumptions about participation rates in 1980, and Statistical Appendix, Table SA1.15 compares labor force growth between 1970 and 1980 with that of the previous decade, assuming reduced migration compared with the 1960–70 period and participation rates at 1970 levels. Statistical Appendix, Table SA1.19 shows country changes by age group.

31. The data in Table SA1.20 suggest that even if migration were to continue at the same level it did during the 1960s and participation rates were to fall to the same extent that they did during the 1960s (a low projection), the labor force would increase by about 173,000 between 1970 and 1980.

Age, sex, and the employment problems

In general, work rates tend to be significantly lower among the younger age groups of the working population than those of older workers. Similarly, females typically have lower work rates than males of corresponding age. Differences in age- and sex-specific work rates in the CARICOM region conform to this general pattern, but the relative magnitudes of the differences appear to be atypically large. A summary of the structure of work rates by age and sex for the CARICOM region in 1970 is given in Table 3.11.

For the region as a whole, there were over two-and-a-half times as many working age males employed in 1970 as females. There are some striking differences in the age and sex structure of work rates between the MDCs and LDCs as a group, as well as between individual countries. For example: (a) the LDCs as a group show higher work rates for every single disaggregated age and sex category; (b) with the exception of males aged over 60, Barbados shows appreciably higher work rates than the other MDCs and than most LDCs for every category; and (c) focusing on the primary work force group of males 25 to 59 years, Jamaica and Trinidad (which together contain two-thirds of the region's total male labor force) show unusually low work rates—further evidence that these two countries had the most serious employment problem in the region in 1970.[32]

The general problem of manpower utilization in the CARICOM states, as measured by work rate data, is thus highly concentrated among females and among the younger members of the working age population. Statistics indicate, however, that almost 80 percent of the nonworking potential labor force did not want a job, the vast majority being females engaged in home duties.[33] This suggests that the actual socioeconomic costs of the employment problem tend to be far more serious in the case of younger males.

TABLE 3.11. WORK RATE BY AGE GROUP AND SEX, 1970
(percent)

	14 years and over			*14–19*		*20–24*		*25–59*		*60 and over*	
Category	*Total*	*Male*	*Female*	*Male*	*Female*	*Male*	*Female*	*Male*	*Female*	*Male*	*Female*
MDC total	43.6	64.8	24.2	23.1	10.3	68.5	33.0	85.1	31.0	50.4	11.7
LDC total	49.4	73.3	29.3	39.3	18.6	86.6	42.5	91.6	35.4	61.2	16.3
CARICOM total[a]	44.3	65.7	24.8	25.8	11.4	70.4	34.1	85.8	31.5	51.7	12.3

a. Weighted average.
Source: Statistical Appendix, Table SA1.22.

32. More recent survey data available for these countries show no real improvement in this respect in the two years following the census.

33. See Statistical Appendix, Table SA1.23.

The composition of those who were said to have wanted work tended to be highly concentrated among those seeking their first job. This was particularly true for the LDCs, where this category was almost two and a half times as great as that of work seekers with previous job experience. Analysis of work seekers by age group and sex[34] shows that the youngest age group (14 to 19 years old) accounted for approximately half of all work seekers in the CARICOM region. There were roughly twice as many males as females in both the 14 to 19, and the 19 and over age groups.

Unemployment rates are disproportionately high in the two youngest age groups. As Table 3.12 indicates, nearly half of those aged 14–19 in the region were unemployed, and one-fifth of those ages 20–24. The unemployment rate falls to a moderate 6 percent or less among those aged 25 or older.

In the 1960s, the population of working age rose by 11 percent; in the period between 1970 and 1980, World Bank projections—based, as already indicated, on an assumption of reduced migration compared to 1960–70—suggest that it could increase by around 30 percent. While the labor force decreased by 46,000 during the 1960s, it is expected to increase by about 416,000 in the seventies. Two-thirds of this increase will be young adults.

The region is therefore faced with an ongoing problem of providing employment for young workers. This problem will become very much more serious during the 1970s, involving major losses of output from this age group on account of unemployment, and related social problems (including the fact that the unemployed will have had no chance to establish regular work habits for the future).

To come to grips with this problem, the output of the school system needs to be matched more closely with the labor input requirements of the economy. At present, too many individuals, especially males around the ages of 14 to 20, are leaving the school system with a set of job aspirations and skills which are largely incompatible with the structure and conditions

TABLE 3.12. UNEMPLOYMENT RATES BY AGE GROUP AND SEX, 1970
(percent)

	14 years and over			*14–19*		*20–24*		*25–59*		*60 and over*	
Category	*Total*	*Male*	*Female*	*Male*	*Female*	*Male*	*Female*	*Male*	*Female*	*Male*	*Female*
MDC total	14.0	13.5	15.3	48.5	49.9	20.2	20.3	5.9	5.9	3.0	1.9
LDC total	7.7	6.7	9.8	25.3	33.1	7.5	10.7	1.7	2.5	1.0	1.1
CARICOM total[a]	13.2	12.7	14.5	45.1	47.2	18.7	19.1	5.5	5.5	2.7	1.3

a. Weighted average.
Source: Statistical Appendix, Table SA1.25.

34. See Statistical Appendix, Table SA1.24.

of the labor market in their countries; the situation seems to be particularly serious in the cases of Jamaica, Trinidad and Tobago, and Guyana.

On the supply side, labor market studies and manpower projects are needed to match the supply of available workers with vacancies, and the education system might be given responsibility for finding its graduates their first jobs. On the demand side, governments might organize schemes of a national service type designed to employ underemployed youth; subsidize on the job training; and stimulate sectors likely to use substantial amounts of labor, such as agriculture and construction.

Trends in the composition of employment

As in many other parts of the world, the kind of work done by those employed in the Caribbean region is strongly linked to their sex. The pattern of occupational groups is very similar in the MDCs and the LDCs. The three main white-collar groups, for example (designated as: professional and technical; administrative and managerial; and clerical and related) together accounted for 16.8 percent of the employed in the MDCs and 15.9 percent in the LDCs in 1970. But this is not the whole story.

THE OCCUPATIONAL COMPOSITION OF EMPLOYMENT. A breakdown by sex shows working women were twice as likely to hold one of these white-collar jobs as men in both groups of countries. (For the MDCs as a whole, 27.6 percent of working women had white-collar jobs, compared with 12.8 percent of working men. In the LDCs, the proportions were 23.1 percent and 10.2 percent, respectively.) Although the ratios for MDC and LDC groups are similar, there are some striking differences within each country group. For example, 36.8 percent of working women in Trinidad and Tobago had a white-collar job, compared with only 23.4 percent of working women in Jamaica.[35] Because the female working population is approximately half that of the male, the actual numbers of workers with white-collar jobs are very similar; 88,123 women and 95,385 men. Table 3.13 summarizes the occupational distribution of the working population.

Opportunities clearly exist for women to hold good jobs. The education system prepares them as fully as it prepares the men. Excess demand for skilled workers and managerial talent may have favored educated women who chose not to emigrate. Despite a general tendency for female employment to fall, the proportion of women in the professional and technical and clerical and related groups has been increasing while almost all other groups (with the marked exception of sales workers in the LDCs) have been declining.[36]

If the effects of migration have been to offer increased opportunities to women, it might reasonably be expected that a marked reduction in migra-

35. See Statistical Appendix, Table SA1.39.
36. See Statistical Appendix, Table SA1.45.

TABLE 3.13. DISTRIBUTION OF TOTAL WORKING POPULATION BY OCCUPATIONAL GROUP, 1970
(weighted averages)

	MDC			LDC		
Working population	*Total*	*Males*	*Females*	*Total*	*Males*	*Females*
Professional and technical	8.0	6.1	12.8	8.0	5.4	13.3
Administrative and managerial	0.9	1.1	0.3	1.4	0.9	0.3
Clerical and related	7.9	5.2	14.5	6.5	3.9	9.5
Transport and communications	1.1	1.0	1.2	0.9	1.1	0.4
Sales workers	7.9	6.0	12.3	6.7	5.0	11.4
Service workers	13.6	6.5	31.2	12.7	5.1	23.7
Farm managers, supervisors, and farmers	12.7	16.6	3.1	31.2	15.4	4.8
Other agricultural workers	11.7	13.9	6.2		23.2	20.4
Production and related workers	26.9	32.4	13.5	25.5	31.2	11.0
Not elsewhere stated	9.2	11.1	4.9	7.0	8.8	5.1
Total	100	100	100	100	100	100

Source: Statistical Appendix, Tables SA1.37, SA1.38, and SA1.39.

tion and the consequent increase in demand for higher level jobs would cause particular problems for women workers.

The working age population is expected to increase rapidly in the future. The occupational groups which have shown the most growth in the past decade for both men and women are the professional and technical, clerical and related, and sales (except for women in the MDCs). The production workers category has also provided an increasing number of jobs for men. It will be important for future policymaking to consider whether declining employment in the other sectors was caused by increased efficiency or reduced economic activity, and to identify the types of occupation which can be most readily expanded to absorb the very large projected increase in the labor force.

THE INDUSTRIAL COMPOSITION OF EMPLOYMENT. The composition of employment by industrial sector differs predictably between the MDCs and the LDCs, corresponding to their stages of development. In the MDCs, a smaller percentage of the working population is involved in agriculture and a larger percentage in manufacturing, as is indicated in Table 3.14. There are, however, marked differences between countries within the MDC and LDC groups. In Trinidad and Barbados only 15 percent of the working population is in agriculture, half the proportion for Guyana and Jamaica. Similar divergences exist among the countries in the LDC group.[37]

37. See Statistical Appendix, Table SA1.40.

TABLE 3.14. DISTRIBUTION OF TOTAL WORKING POPULATION BY INDUSTRIAL GROUP, 1970
(weighted averages)

	MDC			LDC		
Working population	*Total*	*Males*	*Females*	*Total*	*Males*	*Females*
Agriculture, forestry, hunting, and fishing	24.9	31.1	9.8	31.8	39.5	25.2
Mining, refining, and quarrying	2.9	3.9	0.4	0.1	0.1	0.1
Manufacturing	14.3	14.0	15.0	10.2	9.9	8.9
Construction and installation	7.6	10.5	0.7	11.3	16.1	3.1
Electricity, gas, water, and sanitary services	1.2	1.6	0.3	1.3	1.5	0.8
Commerce	10.6	8.4	15.9	11.1	8.3	17.7
Transport, storage, and communications	5.0	5.9	2.5	5.3	6.2	0.9
Services	27.0	18.0	49.1	26.7	15.5	41.7
Not elsewhere stated	6.5	6.6	6.3	2.2	2.9	1.7
Total	100	100	100	100[a]	100	100

a. Because the statistical breakdown for Grenada was noncomparable, the working population of 26,000 has been omitted from this table.

Source: Statistical Appendix, Tables SA1.40, SA1.41, and SA1.42.

The fact that participation rates have fallen rather more rapidly among females than among males, notably in the LDCs, may be explained by the changing economic structure of the LDCs. The trend away from agriculture toward manufacturing and services affects female employment adversely: 25 percent of all women in the LDCs are employed in agriculture compared with only 10 percent in the MDCs. Indeed the occupational group with the largest decline in employment is that comprising farm managers, supervisors, and farmers, with women showing a much greater percentage fall than men.[38] Relatively high female employment levels are positively correlated with reduced fertility; it is, therefore, unsurprising that Barbados, the country with the lowest GRR, showed the smallest drop in females among the MDCs.

As the LDCs develop economically, these distributions by industrial group give an indication of the sectors of employment growth and decline. For example, the figures clearly show the decline of agriculture; to avoid sharp increases in unemployment levels, other sectors, notably manufacturing, need to expand employment. Policy recommendations to increase both agricultural and manufacturing employment are discussed, respectively, in Chapters 5 and 7.

38. See Statistical Appendix, Tables SA1.42, 1.14, and 1.45.

Labor Markets

The present labor market situation in the CARICOM countries combines scarcity of skilled workers with oversupply of the unskilled. In a perfectly competitive labor market structure, the wages of all less skilled workers would fall considerably, reducing the cost of labor relative to capital, thus encouraging more labor-intensive production. It appears, however, that capital costs are still relatively low compared with labor costs, particularly to the larger firms. This may be partially explained by artificially high wages in the organized sector of the labor markets. The evolution of the current wage structure and some of the problems it presents are now examined.

Labor markets for the highly skilled and the brain drain

Fragmentary evidence suggests that professional, technical, administrative, and managerial workers (and, to a lesser extent, skilled manual workers) have become increasingly scarce during the last decade. The disproportionately large emigration, or brain drain, of individuals in these categories during the 1960s, combined with rapidly increasing demand for their services (spurred primarily by the expansion of the public sector), have been the main causes of these scarcities.

The sharp increase in demand for professionals and skilled technical workers can be illustrated by the behavior of their wage rates. In the case of Trinidad and Tobago, for example, the proportion of professional and technical workers in the total labor force remained virtually unchanged at around 6 percent between 1964 and 1971.[39] Meanwhile, the weighted average minimum rates of pay of government employees in the fifteen highest-paid occupational categories rose by 68 percent between 1966 and 1971, compared with increases of 19 percent for daily paid manual workers and 37 percent for the bottom six monthly paid occupations.[40] This substantial widening in the wage structure of the public sector appears to have been even more marked in the private sector.[41] It seems unlikely that this tendency in Trinidad toward greater relative demand for, and hence increased earnings of, highly skilled workers could have been qualitatively different in the other CARICOM states.

Two rough measures of the current relatively scarcity of professional and skilled workers in the various CARICOM countries are: the percentage of all workers in each member state classified as professional and technical or administrative and managerial; and wage indexes for select occupations of professionals and skilled workers, based on the pay rate associated with a general laborer in each corresponding state. Table 3.15 summarizes such

39. Sidney E. Chernick, and others, "Employment in Trinidad and Tobago" (Washington, D.C.: World Bank, 1973; restricted circulation document), Statistical Appendix, Table 1.17.

40. Ibid., Table 9, p. 34.

41. Ibid., p. 32.

TABLE 3.15. INDEXES OF RELATIVE SCARCITY OF PROFESSIONAL AND SKILLED WORKERS

	Workers in highly skilled categories[a]		*Occupational/skill wage index*[b]	
Category	*Professional and technical*	*Administrative and managerial*	*Mechanic*	*Accountant*
MDCS	8.8	1.0	196	530
LDCS[c]	8.2	0.8	273	974

a. As percentage of all workers; unweighted means for each group, 1970.
b. Wage for general laborer = 100 in 1973.
c. Excludes Antigua.
Source: Statistical Appendix, Tables SA1.28a, SA1.28b.

data. The overall pattern suggests that the relative scarcity of professional and skilled workers is acute, and even more so in the LDCS than in the MDCS.

In addition to the 1970 census, other potential sources of relevant data include the types of skills requested by potential employers through employment agencies and trade unions, and the salaries offered; and the skill or occupational composition of work permits requested and granted. St. Lucia is the only country for which either type of information is available. About 45 percent of the work permits issued in St. Lucia during the 1971–73 period were for managers, engineers, and accountants.[42]

It has already been suggested that the rapid expansion in the demand for high-level personnel during the past decade has been largely caused by the growth of public sector employment of the relatively well trained. Although quantified information on this phenomenon is not available, it is interesting to note that in 1970 the proportion of the public sector's work force holding either a diploma or degree was 3.5 times that of private sector employees and the self-employed.

The numbers of highly trained personnel employed in government compared to the private sector may be large, but observations and experiences in the field roughly suggest that their productivity is generally substantial. Further, there is ample room for further growth of the numbers of such personnel in public as well as private employment throughout the region before the point of seriously diminishing marginal returns from their services is reached.

Heavy migration of highly trained and skilled manpower has seriously impeded the accumulation of human capital in the CARICOM region during the past two decades. Fragmentary evidence suggests that average net emigration of professionals from Trinidad and Tobago was, very roughly, 6 percent a year during the 1960s.[43] A comparable order of magnitude for

42. See Statistical Appendix, Table SA1.29.

43. The estimate is based on the assumption that net emigration from Trinidad had the same proportion of professional, technical, and kindred workers as that of Trini-

Barbados does not appear implausible; the size of the brain drain from Jamaica appears to be far more serious.[44] Until recently, none of the LDCs or Guyana had the educational facilities to produce individuals in this skill category; consequently, they were not direct net exporters of such individuals. The brain drain phenomenon may still have impinged upon these countries, however, through the emigration of high level personnel trained abroad.

Much has been written on the brain drain in general and some of the literature refers specifically to certain CARICOM countries. Although the dynamics of the brain drain process in the region are far too complex to be analyzed here, the situation may become somewhat easier in future years as a result of the following factors:

a. The increasing difficulty of obtaining immigrant visas in the highly industrialized English-speaking countries—even for the highly skilled.
b. An apparent narrowing of the potential earnings differentials for the highly skilled between the CARICOM area and international labor markets.
c. The growth of sentiments of nationalism and regionalism among the highly skilled, which will tend partially to counteract the "pull" factors.
d. A growing awareness of the problem on the part of high government officials, and thus a better disposition to deal effectively with some of the important nonpecuniary "push" factors (problems associated with obtaining professional literature or scientific equipment and facilities, for example, or the bureaucratic routine associated with public sector employment).

Intraregional migration may be as damaging as extraregional migration for some of the smaller territories with very limited supplies of skilled manpower. This problem may be expected to abate somewhat in the future as a result of factors analogous to those tending to limit extraregional migration.

Organized labor markets and unemployment

The organized labor markets in the CARICOM countries comprise virtually all public sector jobs and that part of the private sector in which conditions of employment are subject to collective bargaining. They account for between 30 and 50 percent of total employment, and wages and related benefits tend

---

dadians admitted as immigrants to the United States and Canada during the years 1966 to 1970; this proportion being 10 percent (Chernick and others, "Employment in Trinidad and Tobago," Table 1.10). Average annual net emigration from Trinidad during the sixties is estimated at 12,780 (Roberts, "Working Force of the Commonwealth Caribbean at 1970," Table I), of which 10 percent equals 1,278 which equals 6.2 percent of the 20,600 individuals classified in that category in Trinidad on average between 1966 and 1970 (Chernick and others, "Employment in Trinidad and Tobago," Table 1.17). This may be regarded as a rather conservative assessment, in that if the calculations had been based on official estimates of the Central Statistical Office, government of Trinidad, the derived net emigration rate would have been over twice as large.

44. See Statistical Appendix, Table SA1.31.

to be appreciably better than in the unorganized sectors (except for the most highly skilled professional and technical workers). It has been argued that these organized labor markets cause, at least, in part, the high rates of open unemployment in CARICOM countries, especially among the young. This is because conditions of employment are such that the supply of workers is bound to be in excess of demand, and individuals are willing and able to queue for scarce jobs rather than accept inferior ones (particularly those involving agricultural work) in the unorganized sector.

While there is no single reliable source of data on the size of the organized sector, it is possible to make some plausible inferences about its relative importance from country to country on the basis of indirect evidence. The percentage of total employment accounted for by paid workers,[45] based on 1970 census data, ranges from 69 percent in Jamaica to 92 percent in Barbados. The unweighted mean is 82 percent for the MDCs and 80 percent for the LDCs.[46] Barbados appears to have the largest organized sector, followed by St. Kitts and Trinidad. Jamaica, St. Lucia, and Belize, with low ratios of paid workers to total employment, are the opposite extreme. In general, there appears to be a positive association between the degree of unionization and the paid worker ratio for the eight territories for which information is available.

The importance of the size of the organized sector lies in its power to impose conditions of employment (or, for simplicity, wages) in excess of those which would tend to prevail under competitive conditions. Unfortunately, the wage data currently available for interterritorial comparisons cannot provide a direct assessment of the alleged wage gap between the organized and unorganized labor markets for comparable inputs of labor services. The only rough index for this gap is the relative wage differential between the typically organized factory operatives and the more loosely organized agricultural laborers as reported in mid-1973.[47] This proxy index, which is unavailable for Montserrat, averages 2.4 for both MDCs and LDCs and ranges from 1.0 in St. Kitts to 4.8 in Belize.[48] The index shows some positive statistical association with the paid worker ratio, and this association increases appreciably if the extreme observation for Belize is deleted. Although the evidence is far from conclusive, it tends to support the view that there is strength in (relative) numbers in the case of the size and monopolistic power of the organized sector of Caribbean labor markets.

45. This percentage is that proportion of total employment not accounted for by employers or the self-employed.

46. See Statistical Appendix, Table SA1.32.

47. Since there is quite probably a pure (that is, noncomparability of labor inputs) skill differential built into such an index, its value for any single territory is a poor measure of the organized-unorganized wage gap effect. If, however, it is postulated that the skill differential component in the index is constant across territories, its variation between territories might be presumed to be associated with differences in the degree of wage gap between them.

48. See Statistical Appendix, Table SA1.33.

The argument that the wage gap between the organized and unorganized labor market causes unemployment depends on the extent to which the working age population (particularly its younger members) can afford to remain unemployed for long periods of time while waiting for a job opening in the organized market, instead of being forced by economic necessity to find work in the less remunerative unorganized labor markets. Their degree of choice depends on the availability of alternative sources of income during the waiting period, which is in turn related to a host of socioeconomic factors. Three that appear to be particularly relevant in the CARICOM context are family income, casual work in the unorganized labor markets, and illegal activities.

The income earned by other members of their families is the most obvious alternative source of support for work seekers, particularly for the majority of the unemployed who are young. Although there is no direct information on the relationship between the incidence of unemployment and family income, there are reasons to suspect that work seekers are probably concentrated among households in the lower middle to upper lower socioeconomic strata. The poorest families simply lack the means to finance the work-seeker; the relatively well-to-do, on the other hand, can afford to support their children, helping them to get sufficient education and training to keep them out of the labor force throughout most of the period from age 14 to age 20 when they would otherwise be looking for any kind of work. The skills they learn will either increase their chances of employment in the excess demand labor markets (those for the highly skilled) or facilitate quick access to the organized sector. There is some indirect empirical evidence in support of this view; figures for Trinidad in 1970 show that the unemployment rate among individuals with negligible educational attainment (usually a good indicator of family and individual income) was less than one-third of the overall rate and only one-fifth of the rate among individuals with a secondary education certificate and above. Those with incomplete secondary education, however, had an unemployment rate 40 percent greater than the national average.[49]

Occasional employment in the unorganized labor markets seems to be the second important source of support for the unemployed in the CARICOM region who regard seeking work in the organized sector as their main activity. For example, 1970 census data for Jamaica show that at least 27 percent of male work seekers with previous job experience (about one-half of total male unemployment) had worked for two months or more during the preceding year. Although census data for the other territories do not permit similar calculations, it seems reasonable to believe that participation in unorganized labor markets, particularly in agriculture and tourism activities during peak seasons, is quite widespread.

The last source of support for the unemployed may include income from activities excluded from the statistical definition of work, such as prostitu-

49. Chernick and others, "Employment in Trinidad and Tobago," Table 3, p. 10.

tion, drug distribution and theft.[50] It is not possible, however, to provide a quantitative assessment of the extent of size of these sources of income.

It seems reasonable to suppose that the availability of alternative income sources is positively correlated with per capita income, and that this relationship would hold in spite of the appreciable differences in socioeconomic conditions and income distribution patterns between the CARICOM states. Taking the relative wage rate differential between factory operatives and agricultural laborers as a proxy for the wage gap between organized and unorganized markets (the wage gap index), the hypothesis was then tested in terms of a linear relationship between unemployment, the wage gap index, and per capita income.[51] The results yielded strongly and significantly positive coefficients for both independent variables, particularly for the wage gap index. Between them, they accounted for 66 percent of the observed variation in aggregate unemployment rates in 1970 in ten CARICOM states.[52] In the light of this evidence, it appears that the wage gap unemployment hypothesis deserves serious consideration in work on the causes of unemployment and cures for it.

Sources of disequilibrium in the organized sector

It has already been suggested that the wage gap was a consequence of the collective bargaining process, which was a feature of the organized labor market as a whole. Wages for comparable work differ markedly, however, within this market itself in most CARICOM states.[53] Some of the factors affecting the wage determination process in the organized labor markets are examined below.

INDUSTRIAL RELATIONS AND COLLECTIVE BARGAINING. Collective bargaining systems vary widely in the CARICOM region. The variations reflect the extreme diversity of different countries' institutional arrangements; legislation and government regulation of labor relations range from highly elaborate systems, such as that of Trinidad, to virtually nonexistent ones, as

50. While the relationship between unemployment and socially deviant behavior in general and crime in particular are both too complex and too remote from the objective of this study to permit further elaboration, it is perhaps one of the most important aspects of the unemployment problem in the majority of the CARICOM states.

51. $y = b_0 + b_1x_1 + b_2x_2$.
where y is the aggregate rate of unemployment in 1970; x_1 is the wage gap index (recorded in 1973); and x_2 is per capita income in 1970 in current East Caribbean dollars. The corresponding observations are shown in Statistical Appendix, Table SA1.33. Montserrat and Belize were excluded because of the absence of usable data.

52. The numerical results associated with each of these regressions are shown in Statistical Appendix, Table SA1.34.

53. For instance, minimum wage rates for laborers in Trinidad and Tobago's oil industry during 1971 were roughly two and a quarter times greater than those in the rest of the organized manufacturing sector (Chernick and others, "Employment in Trinidad and Tobago," p. 36).

in St. Lucia. The differing organizational structures, ideologies and operating methods of the various trade unions and employers acting as bargaining agents within the region also lead to variations in the process, and in its results. The size of wage settlements in collective bargaining agreements, and consequently the size of the wage gap, thus differs from country to country as a result of institutional factors.

One important exception to this state of affairs is the wage determination process in public sector employment. This not only accounts for a significant fraction of all jobs in the organized labor markets in the region, but also represents a major source of total employment. While the size of the public sector's wage bill in each territory is ultimately limited by fiscal and economic contraints, conditions of employment of government workers seem to be largely determined by institutional and political factors, together with the collective bargaining ability of public servants.[54,55] Fragmentary evidence suggests that the public sector's wage gap[56] tends to be positively correlated with countries' per capita income and to be relatively greater for less skilled occupations within each country. This may be because the richer countries tend to have a more elaborate institutional framework of labor relations and a generally more experienced trade union movement; these factors strengthen the bargaining position of government workers as a group, particularly favoring those at the lower end of the public pay scale whose earnings would be substantially lower in the unorganized sector.

ENCLAVE INDUSTRIES. The most conspicuous cases of extremely wide wage gaps in the region are found in (a) the oil industry in Trinidad and Antigua; (b) bauxite mining in Jamaica and Guyana; and (c) luxury tourism in most of the islands. There is no reliable quantified information on the size of these wage differentials, but indirect evidence and informed estimates suggest orders of magnitude ranging from three to five times the earnings of semiskilled and unskilled workers doing similar work in the unorganized sector.[57] All of these industries have certain elements in common which explain to a large extent their extraordinarily high relative rates of pay.

54. For men, the relative share of government workers in total employment during 1969–70 ranged from 11 percent in Jamaica to 29 percent in Trinidad and Tobago, averaging 18 percent for all 12 states (Roberts, "Working Force of the Commonwealth Caribbean at 1970," Table 5).

55. The traditional links between the trade union movement and political parties in the region undoubtedly play an important, if complex, role in this process.

56. This is the wage differential between the public sector and unorganized sector employment for comparable skill categories.

57. For example, it has already been noted that wages for laborers in Trinidad's oil industry in 1971 were approximately 2.2 times greater than in the rest of the manufacturing sector, which is also by and large unionized. On the other hand, median earnings of paid employees in (typically organized) firms with ten or more workers were 2.4 times as large as in 1965 (Chernick and others, "Employment in Trinidad and Tobago," Table 10, p. 38). Estimates of take home pay for workers in luxury resort

In the first place, local wage costs, even at these relatively inflated rates, are a small fraction of total costs to the firms in question, mainly because of their technological characteristics. The oil and bauxite industries are capital-intensive and employ a disproportionate amount of highly skilled as opposed to semiskilled and unskilled labor. To a lesser extent, this situation is also true of luxury tourism. In the CARICOM countries generally, and especially in the smaller islands, this production-structure effect is augmented by the extremely high import and related costs of other inputs, such as building materials, equipment and food.

In the second place, since all these industries are based on natural resources, their options to relocate are limited. Their demand for local labor is consequently quite inelastic and the unions can afford to push for increasingly higher wages without incurring significant costs in terms of the number of available jobs. In addition to the fact that relatively high wage rates represent a small proportion of firms' costs, most of these firms are owned, controlled, and managed by foreigners. This places them in a relatively weak bargaining position in relation to the unions, which are often supported by governments with which these same employers must deal on many other issues which vitally affect their firms' profitability.

In sum, the evidence generally supports the view that there are wide wage differentials between organized and unorganized labor markets, and that nonwage sources of income are available to those who decide to wait for a well-paid unionized job, rather than taking employment in the low-wage, unorganized sector. These factors combine to induce high rates of open unemployment. The earnings disequilibrium between organized and unorganized labor is not simply a result of trade union monopoly power over labor supply, but also reflects factors such as the presence of foreign employers with highly inelastic demand for local labor. This situation leads to wage gaps within the organized sector in addition to those between it and the unorganized sector. Clearly, any serious attempt on the part of governments to reduce the wage gap by imposing upper limits on negotiated wage rates will collide with the self-interest of the trade unions. In most CARICOM countries, where political and trade union leadership and support are closely intertwined, it seems unrealistic to expect any such move within the foreseeable future. Although distortions in the wage structure help to produce open unemployment, governments are unlikely to limit the unions' freedom to bargain with the enclave industries and expose themselves to the considerable consequent political risks.

---

hotels in St. Lucia and Antigua ranged between 2 to 7 times what they would earn doing similar work in unorganized establishments, depending on whether they performed direct services for the affluent foreign tourist (for example, as waiters and porters), in which case tips would account for most of their earnings, or otherwise (for example, as dishwashers). As a final example, average earnings in Jamaica's mining sector in 1960 and 1965 were approximately 3 times greater than in manufacturing.

Unorganized labor markets and poverty

Many workers, of course, lack the skills to compete for the jobs for which demand is high. They also lack the opportunity to work in the organized sector, or the access to alternative sources of income that would allow them to remain idle, either voluntarily or in the status of seeking work, for long periods of time. These individuals are forced by economic necessity to compete with each other for the relatively few jobs available or else to work in low-skill, labor-intensive activities. As a result, their productivity and earnings tend to be quite low. The bulk of the working poor in the region (particularly those in the LDCs) seem to be engaged in peasant farming and in other types of poorly paid activities, such as handicrafts, petty commerce, and certain types of low-skill personal services (such as domestic work).

Available evidence does not permit a direct assessment of the degree or extent of poverty[58] in the region, but a number of indicators shed some indirect light on the dimensions of the problem. Indicators of the degree of poverty include the infant mortality rate; the child mortality rate; the index of child malnutrition; and an index of underemployment income requirements for the lowest paid workers. Some indicators of the extent of poverty are the proportion of the working population in the lowest paid occupational categories; the ratio of the self-employed to the whole work force; and the proportion of the male working population which has not completed secondary education.[59]

The four indexes of the degree of poverty vary markedly from country to country, but are quite highly correlated for any given country. St. Vincent and St. Kitts seem to suffer the most acute cases of extreme poverty in the region. At the other extreme, the lowest income households of Trinidad, Barbados, and Antigua seem to be relatively better off than their counterparts in the other states. The three extent of poverty indexes also vary quite substantially between countries; the correlation between them is significantly stronger for each country than in the previous set of indexes. According to these indicators, the relative extent of poverty is much greater in Jamaica than in any of the other territories. At the other extreme, poverty in Barbados and Trinidad appears to be limited to a comparatively small fraction of the population.

These indexes may also be used to supplement the crude figures for per capita income in each country, in that they add a distributional element to the picture. For example, while Jamaica had the second highest per capita income in the region, it had the highest value for the child mortality index

58. The degree of poverty refers to deficiencies in such essential requirements as food, clothing, and shelter. The extent of poverty refers to the proportion of poor people in the entire population.

59. The indexes and explanatory notes on their precise definitions and sources appear in Statistical Appendix, Table SA1.35, and in standardized form (in which the CARICOM mean value for each index is used as the corresponding base of 100) in Statistical Appendix, Table SA1.35a.

and for all three extent of poverty indexes, suggesting a highly skewed distribution of income. Antigua, on the other hand, showed better than average values in the five poverty indexes for which information was available, although its per capita income was less than two-thirds that of Jamaica.

The degree of poverty in the CARICOM countries can be put into perspective by contrasting the values of some of the indexes in the region with those for a paradigm country such as Sweden. The region's average infant mortality rate is about four times as great as that of Sweden, ranging from three to eight times greater in, respectively, Trinidad and St. Vincent. With regard to child mortality, the region's average is nine times greater than Sweden's (varying from six- to fifteen-fold, respectively, in Trinidad and Jamaica). The child malnutrition index is fourteen times as large as that of Sweden, ranging from two to twenty-six times larger in, respectively, Antigua and St. Vincent.

Population and Employment from a Regional Integration Perspective: Issues and Options

From a regional integration perspective, the employment problems facing the CARICOM states may be conveniently grouped under three headings: (a) intraregional mobility; (b) the labor market impact of economic integration; and (c) the scope for regional manpower policies.

Intraregional mobility

The issue of freedom of movement between member countries was one of the principal sources of disagreement and conflict among the various governments which participated in the West Indies Federation. Indeed, some authoritative commentators believe that this question played a leading role in the collapse of the federation in 1962.[60] It is thus not surprising that a publication emanating from the Commonwealth Caribbean Regional Secretariat (CCRS) explicitly excluded freedom of movement of labor from the aims of the Caribbean common market, distinguishing CARICOM from ". . . the orthodox definition of a common market . . . in which there is internal free trade, a Common External Tariff and a freedom of movement by the factors of production—namely, capital and labor."[61]

This problem remains qualitatively just as difficult today as it was fifteen years ago. The governments of some territories are concerned that unrestricted intraregional mobility of persons would aggravate their employment

60. See, for example, Gordon K. Lewis, *The Growth of the Modern West Indies* (New York: 1958) and A. McIntyre, "Some Issues of Trade Policy in the West Indies," *New World Quarterly*, vol. 1, no. 2, 1966.

61. Commonwealth Caribbean Regional Secretariat, "From CARIFTA to Caribbean Community," (Georgetown, Guyana: 1972), p. 109.

problems. Are such fears warranted? What are the likely consequences if freedom of movement were allowed? Who would benefit and who would bear the costs? Would substantial net gains accrue as a result of mobility and could these be redistributed in such a way that everyone would be better off?

In the first place, it should not be assumed that the prevailing legal restrictions on interterritorial migration have in fact prevented such population movements from occurring. There is no quantified information on these migratory flows, but the available evidence suggests that it has been substantial during the past few decades.[62] Moreover, it is reasonable to suppose that the pattern of intraregional migration has been, is, and will continue to be dominated by net flows of potential workers in accordance with the structure of expected wage and salary differentials and other conditions of employment in different CARICOM countries. The factors underlying intraregional migration are thus basically analogous to those associated with extraregional migration.

With the exception of some seasonal movements of agricultural labor in recent years (particularly between the Windward Islands and Barbados, and within the Leeward Islands), most intraregional migration appears to be made up of movements of the semiskilled urban young from the urban areas of the poorest countries into those of the relatively rich—particularly into the northwestern coastal areas of Jamaica (the Montego Bay–Ocho Rios strip), Antigua and the areas of greater Port of Spain and San Fernando in Trinidad. The main effects of this intraregional migration are probably to reduce somewhat the problems of low income employment and idleness in the states of origin, and to increase the already serious problems of open unemployment, overloaded infrastructure and inadequate social services in the urban areas of the recipient territories.

Although legal restrictions on intraregional migration are not strictly enforced, they probably deter a significant number of potential migrants; their elimination would probably, therefore, lead to somewhat heavier net migratory flows. It is hard to imagine any realistic way in which host countries could capitalize on the removal of restrictions by taxing or otherwise appropriating any significant part of the benefits accruing either to immigrants or to the labor market competitors they left behind in their home areas. The elimination of legal barriers to intraregional migration would, therefore, probably serve simply to increase both the private and social benefits and costs associated with existing levels of migration.[63]

62. For example, a tally of enumeration districts accounting for 67 percent of the total 1960 census population in Trinidad indicates that roughly 8 percent of this subset (over 42,000 persons) claimed to have been born in some other West Indian country. It is quite likely that this percentage underestimates the true proportion, since in all probability a significant fraction of all such immigrants have not met some or all of the legal requirements associated with their residence in Trinidad, and would be reluctant to admit their extraterritorial origin to the census enumerator.

63. The expected benefits and costs of intraregional migration may be summarized as follows: private benefits—higher expected wages, both for immigrants and their

In sum, the long standing opposition of certain governments to unrestricted movement of persons within the region seems to be justifiable from their own nationalistic point of view. It is not clear, moreover, that any incremental costs and benefits resulting from the abolition of current migratory restrictions would lead to a net gain in the social welfare of the region as a whole. The issue seems to hinge on the comparative net marginal social cost to the region as a whole of idleness among the younger members of the working age population in one group of urban areas (those in the more affluent states, notably Trinidad) and another (those in the poorer territories, especially the Windward Islands). If and when the employment problem is brought under control in Jamaica, Trinidad, and Guyana, the removal of all restrictions to intraregional mobility of persons will then become more clearly advantageous from a regional economic point of view and more likely will become politically acceptable to the governments of all member states.

The labor market impact of regional integration

The impact of regional integration on labor markets appears to have been quite modest. Very broadly, it appears to have raised somewhat the demand for certain categories of professional and skilled workers in full employment labor markets, and to have led to a degree of convergence in wage structures and conditions of employment in the organized labor markets of different countries—notably in the government sector and some capital intensive industries. Its effect on unorganized labor markets has probably been either negligible or slightly negative. The impact would become significantly greater if planned regional projects in agriculture are implemented. The livestock program, for example, is expected to provide directly about 15,600 on-farm jobs, with additional jobs in complementary sectors such as feed and fertilizer production. The region has also been giving consideration to the establishment of rural settlement projects in Belize. These projects would provide scope for intraregional migration without putting further strains on the urban areas of recipient countries. Further favorable effects can be obtained with the adoption of regional manpower policies of the kind suggested later in this chapter.

INCREASED DEMAND FOR SKILLED WORKERS. The suggestion that integration has raised the demand for certain categories of professional and skilled manpower (such as engineers, statisticians, managers, technical personnel, and specialized workers in general) is based on two propositions: (a) that

---

erstwhile labor market competitors in the corresponding countries of origin; public benefits—relief of pressure on urban infrastructure and reduction of social costs associated with the employment problem in countries of net migratory outflow; private costs—lower expected wages for migrant labor market competitors in recipient countries; and public costs—increasing pressure on urban infrastructure and higher social costs associated with the employment problem in recipient countries.

the integration process entails the expansion of certain product markets; and (b) that these enlarged markets elicit a significant supply response from within the region (either by increasing output levels of goods already being produced in one or more of the member states, or by inducing the development of new product lines).

The limited evidence accumulated about the growth of intraregional trade since the inception of CARIFTA in 1968 tends to support these two propositions, and the supply response seems overwhelmingly likely to take the form of greater modern sector activity. More specifically, both new and expanding industries will tend to make more use of capital and skilled manpower than the traditional sector; this will sharply raise the demand for specialized personnel in relation to the region's limited supply, but will produce little if any increase (either directly or through multiplier-type effects) in the demand for unskilled labor.

This trend is likely to widen occupational wage differentials within the region, particularly in Trinidad and Tobago and Jamaica, where the potential for modern sector expansion in response to integration appears to be greatest. To the extent, moreover, that integration-induced industrial expansion leads to greater output of mass-produced items which can easily substitute for labor-intensive goods traditionally supplied from within the region (for example, ready-made garments instead of custom-tailored ones, or aluminum and fiberglass boats instead of hand crafted wooden ones), employment in unorganized handicraft and cottage manufacturing activities may actually be reduced.

CONVERGING WAGE STRUCTURES IN ORGANIZED MARKETS. The integration process is also likely to affect interterritorial wage structures and related conditions of employment in such strongly unionized sectors as those of minerals and government employment. The principal factors underlying the relationship between integration and wage structures seem to be (a) increasing awareness at a national level on the part of trade union leaders and middle- and higher-echelon government workers of the conditions of employment and wage structures prevailing in corresponding sectors of other CARICOM countries; and (b) a tendency on the part of these individuals to link the concept of regional integration with the regionwide application of the objective of equal pay for equal work. Both of these factors, which appears to be fostered by the spirit of the integration process and the institutional mechanisms involved in it, would tend to reduce wage differences between territories for comparable job categories. This would lead to more homogeneous occupational wage structures within the organized sectors throughout the region as integration continues.

With the possible exception of the bargaining demands ultimately incorporated into the collective agreements between the Antigua Workers' Union and the West Indies Oil Refinery since the early 1970s, and some current attempts to draw up regionwide collective agreements by local trade unions bargaining with employers operating in several of the CARICOM states (for example: British West Indies Airways [BWIA], Leeward Island Air Transport

[LIAT], the Hilton and Holiday Inn hotel chains), the available evidence suggests that the trend toward harmonization of conditions of employment is still far from being established. Nevertheless, the regularity and persistence with which this issue is linked to the process of integration by trade unions, employers' associations and civil servants[64] suggests that regionwide patterns of wage settlements will become more common as integration proceeds.

This development could have adverse consequences for employment. The pursuit of the objective of integration through harmonization of conditions of employment make the bargaining agents of workers at the lower end of the regional occupational wage structure more likely to press for agreements which allow their members to catch up with their more highly paid counterparts elsewhere in the region. This would place immediate strains on labor relations in the lower wage countries, leading either to industrial conflict, or to sharp increases in pay in their organized labor market, or both. In the latter two cases the wage gap between the organized and unorganized sectors in these countries would widen with the consequence of restricting labor demand and exacerbating open unemployment. It is not difficult to envisage a subsequent scenario of a regionwide spiral developing as the trade unions in the traditionally higher wage countries (particularly Trinidad and Tobago and Jamaica) strive to regain their relative advantage over the traditionally low wage territories. This potentially disruptive side effect of the integration process deserves careful consideration by the CARICOM Secretariat and the recently created "labor desk" in the CCRS.

The scope for regional manpower policies

The region urgently needs to develop a program to generate, analyze, and disseminate manpower information on a systematic and reasonably current basis. Only Jamaica and Trinidad, among all the CARICOM countries, have attempted such a task through their periodic household surveys.

MANPOWER INFORMATION AND ANALYSIS. The process of generating this sort of information is subject to very marked economies of scale; in particular, tasks such as the design of questionnaires and samples, the preparation of interviewers' manuals and the analysis of the collected data can easily be undertaken centrally for the whole region. The Commonwealth Caribbean population censuses, which have been conducted since 1911, represents a precedent for a regionwide arrangement and an example of its technical and political feasibility. The inauguration of a PREALC[65] subregional office with headquarters in Jamaica could be an important catalyst for the

64. The massive wage increase granted by Jamaica to its civil servants late in 1973 provoked concern in other territories that similar demands would be made by their own public workers.

65. *Programa Regional del Empleo para America Latina y el Caribe*—a regional agency of the International Labour Office's World Employment Program.

expansion of CARICOM's manpower data base[66]—which is, in turn, a prerequisite for an effective manpower policy.

A second urgent need, closely related to the development of an adequate data base, and particularly dependent on it, is the establishment of a regional manpower office in the CARICOM Secretariat. This office should be staffed with specialized technical personnel, should have data processing capabilities and should be charged with (a) giving member states technical assistance in coordinating the collection of manpower data, including helping them to standardize statistical concepts and methodology; and (b) centralizing, compiling, analyzing, and disseminating this information, particularly the composition and regional deployment of the working age population (current and projected), and the characteristics of work seekers and employment opportunities available in each territory (current and projected).

The regional manpower office could also help to promote, coordinate, and disseminate research efforts bearing on the common manpower problems facing member countries, and to synthesize the regional policy implications of such research. The University of the West Indies (UWI), particularly through its Institute of Social and Economic Research and its Census Research Program, has done valuable work in this area; close institutional and operational ties should be established between these and other relevant, specialized research units within UWI and the regional manpower office.

TRAINING. Training is another important aspect of manpower policy, which like the preceding proposals, offers major economies of scale, particularly at higher and more specialized levels of expertise. The University of the West Indies provides a successful precedent for regional cooperation of this kind. In addition, CARICOM has already accepted and incorporated education as one of the areas of functional cooperation among member states; this provides a policy base for efforts to integrate work in this area on a regionwide basis.

The idea of regional cooperation in manpower training is not new. Its scope, however, could usefully be expanded in the immediate future to help meet the rapid rates of growth which are likely to occur among the population group between 15 and 19 years old in the region during the next ten years or so.

In addition to the potential economies of scale to be derived from regional integration of secondary level training, a regionwide program should help to produce a mix of skills which is appropriate to CARICOM's overall needs. At present, structural imbalances, between the demand for and supply of various types of labor skills in the CARICOM states, clearly represent a major

66. A reasonable objective for a manpower information program would be to conduct continuous household sample surveys in all territories, using a basic questionnaire analogous to that of the Commonwealth Caribbean population census to which special purposes modules could be added on a periodic basis. Results could, for example, be published quarterly, with a delay of several months.

waste of manpower resources in the region; certain high-skilled occupations face labor shortages, while at the same time large numbers of persons are either idle or employed in low-skill activities whose marginal productivity is negligible. Regional collaboration in the delivery of secondary level instruction could help to reduce this problem.

The labor markets for various specialized craft skills in most countries in the region are so small that effective national demand is insufficient to absorb the services of more than a handful of trained individuals on a full-time productive basis. Electricians, laboratory technicians, mechanics, and paramedical personnel of various types are examples of the skills in question. Acting alone on a purely national basis, few CARICOM countries can afford to provide training in these skills; consequently, they must either do without them or import them from abroad. Alternatively, countries which do provide training are faced with either excess capacity of the required training facilities,[67] excess supply of persons with such skills in their domestic labor markets, or both. Provision of this type of training on a regionally integrated basis would make it possible to cover a much broader range of skills than any one national program could. At the same time, a regionwide program could take steps to prevent an excessive supply of specific types of skills. This allocative function would be based on, and be a direct practical complement to, the labor market data to be gathered and processed by the regional manpower office.

Specialized training could also expand to include skills and "skill packages" which are currently being provided from extraregional sources. These would include a number of project-specific skills (such as those associated with geological surveying for mineral resources; construction of subterranean sewerage, communications, and transportation systems; and dredging, installation, and expansion of port facilities). Such skills can be fully utilized only intermittently in any one of the CARICOM member states; investment in acquiring them is therefore hardly justifiable from the individual national point of view. It is quite likely, however, that regionally coordinated scheduling of projects using these skills might provide full-time and highly productive employment to individuals trained in them (and to regional firms with such "skill package" capabilities). Regional project programming of this type could have a favorable impact on the skill base of the region's population, and could save some of the foreign exchange currently being paid to extraregional contractors undertaking such projects.

EXTRAREGIONAL MIGRATION. Cooperation and integration in the area of extraregional migration policies and their implementation also offer economies of scale in manpower policy. There are certain objectives in this area that seem to be widely shared among CARICOM states; moreover, to pursue them effectively is beyond the capacity of any one individual country. The main objectives in question are (a) to reduce to a minimum restrictions

67. They are typically of suboptimal size to begin with.

in extraregional countries on immigration into those countries of low-skilled workers from the CARICOM states; (b) to foster the repatriation of CARICOM nationals working abroad whose skills are in short supply in the region. To promote these objectives, it might be worthwhile establishing regionally supported offices which could be assigned the tasks of assembling and maintaining a current registry of citizens of CARICOM countries residing abroad, with the object of identifying suitable potential candidates for re-employment in the region.

Chapter 4

Transport

THE DEVELOPMENT OF AN ADEQUATE REGIONAL TRANSPORT SYSTEM IS essential for the economic integration of the English-speaking Caribbean. Both the openness of the economies of the member states of the Caribbean Community (CARICOM)[1] and the fact that they are so physically dispersed underline the importance of the transport linkages between them.

Although the region has a common heritage of British colonization, common customs and tastes, and even a commonality of social and economic features and problems, it has not developed a cohesive transport network. This is partly because the individual islands were historically encouraged to look to Britain for both trade relations and military and financial support, rather than to forge links with one another. Consequently, the establishment of strong intraregional ties was neglected until relatively recent years. When transport links eventually did evolve—both by sea and by air—they grew in a rather haphazard fashion.

Since the inception of CARICOM, the member countries have been investigating whether and how they should set up regional air and sea carriers. Action has already been taken to reorganize a faltering sea carrier and to

1. On average, the foreign trade sector accounts for more than 40 percent of gross domestic product in the countries that comprise CARICOM. Traditionally, much of this trade has been with metropolitan countries. In 1973, however, as much as 10 percent of total exports was accounted for by trade among CARICOM member countries. The region depends very heavily on foreign trade; imports cover the full range of capital, intermediate, and consumer goods. A major objective of CARICOM is to promote greater regional self-sufficiency, particularly in agriculture (through specialized production by individual member countries in accordance with their resource endowments), and through the development of greater intraregional trade. This objective makes it urgent to provide adequate regional transport services.

rescue a defunct airline. There are still too many air and sea carriers in the region, however. The slow pace of rationalization in the transport sector is a consequence of three factors: the absence of a regional plan for transport; the tendency for nationalistic interests to take precedence over regional needs; and the fact that the geographical configuration of CARICOM makes it hard to organize a logical transport network.

Sea transport in the region consists of three different types of general cargo services—the regionally owned West Indies Shipping Corporation (WISCO), which carries an important proportion of intraregional cargo; the foreign-owned shipping lines, which handle almost all of the bulk commodity shipping (bauxite, petroleum, and petroleum products);[2] and the small, privately owned vessels serving the Eastern Caribbean.

The main exports of the Caribbean countries are agricultural commodities consisting predominantly of sugar, bananas, and citrus fruits. While the bulk of intraregional trade has been in petroleum and petroleum products and manufactures, the Regional Food Plan (RFP) has set a goal of self-sufficiency in food.[3] This goal will greatly affect the shape and size of both intraregional and extraregional trade, and needs to be taken into account in any plans for the development of a regional transport system. The constraints upon and prospects for sea transport in the region must be considered in the light of developments in regional agriculture. The question of subsidies for sea transport also needs to be examined. Services must both increase in volume and improve in quality in the region, and in the Eastern Caribbean in particular—but new and upgraded services priced on a fully commercial basis may well be too costly for the Community's less developed countries (LDCs) unless the strategy for the sector takes their special needs into account.

Three international air carriers are based in the region—British West Indian Airways (BWIA); Air Jamaica; and International Caribbean Airways (ICA). Extraregional services are also provided by foreign carriers. Intraregional service has developed sporadically, but generally in close step with tourism. Leeward Islands Air Transport (LIAT) and its two subsidiaries operate most interisland flights, serving all member countries except Jamaica, Guyana, and Belize. A number of small operators also carry scheduled passengers, charter passengers and freight in the Caribbean, but they are unreliable—a serious drawback for tourists from outside the region. If existing air services were consolidated on a regional basis, it might then be possible to develop the services to currently underserved areas which the region badly needs. Any plan to consolidate regional air services will, however, have to include satisfactory compensation arrangements to current carriers.

One of the more significant recent developments in CARICOM has been

2. Government owned ships are responsible for some shipments of bauxite and products from Guyana and Jamaica.

3. The plan is discussed in greater detail in Chapter 5, which examines agricultural development.

the establishment of a Standing Committee of Ministers Responsible for Transportation (SCMT). This body has broad responsibilities which include the coordination of all aspects of sea and air transport for both passenger and freight movement; the drafting of port and airport plans; and the establishment of the administrative apparatus required to negotiate rate increases with extraregional shipping lines and air carriers.

Any attempts to develop regional transport infrastructure or apply integrated transport policies must, however, take account of the many different aspects of the integration effort and the changing regional economic environment—including new industry, new commerce, economic activity in new locations, and the growth and decline of different kinds of activity. Markets will change, and trade patterns and passenger movements will change with them. An understanding of these structural changes, particularly in terms of their market potential is essential if the region is to plan transport to yield the greatest net benefit for all.

The CARICOM region differs from many other geographical areas in that road, air, and sea transport do not compete within it. Nearly all goods are transported by sea, and nearly all passengers by air. Although cruise ships operate extensively in the region, they do not compete with the airlines' passenger services. The number of travelers using ships which carry both cargo and passengers between the islands has decreased sharply, and this type of service will probably become increasingly uneconomical.[4] The two modes of transport—sea and air—are, therefore, examined separately in this chapter.

Sea Transport

The following discussion of the sea transport system in the Caribbean Community is divided into three parts. First, the various components of the system are introduced and analyzed in terms of ownership patterns and functional divisions. Second, the port system is described. Third, the question of shipping tariffs and rates is examined.

The shipping system

For centuries, shipping patterns in the Caribbean were based on movement between territories in the region and the metropolitan countries (mainly England in the case of CARICOM). Ships would load up in Caribbean ports with the primary agricultural products which provided the foundation of the mercantilist empires of Europe; on their return journeys, they would carry to the West Indies industrial and home-crafted products for the expatriate population of the region.

4. WISCO provided a freight and passenger service until the end of 1975 when the "Federal Maple" was withdrawn from service.

HISTORICAL DEVELOPMENT. New markets developed in England's North American colonies over the years, as they received and assimilated immigrants from Europe, and Caribbean trade and shipping routes took on a triangular pattern.[5] The flow between Britain, the West Indies, and the American colonies of sugar, molasses, distilled spirits, and industrial and crafted products, augmented trade and increased the revenues of British merchant houses. Throughout this period, however, transport and communications flowed mainly between points within the Caribbean and points outside. Apart from stops en route to pick up additional cargo and water, and occasionally to replace crew members who had jumped ship, there was no traffic within the region. It can be argued that the natural isolation of a number of small island colonies worked to the advantage of British imperialism; consequently, this isolation was a state of affairs to be encouraged and preserved.

REGIONALLY OWNED SHIPPING SERVICES. It was not until as late as 1953 that the first effort was made to operate a regional shipping line. In that year, the governments of all the British Caribbean territories, with the exception of Belize, agreed to open a subsidized shipping service from Jamaica to Guyana, calling at all islands en route. The governments were to share the first EC$6 million[6] of losses among themselves; additional losses were to be met by the United Kingdom. This service, operated by charter vessels which proved to be either too expensive or too small, was short-lived; it was significant, however, in that it overcame the inertia that had previously existed. It also paved the way for the establishment of the West Indies Shipping Corporation (WISCO) in 1961 by the West Indies Federation. This new shipping company was to establish, maintain, operate, and contract for the operation of shipping services to transport mail, passengers, and goods within the Caribbean region. Fares, charges, routes, and schedules were subject to ministerial approval. Subsidies were provided for WISCO operations through grants which were payable if operating costs exceeded revenue earned in any year. This practice was justified by arguments for the need to encourage intraregional trade. Unfortunately, the subsidy did not in itself give WISCO an adequate cost advantage; moreover, it operated in isolation without the benefit of other trade promotion policies which were urgently needed. These policies were only brought into effect some years later with the inception of the Caribbean Free Trade Association (CARIFTA) and then CARICOM itself; by that time the low level of trade had made it exceedingly difficult to keep the faltering carrier in operation.

It had originally been intended that WISCO should be controlled by a federal board of five members appointed by the appropriate federal minister. They were to be men with relevant competence, skill, and experience in

5. The first triangular movement was of course that between Europe, Africa, and the Caribbean in the period of the slave trade.

6. For exchange rates for the Eastern Caribbean dollar (EC$) and other related currencies, see Statistical Appendix, Table SA11.20.

trade, industry, finance, or business administration. To provide some diversity of background, it was decided that only four board members could be public officials.

After the dissolution of the federation in 1961, Trinidad and Tobago took the initiative in passing an act in 1962, creating the Regional Shipping Council (RSC). This body assumed the powers which had originally been held by the federal board. Members were nominated by participating governments and the RSC gradually developed as a political body. It became responsible for overall shipping policy, operation of the shipping services, supervision of extraregional services, and negotiations on freight rates with the conferences of ocean shipping lines which determine the rules of ocean shipping. Broad policy questions as well as day-to-day operational matters fell within the purview of the RSC, and social, rather than commercial, criteria became paramount in the decisions it took, with the result that shipping services needed constant subsidies.

In 1973, the governments of the CARICOM countries agreed to replace the RSC with a new body—the Standing Committee of Ministers Responsible for Transportation (SCMT). They gave the SCMT general authority over all regional transport matters. Its maritime responsibilities were to include the planning of future shipping growth, the development of ports, and the negotiation of freight rates proposed by concerns engaged in extraregional shipping. The SCMT now has overall responsibility for shaping regional policy and development for the transport sector.

Despite the establishment of the SCMT, WISCO operations have continued to lose money. It has been argued that the carrier's inefficiency can be traced back to the preemption of managements' authority by the old RSC, but there are other equally important causes.

The advent of containers and pallets, a major development in international shipping, had an adverse effect on WISCO operations. The obsolete cargo-handling equipment and arrangement of holds and hatches of the two WISCO ships, the "Federal Palm" and "Federal Maple," impaired the carrier's efficiency in ports equipped for containerized cargoes. Furthermore, WISCO had to provide a regular service to all ports between Jamaica and Trinidad. The costs of using the same ships to serve ten different ports with widely differing volumes of cargo, the inadequate and sometimes inefficient port facilities in certain islands, and the ships' dual function of carrying passengers and cargo all contributed to the losses sustained by the company.

As time passed, WISCO's losses and the subsidies it needed became increasingly serious. Contributions from member governments to make up operating losses began to lag. It finally became necessary to mount a rescue operation. In 1975, a new agreement was reached by CARICOM member governments which in effect restructured WISCO's operations, putting them on a more commercially viable basis. One of the most significant provisions in the new WISCO agreement is the departure from the historical practice of subsidizing operating losses. It has now been agreed that the company is to set fares at a level high enough to cover operating expenses plus allowable depreciation and financing charges. A special fund is to be established, however, to meet any operating deficits incurred. Contributions to this fund are to be made in proportion to each member's subscribed share capital. Under the new agreement, the management of WISCO is also to assume greater responsibility for day-to-day operations; this should help raise morale and improve efficiency. The management of WISCO is also examining its tariffs to see that distances traveled are adequately reflected in the rates the company charges. Receiving, storage, and delivery charges have been revised to reflect actual costs as closely as possible, and all charges in future are to be in U.S. dollars to avoid currency fluctuations. The company is also examining the extension of service to Belize. Although the new regime should help to improve its operations, WISCO still requires assistance in planning and marketing.

In addition to the restructuring of WISCO, the CARICOM governments agreed in December 1975 to a TT$25 million[7] investment program. The objective of this program was for WISCO to purchase four ships over a five-year period. The first ship—a container vessel—was introduced into the service in 1976. Financing has been secured for the other three units from the Caribbean Development Bank, the European Development Fund, and the European Investment Bank.

EXTRAREGIONAL SERVICES UNDER REGIONAL OWNERSHIP. The need for regional investment in extraregional shipping has been raised at both national and regional levels. The principal justification is the volume of foreign trade and the consequent vulnerability of the region to foreign shipping policies. The difference in the nature of the foreign trade—bulk exports and manufactured, break-bulk imports; the diversity of sources, particularly of imports; and the integration of transport of exports into the export production structure have all operated as constraints.

Two governments have recently entered the field. The Guyana Bauxite Company has, in partnership with a Norwegian firm, A. S. Bulkhandling, formed a shipping company—Guyana Shipping Ltd., which carries bauxite and aluminum from Guyana to North America and Europe, and grains mainly from North America. Jamaica, in partnership with a Mexican company has formed Jamaica Merchant Marines Ltd., initially to transport bauxite and aluminum from Jamaica to the Gulf ports. Significantly, these two companies have been based on a major bulk export commodity.

At the regional level, there have been proposals for study, particularly in light of the Regional Food Plan, and proposals for other joint industrial projects involving, for example, aluminum and steel. A technical committee was set up in 1975 to undertake such a study, but no firm proposals have yet appeared.

SERVICES UNDER EXTRAREGIONAL OWNERSHIP. It has already been mentioned that extraregional shipping is controlled by the international shipping

7. See note 6.

lines through the conference system. Under this system, conferences restrict competition, establish standard freight rates for each given route, determine and regulate shipping schedules, select ports of call, and occasionally enter into pooling arrangements for both cargoes and revenues.

In the English-speaking Caribbean, the West Indian Transatlantic Steamship Lines (WITASS) conference controls services between the region and Europe, including the United Kingdom. The SCMT has established a committee with power to meet with the members of the conference to discuss freight rate issues. The SCMT has had little success, however, in its attempts to lower freight rates by negotiation.

Other conferences control extraregional shipping between the CARICOM countries and other parts of the world. In particular, trade with the East Coast of North America is controlled by the Leeward and Windward islands and Guianas conference. There are also separate conferences for the United States West Coast and for the Far East.

Because of the large size and the diversity of trade between the Caribbean region and the rest of the world, a wide variety of ships is needed to provide ocean shipping services. There are, for example, bulk carriers, specializing in the haulage of specific commodities such as petroleum, bauxite, sugar, and bananas. These ships are usually owned by the organizations that either process or market the commodities carried; it is very hard to estimate the costs or the efficiency of this type of vertically integrated operation. Then there are conventional cargo vessels, usually carrying a somewhat more diversified cargo; in recent years there have also been container cargo vessels, a rapidly expanding category. Finally, there are a few "roll-on/roll-off" ships operated by some of the ocean shipping lines.

The routes that these ocean-going ships follow are usually imposed upon them by factors largely beyond their control. Mooring and pilotage charges are strong inducements for ships to minimize their ports of call. In fact, of the 150 shipping lines serving the Caribbean in 1968, only five called on more than five ports. Ships usually call regularly on the major ports, but only appear to be willing to operate in the smaller ports on the basis of an additional inducement charge. This is a charge intended to compensate carriers for the extra cost and inconvenience of stopping specially on a particular occasion. As bigger ships become the rule, it is almost certain that the inducement charge will become too large to be worth paying, except when the very largest quantities of goods are being shipped. Small-scale production is the norm in the countries in which these ports are located, however, and their major exports are agricultural goods whose output is limited by the finite amount of land suitable for their cultivation. If the CARICOM LDCs are not to be cut off from the rest of the world, therefore, an efficient transfer and feeder system must be developed.

Cruise ships are yet another type of ocean shipping operating in the Caribbean. These ships operate from North American and European ports on regular, year-round schedules; activity is at its peak in the winter season. Cruising is more closely linked to the tourist market than to other shipping activity in the region. It does not, however, compete directly with air services for tourist expenditures, since vacation cruises to the Caribbean are not made in order to arrive at any particular destination; the islands are simply ports of call to give vacationers a brief opportunity to go shopping and sightseeing.

SMALL VESSEL SERVICES. There are two distinct types of small vessels operating in the waters of the Caribbean Community. The first is that of the Guyanese coastal and river vessels, whose service extends as far as Trinidad and Barbados. Then there are the small vessels which operate in the southern half of the Eastern Caribbean; their service extends to the Windward and Leeward islands. For years these small wooden-hulled vessels, powered by sail and auxiliary engines, have been operating on the same routes in this part of the region without any regularly scheduled service. The very cheap form of sea transport they have provided has been made possible by standards of service which leave a great deal to be desired. Delays in shipment are frequent; pilferage and damage to cargo are not uncommon. Because many of the vessels are permanently in a poor state of repair, it can be very difficult to insure cargoes. Moreover, when it is possible to get insurance, the premiums are usually twice those charged for cargo transported on larger ships, and only cover the total loss of both ship and cargo. Compensation is rarely paid for damaged or spoiled cargo.[8]

The governments of the CARICOM countries have recently pledged support for small vessel sea transport, but this type of service needs to be substantially improved and consolidated. The entry of WISCO into this segment of the market might help to bring about the changes which are required.

THE COMPOSITION AND VOLUME OF CARGO SHIPPING. Of the three different types of shipping service described above, WISCO accounts for 20 to 25 percent of total regional traffic. The ocean shipping lines handle a further 30 to 40 percent (together with all the extraregional traffic) and the smaller vessels of the Eastern Caribbean handle the remaining 40 to 50 percent of the intraregional traffic. The low percentage of intraregional traffic carried by WISCO is mainly a result of the company's small capacity.

In the first five years of CARIFTA, intraregional exports increased in value terms from US$45 million in 1967 to US$110 million in 1972. This increase raised the share of intraregional trade in the total trade of the region from 5.7 percent of the total to 9.3 percent. The most recent figures are for 1973; in that year total intraregional exports reached US$120 million, which represents 10 percent of total regional exports. Data on physical flows of maritime traffic are difficult to obtain because trade statistics are usually expressed in value terms, but estimates of intraregional export shipments

8. The small vessels were once organized under the British West Indies Schooner Pool Association which provided insurance, fixed schedules, canvassed cargo, and fixed and published tariffs. More recently most ship owners have withdrawn and the pool is now mainly constituted of agents.

expressed in metric tons have been made by the SCMT. These are presented in Table 4.1. Unfortunately, data were not available for all countries for the same year. Table 4.1 gives some useful indications of established trade patterns, however, which can be related to the supply of, and demand for, port facilities in terms of the tonnages shipped. If it were to be assumed that the data in Table 4.1 were representative of a single year, say 1973, the figures suggest that intraregional general cargo export shipments amounted to around 1.4 million tons. By extension, this implies a total level of intra-CARICOM cargo trade movements slightly in excess of 2.8 million tons in that year, because total cargo movements of exports and imports represent twice the physical volume of export shipments of goods.

Most of CARICOM's extraregional exports go to destinations in the United States, the United Kingdom, Canada, and Europe. Extraregional imports consist mainly of manufactured goods and other general cargo, usually imported from these same countries and from Japan. Bauxite is exported from Jamaica and Guyana to the United States, Canada, and Europe. Sugar is exported—mainly to the United Kingdom—from Belize, Jamaica, St. Kitts, and Guyana. Petroleum is exported by Trinidad and Tobago to various buyers. These products are generally carried in the ships of companies engaged in further processing or marketing. Chemicals, cereals, fertilizers, animal feed, iron and steel, nonmetallic mineral manufactures, paper and paperboard are the principal imports from the United States. Iron and steel,

TABLE 4.1. SUMMARY OF EXPORT QUANTITIES OF CARICOM STATES TO CARICOM
(in metric tons)

	Destination				
Exporter (year)	*Antigua*	*Barbados*	*Belize*	*Dominica*	*Grenada*
Antigua (1973)	—	27	—	19	19
Barbados (1973)	804	—	—	583	956
Belize (1970)	129	129	—	—	—
Dominica (1974)	988	1,035	—	—	17
Grenada (1973)	22	176	—	14	—
Guyana (1973)	2,022	15,867	20	523	1,050
Jamaica (1974)	583	5,069	21,770	278	1,067
Montserrat (1974)	35	35	—	5	—
St. Kitts-Nevis-Anguilla (1972)	113	—	—	—	—
St. Lucia (1974)	98	1,068	—	1,397	622
St. Vincent (1970)	93	1,293	—	14	21
Trinidad and Tobago (1973)	23,459	99,466	272	7,370	27,652
Totals	28,346	124,185	22,062	10,203	31,394

— Not applicable.
Source: National statistics and CARICOM Secretariat.

nonmetallic mineral manufactures, cereals, metal manufactures, dairy products, eggs, fruits, and vegetables are the main imports from Europe.

The rates of growth for extraregional trade can be expected to range from 5 to 10 percent a year for different commodities. It is very difficult to be more precise because of three factors: the uncertainties of world markets; the problems associated with aggregating national trade statistics into region-wide estimates; and the consequences of newly enacted regional policies that will affect both trade and investment.

The port system

The three major ports of the CARICOM region are Kingston, Jamaica; Port of Spain, Trinidad; and Bridgetown, Barbados. Kingston is by far the largest of the three. It is strategically located to serve the Gulf ports of the United States, it is centrally located in the Caribbean Basin, and it is on the trade route between Europe and the Far East through the Panama Canal. Kingston can handle all the most modern types of container ships; within the next year or so, barring severe labor problems, it can be expected to become the chief transshipment port for the whole Caribbean Basin. The present development plan will provide an additional 2,100 feet of dock space for container operations. Two 600-foot berths with two 40-ton lift container cranes and a backup container storage space of 27 acres have

Guyana	*Jamaica*	*Mont-serrat*	*St. Kitts-Nevis-Anguilla*	*St. Lucia*	*St. Vincent*	*Trinidad and Tobago*	*Total* CARICOM
19	6	27	253	44	6	3	423
11,152	1,031	185	708	1,763	1,270	19,132	27,584
—	7,639	—	13	—	—	—	7,910
470	102	147	614	47	111	498	8,919
343	26	4	1	27	18	241	7,872
—	23,109	—	5,242	2,459	6,741	27,902	85,645
7,143	—	59	734	1,695	504	10,875	49,797
6	—	—	24	11	—	12	123
—	—	169	—	—	511	5,828	6,621
125	1,303	9	65	—	1,172	221	6,080
64	19	5	11	41	—	1,764	3,315
535,841	453,478	8,737	19,779	57,691	16,381	—	1,250,126
555,163	486,623	9,342	27,434	64,778	26,614	56,476	1,442,620

been completed. A third berth has also been completed, but dredging to the required depth of 40 feet is still to be undertaken. Work on a fourth berth is nearing completion.

A container terminal, designed to provide 40,000 square feet of space for packing and unpacking containers, together with office facilities, is currently being constructed. The first stage of a fourteen-acre free port area, planned to contain fifty-seven buildings upon completion, has been started. The area is to be protected by a security wall. This program, which is scheduled for completion by 1980, has involved initial financing from commercial sources in Japan, the United Kingdom, Canada, and Jamaica.

Port of Spain and Bridgetown each have eight berths providing 4,400 feet of wharf space, although in Bridgetown 2,700 feet of this space is breakwater. In Port of Spain, oil and bauxite are loaded at separate facilities; Bridgetown offers a sugar loading facility. Port of Spain and Bridgetown currently compete for the role of the second most important transshipment port in the Caribbean. It used to be thought that Port of Spain would assume this role, since its expansion plan was at an advanced stage in obtaining World Bank funding. Progress has been halted for a variety of reasons, however, and Port of Spain's prospects now look uncertain. The position of Bridgetown, by contrast, looks healthy, especially after the recent approval by the Inter-American Development Bank (IDB) of a loan for a project to increase the number of berths and to provide facilities for handling containers and small vessels. Work on this expansion program is now under way. If Trinidad makes no new progress in port development, and if Jamaica's current problems of labor unrest and internal strife do not improve, Barbados may well acquire much more transshipment traffic than was previously envisaged, to the detriment of its two CARICOM partners.

There are four other deepwater ports in the region: at St. Johns, Antigua; St. Georges, Grenada; Castries, St. Lucia; and Kingstown, St. Vincent. Each of these ports has plans for additional expansion which include the provision of transshipment facilities. At present, however, work is only being undertaken at Castries. When this work is finished, Castries will have a container handling facility with refrigerated storage space, a new banana warehouse, and three new berths; the total cost of the project is approximately EC$9.5 million, of which EC$4 million has been provided by commercial banks and the balance by the Caribbean Development Bank (CDB). The amount of traffic on which the expansion plans were based has as yet to be realized; if it does not materialize quite soon, the investment could be adversely affected.

There are no deepwater berths in Belize, St. Kitts, Dominica, or Montserrat. All these places have lighterage ports; ships anchor offshore and load or discharge cargo into barges or lighters which then make the transfer to land. This double handling of cargo is time consuming and costly and leads to pilferage and damage. In addition to these problems, cargo handling and warehousing facilities are inadequate at these ports.

As the discussion in Chapter 5 indicates, both Belize and Guyana are potential sources of much of the region's food. If this potential is to be realized, however, major improvements in port facilities will be necessary. The Government of Belize has discussed plans for major port development with the CDB, but decisions on port development have recently been deferred; more stable shipping patterns—which are expected—are needed before a rational assessment of the requirements of Belize City can be made.

Guyana has no deepwater port, and its rivers are all badly affected by silting caused by strong coastal drift. The Demarara River at Georgetown is currently the main port. Although there are special loading facilities for bauxite, sugar, molasses, and rice, a major disadvantage of this port is that it cannot accommodate vessels with a draft of more than twenty feet at low tide. In fact many vessels rest on the soft mud river floor at low tide and ship sailings must be phased with the tides, a time-consuming and costly business.

If deep water ports were to be constructed at Belize and Guyana, CARICOM would have adequate port facilities for organizing the region's sea transport network on a rational basis.

Shipping tariffs and rates

There are two main components of cargo transport costs. The first is the freight rate applied by the carrier, which generally reflects operating costs (except to the extent that shipping services are subsidized); the second is the port charge. The latter involves two subcomponents—charges levied against the ship itself (which are theoretically passed on to the importer via the freight rate); and charges assessed against the cargo.

It has already been noted that WISCO has always operated with the aid of subsidies because governments believed that the subsidy policy would help to achieve several regional objectives. These objectives were to encourage regional trade, to keep the cost of living down, and to influence the rates charged by the ocean shipping lines. In retrospect, however, it would appear that this policy failed on all three counts. It did not substantially influence the volume of intraregional trade, because transport costs—representing only 5 percent of delivered prices—were the least of the various impediments to trade. The small proportion of total costs represented by the transport cost element also meant that the subsidy to WISCO played an insignificant role in the fight against inflation. Finally, the subsidy failed to influence the rates of the ocean shipping lines because WISCO was simply too small and controlled too little a share of the regional shipping market to have any serious impact on the pricing decisions of these giants.

The failure of WISCO's low freight rates to meet their objectives, combined with the burdensome financial costs that they imposed both on WISCO itself and also on the member governments of the region, have recently led to the virtual abolition of the subsidy practice.

In addition to being artificially low, WISCO's charges were based on a flat rate irrespective of distance; the charge was the same for a shipment from Jamaica to Grenada, a distance of 1,000 miles, as it was from Trinidad to Grenada, a distance of only 100 miles. It was noted earlier that this situation has changed as a result of the new WISCO agreement; it is expected that distance will now be taken into account in the carrier's new schedule freight weight.

In port, a ship pays a fee for the use of a berth. The fee is usually based upon the ship's net registered tonnage (NRT), as are lighterage, pilotage, mooring, and unmooring. These rates are reduced for ships calling for supplies, bunkers, and passengers and, of course, for ships in distress. The ports in Guyana currently assess their charges on the basis of the draft of the vessel rather than the NRT, but there are proposals to change this policy.

When cargo is loaded or unloaded, there is a charge for receiving, storage and delivery (RSD). This charge covers the total cost of handling cargo through the port and reflects the efficiency of the port operations, local wage rates, and lighterage where used. As a result, these charges vary widely, even among ports of a similar size. Table 4.2 shows the RSD charges for WISCO operations published in March 1972. Although these figures are out of date, they illustrate how widely handling costs vary in the region.

A full review of tariff and rate structures in the CARICOM region should be undertaken as part of a general study of the regional transport market.

Air Transport

The first air services in the region were provided by Britain during the latter part of the 1930s. These services involved long, arduous transoceanic flights and demanded courage and endurance on the part of travelers. Inter-island services had not developed at that time but were to evolve with tourism some years later. But when World War II broke out, Britain suspended air services and the region found itself isolated.

TABLE 4.2 RECEIVING, STORAGE, AND DELIVERY CHARGES FOR THE WEST INDIES SHIPPING CORPORATION (WISCO), MARCH 1972
(in U.S. dollars a ton)

Country	*Charge*
Guyana	10.21
Trinidad	8.13[a]
Antigua	8.02
St. Kitts	7.66
Montserrat	6.84
Dominica	6.71
St. Vincent	5.05
Barbados	4.73
Grenada	4.29
St. Lucia	3.22

a. Only US$5.45 if regional produce.
Source: CARICOM Secretariat.

The region's airlines

Given this situation, the government of the United Kingdom then suggested that a British-controlled airline based in Trinidad should be established to serve the area. This proposal was adopted and the government of Trinidad and Tobago became a shareholder of the newly formed British West Indies Airways (BWIA). Gradually, the airline extended its services to cover most of the Windward and Leeward islands. The rate of expansion of service was determined by the timing of airport construction in the territories. By 1944, BWIA service also extended to Jamaica and Belize. After the war, the airline was taken over by British South American Airways which, in due course, was itself absorbed by the British Overseas Airways Corporation (BOAC), later British Airways. This arrangement lasted until 1971, when drastic cuts in services, made in order to reduce losses, led to layoffs for some 700 employees, primarily in Trinidad. The loss ascribed to BWIA in 1971/72 was estimated at US$1.7 million.

The federation of the West Indies at this time called for the establishment of a regional carrier based upon BWIA. The principal shareholders were to be the federation (with 51 percent of the equity) while BOAC, and the governments of Jamaica, and Trinidad and Tobago, were to be minor partners in a venture that was to cost US$32.3 million to establish.

With the dissolution of the federation, the government of Trinidad and Tobago was faced with the problem of maintaining service and avoiding the duplication elsewhere in the region of facilities already operating in Trinidad. The government therefore decided to purchase and operate the airline in cooperation with other regional governments. In the early 1960s, the airline served Miami, Jamaica, San Juan, Martinique, Barbados, Trinidad, Guyana, Grand Cayman, Belize, Grenada, St. Lucia, St. Kitts, St. Thomas, Curaçao, and New York. It also operated under BOAC contract to Bermuda and London. Three Boeing B727 jets were purchased for US$20 million in 1963, and entered service in 1965. The purchase was necessary because a BOAC charter arrangement, which had operated for the previous two years, could not be expected to continue indefinitely. Furthermore, Pan American had introduced jet aircraft on services to the region and had found that jets were more economical than older aircraft. In the late 1960s, service was extended to Toronto, and B727 aircraft were upgraded to B707s. This enabled the company to operate charter services to the United Kingdom and an additional aircraft was acquired.

Since its divestiture by BOAC in 1961, BWIA has been in constant financial difficulty. The government of Trinidad has had to subsidize the airline repeatedly from general government revenues. The airline's accumulated deficit increased from US$7.4 million in 1965 to US$39 million in 1970 and by the mid-1970s stood at more than US$55 million; the government of Trinidad guarantees the interest on the debt.

Poor management has been largely responsible for the size of BWIA's deficit. Various attempts have been made to deal with this problem through arrangements for technical and managerial assistance. Air Canada was approached, and agreed to participate in operating the airline, if the four independent Caribbean governments (Jamaica, Barbados, Guyana, and Trinidad) would designate BWIA as the regional carrier and jointly negotiate their bilateral air agreements. It proved impossible to implement this key condition and Air Canada withdrew. Then the government of Trinidad and Tobago reached an agreement with the Caribbean International Corporation and Trans World Airways, that they would accept share capital, and provide both the additional capital and the technical expertise required to run the airline. In all, some US$4 million of additional capital was thus provided. When it became apparent, however, that this arrangement could not generate the amount of capital required, the shareholding was successively reduced; by 1973 Trinidad was once again the sole owner of the airline. Since then, a number of economy measures have been taken, including a sharp reduction in the concessions to staff and others for free or reduced-cost travel. Measures have also been taken to ensure that BWIA transports, where possible, all airmail from Trinidad, and carries government personnel traveling on business.

The fourth heads of government conference in 1967 recognized that the establishment of a regional airline would help regional development, and a resolution was passed at the fifth conference in 1969 recognizing BWIA's claim to that role. Moreover, the Port of Spain Agreement of June 9, 1976, among the Premiers of the four MDCs, reiterated the need for rationalizing air service in the Caribbean area and recognized the special claims of BWIA to be recognized as the regional air carrier. As yet, however, no regional air carrier has been designated.

Jamaica established its own airline in 1963. The government, BOAC and BWIA were joint shareholders in the company under a five-year agreement. BOAC operated services in the name of Air Jamaica to London, New York, and Toronto; BWIA operated to Miami and provided internal service in Jamaica. When this agreement ended, a new company called Air Jamaica (1968) Ltd. was formed. The Jamaican government formulated a careful development strategy for the airline, based mainly on the projected air transport demand of Jamaica's growing tourist industry. Air Jamaica began as a small company and developed gradually, learning from the experience of BWIA. Air Canada was approached by the government and agreed to provide managerial and technical assistance under contract in exchange for a 40 percent shareholding. The government recognized that the airline had to be operated on a strictly commercial basis with the minimum of outside intervention. Accordingly, reasonable stage lengths were established and short routes were ignored. Carefully planned expansion took place with new routes opening to North America and London. At first, the company depended heavily upon Air Canada but Jamaicans have gradually been assuming control, after having had training under the agreement. Air Jamaica has no aspirations to be a regional carrier; it is instead concentrating its efforts on bringing tourists to Jamaica from North America and Europe.

Leeward Islands Air Transport (LIAT) was formed in 1956 when a nonscheduled service was inaugurated between Montserrat and Antigua. When the present airport was built in Montserrat, BWIA became associated with the venture and designated LIAT to operate its routes in the Leeward Islands. As demand grew, services were gradually extended to the present scale of operations.

In the event LIAT was allowed to develop independently; its management in Antigua was physically isolated from BWIA management and it did not provide an effective feeder service from the international flights operated by BWIA. The parent company did, however, support LIAT in a number of ways, providing finance amounting to some US$2.8 million between 1962 and 1970. This sum was over and above any payments by LIAT for managerial services and administrative expenses. In addition, a small aircraft was lent to LIAT by BWIA without charge, and loans for LIAT were guaranteed by BWIA.

Towards the end of the 1960s, the government of Trinidad and Tobago realized that if LIAT were to provide the region with better service, it would need both to expand its operations and to replace depreciated equipment. It was clear, however, that any program of this kind would involve sums of capital well beyond the financial capacity of BWIA. The government therefore approached Court Lines, which bought LIAT as a going concern in 1971. A condition of the sale was that West Indian governments would be permitted to repurchase up to 49 percent of the airline's equity at the original purchase price from Court Line within two years, should it be considered necessary for local interests to be represented in the airline.

Unfortunately, LIAT's subsequent history continued to be one of losses and indebtedness, caused by three main operating problems: the inadequate reservations system, which proved incapable of handling the volumes of traffic which evolved; the operational difficulties caused by night flying restrictions where a delay of five minutes could mean the cancellation of a flight; and a lack of capacity to service peak demand. In addition, there were management problems. The primary objective of Court Line—to provide transport for its hotels in certain islands—was not consistent with the objectives of some governments; the introduction of the BAC111 also significantly increased the costs of operations. The collapse of the parent company in mid-1974 made the prospects of LIAT bleak. In August 1974, LIAT officially went into receivership. At the initiative of the regional governments, however, a new company, LIAT (1974) Ltd. was incorporated in September 1974 to take over the operations of the old company. A new financial structure was worked out for the airline during 1975; all the CARICOM governments except that of Belize agreed to take equity positions in the new company. Additional support was also secured for the new company through loans from the CDB amounting to some US$5.8 million. These loans financed the purchase of aircraft, spares, and equipment needed to maintain the Eastern Caribbean interisland air transport service at the time.

In order to improve the new company's efficiency, a management study was undertaken by Canadian Airlines Consultants (CANAC). Recommendations for the reduction of routes, management assistance, and increased fares were implemented between 1975 and 1976. The implementation of the first recommendation has resulted in the hiving-off of the islander service and the creation of two subsidiaries—one in the north and the other in the south. Losses on the subsidiaries will be subsidized by the islands served. A standby subsidy arrangement for the main company is to be worked out by the shareholders as a condition of the CDB loan.

International Caribbean Airways (ICA) began as a small charter airline based in Barbados and operating to Luxembourg and London. It was fully owned by the Laker group of the United Kingdom. The airline stimulated the flow of tourists from Europe to Barbados mainly as a result of its low rates. In order to provide the same stimulus to tourism from North America, the Barbados government encouraged the airline to extend its operations. This proved impossible, however, as the U.S. government refused to grant route rights because the airline was not "substantially owned and effectively controlled" by Barbados. This refusal prompted the purchase of the majority shareholding by the government of Barbados. Negotiations for route rights into the United States are still inconclusive, although rights have been secured into Canada.

In addition to the main carriers already mentioned, there are a number of small air service operations in the area. The principal ones are as follows (bases in parentheses): Caribbean United (Trinidad), operating scheduled services to Tobago and Grenada; Carib West (Barbados), carrying charter freight; Air Calypso (Barbados), operating inclusive tours and day charters; Maya (Belize) and Jamaica Air Services (Jamaica), both with scheduled internal services; and Seagreen Air (Antigua), operating charters, freight, and passenger services. There are also several still smaller carriers operating freight and passenger services into the region, together with a number of regionally based companies. Many of the latter operate only a single aircraft, however.

It is possible to travel between any two countries in the CARICOM region on any given day, although it may be necessary to change at one of the main airports. There are only two direct flights a week between Jamaica and Belize, but daily service is available via Miami.

A wide variety of aircraft is used in the region.[9] Although the past development and present organization of the air carriers may to some extent

9. Most intraregional services are provided by small jets, such as the British Aircraft Corporation BAC 111 with 100 seats. Small turbo-props with up to fifty seats, such as the Hawker Siddeley US748, Convair 440, and Fokker F27, are also used. Other services are provided by small aircraft with fewer than ten seats such as the Britten Norman Islander and Beechcraft Bonanza. Freight is carried in the large passenger aircraft as well as in smaller all-freight aircraft such as the Douglas DC7, DC6, DC4, DC3, and Convair aircraft. DeHavilland DHC4 Caribou and Twin Otters are also used. The Boeing B747 is used occasionally for scheduled service to Jamaica, and regularly on charters to Barbados, but the largest passenger jets in regularly scheduled services are the Douglas DC8, the Boeing B707, and the Vickers VC10. These operate mainly on extraregional services. Medium-range jets such as the Douglas DC9 and the Boeing B727 are also used.

account for this factor, the current range of types of aircraft makes it almost impossible for any single company to operate services on an economic basis.

Air travel is the predominant mode of passenger travel in the region. Tourists comprise by far the majority of arrivals in CARICOM countries, and the future of regional air traffic is inescapably linked to the prospects for the regional tourist market. Available tourist data suggests that most visitors to the Caribbean travel to a single destination. The MDCs already enjoy adequate transport links with countries of tourist origin outside the region, but intraregional connections are still required for the growth of the tourism sector in the Eastern Caribbean. The alternative, that is, for the smaller countries to develop direct transport links with countries of tourist origin, would be an extremely expensive one; it would not only be generally difficult to justify from a national perspective, but would also be of negligible benefit from the point of view of regional development.

Initiatives at regional collaboration are already under way. The SCMT has reactivated a long standing working group on rationalization of air transportation to elaborate possible areas of collaboration between the existing nationally owned airlines. Further, the governments of the MDCs established a governing committee in mid-1976 to elaborate and implement areas of cooperation between the national airlines.

Airports in the region

Jamaica, Antigua, Barbados, and Trinidad provide the major external air linkages for the CARICOM region. Nearly all passengers flying from Europe or North America, the two principal external markets, pass through the airports of these four islands. The airports at Guyana, St. Lucia, and St. Kitts can also handle extraregional air traffic, although to a lesser extent. Their facilities include runways between 7,000 and 11,000 feet in length, together with adequate air traffic control, navigational aids and operating equipment. They serve primarily as interchange points between extra- and intraregional services. Seven smaller airports are located in Belize, Tobago, St. Lucia, Grenada, St. Vincent, Dominica, and Montserrat. These airports have runways between 4,000 and 6,000 feet in length, and have less sophisticated navigational aids and operating equipment. In particular, the airports at Grenada, St. Vincent, Dominica, and Montserrat are severely restricted in terms of their operating efficiency; some of them have unusual features, such as roads and pedestrian walkways crossing the runways. Finally, there are several smaller feeder airports; these generally have runways of less than 3,000 feet in length, a few of which are unsurfaced. They have extremely limited navigational aids, are for the most part restricted to daytime operation, and accommodate only very small aircraft which usually carry fewer than ten passengers.

The pattern of airport investment has been closely associated with the development of tourism. There has been some overinvestment in airports capable of handling large commercial aircraft, reflecting the absence of a regionwide approach to planning in both tourism and air transport. Independent decisions to increase the flow of tourists and thereby to improve foreign exchange earnings have led to separate programs for airport development. If the primary aim of these individual investments has been to increase tourism in terms of visitor nights, then these uncoordinated airport programs have been successful. If, however, their primary objective has been to improve either net regional earnings or overall balance of payments receipts, then their benefits are much more questionable. In fact, in several cases, the retained earnings from tourism have been insufficient to cover the interest charges on airport investments during their construction; it may therefore be argued that these investments have reduced the welfare of several of the islands.

Much of the infrastructure required for an efficient regional transport network is nevertheless already available. Although some very serious deficiencies exist, particularly at the secondary level, the solution to this problem is not the construction of a number of new and competing major international airports.

Some new development may be necessary, but existing infrastructure can quite effectively provide most of the feeder services needed at the existing major linkage points. The direction of future airport development should be planned in accordance with the growth of regional markets, and this primarily means the markets for tourism. A realistic assessment of the region's air transport market will undoubtedly rule out a number of plans for growth, because of the small size of some of the island economies relative to their aspirations.

Toward a Regional Transport Strategy

Throughout this survey of transport in the Commonwealth Caribbean, a number of problem areas and issues have been identified and discussed. The prospects for solving these problems and resolving these issues are generally favorable, but determination and foresight will be needed on the part of the governments in the region. Above all, the area must develop an agreed, operational, regional transport policy. This policy must specify both regional objectives and the instruments employed to achieve them; it must be endorsed by, and produce a major commitment from, each of the regional governments; and both the CARICOM Secretariat and the CDB should help formulate it and support it.

The transport sector influences the whole spectrum of economic and social activity in the region. The formulation of effective policy in this sector will therefore require both knowledge of plans, targets, and magnitudes of indicators in most of the other sectors, and the capacity to coordinate and incorporate this information into the planning process. Most of the necessary information on the supply of transport infrastructure is currently available, but information on demand is weak, especially with regard to the size of regional transport markets. In order to obtain adequate information about these markets, it will be necessary to analyze a number of sectors (notably agriculture, tourism, and industry) together with trends in intraregional and extraregional trade. Without these analyses, it will be impossible to frame a coherent policy for the region.

In the case of sea transport, the main specific tasks for policy appear to be to establish an official intraregional carrier, to coordinate intraregional services provided by the three types of shipping operation, to streamline Eastern Caribbean small shipping operations in ways which avoid any major disadvantages to the LDCs, and to redesign WISCO to meet regionwide economic requirements. All these tasks should be conducted in the light of adequate information on transport markets.

Improved management, together with better technology in the form of specialized ships (complete with the expertise necessary for their operation), are urgently required in the region. Technical assistance should be sought in the near future for these requirements. Special emphasis should be placed upon the upgrading of managerial skills and the design and implementation of better structures of organization, together with improvement in operating and planning systems.

For the moment, the effort to develop a regional shipping line should be concentrated upon the provision of intraregional services. Extraregional shipping based on the major regional exports should be studied but the premature operation of extraregional services in the linear trade should be avoided in the face of strong competition from the powerful conferences which could lead to large financial losses. Such investments should therefore be postponed until all its aspects have been thoroughly studied.

Port development requires close and immediate scrutiny by the SCMT. What appears to amount to the independently planned duplication of container facilities in Jamaica, Barbados, Trinidad, and St. Lucia needs special examination in the light of regional demand forecasts for transshipment facilities. The SCMT should also devise (or at least endorse the establishment of) criteria and procedures for cost sharing among member countries, so that those countries which stand to lose if they limit their transport investment plans may in some way be compensated for income, employment, and development opportunities foregone when policy decisions are made. This task will require substantial inputs of technical assistance in planning and program evaluation.

In many respects, the problems of air transport in the region are similar to those of sea transport. It should not be surprising, therefore, if some of the proposed solutions appear similar.

The SCMT should conduct a major reevaluation of airport development plans in order to fit them into the framework of a logical regional transport plan. Plans which are too ambitious should be scaled down where necessary; the principal objective should be to develop an efficient network of trunk and feeder routes and services.

The regional air transport system must efficiently meet the demands of the tourist industry in the region. This objective can be achieved in various ways, one of which might be the consolidation of the existing airlines into a single entity and the establishment of a regional management and service company. There are obstacles and costs involved; these must be evaluated and action must be taken before existing deficiencies become worse. Routes and schedules must be improved soon, to stop customer relations on LIAT flights from becoming even worse than they are now. Computerized bookings may soon become not merely feasible, but essential, if the greater traffic that increased tourism will bring is to be handled competently.

Investment in air transport is massive and requires substantial supporting investment in ground transport and other services. Because it is so large, and cannot easily be deployed elsewhere if mistakes are made in demand forecasts, investment policy must put regional considerations above the national interest of any individual country, if air transport is to make a positive contribution to regional integration.

Throughout this chapter, no mention has been made of road or rail transport. The reason for this is that new roads and railroads, while perhaps important from a national point of view, have no direct relevance for intra-regional transport. They may, however, contribute indirectly to regional development as a whole, to the extent that they open up outlying regions in member countries and permit agricultural produce to reach export shipment points. Efficient road and rail development will be needed if the Regional Food Plan is to succeed. Close examination of the suitability of existing ground links will be a necessary part of agricultural, tourism, and transport planning in the region.

Chapter 5

Agriculture

AGRICULTURE IN THE CARIBBEAN REGION HAS TRADITIONALLY TAKEN TWO main forms. First, large private estates or plantations, making use of most of the best land, have been the sources of the region's traditional exports—primarily sugar, but also bananas and citrus fruits—while, secondly, large numbers of peasant farms, occupying a small proportion of the total land area, have mainly produced subsistence crops, contributing only marginally and inefficiently to output for export. This pattern has changed significantly in recent years.

The following discussion is divided into two parts. The first surveys the problems of, and prospects for, regional cooperation and integration, after an opening assessment of recent trends in output and trade. The second portion examines the two chief crops—sugar and bananas—in terms of trends, prospects, and policies.

Integration Problems and Prospects

Before considering the major structural problems facing Caribbean agriculture, and moving on to a discussion of the prospects for integration and cooperation and their various manifestations, it is useful to consider the changing pattern of output and trade.

Recent trends in output and trade

What are the significant changes that have been taking place in Caribbean agriculture in recent years? Most sugar plantations are now publicly owned, and a higher share of total production comes from small cane growers.

Small farms also account for a larger share of the production of bananas, citrus fruits, and coconut products.

At the same time, work in agriculture, especially wage labor on the estates, is in evident decline as an occupation. Its unattractiveness has been heightened by the continuing use of traditional methods, deteriorating local communities, and the growth of new capital-intensive industries which, when combined with powerful trade unions, can offer high wages and relatively pleasant working conditions for a small proportion of the urban labor force. In addition, education—which has greatly expanded in recent years—has been heavily biased against agriculture in content and orientation, and indirectly initiates the rural-to-urban drift through the practice of removing the brighter youngsters to the urban areas for secondary and tertiary training. Consequently, few young people wish to enter agriculture; instead they drift into the urban sector, despite its shortage of jobs. This tendency has aggravated already serious social problems caused by high urban unemployment.

The general movement away from the land has meant that agricultural output has stagnated, failing either to match population growth or to maintain former export production levels. Per capita production of food has declined in the last decade, with the result that the region's negative trading balance in respect of foodstuffs has continued to increase. Agricultural production for export fell by about 40 percent from the mid-1960s to the mid-1970s. During the 1960s alone, the area of land under cultivation fell by about 500,000 acres, a reduction of about one-quarter of the 1960 acreage.[1]

Although agriculture's importance in the national economies of the countries in the region has declined in recent years, it still remains one of the most important sources of employment, income, and foreign exchange. Taking the region as a whole, the sector accounts for about 10 percent of gross domestic product and employs about 30 percent of the labor force; a higher proportion of the total population, probably about 50 percent, lives in the rural areas.

The importance of agriculture in the economy varies sharply between one Caribbean Community (CARICOM) member country and another. Agriculture plays an especially important role in the islands which are members of the Eastern Caribbean Common Market (ECCM), in Guyana, and also in Belize, but is a rather less significant source of income and employment in Trinidad and Tobago, and Barbados. In the case of Jamaica, the role of agriculture is less clearcut, as it produces only 8 percent of output while providing almost 30 percent of employment, and the disparity between agricultural and nonagricultural income is, therefore large. Table 5.1 shows these differences within the region.

The region as a whole, and the small islands in particular, depend heavily

1. Historical production and land use data are not readily available. The estimate on land under cultivation is based on information supplied by government agriculture officers in the region and World Bank staff.

TABLE 5.1. AGRICULTURAL EMPLOYMENT AND OUTPUT, SELECTED TERRITORIES, 1960 AND 1970
(percentage of total)

	1960		*1970*	
Territory	*Employment*	*Output*	*Employment*	*Output*
Barbados	26	28	16	14
Guyana	37	26	29	19
Jamaica	39	12	29	8
Trinidad and Tobago	21	12	16	5
ECCM	46	36	32	22

Source: Statistical Appendix, Tables SA7.1 and SA7.2.

on food imports. At the same time, the export of a few traditional crops accounts for a large proportion of foreign exchange earnings. By 1972, for example, that proportion was three-quarters for the LDCs, about one-half for Barbados and Guyana, but less than 20 percent for Jamaica and Trinidad and Tobago.

The two major export crops (discussed in detail in later sections of this chapter) are sugar, produced in the four MDCs, Belize and St. Kitts, and bananas, grown in Jamaica and the Windward Islands, and now also from Belize. Citrus fruits are also important exports for the region generally. A number of other crops are significant for individual countries (pimento in Jamaica, nutmeg in Grenada, and arrowroot in St. Vincent, for example), though these do not loom large in regional statistics. As Table 5.2 and Figure 2 demonstrate, production and exports of sugar, bananas, and citrus fruits have all been on a generally declining trend since the mid-1960s.

Since 1965, the volume of sugar exports has fallen by one-fifth and that of banana exports by almost one-half. Fortunately for the region, export prices, particularly for sugar, have risen substantially over the last few years, so the value of agricultural exports has in fact risen despite the decline in output. This increase has been too small, however, to offset the even more rapid rise in food and foodgrain imports. As Table 5.3 indicates, the region has now a net deficit on its agricultural trade.

TABLE 5.2. MAIN AGRICULTURAL EXPORTS, BY VOLUME, 1965–74

Commodity	*1965*	*1966*	*1967*	*1968*	*1969*	*1970*	*1971*	*1972*	*1973*	*1974*
Sugar (thousands of long tons)	1,190	1,100	1,080	1,130	1,050	970	1,020	950	840	940
Bananas (thousands of long tons)	358	342	338	319	305	253	249	246	200	169
Citrus (millions of pounds)	n.a.	142	135	117	116	103	110	99	62	81

n.a. Not available.
Sources: National trade statistics and commodity associations.

Figure 2. Index of Main Agricultural Exports, by Volume (1966 = 100)

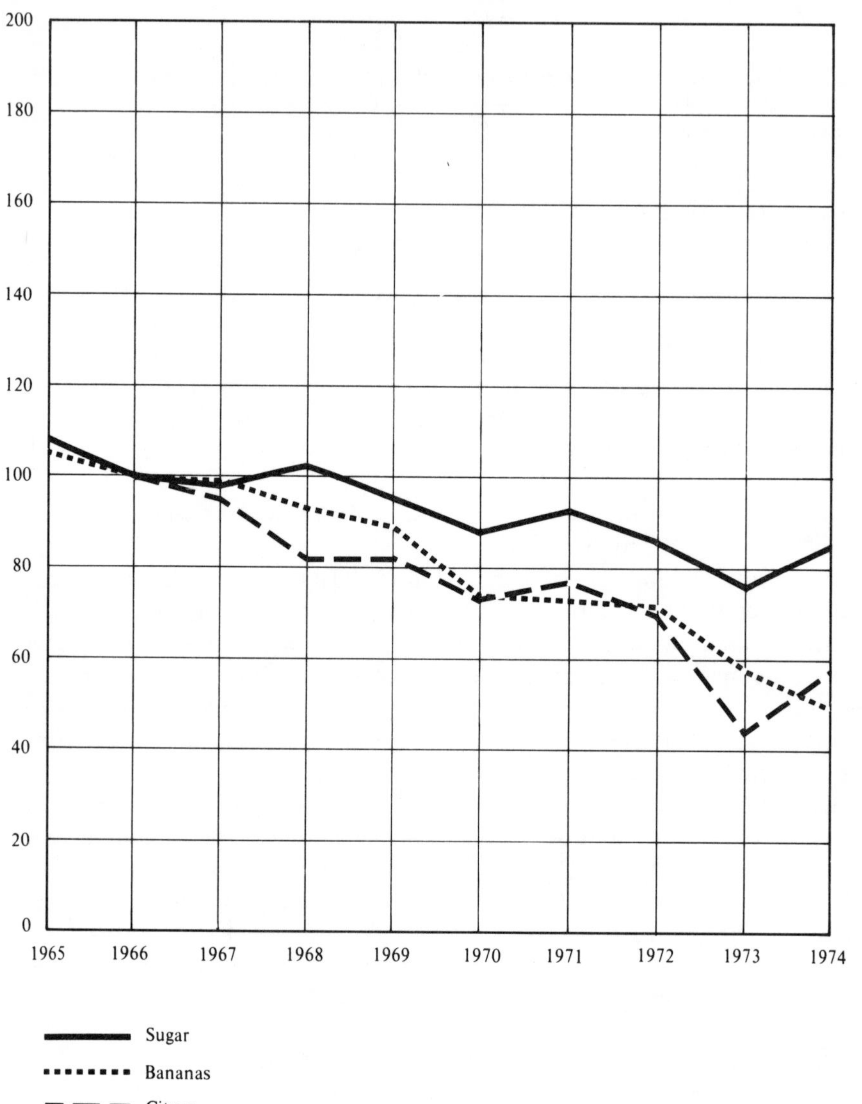

TABLE 5.3. AGRICULTURAL EXPORTS AND IMPORTS, 1965–73
(millions of Eastern Caribbean dollars)

Category	Year 1965	Year 1973	Average annual growth rates, 1965–1973 (percent)
Agricultural exports from region	394	527	3.7
Agricultural imports into region	328	722	10.5
Net surplus (+) or deficit (−)	+66	−195	—

— Not applicable.
Sources: National trade statistics; commodity associations; and CARICOM Secretariat.

The composition of the import bill (Tables 5.4 and 5.5) gives an indication of the major food deficiencies of the region. The most important imported items are animal proteins; meat, dairy and fish products, and animal feed, make up more than 50 percent of the total value of food imports. Fruits and vegetables account for only about 9 percent of the import bill and oils and fats for about 4 percent.

Major structural problems

Agricultural development in the CARICOM countries is beset by fundamental problems associated with the structure of the industry as a whole, together with technical and institutional weaknesses. Many of the structural problems are historical in origin, although they have often been exacerbated by government policies toward agriculture over the last decade. The distribution of land holdings and the ways in which land is held represent a basic obstacle to development. Traditionally, land holdings in the Caribbean have

TABLE 5.4. COMMODITY COMPOSITION OF REGIONAL FOOD IMPORTS, 1972
(millions of Eastern Caribbean dollars)

Commodity	Amount	Percentage
Meat	82.6	13.6
Dairy products	85.2	14.0
Cereals	158.6	26.0
Fish	36.3	6.0
Animal feed	30.5	5.0
Subtotal	393.2	64.6
Fruit and vegetables	56.8	9.3
Oils and fats	24.9	4.1
Others	134.2	22.0
Total	609.1	100.0

Source: World Bank staff estimates based on national trade statistics.

TABLE 5.5. DEGREE OF REGIONAL SELF-SUFFICIENCY, SELECTED PRODUCT GROUPS, 1972
(percentage of local production to consumption)

Commodity groups	*Jamaica*	*Trinidad and Tobago*	*Guyana*	*Barbados*	*Total* CARICOM
Meat					
Beef	54.2	71.6	93.4	24.4	56.8
Mutton[a]	72.9	23.5	100.0	14.9	61.3
Pork	0.6	6.3	100.0	15.0	2.7
Poultry	87.9	72.2	100.0	97.4	85.4
Processed[b]	71.0	99.3	100.0	30.0	76.6
Dairy products					
Milk	43.0	15.6	31.9	14.6	27.7
Butter	...	11.1	23.1	...	4.6
Cheese	...	...	...	...	...
Eggs	88.0	82.9	82.0	83.6	85.7
Fish	39.3	82.2	98.5	71.6	57.7
Cereals					
Rice	0.7	20.3	100.0	...	86.3
Corn	6.1	...	38.3	35.7	12.9
Wheat and flour	...	...	...	...	...

... Zero or negligible.
a. Includes miscellaneous meats.
b. Production data not shown separately.
Source: United Nations Caribbean Regional Integration Advisors' Team, "Planning to Meet the Caribbean's Growing Food Needs," Port of Spain, Trinidad and Tobago, November 1975, p. 7.

taken the form either of very large estates involved in commercial, export-oriented agriculture, or of very small farms holding a small share of the total acreage of land under cultivation. It is estimated that 95 percent of the roughly 350,000 farm holdings in the region are less than 25 acres in size. These smallholdings account for less than 30 percent of total farm acreage, while holdings of 100 acres or more, representing about 2 percent of all holdings, account for more than 50 percent of the total acreage.[2]

The small size of holdings worked by peasant farmers has meant that they frequently supplement their farm income with employment outside agriculture. For instance, between 50 and 60 percent of farmers with less than five acres are occupied in agriculture on a part-time basis only. This state of affairs has led to intensive use of available land, but poor agronomic practices. Since they can survive without frequent regular supervision, mixed stands of such tree crops as bananas, cocoa, and nutmegs are common on these smaller plots. Yields are low, however, for three reasons: poor cultivation practices in terms of replanting time and density of plants; poor and inadequate use of inputs such as fertilizer; and the absence of proper soil conservation and irrigation methods.

2. See Statistical Appendix, Table SA7.12.

This situation is made worse by the fact that an individual's land frequently consists of several small plots in different locations. This problem, which is most acute in the Windward Islands and in Jamaica, stems from the system of joint inheritance whereby each child in the family receives a portion of land. As a result, a farmer may inherit a small piece of land which is not adjacent to any other land he may own. The complex pattern of ownership, and the traditional attachment to such inherited family land, make it difficult for him to expand his holdings in a single block. This pattern of fragmented holdings leads to obvious inefficiencies in moving from plot to plot; moreover, improvement schemes such as weed and pest control programs, which depend upon cooperation between farmers with adjacent holdings, are very hard to operate.

The combined effect of small size holdings, insecurity of tenure, sporadic provision of complementary services, and poor agronomic practices, is that smallholders are one of the poorest groups in the region. Since this group represents a significant proportion of the total labor force, its low income has an adverse general effect on the distribution of income throughout the region.

Major inefficiencies in land use also occur in estate agriculture, primarily because of the volume of land which remains uncultivated. Estates typically cultivate one crop on the most suitable sections of their total holding so that while output for acre of cultivated lands might be high, output per acre of land owned is typically much lower. Land which becomes too marginal for the main crop is simply allowed to lie idle. Another source of inefficiency in the use of estate lands is that the particular export crop, related as it often is to the needs of the parent company, is not necessarily the most appropriate crop for the land.

Estates are also plagued by a chronic shortage of labor. This is caused by three main factors: the social stigma attached to plantation work; the high wages paid to the small section of the labor force working in modern capital-intensive activities; and the comparatively more strenuous nature of agricultural work. Workers leave the agricultural sector in search of these high wages, even at the risk of unemployment or underemployment in the towns. The labor shortage has led to the adoption of cultivation and harvesting practices which have cut total output. The most striking example of this has been in the sugar industry, with the movement from green cane harvesting to the harvesting of burnt cane. The cutting of green cane by hand requires handling of the cane leaves and tops as well as the cane itself; if the leaves and tops are burnt off first, a worker can cut almost twice as much cane in a day. Persistent labor shortages have encouraged the increasing use of this practice in the region. Because the sucrose content of the cane declines rapidly after burning, however, the practice reduces yields—a state of affairs which has been reflected in the decline in the region's output of sugar per acre.

In periods of prolonged sugar crises, such as in the late nineteenth century and late 1930s and early 1940s, some large sugar estates have shifted to production of bananas, but reverted to sugar when the crises ended.

The present system of land tenure—large privately owned estates on the one hand and smallholdings on the other—makes for inefficiency in land use. The problem is thus the size of holdings and the institutional form of ownership. Land reform which focus on both aspects of the problem is crucial if agricultural production is to be restored. The encouragement of family farms could be one institutional form. There is evidence that small farms using family labor may actually fare better, in net cash terms, than the larger farmers who have to rely on hired labor and are faced with the pressure of rising costs. If it is true that workers on family farms are more interested in getting a reasonable average income over time, than in getting the largest possible income at any one time, then the creation of viable family units should help to reduce the outflow of labor to the urban sector. Some programs already have been initiated whereby governments have put some of their own land under farm settlement (Black Bush Polder in Guyana, for example; there are similar schemes in Jamaica and Trinidad), or have acquired some estate land and redistributed it on a leasehold basis (this has been done in Jamaica, Trinidad, and Grenada). The total amount of land involved has been fairly small so far, however, and the schemes have often suffered from inadequacies in both extension services and production credit for the new settlers. Moreover, it appears that the average size of plot distributed to beneficiaries of the programs is often too small to be combined with those of other family members into a unit which could provide a reasonable income to a farm family. For instance, Grenada's "land for the landless" program has acquired 3,500 acres (about 5 percent of the island's cultivable land) since it was launched in 1971, but half of this has been distributed as half-acre lots designated for housing and the remainder has been apportioned in lots of little more than one acre.[3]

The region, particularly Guyana and Jamaica, has also experimented with other institutional forms, such as cooperatives and state farms. The sugar cooperatives on the Frome and Monymusk estates, and food farms such as Hounslow in Jamaica, are examples of these two forms of organization. These programs, however, have not been sufficiently successful to provide a model.

Clearly, a vigorous program of land reform is essential if agriculture is to revive in the CARICOM countries. Most governments are fully aware of the need for aggressive reforms, but it is difficult to make progress in such a sensitive area of policy. Delaying action, on the other hand, could have very damaging long run economic consequences. Measures should be taken to encourage the consolidation of smallholdings into farms of sufficient size to achieve economies of scale. These farms should probably be no less than five acres in size. New arrangements which would avoid the tendency to fragmentation should be sought for owning and operating large estates. But those large estates, where labor relations have been difficult and management

3. See J. S. Brierley, "Small Farming in Grenada, West Indies," *Manitoba Geographical Studies*, 4 (1974).

deficient, should be encouraged to break up. Programs will also be required to ensure the provision of adequate services for the new settlements, including extension, credit, and marketing facilities.

Regional integration: the history

The regional integration effort has hardly touched agriculture, for a number of reasons. Agricultural exports from the Caribbean go to destinations outside the region, rather than to other countries within it; the advantages of specialization and associated economies of scale are less obvious in agriculture than they are in industry; and the countries of the region have broadly similar weather, topography and soils, leading to a high degree of intraregional competition, rather than to complementarity in the crops produced. National economies in the Caribbean are basically open and export-oriented; these characteristics, together with the limited size of the regional market, reduce the scope for benefits from integration exclusively based on the region. Nevertheless, CARIFTA member countries could profitably specialize in different agricultural products because individually they have comparative advantages in resource endowments, especially in the form of the relatively large land resources of the continental territories of Guyana and Belize.

Since the formation of CARIFTA in 1968, there has been some growth in the relative importance of intraregional agricultural trade, at least for the MDCs, as Table 5.6 shows. Such trade still constitutes only a small part of the total, however—around 10 to 15 percent for the MDCs. There is no evidence of similar growth for the LDCs, with the possible exception of St. Vincent. The major item traded within the region is rice exported from Guyana (with a total value of about EC$20 million[4] in 1971, or over one-

TABLE 5.6. INTRAREGIONAL AGRICULTURAL TRADE OF MDCS, 1967–73
(millions of Eastern Caribbean dollars and percentage of total agricultural trade)

	Exports				Imports			
	1967		*1973*		*1967*		*1973*	
MDC	*Value*	*Percent*	*Value*	*Percent*	*Value*	*Percent*	*Value*	*Percent*
Barbados	3.5	7.0	7.6	15.7	4.6	12.8	11.9	13.1
Guyana	17.6	18.0	25.4	21.7	1.1	2.9	10.6	18.2
Jamaica	1.1	0.7	12.8	7.0	4.2	3.3	22.9	8.2
Trinidad	5.3	8.7	20.9	22.7	11.6	12.0	16.1	8.8
Total	27.5	7.7	66.7	15.2	21.5	7.2	61.5	10.0

Source: National trade statistics.

4. For exchange rates for the Eastern Caribbean dollar (EC$) and other related currencies, see Statistical Appendix, Table SA11.20.

third of intraregional agricultural exports of the MDCs). Other items include coconut products, vegetables, processed food, and citrus fruits (especially oranges).

Apart from regional arrangements among producers of sugar and bananas, and bilateral rice marketing agreements with Guyana which predate CARICOM, the two major instruments of regional agricultural cooperation to date have been the Agricultural Marketing Protocol (AMP) and the Oils and Fats Agreement (OFA). There is also an arrangement for the sugar-producing countries to supply the demand of the nonsugar producing territories at a price equal to the lowest contractual price. The AMP represents a cautious approach to intraregional trade promotion for a limited range of commodities only. The protocol covers twenty-two items comprising vegetables, fruits (oranges and pineapples), and some meat products (pork, poultry, eggs).[5] It requires each territory to declare its estimates of surpluses and deficits of the twenty-two items twice a year, and the AMP committee of officials then allocates markets among all the territories. In practice, priority is given to the surpluses of the LDCs over those of the MDCs, and the AMP committee will authorize member countries to import from outside the region only when regional supplies are not available. The Protocol also provides for the fixing of minimum f.o.b. export prices for each six-month period.

Operations under the AMP have not been entirely satisfactory. The information provided by member countries about their surpluses and deficits has often been very inaccurate, and information on market opportunities has not been systematically relayed back to the territories producing particular crops. Information on the costs of production of different crops is scanty, so the minimum prices under the Protocol tend to be fixed broadly on the basis of the prices of imports and exports over the previous six months, together with what little information is available on future prospects, and the negotiating skill of the exporters. Prices are sometimes set above the costs of production in importing countries, with the result that they artificially reduce the amount of regional trade by encouraging import substitution within each country. A case in point is the importation of sweet potatoes into Trinidad from St. Vincent. In addition, the MDCs appear to use the Protocol as a means to restrict the quantity of imports from within the region, particularly in the case of processed and semiprocessed products. By not declaring a deficit for such products, even when they have one, they are able to exclude regional imports and thus encourage domestic import substitution.

It is hard to assess the actual effect of the Protocol on intraregional trade, because of the absence of statistical information. Available evidence suggests

5. The full list of commodities covered by the AMP is as follows: carrots, peanuts, tomatoes, red kidney beans, black peppers, sweet peppers, garlic, onions, potatoes (sweet), potatoes (not sweet), string beans, cinnamon, cloves, cabbage, plantains, pork and pork products, poultry meat, eggs, okra, fresh oranges, pineapples, and pigeon peas. In 1976, processed products were excluded from the list so that pork is interpreted as fresh pork.

that it has had some limited success, however uneven, but that the amounts traded are too small for its impact to be of much significance. Trade has been concentrated in about ten products. For example, intraregional trade in vegetables on the AMP list in 1972 was estimated at less than 7 million pounds valued at EC$2 to 3 million, compared to total regional imports of vegetables and root crops of about 180 million pounds. Likewise, there is no evidence of significant intraregional trade in meats and eggs. Only in the case of citrus fruits is intra-CARIFTA trade large enough for the deficits of importing countries, especially Barbados, to come close to being matched by surpluses elsewhere. Perhaps the single most conspicuous feature of the Protocol is the number of products for declared deficits which remain in excess of declared surpluses or for which there are no surpluses to declare.

Output information is not available for the LDCs, but the Protocol did not apparently raise output enough for them to export much to the MDCs, despite the privileged position the Protocol gives them in MDC markets. Among these countries, only St. Vincent can be considered a significant exporter of vegetables, while Dominica and Grenada are lesser participants.[6] Most of the intra-CARIFTA trade that does take place appears to originate in Jamaica (meat), or Guyana and Trinidad (citrus fruit).

Because of the relative lack of success of the AMP, particularly as it relates to agricultural production in the LDCs, the Guaranteed Market Scheme (GMS) was initiated in 1972. Under this agreement, the MDCs (Barbados, Guyana, Jamaica, and Trinidad and Tobago) are required to purchase specified amounts by volume of six particular commodities, at a negotiated price, from individual LDCs. It is still too early to judge the effects of the scheme, but the number of commodities covered is small, and major increases in the agricultural exports of the LDCs are unlikely until action is taken to remedy the basic problems of the structure of the agricultural sector in each island.

A specialized working group of officials was established in July 1975 to review the operations of the Protocol and make recommendations for its improvement, including a new formula for fixing prices. The resultant formula for fixing prices implemented in 1976 has two basic elements—a cost of production, and a fixed profit per acre.

The OFA is quite important for the region. The agricultural and manufacturing activities of the oils and fats industry taken together represent an estimated 5 percent of regional gross domestic product, and trade within the region is greater than are imports from outside it. The principal suppliers of oils and fats products are Dominica, St. Lucia, and St. Vincent. The arrangement, however, has by no means replaced imports. Intraregional trade is almost exclusively in coconut products (raw oil, refined oil, and margarine), whereas extraregional imports consist mostly of such substitute products as soybeans and other vegetable oils, hydrogenated oils and fats, and lard. Indeed, the regional deficit has risen as consumption has grown,

6. See Statistical Appendix, Table SA7.15.

while regional copra production has been sluggish.[7] At the same time, the price levels used to protect domestic industry have tended to exceed world prices, and factories have been operating well below capacity. As long as the world prices of substitutes, such as soybean oil, are comparatively low, there is an incentive for a number of countries to rely on extraregional supplies of refined products; the demand for imports also reflects established consumption habits in the region, which tend to favor some products other than coconuts, particularly in the case of edible oils.

Regional cooperation: future prospects

It has already been emphasized that sustained growth in the agricultural sector requires action to deal with major technical and structural obstacles at the national level. The CARICOM governments should not regard a program for increased regional integration as a substitute for the difficult policy decisions which have to be made within each member country. It would nevertheless be useful to set general policy objectives for the region's agriculture, because they could provide a coherent framework for national programs. The preparation of a Regional Food Plan (RFP) already represents some progress towards such a framework.

The RFP has been designed specifically to reduce the region's rapidly rising food import bill. The main elements of the production program under the RFP, approved by the second conference of CARICOM Heads of Government in December 1975, are as follows:

a. Preliminary proposals for a regional livestock program aimed at achieving a significant level of self-sufficiency in all meat products over the next ten years.
b. Important food production projects to be undertaken by a specially created Caribbean Food Corporation. These include the production and processing of fish, the production of grains and the production of fruits and vegetables.
c. Projects to supply the region with vitally needed agricultural inputs, by bulk purchasing and distribution of agricultural chemicals including fertilizers, and the production of seeds and other propagating materials.[8]

The Caribbean Food Corporation (CFC), established in 1976, is the major regional institution involved in implementing the RFP, including the control of regional projects. Shares in the CFC are held by all the CARICOM governments.

The largest component of the RFP would be the regional livestock program. The initial proposals are designed to replace, over the next ten years,

7. See Statistical Appendix, Table SA7.18.

8. Working Party on Food Production, "Progress Report on the Regional Food Plan" (Georgetown, Guyana: CARICOM Secretariat, April 1976). The working party was established by the heads of government of the four MDCs.

the 1973 level of imports of virtually all livestock products, and to meet a high proportion of the extra demand which will appear by 1980. This would require achieving the following annual production levels by the tenth year of the plan:

a. Production of an extra 574 million pounds of fresh milk, to replace the 1973 level of imports of milk and milk products (excluding butter and cheese). This is estimated to require an extra 164,000 cows on 317,000 acres of improved pastures. (Total regional production of fresh milk in 1973 was only 170 million pounds.)
b. Production of an extra 26 million pounds of beef as a by-product of the dairy industry. A proposal for a specialized beef herd to produce an extra 25 million pounds has been temporarily deferred, in view of the heavy demands it would make on scarce land resources. (Regional production of beef products in 1973 was 41 million pounds, with a further 32 million pounds imported.)
c. Production of an extra 12 million pounds of mutton and lamb, to completely replace current imports and cater for the expected increase in demand to 1980. (Total 1973 production in the region was approximately 5 million pounds.)
d. Introduction of the production of eggs for hatching within the region. This would require an estimated annual production of 77 million hatching eggs by the tenth year of the plan. (At present, approximately 36 million hatching eggs are imported each year.)
e. Expansion of production to maintain the high current level of regional self-sufficiency in pork, poultry, and eating eggs.
f. Development of a regional breeding program for the dairy, beef, and sheep and goat industries, to avoid the high cost of importing breeding animals and to develop breeds more suitable to the regional conditions.[9]

Total resource costs of the program (excluding the possible specialized beef production) would include an estimated capital cost of EC$530 million, largely for the development of the dairy industry; an extra 15,600 jobs in direct farm employment; and the use of 366,000 acres of land (excluding the animal feed component). Other activities in the region developing out of the program could include the expansion of fertilizer production and the use of hides and skins for leather production.

A number of the projects in the RFP have already been tentatively allocated between member countries, based on their anticipated comparative advantage in particular sectors. The dairy industry would be largely concentrated in Guyana and Belize, which have the largest areas of land not in use, and in Trinidad and Jamaica, which also have some land available and which are the largest importers of dairy products. The beef industry,

9. "Progress Report on the Regional Food Plan," April 1976, and "A Preliminary Design for a Regional Livestock Complex," (Georgetown, Guyana: CARICOM Secretariat, November 1976).

should it be developed, would be concentrated in Guyana, Belize, and Jamaica; most of the corn and soya feedstuffs for the industry would be produced in the two continental territories. The project for production of hatching eggs has a relatively small land requirement and would seem ideally suited to the ECCM countries. Each unit would become self-sufficient in small stock.

As of the later 1970s, however, the RFP is mainly a series of tentative proposals on paper. Much detailed work needs to be done on the preparation and economic appraisal of individual projects before large-scale implementation can start. The communication aspect of the development and implementation of the plan will also be crucial. A limited start in this direction was made in 1976, with the employment of an agricultural information specialist in the CARICOM Secretariat. Bilateral assistance is also being sought. In addition, two major barriers to increased livestock production must be removed quickly if the rate of expansion implied in the RFP is to be achieved.

The first of these barriers is the shortfall in the region as a whole of breeding animals of adequate quality. Some countries are trying to increase their dairy herds by importing bred heifers from temperate zone dairy countries, but this process is expensive and slow; it also involves severe problems with the management of animals bred for cooler climates. In some areas, semen from high quality dairy bulls is imported and used to upgrade local cows, which have adapted to the area and have developed resistance to the heat of the climate. This is a relatively inexpensive program, but it has been implemented very slowly because of inexperienced local management. In any case, the poor initial quality of native cows means that it will take many years to upgrade local cattle. A more efficient alternative might be to use semen from top quality dairy bulls adapted to tropical conditions to breed large numbers of high producing dairy cows in temperate countries. The resulting crossbred heifer calves could then be transported by air freight to the region and raised under tropical conditions to form the basis of commercial dairy herds. Alternatively, bred heifer calves could be imported from temperate zone dairy countries to be raised in the region and then crossbred locally.

The second major barrier to expansion is the inadequate number of skilled personnel for livestock management in the region. Cooperation on a regional basis to set up education and training programs in livestock control would be a helpful first step in a more general effort to improve agricultural training. This suggestion is discussed further below.

The preliminary design for the livestock program estimates the extra feed inputs required by the expanded dairy, poultry, and pork industries at over 1,000 million pounds of mixed (corn and soya) feeds, which would require about 330,000 acres of land. Because these acreage requirements are far in excess of immediate plans for the production of corn and soya beans in the region, it has been suggested that much of the feed inputs needed should be imported from outside the area. If the livestock industry were to expand as rapidly as envisaged in the plan, Guyana and Belize clearly could not develop the necessary large new supplies of feedstuffs within the required time frame. On the other hand, prolonged reliance on imports of feedstuffs would make the industry vulnerable to fluctuations in world feed prices and would involve large foreign exchange costs. In the longer run, because the natural resources of Guyana and Belize include large areas of land which are not in use; these countries will be able to specialize in the land-intensive production of animal feeds, which could in turn be used to supply the livestock industries of the island territories.

A modest step in this direction has already been taken, with two projects for the production of corn and soya beans nearing completion in Guyana and Belize. The projects will be operated by the Caribbean Food Corporation and it is proposed that they be regionally financed, initially with Trinidad and St. Kitts and Nevis participating in the Guyana project, and Jamaica in the project in Belize. The two projects together will use 17,500 acres, only about 5 percent of total additional regional requirements under the livestock plan. Nevertheless, if the projects are successful, they could point the way to greater regional participation in the development of underused land in the two continental member countries.

Regional cooperation in institutions: marketing, extension, research and education

Agricultural productivity and income depend significantly on infrastructure, including feeder roads and other transport and marketing facilities; on credit and extension services; and on education and research programs relevant to the needs of the region's farmers. Extension services, education, and research are especially important for the small farmers who constitute one of the poorest groups in the community; this group is particularly difficult to reach through extension services, however, and it has therefore derived little benefit from existing research and promotion activities.

The extension services in the region are grossly inadequate. Field extension officers are poorly trained; individual officers are expected to serve too many farmers; transport is inadequate, and teaching aids are poor. The attrition rate among officers is high, a situation which could be corrected by more adequate salaries and greater recognition of their services, in terms of their civil service grades. Since only a very few secondary schools in the entire region provide agricultural training, new extension officers are recruited from among candidates with some senior secondary education; appointees are given special on-the-job training. Appointees achieve an uneven level of competence in subject matter, and their knowledge of extension methods is weak.

The establishment of a Regional Agricultural Training Center would help to correct these problems. Appropriate objectives of a Center might be: to upgrade present staff; to provide for the continuing introduction of new technology and scientific advances; and to ensure ongoing communication between the extension services of the participating countries. The new Center could be located near an existing agricultural research center or agricultural school. It would be essential for a training program to offer refresher training for previously trained officers; the training staff would have to be sensitive to the special needs of Caribbean agriculture; and the Center would have to concentrate on training the trainers (that is, the officers who would then train farmers). Finally, the impact even of well-trained graduates from such a Center would only be effective if they were genuinely committed to the aim of developing a more productive agricultural sector.

Agricultural research at the regional level, and in individual CARICOM member countries, falls far short of even the most urgent needs. The applied research necessary to make better use of technology familiar to the developed regions of the world has not been done. The findings of research in other developing areas are not transmitted. The countries of the region have no research program adequate to deal with national agricultural problems, and they have failed to utilize such useful research information as has emanated from the Regional Research Center (RRC). Each of the countries has one or more competent researchers, but staff, facilities, and budgets are all extremely limited. The Regional Center at the University of the West Indies has little visibility in the region, and its activities do not seem to begin to meet regional needs.

Most research into export crops (sugar, bananas, coffee, cocoa, and citrus fruits, for example) has been done by commodity associations.[10] Small growers of these commodities are ignorant of these research findings and, in any event, the special problems of small growers receive little attention from researchers. Even so, research programs for export crops are less seriously deficient than are those for commodities grown for internal consumption, or those for the entire range of livestock enterprises and products (meat, milk, eggs, and fish).

In the light of these fundamental shortcomings, the recent establishment of the Caribbean Agricultural Research and Development Institute (CARDI), is a welcome development, which promises to revitalize applied agricultural research in the region with the emphasis on urgent problem solving. It merits strong financial support from every member government, as well as assistance from international sources of funds. The Institute's current terms of reference might usefully be extended to include the establishment of formal links with other international research institutes. This step would help make promising findings available to researchers in the Caribbean for local testing and exploration of additional areas of research, such as studies of production cost estimation methods of management systems, and of feed supplies and livestock nutrition. The placement of field officers to work full time in individual member countries so as to ensure the prompt testing of the applicability of research findings and innovative procedures in each country, is an important

10. A study (*Caribbean Technology Policy Studies*, forthcoming) by the Institute of Social and Economic Research (Mona) and the Institute of Development Studies (University of Guyana), has found that research by these bodies has concentrated the application of labor saving techniques, but that the quality and impact varied with specific research directors.

feature of CARDI's program, but its effectiveness will depend on each country maintaining a research program of its own.

Proper education at all levels can augment extension services and the general ability of farmers to use land more productively. The educational system in the region is seriously deficient in this respect. Agricultural education at the post-secondary level is now provided in three countries (Jamaica, Trinidad, and Guyana) and additional education at professional levels is provided by the Faculty of Agriculture of the University of the West Indies. A program for the training of veterinary assistants in Guyana under the sponsorship of the Pan American Health Organization (PAHO) produced its first graduates in 1977. This should greatly assist the livestock program. Agricultural education at lower levels is currently either nonexistent or trivial; it should be incorporated into school systems at all ages and levels as a matter of urgency. The content of programs suitable for local conditions, and the best way to set such programs up, should be studied at the national level by the countries of the region.

Agricultural marketing arrangements throughout the region, and especially in the LDCs, are well known to be inadequate. Some years ago, a major effort was initiated with the assistance of funds from the United Kingdom and the Caribbean Development Bank (CDB) in the LDCs, and with the help of other external assistance in the MDCs, to improve transport facilities through the creation of feeder roads, main roads, and port and airport facilities. Much less attention has been given to the improvement, upgrading or—in the case of the LDCs—outright creation of other facilities for the distribution of agricultural products such as inland cold storage, reception points in the countryside, transport fleets, and refrigerated transport facilities for transfer of goods between islands. The level and quality of services provided at each end of a marketing route often differ sharply from one country to another, or even within a given country; this means that perishable products suffer alarming rates of losses in both quantity and quality.

A feasibility study of a comprehensive range of agricultural marketing facilities and services needs to be undertaken on a regional basis. The range would include the storage and transport facilities needed, such as collection points for agricultural produce (especially in the LDCs); port facilities, including cold storage; and air transport facilities for perishable products. It would also include a uniform regional system of standards for quality control and a regional marketing agency for the purchase in bulk of agricultural inputs from outside the region—items such as fertilizers, chemicals, and animal feed, for example. The operation of these facilities and services should involve all the marketing boards of the member countries, the regional secretariat, and the commodity associations.

The Chief Crops: Prospects and Policies

The preceding discussion has surveyed the problems of, and prospects for, regional integration in the area of Caribbean agriculture. Having established this framework, it is now possible to make a similar survey of the prospects for, and policies relating to, the chief crops of the Caribbean: sugar and bananas.

Sugar

The following discussion of sugar production in the Caribbean is divided into three parts. First, recent market developments are described and assessed. Second, an examination is made of problems and constraints in production. Finally, an analysis is made of suggested national policy actions.

RECENT MARKET DEVELOPMENTS. The sugar industry has been the economic mainstay of the West Indies and Guyana for centuries. The history of the West Indies cannot be separated from that of sugar in the region; the culture and institutions associated with the industry have left their imprint even on those territories which have ceased to produce sugar. Four islands have stopped producing sugar since World War II: St. Lucia, St. Vincent, Grenada (which still maintains a small plant), and Antigua.[11] Active industries still operate in Barbados, Guyana, Jamaica, St. Kitts, Trinidad, and Belize; all these countries, with the exception of Belize, are members of the West Indies Sugar Association (WISA).

Sugar is the most important agricultural product of the Caribbean region. It is also the chief agricultural export of the six countries with active industries, contributing, for example, close to EC$310 million in foreign exchange earnings in 1972 (the figure includes the value of exports of such derived products as rum and molasses). This total represented more than 55 percent of the region's total agricultural exports in that year. The relative importance of sugar to the national economy varies considerably from country to country. The share of sugar exports in the agricultural exports of countries, and in their total exports, ranged in 1972 from 98 percent and 41 percent, respectively, for Barbados to 45 percent and 5 percent, respectively, for Trinidad. Comparative percentages for the other producers were: Jamaica—64 and 13; Guyana—72 and 37; St. Kitts—97 and 64; and Belize—58 and 51.

Sugar is also one of the most important sources of employment in the region, directly employing more than 150,000 workers. The industry also generates considerable indirect employment. Some 54,000 farmers earn a livelihood from sugar cane production in the various territories, producing approximately 30 percent of the cane milled.

The total of regional sugar production has been declining in recent years. The production level was about one million long tons in 1975, compared with the all-time high of 1.3 million long tons in 1965. Production has fallen, in spite of the fact that there are secure markets for exports of

11. The latter three states are currently reconsidering the reestablishment of the sugar industry with the principal aim of satisfying domestic demand for sugar.

Caribbean sugar, and in the face of large increases in regional demand. Even more surprising is the fact that the total acreage under cane cultivation has actually grown during recent years, from about 440,000 acres in 1965, to about 500,000 acres in 1974. The decline of output can largely be attributed to increases in costs, which, until 1974, were more than proportional to the increase in the price of sugar.

Until the early 1970s, the traditional export markets for Caribbean sugar were all regulated by special quota arrangements, amounting to a total theoretical quota of 1.2 million tons at the end of 1973. Most of this total (62 percent) was accounted for by the United Kingdom under the Commonwealth Sugar Agreement (CSA), with the remainder going to the United States under the U.S. Sugar Act, and to the world market under the International Sugar Agreement (ISA).

The existing institutional arrangements were, however, radically altered during 1974. From 1971 to early 1974, the Caribbean region had received a price of EC$293 per long ton for sugar exported to the United Kingdom under the CSA. This price was renegotiated twice during 1974, however, eventually reaching EC$650 per ton. The new price remained in effect until June 1975. When the United Kingdom joined the European Economic Community (EEC), the Lomé Convention of February 1975, negotiated between the EEC and the African, Caribbean, and Pacific (ACP) states, replaced the CSA. Under the Convention, which remains in force until 1980, ACP sugar producers can supply up to 1.4 million long tons per annum to the EEC.[12] The price received will be indexed to the basic support price paid by the EEC to its own sugar beet producers. The market guaranteed for each country was to be limited to the amount it shipped to the Community during the year July 1975 to June 1976. It is expected that exports from CARICOM countries will be distributed as shown in Table 5.7. In the case of the U.S. market, the Sugar Act expired in 1974 and was not renewed; as a consequence, the United States is now effectively part of the unregulated world market.

The negotiated price of sugar to the EEC fell from £260 sterling per ton c.i.f. in 1975 to £188 per ton c.i.f. in 1976.[13] The long-term price stability which was envisioned under the Convention has not materialized. The region, had on the basis of the earlier price, established a cost structure which it will find difficult to maintain. This situation provides a strong argument for rationalizing regional sugar production, so that average costs are reduced. Cost reduction will require further action, mainly at the

12. The EEC has retained the right to export an equivalent tonnage to the free market, if it cannot absorb all the guaranteed imports. Should it do so, this would undoubtedly force down the free market price.

13. Conformity of the price to the provision of Article 5 of the Protocol which indexed the price of ACP sugar to beet sugar has been questioned. The issue was submitted for resolution to the European Court of Justice by the ACP under Article 81 of the Lomé Convention.

TABLE 5.7. ESTIMATED VOLUME OF SUGAR EXPORTS FROM CARICOM COUNTRIES TO EEC, JULY 1975–JUNE 1976
(thousands of tons)

Country	*Volume*	*Percent*
Barbados	50	11.0
Guyana	160	35.1
St. Kitts	15	3.3
Belize	40	8.8
Jamaica	120	26.4
Trinidad and Tobago	70	15.4
Total	455	100.0

Sources: National trade statistics and CARICOM Secretariat.

national level, to remove the major causes of the current decline in sugar productivity.

PROBLEMS AND CONSTRAINTS IN PRODUCTION. It is difficult to generalize from the specific problems which individual national sugar industries face, given the differences between their natural endowments and industrial structures. There are, however, some general problems which affect them all, although in varying degrees.

In some territories, such as in Barbados, both the overall acreage planted to sugar and the acreage reaped have recently fallen, partly in response to programs of diversification in agriculture. Furthermore, there has been a decline in yields per acre. The number of tons of cane reaped per acre consistently decreased from more than thirty tons in the early 1960s to about twenty-seven tons in 1972. Important factors contributing to this decrease included poor cultivation practices, such as delays in replanting and reductions in the use of fertilizer (perhaps partly a result of reduced profit margins); and lack of proper water management and control (in some dry countries, such as Jamaica and St. Kitts, water resources are limited but existing sources are not fully exploited, and in others, such as Guyana, water drainage is a serious problem because of the periodic floods). The number of tons of cane required to produce a ton of sugar (the conversion ratio) also increased regionally from less than ten in 1963 to more than eleven in 1972. This was because burning of the cane before harvesting became widespread and the grinding season became too long. Both these practices, which were adopted in response to recurrent labor shortages, reduce the sucrose content of harvested cane.

On a worldwide basis, the levels of yield achieved in the region are low. Average yields of sugar per acre are only 2.5 tons in CARICOM, compared with 3.2 tons per acre in the Dominican Republic and 4.9 tons in Australia. In addition to the farming practices just described, the high proportion of

Caribbean output in the hands of small growers, who can generally only achieve relatively low sugar yields, contributes to the problem.

The history of the sugar industry has had a profound effect on the social and political development of the Caribbean, and is to some extent responsible for the prevailing unpopularity of all agriculture throughout the region. The stigma which became associated with working in sugar is still very much alive; together with the generally unpleasant nature of much of the work, this has contributed to the currently unsatisfactory state of labor supply, and labor relations in general. Shortages of labor are now common, especially at harvest time, when much of the cane cutting is done by hand. Some territories, such as Barbados, import labor from neighboring territories to overcome this. Indeed, there appears to be a strong preference for migration among unskilled sugar workers. It has been common in recent times for them to migrate to Puerto Rico or the United States to harvest cane, rather than to stay in their own country to do the same job.

Because a relatively high proportion of the local labor force in each country is still employed in the sugar industry, and because the industry is highly unionized, wage settlements and other terms of employment are often influenced by general social and political factors, and may in turn have important political and social effects. Wage demands in recent years have sometimes been high in spite of the levels of unemployment, and the difficulty many companies experienced in making any profits until 1974. Part of the explanation may lie in the mutual distrust which is common between management and labor. More important, the expectations and demands of the sugar laborer are to an increasing extent influenced by the high wages paid in the enclave sectors of national economies—tourism in the Windward and Leeward islands and Barbados, bauxite in Jamaica and Guyana, and oil in Trinidad and Tobago. There has, therefore, been a fairly consistent increase in labor costs throughout the industry, despite the low level of productivity (for all field operations in Belize and Jamaica, productivity is on average two-fifths of that in Louisiana).[14]

In the light of these labor problems, an important recent development in the industry has been the increasing number of smallholders. These now supply about 30 percent of total cane deliveries. There are now more than 55,000 cane farmers, employing an estimated 40,000 people. (These figures do not include self-employed small farmers and smallholders, the latter defined as those farming less than 10 acres.) The circumstances of these farmers vary greatly; many only farm part-time, some grow only 2 or 3 acres of cane, others grow 200 acres or more. Despite their important contribution to total output, the problems of smallholders have not been systematically examined or dealt with. The relatively low current productivity of smallholdings suggests that their output could rise considerably. For example, in Barbados, smallholders get an average of thirteen tons of cane an acre, against more than twenty-six tons on estates. Extension,

14. See Statistical Appendix, Table SA7.50.

marketing, and technology services for smallholders are usually provided by the company controlling the factory which processes their cane; this fact probably accounts in part for the widely varying standards of smallholder farming in the region. It should be noted, however, that in many instances, smallholders using family labor may actually fare better, in net cash terms, than larger farmers who have to rely on hired labor for a few peak work months during the year, and face the full force of rising labor costs.

To place matters in a global perspective, it is important to note that the West Indies are high cost producers of sugar compared with other producing countries in the world. Costs of production per ton have been consistently more than 30 percent higher in the West Indies than in such other Commonwealth countries as Australia, Fiji, or Mauritius. It should be noted, however, that the gap between the two groups of producers has been reduced since 1970.[15] Costs of production rose by about 75 percent in the other Commonwealth countries between 1970 and 1974, but by only 45 percent in the West Indies. This narrowing of the gap is mostly due to very substantial wage increases in the other Commonwealth countries (in Australia, for example, the increases were twice as large as they were in the West Indies in both 1973 and 1974).

The loading stage of the harvesting process is quite highly mechanized; for example, about one-third of all cane reaped in 1972 was loaded mechanically. On the other hand, mechanical cane harvesting itself is most uncommon, with only 1 percent of cane being harvested mechanically.[16] Chopper harvesters are being used in all territories on an experimental basis, but harvesting costs per acre are very high. Moreover, a significant part of the traditional cane lands of the islands cannot accommodate the field layout necessary for full mechanization (this is particularly the case in St. Kitts and Barbados). In Barbados, for example, the most optimistic estimates call for 10,000 acres, or 20 percent of the total, to be reaped mechanically within the next few years and set about 60 percent of total acreage as the maximum which might eventually be suitable for mechanical reaping.

NATIONAL POLICY MEASURES. At the national level, all CARICOM sugar producing countries need to consider certain fundamental institutional changes. High priority should be given to land reform, which may offer a solution to some of the social and economic problems which beset the sector. Family farms and cooperatives of an intermediate size promise to be more viable than the traditional large estates, or than family farms of less than five acres (which are simply too small to be economical). Governments should consider instituting land reform programs including the provision of long-term finance and advice to family farmers for the expansion of cultivated acreage. The larger sugar estates, on the other hand, in which the labor relations problems of the industry are concentrated, should be reorganized.

15. See Statistical Appendix, Table SA7.54.

16. Trinidad is the only territory where mechanical harvesting is significant (accounting for 8 or 9 percent of total cane reaped in that country).

As land distribution is consolidated in this way, a comprehensive program is also needed to improve physical access to farms (a problem that varies greatly from country to country), and to expand extension services to provide technical assistance and advice to the small farmer. This assistance could be linked to the supply of such inputs as fertilizer, which in the past have been partly misused or underutilized.

Any program which raises the number of independent producers serving a market increases the importance of the price mechanism. Consequently, as land reform proceeds, the success of the sugar industry will increasingly depend upon the incentive provided by the size and rate of growth of net income to the average family farmer or cooperator. The margin between the factory price of cut cane and the aggregate cost of leased equipment, of inputs such as fertilizer, and of mortgage or rent payments for land, must be sufficient to provide an appropriate incentive to the small farmer. To encourage improved techniques of farming, it may be necessary initially to subsidize the price of any inputs that are new to farmers using them.

Any program to increase profitability in the industry should include a careful reassessment of domestic consumer prices for sugar. Although the effect of a moderate price rise on the overall cost of living would be small, it might still be argued on equity grounds that the present pricing policy, which effectively subsidizes the consumer for purchase of a necessity, is progressive. This subsidy, however, is at the expense of the producer. Given the importance of sugar as a source of employment, especially in the future as land reform progresses, the argument on equity grounds against increased domestic sugar prices becomes far less compelling. This is because higher average prices and consequently greater farmer incentives could lead to a significant increase in rural employment.

Stable prices are of special help to the small farmer; stability of input and crop prices also make him more willing to experiment with specialized as opposed to mixed cropping, and with improved farming techniques. Stabilized producer prices are quite compatible with the policy some governments have pursued recently, when market prices rose rapidly, of taxing away as much as 85 percent of the windfall gains with highly progressive export taxes. This experience shows that price stabilization can, at times, be anything but a drain on government resources. The long-run success of such a policy depends on choosing appropriate base prices and adjustment factors.

The West Indies Sugar Association (WISA) represents all the sugar producing countries of the community, except Belize. Its main function has been to administer the quotas granted under the terms of the various sugar agreements, since these quotas were awarded to WISA and not directly to individual countries. The Association is also responsible for a research program carried out in Barbados.

Although it has established links with the cane farmers' organizations and with the trade unions, WISA is not directly involved with the organization of sugar production. Neither is any other regional body. Recent developments in regional economic integration and changes in international marketing arrangements prompted some institutional reform in the sugar industry. The functions of WISA were transferred to the CARICOM Secretariat and to a working party of regional officials on the long-term development of the sugar industry. In addition to the marketing of sugar, there might be scope for economies of scale from regional action in the purchasing of such imported inputs as fertilizers, and in research and development.

A major weakness of the sugar industry in the region is the limited development of by-products. There have been experiments with using sugarcane for animal feeds (Comfith, a process developed by Canadian agricultural engineers), the production of bagasse board and the use of bagasse for fuel. Further research and development, and the commercialization of the use of by-products, could, however, greatly enhance the attractiveness of sugar.

Sugarcane has been and continues to be one of the crops best adapted to the ecological conditions of the Caribbean region. Many countries have become increasingly anxious to diversify agriculture away from its dependence on sugar, for a combination of economic and social reasons; the economics of the shift from sugarcane to other crops are, however, still largely unexplored. The main candidates to replace sugar, in the short run, are the commodities emphasized in the RFP—livestock products, grains, fruit and vegetables—or other export crops.

Several factors must be taken into consideration when discussing the external demand aspects of possible alternative export crops. A number of possible export crops with market potential (citrus, cocoa, or coffee, for example) are not ecologically suited to sugarcane lands; the banana is an ecologically feasible, if limited, substitute but its export potential is limited; several other possible export crops do not have large enough potential markets to make use of more than marginal amounts of the land now planted with sugarcane.

On the supply side of the equation, inputs of domestic agricultural resources are currently well below what is available. More than 500,000 acres of farm land have been abandoned in the last five or six years; this land could be brought back into cultivation. In addition, large tracts of land are available in several countries, especially in Guyana and Belize, although the costs of development are high. Finally, the high rates of unemployment and underemployment in agriculture suggest that, with the right social and economic incentives, large amounts of labor would also be available. Thus, while other crops might be more profitable per acre than sugar[17] from the point of view of resource supply, the production of crops for import substitution or the increased production of crops for export do not necessarily imply competition with sugarcane for the use of natural resources.

The evidence suggests, therefore, that other crops need not be directly

17. A recent study in Trinidad indicated that, on the average, net returns from one acre to family labor were as follows (in EC$): sugarcane 146, dairy production 425, sweet potatoes 300, tomatoes 600 to 1,200, oranges 120 to 400, cassava 250.

substituted for sugar to any significant degree in the short or medium term, since there is no real competition between sugarcane and other crops for the use of inputs such as land and labor.[18] In the longer run, sugar industry policy should be designed to complement the region's new import substitution initiatives.

Bananas

The following discussion of banana production covers four main topics: export trends; production problems; marketing and organizational problems; and policy recommendations.

EXPORT TRENDS. Bananas are currently exported by five countries in the region: Jamaica, and the four Windward Islands (Dominica, Grenada, St. Lucia, and St. Vincent). Other territories produce small quantities only, for domestic consumption, although Belize has exported small amounts in recent years and is currently initiating a large expansion program; this should enable it to export substantial quantities within the next few years. The discussion which follows refers mainly to the five traditional exporting countries.

After sugar, bananas are the region's second most important agricultural product. It has been estimated that some 140,000 persons in the five exporting countries are directly dependent upon the banana industry. There are some 68,000 growers in the region; approximately half of them live in Jamaica, and the other half in the Windward Islands, which are much more dependent on bananas than Jamaica, as is indicated by Table 5.8, which presents data on the share of banana exports in total exports. For the region as a whole, banana exports account for around 8 percent of the total value of agricultural exports.

As in the case of sugar, production of bananas for export has been declining in the last few years, as is shown in Table 5.9. Fortunately for the region, the price received for the exported fruit was relatively high during 1973 and 1974, so the full impact of the fall in output was not felt. Unfortunately recovery in production, particularly in the Windward Islands in 1976, was accompanied by a fall in prices due to competition on the United Kingdom market and a cutback in exports to forestall further price decline.

18. More than 510,000 acres of land are currently under sugarcane cultivation. Production amounted to about 1.1 million tons in 1972, giving a yield of 2.2 tons per acre. Increasing the yield to 3.0 tons per acre (which is less than the yield levels obtained in the early 1960s), and raising the ratio of acreage reaped to total acreage under cultivation back to the former level of 95 percent, the target of 1.2 million tons of sugar for the region could be obtained from about 400,000 acres under sugarcane cultivation. This would mean the release of more than 100,000 acres of land for other crops. Conversely, the 500,000 acres would, under the suggested target figures for yields and reaping ratios, bring total production to nearly 1.5 million tons of sugar, thus adding to foreign exchange earnings.

TABLE 5.8. SHARE OF BANANA EXPORTS IN AGRICULTURAL AND TOTAL EXPORTS, 1968–74
(percentage)

	Total agricultural exports			*Total merchandise exports*		
Country	*1968*	*1971*	*1974*	*1968*	*1971*	*1974*
Dominica	99.1	73.6	66.8	91.8	64.2	62.2
Grenada	40.6	19.6	14.9[a]	39.4	19.4	11.2[a]
St. Lucia	92.5	81.4	82.2	82.4	76.1	68.6
St. Vincent	67.2	56.6	55.2[b]	60.3	55.6	53.3[b]
Jamaica	20.4	17.9	9.1	7.7	4.3	1.8

a. 1973.
b. 1972.
Source: Statistical Appendix, Tables SA7.56, SA3.3, SA3.7, SA3.8, SA3.11, SA3.12.

The short-term prospects of the banana industry hinge on the manner of application of Protocol 6 of the Lomé Convention.

PRODUCTION PROBLEMS. Yields per acre of bananas are believed to be extremely low in the Caribbean compared to the yields obtained in Central America, Africa, or the French Antilles. On a pure stand basis, average yields for the region probably do not exceed three to four tons an acre, compared to more than ten to twelve tons an acre in the French Antilles. Yields vary a great deal, of course, from grower to grower; some farmers obtain yields well above ten tons per acre in pure stand, while others may only get one to one-and-a-half tons per acre in mixed cropping. It is very hard to compare the returns per acre to farmers using different systems of production. In the case of mixed cropping, bananas are only one of several items produced on each acre, and consequently represent only part of the total return per acre. The traditional criticism of mixed cropping—that it lowers yields per acre and hence total returns—may, however, be mistaken;

TABLE 5.9. EXPORTS OF BANANAS, BY VOLUME AND VALUE, 1965–74

Category	*1965*	*1966*	*1967*	*1968*	*1969*	*1970*	*1971*	*1972*	*1973*	*1974*
Volume (thousand long tons)										
Jamaica	180	180	173	138	136	135	126	127	108	72
Windward Islands	178	162	165	180	169	118	123	119	93	96
Total	358	342	338	318	305	253	249	246	201	168
Value (million Eastern Caribbean dollars)										
Jamaica	29.3	30.2	32.0	33.1	29.9	28.4	28.1	28.4	35.3	25.9
Windward Islands	21.7	21.9	23.3	29.0	30.2	19.0	19.5	17.7	26.6	45.1
Total	51.0	52.1	55.3	62.1	60.1	47.4	47.6	46.1	61.9	71.0

Source: National trade statistics (see Table SA7.56 of Statistical Appendix for island by island breakdown).

in some situations, mixed cropping may actually benefit the farmer, because it spreads his risk over a number of products.

In any event, production of bananas in the region can be considered poor by any standard, and the three consecutive drought years from 1970 to 1973 proved disastrous to the producing countries. Bad weather represents only a partial explanation, however, of the low yields of Caribbean growers. Other causal factors have included poor cultivation practices, in terms of replanting time and plant density; inefficient or insufficient use of inputs; lack of proper soil conservation and irrigation methods; and inefficient land utilization. In many instances, bananas are grown on land which is either ecologically or topographically unsuitable for the crop, or both, while other suitable land of good quality is left unplanted.

MARKETING AND ORGANIZATION PROBLEMS. The industry is entirely dependent on the United Kingdom market, which is the sole outlet for all exports of bananas from the Windward Islands and Jamaica. As the industry's export performance has deteriorated, however, its share of the United Kingdom market has fallen from 97 percent in 1967 to about 75 percent in 1972. Meanwhile, the absolute size of United Kingdom demand is itself decreasing, because of switches to other fruits. Further, as the Caribbean countries have failed to meet its full requirements, the United Kingdom has found alternative suppliers (the Ivory Coast and Surinam) which are now strongly established.

The banana industry is structured along the same lines in all five producer islands. Banana farmers are organized in local growers' associations which buy the fruit from the grower. The associations operate a number of buying points and a transport system; they also provide some services, such as the supply of inputs (including planting material, fertilizers, and spraying services). The local growers' associations are grouped into larger organizations which handle relations with banana marketing agencies, and organize research on production problems. The two organizations involved are the Windward Islands Banana Growers' Association (WINBAN) and the Jamaica Banana Board.

These two producer associations negotiate purchasing contracts with the marketing companies who handle all stages of the export of the bananas, as far as the wholesaler in the United Kingdom. The companies are Geest Industries for the Windward Islands, and Fyffes (a subsidiary of United Fruit) and the Jamaica Producers Marketing Company for Jamaica.

Various problems have always hampered the smooth functioning of the marketing system. The large numbers of small farmers, and their wide geographical dispersion over the islands, require an extensive network of feeder roads to collect and transport bananas. Although some efforts are being made to improve it, the transport system is currently inadequate, and contributes significantly to the high level of wastage of harvested fruit. In Jamaica, for instance, only 75 percent of the fruit offered in 1970 was actually shipped. The wastage may be even higher in some of the Windward Islands. High costs of transport, both from farms to packing plants within the islands, and from the islands to the United Kingdom market, together with the high overhead costs of the growers' associations (partly because of the large number of smallholders to be serviced), have seriously reduced the prices paid to growers. It is estimated that growers receive only between 10 and 15 percent of the final retail price of bananas in the United Kingdom. This situation was made worse by competition among the three marketing agents to increase their shares of the market, a situation which led to the price wars of the mid-1960s. The relationships between the marketing agents and producers' associations have generally been poor and have been based on mutual distrust, especially in the case of Jamaica.

Until recently, the United Kingdom government took little part in the banana trade except to secure adequate protection against imports of bananas from non-Commonwealth areas, and to ensure minimum increases in the retail price of bananas. Traditionally, it was not involved in the negotiations between marketing agents and the producers' associations. (Under the French system, by contrast, price negotiations include all concerned parties: producers, marketing agents, ripeners, wholesalers, retailers, consumers, and the government.)

In 1972, however, WINBAN and the Jamaica Banana Board decided to create the Commonwealth Banana Exporters Association (CBEA), which Belize was invited to join. Among CBEA's objectives was to seek concrete proposals from the United Kingdom government for adequate protection of the Commonwealth banana industry in the light of Britain's entry in the EEC, and to have the British government give further consideration to the establishment of a Banana Committee which would ensure proper rationalization of the United Kingdom market, and consequently a fair return to the grower. This Committee was created in 1973, with the participation of the British government, CBEA, and the marketing agents. The Association also decided to explore common approaches to such questions as the rationalization of the supply of cardboard boxes; purchases of plastic field boxes; the study of findings of research schemes; tendering for fertilizers and for leaf spot control; and contract negotiations. To date, however, there has been little progress towards any kind of integrated approach to solving the production and marketing problems of the banana trade of the West Indies. In any case, the banana trade with the United Kingdom has come under Protocol 6 of the Lomé Convention. Protection from other ACP banana producers can only be under the "common organization of the market of the European Community" provision; it can be invoked only by decision of the EEC at large.

POLICY RECOMMENDATIONS. The main problems of the industry are in production and marketing. A regional strategy should aim to restore the production levels of the years from 1966 to 1969, representing an export equivalent of about 340,000 to 350,000 long tons; this would correspond to the current volume of demand in the United Kingdom market. To this end, development plans for the industry should be incorporated in the overall RFP. These plans should include measures to raise productivity through expanded research and extension services, and to improve managerial expertise at all levels. Higher output from farms will require expenditures on land improvement, such conservation measures as terracing, and the provision of feeder roads. At the same time, a regional strategy should aim at a satisfactory implementation of Protocol 6 of the Lomé Convention, and to strengthen the bargaining power of the region in relation to the United Kingdom market and the marketing agents, so as to get the farmer the highest possible prices. This in turn will give him a real incentive to expand production. The regional strategy should begin to focus on the EEC market rather than be limited to the declining U.K. market.

The overall structure of the industry, the traditionally limited role of the British government in price negotiations, the absence of strong regional cooperation between Jamaica and the Windward Islands in the banana trade, and the relative power of the marketing agents, have all contributed to the traditionally weak bargaining power of West Indies banana producers in trade negotiations. As a result, many of the problems currently faced by the various participants in the business, for which growers are not necessarily responsible, are eventually transferred to them through the price mechanism. The underlying principle for a successful strategy for producers, therefore, is that they, through their representatives, should have access to the control and supervision of the product throughout the entire channel of distribution, up to the level of the determination of price. This requires the involvement of the growers in all aspects of the trade, on a basis of parity with all other parties concerned: retailers, marketing agents, and the British government. The role of the Banana Committee should therefore be greatly expanded; it should develop into a full scale regulatory agency for banana marketing, possibly along the lines of the organization presently in operation in the French market.[19] Increased participation from the British government and other marketing agents, especially retailers, is essential. Joint price negotiations involving all parties concerned (the CBEA, marketing agents, the British government, independent ripeners and retailers) should be held periodically; import quotas should be allocated to each source of supply at the same time.

As the overall idea underlying the present recommendations is to increase the control and responsibility of Caribbean producers over a larger part of

19. The organization of the banana trade for the French market is highly structured. The import regime is managed by the Comité Interprofessionel Bananier (CIB) and its Comité Restraint (CRIB) which group all parties involved: producers, importers, ripeners, retailers, and representatives of ministries concerned (Agriculture, Finance, Foreign Affairs, Overseas Departments). CIB's role is: (a) to fix the amounts of bananas to be marketed for a period of two months; (b) to check the execution of policy decisions; and (c) to take appropriate measures in case of unexpected market distortions. The CIB is assisted by the Groupement d'Investissement Economique Bananier (GIEB), created in 1970, whose function is to ensure proper supplies of bananas, while maintaining prices at levels satisfactory to producers and other agents. It is entitled to set an annual weighted average price to be attained at the wholesale level, as well as monthly price objectives. The GIEB regulates the distribution of all import licenses.

the banana trade, it is suggested that the region initiate a substantial effort to promote and advertise bananas in the United Kingdom market. This has already been done in many other countries and it could help to increase Britain's per capita consumption of bananas.

Increased regional cooperation could also be extended to provide economies of scale in the supply of nonlabor inputs, most of which are imported from outside the region. A regional policy for the supply of major inputs could be established and operated by the CBEA; it could cover bulk buying of fertilizer and chemicals, and contract negotiations for the supply of cartons, boxing equipment, handling material, and other necessary inputs.

Research and extension activities could also be more closely integrated than in the past, to avoid unnecessary duplication of activities. In the case of research, a regional effort would also greatly benefit from close relationships with similar institutions in other producing countries, especially in the French Antilles. Because conditions are similar in the two areas, research results might be exchanged with relative ease to the benefit of all concerned.

Chapter 6

Tourism

THE COMMONWEALTH CARIBBEAN HAS ATTRACTED VISITORS FROM EUROPE and North America for many years. At first, most visitors to the region traveled long distances by boat to spend the winter in private homes or guest houses. This state of affairs began to change after World War II, although Caribbean tourism grew slowly during the immediate postwar period.

The following discussion of tourism in the Caribbean is divided into five parts. First, there is an overview assessing the historical background, recent problems, and prospects and policies for regional cooperation. Second, there is an analysis of the demand for, and supply of, tourist facilities in the Caribbean. Third, there is a special review of the seasonal factor as it affects price competitiveness of tourism in the area. Fourth, the growth prospects and constraints for tourism are outlined and assessed. Fifth, there is a summary analysis of both the benefits and the costs of tourism to the region.

Background, Problems, and Prospects

The advent of the jet set in the mid-1950s ushered in a new era of glamor for the Caribbean. This social group gave the region the image of an exclusive tourist haven where the wealthy could escape the rigor of northern winters by sunbathing on secluded beaches, snorkeling around coral reefs in clear turquoise seas, and dancing under starlit, tropical skies. The hotels built to accommodate the new tourists catered to their desire for ostentation, providing them with a luxury that very few could afford. The exclusiveness of the region's resorts was ensured by very high prices in winter, which hoteliers were able to charge because of both the seasonal scarcity of the tourist assets the Caribbean could offer, and the wealth of the market to which they catered. In summer, there were many alternative activities to attract the international tourist; consequently, hotel owners or managers closed down their hotels for the summer season, because of the relatively low demand and to satisfy their own desire for some leisure.

Patterns of growth

The first islands to become major tourist destinations were those which already had adequate public services and strong traditional ties with a developed country. In the northern part of the Caribbean, easy access by boat, and later by plane, from the United States also helped the growth of tourist traffic. The islands which first satisfied these criteria were Cuba (and, to a lesser extent, New Providence in the Bahamas) in the north, and Antigua and Barbados in the east. Cuba's heyday ended abruptly, however, when Fidel Castro assumed power in 1959. This event was of substantial benefit to the tourist industry in the Bahamas, Jamaica, and Puerto Rico, coinciding as it did with a number of developments which served to stimulate the general growth of tourism—and that of tourism in the Caribbean in particular.

In the early 1960s, rapid economic growth in the industrialized countries gave many people levels of income well above their everyday needs. At the same time, air travel was beginning to serve an increasing number of destinations at lower costs than before, and new social attitudes towards vacations encouraged tourism throughout much of the world. In the Caribbean, these developments led to a diversification as well as a general expansion of regional tourism. As the number of tourists grew, so new areas opened up; islands which had not previously been tourist centers began to compete for a share of the rapidly growing market. Off the Venezuelan coast, Curaçao and Aruba evolved from cruise ports of call into destination resorts. As formerly exclusive areas became better known, so the very wealthy tourists discovered new hideaways, thus extending tourist routes progressively further south and to less developed islands.

A sustained tourism boom was forecast in the latter part of the 1960s because the new wide-bodied jets were expected to stimulate group travel and to reduce air fares. Exchange controls were reduced or dismantled, and economic growth in North America and Europe was expected to remain strong. Further, President Lyndon Johnson's 1968 balance-of-payments message, urging U.S. citizens to confine their travel to the Western Hemisphere, was of special benefit to the Caribbean. This combination of events led to a fast rate of growth in the provision of accommodation in the Caribbean, a development which was further stimulated by the investment incentives offered by many governments. The predominant trends were toward larger, chain-managed hotels, self-catering accommodation, and condominia. Charter operations from Canada, from Europe and from the United States became popular at about the same time.

All did not go according to plan, however. In spite of such promotion and marketing efforts as attempts to attract more off-season traffic, and to achieve greater diversification of visitor origins, the growth of tourism demand in the Caribbean has still not matched expectations.

Recent problems

What happened? There are several explanations for the failure of tourism to grow in the years since 1968. The new wide-bodied aircraft, which had been expected to introduce mass tourism to the region, were used mainly on the North Atlantic routes, where excess capacity led to a price war. The highly diversified structure of air fares effectively undercut the Caribbean's price advantage for scheduled flights and the generally high cost of accommodation, food, and internal transport in the Caribbean made the total holiday package in the region less competitive than those available in Europe. North America also became a stronger competitor for European tourists. Summer tourism in the Caribbean suffered much more severely as a result of these developments than did winter tourism. Although the summer is absolutely less important than the winter in terms of its share of overall tourism earnings, it contributes significantly to annual fixed costs; any decline, therefore, has adverse effects on the profitability of the industry.

In addition, the popularity of Caribbean holidays has typically been affected by the existence of special concessionary air fares; by currency realignments and internal inflation rates, which have altered the ability of tourists to afford Caribbean vacations; by the directions of overseas investment flows, which have induced a mix of business and vacation travel; and by the decisions of tour wholesalers, made in an international context, about the marketability of a Caribbean vacation. These factors, which have been particularly important for European tourists, but have also affected demand from other areas, have varied sharply in strength in recent years. Fluctuations in tourism demand have been the result.

During the early 1970s, Caribbean tourism was also badly hurt by the simultaneous impact of the energy crisis and of sporadic civil disorders accompanied by violence in some of the islands: average annual occupancy levels fell drastically, for example, between 1968 and 1972. Later, the energy shortage eased somewhat and vacationers were slowly forgetting the violence of several years ago—at least until further turmoil in Jamaica and elsewhere. As of the later 1970s, however, much of the ground lost had not yet been recovered.

Tourism has provided the Caribbean region with a significant portion of its foreign exchange earnings and has created jobs for many West Indians, but it is not viewed by the people of the region as any kind of solution to their economic problems. Tourism in fact probably has as many critics in the Caribbean as it has defenders, and with some historical justification. While advocates of tourism have made much of the foreign exchange inflows and alleged multiplier effects it creates, its critics have pointed out the social costs which accompany the expansion of tourism—social tension, the alienation of land caused by the movement of small farmers into the tourist labor force, the frustrations engendered in the local populace by the lifestyles of affluent visitors, and the erosion of dignity and perpetuation of servitude involved in employment in the tourist sector. The income benefits arising from the industry are, moreover, much smaller than they seem. This is the result of very high leakages of earnings from tourist dollars, as expressed in terms of the import costs of inputs used in the industry, repatriation of profits on foreign capital, interest payments on foreign loans, and the cost of wages paid to expatriate management personnel.

These drawbacks are indeed real, are important for the people of the region, and formerly were frequently discounted or ignored by both investors and planners. In addition, it is very difficult to measure either the overall social benefits of tourism or its social costs because the factors involved are hard to quantify or to analyze properly. The ambivalent attitude of the more developed countries (MDCs) in the region toward tourism, seems recently to have hardened into resentment. Trinidad places tourism very low among its development priorities. Barbados, which depends heavily on tourism, is seeking to diversify its economy in order to become less dependent on the industry. Jamaica, although still seeking to attract tourists, has taken steps to bring a number of larger hotels into public ownership. The MDCs, with their relatively diversified economies, can perhaps afford to take a critical stand with respect to tourism; the less developed countries (LDCs), that is, the islands of the Eastern Caribbean, cannot. To them, tourism offers one of the very few available opportunities to develop their economies.

Regional cooperation in tourism development

A limited amount of cooperation already takes place between Caribbean Community (CARICOM) states in the development of tourism but this has been restricted to tourism promotion and research. With respect to tourism promotion, a number of governments are members of the Caribbean Tourism Association (CTA) and the Eastern Caribbean Tourism Association (ECTA). The CTA is a New York based organization sponsored by most of the Spanish, French, Dutch, and English Caribbean islands involved in tourism. It is one of the major promotional agencies for Caribbean tourism in North America. The ECTA is supported by the Eastern Caribbean islands and has responsibility for tourism promotion in the United Kingdom.

In the area of tourism analysis, the most significant cooperative development was the establishment in 1973 of the Caribbean Tourism Research Centre (CTRC) in Barbados. The CTRC is supported by some twenty governments. Its primary objective is to conduct fundamental studies and analyses of Caribbean tourism with a view to reducing the social costs and increasing the benefits of the sector to the regional economy. The CTRC has already undertaken and published a number of critical studies of the tourist industry; provided advice for small hoteliers; and run training courses for government personnel. One side effect of the establishment of the CTRC has been the decision of the Organization of American States (OAS) to channel assistance to the Caribbean in tourism development through it. Under an agreement with the CTRC and the Barbados government, the OAS has in fact established a technical unit within the CTRC, staffed by about four professionals.

Prospects and policies

Careful planning and an appropriate mix of policies can remove many of the less desirable consequences of tourism. Furthermore, the region generally has a strong comparative advantage in resort tourism, although some islands are better endowed than others. Finally, because a decline in tourism —or even a stabilization at the low level of activity of the mid-1970s—will lower per capita incomes and living standards, it is likely that efforts to develop tourism will continue to be required in the CARICOM countries over the long run.

The greatest single need in the region is to improve the links between the tourism sector and the rest of the economy. The development of such links presents a real opportunity to introduce regional cooperation. Up to now, tourism development in the Caribbean has been primarily the result of independent private initiatives by foreign investors who have established strong ties between their tourist operations in the Caribbean and suppliers in the developed countries. A few tourist projects have been initiated by local interests, both private and public, but these have had to rely on foreign suppliers of project inputs. These suppliers can currently offer economies of scale which cannot be matched in the region because of poor coordination of production. Links with other sectors of the regional economy can be developed, but coordination between the islands is needed in order to realize the economies of scale which specialized production of inputs, and standardized hotel design and service could provide. It might be advantageous, for example, to locate production of particular inputs on one island, which would supply the tourist industries of others. Items which might be handled in this way are furniture, small items of equipment, fittings, uniforms, linens, and foodstuffs. This kind of increased economic benefit from tourism can only come about, however, if the tourism sector as a whole is guided by plans and strategies geared to national and regional objectives. In the future, the way in which tourism projects are designed will determine the regional distribution of their benefits. Without drastic policy measures, however, the process of altering the current income distribution from Caribbean tourism will be very slow. Given the excess capacity which currently exists in the hotel industry, the first priority should be to raise demand to an acceptable level before making any plans to augment existing supply.

Demand for and Supply of Tourist Facilities in the Commonwealth Caribbean

Over the period between 1968 and 1974, tourism to all Caribbean countries grew at an average annual rate of 7.9 percent. Table 6.1 shows the volume and rate of growth of annual tourist arrivals in the Caribbean as a

TABLE 6.1. TOURIST ARRIVALS IN ALL CARIBBEAN COUNTRIES, 1968–74

Category	*1968*	*1969*	*1970*	*1971*	*1972*	*1973*	*1974*
All Caribbean countries							
Tourist arrivals (thousands)	3,748	4,462	4,477	4,789	5,261	5,636	5,918
Annual growth rate (percentage)	—	19.1	0.3	7.0	9.9	7.1	5.0
CARICOM							
Tourist arrivals (number)	609,676	669,890	733,101	852,069	946,405	977,672	992,400
Market share (percentage)	16.3	15.0	16.4	17.8	18.0	17.3	16.8
Annual growth rate (percentage)	—	9.9	9.4	16.2	11.1	3.3	1.5
LDCS							
Tourist arrivals (number)	143,091	161,948	179,062	191,131	212,879	210,185	199,585
Market share (percentage)	3.8	3.6	4.0	4.0	4.0	3.7	3.4
Annual growth rate (percentage)	—	13.2	10.6	6.7	11.4	−1.2	−5.0

— Not applicable.
Source: World Bank staff estimates based on national tourism statistics.

whole, in the CARICOM countries as a group, and in the LDCs during the period. It also shows the shares of the total Caribbean tourism market accounted for by CARICOM as a whole and by the LDCs.

Volume and growth of demand

From 1968 to 1972, the CARICOM countries enjoyed an increasing share of the Caribbean tourism market, but between 1972 and 1974 the market share of the ten CARICOM countries fell to a level only slightly higher than it had been in 1968.[1] Most of this decline was caused by the rise in transport costs precipitated by the energy crisis. Both Table 6.1 and Table 6.2 (which provides a breakdown by individual country) suggest that tourism in the LDCs was particularly hard hit; the market share of these countries declined from 4.0 percent in 1972 to 3.4 percent in 1974. The inefficiency and inconvenience which characterize the air transportation system in the Eastern Caribbean (described in detail in Chapter 4), together with rising costs of access to these islands, have combined to reduce tourism to the Windward and Leeward islands. This is an unfortunate outcome, because these countries depend heavily upon tourist receipts, not only for income and foreign exchange, but also for employment.

1. Data for Guyana and Belize were not available for this analysis.

TABLE 6.2. SHARES IN CARICOM TOURIST ARRIVALS AND RATES OF GROWTH, 1968 AND 1974

Country	*Tourist arrivals (number)* 1968	1974	*Average annual growth rate (percentage) 1968–74*	*Share of CARICOM arrivals (percentage)* 1968	1974
LDCS					
Antigua	58,813	71,122	3.2	9.6	7.2
Dominica	9,977	17,097	9.4	1.6	1.7
Grenada	23,164	14,723	−7.3	3.8	1.5
Montserrat	6,215	10,754	9.6	1.0	1.1
St. Kitts, Nevis, and Anguilla	9,797	13,251	5.2	1.6	1.3
St. Lucia	22,653	51,816	14.8	3.7	5.2
St. Vincent	12,472	20,822	8.9	2.0	2.1
Subtotal	143,091	199,585	5.7	23.5	20.1
MDCS					
Jamaica	258,460	432,987	9.0	42.4	43.6
Barbados	115,695	230,718	12.2	19.0	23.2
Trinidad and Tobago	92,430	129,110	5.7	15.2	13.0
Subtotal	466,585	792,815	9.2	76.5	79.9
Total CARICOM	609,676	992,400	8.5	100.0	100.0

Source: World Bank staff estimates based on national tourism statistics.

By contrast, Barbados enjoyed a six-year period of sustained growth at the high average annual rate of 12.2 percent. This state of affairs is the consequence of a number of factors. These include the island's reputation for stability; the diverse range of facilities it offers (which attract different segments of the tourist market); and, perhaps most important, the fact that the Barbados airport is a major gateway to the Caribbean. A visitor to the Caribbean must change planes in Barbados; the highly attractive local tourist assets and the ample supply of accommodation argue strongly in favor of the tourist's terminating his or her journey there.

Jamaica, which also enjoys gateway status and has long been an established tourist destination, experienced an average growth rate of 9 percent a year between 1968 and 1974. Because it depends heavily on the U.S. tourist market, the island tends to compete more with the Bahamas, Puerto Rico, and the Virgin Islands of the United States than it does with the Eastern Caribbean. The social unrest that has recently beset Jamaica nevertheless led to a 9 percent decline in tourism in 1975—a decline which has persisted.

The Caribbean region has long been a favorite destination for travelers from the United States (who represented 51 percent of CARICOM tourist arrivals in 1974). These travelers have heavily influenced both the general nature of tourism development in the region, and the design of hotel and other accommodation facilities. To a smaller, but increasingly important extent, Canada has been providing the Caribbean with more and more tourists. Canadian arrivals accounted for approximately 15 percent of total arrivals in CARICOM countries (excluding Belize and Guyana) in 1974. Demand from within the region has increased rapidly as well. Most of this last development is favorable, in that it contributes to total demand, but at the same time it reduces the capacity of Leeward Islands Air Transport (LIAT) to carry tourists from outside the region to Eastern Caribbean destinations. In addition, West Indian business travelers generally spend less than extra-regional travelers on vacation, consequently reducing overall per capita tourism earnings.

Information is not available on the number of islands visited by the average tourist, but most visitors appear to be single-destination, long-stay travelers in search of sun, sea, and sand. A particularly significant development is the one-stop tour charter (OTC). The effect of the OTC is to reduce the host country's control over the market image of its tourism product.[2] Product differentiation is, however, vital to the competitiveness of each island with its neighbors. The OTC gives tour operators virtual control over a considerable proportion of the geographic distribution of Caribbean tourist demand, and their interests are not necessarily in harmony with the national interests of many of the countries in which they operate. The ability of countries to attract tourists is highly dependent upon the organization and efficiency of the regional air transport system, the characteristics and deficiencies of which were discussed in Chapter 4.

Taking the Caribbean as a whole, the average tourist's length of stay ranges between five and eight days. In general, visitors stay longer in the MDCs than in the LDCs, although tourists to the LDCs have been showing a tendency to increase their length of stay. Jamaica experienced a decline in length of stay from nine to eight days between 1968 and 1972, but this average rose again to eight days by 1974. The long average length of stay in Grenada (and its apparent increase from seven to thirteen days), combined with a fast growth of arrivals through 1973, marked a successful period of tourism development in that country.[3] Antigua has a very short average length of stay, reflecting a mixture of visitors which includes some destination tourists, together with overnight visitors on their way elsewhere. This is because Antigua's airport is a crossover point for a number of international airways. From the data available, the length of stay appears to be longer in winter than in summer throughout CARICOM.

Table 6.3 shows the absolute and relative volume of tourism in the region for 1974 in terms of numbers of bednights (the number of tourists multiplied

2. See Timothy Prime, "Prospects for Tourism for the Next Five Years," in *Development Prospects and Options in the Commonwealth Caribbean*, ed. Edith Hodgkinson (London: Overseas Development Institute, 1976).

3. At the beginning of 1974, however, a combination of labor stoppages and civil strife brought havoc to the country's tourist trade, causing arrivals to drop to less than half the 1973 level. Since that time, tourism has been regaining lost ground, but will require time to reach its former peak levels.

TABLE 6.3. VOLUME OF TOURISM, 1974
(bednights and arrivals)

Country[a]	Bednights (thousands)	Share in CARICOM (percent) Bednights	Share in CARICOM (percent) Arrivals
Jamaica	3,680	45.9	43.7
Barbados	2,538	31.7	23.2
Trinidad and Tobago	710	8.9	13.0
Antigua	284	3.5	7.2
St. Lucia	181	2.3	5.2
Grenada	177	2.2	1.5
St. Vincent	167	2.1	2.1
St. Kitts, Nevis, and Anguilla	119	1.5	1.3
Montserrat	86	1.1	1.1
Dominica	68	0.8	1.7
Total CARICOM	8,010	100.0	100.0

a. In descending order of bednights, 1974.
Source: World Bank staff estimates basel on national tourism statistics.

by the number of nights stayed). The analysis in terms of bednights shows that Jamaica, Barbados, and Trinidad and Tobago together accounted for almost 87 percent of the tourist bednights spent in the CARICOM group of islands in 1974. The seven LDCs together only accounted for 13 percent. Grenada is shown in sixth place in the table in terms of share of total bednights; it had been in fourth place in 1972.

Growth of accommodation

On the basis of partial evidence, it would appear that there was no serious shortfall in accommodation up to 1968. A comparison of growth rates in supply (number of beds) and demand (tourist arrivals) presented in Table 6.4 indicates that, by the end of 1973, a situation of excess supply had occurred in most CARICOM countries. This excess of supply may be the result of the very rapid expansion of apartment and cottage accommodation, but it is not possible to say whether the rate of growth of tourist arrivals would have been achieved without the apartments and cottages. The important question is whether these components of supply also diversified demand, or whether they merely encroached upon a limited market. This point merits further investigation because of its policy implications for the future.

In addition to the clear trend towards greater investment in self-service accommodation, investment has been concentrated in the larger hotels since 1967. Table 6.5 provides estimates for the increases in hotel accommodation by size of hotel in Jamaica between 1967 and 1975. Comparable information is not available for other islands, but impressions gained from interviews suggest that a similar trend to larger and higher category hotels has changed the characteristics of accommodation in most of the islands. The main exception is the rapid growth of guest houses. This phenomenon reflects both expectations about the growth of tourism and the limited investment options of local entrepreneurs; local investors are more easily able to finance guest houses and small hotels than larger, more complex units. The same reasons

TABLE 6.4. AVERAGE ANNUAL GROWTH RATE OF ACCOMMODATIONS, 1968–73
(percent)

	Category of Accommodations				
Country	*Hotels*	*Guest houses*	*Apartments and cottages*	*Total beds*	*Tourist arrivals*
LDCS					
Antigua	5.3	–4.8	n.a.	5.8	4.5
Dominica	30.7	9.3	n.a.	26.8	9.2
Grenada	18.3	15.1	26.2	19.8	7.7
Montserrat	7.8	34.1	6.9	7.9	11.5
St. Kitts, Nevis, and Anguilla	13.7	n.a.	n.a.	22.7	8.8
St. Lucia	39.1	n.a.	32.4	38.8	15.1
St. Vincent	11.1	11.7	n.a.	16.1	5.9
All LDCS	16.6	14.5	28.2	17.8	8.0
MDCS					
Barbados	2.0	–3.3	20.0	7.0	10.1
Jamaica	13.6	6.0	17.5	14.2	13.9
Trinidad and Tobago	6.2	1.5	n.a.	5.6	6.6
All MDCS	9.6	1.6	18.5	11.0	10.5
All CARICOM	11.3	5.0	19.9	12.5	9.9

n.a. Not available.
Source: Shankland and Cox Partnership, *Tourism Supply in the Caribbean Region* (Washington, D.C.: World Bank, November 1974), pp. 51–54.

TABLE 6.5. TRENDS IN HOTEL SIZE IN JAMAICA, 1967–75

	1967		*1972*		*1975*[a]	
Hotel size	*Number of hotels*	*Number of rooms*	*Number of hotels*	*Number of rooms*	*Number of hotels*	*Number of rooms*
Under 50 rooms	59	1,369	67	1,679	71	1,813
50–99	14	952	19	1,268	20	1,348
100–199	8	986	12	1,567	13	1,707
Over 200	1	202	5	1,966	14	5,341

a. Estimated.
Source: World Bank staff estimate based on Jamaican tourism statistics.

have encouraged investment in self-catering accommodation; the outlay for cottages is often small, and the financial returns on condominia are fast enough to attract local investment funds.

In most of the Caribbean, the larger the size of the unit of accommodation, the less likely it is to be locally owned. Large luxury hotels thus have high percentages of foreign ownership, whereas guest houses are frequently owned by nationals.[4] Resort cottages and condominia are not subject to this generalization, as they are frequently owned by foreigners. A high degree of local ownership on a given island tends to reflect poor growth prospects caused by limited tourist assets, difficult air access, or unfavorable local attitudes toward tourism.

The patterns of investment in, and ownership of, accommodation reflect the sources of funds and types of financing which have been available in the region over recent years. The Caribbean Development Bank (CDB) has financed projects in Antigua and Grenada. The Commonwealth Development Corporation (CDC), together with Commonwealth Holiday Inns of Canada (CHIC) and an affiliate of Air Canada, owns and manages hotels in Antigua, Grenada, St. Lucia, and St. Kitts.[5] The CDB and CDC have financed infrastructure, including transport and public utilities directly beneficial to tourism, as have the United Kingdom's Overseas Development Administration (ODA) and the Canadian International Development Agency (CIDA) under the bilateral assistance programs of those countries. Both ODA and CIDA have financed tourism-related studies in the area. They have also provided technical assistance, particularly for training. The Inter-American Development Bank (IDB) has made loans to development banks in Barbados and Jamaica, portions of which are allocated for small hotels. Among the local sources of funds, Caribbean governments have invested directly in hotels for business visitors; these hotels are operated by chains under management contracts. Commercial banks have generally provided financing for hotels to creditworthy borrowers as a normal business service.

The availability of loan funds has depended on monetary and credit policies. The commercial banking system financed a considerable portion of new hotel investments in the late 1960s in Barbados, the financial center of the Eastern Caribbean group of CARICOM countries. Subsequent debt repayment problems and a tight money market led to a sharp reduction in the volume of new lending. Commercial credit and development bank financing are hard to obtain in most of the islands; consequently, local investors have had to rely on their own resources. Limited managerial skills and the high price of resort land have tended to concentrate local investment in small units of accommodation, or in condominia which can be sold quickly

4. The exception is local government-owned chain hotels, such as the Hiltons in Barbados and Trinidad and, in Jamaica, the Sheraton in Kingston and the Holiday Inn at Montego Bay.

5. For further details see Commonwealth Development Corporation, *Caribbean 1972*, (London, 1973), pp. 9–10.

if the owner needs to restore his liquidity. Apartment complexes have also attracted local investors since they do not require the managerial skill or working capital needed for a hotel.

In general, however, because public and multilateral funds are scarce in the islands, and since competition for commercial bank funds is fierce, accommodation has been mainly financed by foreign private sources. Foreign investment has been attracted into the tourist sector by legislation providing such incentives as duty-free imports during the construction stage, and tax holidays for the first several years of operation of a hotel. In Jamaica, additional measures have included the guaranteeing of foreign debt, and the provision of preferential incentives for hotels big enough to play host to conventions. In almost all cases, whatever the category of hotel or type of accommodation, profit on current operations is only one motive for hotel investment. Other motives include: the expectation of an eventual profit as a result of inflation; expectations of capital appreciation; the availability of tax relief, either through tax holidays under incentive legislation or through a tax writeoff on losses (particularly where double taxation agreements are in operation); the appeal of investment in accommodation as a means of livelihood, or official residence in a particularly beautiful part of the world; the attraction of tourism as a source of opportunity to meet people; in individually owned hotels—a motive which is not as uncommon as it might seem—the psychological appeal of handing out largesse and hospitality as the innkeeper of a particularly excellent establishment; and, in the case of larger hotels, the opportunity to organize vertically integrated production, transport, or marketing services with the hotel as the eventual outlet.

Recent operating problems

The effects of the construction boom which began in 1968 continue to be evident. Hotels were often financed at short-term market interest rates and with very low equity to loan funds.[6] Investment proposals and management contracts were agreed upon by governments with virtually no screening. Projects were accepted uncritically. Government incentive schemes were often hastily made even more magnanimous in the cut-throat battle for investment capital. Inexperienced small investors also began to proliferate as profit expectations from tourism became greater than those from alternative investments. Physical and economic plans to control the location and type of project being undertaken were not available. Governments failed to anticipate the need for programs to develop the infrastructure for tourism; to set up employee training schemes; to strengthen public sector institutions; or to arrange adequate promotion and marketing services. The requirements of the tourism sector did not lead to increased local production of inputs or the development of import-substitution industries. Instead, they were

6. World Bank analysis suggests that the terms of lending that would ensure the financial viability of hotel projects differ somewhat from conventional loan terms.

translated into higher import demand. Fiscal measures to realize benefits from tourism development were neglected. Among the LDCs, Antigua, Grenada, and St. Lucia match this description rather more closely than do the others. Jamaica, and to a much lesser extent Barbados, are also examples.

Job creation is a prime public sector objective in tourism development. Efficient service is also both a determinant of hotel profitability and an essential ingredient in the tourist's impression of his or her stay. Hotel schools exist in Jamaica, Barbados, and Trinidad, and the last two named have absorbed candidates from other islands. More places at hotel schools are obviously necessary, although many managers prefer on-the-job training at the lower levels of skills. The rapid expansion of tourist accommodation has not been accompanied by a similar expansion in management training. The International Labour Organization (ILO) currently plans hotel training schools for the region (with headquarters in Antigua) to provide training for middle management levels and above. The University of the West Indies Faculty of Business Administration is an excellent training source for hotel managers, although it is often neglected by candidates. The university, however, unlike several in the United States, has only recently introduced a degree in tourism development and hotel management, despite the importance of tourism in the Caribbean.[7] The alternative to specialized hotel management courses is the long process of promotion in the large hotels which normally has little appeal to the bright student in less developed countries, since training opportunities and promotion are often greater and faster in other occupations. In the larger or more luxurious hotels, top management still tends to be expatriate, but some chains are increasingly using local staff in their hotels. Where a gap exists in middle or top management, many hotels fill it with expatriates on work permits. The regulations for, and duration of, these permits vary from island to island and from time to time, causing considerable insecurity in the hotels and the staffs. Often only third-rate candidates apply for a job in which their future is guaranteed for a year or less. The costs to the hotel are considerable and the effectiveness of the appointee is limited by the short duration of his or her contract. Problems also occur, although less frequently, as a result of the appointment of local people who are not properly qualified to fill the job because they lack sufficient experience and training. The adverse consequences of poor management are endless in a hotel operation; it is, therefore, essential that appointees be properly qualified. At the same time, however, the continued absence of local personnel from the higher echelons of hotel staffs will simply perpetuate the criticism that only menial jobs are reserved for local people.

Wage levels in the tourism sector tend to compare favorably with those in most other unskilled or semiskilled occupations. The regional pool of unemployment or underemployment is so large, however, that the impact of

7. American examples would include Cornell and Michigan State. The degree course is offered at the Bahamas campus.

tourism wages on other activities is likely to be minimal.[8] While they compare favorably with earnings for the unskilled and semiskilled in other sectors—particularly when tips are included—tourism wage rates in the CARICOM countries tend to be rather low on an international comparative basis.[9]

The opposite appears to be true of construction costs, which dictate the final room price to tourists; they tend to be distinctly high on a comparative international basis. An excellent study of this complex subject is contained in an appendix to the Doxey report for Barbados, which appears to be applicable to the region as a whole.[10] Land in tourist areas tends to be among the most expensive in the islands.[11] An exception is the land in certain tourist development areas that are controlled by governments, for example, the Frigate Bay and Rodney Bay areas of St. Kitts and St. Lucia. In such instances prices are considerably below the market value of resort land elsewhere. Another exception is Antigua, where land values seem unduly depressed. At the other extreme, prime land in Grenada has reached the very high levels of the Bahamas and Barbados. With the exception of Jamaica, the CARICOM governments insist upon the provision of public access to beaches. The high cost of land and construction leads to a high room cost for all categories of tourist accommodation, which is only minimally compensated for by relatively low wage rates.

By 1974, the investment boom had virtually evaporated. In the years which have followed, demand has been below expectations and hotel occupancy rates have fallen below projected levels. Some hotels in a number of islands have been forced to close down. Unfortunately, because most owners and managers regard financial information as confidential, only a few studies of hotel finances have been carried out in the region, and the information in them has not been made generally available. The subject of hotel profitability is closely linked, however, to national and regional prospects for economic growth, and to broad planning and marketing decisions. It cannot reasonably be neglected for much longer.[12]

To the extent that it is possible to draw conclusions about profitability

8. Unquestionably, hotel work is more pleasant than cutting sugarcane, so that wage rates in themselves cannot be held responsible for attracting cane cutters or other workers away from agriculture. Almost any alternative employment opportunity would have the same effect. Domestic servants may be an exception, and maids are undoubtedly becoming more scarce in the Caribbean. As in agriculture, however, the hours are long and the wages low, with very little leisure time.

9. Low productivity of staff may entail higher maintenance and replacement costs rather than a high employee room ratio.

10. Carlson L. Jenkins, "The Impact of Tourism on the Construction Industry in Barbados," Appendix 2 in George V. Doxey and Associates, *The Tourist Industry in Barbados* (Ontario, Canada: Dusco Graphics, n.d.).

11. Data were mainly compiled from interviews.

12. For further discussion of hotel profitability in the region, see Caribbean Tourism Research Centre, *Profits and Performance in the Caribbean Hotel Industry* (Barbados, 1976).

from available data, it appears that luxury hotels tend to be more profitable than those at the lower end of the scale. A study carried out in Barbados indicated that "A" category hotels and apartments suffered losses in 1972. The operations of chain hotels managed under contract are often subsidized by the investor in the short term, but investors can probably expect to recoup their losses from the eventual and almost inevitable capital gains obtained from the investment. Guest houses operated by families generally fulfill the limited expectations of their owners, without necessarily being profitable by true accounting measures.

Since about 1970, operating costs, which were already high, have tended to rise further while revenues have suffered some decline. The limited resource base of the islands; their shortages of skills and dependence on imports; speculative land prices; structural inefficiencies in the tourism sector (the absence of facilities for local servicing and maintenance of equipment, for example); and, of course, inflation; have all combined to make hotel construction and operation a high-cost and a rising-cost venture. Relatively low payroll costs in relation to revenues are partially offset by the high cost of imported management. At the same time, average room revenues seem to have been falling. High published hotel rates do not reflect the actual picture in the sector. Hotels are facing stiff competition from cheaper self-catering accommodation; they are consequently cutting their published rates in a scramble for higher occupancy. Furthermore, the growing popularity of group and charter travel means that more tourists are paying the discounted rates which charter organizations can demand from hoteliers. In the case of tourists who do in fact pay full rates, the prices charged by Caribbean hotels are already high and cannot be raised further if the region is to remain competitive in international markets. Most hotels can reduce their operating costs somewhat, though often at the expense of quality of service and maintenance. The newer and larger hotels, with their higher fixed costs, find it hard, however, to reduce overall operational outgoings. Older hotels, less burdened by amortization payments, have greater liquidity with which to survive a squeeze on profits. To a considerable extent, the survival of certain hotels depends on how long such a squeeze lasts.

In the absence of the information needed to calculate hotel profitability directly, an analysis of occupancy rates in CARICOM islands provides some indication of the industry's economic health. Even occupancy rates are difficult to calculate accurately, but it is possible to estimate overall utilization of accommodation. This can be done by comparing the number of bednights actually spent on an island in one year with the number of beds offered that year. The estimates are inevitably imperfect; in particular, they do not include figures for domestic tourism, or for foreigners who stay on yachts, in tents, or in private homes. The margin of error is likely to be greater in cases where nonhotel accommodation is plentiful and often goes unrecorded in supply statistics, as is the situation in, for example, Montserrat. In order to make judgments about the extent to which any particular occupancy rate satisfies the minimum profitability requirements of those offering various types of accommodation, a set of break-even occupancy rates for different types of accommodation has been estimated.[13] These rates are based on interviews with hoteliers and on financial data. They take into account the age and type of recent investments in the CARICOM countries. Tentative break-even rates would seem to be 60 percent bed occupancy for hotels, 50 percent for apartments and cottages, and 40 percent for guest houses. These compare with the data shown in Table 6.6, which presents calculations of average annual bed occupancy in CARICOM countries in 1968, 1972, and 1974.

Table 6.6 suggests that average occupancy has declined over the 1968 to to 1974 period and that excess capacity exists in all islands. As the figures in Table 6.6 are aggregated for all types of accommodations this may disguise the fact that some types may actually have adequate percentage utilization while others have considerable excess capacity. Wide variations in percentage utilization of different types of accommodation are most likely to occur in those islands on which there are a large number of small units and several large, heavily promoted, and often vertically integrated hotels.

TABLE 6.6. ESTIMATED OCCUPANCY RATES FOR TOURIST ACCOMMODATIONS, 1968–74
(percent)

	Annual bed use		
Country	*1968*	*1972*	*1974*
LDCS			
Antigua	32	21	29.5
Dominica	73	36	28.1
Grenada	59	72	26.2
Montserrat	58	69	46.4
St. Kitts, Nevis, and Anguilla	24	24	31.7
St. Lucia	38	18	16.9
St. Vincent	38	40	44.7
All LDCS	40	35	26.2
MDCS			
Barbados	36	48	82.3
Jamaica	66	50	45.9
Trinidad and Tobago	53	50	56.9
All MDCS	55	50	54.7
All CARICOM	52	46	44.9

Source: World Bank staff estimates based on national tourism statistics.

13. Break-even is often somewhat loosely defined, but could be said to mean the average hotel occupancy rate which generates sufficient revenues to cover current operating costs and capital expenditures. The high double room occupancy rate in resort hotels in the Caribbean tends to minimize differences in room and bed occupancy rates.

Annual averages also conceal the possibility of peak occupancy rates during specific periods.

Hotel operations were probably not making significant profits for their investors in 1972, and revenues were probably well below investor expectations. Demand weakened further in 1973 and 1974, and inflation greatly increased operating costs. Since prices are already high, further increases would seem likely actually to reduce tourist demand in most islands—even in winter. The achievement of profitability will probably require intensive cost controls, improved managerial efficiency, and flexible public sector policies.

Seasonality and the Price Competitiveness of Caribbean Tourism

There are two tourist seasons in the Caribbean: winter, from December 6 to April 15; and summer, covering the remaining eight months. "Shoulder" or mini-peak seasons do exist (carnival time in Trinidad, for example), but are not uniform. The price of a hotel room in the Caribbean is about 30 percent lower in summer than in winter. Seasonal pricing recognizes that winter and summer vacations attract different types of tourist with different attitudes towards the prices they are prepared to pay.

The economics of seasonal demand

Promotional efforts throughout the Caribbean have concentrated in recent years on attracting lower income summer tourists (to such places as the Bahamas, Coombay, Barbados, and Bonanza).[14] On the basis of only partial data, lower prices appear to have increased summer demand. The CARICOM countries receive between 36 percent and 43 percent of their tourist arrivals in the four winter months.[15] On the whole, however, the distribution of tourists is remarkably even throughout the year and there is relatively little difference between winter and summer levels of tourist arrivals in the Caribbean.[16] The monthly hotel occupancy rates in 1972 for several CARICOM islands also confirm the lack of significant monthly variations. The particularly low monthly variation in Trinidad and Tobago reflects business travelers' use of hotels, which offsets seasonal tourist peaks. May, October, and November, the months immediately before or after a peak season, are

14. Given a year-round climate without variation there is no obvious reason for seasonality. Seasonality is, however, typically dictated by conditions in the country of tourist origin rather than destination, for example, climate, holiday patterns, and so on.

15. Statistical Appendix Table SA9.3 gives comparative figures for tourist arrivals by season in different CARICOM islands.

16. In Yugoslavia, by contrast, which is by no means atypical in the Mediterannean, 57 percent of total tourist nights in the whole year are concentrated in July and August, while 85 percent of total tourist nights occur in the four months from June to September.

the slackest tourism periods in the region as a whole. In Antigua and Jamaica, summer visitors have increased at a faster rate than winter visitors, while in Barbados, where tourism has grown at a fast overall annual rate, winter tourism has recently shown the more rapid rate of seasonal growth.

The financial basis of hotel operations differs markedly from the winter to the summer seasons. The occupancy percentage required to reach the break-even point is generally considerably lower in winter than it is in summer. The 30 percent discount is applied only to the room portion of a Caribbean vacation; prices of all other goods and services remain more or less constant.[17] Hotels pay just as much for goods and services used in their summer operations as they do in winter; price reductions are achieved by stripping variable costs to a minimum. The ratio of employees to rooms is reduced; items such as sports facilities (included in the room cost in winter) have to be paid for separately; and certain cosmetic attractions of winter luxury tourism are eliminated or reduced in quality. Free drinks and portable room accessories fall into this category. Food prices decline only because a somewhat lower quality menu is served in summer. In summer, the hotel's operation is thus restructured to reduce the variable portion of operating costs.

A summer season was resisted by hotel owners until the chain hotels, which are geared to a year-round operation, moved into the Caribbean. As operating costs rose and squeezed winter profits; as both demand and supply expanded; as competition for trained staff increased; and as debt servicing increased and remained constant throughout the year; the importance of the summer season grew. Some observers fear that the region will lose its sophisticated image, and hence its freespending winter guests, as the idea of a Caribbean vacation becomes more commonplace. So far, however, traditional hotels appear to have retained their winter demand; in many ways they seem to represent the most attractive year-round form of tourist accommodation. They appeal to the rich tourists in the winter. In the summer, they attract the less wealthy but discerning traveler, who recognizes the greater attractiveness of their accommodation, facilities, and service.

Discussions which are confined to the inflow of tourists at different times of the year ignore some more fundamental aspects of seasonality. The increased size of the tourist sector, the income it generates, and the heavy economic dependence of the islands on it, have all led those concerned with policy towards tourism to consider the wider benefits of seasonality, as well as the narrow issue of the seasonal profitability of hotels. In this connection, the summer season is important as a means of avoiding massive seasonal unemployment.[18] It provides jobs, both in hotels and other forms of accom-

17. Although price differentials are ably handled by hotels in the Caribbean and fully exploit the scarcity of sun, sea, and sand in northern countries in winter, hotels seem to be unfamiliar with more imaginative and less conventional promotion ploys designed both to attract and extend a tourist's stay, for example, a seventh night free.

18. Which has often coincided with the low season—and, therefore, seasonal unemployment—in agriculture.

modation, and also in the dependent services sector. There is a growing tendency to share underemployment among hotel employees by rotating staff rather than dismissing them. In this way, the incomes of most employees are reduced in summer but are not totally cut off, and individual hotels maintain efficiency by retaining the core of their staff on a year-round basis.

Depending on the type of visitor, the category of hotel, the spending attractions outside it, and other factors, tourists spend between 20 percent and 50 percent of their total expenditures outside their accommodation. If hotels were to close in the summer, therefore, the incomes of many of those working in production and service activities throughout the economy might suffer. The few expenditure surveys carried out in the Caribbean show that winter visitors spend more on average than summer visitors, but also that they spend a considerably higher proportion of total expenditures within the hotel or on self-catering accommodation. If spending on accommodation is deducted from total expenditures, summer visitors spend only 10 percent less than winter visitors on food, local transport, souvenirs, entertainment, and other purchases outside the hotel. The social value of summer tourism, therefore, is very great. Furthermore, the hotel seems to act as a loss leader for other sectors which benefit from tourist spending and which do not cut their prices in summer. The real costs of the summer operation are therefore borne by hotel employees through their reduced summer incomes and by hotel investors. Operations for the whole summer often succeed only in covering operating costs.

The competitiveness of Caribbean holidays

The relative success of cheaper summer tourism might suggest that the Caribbean islands should continue the trend to lower-cost accommodation, but any such decision needs to be based on an assessment of the net benefits to the economy of each category of accommodation. Present economic uncertainties make price the main area of concern for all categories; at the same time, price controls are not applied and few islands even inspect accommodation to check that it conforms to specific standards (which in any case have not yet been defined for different categories of accommodation). There is, therefore, no policing of standards and the market is left to regulate prices, although Jamaica has sought to remedy this weakness through the creation of the Tourism Product Company in 1975. Any pricing strategy should thus consider the following three questions:

a. Are first class and self-catering accommodation competitive in their prices, both between different locations in the Caribbean, and between Caribbean locations and selected locations elsewhere?
b. Is the price differential between different types of accommodation sufficient to offer a genuinely diverse supply and therefore to expand demand, or do overlapping prices cause competition between different types of accommodation?
c. Do price differentials between islands reflect both different cost struc-

tures and different tourism resource endowments, or are they the result of different cost structures not specifically related to tourism?

Unfortunately, these questions are easier to pose than to answer. Furthermore, the price of accommodation is only a part of the total cost of a holiday. Given the distance of the CARICOM countries from the homes of visitors, the cost of air fares obviously represents a large proportion of the total price of a holiday. In summer, seasonal discounts are available on hotels, but not on air fares—because the Caribbean off-season coincides with the peak North Atlantic and North American domestic tourist seasons. At this time of year, aircraft can always be deployed elsewhere, and do not need to operate at reduced fares in attempts to fill flights to the Caribbean. Discounts on the normal economy excursion fares are available to certain destinations—chiefly to Barbados and to Jamaica—but these apply mainly to flight made in "shoulder" periods rather than those in the off or peak seasons. During the period shortly before the energy crisis, charter flights became the primary means of reducing air fares for tourists from Europe (in particular the United Kingdom) and from Canada.

Hotel discounts reduce the price of a total holiday package to only a minimal degree for Europeans, because of the heavy weight of the air fare in their total costs. The Caribbean thus remains a destination which appeals to a relatively wealthy segment of the European market, even in summer.[19] Summer hotel discounts considerably reduce the total cost of Caribbean holidays for North American tourists, however, and the region is therefore beginning to appeal to the less wealthy on that continent. Demand from Canada, in particular, seems to have precipitated a decline in the price of a Caribbean holiday for Canadians: summer hotel discounts stimulated air charters from Canada which, in turn, stimulated demand for even cheaper accommodation (self-catering, for example), thereby substantially reducing the total cost, in real terms, to the tourist. Once constructed, the cheaper accommodation has provided stiff competition for the already-expanding hotel supply, and has initiated a price war which has to some extent carried on even in the winter season.

In an attempt to establish the price competitiveness of Caribbean tourism, the following four comparisons have been made: comparative costs of tour packages from Toronto and London to the Caribbean and competing destinations; standard air fares from Washington, D.C., to different destinations; the comparative costs of different types of accommodation within the CARICOM group (mainly Hilton and Holiday Inn hotels); and, although they are only tangentially relevant because of the limited number of business visitors to the islands, daily allowances for travel expense purposes.[20]

Standard return air fares from North America give the Caribbean a con-

19. The relatively low tourist densities and the seclusion of many hotels compared to many Mediterranean resorts heighten the appeal to higher income European tourists in summer.

20. Details of the comparisons are shown in Statistical Appendix, Tables SA9.10–9.13.

siderable competitive edge over most competing destinations, simply because fares are based in a per mile rate. Although air fares from the east coast of the United States to Bermuda, the Bahamas, and Mexico are much lower than fares to all CARICOM countries except Jamaica, the further the traveler flies, the greater his or her costs. Before the energy crisis, the wide range of excursion, youth, and group rates available for most European destinations reduced the overall costs of air travel on the North Atlantic route well below standard fares, and brought them down to a level competitive with fares to the Caribbean, despite the Caribbean's proximity to the United States. Later, however, transatlantic air fares have increased more than have those to the Caribbean and have also become less varied. As a result, the Caribbean has partly recovered its competitive edge in the North American market. This advantage could again be eroded, however, if the airbus concept becomes generally accepted on the North Atlantic route.

A comparison of package prices reveals that the Caribbean is among the more expensive destinations for Europeans, even with seasonal pricing in summer. An analysis of the comparative costs of Sunflight Tours from Toronto to destinations in the Caribbean, Honolulu, Mexico, and the Mediterranean, at different times of the year, suggests that price differentials between destinations are probably too marginal for price, rather than destination preference, to be the basis for a decision as to where to spend a holiday.[21]

Analysis of the price of different categories of accommodation in the CARICOM islands suggests that the quantitative increase in price for luxury accommodation over "A" category is justified by the qualitative improvement in facilities. The price of self-catering accommodation overlaps widely with both "A" and "B" categories. Certain areas of the Caribbean (particularly Freeport in the Bahamas and, possibly, Jamaica) have cut prices drastically on lower category and self-catering accommodation, but first-class accommodation still sells for a considerably higher price than elsewhere. The most spectacularly wide range of prices (in terms of seasonal differences and variety of accommodation as well as rate structure) occurs in Jamaica and in Barbados—though the expansion at the lower end of the price range seems to be more recent in the former. The highest prices throughout the CARICOM region—and probably in the whole Caribbean—can be paid in Jamaica: up to US$120 a day, single, full board. At most accommodation levels, Barbados tends to be more expensive than other islands, partly because of its greater number of high-quality luxury accommodation units and its established tourist image. The constancy of the findings at different price levels suggests that costs are generally higher in Barbados than in the rest of CARICOM, or even throughout the rest of the Caribbean.

The wide range of prices indicates the variety of accommodation available, but also suggests a lack of concern for price competitiveness, except

21. Package prices, however, appear to be sufficiently attractive, particularly in the off-season, to make inroads into Canada's thriving domestic tourism market.

in the summer season. Analysis of the structure of prices reveals a heavy preponderance of first class and luxury accommodation—far more than in the world's other major resort area, the Mediterranean, and more than in most other tourist destinations. Furthermore, some of the world's most expensive and exclusive hotels are in the region, particularly in Jamaica and Barbados. In general, the quality of the resort assets justifies high priced accommodation.[22] Recent adverse developments have, however, forced prices downwards in almost all categories of accommodation, with the exception of those of luxury hotels.[23]

At the same time, because transatlantic air fares have risen more rapidly than those to the Caribbean and because controls on the price, frequency, and capacity of charter operations have been tightened, the Caribbean has begun to recover its competitive position in the North American market. Furthermore, high rates of inflation in Europe have reduced the dollar's purchasing power there. This fact, together with air fare costs, seems to be deflecting long-haul travelers to shorter-haul destinations. As part of this process, the average length of stay in the Caribbean appears to be increasing slightly. For the moment, therefore, the Caribbean has regained its price competitiveness for tourists from North America; but it has become even more expensive for Europeans. In the last two years, overall demand has become weaker—more for summer than for winter tourism.

Growth Prospects and Constraints for Caribbean Tourism

The Caribbean has an excess supply of tourist accommodation over current levels of demand. Forecasts of future tourist demand are subject to a large margin of error; they are based upon a very wide range of variables in the economic sectors which principally determine market demand, and are likely to be influenced by the fact that the future—in particular the future of air transport—is full of uncertainty.

Structure of demand and supply

Unlike the producers of many primary and manufactured products, owners of tourist facilities often appear to be unaware of the extent to which the demand for their facilities and services responds to price; they are also frequently unaware of important information on the supply side, such as the quantity and quality of facilities in direct competition with them in any given season. Unprecedented world-wide inflation, recession, and unemployment have made the task of forecasting future demand even more difficult. It can

22. The room cost in a luxury hotel includes a share in a virtually private beach; the use of recreation facilities, which can include golf, tennis, riding, and sailing; and sunshine, attentive service, and natural beauty for the duration of the stay.

23. In some cases, hotel prices are being held at current levels despite inflation and in others, prices are actually being reduced below those of the previous season.

be expected, however, that tourism demand is likely to be dampened in those parts of the world which have experienced—or expect to experience—recession, a slowdown in economic growth, or high rates of inflation. It is unclear, moreover, whether tourism is now to be regarded as an integral part of consumer expenditures or as a part of discretionary income; if it is the latter, adverse economic circumstances, which lower discretionary income, are likely to damage tourism prospects.

Any comprehensive market analysis requires two separate demand forecasts for the CARICOM region: one for Jamaica, and one for the rest of the islands. Jamaica is close to the United States and is heavily dependent on it as a source of tourists; it, therefore, has more in common with the rest of the northern Caribbean than it has with the countries of the Eastern Caribbean. A number of features, however, are common to the entire region: some of them are positive and others are negative.

On the positive side, winter tourism, especially at the luxury level (visits to small, exclusive, enclave-type hotels), may be relatively unaffected by any general recession, since the wealthy are usually well protected against adverse economic conditions. In addition, the energy crisis may persuade North American vacationers to switch from the private car to public air transport, and the price of travel should encourage them to make relatively short-distance vacation journeys. Furthermore, because of higher increases in air fares on the North Atlantic routes than on the Caribbean routes (about 40 percent and 20 percent increases respectively), the region has been regaining its competitive advantage based on proximity to the North American market. General changes in the structure of air fares are more likely to reduce demand on North Atlantic routes than on those to the Caribbean. Persistent excess capacity in hotel accommodation and the expansion of self-catering accommodation have combined with the slow growth of demand since 1973 to reduce prices for accommodation. This turn of events has further increased the Caribbean's competitive advantage over other areas. The Canadian market looks healthy, particularly in the light of the resilience of charter operations there. Demand for self-catering accommodation at the bottom end of the tourist scale should also remain strong, particularly in winter.

Some generally adverse factors affecting Caribbean tourism can also be identified. The energy crisis prevented the U.S. Civil Aeronautics Board (CAB) from making a decision in 1974 about the introduction of a one-stop inclusive tour charter which would have stimulated short-haul group travel from the United States. Both convention and incentive business travel depend on the level of profits as well as on corporate tax measures. Should profits decline, taxes be raised, and loopholes be closed, group business travel, on which Caribbean tourism partly depends, could be severely affected. The cost of travel from Europe has risen more sharply than the prices for accommodation have fallen. European demand has not, therefore, flourished as seemed possible when charters were first initiated. New oil wealth in Venezuela, and generally closer ties between the Caribbean and Latin American countries, may partially offset the slow growth of wealth in other sources of tourism demand, but the population sizes and income groups involved are relatively small. Furthermore, the competition for tourists is likely to be even greater in the future, not only among traditional suppliers of tourism facilities, but also from new ones that are opening up around the Caribbean itself. These would include the Dominican Republic, Haiti, the Caribbean coast of Mexico, and possibly even Central America. Perhaps most important is Cuba's recent re-entry into the tourist market. These areas are without the stigmas attached to traditional Caribbean tourism destinations; also, because they produce more of the goods needed for the hotel industry at home, they will presumably be able to offer accommodation at a relatively low cost.

Jamaica must be concerned about its generally high prices compared with those of nearby competitors, and about the problem of maintaining the level of travel to the island. Demand for summer tourism is likely to weaken because tourists have many attractive alternative options. The closing of a number of hotels on the north coast in September and October of 1974, for example, indicated a weakening of demand in the off-season. Jamaica's main concern, however, must be the possibility that Cuba may again become a major tourism destination, because of the latter's proximity to the United States. Tourism in the Eastern Caribbean has depended significantly on travelers from Europe; increased fuel costs and internal inflation in Europe, particularly in the United Kingdom, are likely to restrict travel to the area on scheduled airlines and severely to curtail the growing charter market. The Eastern Caribbean is likely to benefit less than Jamaica from the fact that fares to and from North America are becoming more competitive with those to and from Europe, simply because of its greater distance from North America. Finally, the Eastern Caribbean is highly dependent on foreign airlines for air services.

Over the longer term, the Caribbean's superb resort assets, its warm climate throughout the year, its location reasonably close to such important sources of tourists as the United States and Canada—together with the growth of incomes and scarcity of beaches in these countries (as well as a rather harsh climate in Canada)—will ensure the eventual recovery of demand for tourism in the region. In fact, over the longer term, demand seems likely to meet a physical constraint before it can be satisfied, although the relatively small size of the industry in most islands makes it unlikely that such a growth constraint will arise over the next five years. An indication of the room for potential expansion of the CARICOM tourist sector can be drawn from the physical plan for Barbados, one of the smaller islands. The plan estimates that the present number of beds can be expanded by 125 percent before physical limitations occur, and the island's present tourist capacity is already well above that of all the LDCs of the region combined.

The role of transport

The extent to which transport meets tourist needs is the most serious present limitation on the growth of tourism in the LDCs. While direct air access cannot guarantee growth, it certainly appears to be a major factor influencing investors when they decide where to locate tourist facilities. For example, in the case of St. Kitts, the Frigate Bay Development Corporation began to receive firm investment proposals only after a decision was made to build a runway suitable for jet aircraft. Antigua's early growth can be attributed to its airport (built by the U.S. Army), and also to its location at the crossroads of several air traffic routes. As a result the island is both an interchange stopover and a resort destination. The growth of tourism in St. Vincent and the Grenadines has been limited by poor air access. Access is equally poor in Grenada, although tourism growth there was very promising until 1973. St. Lucia has a jet airport which is one and a half hour's drive from hotels in the northern section of the island. The alternative entry point is the small airport at Castries, which cannot accommodate jet planes; in order to use it, the tourist has to stay overnight in either Antigua or Barbados. Nonetheless, St. Lucia's tourist industry has grown rapidly in recent years, despite the considerable personal discomfort undergone by travelers.

If resort assets are particularly good, dynamic growth rates can be achieved in the early stages of tourist development, even in such areas of poor access as St. Lucia. A major further expansion of tourism, however, becomes extremely difficult unless the problem of air access is overcome. It is equally important that airports be near the resorts at which tourists stay, because most flights to the Eastern Caribbean are from four to ten hours' flying time from the islands. After a flight of this length, travelers are often unwilling to resign themselves to the additional discomfort of a long drive over the mountains from the jet airport to the hotel area, as they have to do in St. Lucia and Dominica. Additionally, travelers feel that a night spent at a stopover at either end of the trip is a loss of holiday time, even if the stopover is at another island.

The stopover becomes even less attractive when interisland transport is unreliable. As Chapter 4 has noted, the problems of Leeward Islands Air Transport (LIAT) and the other smaller short-haul carriers which operate in the Caribbean are enormous. The frequency of takeoff and landing makes operations very costly. Night flying is prohibited in some islands; landing approaches are often difficult; climatic problems abound. Efforts to coordinate interisland transport with international departures and arrivals make scheduling complicated. The combination of difficult flying conditions and complex schedules leads to frequent delays. The limited availability of spare equipment makes cancellations frequent. An improved service is badly needed and would greatly encourage tourist mobility between islands.

There are three basic requirements for the establishment of direct air services between a country outside the region and a given island; first, a sufficient volume of passenger demand for the service; second, adequate airport infrastructure, especially a runway capable of accommodating jets; and, third, the existence of bilateral agreements between the island and the extraregional country to provide a scheduled service. At present, the United Kingdom negotiates bilateral air agreements on behalf of the Associated

States. The United Kingdom represents many varied interests, and those of the Commonwealth Caribbean LDCs are not necessarily paramount at all times. All the LDCs except Antigua depend, moreover, for tourist inflows on scheduled services to another airport in the region and on interisland transport from that airport. Current arrangements virtually exclude them from the decisionmaking process about air access, which is the life blood of tourism.

Airport facilities are currently inadequate for tourism growth in Grenada, St. Vincent, the northern part of St. Lucia, Dominica, and Montserrat.[24] Where the numbers of tourists and the sizes of groups are not large, an improvement in interisland transport, between Barbados and Antigua and the LDCs, for example, might be an effective substitute for direct air access. The present inefficiency of services makes such an improvement necessary, in any case. Any more substantial investment in airport infrastructure should only be undertaken after careful planning to establish the optimum future scale of tourism at a given location. The volume of traffic may be too small to justify an airport, if the investment is appraised by conventional cost-benefit analysis.[25] Whether this type of analysis is appropriate, whether foreign aid on noncommercial terms can be obtained, and whether tourism is in fact an island's most viable development option, are all subjects which need to be examined further.

On a related point, none of the LDCs has good berths for cruise ships, although the current expansion of St. Lucia's port facilities should help to attract more of this type of traffic. The Caribbean Development Bank (CDB) has approved loans for port improvement in Dominica, St. Kitts, and Montserrat, and is considering financing similar projects in Antigua, Grenada, and St. Vincent. The Eastern Caribbean is ideally suited for cruising throughout the year; the islands are close to one another and offer varied attractions. Given an improved infrastructure, together with more and better hotels and recreational facilities, the prospects for the growth of cruise traffic seem bright. Few islands, however, currently make specific provision for cruise visitors in their tourist facilities. Though the need for better planning to attract these visitors is evident, an in-depth analysis of the costs and benefits of cruise traffic, social as well as financial, is needed equally urgently. This area of activity seems especially worth investigating in the light of the increasing popularity of combined fly and cruise holidays.

A related area is that of yacht cruises. Some CARICOM islands, in particular Antigua, Grenada, St. Vincent, and the Grenadines, offer excellent facilities and are currently used by yacht operators. These are seldom seen as a part of tourism and no efforts are made for the islands to benefit from these activities.

The overall growth of the market for tourism is a factor beyond the

24. The international airports in Jamaica (at Montego Bay and Kingston) have been expanded, as well as Seawell airport in Barbados.

25. The construction costs in Dominica, for example, would include the costs either of leveling mountains or of reclaiming sea land, in order to obtain a suitable site.

control of CARICOM governments. Quite apart from the fact that demand is heavily influenced by conditions in countries of tourist origin, the islands' dependence on foreign airlines and on international air agreements makes it impossible for them to influence the price of travel to the Caribbean or the capacity of the services provided. In contrast, however, the nature of the final product sold to the tourist is determined by numerous factors which are, in fact, subject to public and private sector policies and controls in the islands themselves. Both the price and the quality of the final product can be influenced. The organization and administration of policy for tourism can play a major part in the success of individual tourist projects. Tourism cuts across a number of different economic sectors—retailing, transport, and production, for example—so that the creation of a ministry of tourism, as in Barbados, can be very helpful. Under such an arrangement, policies for the sector can be debated at interministerial level, and transdepartmental issues can be fully aired. Jamaica, as might be expected, has the appropriate institutions and particularly highly qualified management and staff in both the public and private sectors. In recent years, however, planning has been badly coordinated, owing to a separation of the responsibilities for the current management of the sector and its future development. This has been a serious weakness, and has led to an overexpansion of tourist accommodation.[26]

As a broad generalization, most LDC governments have left tourism to develop without official intervention. The islands have become self-governing very recently; faced with the complexities of managing a tourism sector, governments have become acutely aware of their own lack of expertise, and of the heavy demands made on their limited manpower. In LDCs where foreign investors have brought in technical knowhow, the private sector has often helped to improve techniques for marketing and promoting tourism to the benefit of national economies.[27] Nevertheless, only if the public sector in each island recognizes the need, both for controls and for appropriate incentives (to attract investment and to induce lower prices of tourism inputs and final products), will the sector expand and its quality be maintained or improved. Any public sector policies, however, need to be framed in close cooperation with the private sector; the benefits of cooperative policies have been observed in many of the Caribbean islands.

Benefits and Costs of Tourism

Opinions differ widely about the extent to which tourism contributes to development. There are those who would be willing to accept zero growth

26. Trinidad and Tobago are excluded from this discussion because the sector is small in Tobago, and Trinidad has taken a deliberate policy decision to curtail tourism growth.

27. The interests of the private sector do not necessarily, of course, coincide with those of the public sector, nor with the national interest in those cases where the latter two are not identical.

in the national economy, or even a decline, rather than rely on increased tourism to achieve economic gains. Subscribers to this school of thought tend to emphasize the social costs of tourism, frequently citing a number of maladies which are hard to quantify.

The benefits

A more moderate approach might be to suggest that the rapid recent growth of tourism has made it hard for governments in most of the Caribbean islands to reorganize the elements of domestic output to meet a larger proportion of the components of tourism demand from local resources. As a result, the net benefits from tourism have often been below their potential levels. Furthermore, partly because the public sector has failed to tackle the problem of how best to distribute the benefits of tourism, the interests of local people have often been neglected and benefits have been distributed inequitably, favoring the investor, who has generally been foreign.

Whatever view of the issue is taken, it remains important to attempt to quantify the contribution that tourism makes to national economies in the Caribbean region in order to put decisions on tourism policy into an objective context.

One useful measure of the contribution of tourism to economic growth is the percentage of gross national product which it represents. Value-added estimates for tourism are scarce but some crude World Bank staff estimates of the share of tourism in gross product, based on available information for selected islands, follow[28]:

Island	*Definition of gross product*	*Contribution of tourism (percent)*
Antigua	GDP	40–50
Bahamas	GDP basis	77
Barbados	GDP	20
Jamaica	GDP	6

Some of these estimates make allowances for the added value of all tourist expenditures. The Jamaican estimate, however, includes only value added in the hotel sector, while services, as a group, make up over 35 percent of gross domestic product (GDP); part of this component must logically be generated by tourism.

Although estimates are not available for the other CARICOM countries, the contribution of tourism to GDP is likely to be high—possibly at the lower level shown above for Antigua—in islands whose economies are not

28. One of the problems entailed in calculating value added in tourism is that tourism expenditures cover a cross-section of GDP components, and the financial data on which to base calculations on the income method are not generally available. Furthermore, as tourism is a sector of final demand and input/output tables are generally not available, a difficulty arises over the elimination of intermediate goods when using the production method.

diversified and in which the tourist sector is significant. Tourism's contribution is probably at this level in Grenada and Montserrat, followed by St. Lucia and St. Vincent and then by St. Kitts–Nevis–Anguilla. Trinidad and Tobago is at the bottom end of the scale. When more information is available, a careful quantified analysis should be undertaken to establish the contribution of tourism to these countries' economies. In any assessment, it is worth remembering the low opportunity cost of some of the factors of production employed in tourism, such as unskilled labor and beach lands.

The most conspicuous benefits and costs of tourism are the foreign exchange revenues earned and the costs of imported goods and services. The main difficulty in assessing the balance-of-payments impact of a prospective tourist project is the leakage of foreign exchange. This can be measured in terms of the percentage of each dollar of revenue received from tourist expenditure that is repatriated overseas in the first round.[29]

Unfortunately, no comparable estimates are available for the leakage from other sectors. Given the limited natural resource base of the region and the openness of the economies of its countries, however, it is probable that the import content of almost any economic activity in the CARICOM region is high.

Tourism also contributes directly to employment. The ratio of employees to rooms is the indicator normally used to measure this function. The ratio has varied somewhat in the recent past because of changes in the importance of different types of accommodation. As labor has become unionized, moreover, management has probably made greater efforts to extract more productivity from its work force. The indirect contribution of tourism to employment is harder to measure. A number of nontourist activities undoubtedly also benefit from an investment in hotel accommodation, but because many interrelated services are not totally dependent on tourism, the industry's contribution to employment in them cannot be assessed with any accuracy.

Table 6.7 shows the estimated numbers of those directly employed in tourist accommodation in the early 1970s; the implicit employee-room ratio; the ratio of peak to off-season employment; and the number of jobs that will be generated by accommodation at present under construction. Employment estimates refer only to jobs in tourist accommodation and exclude, for want of a satisfactory way to estimate it, employment created by tourist expenditures on purchases of transport, entertainment, food and beverages outside the hotel, and other goods or services.

The costs

The visible costs of tourism that concern governments are mainly the inflated price of land; high wages in tourism which may attract relatively

29. Leakage from one dollar of tourist expenditure, calculated from a number of sources, is as follows: Barbados, 42 cents; Bermuda, 30 cents; Cayman Islands, 30 cents; Puerto Rico, 21 cents; Jamaica, 34 cents; and St. Vincent, 50 cents (first class hotels) and 35 to 40 cents (other accommodations).

TABLE 6.7. TOURISM EMPLOYMENT ESTIMATES AS OF THE EARLY 1970S

Island	*Number employed in existing accommodation*	*Employee to room ratio*[a]	*Peak to off-season employment ratio*	*Number to be employed in accommodation under construction in 1977*[b]
LDCS				
Antigua	1,037	0.94	1.45	448
Dominica	162	1.19	n.a.	12
Grenada	370	0.48	n.a.	81
Montserrat	146	1.33	1.51	n.a.
St. Kitts, Nevis, and Anguilla	144	0.64	1.28	30
St. Lucia	1,600	1.95	1.79	20
St. Vincent	207	0.98	1.29	198
Subtotal	3,666	—	—	789
MDCS				
Barbados	4,069	1.83	1.59	250
Jamaica	9,585	1.05	1.54	2,140
Trinidad and Tobago	2,437	1.50	n.a.	288
Subtotal	16,091	—	—	2,678
Total CARICOM	19,757	—	—	3,467

— Not applicable.
n.a. Not available.
a. The source is generally the Shankland Cox study, but the data are difficult to obtain and in some cases seem inaccurate. For example, the figures seem to be very low for Grenada and very high for St. Lucia, though the latter's luxury resort accommodation requires a high employee-room ratio.
b. The estimate was obtained directly for Jamaica. For other countries, the following factors were applied: one employee per hotel room and 0.5 employees per guest house and apartment room, for each unit of accommodation known to be under construction. These factors may be low, but given low occupancies in 1972 and those that were expected in 1977, variable costs are likely to be reduced as much as possible.
Source: World Bank staff estimates based on national statistics.

badly paid workers out of menial but essential jobs; the cost of investment in infrastructure required for tourism development; and the high bills for imports of food and hotel equipment which make demands on foreign exchange. While the government has been required to provide infrastructure, some of it costly (an airport and port, roads, sewerage, public utilities, water and gas, for example), these infrastructure investments have, of course, benefited the local population and would often have been essential in any case. Economies of scale stemming from heavy tourist demand have sometimes made it possible to extend utility services to the local population at a lower cost per unit than would otherwise have had to be charged. The sudden increase in value of an unimproved site, solely because of its desirability for tourism development, represents a considerable appreciation of national wealth which is seldom exploited by governments. Too often, windfall gains have gone to private sector speculators without any benefit accruing to the government; appropriate fiscal policies could change this state of affairs.

All food imports by hotels are, of course, paid from tourists' foreign exchange expenditures. The sight of foreign foods in hotels and in local supermarkets has probably increased local consumption of foreign foods.[30] At the same time, however, some local food is consumed in hotels; since it is paid for by tourists' foreign exchange, this could be considered a windfall export. Traders' margins and local taxes on all foodstuffs are paid by hotels to local intermediaries and the government, whether the food is imported or of local origin.

It remains true, however, that potentially profitable linkages between tourism and other sectors are notoriously weak, and that this is particularly true in the case of agriculture. Not even Jamaica, with its highly developed agricultural base, has been able to produce, market, and distribute a significant quantity of food supplies for hotels on a regular basis. The production of the right foods in the appropriate quantities at the right time of year is only half the problem. Agricultural Marketing Corporations (AMCS) have had only limited success in most islands. The hotel industry criticizes them frequently, complaining about lack of quality control, inadequate packaging, interruptions in deliveries, variations in prices, and lack of guaranteed volume. Agriculture is not the only sector where links with tourism could be better than they are at present; opportunities clearly exist to gear local manufacturing more closely to the accommodation sector. Furniture, small fixtures (such as door knobs and light fittings), ceramics, rush mats, textiles, and other items could all be locally produced, although it is not clear whether production would be at a lower unit cost than that of imported products.

The negative aspects of tourism development, other than the economic ones, range from the alienation of local culture[31] and the corruption of moral values,[32] to the feeling of exclusion from participation at all but the

30. An indirect benefit is that the diet of the local population has improved considerably as a consequence.

31. According to the Caribbean Ecumenical Consultation for Development: "Centuries of colonial domination have prevented the emergence of a positive affirmation of the unique potentials of this pluralistic Caribbean society. Different cultural backgrounds are now being welded into an integrated culture which incorporates, but also transcends, each of the individual contributing streams. At this crucial stage, large scale tourism might prove to be a serious hazard to the process of cultural metamorphosis which the Caribbean countries are going through.

"New developments for tourism must exploit the natural attributes of the site, be of the right density, scale and character to reflect the essence of the overall location. Architecture should ideally echo the culture of the host country, and not degenerate into a depersonalized, international mass produced concept of box-like constructions that give no indication of their whereabouts; that could be anywhere in the world—from Moscow, Chicago to Toledo or Cairo." See the Caribbean Ecumenical Consultation for Development, *The Role of Tourism in Caribbean Development*, Study Paper no. 8.

32. Two of the main problems facing one ministry of health are the eradication of drug abuse and the elimination of venereal disease. Both problems were attributed partly to tourism and partly to migration, given the heavy traffic between the island and the United States, Canada, and Europe.

least skilled levels and in all but the smallest units of accommodation. Until recently, only the most sophisticated travelers used local hotel facilities; this situation is now changing and Jamaica, for one, is now actively encouraging domestic tourism through off-season discounts for Jamaicans. There is a trend towards greater involvement of locals in tourism. Jamaica has again taken the initiative with a program of welcome for visitors that introduces tourists to local residents with similar interests and also through a public education campaign called "Tourism is My Business and Yours Too," designed to improve local attitudes to tourism.[33] In this connection it is often forgotten, however, that where income distribution is skewed and unemployment is high, outbursts of crime and violence against tourists reflect not only social problems related to tourism development, but also the local socioeconomic context.

One cost of tourism development which could have serious consequences if it is not controlled is that of pollution, together with the related problem of the indiscriminate exploitation of national resources. In some areas, the very assets that now attract tourists are being destroyed rather than preserved or protected. Physical planning is still embryonic in most islands; only when planning becomes a major ongoing activity, and is accompanied by strict zoning regulations and building codes, will the islands' natural assets be assured of adequate protection. The current spoilation of natural resources includes depletion of lobster beds and fish populations; pollution of the sea and beaches; the disruptive effect of sudden increases in population on local production and service activities, on public utilities, and on the lifestyle of local residents; and unacceptable traffic densities created by tourists and cruise visitors. The need to take steps to protect natural assets in tourist areas is heightened by the importance attached to an attractive, unspoiled environment for their vacation by tourists themselves, and by public opinion generally in the developed countries.

The tourism sector will probably always remain controversial, but the greater the linkages to other sectors, the greater the compatibility between tourism and local culture, and the more equitable the distribution of benefits from tourism, the more acceptable and effective the sector will become as a development tool in the Caribbean.

33. Barbados on the other hand has begun a campaign to exhort tourists not to offend local sensibilities.

Chapter 7

Industry

THE DEVELOPMENT OF MANUFACTURING IN THE TWELVE COUNTRIES OF THE Commonwealth Caribbean has been heavily influenced by the fact that most of them are relatively small. Jamaica's population of nearly 2 million people, by far the largest in CARICOM, is about twenty-five times that of the average of the eight less developed countries (LDCs) in the region. The generally small size of national units has led to a broadly similar pattern of industrialization in Caribbean countries, although the timing and extent of their industrial development have varied. This variation is largely accounted for by the different sizes of national markets and the consequently differing opportunities for import substitution. The extent of industrialization ranges from the relatively developed manufacturing sectors of the more developed countries (MDCs), especially Jamaica and Trinidad, to the very simple industries established in most of the LDCs.

The Structural and Policy Background

Because of the overwhelming regional preponderance of the four MDCs in the sector, any general survey of manufacturing in CARICOM as a whole will be implicitly or explicitly dealing with their problems most of the time. The following discussion first presents an overview of the scope and structure of manufacturing and of industrialization policies. Subsequent sections of this chapter analyze the CARIFTA experience, the options for industrialization in CARICOM, and prospective areas for integrated policy development. To provide a balanced perspective, however, the last section of the chapter examines separately the special problems of the eight LDCs.

The scope and structure of manufacturing

The MDCs—Jamaica, Trinidad and Tobago, Guyana, and Barbados—account for 86 percent of the population of the region, 91 percent of its total gross national product (GNP) and 94 percent of its manufacturing gross domestic product (GDP). The eight LDCs together account for only 14 percent of the population, and a much smaller proportion—6 percent—of CARIFTA's manufacturing GDP. More than half the manufacturing GDP of the least developed group is, moreover, produced in Belize, the largest country in this category with 20 percent of the population of the LDCs.[1]

By 1970, manufacturing accounted for an average of more than 12 percent of GDP in the MDCs, the range extending from 10.8 percent in Barbados to 13.6 percent in Jamaica, the largest country in terms of both population and manufacturing output. In the LDCs, the average contribution of the manufacturing sector to the GDP was about 8 percent by 1970, but the bulk of the total was accounted for by Belize, where the contribution of manufacturing to output was 15.6 percent. In the remaining seven LDCs, manufacturing output averaged 5 percent of total GDP.[2]

The growth and structure of industrial production in the CARIFTA countries can be viewed in terms of three successive layers of products.[3] The first group of products is one which became economic at an early stage of industrialization, as a result of a combination of factors—considerable labor intensity, simple technology, economical small scale production, and, in many cases, the high cost of transport from external production centers. Clothes, low-quality furniture, aerated drinks, cement blocks, and tire retreads are examples of this group. Most of the LDCs produce goods of this type, although they are not self-sufficient in all of them.

The second group consists principally of consumer goods, typically requiring larger scale production and more technology than the first group. Semi-mass production shoes, margarine, beer and other alcoholic beverages, cigarettes, soap, and various mixing and packaging operations, such as those involving paints, fertilizers, cosmetics, pharmaceuticals, and paper products are examples of this group. Guyana and Barbados have reached this stage of industrialization, while one or two of these industries are to be found in some LDCs.

A third and final group of intermediate and consumer goods, requiring still larger scale production and greater technology, can be divided into two subcategories. The first of these consists of basic mass-consumption intermediate products, such as woven textiles, cement, bottles, tin cans, and some structural steel items. The second subcategory is that of locally assembled consumer durables; these are the "screwdriver" industries covering such

1. See Statistical Appendix, Table SA10.1.

2. See Statistical Appendix, Table SA10.2.

3. Statistical Appendix, Table SA10.3, giving physical output of selected manufactures in the MDCs, and Table SA10.5, listing products benefiting from protection, illustrate the point.

activities as the assembling of bicycles, domestic electric appliances, and motorcars. Jamaica and Trinidad have reached this stage, but they have not yet proceeded to more skill-intensive activities, such as light engineering, or larger-scale industries, such as the manufacture of pulp and paper, or of basic industrial chemicals.

Manufacturing tends to depend heavily on imported inputs. On the whole, the local value added is small, and few linkages (production processes in which domestically produced inputs are used in domestic final manufactures) have been generated within the domestic economy.[4] There are two main reasons for this state of affairs: in the first place, neither raw materials nor intermediate industries exist locally; in the second, as will be subsequently discussed, the incentive system currently in operation encourages imported manufacturing inputs. Available data indicate that there has been little change over time in the import dependence of manufacturing.

The small size of domestic markets inhibits the establishment of intermediate manufacturing, which, to be efficient, needs to operate on a reasonably large scale. Market size is reduced still further for individual items by product differentiation. Many local assembly activities are of the branch plant type, in which various makes or brands of product are assembled from imported components. The local assembly of twenty types of automobiles in a market with annual sales of only 2,000 units in Trinidad provides a striking example. To produce the basic parts for such products locally would be thoroughly uneconomical, because these components are not standardized. Product differentiation also tends to lead to higher import bills, because the quantities ordered of each of the many brands in use are individually too small to attract supplier discounts or bulk rate reductions in transport or other shipping and handling charges made by suppliers.

The constraints imposed on industrial development by a limited domestic market can be countered by manufacturing for export. In most CARIFTA member countries, however, exports of manufactured goods represent only a small percentage of manufacturing gross domestic product (for example, 4.4 percent on average for the region in 1970). Manufacturing exports form a significant proportion of total manufacturing output in only two of the LDCs, St. Kitts (34.6 percent) and Dominica (9.7 percent). Among the MDCs, Barbados stands out.[5]

Most local manufacturing output is thus for domestic sale. Imports nevertheless predominate in total domestic manufacturing sales—and the share of local production in domestic markets for manufactures has generally been static or even falling. This is consistent with a pattern of import-intensive

4. See Statistical Appendix, Tables SA10.6 and 10.7, for the share of imported and local materials and services in a sample of firms and industries in, respectively, Guyana and Trinidad.

5. See Statistical Appendix, Table SA10.2. These figures, however, include neither sugar milling—important in a number of CARIFTA member countries—nor Trinidad's refining activities related to petroleum-based chemicals.

industrialization, where the replacement of assembled by unassembled manufactured imports has little effect on the import bill.

Industrialization policies

Manufacturing has been actively encouraged since the 1940s through a combination of government measures in individual CARIFTA countries, with emphasis on import substitution. Steps to promote industry only developed a regional flavor in the late 1960s.

The instruments used by the Commonwealth Caribbean countries to encourage manufacturing include fiscal incentives, and both quantitative and tariff restrictions on manufactured imports. Tariff concessions are used to lower the cost of imported manufacturing inputs. A number of industrial development corporations have been established to administer and guide the process of industrialization. The use of quotas on important categories of manufactured imports has been widespread.[6] Indeed, with some exceptions, quota protection has been central to industrial development in the Commonwealth Caribbean, at any rate in the MDCs. Tariff protection has been used as a secondary means of protection for a smaller number of items, or has been redundant. Among the LDCs, however, only Belize has imposed major quantitative restrictions on industrial imports.

In all the MDCs, negative lists (lists of goods for which import licenses are required) were originally established on a pragmatic basis by trade ministries, as specific new products came into local production in these countries. In principle, the criteria for the imposition and continuation of protective measures are the availability of local supplies in sufficient quantity and quality, and at an acceptable price. In practice, the quantity of local supplies has proved the important criterion. Although protection was initially imposed on "infant industry" grounds, quota protection has been continued on a discretionary basis, either because local producers have never been able to achieve cost levels competitive with world prices, or because they have been able to bring pressure to bear on governments by arguing that the removal of protection would produce politically unacceptable levels of unemployment. In most cases, controls have taken the form of discretionary import licenses for marginal imports. Price minima[7] are also used, for example, on many clothing items; Guyana only permits certain products to be imported through such specially designated government organizations as the External Trade Bureau.

The ad valorem tariff rates in force in national schedules prior to the advent of the CARICOM Common External Tariff (CET) in 1973 were, for the most part, modest in comparison with those of many other developing

6. See Statistical Appendix, Table SA10.5.

7. Price minima assure that the only imports allowe[illegible]nd allowed freely) are those whose unit price—hence quality—is too high to provide substantial direct competition for local production.

countries.[8] Some specific rates, however, particularly those on beverages, cigarettes and cement, tended to have a higher ad valorem equivalent. Consumption taxes also often contained a protective element, particularly in the case of Guyana (which also had the highest protective tariff). The LDCs and Barbados had the lowest protective tariff while Jamaica and Trinidad occupied a middle position. The Commonwealth Caribbean countries also offered substantial Commonwealth preferential margins consisting, for the most part, of some 5 percentage points on general rates up to 20 percent; some 10 percentage points on general rates between 25 and 35 percent; and some 20 percentage points on the 40 percent general rate.[9]

The industrial development corporations have been credited with an important role in fostering Caribbean industrial growth. Apart from their administrative role in the incentive system, and their general function of identifying industrial possibilities and attracting local and foreign investors, they are responsible for developing industrial sites and building factory shells for subsequent leasing to private firms. In a number of cases, rentals have been at subsidized rates. During the 1960s, a large number of new establishments, usually in the light manufacturing sectors, were housed in government-built factories.

Governments have seldom provided capital, either free or at preferential rates, to promote industry. On the other hand, fiscal investment incentives have been common.[10] For approved ("pioneer") activities, the general rule has been to grant income tax holidays averaging five to ten years, with provision for losses to be carried over, together with liberal allowances for duty-free imports of investment goods and, in many cases, of intermediate inputs. In the case of export incentives, only Barbados and Jamaica have had substantial legislation. This has consisted of broadly similar fiscal packages, available to industries (such as the garment industry) exporting 100 percent of their output. These industries would not necessarily be granted pioneer status if they were producing for the domestic market.[11]

In addition to fiscal incentives to pioneer industries, Trinidad and Tobago began, in the early 1960s, the practice of allowing duty-free imports of intermediate inputs to approved firms in approved industries (not necessarily those with pioneer status). This was done as a means of promoting industrial growth.[12] Jamaica followed suit extensively, and Barbados and Guyana did so more selectively. This concession has come to be extended to

8. See Statistical Appendix, Table SA10.5. National rates for LDCS, not given in Table SA10.5, are comparable to the common external tariff rate adopted by the ECCM in 1972, and presented in the table.

9. See the explanatory notes to Table SA10.5 for details of the Commonwealth preference rate.

10. The salient details of fiscal investment incentives prior to CARICOM harmonization are set out in Statistical Appendix, Table SA10.8.

11. In recent years, Trinidad has offered a small tax concession on export profits, based on a complicated formula, but the provision has hardly been used.

12. Under provisions of the customs code.

the majority of manufacturing establishments in the organized sector in Trinidad and Tobago, in Jamaica, and, to a lesser extent, in Barbados. The major exceptions are those industries where major existing local inputs have been identified. Examples would include such food items as processed milk products, and some cotton textile fabrics.

It has not been possible to examine whether this approach has actually inhibited industrial linkages, but it appears likely that this has occurred. Duty-free importing of capital goods tends, moreover, to promote the use of capital-intensive techniques and the production of goods best suited to them. If local manufacturing employment and linkages are to be encouraged (subject to reasonable levels of productive efficiency), these incentives need to be applied with caution. In view of their questionable side effects, and since quantitative restrictions in any case guarantee a local market for domestic producers, the further use of such special provisions for the duty-free import of inputs and capital goods is arguably redundant.

It has been noted that the process of industrial growth in CARICOM countries has basically involved import substitution in the case of final products, but great import intensity in the case of inputs. As a result, linkages have been few and employment effects less than might have been anticipated. The emphasis on import substitution, rather than export promotion, and the small size of the domestic market clearly limit the expansion of output in situations where economies of scale are needed for reasonably efficient production. Linkages nevertheless appear to be equally weak in such activities as agriculture, where the scale of operations need not be an impediment to expansion.

While there is no single regional viewpoint, many economists in the region have taken views similar to those just stated. The Commonwealth Caribbean Regional Secretariat (CCRS) identified the problem in the following manner:

> . . . the rapid growth of the manufacturing sector which has taken place in the last decade or two in the four independent countries has been accompanied by certain undesirable features: too heavy a dependence on foreign capital, foreign technology and foreign inputs (that is, raw materials and components), the excessive capital-intensity (and therefore the limited impact on employment) of foreign technologies used; the creation of insufficient "linkages" between this sector and other sectors of the economy (particularly agriculture); a drain abroad of profits, dividends, interest, royalties, license fees, and management charges because of heavy dependence on foreign capital and foreign enterprise; and insufficient expansion of exports of manufactures to countries in the outside world—a very important objective for small countries such as those in the Caribbean.
>
> All of this has occurred in the context of heavy direct and indirect subsidization and protection . . . relatively to the governmental encouragement given to agriculture, particularly domestic agriculture.[13]

13. Caribbean Community Regional Secretariat, "From CARIFTA to Caribbean Community" (Georgetown, Guyana: 1972), pp. 12–13.

Since the CARICOM countries are of small size, they may choose to encourage manufacturing activities in which scale is not important, to stimulate manufacturing through participation in regional or foreign export markets, or a combination of these two approaches. The region's own analysis emphasizes the enlargement of regional markets, not only as a source of economies of scale in industry, but also as a way to create the linkages on which dynamic industrial development is based; at the same time, however, regional commentators do not shut the door on extraregional exporting.

The CARIFTA Experience

For two reasons, it is as yet too early to judge the effects of CARIFTA on patterns of trade in manufactured goods.[14] In the first place, entrepreneurs typically require some time to react fully to new trading situations; there is a significant lag between the time when investment decisions affecting trade are made, and the time at which they come to fruition. In the second place, a number of exceptions were built into the CARIFTA agreement, a factor which reduced the extent of its impact.

Regional trade in manufactures

In the case of the trade of CARIFTA countries with the whole world, the share of manufactures in total imports has tended to be static or slowly rising, while the share of manufactured exports in total exports has remained unchanged. On the other hand, the composition of intra-CARIFTA trade, with some exceptions, shows a marked and steady rise in the share of both imports and exports of manufactured goods. This trend was apparent before, as well as after, the establishment of CARIFTA.[15] The growth of trade in manufactures cannot, therefore, be associated exclusively with the advent of CARIFTA.

Since 1967, the share of the various CARIFTA countries in intra-CARIFTA trade in manufactures has shown a highly skewed pattern which partly reflects relative country sizes (see Table 7.1). Exports are dominated by Trinidad, and to a lesser extent Jamaica, while the LDCs are hardly represented. The pattern is also lopsided in importing, but in the opposite direction, with the smallest group, the LDCs, accounting for almost one-third of the total. The third column in Table 7.1, which expresses the share of each country's manufactured exports to all other CARIFTA members made up by exports to the LDCs, demonstrates the high reliance of Barbados and Trinidad on the small LDC markets.[16]

14. For a description of CARIFTA trade policies, see Chapter 2.
15. With the exception of growth in export of petroleum-based products from Trinidad.
16. The main effects of CARIFTA on levels and directions of trade, and on domestic levels of manufacturing activity, are presented in Statistical Appendix, Table SA10.12.

TABLE 7.1. SHARES IN REGIONAL TRADE IN MANUFACTURES,[a] 1971
(percent)

Country	*Imports*	*Exports*	*Share of regional exports going to* LDCS	*Share of total exports going to region*
LDCS	31	1	29	14
Barbados	18	6	59	35
Guyana	16	8	22	96
Jamaica	18	23	14	35
Trinidad	17	62	35	76
Total	100	100	31	56

a. Standard International Trade Classification 5–8.
Source: Statistical Appendix, Table SA10.4.

A country opening its economy to foreign trade can expect export and import levels to change, and to affect levels of domestic activity. Information on the relationship, over time, of the intra-CARIFTA trade balance to manufacturing GDP, gives an indication of the effects of changes in trade patterns on various countries.[17] As Table 7.2 shows, the ratios do not change much

TABLE 7.2. INTRA-CARIFTA TRADE BALANCE,[a] 1963, 1967, 1973
(percentage of manufacturing GDP[b])

Country	*1963*	*1967*	*1973*
ECCM	−100	−176	−156
Barbados	− 14	− 17	− 14
Guyana	− 14	− 20	− 18
Jamaica	0	+ 2	0
Trinidad	+ 18	+ 17	+ 14

a. + indicates positive, − indicates negative, trade balance.
b. Gross Domestic Product.
Source: Statistical Appendix, Tables SA10.11 and SA10.12.

The table shows the share in domestic markets of local manufacturing production and imports from CARIFTA and non-CARIFTA trading partners; the shares in output of local production and exports to CARIFTA and non-CARIFTA trading partners; the ratio of the trade balance to output; and the ratio of exports to imports for 1963, 1967, 1971, and 1973.

17. The larger the growth in the ratio of imports and exports to production, the greater—other things being equal—the trade creation effect (the maximization of comparative advantage). Of course, this is not necessarily so in the present situation, where growing CARIFTA trade ratios may simply represent diversion from lower cost world sources.

in the case of the MDCs, while that of the LDCs increases markedly before CARIFTA's establishment in 1968, and falls back to a lower level thereafter. The negative intra-CARIFTA trade balance of the LDCs worsened appreciably, as imports increased in relation to exports, and in relation to the output of manufactures. For the LDCs, imports from the MDCs, mostly from Trinidad, became more important in relation to (a) the LDCs' exports to CARIFTA; (b) the LDCs' nonexported output of manufactures; and (c) the LDCs' domestic markets for manufactured goods. While the LDCs were able to export an increasing proportion of their output to markets outside the region, the MDCs clearly gained in intra-CARIFTA trade.[18]

The fact that the MDCs did better in LDC markets than the LDCs did in MDC ones is not simply a consequence of the establishment of CARIFTA. The trend was noticeable before 1967, and subsequent developments represent its continuation. The MDCs (in particular Trinidad) were apparently becoming sufficiently industrialized in the early 1960s to benefit from a modest margin of Commonwealth preference and their distinct locational advantage in supplying LDC markets. It would appear, nevertheless, that CARIFTA gave a further impulse to intraregional trade after 1967. The share of regional imports in CARIFTA's manufacturing output grew from 7.9 percent in 1963 to 9.1 percent in 1967 and accelerated to 14.9 percent in 1973.[19]

*The composition of intra-*CARIFTA *trade*

Overall, intra-CARIFTA trade covered a broad range of products, while extra-CARIFTA exports were relatively few.[20, 21] In general, those products least represented in trade tended to be among the more import-intensive items, such as cigarettes, animal feeds, and assembly products, which were unable to comply with CARIFTA rules of origin. There is a marked absence of trade in resource based manufactures. These are limited to manufactured fertilizer

18. The size of the trade balances also shows the importance of the whole of the Commonwealth Eastern Caribbean, throughout the period, as a market for Trinidad manufactures. The relatively large decline of the LDC trade balance and the very minor changes in the MDC balances are caused by the different sizes and rates of growth of output of trading partners. Thus, for instance, in the period 1967–71 very modest gains in the Guyanian and Trinidadian trade balance ratios are the complement of the sharp decline in the LDC ratios.

19. See Statistical Appendix, Table SA10.11.

20. See Statistical Appendix, Tables SA10.13 to 10.16, which give details of the total trade of the MDCs in manufactures by major product group, and by individual CARIFTA trading partners (the LDCs counting as one trading partner) for the latest year available. Table SA10.17, using the data of Tables SA10.13 to 10.16, gives indicators of comparative advantage as shown by significant positive trade balances of different MDCs in selected products important in intra-CARIFTA trade.

21. An interesting corollary to this trend is the tendency for intra-CARIFTA trade to be the result of marginal exporting by firms principally serving domestic markets. Extra-CARIFTA exports, on the other hand, are heavily concentrated in establishments specializing in exports, often to one country.

exports from Trinidad, simple wood products and some flat glass from Guyana, agricultural lime from Barbados, and a small amount of aluminum in primary form from Jamaica.

Not surprisingly, there is a group of products which is only produced in, and exported from, the more industrially advanced MDCs, notably Jamaica and Trinidad. These are, for the most part, intermediate industrial products where only the market size of Jamaica and Trinidad has been able to justify minimal scale.[22] Among the most important items are cement, glass bottles, cans, crown corks, and some assembly items (such as refrigerators and television sets).

In spite of the broad base of intra-CARIFTA trade, there is a considerable degree of product concentration. In particular, two product groups—perfumes, cosmetics and cleansing products, and clothing—account for at least 30 percent of each MDC's intra-CARIFTA trade in manufactures. A few other product groups account for much of the remainder. They include paper articles, paints, medicinal and pharmaceutical products, textile fabrics (either locally woven or finished), and footwear.

Three main factors help to explain the pattern of trade that has developed. In the first place, and not surprisingly, the variety and type of products exported by different countries correlate with their level of industrial development. In the second place, transport costs and information barriers constrain trade between Jamaica and the Eastern Caribbean. This is one reason why Trinidad has been better able than Jamaica to profit from the exports of such items as cement, glass bottles, and cans, which are not produced in the other countries of the region.[23]

In the third place, the pattern of trade is influenced by the country-by-country imposition of special levels of protection against third country imports. It is clear that trade in some items tends to be heavily concentrated on countries giving quota protection to those items against extraregional producers. Among the most prominent examples of such items are canned meat, processed vegetables, sugar confectionery, perfumes and cosmetics, tires, cotton fabrics, and refrigerators. Quotas no doubt affect the level of trade in many other items, notably clothing, footwear, and processed foods, but the existence of MDC exports of these products to unprotected markets suggests that they are, to some extent, competitive in their own right.

Table 7.3 presents data suggesting that levels of protection may have played an important part in generating intraregional trade. The figures in Table 7.3 show the changing shares (between 1967 and 1971) of imports from CARIFTA and extraregional sources in domestic markets and of exports to CARIFTA and extraregional destinations. The growth in the shares of

22. See Statistical Appendix, Table SA10.19, which classifies items of this kind as "monopolistically available products."

23. Some of these items, and such other goods as processed milk and paints, are produced by only one or a few foreign firms. The extent of intra-CARIFTA trade in these products is clearly related to the decisions of these extraregional corporations.

TABLE 7.3. INDEX OF GROWTH IN IMPACT OF CARIFTA TRADE IN MANUFACTURES, 1967–71 (1967 = 100)

Country	Growth in share of imports in domestic market		Growth in share of exports in domestic output		Ranking of degree of protection to industry
	CARIFTA	Non-CARIFTA	CARIFTA	Non-CARIFTA	
ECCM	113	99	65	420	1
Barbados	112	103	190	938	2
Guyana	159	95	464	15	3
Jamaica	300	106	155	94	4
Trinidad	288	99	143	66	5

Source: Statistical Appendix, Table SA10.11 for the first four columns. The last column is a simple ranking based on the number of nontariff barriers for each country recorded in Statistical Appendix, Table SA10.5 (no, or few, nontariff barriers are assumed in the ECCM); 1 is least protective; 5 is most protective.

imports from CARIFTA sources in the domestic markets of different countries closely correspond in ranking with the degree of protection afforded by those countries to local (and CARIFTA) producers against third-country imports. This pattern is not evident, however, in the growth of the shares of non-CARIFTA imports in countries' domestic markets or in the growth of the shares in countries' domestic output of exports, either to CARIFTA or non-CARIFTA destinations. Thus, CARIFTA member countries import more goods from other CARIFTA countries in line with the levels of protection they impose against third-country imports, but increases in both non-CARIFTA imports and exports are related to overall competitiveness regardless of destination.

There is no clear pattern of comparative advantage in CARIFTA countries' trade in manufactured goods. The nearest situation to a classical version of comparative advantage, where a country exports items it can produce relatively cheaply in exchange for imports of items which are relatively expensive to produce domestically, is that relating to some of Jamaica's trade. In that instance, clothing and shoes are imported from the other MDCs, in return for such items as razor blades, cables, and other metal and mechanical products. The tendency is not pronounced however, and there are cases where countries have export strength outside, but not within CARIFTA. Barbadian jewelry, and Jamaican clothing and processed fruit, are examples of such cases. This situation is not surprising and reflects the fact that the countries of the region have broadly similar factor endowments.

Indeed, much of intra-CARIFTA trade is complementary rather than compensatory. In other words, many products are consumed in all MDCs and are traded between them because of accidents of location and specialization, rather than because a given country can produce a particular item at a uniquely attractive cost and price. The economic advantages arising from such trade flows may be ephemeral. In many cases, it is likely that overall production could become more efficient through greater specialization by individual producers within product groups (which would give each of them economies of scale based on longer runs), or simply by greater competition. In the case of clothing, for instance, it is likely that gains have been secured both by specialization and by competition, but in the case of cosmetics and soaps—the other main product group traded—the gains may be less real, in the sense that consumers are merely offered an increased choice. In principle, this may represent a welfare gain, but too much product differentiation may reduce the region's ability to develop linkages between the production of finished goods and the inputs they require. This is because the individual markets for the various finished items may be too small for it to be economical for local enterprises to produce the small numbers of different inputs that each requires.

This brief review of the development of regional trade in manufactures suggests three conclusions. First, that the MDCs, particularly Trinidad, have taken an increasing share of the LDC market for manufactures. Second, that there is some evidence that the advent of CARIFTA has accelerated the preexisting growth of regional trade in manufactures, but that it does not appear to have had much effect on the pattern of investment. Third, that a significant proportion of regional trade is accounted for by consumer goods, a sector in which product differentiation is high and linkages are poor.

The Options for Industrialization in CARICOM

The main reasons for industrialization in the Caribbean region are threefold: first, to create employment (the reason most emphasized in the region); second, to contribute to the growth of output; and, third, to raise foreign exchange earnings (the reason least emphasized in the region). In addition, it has been strongly believed in the region that industrialization of the right kind plays an important and dynamic role in economic development. Industrialization which creates sectoral linkages—national or regional—will, it is believed, bring new resources into use and reduce dependence on the outside world.

The region's integration efforts are based on political and cultural, as well as economic, interests, which are thus difficult to separate. A particular, immediate, and specific, political and economic objective of integration is that of spreading equitably the fruits of growth within the region. Finally, although there is a general commitment to integrate, it may be noted that the strength of this commitment varies between national governments. The available economic options have to be viewed against this background.

Prospects for import substitution

The development of an industrial sector through import substitution should go hand in hand with the promotion of economically efficient linkages both within the industrial sector, and between industry and other sectors of the economy. A reasonable degree of efficiency and an adequate scale of operations are also needed in the relatively small Commonwealth Caribbean market.

In fact, however, import substitution in manufacturing has been accompanied by relatively few local linkages with other sectors of the economy. Instead, it has relied on imported inputs. As import-substituting industry is, however, protected, the nonindustrial sectors, in effect, subsidize industrial development. They do this by buying high-priced industrial goods, through price controls on nonindustrial products, or by paying taxes at higher rates than tax-exempt industries.

The problem is not merely that there are too few linkages, but also that industry is favored at the expense of other sectors of the economy. What might be called the Brewster-Thomas strategy for heavy industry development[24] might help to create linkages, but at a high cost to the rest of the economy. This is because import substitution, even on a regional basis, does not allow for sufficiently large scale production. It has been argued that the presence of heavy industries in Latin American countries lays the basis for the subsequent transformation of their economies. The historical verdict of many economists, however, is that such industries tend to inhibit transformation because of their high costs in credit, incentives, and protection policies, costs which are paid for by other sectors. Import substitution in heavy industries would be very expensive for the Caribbean region with its small population of 4.5 million people; it would place a heavy burden on other sectors of the regional economy. Mature economies are able to display the full range of heavy industries only by virtue of their large size or of their specialization of production in the international economy.

The benefits of linkages may be outweighed, therefore, by the high costs of large scale production. There is an additional problem about the linkages which Brewster and Thomas suggest in the industries which they examine in detail. They suggest that the more important linkages would be backward rather than forward ones. An examination of the integration industries gives a sense of insufficient linkages with the primary sector.[25] Some key industries —steel and automobile production in particular—remain import dependent. Others rely on domestic inputs to a greater degree, but not on inputs from agriculture, which remains the region's primary resource. In addition to agriculture, the region's known potential for basic materials lies in bauxite, petroleum, and natural gas.

It would be possible to develop linkages beneficial to the agricultural sector by emphasizing agricultural processing, either for local or for export

24. Brewster and Thomas have argued that the region should move towards economic integration through production of those key intermediate goods, steel, textiles, paper, chemicals, and so on, characterizing the output of mature economies. See Havelock Brewster and Clive Y. Thomas, *The Dynamics of West Indian Integration* (Mona, Jamaica: Institute of Social and Economic Research, University of the West Indies, 1967).

25. See Statistical Appendix, Table SA10.9.

markets. In any event, the fact that a developing economy is not vertically integrated need not and, given extreme diseconomies of scale, should not automatically lead to a strategy of import substitution based on the development of heavy industries. The following discussion reviews the prospects for, respectively, processed agricultural products; textile production; the wood and pulp and paper industries; cement, glass sheet, and chemical production; and the steel, motor vehicle, and engineering industries.

Processed agricultural products figure prominently in the import bills of the countries of the region and appear to offer valuable opportunities for substitution in industry and agriculture. Most of the region's current processing capacity for dairy, meat, vegetable, and fruit products is located in Jamaica and Trinidad. Operations are generally on a small scale, and each plant produces a wide variety of goods: this factor inhibits specialization. An even more serious problem, however, is that it is difficult to obtain agricultural inputs from local sources which are acceptable in terms of quantity, quality, and price. As a result, the food industry is largely import-dependent.[26] (As was noted in Chapter 6, this is a particular problem for tourist industry food requirements.)

Ample opportunities exist in the region for import substitution which would justify the development of a number of new plants, each of which would cater to local agricultural specializations. The problem of supply remains a formidable obstacle, however. It is particularly critical in the LDCs and obstructs the development of a promising industry.[27]

Two mills in Jamaica and Trinidad, each over twenty years old, constitute the region's existing capacity in textile production.[28] With modern integrated mills of an acceptable size producing some 15 to 30 million square yards of fabrics annually, a demand forecast of some 140 million square yards for woven cotton and man-made fiber textiles in the late 1970s would seem to justify substantial extra capacity. The Caribbean market has traditionally been furnished with fabrics from all over the world, however, and consumers have developed sophisticated and varied tastes. Production costs grow substantially as mills produce a wider range of goods. For this reason, a 1969 United Nations Development Organization (UNIDO) study recommended that the region invest in two integrated mills, a cotton mill producing 25 million square yards annually, in six basic product lines, and a polyester and

26. Consumers, moreover, have acquired tastes for foods which are not locally available, in particular those from temperate zones.

27. A prefeasibility study of the canning industry carried out by the Economist Intelligence Unit (EIU) found local agricultural prices to be a principal problem. See Economist Intelligence Unit, *Eastern Caribbean and British Honduras Industrial Survey* (London, 1972).

28. Brewster and Thomas, *Dynamics of West Indian Integration*, estimated additional regional capacity requirements in integrated cotton and synthetic mills. This was followed up by a UNIDO prefeasibility study in 1969. A recent survey of the textile and garment industry is contained in Earl Baccus and Geoffrey Shepherd, *A Protective Regime for the Textile Industry in the Commonwealth Caribbean* (Georgetown, Guyana: CARICOM Secretariat), 1973.

cotton mill producing 15 million square yards in five lines.[29] In fact, the investment plans of individual MDCs may already go beyond this target.

The UNIDO recommendations would generate an annual demand of some 14 million pounds for cotton, and of just over 3 million pounds for polyester. If both Trinidad and Jamaica were to invest in a polyester and cotton mill, demand for polyester fibers might approach some 4,000 tons per annum. Such an eventuality might justify a small polyester extrusion and spinning plant which could eventually be fed by the local petrochemical industry.

Both the Brewster and Thomas study and an Economist Intelligence Unit (EIU) survey prepared in 1972 under the sponsorship of the Caribbean Development Bank (CDB) identified regional import substitution possibilities in the production of shoes.[30] Brewster and Thomas also pointed out the possibilities of backward integration by developing a regional meat complex, which could supply hides for the use of the region's single tannery in Jamaica.[31] Plant scale, in this instance, is not as critical a factor as in the production of textiles, and the region could probably support a number of extra shoe producers. Again, however—and particularly in the case of tanneries—there arise the conflicting claims of broad consumer tastes and efficient specialization by a limited number of firms.[32] As in the case of textiles, import substitution means either the restriction of consumer tastes or the higher costs of product differentiation.

Past studies have paid little attention to the wood industry. Guyana and Belize have substantial forestry reserves—largely tropical hardwoods with limited value for construction purposes—which could well substitute for present regional imports to such industries as furniture manufacture. Brewster and Thomas, UNIDO, and other United Nations organizations, have given some attention to a possible regional pulp and paper industry which does not exist at present.[33] The industry could be based on the forestry resources of Guyana or Belize and/or on bagasse from the sugar industry. According to estimates by Brewster and Thomas, the regional market for newsprint would be some 25,000 tons per annum in 1975.[34] Estimates of the conse-

29. Brewster and Thomas, on the other hand, had suggested that the region could become self-sufficient in cotton textiles with four integrated mills and a substantial reduction of the range of products that consumers could buy. Four new mills are being planned in the region; two in Guyana and one each in Jamaica, and Trinidad and Tobago.

30. See Economist Intelligence Unit (EIU) *Eastern Caribbean and British Honduras Industrial Survey*, prepared for the CDB (London, 1972).

31. Brewster and Thomas, *Dynamics of West Indian Integration*, p. 255.

32. Indeed the attitude of Jamaican shoe manufacturers to the local tannery mirrors that of Jamaican and Trinidadian garment manufacturers to the local textile mills: the complaint is that the local product is overpriced, underdesigned and of low quality.

33. The Caribbean Development Bank (CDB) has identified the pulp and paper industry as one with potential for development in a regional industrial programming frame. In 1977 a prefeasibility study began to identify activities which could be located in different territories. A major objective of this study is to provide a model approach to regional industrial programming. Allocation of industrial activities will be based on prefeasibility studies of particular subsectors.

34. Brewster and Thomas, *Dynamics of West Indian Integration*, p. 178.

quences of small-scale operations in modern integrated mills suggest a substantial cost penalty for such a small size.[35] The conclusion reached by UNIDO was that a regional paper mill would only be viable with additional export markets. The most profitable type of production appears to be in the field of substituting for imports in packaging paper.

The regional cement market is characterized by an excess of consumption over regional production.[36] If investment intentions are realized, there will probably be some excess capacity by the late 1970s. The benefits of economies of scale are substantial in cement production, but the whole regional market would not now justify an optimally sized plant.

Brewster and Thomas estimated that the regional market would justify a plant producing some 6,000 tons of glass sheets by 1975. Recent estimates of economies of scale in glass production suggest that this level of output is below the minimum acceptable level of operation.[37] This is the case even allowing for the substantial transport cost advantage that a regional producer could expect to have, particularly in its home market.

Economies of scale are important in the production of many chemicals. Petrochemical production could not, for instance, be based solely on the regional market, in spite of the Trinidadian resource base. A 1972 feasibility study for caustic soda production (principally used in the region as an input to aluminum smelting), by De Castro and Dolly, found that production was justified if a sufficiently large market for the accompanying by-product, chlorine, could be found.[38] This would most probably occur if polyvinylchloride were to be produced (but this process would also require inputs of ethylene from the petrochemicals industry).

The production of steel from imported iron ore was suggested by Brewster and Thomas on the basis of a 300,000 ton steelmaking, and a 200,000 ton steelrolling capacity. Steelmaking might be appropriate for the region, but rolling involves substantial product diversification at the rolling stage, and would entail substantial costs—large enough to call into question the economics of the enterprise.[39] Current reports are that Trinidad is considering

35. Data from *Asia Industrial Survey for Regional Co-operation* (Bangkok: U.N. Commission for Asia and the Far East [ECAFE]), 1972, suggest that unit costs in a mill of 50,000 tons per year (TPY) capacity are some 66 percent higher than in a mill of 500,000 TPY capacity. The CARICOM region would also face a shortage of suitable soft wood unless specific production programs are initiated or more appropriate technologies can be found.

36. See Statistical Appendix, Table SA10.10.

37. The *Asia Industrial Survey* data support the estimate that one glass process, for instance, when associated with a 10,000 TPY capacity, results in unit costs 40 percent higher than in a plant producing 25,000 TPY and 100 percent higher than in a plant producing 100,000 TPY.

38. See the study by Steven DeCastro and Montgomery Dolly (Mona, Jamaica: 1972).

39. According to Pratten, a 250,000 ton capacity in steelmaking incurs a unit cost penalty of some 25 percent over one million tons and 33 percent over two million tons. See Clifford F. Pratten, *Economics of Scale In Manufacturing Industry* (Cambridge: Cambridge University Press, n.d.), p. 105.

electric arc furnace steel production on the basis of imported iron pellets.

The motor vehicle industry of the region consists, essentially, of the present Trinidadian assembly capacity, amounting to some 6,000 units a year (out of a regional market of some 25,000 units a year), none of which are exported. It also comprises a small plant producing "hustlers" (small vehicles with fiberglass bodies) in Antigua, and a plant producing a similar light vehicle in Guyana. In addition, Jamaica and Trinidad produce tires and batteries and other minor accessories. Jamaica has, from time to time, given some consideration to the possibility of local motor vehicle assembly. As with many other consumer-oriented industries, product diversity presents an obstacle to import substitution. Additional serious obstacles are posed, however, by the nature of the international motor industry. While local motor vehicle assembly can often be fairly efficient in developing countries, progressive import substitution is frequently hindered. The explanation is that when the foreign manufacturer deletes the components which a developing country has started to produce locally from the completely knocked-down (CKD) kit he exports, the deletion allowance, which he subtracts from the price of the CKD kit, is less than his average cost of production for that component. The cost of import substitution in motor vehicles thus escalates, irrespective of whether or not the import-substituting country is or can be an efficient producer.[40]

The engineering industry does not face the same problems of large scale production which beset many of the industries already discussed. The development of engineering skills has important external economies, both for industrial development in general, and for the adaptation of technologies to local conditions in particular. If engineering is to be developed, in part at least, through backward integration, the output of the component industries must become more standardized. It would, therefore, be best to start with the least oligopolistic (and least product-differentiated) industries. Bicycle assembly has been suggested by the EIU survey as a potential industry for the LDCs; other candidates could be the production of electric fans, and of gas and electric cookers.

A constant feature of this survey of possibilities for import substitution, has been the serious problem of the absence of the demand required for the economical operation of large scale units of production. This should come as no surprise, given the small size of the regional market, but it should be emphasized that the crude scale estimates used in the discussion have been based largely on advanced country data, and have not always fully considered the effects of local raw materials or transport costs on estimates of regional viability. Product differentiation has, however, compounded the

40. But for this factor, a broad range of ancillary light engineering items would be strong candidates for import substitution. Some of the central items, however, such as the body, engine block, and gearbox, require production on a substantial scale if they are to be at all cost competitive.

problem of market size. In the case of some products, such as shoes, textiles, or motor vehicles, a certain degree of product homogeneity can be imposed on the market. In others, such as in the case of steel and paper products, production runs are inevitably limited by the nature of demand. In addition, the distinction might be drawn between import substitution, that is, local production of previously imported items, and import replacement, that is, local production of items more appropriate than the imports they replace, for example, mango juice instead of apple juice. While the potential for import replacement is strongest in processed foods, it also exists in the case of such items as local soaps based on the coconut industry.

The greatest opportunities for long run import substitution, import replacement, and sectoral linkages, exist in processed agricultural products. In addition, judicious import substitution, on the basis of specialization within the region, should be possible in the case of textiles, leather and shoes, and engineering goods. The heavier intermediate industry goods that have been discussed seem to involve far more fundamental problems associated with economies of scale.

An additional point might be made about methods of identifying the possibilities for import substitution. In the past, the standard method has been based largely on scrutiny of the import bill. At the present time, the more obvious items in the import bill have already been accounted for, and the EIU survey was able to come up with only a surprisingly short list of possible exports from LDCs to MDCs. One way of overcoming this problem—and also of dealing with the problem of product differentiation—is to undertake in-depth studies of product groups at the regional level. The domestic electric appliance industry, for example, might be the subject of a study to examine strategies for project standardization during subsequent backward integration processes.

Export promotion

Exporting outside the region must be considered in an industrialization strategy, because the small size of the local market limits the expansion of manufacturing through reasonably efficient import substitution. If sectoral linkages are to be developed, moreover, it should be kept in mind that these will be partially dependent on exporting—even in the cases of some of the more promising forms of regional import substitution. For example, the region might eventually export garments made of locally produced polyester fibers and polyester and cotton fabrics, or locally produced plastic or paper articles. Alternatively, the region might export fertilizer but also consume part of its output locally.

The region can also benefit from enclave-type exporting even though this activity is often undertaken by firms which tend to shift investment rapidly from location to location, with the result that little value is added locally. As long as unemployment and underemployment keep the opportunity cost of labor down (and as long as the costs to the economy of the enclave industries remain chiefly labor costs), these activities are justified. At the same time, of course, governments can require enclave firms to pay taxes and train local labor if they judge the contribution of such industries to be too small. To encourage enclave exports is not inconsistent with taking longer-term steps to transform the structure of the economy by developing stronger internal linkages.

Some countries of the region are pessimistic about the prospects for exports; it is believed that local production and marketing costs are too high, and that foreign trade barriers may sometimes be too great for exporting efforts to succeed. In fact, however, the countries of the region are in quite a good position to compete with other low-wage countries in the markets of the North American eastern seaboard by virtue of their labor costs, proximity, and language.[41] The modest export success of Barbados (and of St. Kitts and St. Lucia) lends support to this belief; it also suggests that developed country markets can be penetrated. Pessimism about exporting may, in some cases, be the result of high levels of domestic protection, which give manufacturers little incentive to seek external markets. The increased emphasis on export incentives in the region should help change this attitude.

In the case of Barbados and the LDCs, exports are likely to continue to consist of the products of enclave industries, especially of garments and electronic assembly items. Trinidad and Jamaica seem less likely to attract more enclave exporters, not only because their governments view these industries with suspicion but also because other CARICOM, or indeed other Caribbean, locations with lower wage costs may prove more attractive. Exports from the larger and industrially more advanced countries are more likely to be resource based (including petroleum-based products) and to supply both regional and extraregional markets.

The region must, however, develop a strategy and a unified approach. This strategy would include the identification of specific markets and specific products, the development of procedures for sharing marketing information, and the establishment and supervision of standards for the market, and arrangements for joint supply of orders by several producers in different territories.

Prospective Areas for Integrated Policy Development

Unharmonized tariffs on inputs, and differential quota regimes for outputs, make CARICOM a disguised free trade area rather than a common market or customs union. Until quota regimes are harmonized (and this is unlikely before the end of the transitional period in 1981), the CARICOM experience will probably differ little from that of CARIFTA.

41. Preferential arrangements, such as the Lomé Convention, increase the potential for exporting to developed countries. In the longer term the market of certain developing countries also hold out potential.

Intraregional trade liberalization under CARICOM

Some minor changes can, however, be expected within CARICOM. The Common External Tariff (CET) will increase levels of tariff protection in the previously low-tariff areas, that is, in Barbados and the LDCs, to the levels of the other MDCs. Consequently, Barbados and the LDCs are likely to import less from extraregional sources and more from CARICOM countries. This tendency can be expected to be strongest in such items as cosmetics, clothing, and alcoholic beverages. In these cases, the CET is high and the MDCs are strong regional exporters. The landed prices of both regional and nonregional imports will consequently rise in Barbados and the LDCs.

Important provisions to favor industrial development in the LDCs were built into the new CARICOM arrangements. The new incentives for LDC exports to MDCs are, however, less valuable than they may appear to be. The LDCs are not very competitive with the MDCs in terms of costs, and the industries in which they might be the most competitive (such as the garment industry) are also those which are best developed in the MDCs. The combined effect of preferential incentives for LDCs, and moratoria on the granting of incentives to certain industries in the MDCs, will be too small, in most cases, to alter the situation.

Furthermore, an investor with complete freedom to choose a location in CARICOM from which to serve the region would, as yet, be unlikely to choose an LDC. The politics of regional integration are still quite risky in the eyes of businessmen. Other things being equal, they will choose to locate in the larger countries where, in the event of a complete or partial failure of the regional movement, the local market will provide a fallback level of demand.

Some of these comments apply, though to a lesser extent, to Guyana and Barbados. A reasonably large market and a significant level of industrial development are powerful locational advantages, particularly if investments are to be made in a small number of regionally based industries. Trade liberalization will help sustain rather than counter these advantages.

The other major question arising from the CARICOM arrangements, is that of the changes they may produce in the pattern of investment. Will trade liberalization encourage investment in regionally based industries? This is improbable, or likely at the margin only, since the CET is quite low, particularly for intermediate goods. Such investments are, on the whole, unlikely in the absence of regional quantitative restrictions.[42] The MDCs, meanwhile, appear to be developing large new industrial projects which would clearly benefit from a regionally integrated approach, but which nevertheless seem to be designed on the basis of national markets; small amounts of possible regional exports are being considered, but they represent only a marginal factor.

Investment on a national, rather than a regional, basis will create tensions

42. The region has accepted the need for regional quantitative restrictions. In mid-1976, the prime ministers of the MDCs set up a team of regional officials to study this question. The work is still under way.

within CARICOM because of current distortions in the structure of protection. Two important examples already exist. In the field of textiles, Jamaica and Trinidad, trying to protect their existing mills, do not permit their own garment manufacturers to import competing fabrics free of duty. Other countries in the region, however, are allowed by the rules of CARICOM (expressed in the Exemptions List) to export garments to Jamaica and Trinidad, incorporating fabrics which had previously been imported free of duty into Jamaica and Trinidad. Jamaica has a similar conflict of policy with regard to leather tanning and shoe production. These problems are new to the region, because it has hitherto produced few intermediate goods.

Industrial programming

The past experience of CARIFTA and CARICOM suggests that the region must try much harder than it has done to coordinate regional planning. The objective should be to make the best use of the region's industrial potential for import substitution and exporting. This goal will require a regionwide agreement covering the timing, location, and capacity of new investments likely to affect part or all of the market. Although regional industrial programming is not a new concept, it has hitherto been observed more in principle than in practice. This is because it raises, in more intense form, all the problems of national planning in developing economies. Attempts at industrial programming in regional groupings of developing countries have not been conspicuously successful in the past.[43]

Policy prescriptions for regional programming are difficult and dangerous. The central problem is how to share out the new capacity that the regional market would justify. This has been done in various ways. These have ranged from integration "rounds" in the Central American Common Market (in which countries took new industries more or less in turn), to compulsory consultation (in, for example, the Central African Customs and Economic Union), to collaboration, as in the Regional Cooperation for Development among Pakistan, Turkey, and Iran. Probably the best approach is to avoid rigid rules and to rely on a spirit of cooperation. This spirit still has to make itself manifest in CARICOM.

The region could attempt to find common ground for regional planning in a number of ways. The LDCs could improve communications with each other, possibly through regular meetings or obligatory mutual consultation. The Community Secretariat has initiated work on a long-term perspective plan for industry, but the resources it is able to devote to this effort are very small compared with those it must apply to the implementation of CARICOM trade measures. As Brewster and Thomas have pointed out, the region's favorite method of dealing with a problem has been to arrange an "*ad hoc* meeting of experts" (whether these experts are from within the region or

43. The trade liberalization approach, by contrast, involves fewer conflicts related to the existing industrial structure and requires fewer fundamental planning decisions.

from outside).[44] As a result, the region has not studied its problems with any continuity.

There are good reasons for arguing that trade liberalization should not proceed faster than regional planning. If it does, the position of the industrially weaker members of CARICOM may be further eroded. It is probably inevitable that regional levels of protection will eventually be higher than they need to be for the MDCs. It is by no means clear, however, that increased regional protection is in the interests of the LDCs unless strong compensating measures are taken to provide them with export markets in the MDCs.

Incentives

Even in the absence of serious attempts at regional planning, there are three other areas where CARICOM might make some progress. The first is that of efficiency. Harmonized fiscal incentives put no premium on efficiency, and could even reduce it in terms of the types of industrial activity they encourage. For this reason, some consideration should be given to the introduction of more formal criteria for measuring efficiency in the incentives system.

Secondly, it has been suggested (see the discussion in Chapter 2) that the harmonized fiscal incentives to exporters have a number of weaknesses. They do not apply as long as a firm is enjoying an investment incentive tax holiday; they are not likely to have much of a quantitative impact on export prices; and they fail to encourage firms which wish to export only a small proportion of their output. The first objection could be overcome if incentives to firms which were undertaking new investment, and had some export potential, were to be made contingent on a certain level of export performance. The second and third objections could be met by setting income tax rebates on profits at higher rates, and by preventing rebates from discriminating between different ratios of exports to total sales. These measures would, of course, entail a partial rewriting of the harmonization agreement; in view of the difficulties experienced in arriving at the original agreement, this might not be politically feasible.

The third area for potential progress lies in a revision of the present incentive system's explicit encouragement of the use of imported, rather than local, inputs in industrial production. To withdraw concessions on some capital goods imports (such as machinery that cannot be produced in the region) would probably have little effect. The national exemptions lists, on the other hand, permit the import of many products for which regional substitutes could, in the medium term at least, be developed. The most obvious examples of this are in the food industry, which is highly import-dependent. The removal of the food industry from the Exemptions List would not alone solve many of the supply problems of agriculture, but it would be a begin-

44. Brewster and Thomas, *Dynamics of West Indian Integration*, p. 29.

ning. The longer-term growth of some regional industries—for example, textiles, paper packaging materials, and leather—will also require the removal of the present strong incentives to import.[45]

Manufacturing in the LDCs

Although the small size of domestic markets is the main impediment to industrial development in the LDCs, other elements of their factor endowments also create difficulties. Outside the agricultural sector, the LDCs are poorly endowed with raw materials. They have few metallic minerals or construction materials. Apart from Belize, with its substantial forestry resources, only St. Vincent has small amounts of usable timber resources. Although literacy rates are high, education has stressed the liberal arts along British lines. Technical education is gaining some ground but, by and large, the work force lacks industrial skills and attitudes. In some cases, notably Antigua, the rudiments of industrial and engineering skill seem to have been fostered by the growth of the tourism industry and associated construction activities. Given the small scale of nearly all manufacturing activity, entrepreneurial talents have not developed much. The underdevelopment of industry and of human capital go hand in hand, and the absence of appropriate skills may hamper the growth of manufacturing over the years to come. Basic infrastructure facilities seem on the whole to be adequate for the development of light manufacturing, although certain aspects of the internal and external transport system are less than ideal.

Structure and organization of industry

The pattern of local manufacturing production is largely explained by two factors: the constraint imposed by small size; and the protective effect of transport costs. Apart from the resource-based industries, local production is dominated by semitradable and nontradable goods. These goods are characterized by a high ratio of weight to value, and include cement blocks, low-cost furniture, and bottled drinks. The more labor-intensive goods with lower ratios of weight to value, such as clothing, are not dominant. Businesses typically employ very few workers, usually between five and twenty employees. Some comparatively large establishments have been set up to process agricultural raw materials. Their activities include the extraction of lime juice, coconut oil processing, and the manufacture of coconut byproducts. Since the late 1960s, a few exporting businesses of the enclave type have been established in some countries. Prominent among these are a workwear

45. The proposed new origin system, which removes the Basic Materials List and, in certain cases, provides for the use of regionally produced "starting" materials, should assist in meeting this goal. The proposals could be further amended to offer still greater protection.

garment firm in Belize, a television assembly plant in St. Kitts, and firms assembling display materials and electronic components in St. Lucia.

The estimates in Table 7.4 illustrate the very small share of the LDCs in the manufacturing activity of CARIFTA, and the small share of manufacturing in total LDC economic activity (Belize is the most important exception).

No reliable information exists on the evolution of manufacturing activity in the LDCs. The slow growth of GDP in the 1960s, together with evidence from census data for the ECCM countries that manufacturing employment was stagnant, support the inference that the sector contributed little to the economy during the decade.

A complementary feature of small average establishment size is relative labor intensity. This is borne out by the figures of GDP per employee in manufacturing.[46] Indeed, contrary to the experience of many other developing countries, GDP per employee in the manufacturing sector of the CARICOM LDCs tends to be well below the average for the economy as a whole. This may partly reflect the relative capital intensity of other sectors of the economy (for example, in the hotel sector) but it is basically a consequence of the almost complete absence of medium-to-large capital-intensive establishments.

The few publicly owned businesses in LDC industrial sectors (for example, coconut oil and soap manufacture in Antigua) have not been successful because governments have no more entrepreneurial experience than the private sector. There is little systematic information about the nature of private ownership. The enclave industries are, of course, owned and managed by foreigners. As a result of the fairly high rates of migration within the region, there are also some enterprises owned and run by nationals of other CARIFTA countries.

TABLE 7.4. LESS DEVELOPED COUNTRY (LDC) MANUFACTURING ACTIVITY AS PERCENTAGE OF CARIFTA MANUFACTURING, GROSS DOMESTIC PRODUCT (GDP), AND EMPLOYMENT

	Share in CARIFTA *total*			*Share in national economy*	
Country	*Population*	*Market for manufactures*	*Manufacturing* GDP	*Manufacturing* GDP *as percentage of total* GDP	*Manufacturing employment as percentage of total employment*
ECCM	11	7	2	5	10
Belize	3	3	3	8	15
MDCS	86	90	95	13	17
Total CARIFTA	100	100	100	—	—
Average	—	—	—	12	17

— Not applicable.
Source: Statistical Appendix, Tables SA10.1 and SA10.2.

46. See Statistical Appendix, Table SA10.2.

The small size of the LDCs, together with the nature of their colonial history, has had some notable consequences for the distribution system for manufactures, which in turn affect the prospects for local manufacturing. Most of the imports of manufactured consumer and intermediate goods (mainly used in the construction industry), are accounted for by large trading houses which often retail directly. These trading houses may have foreign ownership, and usually have some foreign management. The nature of the management and the oligopolistic position of the trading houses, have led to a preference for traditional sources of imports (chiefly the United Kingdom and Canada) over newer and probably cheaper ones, such as the countries of the European Economic Community and Japan, or semi-industrialized, low-cost exporters. As a result, the LDCs tend to pay higher prices for imports than the MDCs pay—reflecting not only the reliance of the LDCs on traditional sources, but also their inability to obtain the best prices from these sources. In addition, the trading houses are likely to discriminate against local and CARIFTA sources of supply, because of the relative convenience of present trade channels.

Past industrialization policies

The governments of the LDCs suffer extreme diseconomies by virtue of their smallness. Although industrialization has been an important nominal policy objective since the 1950s, and although various pioneer industry laws were passed in the early 1960s, policy towards the sector has thus rarely been pursued in a concerted or coherent manner. This situation may be changing, as most of the LDCs formally pass responsibility for industrial promotion from trade ministries (whose special concern has traditionally been the regulation of internal and external trade) to especially created industrialization bodies. The absence of an industrialization policy has nevertheless been as much a consequence of the absence of obvious opportunities for industrial development, as of inadequate administrative resources.

In principle, the packages of incentives available in the LDCs are potentially as powerful as those offered in the MDCs and other developing countries. Incentives legislation offers tax holidays for five to ten years. There are few formal controls on foreign investment. Tariff protection on output is, by the standards of developing countries, modest. The LDCs provide nontariff protection of certain activities through the use of negative lists. Although manufactured goods do not figure prominently on these lists, the few domestic market oriented industries which do not enjoy considerable natural protection as a result of high transport costs do in fact seem generally to have been accorded negative list treatment instead.

CARIFTA *and the* ECCM

The CARIFTA Agreement which came into effect in 1967 was a conventional free trade agreement based largely on the European Free Trade Association (EFTA) model. Its main principle was the immediate introduction of internal trade free of tariffs and quotas for goods from member countries which could satisfy CARIFTA origin criteria. Qualifying this basic principle were reserve lists of sensitive items for which member countries required longer periods over which to phase in their abolition of tariffs. One of the major concessions to the LDCs came in this part of the Agreement. They were allowed to have rather more products on their reserve list than the MDCs and were given a ten-year phasing-in period (compared to five years for the MDCs). The other important concession to the LDCs in the Agreement was a provision which allowed them to introduce tariff protection against the MDCs on infant LDC industries competing with industries which already existed in MDCs. It is important to stress CARIFTA's limited impact on LDC import patterns. The LDCs were allowed to retain their essentially modest external tariffs and, since they were not making extensive use of quantitative restrictions (QRs) to control manufactured imports, the extent of trade diversion from world to CARIFTA sources was limited by the modest tariff levels and the rules of origin. On the other hand, the higher levels of protection implicit in the extensive quota systems of the MDCs provided, in principle, much better ground for trade diversion.

The Eastern Caribbean LDCs (the LDCs less Belize which, in any case, did not join CARIFTA until 1971) formed the ECCM in 1968, to provide themselves with a slightly larger market to help them to face the MDCs as a unit. The ECCM regulations mirrored those of CARIFTA with the major exceptions that internal free trade was absolute and immediate, and an eventual Common External Tariff (CET) was agreed in principle; the free movement of capital and labor was also part of the agreement. The CET was introduced on October 1, 1972, among all the ECCM members except Antigua and Montserrat. Antigua accepted the CET later while Montserrat has maintained its own tariff. This CET, based to some extent on its national predecessors, is modest in giving higher rates of protection—in the range of 20 to 40 percent ad valorem—to products which were currently being produced locally, or might be in the future, and to luxury items. The ECCM provisions thus created a common market equivalent in size to Barbados, which has experienced substantial light industrialization. Three characteristics of the ECCM Agreement may limit its effectiveness, however: the first is that there is no common Quantitative Restriction (QR) policy at yet and QRs have been the backbone of industrialization elsewhere;[47] the second is that the rules of origin severely limit the amount of light manufacturing that can qualify for area treatment; and the third is that the LDCs have contractual obligations, within the limitations of Article 39 of CARIFTA, succeeded by Article 56 of CARICOM, to extend free trade treatment to MDC goods.

Trade statistics for the LDCs for the period up to 1971 show no evidence of a positive effect of either CARIFTA or ECCM on trade. Table 7.5 indicates that, over the first four years of CARIFTA, and the first three years of ECCM,

47. The ECCM agreement commits member countries to work towards a harmonization of external QR policy, but the provision is relatively weak.

TABLE 7.5. TRADE OF SELECTED[a] ECCM COUNTRIES, 1967 AND 1971
(thousands of Eastern Caribbean dollars)

Category	1967 Amount	1967 Percent	1971 Amount	1971 Percent
Imports				
From ECCM	0.9	1.0	1.1	0.6
From other CARIFTA	16.5	17.5	36.6	19.6
Total	94.1	100.0	186.7	100.0
Exports				
To ECCM	0.7	1.8	0.6	1.6
To other CARIFTA	2.6	6.7	3.1	8.1
Total	38.7	100.0	38.2	100.0

a. Dominica, Grenada, St. Lucia, Montserrat, and St. Kitts.
Source: National trade returns and CARICOM Secretariat trade estimates.

LDC trade was characterized by (a) a large and growing overall deficit; (b) a negligible and possibly declining share of LDC trade in total trade; (c) a comparatively large and increasing share of MDC manufactured goods in LDC imports; (d) only a small increase in LDC exports to MDCs (the 19 percent increase in current dollar terms over the four-year period hardly constitutes dynamic growth); and (e) a rapidly growing trade deficit with the MDCs. The trade figures do not suggest that either the ECCM or CARIFTA have made a positive contribution to the growth of LDC trade unless it is assumed that the situation would have been worse without it.

Fragmentary evidence suggests that the product composition of LDC imports from MDCs may have undergone some change. The share of manufactures in total imports from MDCs seems to have grown from around 30 percent in 1967 to around 45 percent in 1971. This development is consistent with the differential effects of trade liberalization on generally higher tariff manufactures and lower tariff raw materials. There is also some evidence that a mild degree of trade diversion, affecting an estimated 3 percent of the total LDC import bill, was accompanied by marginally higher import prices.[48]

The tentative conclusion is that CARIFTA and the ECCM have been, and

48. The 3 percent figure was calculated simply by expressing the increased share of manufactures in imports from MDCs (30 to 45 percent) as a percentage of the total import bill. If, in turn, it is assumed that the LDC tariffs allowed, c.i.f., prices of MDC products to be no more than 20 percent of that of imports from other sources (an upper estimate), it could be further stated that this trade diversion entailed a rise in the import bill of the LDCs of less than 1 percent (that is, 20 percent of 3 percent). The rising price would be reflected in a fall in customs revenues rather than an increase in prices to the consumer. The example is illustrative in the sense that the precise extent, if any, of the increasing share of manufactures from MDCs in LDC imports is unclear, but the price effect has certainly been small.

may continue to remain, relatively unimportant in promoting industrialization in the LDCs. The potential costs and benefits for the LDCs in the package of measures associated with CARICOM appear more important, however. The costs are associated with the need to adopt a common protective policy, while the benefits result from a broad range of newly introduced measures.

Future directions for industrial development

The prospective costs and benefits of CARICOM depend on the nature of the comparative advantage of the LDCs. The elements of this advantage have already been discussed and it is clear that, until agriculture can produce at lower cost, there is likely to be little competitive advantage in resource-based products. The small size of local markets obliges manufacturers to turn to foreign markets, in which it is difficult for the LDCs to be competitive. A comparison of cost structures in the LDCs with those in the MDCs or the outside world is difficult, because the absence of an established manufacturing sector means that such a comparison must be hypothetical and based on elusive notions such as the cost of entrepreneurship and the level of productivity.[49]

While wages in the LDCs are low by the standards of Trinidad and Tobago, and Jamaica, they are not particularly low by the standards of other developing countries. It is probable that the comparatively good labor relations prevalent in the LDCs would give the LDCs an important advantage relative to Jamaica and Trinidad. Barbados and Guyana, however, are closely comparable in both wage levels and industrial relations. The LDCs suffer distinct disadvantages at the skilled labor level and at all levels of management, however, which may outweigh any advantages they may have in wages for unskilled labor. Skilled and managerial inputs are sufficiently important in most industries to make the higher costs of filling these positions with expatriates (or alternatively of jeopardizing productivity by employing unqualified locals) a major factor in overall costings.[50]

Although basic infrastructure costs (factory shell rentals, electricity, and communications) are similar in all the CARICOM countries, industry in the LDCs would face special cost penalties in many of the external services associated with manufacturing—engineering and accountancy services, for example—because they lack a modern commercial and industrial sector. It is probable that only the most raw labor-intensive industries in the LDCs would prove competitive in exporting.

The ECCM offers some limited industrialization possibilities. A foundry industry, for example, might provide both useful inputs to other infant in-

49. The EIU costings were hypothetical in this sense, and thus based on tenuous assumptions. The assumptions are easiest for enclave industries where practically the only local input is raw labor, which can be costed with relative ease.

50. The prospectus industries of the EIU study require largely expatriate management and skills and, as a result, these two categories of labor in most cases account for a greater cost than operative labor.

dustries and foster entrepreneurship. There are also possibilities of linkages with the tourism industry in such activities as the manufacture of furniture for hotels and of handicrafts for tourists. In general, however, the market will remain small and will probably grow relatively slowly.

Cost differences are small between the ECCM, and higher wage countries such as Antigua also tend to be industrially the most experienced. Transport costs, moreover, provide a degree of national protection to each country. Under these circumstances, it appears that measures to promote trade liberalization within the ECCM are worthwhile in terms of their effect on trade, and of increasing the solidarity of the ECCM.

The advantage of CARICOM to the LDCs is that it presents a larger, well-protected market in which their export marketing problems might be reduced by the use of existing well-established channels of trade and communications. Exporting to CARICOM could provide useful practice for subsequent export marketing in the world at large. Any evaluation of LDC prospects in CARICOM, however, must take account of both the prospects for LDC manufactured exports to the MDCs (benefits), and the trade diversion effects of CARICOM, particularly in manufactures (costs).

Without a strong cost advantage, investments oriented to the CARICOM market will in principle tend to be located in one of the larger MDC markets. This is because investors will want the secure fallback position of a larger market in the event that regional arrangements should run into difficulties. Possible exceptions to this situation are investments that may be made in LDCs to circumvent trade restrictions in MDCs. It is believed, for instance, that one or two investments in the garment industry have been made in LDCs because garment producers in Trinidad fear increasing restrictions on duty-free fabric imports aimed at protecting Trinidadian textile production.

There is reason to believe that the major concessionary mechanisms for LDCs built into CARICOM agreements may be less effective than would appear on the surface. The provisions for protection of LDC industries against competition from MDCs in LDC markets appear to be adequate, as long as the MDCs are favorably disposed towards LDC requests for such protection. Seven enterprises have already received protection under this provision. Investment and export incentives are, however, less satisfactory. The maximum LDC tax holiday of fifteen years, compared with nine in the MDCs (ten in Barbados), does not have much of a differential impact on production costs. Since the typical project has a life of ten years, and since a developing country entrepreneur tends in any case to take a short-term view and to use a high discount rate, the extra years of tax holidays mean little. In addition, such generous tax holidays mean that manufacturing may not contribute significantly to tax revenue in the LDCs for many years to come.

While LDCs are allowed to give some government assistance to exporters to MDCs, they are unable to give fiscal incentives if exporting firms already benefit from a tax holiday. Alternative forms of export aid, such as direct subsidies, to the extent that they can be provided under the terms of the fiscal harmonization agreement, may prove too great a fiscal burden for LDC governments to consider.

Future policy initiatives

The establishment of an industrial development corporation at the ECCM level, to promote coherent industrial growth in the LDCs, would seem to be an important objective of policy, both from a regionwide point of view and from the more specific viewpoint of the LDCs. The existing industrial promotion unit in the ECCM Secretariat should be strengthened and encouraged to play a more active role than it has in the past.

The LDCs may wish to consider how far they can and should move towards closer integration within ECCM. In spite of the CET, there is at present no harmonized protective regime; both the rating of duty free concessions on imports of materials for user industries, and national quota protection measures are discretionary. The achievement of harmonized levels of protection on inputs and a common quota regime would allow rules of origin to be scrapped within ECCM, and this would increase internal trade possibilities and possibly increase competition between importers.

There may be considerable pressure to agree to a common CARICOM quota regime that is likely to be highly restrictive (reflecting present national regimes in the MDCs). Such a regime could increase the level of LDC import prices significantly. Acceptance by the LDCs of some common QR regimes or other protective policy might be negotiated in exchange for increased market opportunities for LDC products in MDC markets. The LDCs have a case for asking that the five CARIFTA-oriented prospectus industries identified in the EIU survey be added to Annex II of the Georgetown Accord (that is, that CARICOM incentive status for these industries be reserved for the LDCs).

The LDCs have allocated thirty-five industries among themselves. They should proceed to undertake the necessary feasibility studies, refining the list where necessary, and bargain from the MDCs not only Article 56 treatment, but specific commitments to direct participation in the equity of some of those ventures.

Policy prescriptions for extraregional exporting are more difficult, since the necessary entrepreneurial ability cannot be created overnight. A start can be made, however, through the creation or promotion of appropriate institutional arrangements. The industrial promotion unit of the ECCM Secretariat will need to consider how the effort to attract foreign entrepreneurs can best be organized. Consideration could be given to the establishment of small overseas branches of the unit which could seek to make contracts with foreign department stores and industries, with a view to subcontracting assembly operations. Given the special nature of the problems of the LDCs, the institutional approach may prove more valuable than one directly related to the price mechanism. A revision of the currently overgenerous incentives to invest, making them conditional on extraregional exporting, should be given serious consideration. The LDCs could also encourage interest in a CARICOM-wide approach to exportation at the CARICOM level.

Appendix A

The Distribution of Benefits from Integration

THE COMMONWEALTH CARIBBEAN INTEGRATION MOVEMENT HAS BEEN strained because of the dissatisfaction of many of the less developed countries (LDCs) with the lack of evident benefits from their participation in the Caribbean Community (CARICOM). Despite the special treatment accorded them in the CARICOM treaty, the LDCs argue that, under the present arrangements, their weak economies have served merely as outlets for packaging industries in the MDCs, and that few, if any, new production and trade opportunities have materialized. This contentious issue merits some discussion.

All integration schemes established so far among less developed countries have faced the problem of how to distribute equitably the benefits arising from economic integration. The term "equitable" is not easy to define precisely and is left vague in the Treaty establishing the Caribbean Community. Article 4 of that Treaty states that the objectives of the Community are: "The sustained expansion and continuing integration of economic activities, the benefits of which shall be equitably shared taking into account the need to provide special opportunities for the less developed countries."

The ways in which the benefits of an integration scheme are distributed are difficult to calculate, in principle or in practice. Both the benefits and costs of integration are made up of multiple elements, including both direct changes in per capita income and indirect changes in the economy's productive potential.

Theoretically, it might be expected that the poorest areas within an integrating community would be stimulated most from an elimination of barriers to trade, since they would tend to have relatively low wages and would therefore be able to attract new industry from their richer partners. It might also be expected that the consequent increase in the demand for labor, and in incomes, in these areas would help to equalize living standards among member countries. In most integration schemes, however, the poorer members tend to lack infrastructure and financial and manpower services. This problem may more than offset low wage costs, so that new industry in fact gravitates to more developed, rather than least developed, centers.

Unless the establishment of a common market is accompanied by specific distributional measures, the income gap among the member countries may thus in fact widen instead of narrowing. To deal with this issue, the Caribbean Community has devised several schemes to favor the LDCs. Special provisions for the LDCs comprise measures to (a) facilitate LDC exports to the Common Market; (b) confer particular benefits on the LDCs in certain policy coordination instruments; and (c) promote a greater flow of resources into the LDCs. Most of these special instruments were introduced as a "new deal" in 1973, when the Common Market was formed. In sum, the objective of the special regime for the LDCs is to facilitate the transfer of capital to their productive sectors. The Caribbean Common Market does not impose an obligation on member countries to allow freedom of movement of persons, but it has sought an effective substitute for such movement in a planned and regulated movement of both public and private sector capital from the MDCs to the LDCs.

Available evidence suggests that in the first five years of integration the LDCs did not benefit as greatly as was hoped, although they have probably not lost by participating in the Caribbean Free Trade Association (CARIFTA) and the Caribbean Community (CARICOM). While the exports of the Leeward and Windward islands to the region increased by 20 percent during the 1967–71 period, their imports from the region increased by 90 percent. The intra-CARIFTA trade deficit of the Eastern Caribbean Common Market (ECCM) countries more than doubled from EC$23 million in 1967 to EC$47 million in 1971. At the same time, however, the share of imports from the region in their total ECCM imports, and the share of exports to the region in these countries' total exports, increased roughly in proportion, from 18 to 24 percent and from 10 to 13 percent respectively.

The product composition of LDC imports from MDCs also seems to have changed. Manufactures accounted for 45 percent of total LDC imports from MDCs in 1971, compared with 30 percent in 1967. This development is apparently a consequence of trade diversion, as it seems to have been accompanied by higher relative import prices, but the resource cost to the LDCs is estimated at less than 1 percent of their import bill.

Looking ahead, some additional costs may have to be borne by the ECCM countries with the adoption of the CARICOM Common External Tariff (CET). While 60 percent of the CARICOM CET rates are the same as in the ECCM schedule, the remaining 40 percent of the ECCM schedule is relatively low in comparison with tariffs in developing countries in general. A rough estimate of the future trade diversion cost has been made for St. Kitts–Nevis–Anguilla. Assuming that the share of its intraregional imports will increase from 15 percent (as of 1973) to 25 percent and the price rise associated with trade diversion is the difference between the ECCM and the CARICOM CETs, the resource cost is equivalent to 3 percent of the total import bill. The amount is not negligible, since in a typical LDC open economy this cost corresponds to about 2 percent of gross domestic product (GDP). Such a sharp shift in import sources, however, would only be expected to occur after tariff harmonization had been in effect for several years.

On the positive side, the LDCs have benefited from Caribbean Development Bank (CDB) loans and have shared in the provision of regional common services; one of the islands, St. Vincent, has gained some advantage from the Agricultural Marketing Protocol (AMP). On the whole, the integration experience so far has produced both small costs and small benefits for these countries. The very difficult economic circumstances which the LDCs have confronted the past few years has, moreover, swamped the impact of CARICOM trade arrangements on their economic welfare. More time will be needed before a clear evaluation of the benefits and costs of integration can be made.

Although the judgment is hard to prove, existing regional economic integration programs do not seem to give adequate recognition to the dangers of polarization between the MDCs and the LDCs. The special regime for the LDCs does not, by itself, appear strong enough to avert, let alone reverse, the trend. The competitive advantages of the MDCs include the size of their internal market; their attractive comparative transport costs; their levels of business supporting services; their social and educational amenities; and other factors. There is a real risk that, despite the "new deal" for the LDCs, the establishment of a common market will result in the concentration of economic activity in those countries that already have a headstart in the development process.

Supplementary measures of assistance to the LDCs, designed to reduce the risks of economic polarization are well worth examining. In agriculture, the LDCs do not have any cost advantage relative to the MDCs. In these circumstances, some specified products should be given preference for LDC exports to the MDCs, by expanding the coverage of guaranteed markets under the AMP. In industry, the situation is similar to that prevailing in agriculture. Unless special concessions are granted to the LDCs over and above what is included in the Annex to the Common Market Treaty, it is very difficult to envisage a substantial expansion of industrial production and associated intraregional exports in the LDCs. Even before regional industrial programming is set in hand, the industry subsectors reserved to the LDCs might be extended by adding those industries which require the whole CARICOM market. The fact that these reserved industries would not be eligible for tax incentives if they are located in the MDCs, is not necessarily a guarantee that they will be located in the LDCs.

A more effective way to transfer resources for industrial development from the MDCs to the LDCs would be the adoption of a scheme that would allow Caribbean corporations to deduct a certain percentage of their income tax liabilities on condition that they establish, or invest in, specified industries in the LDCs. A precedent for such a scheme is to be found in Brazil's Article 34/18, which successfully contributed to the industrialization of northeast Brazil. Joint ventures between MDC and LDC nationals should be sought, and the CDB should be encouraged to extend loans for these enterprises. Such a tax credit mechanism is a much more powerful instrument than exemption from income tax. Income tax exemptions for new industries make a profitable new venture more profitable, but do nothing to reduce the loss to an enterprise if the new venture turns out to be unprofitable. On the other hand, by reducing the amount of equity the entrepreneur has to supply for a given venture, the tax credit mechanism automatically reduces the size of a prospective loss. The scheme is ideally suited to circumstances where the principal obstacle to industrial investment is uncertainty about future costs and markets, rather than the sheer absence of profitable investment opportunities; this is the situation in the CARICOM LDCs. The cost that the MDCs have to bear in terms of foregone income tax revenues would be compensated in time by profit remittances, and through purchases in MDC markets by the newly established LDC firms.[1]

In the future, the LDCs will continue to gain from participation in common services and from functional cooperation, especially if the recommendations of the ECCM's task force on common services are implemented. There are also intangible benefits to be derived from joint actions and common policies toward the outside world; common trade negotiations with the European Economic Community (EEC) on the Lomé Convention represent a case in point.[2]

1. This scheme is similar to the proposal made by UNCTAD: "One procedure whose application might be considered would be to oblige the exporters in the more advanced countries to invest in the less developed countries a certain proportion of the value of their exports to those countries. Thus, an exporter in country A would receive, for example, 95 percent of the value of his exports to country B; the remaining 5 percent would be withheld and he would have to invest it in some enterprise or in some new project in country B. If after a certain period of time, say one year, he has not invested the sums withheld, they would be added to the capital of the grouping's subregional bank, for financing projects in country B. Although the increase in the financial resources of country B is by no means a negligible consideration, the important aspect is the fact that entrepreneurs in the more advanced countries are forced to seek new investment opportunities in the less developed countries. Indeed, it is frequently the case that the main problem of these countries is not so much the shortage of financial resources, as the lack of investment projects." See "Current Problems of Economic Integration—The Distribution of Benefits and Costs in Integration among Developing Countries" (Geneva, 1972), p. 87. The drawback of the UNCTAD proposal, which, in effect, amounts to a reimbursable export tax, is that it puts too much of a burden on the exporter, whose opportunity cost of the foregone export revenue is not zero. In the extreme case, it can be detrimental to intraregional exports, and thus contrary to the objectives of integration.

2. Negotiations between the EEC and forty-six African, Caribbean, and Pacific (ACP) states and subsequently expanded to fifty-two states resulted in the signing of the Lomé Convention in 1974. The five-year agreement provides ACP states with economic aid, trade preferences for exports of manufactured goods and noncompeting agricultural exports, a price stabilization fund for twelve primary commodities, and sugar arrangements which replaced the expired Commonwealth Sugar Agreement (CSA). The Commonwealth sugar producers agreed to market in the EEC up to 1.4 million long tons of sugar a year up to 1980. The 1975 price was set at £245 per f.o.b. long ton. After that, the Commonwealth producers obtained a price indexed to the EEC's support price of £150 per long ton. In any event the impact of the Lomé Convention upon the Commonwealth Caribbean has been much less beneficial than anticipated.

The administrative capability of the LDCs to formulate and implement projects is a critical constraint on their development. The removal or reduction of this constraint should be a specific objective of the integration movement. Initiatives for the identification, establishment, and financing of common services and pools of experts could prove a useful first step in this direction if they were to extend to productive projects. The Caribbean Food Corporation (CFC) should also be used to remove entrepreneurial and managerial bottlenecks in food production.

The provision of sustainable improvements in the standard of living in the less developed member countries of the region is one of the most challenging of all the objectives of CARICOM. In the final analysis, indeed, it is perhaps this objective which will determine the success or failure of the integration movement. Action of the kind discussed above, designed to improve the distribution of economic benefits between the MDCs and the LDCs, is therefore a matter of the highest priority.

Appendix B

A Statistical System for Caribbean Integration

AS ECONOMIC INTEGRATION PROCEEDS IN THE COMMONWEALTH CARIBBEAN, it will become increasingly necessary to develop a comprehensive, regular, and up-to-date statistical evaluation of the economic progress of the region and its member countries.[1] An evaluation of this kind is currently made difficult by the fact that the twelve member countries of the Caribbean Community (CARICOM) are at markedly different stages of statistical development, and because available data exhibit some serious deficiencies and a number of fundamental inconsistencies. Appendix B discusses a strategy for moving towards an integrated statistical system for the Community as a whole.

Such a strategy implicitly assumes that it is better to organize the development of statistical work around a general framework rather than through a series of more or less unrelated efforts. In this context, it is important to note that while the framework discussed here is comprehensive in a macroeconomic sense, it is by no means all-embracing; a good deal of the statistical work to be done in the Caribbean will inevitably proceed independently of it. The existence of a clearly defined and agreed framework does, nevertheless, have a number of important advantages, three of which are suggested below.

First, since statistics in the less developed countries (LDCS) are presently very poor, and since the expertise available to improve them is certain to be limited, a common upgrading program for all eight LDC countries is likely

1. This appendix is an expansion of Alan R. Roe, Jeffery L. Round, and others, "A Framework of Economic Statistics for the Caribbean Common Market," a report to the Caribbean Community Secretariat (Georgetown, Guyana: December 1975; processed). The authors wish to thank the United Nations Development Programme for financial assistance, and their collaborators on the project, Eric Armstrong and Eustace Liburd.

to be more effective than the alternative of a series of independent programs. This is partly a matter of organization but it will also be helped by agreements on statistical priorities, concepts, and definitions. Since the eight countries are much alike, the data from one can, moreover, reinforce statistical strengths in others. A common program can provide a framework for reinforcement of this kind, and can promote a degree of standardization across countries. Similar consequences can be expected, though perhaps to a lesser extent, for the four more developed countries (MDCs).

Second, the data framework proposed here has the advantage that it links a number of crucial accounting identities. The use of these identities can readily reveal the points at which existing data are inadequate, and can consequently suggest priorities for improvement. In addition, a good deal of existing information in the region could be of much more analytical value than it is at present, if it were to be integrated with data relating to other parts of the regional macroeconomic system so as to reveal interdependencies. A good example might be the data on income distribution which exist in some Caribbean countries. By its very existence, an agreed framework would provide a focus for the collation of existing data and would therefore enormously increase their value for analysis.

Third, and perhaps most important of all, the process of regional decision-making, including long-term planning, clearly requires a body of data which is fairly standardized among countries. To be of real value, this body of data needs to reveal the interdependencies involved in the analysis of particular policy alternatives. Obviously, regional decisions can be made in the absence of such a body of data, but they are likely to be much less informed and hence much less effective.

The following discussion begins with an outline of an elementary statistical framework for the region. The framework serves both to suggest some elements of the economic structure of the CARICOM regions and to indicate areas where statistical information is weak. The section then examines the present statistical capabilities of the twelve member countries. It should be noted at the outset that the situation varies enormously from country to country: Trinidad, for example, has produced national accounting information which is as sophisticated as that of any third-world country, while many of the LDCs have no official estimates for even the broad national accounting aggregates. The remainder of this Appendix consists of two further sections discussing, respectively, priorities for statistical development, and some priorities for future work in both LDCs and MDCs.

Economic Structure and Statistical Development

A data system which will adequately represent the Caribbean region clearly needs to reflect the economic structure of the region and the manner in which that structure is expected to evolve over time. The analysis presented in this section develops a fairly aggregative macroeconomic data system which not only describes the present economic structure of the region but also provides a basis for discussing the regional data framework ultimately proposed in the subsequent section.

A model statistical framework for the region

The macroeconomic data system is shown in schematic form for a three-country situation in Table B.1. The schematic cell entries in this table represent the appropriate interrelationships between the categories described in the rows and columns at the intersection of which the cells are located. A numerical form of this table for the Caribbean region is shown in Table B.2, which has been completed as fully as the currently available data permit. The table includes familiar information about the major macroeconomic aggregates (consumption, investment, and so on) of each country together with data showing the interrelationships between member countries from the

TABLE B.1. BASIC REGIONAL DATA SYSTEM FOR CARICOM, SCHEMATIC FORM FOR THREE-COUNTRY CASE

Category		*Intra-*CARICOM *exports to* Country A (1)	Country B (2)	Country C (3)	*Exports to rest of world* (4)
Intra-CARICOM imports from					
Country A	(1)	0	1.2	1.3	1.4
Country B	(2)	2.1	0	2.3	2.4
Country C	(3)	3.1	3.2	0	3.4
Imports from the rest of the world					
Consumption goods	(4)	4.1	4.2	4.3	
Government goods	(5)	5.1	5.2	5.3	
Investment goods	(6)	6.1	6.2	6.3	
Intermediate goods	(7)	7.1	7.2	7.3	
Indirect taxes on					
Consumption goods	(8)	8.1	8.2	8.3	
Investment goods	(9)	9.1	9.2	9.3	
Intermediate goods	(10)	10.1	10.2	10.3	
Adjustment (f.o.b. to c.i.f.)[a]	(11)	11.1	11.2	11.3	
Total	(12)				12.4
Domestic value-added (equals GDP at factor cost)	(13)	13.1	13.2	13.3	
Total supplies (at market prices)	(14)	14.1	14.2	14.3	

Note: For explanation of empty cells, and for a general explanation of the format shown, see text discussion.

a. "Free on board" to "cost, insurance, and freight."

Source: See text discussion.

point of view of commodity trade. No attempt has been made to chart the economic integration of the twelve countries in the somewhat less important areas such as capital transfers, labor migration, and so on, but this is indeed an area of possible extension which occupies the bulk of the discussion in the following section.

Considering first the schematic version of the system shown in Table B.1, where the rows, columns, and cells are numbered accordingly, the total demands placed upon the output of, for example, country A are shown in cell 1.8 of row 1. The parts of that demand accounted for by sales to other CARICOM countries are shown in cells 1.2 and 1.3, while cell 1.4 records the value of exports to the rest of the world. The row is completed by entries relating to other final uses of the output of country A, namely consumption, government spending, and investment (including stock building). Similar information is recorded for countries B and C in rows 2 and 3 respectively,

Private consumption (at market prices) *(5)*	*Government consumption (at market prices)* *(6)*	*Gross domestic investment (at market prices)* *(7)*	*Total demands (at market prices)* *(8)*	*Total* *(9)*
1.5	1.6	1.7	1.8	
2.5	2.6	2.7	2.8	
3.5	3.6	3.7	3.8	
				4.9
				5.9
				6.9
				7.9
				8.9
				9.9
				10.9
				11.9
12.5	12.6	12.7	12.8	12.9
				13.9

TABLE B.2. BASIC REGIONAL DATA SYSTEM FOR CARICOM, FULL AGGREGATION
(millions of Eastern Caribbean dollars)

	Exports to CARICOM							
Purchases	*Trinidad*	*Jamaica*	*Guyana*	*Barbados*	*St. Lucia*	*St. Vincent*	*Mont-serrat*	*Gren*
Imports from CARICOM								
Trinidad	—	43.3	36.1	22.5	8.7	6.3	1.3	
Jamaica	17.4	—	7.2	5.7	1.1	.7	.1	
Guyana	13.9	15.5	—	5.8	1.2	.9	—	
Barbados	6.4	2.0	1.6	—	3.6	2.2	.4	
St. Lucia	0.8	1.2	0.4	0.5				
St. Vincent	0.8	0.0	0.1	0.9				
Montserrat	0.0	0.0	0.0	0.0				
Grenada	0.6	0.0	0.1	0.1				
Dominica	0.5	0.0	0.1	0.4				
St. Kitts, Nevis, and Anguilla	0.0	0.0	0.0	0.0				
Antigua	0.1	0.2	0.9	0.2				
Belize	0.2	1.4	0.1	0.2				
Total CARICOM	41.0	63.4	46.6	36.5	14.7	10.3	2.0	
Other imports and duties								
Adjustment (f.o.b. to c.i.f.)	2.7	1.4	3.0	2.4				
Duties on consumption	29.1	189.1	45.8	36.4	9.5	5.3	1.5	
Duties on production	16.8	41.8	17.8	25.1	3.9	3.1	0.8	
Duties on investment	19.8	26.6	7.4	3.0	1.3	0.8	0.1	
Imports of consumption goods	346.7	501.5	93.3	121.6	25.9	15.3	3.6	
Imports of investment goods	264.3	356.6	98.7	40.4	15.2	7.0	1.4	
Imports by governments	49.0	52.8	9.3	10.0	1.2	1.1	0.3	
Imports of intermediate goods	808.8	384.0	67.9	116.8	10.0	3.0	1.2	
Domestic value-added (equals GDP at factor cost)	1,944.4	2,897.3	490.3	357.0	73.6	36.6	11.7	
Total supplies	3,022.6	4,484.9	890.1	749.2	155.3	82.5	22.6	1

— Not applicable.
Note: For explanation of empty cells, and for a general explanation of the format shown, see text discussi
Source: See text discussion.

Sales									
Dominica	*St. Kitts, Nevis, and Anguilla*	*Antiqua*	*Belize*	*Total* CARICOM	*Exports to rest of world*	*Consumption (market prices)*	*Investment*	*Government consumption spending*	*Total demands*
3.8	2.6	3.7	0 5	137.2	610.8	1,294.8	633.3	338.4	3,014.5
.7	.7	1.0	7.0	42.7	1,082.2	2,186.8	752.1	420.3	4,484.2
.5	.6	1.0	0.04	40.8	277.2	341.0	111.8	108.9	879.8
1.5	1.5	2.3	0.0	24.0	235.4	287.8	93.0	94.0	734.2
				3.1	20.9	75.7	42.5	12.9	155.1
				1.8	8.8	42.8	17.8	11.1	82.3
				0.0	2.7	13.1	4.0	2.6	22.4
				0.7	21.1	64.6	20.3	15.5	122.2
				1.2	14.6	40.5	13.8	10.0	80.1
				0.0	12.2	30.2	17.9	8.2	68.6
				1.3	26.8	64.5	12.9	12.0	117.5
				1.9	37.0	111.0	41.9	13.9	205.7
6.7	5.6	8.1	7.6	255.1	2,349.7	4,552.8	1,761.3	1,047.8	9,966.6
				9.5					
6.0	3.4	6.8	6.8	447.5					
2.6	4.3	3.4	7.4	131.2					
0.5	0.4	0.6	0.8	61.8					
14.2	13.5	20.3	35.2	1,210.8					
6.3	5.1	6.9	11.0	818.8					
0.9	0.8	1.2	1.6	129.7					
5.0	5.5	14.6	8.7	802.4					
38.2	29.9	55.7	130.8	6,129.6					
80.4	68.4	117.6	209.4	9,996.2					

and the system can clearly be extended to a larger number of countries by the addition of further rows and columns. All entries in rows 1, 2, and 3 are valued at market prices so that the sum of these three row totals can be interpreted as gross domestic production at market prices plus the sum of imports; that is, the total of goods and services available for disposition in the countries concerned.

The columns of the table record the manner in which the demands on each country are met. Thus, for example, in column 1, imports into country A from CARICOM (cells 2.1 and 3.1) and imports from the rest of the world disaggregated by type of good (consumption goods, investment goods, and so on), are all distinguished. The domestic contribution to total supplies is indicated by the value-added of country A shown in cell 13.1. Since row entries are valued at market prices, indirect taxes must be added within the columns so as to ensure comparability of row and column totals. Similarly, an adjustment (see row 11) has to be made to ensure that the totals in both rows and columns are shown on c.i.f. basis.

Table B.2 shows the results of an attempt to quantify a version of Table B.1 for the twelve countries of CARICOM. On the assumption that import data are normally more reliable than export data, a representation of CARICOM imports was assembled according to country source, using the 1972 import statistics of the four MDCs. Since 1972 trade data were not available for most of the LDCs, a representation of LDC imports from MDC sources was then constructed using the MDC export data adjusted (more or less arbitrarily) to a c.i.f. basis. The table has blanks in that part of the trade matrix showing LDCs' trade with other LDCs. This has been done to simplify the assembly of data, but it could also be justified on the grounds that intra-LDC trade is known to be less than 1 percent of intra-CARICOM trade as a whole. Nevertheless, individual elements of this trade will be of significance to particular countries, and should, therefore, be incorporated in any subsequent work on a scheme of this type.

All other data shown in Table B.2 have been drawn from national sources or from the CARICOM Secretariat. The presentation is, of course, highly simplified: it involves no disaggregation of commodities, productive activities, types of factor payments, or institutions. It nonetheless provides a considerable amount of information about the structure of the Caribbean economy and represents a useful skeletal basis for any regional data system. Some illustrations of this point can now be provided by a discussion of two further tables, both of which are constructed wholly from information contained in Table B.2.

Table B.3 shows the country shares of each item of commodity demand identified in Table B.2. The extent to which Jamaica and Trinidad dominate all five components of demand is very striking. Overall, they account for 75 percent of total Caribbean demand, with Guyana adding a further 9 percent and Barbados a further 7 percent. It is only in the case of CARICOM exports (column 1) that Trinidad usurps Jamaica's position with about 54 percent of the total; Jamaica's share of this component is only of the same order of magnitude as that of Guyana. This clearly illustrates the severe

TABLE B.3. SHARES OF DEMAND ELEMENTS BY CARICOM COUNTRY, 1972
(percentages of column totals)

Country	CARICOM *exports* *(1)*	*Other exports* *(2)*	*Private consumption* *(3)*	*Government consumption* *(4)*	*Investment* *(5)*	*Total demands* *(6)*
Jamaica	16.8	46.1	48.0	40.1	42.7	45.0
Trinidad	53.8	28.0	28.4	32.3	36.0	30.3
Guyana	16.0	11.8	7.5	10.4	6.4	8.8
Barbados	9.4	10.0	6.3	9.0	5.3	7.4
St. Lucia	1.2	0.9	1.7	1.2	2.4	1.6
St. Vincent	0.7	0.4	0.9	1.1	1.0	0.8
Montserrat	...	0.1	0.3	0.3	0.2	0.2
Grenada	0.3	0.9	1.4	1.5	1.2	1.2
Dominica	0.5	0.6	0.9	1.0	0.8	0.8
St. Kitts, Nevis, and Anguilla	...	0.5	0.7	0.8	1.0	0.7
Antigua	0.5	1.1	1.4	1.2	0.7	1.2
Belize	0.8	1.6	2.4	1.3	2.4	2.1
Total[a]	100.0	100.0	100.0	100.0	100.0	100.0

... Zero or negligible.
a. Totals may not add to 100.0 because of rounding.
Note: See text discussion.

disadvantage which Jamaica faces in intra-CARICOM trade by virtue of her geographical location.

Similar comparisons are set out in Table B.4, but this time for certain selected rows of Table B.2, so as to show countries' percentage shares in row totals. The last column of Table B.4 shows that the four MDCs account for approximately 93 percent of total Caribbean production (value added). Comparison of columns 3 and 6 shows that the LDCs share of consumption goods from the rest of the world is inevitably greater than their share of production, while the opposite is true for the MDCs. The shares of duties paid by the LDCs are also significantly higher than their shares of production, which is indicative of their high dependence on imports, and especially imports of consumption goods, which generally bear the higher tariffs. But the most striking feature of Table B.4 is the large discrepancy between the shares of CARICOM imports of the LDCs and their shares of total production; the former being considerably in excess of the latter in all cases (as can be seen by comparing columns 1 and 6). Similar discrepancies apply in the cases of Guyana and Barbados. Jamaica and Trindad are the only countries where this discrepancy is reversed.

These are only a few examples of the many structural features of the economy of the region which are reflected even in this highly aggregated version of a regional data system. Experience with the model suggests three main conclusions concerning the form of the system. First, although the scheme defined above is extremely simple, it does provide a useful definition of the structure of the Caribbean economy, its internal interactions, and several of its latent problems. It also provides the basis for initial experiments in modeling and economic forecasting for the region. Second, although the numbers are admittedly crude, experience in putting them together has indicated that it should be possible for a relatively short-term research effort to complete most cells of the basic matrix presented in this Appendix to tolerable degrees of accuracy. Third, the arrangement of these data in the format of Table B.2 is far more illuminating than that which is conventionally applied.

The present state of statistics in the region

At first sight, the current state of regional statistics is somewhat discouraging, since only two of the twelve members of CARICOM (Guyana and Jamaica) have in fact published any official national accounts data for recent years. The eight LDCs have never produced any official national accounts data, Barbados ceased to do so in 1966, while the last official published estimates for Trinidad relate to 1962. The only reasonably up-to-date economic statistics which are available for all CARICOM members are therefore the trade statistics. To this source should be added statistics on government expenditures and revenues, preliminary figures on employment and population from the 1970 population census, and certain monetary statistics. Taking the picture for CARICOM as a whole, however, the degree of statistical development is poor.

TABLE B.4. SHARES OF SUPPLY ELEMENTS BY CARICOM COUNTRY, 1972
(percentages of column totals)

Country	CARICOM *imports* *(1)*	*Indirect taxes* *(2)*	*Consumption goods, imports from rest of world* *(3)*	*Investment goods, imports from rest of world* *(4)*	*Intermediate imports from rest of world* *(5)*	*Domestic value-added* *(6)*
Jamaica	24.9	40.2	41.4	43.6	44.1	47.3
Trinidad	16.1	25.9	28.6	32.3	26.0	31.7
Guyana	18.3	11.1	7.7	12.1	8.5	8.0
Barbados	14.3	10.1	10.0	4.9	14.6	5.8
St. Lucia	5.8	2.3	2.1	1.9	1.3	1.2
St. Vincent	4.0	1.4	1.3	0.9	0.4	0.6
Montserrat	0.8	0.4	0.3	0.2	0.2	0.2
Grenada	4.7	2.0	1.6	0.7	0.9	1.1
Dominica	2.6	1.4	1.2	0.8	0.6	0.6
St. Kitts, Nevis, and Anguilla	2.2	1.3	1.1	0.6	0.7	0.5
Antigua	3.2	1.7	1.7	0.8	1.8	0.9
Belize	3.0	2.3	2.9	1.3	1.1	2.1
Total[a]	100.0	100.0	100.0	100.0	100.0	100.0

a. Totals may not add to 100.0 because of rounding.
Note: See text discussion.

Despite this picture of statistical underdevelopment, a number of encouraging considerations should be borne in mind in developing a framework for a regional statistical system. These include the following seven points:

First, although Trinidad has published no national accounts since 1962, there is a preliminary report on work that has been going on for several years in the National Accounts Division of the Ministry of Planning, and now in the Central Statistical Office, to compile a new series. Preliminary results from this work suggest that the new series will incorporate a great deal of detail not normally available in developing countries, notably on the cost and import structures of different categories of goods, and on the institutional recipients of particular factor payments.

Second, after many years during which the statistical deficiencies of the LDCS have been addressed in a partial fashion, proposals to deal with these deficiencies more systematically now seem to be gaining momentum. The CARICOM Secretariat, with the assistance of the United Nations Development Program (UNDP), is helping develop a regional statistical system. The Eastern Caribbean Common Market (ECCM) Secretariat, also with UNDP support, has inaugurated a new program of technical assistance and support for statistics in that area.[2] The program entails data collection services which would meet many of the requirements of the data framework described earlier. The program is therefore incorporated in the recommendations for the ways in which further statistical work in the area should be organized, set out later in this Appendix.

Third, despite the absence of up-to-date national accounting information in Barbados, it is planned to take up this work anew.

Fourth, although the poor national accounting information for the area is reflected in even more incomplete input-output data, steps have already been taken to improve this situation in at least two countries. The work in Trinidad mentioned above readily lends itself to the compilation of conventional or modified input-output information. In addition, the Ministry of Economic Development in Guyana has prepared input-output information for use in the (1977–82) Development Plan.

Fifth, the Eastern Caribbean Currency Authority (ECCA) is strengthening its work on balance of payments information for the area. Since even the most aggregative system of data requires far more comprehensive data of this type, this is a welcome development.

Sixth, the Caribbean Community Secretariat has now published a Digest of Regional Trade Statistics. It is hoped that the Digest will be expanded gradually to encompass a wider range of statistics.

Finally, the financial data available for the region is currently being brought together in a useful way in two countries (Trinidad and Jamaica), by a fairly comprehensive program of work on flow of funds accounts. This

2. ECCM Secretariat, "Interim Proposals for Technical Assistance and Financial Support for Statistics in the ECCM," (Antigua, 1975).

provides a useful basis for beginning to quantify the capital-flow component of Caribbean interdependence, especially if a separate CARICOM account is identified in the eventual system.

To summarize, therefore, the twelve countries of the region have a generally poor level of statistical development and their progress towards improvement of their statistical systems is uneven. At the same time, a number of promising initiatives are contributing to a coordinated statistical program for the region. The data system shown in its most aggregated form in Table B.2 has been suggested as a basis for this coordination; the next section examines what this might entail in greater detail.

Priorities for Statistical Development

The previous section described the wide variations in the state of statistical evolution among the CARICOM member countries. The extent of these variations suggests that priorities for future statistical development must be considered separately for the MDCs and the LDCs, since the two groups will be starting from very different levels. Before considering separate priorities in this way, however, a number of more general points must be discussed.

The United Nations System of National Accounts (SNA) has been criticized since its inception in 1968 as inappropriate for developing countries. The principal objection has been that the system is too complex to be implemented, given the circumstances of the typical developing country. Without going into the debate it is, nevertheless, the case that some of the approaches suggested in the SNA guidelines have proved to be successful and to be of much practical merit. For example, the SNA gives the highest priority to the execution of a set of commodity balances for the economy (matching commodity supplies and demands), to which most other accounting variables are geared. Previous experience, particularly with systems for Sri Lanka[3] and Swaziland, has shown that this is a useful and practical approach; this conclusion is confirmed by the experience of the Statistical Office in Malaysia, where an advanced system is being implemented.

A commodity balance approach forms the core of the data system shown in Table B.2, and should ideally form the core of any integrated statistical effort within CARICOM. It is clear, however, that there is potentially much more to a regional statistical information framework than a set of commodity balances. In this section, a much more comprehensive scheme is therefore presented, and issues such as appropriate disaggregations are discussed. The purpose of this analysis is not to put forward a system which is capable of implementation in the near future or even in the medium term, but to define a structure which can be of assistance in identifying, and discussing, priorities for improvement.

3. See Graham Pyatt, Alan R. Roe, and others, *Social Accounting for Development Planning with Special Reference to Sri Lanka* (Cambridge University Press, 1977).

One version of a comprehensive regional data framework is set out in Table B.5. It is purposely a general system and so it can accommodate a range of requirements of varying complexity. The system described has been compared with a number of alternatives and has emerged as being one of the more tractable amongst them, bearing in mind the state of the current statistical base.

It is also worth re-emphasizing that the framework is concerned with macroeconomic accounting, and therefore has as its antecedent the United Nations SNA. Many socioeconomic tabulations and data series are not embodied within a macroeconomic framework, however, but nevertheless ought to be consistent with it. Examples are manpower statistics, or even population and age cohort series, neither of which formally fits into a macroeconomic framework.

The broad structure of the regional statistical framework can perhaps best be discussed in terms of nine classes of account: factor accounts; institutions' current accounts (private sector); institutions' current accounts (government and public corporations); institutions' capital accounts (private sector); institutions' capital accounts (government and public corporations); production accounts (commodities); production accounts (activities); rest of world accounts (current); and rest of world accounts (capital).

These basic accounts are fairly easily identifiable with the accounting structure of international systems such as the SNA, in which accounts are separately determined for production, income and outlay, and external transactions, with distinctions usually being made between current and capital transactions, and between public and private sectors. In the accounts listed above, a clear distinction has been made between factor accounts, which receive value added from domestic production activities together with net factor income from abroad, and institutions' income and outlay (current) accounts, which serve in the first instance as recipients of this factor income. This procedure has the advantage of distinguishing between the factoral and the institutional distributions of income.

The way in which the money transactions and transfers between the systems of accounts occur, is shown schematically in Table B.5. As in Table B.2, the preferred presentation is in terms of a matrix, whose rows show receipts and whose columns show outgoings. Thus, for example, the cell connecting the first row for factor accounts, and the seventh column for production activity accounts, shows value added both as an incoming to factor accounts and as an outgoing from production activity accounts. In this way, the framework portrayed by the matrix in Table B.5 identifies the interrelation of the system of nine accounts specified above. Only row totals are shown in the table, although there are also totals for the columns, which, because of accounting balance, must exactly match the corresponding row totals. Again, taking the factor accounts as an example, total factor incomes comprise domestic factor income plus net factor income from abroad. This total factor income is then shown as being "paid out" to institutions' current accounts in column 1. The total must match, by the convention of accounting balance, the total factor income generated either domestically or abroad.

TABLE B.5. A SYSTEM OF REGIONAL ACCOUNTS

Category		Factor account (1)	*Institution current account* Private (2)	Public (3)	*Institution capital account* Private (4)	Public (5)
Factor account	(1)					
Institution current account						
Private	(2)	Receipts of factor incomes by private institutions	Current transfers between institutions (taxes, dividend payments, and so on)			
Public	(3)	Receipts of factor incomes by public institutions				
Institution capital account						
Private	(4)		Private savings		Capital transfers between institutions	
Public	(5)			Public savings		
Production account						
Commodity	(6)		Institutions requirements of goods and services			
Activity	(7)					
Rest of world account						
Current	(8)					
Capital	(9)					

Note: See text discussion.

Production account		*Rest of world account*		
Commodity (6)	*Activity (7)*	*Current (8)*	*Capital (9)*	*Total (10)*
	Value added in production	Net factor incomes from rest of world		Total factor incomes
		Net nonfactor incomes from rest of world		Total private sector receipts
	Indirect taxes on production plus all import duties	Net nonfactor incomes from rest of world		Total public sector receipts
			Net capital transfer from rest of world	Total capital inflows
Commodity trade within CARICOM	Intermediate commodity requirements	Exports to rest of world		Total commodity requirements
Supplies of commodities from CARICOM activities				Total CARICOM outputs
Imports from rest of world				Total from rest of world
		Current balance of payments deficits		Current balance of payments deficits

The cell entries in this double entry accounting system are largely self-explanatory. The familiar macroeconomic aggregates are also identifiable from the table: gross national product (GNP) equals total factor incomes, while gross domestic product (GDP) is shown as the total value added in domestic production. It is particularly important, however, to note the emphasis given within these broad classes of accounts to certain disaggregations, and the ways in which Table B.5 is related to an accounting system which explicitly recognizes intraregional transactions. As will shortly be seen, these questions are not independent. The former will, however, be examined first.

The distinction drawn between commodity and production activity accounts is designed simply to effect a set of commodity balances in the spirit of the United Nations SNA. By so doing, producing units can be distinguished from the commodities which they produce, so that producing units may also be classified according to other criteria such as type of ownership or scale of operation. In effect, the nine accounts shown in Table B.5 are really "sets" of accounts, and embody many potential disaggregations within them. Factors, for example, may be disaggregated according to types of labor (location, skill, employment status, and so on) or of capital. Institutions, first disaggregated by household, companies, and government, may be further disaggregated in several ways. Separate accounts can be identified for households with varying income levels or other distinguishing socioeconomic characteristics. The nature of ownership can serve to disaggregate company accounts, while government accounts may be broken down according to the organizational structure of government.

Turning to the question of regional linkage, the framework shown in Table B.5 could, with only minor modifications, represent the accounts of any one of the twelve member countries of CARICOM. Since the framework is intended to represent a regional accounting system, a further fundamental disaggregation implicit within the accounts shown in the table is one by a member country. Leaving aside the potential disaggregations referred to in the previous paragraph, the regional disaggregations of nine broad classes of accounts is not hard to visualize.

The accounts of each member country can be arranged so that all the accounts of one type (for example, factor accounts, or commodity accounts) are placed adjacent to one another, thus forming a twelve row and twelve column disaggregation of that set of accounts in the table. This could be illustrated by dividing the first row and column of factor accounts in Table B.5 into twelve separate rows and columns. The result is that for any one member country's accounts the original destination of the transactions can be determined both by sector and by country.

At first sight, this suggestion seems likely to lead to an enormous table and a very large data requirement involving nine rows and columns as, for example, shown in Table B.5. This is not in fact the case, however, since most of the twelve-by-twelve matrices created by country disaggregation (comprising the cells of Table B.5), would be heavily diagonal, implying that *inter*country transactions are small or nonexistent. For example, all the savings entries in Table B.5 (elements 4.2 and 5.3) are merely transfers from the current account of an institution in each country to that same institution's capital account in the same country. No intraregional transfers are involved.[4]

In the extreme case where no interconnections of any sort exist between the group of countries, all nonzero cells of Table B.5 would appear as diagonal matrices when disaggregated by country. It follows that the degree of integration is indicated by the degree of nondiagonality of the various cells (submatrices) of the table. The most important example of interaction between member countries represented in the table in this way is, of course, commodity trade. Other important examples are current transfers, capital transfers, and factor payments. These are ignored for the moment, however, principally because such interactions are very hard to identify from available data, and in any case are probably slight. Commodity trade between member countries has already been covered in the simple system of regional accounts shown in Tables B.1 and B.2, but it is noteworthy that such a trade matrix would also be represented in this full regional accounting system at the intersection of the row and column for the commodity accounts. The system has been especially designed to accommodate commodity balances within a regional framework in such a way as to minimize complexity on the one hand and to maximize the possibility of effective data gathering on the other. In particular, this system distinguishes region of origin and region of destination in the commodity balances only in this one trade matrix; this is a significant simplification compared with many alternatives that are available.[5]

Table B.5 in a reasonably disaggregated form can be viewed as an objective of statistical development for the CARICOM region. In due course, with greater regional integration and with more sophisticated and better coordinated data collecting facilities, a framework such as the one briefly outlined in this section can monitor economic development very effectively. Greater integration in terms of commodity trade, or current and capital financial transfers, will be directly reflected in the regional accounts. In the early stages of statistical development, it is unrealistic to suppose that more than a small amount of data on interrelationships between countries will become available, apart from statistics for commodity trade. An intermediate situation would require information relating in a summary way the position of one country in relation to the rest of CARICOM and the rest of the world for items such as capital or current transfer payments, or flows of factor

4. To the extent that inter-country capital transfers do occur, they are shown in the capital transfers cell of Table B.5.

5. The obvious alternative is to show trade in each commodity by both country of origin and the use to which this is put in each country of destination. While this has analytical advantages over what is proposed here, it places impossibly heavy demands on data. For example, if the system has 10 commodities, then the trade matrix in Table B.5 has 120 rows and 120 columns, although of course, the structure would necessitate a large number of zero entries. If, on the other hand, a separate trade matrix is identified for each final and intermediate demand category then there would be many more entries that would need to be determined.

incomes. Even this situation can be easily accommodated within the framework of Table B.5. Its advantages are manifested by the relatively few cells where intraregional flows and transfers have to be recorded. The statistical developments already under consideration and outlined earlier in this Appendix can be incorporated as and when they become effective, without destroying the consistency of the system as a whole. Indeed, statistical evolution can largely be viewed as a disaggregation of a system which is already capable of being compiled in aggregate form, albeit with large errors, for all twelve CARICOM countries. An increasing degree of disaggregation will improve both the analytical value of the system and the accuracy with which aggregative concepts can be estimated.

Some Priorities for Future Work

In the light of the relatively poor state of macroeconomic statistics within a substantial part of the CARICOM area, a sensible strategy for statistical development at the regional level is to work quickly towards a degree of cross-country comparability in relation to a minimum list of economic variables. These might include, for example, those identified in Table B.1. At a second stage, that list might be extended through a program of statistical development agreed among member countries. The data framework discussed in the previous section is so arranged that this second stage, in effect, involves the disaggregation of totals which are capable of estimation, at least tentatively, during the first stage. Thus, differential rates of statistical development in different countries need not destroy intercountry comparability since this could always be restored by appropriate re-aggregation. A strategy of this type has substantially different implications for the LDCs on the one hand, and the MDCs on the other, and in this section some of the potential implications are examined.

The position of the LDCS

Data bases are generally poor in the LDCs and their statistical organizations are normally limited to a handful of people. If a data system is to operate successfully in these countries, therefore, a minimum program for the collection and organization of basic statistics must be established. The ECCM is already mounting this minimum program and its efforts deserve strong support. The program is essential as a means of giving proper weight to the position of the LDCs in any quantitative analysis of the situation in the region, whether for planning or for other purposes.

It is clear, however, that the program of routine work and special projects which is incorporated in the ECCM proposal will of necessity only produce a reasonably complete macroeconomic picture over a period of several years. Given the need to have available at least some data on the overall macropicture relatively quickly, the ECCM program must be supplemented by some additional statistical work geared specifically to short-term analytical requirements. It is also extremely important that statistical development planning in the LDCs should, from the start, take place in the light of advice from those who need to use the additional data to be generated for analytical purposes; in this way, it should be possible to ensure that plans are relevant to priority needs.

The various proposals for LDC statistical development have a number of organizational implications. These would include the establishment of new statistical offices (or the expansion of those offices which already exist), and the possible establishment of a Regional Statistical Centre for the LDCs to obtain certain economies of scale in meeting some of their common statistical needs. This discussion will concentrate, however, on the existing data sources which might be used to produce tentative estimates of some parts of the proposed data system.

The six main sources of information currently available and which may be useful for compiling national accounts in most of the LDCs are: the Accountant General's annual statements which give the actual revenue and expenditure of the government; the overseas trade reports; the annual accounts and reports of the various agricultural associations; the income tax returns of individuals and companies; the pay-as-you-earn returns of employers; and other sources. Each will now be examined in turn.

The Accountant General's annual statements provide the first main source of information. These statements will indicate the major governmental components of GDP—personal emoluments, transport and subsistence allowances and rent, together with expenditures on goods and services. In the case of wages, the situation is normally somewhat more difficult, particularly for the Ministry of Agriculture and the Ministry of Communication and Works. It may, therefore, be necessary to extract from the detailed vote books of these ministries the elements of wages and purchases from other sectors. The main items involved would be forest maintenance, afforestation, expansion of economic crops, experimental plots and plant nurseries, and maintenance and construction of roads, bridges, and buildings. This list is by no means exhaustive and it may be necessary to extract data from the vote books of other departments (the medical and education departments, for example), in cases where large sums are involved and there is doubt about the nature of the expenditure. It will also be necessary to examine carefully the statements of advances and deposits to separate out those items which include factor payments or are of a capital nature. There are several instances where capital expenditure is financed from advances. The Crown Agents and the intergovernmental accounts usually indicate the main receipts and payments to and from the United Kingdom and the CARICOM countries. The revenue sides of the statements are extremely detailed; if they are read in conjunction with the overseas trade report, it is not very difficult to allocate receipts in respect of imported goods, for example, import duties and consumption taxes. The other receipts can be allocated fairly accurately on the basis of the description of the tax or fee.

The overseas trade reports provide a second source of information. Using the current United Nations SNA, together with the previous edition formulated in 1952, it is possible to obtain many of the data required for estimating expenditure on consumption, intermediate, and capital goods from the overseas trade report. This source will also provide information on sales to the rest of the world in respect of agricultural, manufactured and other commodities.

Third, there are the annual accounts and reports of the agricultural associations for bananas, cocoa, nutmegs, arrowroot, citrus, and so on. These indicate the sales of the agricultural export crops and payments to farmers, in addition to the expenses of these associations for activities such as purchasing, grading, or selling these commodities. There is invariably a discrepancy between the sales recorded by these associations and those recorded in the overseas trade report. In such instances, it is desirable to use the associations' figures for sales since they are considered to be more accurate.

Fourth, the income tax returns of individuals and companies provide valuable data for estimating the output and cost structure of the productive sectors in the absence of surveys of establishments. These sources will not provide a complete picture of total productive activities, however, and it will be necessary to turn to others for supplementary information or for indicators which can be used to estimate the output and cost structure of the sectors.

Fifth, the pay-as-you-earn returns will supplement the information obtained from the income tax returns, for example, in cases where returns have not been made by employers or where the returns submitted do not supply sufficient data on wages and salaries paid. In any event, this information can be used to cross-check the data on wages and salaries obtained from the income tax returns already mentioned, or that supplied in respect of the National Provident Fund.

Finally, there are other sources which may be utilized. The three sectors which present the greatest difficulty in terms of estimating output are domestic agriculture, services, and transport. The Ministry of Agriculture will usually have information for some of the principal crops and for fishing, but data on the minor crops, such as vegetables, breadfruits, mangoes, and so on, will rarely be available, and it will be necessary to make informed guesses with the help of officials in the ministry. With respect to services, the Labor Department, the Inland Revenue Department, and the Registrar General's Department can usually give an estimate of the number of persons involved in activities such as domestic service, construction, medicine, and the law. Wage rates collected by the Labor Department can be useful not only for estimating wages in the services sector, but also in the construction sector. Expenditure by tourists in hotels can be estimated either by using income tax returns or the hotel occupancy tax. In the absence of a survey of tourism, however, an estimate must be made of tourists' expenditure outside their hotels. The number and category of motor vehicles registered can be easily obtained from the appropriate government department, but in most cases it will be necessary to estimate the output and cost structures of the transport sector, using the advice of officials in the Inland Revenue Department.

Careful use of the sources and methods listed above should be able to produce reasonable orders of magnitude in respect of many of the items in a basic accounts system, and to provide a basis for a minimum degree of disaggregation. Naturally, as firm figures became available from the program of survey work, they could replace the preliminary estimates; at the same time, the survey program itself should be informed by the knowledge about data inadequacies generated by the rough and ready exercises. This approach to statistical development would help to ensure that adequate information was available for planning and, in the meantime, would provide a body of approximate data against which to test modeling techniques.

The priorities for the MDCS

Three of the four MDCS—Trinidad, Jamaica, and Guyana—are sufficiently advanced statistically to have broad aggregative national accounting systems which can be derived from existing published or otherwise available data. Three specific points of difficulty, however, need to be examined and dealt with.

First, although all four MDCS already produce summaries of import data according to economic function for consumption, investment, or intermediate purposes, in some cases these are disaggregated further. There is no agreement on a standardized definition of these categorized items. An agreement will be necessary, since the distinction is a fairly basic one from the planning viewpoint. Similarly, although this functional classification is carried out for all imports, it is not carried out separately for imports from CARICOM. This must be done by all four countries since the classification is important in explaining the evolution of the CARICOM trading structure. If, in the shorter term, resources do not permit country-by-country functional classification of imports from CARIFTA, then thought might be given in the four countries to providing standardized summaries of CARICOM trade in their annual overseas trade reports. At present, Barbados produces a summary using a two digit commodity classification, Trinidad uses a three digit commodity classification, and Jamaica and Guyana produce no summaries of CARICOM trade on an annual basis. A summary using the Trinidad three digit classification would permit researchers to produce the aggregations needed for planning purposes, assuming that the statistical offices themselves did not have the resources to do this.

Second, the balance of payments data currently available in the four countries do not permit the separation of CARICOM from non-CARICOM items, in respect of flows other than traded goods and services. It is not clear whether it would be possible to make this distinction on the basis of existing documentation of foreign payments and receipts. If an effort to make it were to be conducted in the MDCS, however, it would supply information which would be useful when balances of payments data systems are set up in the LDCS.

Finally, it is clearly important to try to link the import structure (however aggregated or detailed this may be) with the duties paid (or payable), on each separate import category. This is rather difficult to do in respect of duties actually paid, but in some cases the existing documentation and computer listings of the trade data might permit some linking of relatively detailed import data with the duties payable in respect of the imports. If summaries of imports at the three digit level could be linked with the duties payable on them, the accuracy of any work conducted on the effects of tariff policy in the region would be greatly improved.

Turning to the question of disaggregation, Trinidad is clearly already in a position to supply much of the data required, by even the fullest disaggregation of the data system suggested earlier. The major exception is in the disaggregation of the household sector, especially by income. Even here, Trinidad does have recent household budget survey data which might possibly be capable of integration with her new national accounts system, despite the inconsistencies which will inevitably exist because of the deficiencies of survey information of this type (under-recording of income, for example). It would be desirable to attempt this integration and then to conduct some analytical work to demonstrate the usefulness of the detail the system provides.

Efforts are currently being made to recast the Jamaican national accounts. Although adoption of Trinidad's system is unlikely, some degree of consistency between the two would be desirable. The same point applies to the proposed work in Guyana on input-output data. It would be especially advantageous if both Guyana and Jamaica were to draw on the advice and collaboration of those responsible for the Trinidadian work wherever possible, incorporate similar classifications and disaggregations, and distinguish CARICOM commodity sales and purchases from those destined to and originating from the rest of the world.

The position of Barbados is rather different in that work on national accounts is only now recommencing after a lapse of several years. While it is felt that calculation of broad aggregates must take priority in this work, the importance of obtaining commodity detail which is useful for analytical purposes should also be stressed. Calculating national accounts aggregates will inevitably involve considerable commodity detail; the needs of regional planning and the desirability of developing intraregional comparisons ought to be borne in mind in organizing the calculations and disseminating the results.

Conclusions

The philosophy underlying this Appendix is that the development of a system of statistics which documents the progress of CARICOM's integration can itself contribute usefully to the integration process, by helping analyze problems and formulate appropriate regional policies. Such a system should be geared to an agreed framework which should be general enough to encompass all the main issues, and flexible enough to be able to take account of the wide variations in statistical capabilities among countries.

Attempts to assemble data for the whole of CARICOM into a consistent macroeconomic framework show that the task is possible, provided one works with reasonably aggregative data, and that the framework can be of great value in illustrating the nature of the interactions between member countries. At this stage it is perhaps an act of faith to argue that Table B.2 can be produced on a reasonably disaggregated basis. Nevertheless, since the statistical base will improve in most of the twelve member countries independently of what happens on the integration front, the cost of accepting the proposals made in this Appendix would appear to be a marginal re-ordering of national priorities for statistical development, and the acceptance of a degree of standardization of concepts and definitions. Provided that these small costs can be accepted, the task of a central research team in compiling a disaggregated version of Table B.5, in whatever detail considered appropriate at the time, would be quite straightforward.

The proposals in this Appendix have more serious implications for the LDCs, where statistical developments are beginning more or less from scratch, than they have for the already reasonably developed statistical services of the MDCs. It is significant to note in this context that the ECCM subgrouping of CARICOM has clearly accepted the principle of an intergrated approach to statistics. While the data to emerge from the ECCM effort can eventually be expected to meet the needs of the framework proposed here, it is important that the priorities for statistical development should be kept constantly in view by an ongoing, albeit modest program of analysis, based on the regular quantification of a comprehensive framework of the kind identified in this discussion. In this way the gaps in the data can be regularly re-evaluated; at the same time analysis based on the data can evolve, and can interact with, and further improve the statistical program itself. Any regional statistical research unit established to coordinate the statistical developments in ECCM with the requirements of analytical work could discharge a similar, but rather more modest, role in relation to the MDCs. The central purpose here would be to organize the assembly of the already existing data into a common format and to press for greater consistency in concepts, definitions, and coverage of data.

This Appendix has put forward an approach to statistical development in CARICOM which recognizes the different capabilities of different countries, does not require any fundamental revamping of existing statistical arrangements beyond those already in process of development, and does not envisage any grandiose proliferation of data. In particular, the approach to trade flows implicit in Table B.5 demands less in the way of data collection than any of the alternative systems considered, but still retains considerable analytical merit. It is inevitable that trade flow matrices will be central to any quantitative discussion of CARICOM interactions for several years to come. An attempt has also been made to include other crucial areas of interaction in the system outlined here—notably inter-country factor payments and capital transfers. While these remain relatively modest in size, their role in the overall system can be dealt with, using the approach presented here, by aggregation; any less comprehensive approach must inevitably omit them.

Statistical Appendix

Table SA1.1. Proportion of Total Population under 15 Years, 65 Years and above, and Dependency Ratio, 1960 and 1970

Territory	Proportion under 15 years		Proportion 65 years and over		Dependency ratio (per 100)	
	1960	1970	1960	1970	1960	1970
Jamaica	41.2	46.1	4.3	5.5	83	107
Trinidad and Tobago	42.4	42.1	4.1	4.4	87	87
Guyana	46.3	47.1	3.4	3.6	98	103
Barbados	38.3	37.1	6.4	8.3	81	84
Windward islands						
St. Lucia	44.3	49.6	4.8	5.3	96	122
Grenada	47.7	47.1	5.2	5.9	112	113
St. Vincent	49.2	51.2	4.2	4.8	115	127
Dominica	44.7	49.1	5.5	5.9	101	122
Leeward islands						
Antigua	42.8	-	4.5	-	90	-
St. Kitts	45.7	-	5.0	-	103	-
Montserrat	42.7	39.8	8.2	9.9	104	99
Belize	44.6	49.3	4.2	4.3	95	116
All countries	44.3	46.4	3.5	4.4	92	103

Table SA1.2. Population Trends, 1911–70

Country	1911	1921	1946	1960	1970
Jamaica	831,383	858,118	1,237,063 /1	1,609,800	1,854,302
Trinidad and Tobago	333,552	365,913	557,970	828,000	931,071
Guyana	296,041	297,691	369,678	560,400	699,848
Barbados	172,337	156,774	192,800	232,300	235,229
MDCs				3,230,500	3,720,450
Windward islands					
St. Lucia	48,637	51,505	70,113	86,100	99,806
Grenada	66,750	66,302	72,387	88,700	92,775
St. Vincent	41,877	44,447	61,647	79,900	86,314
Dominica	33,863	37,059	47,624	59,000	69,549
Leeward islands					
Antigua	32,269	29,767	41,757	54,060	65,000
St. Kitts	43,303	38,214	46,243	50,900	44,885 /3
Montserrat	12,196	12,120	14,333	12,200	11,458
Belize	40,458	45,317	59,220	90,100	119,934
LDCs				520,960	589,721
All countries	1,952,606	2,003,227	2,770,835	3,751,460	4,310,171

/1 For 1943

/2 Provisional 1970, census estimates

/3 For St. Kitts-Nevis; figures for other years include the population of Anguilla. The estimated population of St. Kitts-Nevis alone for 1960 is 50,000.

Table SA1.3. Intercensal Population Growth Rate, 1911-21 to 1960-70

Country	1911-1921	1921-1946	1946-1960	1960-1970	1911-1970
Jamaica	+ 0.3	+ 1.6/1	+ 1.6/1	+ 1.4	+ 1.4
Trinidad and Tobago	+ 0.9	+ 1.7	+ 2.8	+ 1.3	+ 1.8
Guyana	+ 0.1	+ 0.9	+ 2.9	+ 2.3	+ 1.5
Barbados	- 0.9	+ 0.8	+ 1.3	+ 0.2	+ 0.5
Windward islands					
St. Lucia	+ 0.6	+ 1.2	+ 1.5	+ 1.5	+ 1.2
Grenada	- 0.1	+ 0.4	+ 1.5	+ 0.4	+ 0.6
St. Vincent	+ 0.6	+ 1.3	+ 1.9	+ 0.8	+ 1.2
Dominica	+ 0.9	+ 1.0	+ 1.7	+ 1.5	+ 1.2
Leeward islands					
Antigua	- 0.8	+ 1.4	+ 1.9	+ 1.9	+ 1.2
St. Kitts2/	- 1.2	+ 0.8	+ 1.5	- 0.8	-
Montserrat	- 0.1	+ 0.7	- 1.2	- 0.6	- 0.1
Belize	+ 1.1	+ 1.1	+ 3.1	+ 2.8	+ 1.8
All countries	+ 0.2	+ 1.3	+ 2.2	+ 1.4	+ 1.4

/1 For 1921-1943 and 1943-1960

/2 St. Kitts-Nevis-Anguilla up to 1960 and St. Kitts-Nevis for 1960-70.

Table SA1.4. Growth Rates by Age Group, 1960-70
(Percent per year)

Country	0-14 Years	15-24 Years	25-54 Years	55+	All ages
Jamaica	+ 2.6	+ 0.9	- 0.7	+ 3.2	+ 1.4
Trinidad and Tobago	+ 1.1	+ 2.4	+ 0.2	+ 2.1	+ 1.3
Guyana	+ 2.4	+ 3.7	+ 1.0	+ 2.2	+ 2.3
Barbados	- 0.2	+ 1.7	- 1.4	+ 2.2	+ 0.2
Windward islands					
St. Lucia	+ 2.6	+ 0.8	- 0.4	+ 2.2	+ 1.5
Grenada	+ 0.3	+ 2.0	- 0.9	+ 1.5	+ 0.4
St. Vincent	+ 1.2	+ 1.3	- 0.9	+ 2.0	+ 0.8
Dominica	+ 2.4	+ 1.7	- 0.5	+ 1.9	+ 1.5
Leeward islands					
Antigua					
St. Kitts					
Montserrat	- 0.6	+ 0.2	- 0.1	+ 1.3	- 0.6
Belize	+ 3.9	+ 3.5	+ 0.7	+ 1.2	+ 2.8
All countries	+ 2.0	+ 2.0	- 0.2	+ 2.7	+ 1.4

Table SA1.5. Components of Population Growth, 1946–60 and 1960–70

Country	Total growth		Natural increase		Net migration	
	1946-1960	1960-1970	1946-1960	1960-1970	1946-1960	1960-1970
	Average Annual Rate					
Jamaica	+ 1.6	+ 1.4	+ 2.3	+ 3.0	- 0.7	- 1.6
Trinidad and Tobago	+ 2.8	+ 1.3	+ 2.7	+ 2.7	+ 0.1	- 1.4
Guyana	+ 2.9	+ 2.3	+ 2.9	+ 3.1	+ 0.0	- 0.8
Barbados	+ 1.3	+ 0.2	+ 1.9	+ 1.8	- 0.6	- 1.6
Windward islands						
St. Lucia	+ 1.5	+ 1.5	+ 2.4	3.1	- 1.0	- 1.8
Grenada	+ 1.5	+ 0.4	+ 2.7	2.4	- 1.1	- 2.0
St. Vincent	1.9	+ 0.8	+ 2.9	2.9	- 1.0	- 2.3
Dominica	1.6	+ 1.5	+ 2.4	2.9	- 0.9	- 1.5
Leeward islands						
Antigua	+ 1.9	+ 1.9	2.3	-	- 0.5	-
St. Kitts	+ 1.5	- 0.8	2.4	-	- 1.2	-
Montserrat	- 1.2	- 0.6	1.3	-	- 2.2	-
Belize	+ 3.1	+ 2.8	3.1	+ 3.3	- 0.1	- 0.5
All countries	+ 2.2	+ 1.4	2.7	2.8	- 0.6	- 1.5

Table SA1.6. Crude Birth Rate and Gross Reproductive Rate, 1946, 1960, 1965, and 1970

Country	Birth Rate				GRR	
	1946	1960	1965	1970	1960	1970
Jamaica	30.6	42.1	40.6	34.5	2.77	2.71
Trinidad and Tobago	38.4	39.7	32.8	26.5	2.65	1.81
Guyana	35.0	41.6	39.0	33.9	3.04	2.45
Barbados	31.7	33.8	27.1	20.9	2.29	1.35
Windward islands						
St. Lucia	37.8	49.2	47.1	42.8/2	3.29	3.04
Grenada	32.7	45.3	32.7	29.8/2	3.22	2.40
St. Vincent	38.7	49.9	43.1	36.1/2	3.53	3.03
Dominica	36.2	46.9	43.7	39.3/2	3.31	3.20
Leeward islands						
Antigua	37.0	34.7	29.4	-	-	-
St. Kitts-Nevis	31.8	42.8	32.6	25.1	3.16	1.78
Montserrat	22.0	29.5	32.4	26.4	2.47	2.32
Belize	34.5	45.2	47.0	41.2/1	3.29	3.05
All countries	34.5	41.1	38.2	31.8	2.81	2.39

/1 For 1968

/2 For 1969

Table SA1.7. Crude Death Rate and Expectation of Life at Birth, 1960 and 1970

Country	Crude Death Rate		Life Expectancy: Males		Life Expectancy: Females	
	1960	1970	1960	1970	1960	1970
Jamaica	8.9	7.7	62.6	66.1	66.6	70.0
Trinidad and Tobago	8.0	7.4	62.2	67.2	66.3	70.3
Guyana	9.2	6.8	59.0	63.6	63.0	67.5
Barbados	9.1	8.7	62.7	65.9	67.4	70.9
Windward islands						
St Lucia	14.9	8.5	55.1	58.7	58.5	61.9
Grenada	11.6	8.9	60.1	64.2	65.6	69.6
St. Vincent	15.1	9.7 /1	58.5	62.4	59.7	63.2
Dominica	15.4	9.3	57.0	60.8	59.2	62.6
Leeward islands						
Antitua	10.0	--	60.5	64.5	64.3	68.0
St. Kitts	13.5	7.6	58.0	63.6	61.9	67.5
Montserrat	11.6	10.5	58.8	61.8	62.5	65.5
Belize	7.9	6.3 /1	58.0	63.6	61.9	67.5
All Countries	9.3	7.6	61.3	65.4	65.3	69.1

1/ For 1969

Table SA1.8. Estimated Future Population of Caribbean Countries, 1970–85

Country	1970	1975			1980			1985		
		Projection			Projection			Projection		
		I	II	III	I	II	III	I	II	III
Jamaica	1,854,300	2,124,368	2,036,247	1,977,500	2,448,128	2,251,590	2,120,564	2,827,952	2,511,548	2,300,611
Trinidad	931,071	1,035,555	992,308	970,684	1,153,766	1,062,450	1,016,793	1,281,134	1,152,078	1,068,608
Guyana	699,848	803,784	786,843	775,441	925,954	889,690	864,951	1,063,718	1,007,044	968,187
Barbados	235,229	248,939	237,893	229,601	266,374	242,652	224,850	286,250	253,114	220,698
St. Lucia	99,806	114,160	108,151	105,347	132,239	118,701	111,932	154,364	132,538	121,626
Grenada	92,775	104,755	98,800	95,823	121,294	107,981	101,324	141,195	119,875	109,215
St. Vincent	86,314	99,436	93,339	84,242	116,716	102,847	88,978	138,164	115,665	93,167
Dominica	69,549	79,975	76,900	73,824	93,277	86,251	79,224	109,626	98,202	86,778
Antigua /1	65,000/1	71,000	68,000	--	79,000	73,000	--	88,000	78,000	
St. Kitts	44,885	47,106	44,271	--	51,082	44,913	--	56,499	46,760	--
Montserrat	11,358	12,266	12,266	--	13,533	13,533	--	15,088	15,088	--
Belize	119,934	138,889	135,935	132,989	162,738	156,145	149,552	191,732	181,145	170,558
	4,310,069	4,880,233	4,690,953	4,569,788	5,564,101	5,149,753	4,889,614	6,353,722	5,711,057	5,279,296

ASSUMPTIONS INVOLVED IN THE PROJECTIONS

Country	Fertility (TFR)		Mortality (e_0^o)		Migration (annual 1970-1985)		
	1970	1985	1970	1985	I	II	III
Jamaica	5.535	4.063	68.0	71.0	0	-15,000	-25,000
Trinidad	3.710	2.708	68.7	71.7	0	- 8,000	-12,000
Guyana	5.010	3.600	65.5	69.5	0	- 3,000	- 5,000
Barbados	2.770	2.375	68.4	71.3	0	- 2,000	- 3,500
St. Lucia	6.215	4.755	60.3	64.8	0	- 1,000	- 1,500
Grenada	4.915	3,760	66.7	71.1	0	- 1,000	- 1,500
St. Vincent	6.200	4,743	62,8	67.3	0	- 1,000	- 2,000
Dominica Antigua	6.545	5.007	61.7	66.2	0	- 500	- 1,000
St. Kitts	3.635	2.781	63.6	68.1	0	- 500	--
Montserrat	4.755	3.637	63.6	68.1	0	0	--
Belize	6.245	4.777	65.5	70.0	0	- 500	- 1,000

1/ Approximate estimates.

Projections based on the following assumptions:

I = No migration during 1970-80
II = Net migration at a reduced rate compared with 1960-70
III = Net migration at more or less the same level as during 1960-70

Table SA1.9. Distribution of the Population of Caribbean Countries, by Age and Sex, 1970

Ages	Jamaica	Trinidad	Guyana	Barbados	St. Lucia	Grenada	St. Vincent	Dominica	St. Kitts	Montserrat	Belize
MALES											
0-14	429,656	196,621	165,735	43,768	24,989	21,934	22,390	17,204	10,863	2,285	29,861
14	21,412	11,630	9,208	2,860	1,186	1,336	1,198	869	639	126	1,502
15-19	80,677	51,195	39,509	12,829	4,634	5,131	4,424	3,235	2,393	541	6,276
20-24	60,194	39,856	27,711	9,875	2,935	3,212	2,727	2,269	1,070	460	4,091
25-34	88,980	51,801	35,599	10,532	3,794	3,482	2,984	2,515	1,089	464	5,878
35-44	76,036	40,228	29,485	8,835	3,259	3,114	2,600	2,271	1,266	343	4,999
45-54	67,023	37,085	22,653	9,086	3,238	2,639	2,256	2,166	2,596	386	3,648
55-64	55,623	24,726	15,993	8,664	2,339	2,287	1,938	1,759	1,644	465	2,887
65+	45,113	18,000	111,167	6,881	1,949	1,893	1,473	1,549	1,124	430	2,451
14+	495,058	274,521	191,325	69,562	23,334	23,094	19,600	16,633	11,945	3,215	31,732
All Ages	903,302	459,512	347,852	110,470	47,137	43,692	40,792	32,968	21,045	5,374	60,091
FEMALES											
0-14	425,156	195,092	164,011	43,422	24,538	21,787	21,813	16,914	10,991	2,270	29,307
14	21,604	11,785	9,261	2,910	1,215	1,376	1,187	852	670	129	1,491
15-19	85,969	53,350	39,874	12,879	4,960	5,287	4,677	3,563	2,404	535	6,289
20-24	68,262	41,682	28,924	9,567	3,839	3,543	3,239	2,599	1,188	433	4,164
25-34	97,926	55,131	37,627	12,121	4,929	4,277	3,990	3,210	1,492	437	5,865
35-44	85,814	43,337	30,541	12,034	4,487	4,102	3,644	2,881	1,787	444	5,029
45-54	72,642	35,924	21,995	11,626	3,752	3,498	3,046	2,719	1,932	567	3,578
55-64	58,214	23,703	15,087	10,502	2,840	3,049	2,396	2,143	2,003	591	2,920
65+	57,017	23,340	13,937	12,608	3,324	3,540	2,717	2,552	2,043	807	2,691
14+	547,448	288,252	197,246	84,247	29,346	28,672	24,896	20,519	13,519	3,943	32,027
All Ages	951,000	471,559	351,996	124,759	52,669	49,083	45,522	36,581	23,840	6,084	59,843

Table SA1.10. Estimated Population of Caribbean Countries by Age and Sex, 1980[1]

Ages	Jamaica	Trinidad and Tobago	Guyana	Barbados	St. Lucia	Grenada	St. Vincent	Dominica	St. Kitts	Montserrat/2	Belize
MALES											
0-14	475,486	184,874	185,206	36,015	27,546	21,933	23,662	19,938	7,698	2,494	35,382
14	30,974	13,543	11,966	2,845	1,867	1,489	1,585	1,220	743	165	2,218
15-19	147,932	69,936	58,869	14,977	8,705	8,088	8,003	5,850	3,928	813	10,374
20-24	111,138	58,317	48,258	13,730	6,331	7,081	6,470	4,765	3,373	680	8,030
25-34	115,432	78,286	58,872	18,684	5,294	6,356	5,051	4,393	2,471	976	8,993
35-44	73,676	43,601	28,998	8,206	1,994	1,919	1,331	1,649	321	449	4,778
45-54	67,225	34,836	25,216	7,825	2,243	2,249	1,709	1,755	841	322	4,282
55-64	54,763	29,877	19,167	7,635	2,557	2,130	1,763	1,767	1,289	334	3,082
65+	58,309	23,719	15,948	9,160	2,261	2,327	1,904	1,768	1,580	490	2,972
14+	659,449	352,117	267,293	83,063	31,252	31,640	27,816	23,165	14,543	4,229	44,728
All Ages	1,103,961	523,448	440,533	116,233	56,931	52,084	49,893	41,883	21,498	6,558	77,892
FEMALES											
0-14	468,938	182,563	180,821	35,260	26,869	21,569	22,639	19,457	7,631	2,459	34,273
14	30,916	13,620	11,760	2,781	1,795	1,423	1,556	1,238	707	156	2,177
15-19	148,135	70,080	58,229	14,821	8,371	7,791	7,821	5,763	3,787	775	10,209
20-24	113,903	59,420	48,833	14,005	6,353	7,161	6,196	4,454	3,508	701	8,001
25-34	132,453	83,625	63,094	18,480	6,765	6,686	5,813	5,049	2,507	949	9,518
35-44	77,992	47,235	33,228	9,517	3,385	2,646	2,404	2,371	679	425	5,141
45-54	73,466	37,885	27,601	10,487	3,585	3,221	2,763	2,378	1,337	422	4,541
55-64	61,847	30,224	19,578	9,970	3,152	2,998	2,519	2,321	1,634	511	3,180
65+	70,897	27,971	17,774	13,879	3,292	3,825	2,800	2,572	2,332	734	3,391
14+	709,607	370,059	280,097	93,940	36,696	35,751	31,871	26,148	16,491	4,672	46,157
All Ages	1,147,629	539,002	449,158	126,419	61,770	55,897	52,954	44,367	23,415	6,975	78,253

1/ Assuming a reduction in migration during 1970-1980.
2/ Assuming zero migration.

Table SA1.11. Population Growth in Caribbean Countries, 1960–70, by Age and Sex

Ages	Jamaica	Trinidad and Tobago	Guyana	Barbados	St. Lucia	Grenada	St. Vincent	Dominica	St. Kitts	Montserrat	Belize
							MALES				
0-14	97,040	20,272	34,822	- 519	-5,722	888	2,442	3,649	780	305	9,610
14											
15-19	12,305	11,765	14,104	2,426	501	-1,393	825	669	1,817	-111	2,475
20-24	3,361	7,736	7,033	2,041	- 102	4,621	24	281	1,291	146	733
25-34	- 3,531	2,109	2,206	- 248	- 423	- 441	- 642	- 328	380	99	276
35-44	- 4,815	4,449	3,107	-1,788	- 513	148	- 228	- 136	- 731	- 53	952
45-54	- 4,779	1,967	1,375	-1,669	198	- 268	- 97	- 45	- 549	- 73	165
55-64	13,702	4,908	2,609	1,925	566	484	545	376	539	129	582
65+	16,580	3,624	3,468	2,783	495	366	362	335	220	135	639
14+											
All Ages	129,863	47,932	68,724	4,951	6,444	3,032	3,231	4,801	3,747	- 33	15,432
							FEMALES				
0-14	95,264	20,390	35,696	-1,173	5,696	565	2,456	3,677	550	-338	9,189
14											
15-19	9,533	11,912	13,395	2,078	644	1,231	986	799	1,436	-125	2,321
20-24	225	8,530	7,445	586	249	36	- 90	108	307	19	610
25-34	-14,538	2,822	2,603	-2,836	- 535	-1,090	- 727	- 328	824		- 115
35-44	- 4,963	- 576	4,149	-2,223	- 106	- 63	- 130	- 121	- 61	-109	724
45-54	- 42	3,569	2,484	-1,300	293	- 304	42	51	- 260	-155	- 28
55-64	13,267	4,510	2,196	980	357	232	147	180	486	- 89	594
65+	15,879	4,025	2,826	1,839	656	459	451	466	175	16	702
14+										105	
All Ages	114,625	55,182	70,794	-2,049	7,254	1,066	3,135	4,832	3,457	-676	13,997

Table SA1.12. Population Growth in Caribbean Countries, 1970–80, by Age and Sex[1]

Age	Jamaica	Trinidad and Tobago	Guyana	Barbados	St. Lucia	Grenada	St. Vincent	Dominica	St. Kitts	Montserrat	Belize
MALES											
0-14	+ 45,830	-11,747	+19,471	- 7,753	+2,557	- 1	+1,272	+2,734	-3,165	+ 209	+ 5,521
14	+ 9,562	+ 2,480	+ 2,758	- 15	+ 681	+ 153	+ 387	+ 351	+ 104	+ 39	+ 716
15-19	+ 67,255	+18,741	+19,360	+ 2,148	+4,070	+2,957	+3,579	+2,615	+1,535	+ 272	+ 4,098
20-24	+ 50,944	+18,461	+20,547	+ 3,855	+3,396	+3,869	+3,743	+2,496	+2,303	+ 220	+ 3,939
25-34	+ 26,452	+26,485	+23,273	+ 8,152	+1,500	+2,874	+2,064	+1,878	+1,382	+ 512	- 3,115
35-44	- 2,360	+ 3,373	- 487	- 629	-1,265	-1,195	-1,269	- 622	- 945	+ 106	- 221
45-54	+ 202	- 2,249	+ 2,563	- 1,261	- 995	- 390	- 547	- 411	- 755	- 64	+ 634
55-64	- 860	+ 5,151	+ 3,174	- 1,029	+ 218	- 157	- 175	+ 8	- 355	- 131	+ 195
65+	+ 13,196	+ 5,719	+ 4,781	+ 2,279	+ 312	+ 434	+ 431	+ 219	+ 456	+ 60	+ 521
14+	+164,391	77,596	+75,968	+13,501	+7,918	+8,546	+8,216	+6,532	+2,598	+1,014	+12,996
All Ages	+200,659	+63,936	+92,681	+ 5,763	+9,794	+8,392	+9,101	+8,915	+ 453	+1,184	+17,801
FEMALES											
0-14	+ 43,782	-12,529	+16,810	- 8,162	+2,331	- 218	+ 826	+2,543	-3,360	+ 189	+ 4,966
14	+ 9,312	+ 2,195	2,499	- 129	+ 580	+ 47	+ 369	+ 386	+ 37	+ 27	+ 686
15-19	+ 62,166	+16,730	+18,355	+ 1,942	+3,411	+2,504	+3,144	+2,200	+1,383	+ 240	+ 3,920
20-24	+ 45,641	+17,738	+19,909	+ 4,438	+2,514	+3,618	+2,957	+1,855	+2,320	+ 268	+ 3,837
25-34	+ 34,526	+28,494	+25,467	+ 6,359	+1,836	+2,409	+1,823	+1,839	+1,015	+ 518	+ 3,653
35-44	- 7,822	+ 3,898	+ 2,687	- 2,517	-1,102	-1,456	-1,240	- 510	-1,108	- 19	+ 112
45-54	+ 824	+ 1,961	5,606	- 1,139	- 167	- 277	- 283	- 341	- 595	- 145	+ 963
55-64	+ 3,633	+ 6,521	4,491	- 532	+ 312	- 51	+ 123	+ 178	- 369	- 80	+ 260
65+	+ 13,880	+ 4,631	3,837	+ 1,271	- 32	+ 285	+ 83	+ 20	+ 289	- 73	+ 700
14+	+162,159	+81,807	-82,851	+ 9,693	+7,350	+7,079	+6,975	+5,629	+2,972	+ 729	+14,130
All Ages	+196,629	+67,443	+97,162	+ 1,660	+9,101	+6,814	+7,432	+7,786	- 425	+ 891	+18,410

1/ Assuming reduced migration during 1970-1980

Table SA1.13. Labor Force in Caribbean Countries, 1970 and 1970, by Sex

Country	Total 1960	Total 1970	Males 1960	Males 1970	Females 1960	Females 1970
Jamaica	651,354	586,767	399,308	386,702	252,046	200,065
Trinidad and Tobago	278,147	287,976	203,732	216,589	74,415	71,387
Guyana	174,730	183,744	134,828	147,689	39,902	36,055
Barbados	92,200	91,073	53,501	54,477	38,699	36,596
Windward islands	106,951	102,572	64,917	64,547	42,034	38,025
St. Lucia	31,372	28,988	20,001	18,652	11,371	10,336
Grenada	27,314	28,682	16,392	17,482	10,922	11,200
St. Vincent	24,856	23,731	15,196	15,203	9,660	8,528
Dominica	23,409	21,171	13,328	13,210	10,081	7,961
Leeward islands						
Antigua	18,212		11,467		6,745	
St. Kitts	19,616	13,053	11,773	8,064	7,843	4,989
Montserrat	4,332	3,988	2.439	2,554	1,893	1,434
Belize	27,006	32,753	22,123	26,816	4,883	5,937
All countries 1/	1,354,336	1,301,926	892,621	907,438	461,715	394,488

1/ Excluding Antigua.

Table SA1.14. Labor Force Participation Rates of Caribbean Countries, 1960 and 1970

Country	Total 1960	Total 1970	Males 1960	Males 1970	Females 1960	Females 1970
Jamaica	66.8	55.9	87.8	77.5	48.4	36.3
Trinidad and Tobago	56.1	51.0	83.3	78.6	29.6	24.7
Guyana	55.7	47.1	87.3	76.9	25.1	18.2
Barbados	62.2	59.1	84.1	78.2	45.7	43.4
St. Lucia	62.6	54.7	88.8	79.3	41.2	35.0
Grenada	56.3	55.1	79.2	75.2	39.2	38.8
St. Vincent	58.2	52.9	81.5	76.8	40.2	34.0
Dominica	67.8	56.6	87.0	78.8	52.5	38.6
St. Kitts	61.3	53.3	84.2	74.0	43.5	36.7
Montserrat	57.2	55.5	82.2	79.1	44.0	36.2
Belize	51.7	51.1	86.9	84.0	18.3	18.4
All countries 1/	61.5	53.4	86.1	77.9	39.6	30.9
STANDARDIZED PARTICIPATION RATES /2						
Jamaica	63.8	55.9	84.6	77.5	44.8	36.3
Trinidad and Tobago	54.6	51.0	81.2	78.6	29.4	24.7
Guyana	53.6	47.1	84.3	76.9	24.0	18.2
Barbados	60.0	59.1	79.5	78.2	44.0	43.4
St. Lucia	60.7	54.7	86.3	79.3	40.3	35.0
Grenada	54.6	55.1	75.8	75.2	37.4	38.8
St. Vincent	56.4	52.9	78.5	76.8	38.8	34.0
Dominica	66.0	56.6	84.1	78.8	51.2	38.6
Montserrat	61.1	55.5	82.5	79.1	47.8	36.2
Belize	51.1	51.1	84.6	84.0	18.1	18.4
All countries 1/	59.3	53.4	83.2	77.9	37.5	30.9

1/ Average excluding Antigua and St. Kitts.

2/ Undirect standardization method using 1970 pattern of participation rates.

Table SA1.15. Change in Labor Force Size, 1960–70 and 1970–80, Medium Projection*

Country	1960	1970	1980	1960-1970	1970-1980
Jamaica	651,354	586,767	764,284	-64,587	+177,517
Trinidad and Tobago	278,147	287,976	369,312	+ 9,829	+ 81,336
Guyana	174,730	183,744	270,422	+ 9,014	+ 86,678
Barbados	92,200	91,073	107,628	- 1,127	+ 16,555
St. Lucia	31,372	28,988	36,435	- 2,384	+ 7,447
Grenada	27,314	28,682	38,626	+ 1,368	+ 9,944
St. Vincent	24,856	23,731	32,617	- 1,125	+ 8,886
Dominica	23,409	21,171	28,825	- 2,238	+ 7,654
St. Kitts	19,616	13,053	17,338	- 6,563	+ 4,285
Montserrat	4,332	3,988	5,267	- 344	+ 1,279
Belize	27,006	32,753	46,482	+ 5,747	+ 13,729
All countries 1/	1,354,336	1,301,926	1,717,236	-52,410	+415,310

1/ Excluding Antigua.

* Assuming net migration at a reduced rate compared with 1960-1970, participation rates at 1970 level.

Table SA1.16. Labor Force Rates of Caribbean Countries by Age and Sex, 1970

(Percent)

Age	Jamaina	Trinidad and Tobago	Guyana	Barbados	St. Lucia	Grenada	St. Vincent	Dominica	St. Kitts	Monteserrat	Belize
							MALES				
14	04.79	16.53	12.44	10.57	10.15	04.59	06.42	06.76	07.9	10.87	26.27
15-19	60.04	56.74	57.05	60.32	69.05	51.20	66.57	66.46	56.7	74.68	70.44
20-24	89.53	91.90	91.60	94.86	93.83	94.61	92.34	95.64	95.2	94.56	95.06
25-29	93.06	96.20	95.54	95.27	94.98	96.74	95.28	95.90	94.6	95.59	97.08
30-34	93.58	96.95	95.80	96.26	95.19	96.14	95.93	95.81	93.4	95.31	97.10
35-39	93.66	96.99	95.81	96.27	96.48	96.60	94.98	96.05	95.2	93.75	97.73
40-44	93.05	96.57	95.23	96.50	94.08	95.60	94.85	95.14	94.4	93.99	96.36
45-49	92.54	95.30	94.19	96.00	94.03	93.98	93.82	94.20	94.4	93.08	96.70
50-54	89.94	92.45	90.39	94.02	89.09	90.45	90.07	92.07	91.2	86.87	94.79
55-59	87.02	86.72	83.38	89.02	87.00	87.74	84.94	87.38	87.5	83.27	90.96
60-64	77.12	70.22	61.44	76.13	76.13	79.39	74.61	77.48	79.3	70.79	85.99
65+	49.29	29.70	30.73	38.72	49.00	55.31	47.72	49.71	49.2	53.02	59.20
All Ages	77.54	78.63	76.86	78.25	79.31	75.16	76.83	78.77	74.0	79.14	84.06
							FEMALES				
14	02.03	04.78	03.21	07.26	03.85	02.28	03.27	03.05	02.8	04.22	04.78
15-19	34.58	22.17	16.96	42.40	41.01	33.21	37.29	43.87	36.8	52.90	21.47
20-24	55.38	38.11	26.14	68.10	50.43	58.96	45.45	57.98	60.4	64.90	29.95
25-29	50.19	31.22	20.19	60.66	41.31	51.80	42.86	45.87	52.8	55.88	20.59
30-34	45.32	27.27	18.41	56.42	38.98	49.04	40.93	42.83	51.1	53.77	18.47
35-39	43.07	27.30	19.86	54.50	36.92	48.90	42.97	41.78	48.6	40.28	17.56
40-44	41.51	27.53	21.94	52.91	36.35	47.35	39.73	40.10	45.8	44.63	16.84
45-49	40.27	26.13	22.20	50.24	37.52	47.87	41.13	43.34	44.5	41.76	17.24
50-54	34.90	24.65	20.37	46.85	33.65	42.86	34.73	40.68	40.0	30.61	16.78
55-59	31.37	22.22	17.98	40.46	34.03	37.98	30.07	37.50	36.4	31.68	16.26
60-64	22.87	15.40	12.06	32.05	27.92	30.84	24.85	30.05	29.1	21.88	13.78
65+	09.59	05.45	05.12	10.87	13.78	15.42	09.94	14.93	13.5	09.42	07.21
All Ages	36.33	24.70	18.20	43.44	35.03	38.85	34.04	36.83	36.7	36.25	18.44

Table SA1.17. Growth of the Labor Force, 1970–70: Natural Increase, Migration, and Changes in Participation Rates

Countries	Natural increase	Net effect of migration	Net effect of population growth	Effect of participation rates	Net growth of labor force
Jamaica	+149,602	-132,369	+17,233	- 81,820	-64,587
Trinidad and Tobago	+ 88,346	- 57,853	+30,493	- 20,664	+ 9,829
Guyana	+ 62,957	- 28,161	+34,796	- 25,782	+ 9,014
Barbados	+ 20,302	- 19,961	+ 341	- 1,468	- 1,127
Windward islands					
St. Lucia	+ 8,712	- 7,898	+ 814	- 3,198	- 2,384
Grenada	+ 9,870	- 8,771	+ 1,099	+ 269	+ 1,368
St. Vincent	+ 9,450	- 9,053	+ 397	- 1,522	- 1,125
Dominica	+ 6,088	- 4,838	+ 1,250	- 3,488	- 2,238
Leeward islands					
Antigua					
St. Kitts					
Montserrat	+ 1,361	- 1,140	+ 221	- 565	- 344
Belize	+ 7,858	- 2,046	+ 5,808	- 61	+ 5,747
TOTAL	364,546	-272,090	+92,452	-138,299	-45,847

Table SA1.18. Participation Rates for Men in Selected Age Groups, Caribbean Countries and Average for Industrialized, Semi-industrialized, and Agricultural Countries

Country	Age Group			
	15-19	20-24	50-64	65+
Jamaica	60.0	89.5	82.1	49.3
Trinidad and Tobago	56.7	91.9	78.5	29.7
Guyana	57.1	91.6	72.4	30.7
Barbados	60.3	94.9	82.6	38.7
St. Lucia	69.1	93.8	81.6	49.0
Grenada	51.2	94.6	83.6	55.3
St. Vincent	66.6	92.3	79.8	47.7
Dominica	66.5	95.6	82.4	49.7
St. Kitts	56.7	95.2	83.4	49.2
Montserrat	74.7	95.6	77.0	53.0
Belize	70.4	97.1	88.5	59.2
Industralized countries	72.4	91.5	85.6	37.7
Semi-industralized countries	70.3	91.8	88.9	61.0
Agricultural countries	78.4	91.2	91.6	70.1

Table SA1.19. Labor Force by Age and Sex, 1970 and 1980, and Growth during 1970–80*

Age	Jamaica 1970	Jamaica 1980	Jamaica 1970-1980	Trinidad and Tobago 1970	Trinidad and Tobago 1980	Trinidad and Tobago 1970-1980	Guyana 1970	Guyana 1980	Guyana 1970-1980	Barbados 1970	Barbados 1980	Barbados 1970-1980
MALES												
14-19	49,609	90,147	40,538	31,126	41,198	10,072	23,790	35,074	11,284	8,046	9,335	1,289
20-24	53,849	99,501	45,652	36,630	53,593	16,963	25,383	52,683	27,300	9,368	13,024	3,656
25-29	46,268	61,651	15,383	27,223	43,001	15,778	18,473	34,063	15,590	5,453	10,427	4,974
30-34	36,742	46,025	9,283	22,788	32,471	9,683	15,580	22,244	6,664	4,628	7,441	2,813
35-39	35,823	38,115	2,292	20,053	22,740	2,687	14,842	19,444	4,602	4,135	4,014	-121
40-44	35,162	30,689	-4,473	18,883	19,464	581	13,326	12,761	565	4,381	3,895	-486
45-49	31,444	31,406	-38	18,595	17,091	-1,504	11,795	12,400	605	4,128	3,653	-475
50-54	29,720	29,938	218	16,246	15,626	-620	9,157	10,893	1,736	4,500	3,780	-720
55-59	25,952	24,888	-1,064	12,278	14,152	1,874	7,923	8,778	855	3,979	3,297	-682
60-64	19,898	20,176	278	7,421	9,520	2,099	3,988	5,160	1,172	3,195	2,993	-202
65+	22,235	28,791	6,556	5,346	7,045	1,699	3,432	4,901	1,469	2,664	3,547	883
All Ages	386,702	501,327	114,625	216,589	275,091	59,312	147,689	218,401	70,712	54,477	65,406	10,929
FEMALES												
14-19	30,229	51,852	21,623	12,427	16,188	3,761	7,085	10,253	3,168	5,676	6,489	813
20-24	37,810	63,079	25,269	15,887	22,645	6,758	7,561	12,765	5,204	6,519	9,537	3,018
25-29	27,249	37,725	10,476	9,348	14,989	5,641	4,124	7,507	3,383	3,802	6,680	2,878
30-34	19,772	25,963	6,191	6,870	9,712	2,842	3,167	4,774	1,607	3,302	4,213	911
35-39	19,069	18,525	-544	6,177	6,878	701	3,232	3,566	334	3,171	2,530	-641
40-44	17,242	14,520	-2,722	5,704	6,067	363	3,131	3,351	220	3,289	2,580	-709
45-49	14,802	15,236	434	5,050	5,203	153	2,684	3,257	573	2,798	2,546	-252
50-54	12,526	12,436	-90	4,098	4,424	326	2,018	2,633	615	2,838	2,539	-299
55-59	9,536	9,882	346	2,943	3,671	728	1,577	1,957	380	2,238	1,944	-294
60-64	6,361	6,940	579	1,611	2,110	499	762	1,048	286	1,593	1,655	62
65+	5,469	6,799	1,330	1,272	1,524	252	714	910	196	1,370	1,509	139
All Ages	200,065	262,957	62,892	71,387	93,411	22,024	36,055	52,021	15,966	36,596	42,222	5,626

* Assuming net migration at a reduced rate compared with 1960-70, participation rates at 1970 level.

(Table continues on following page.)

Table SA1.19. (continued)

Age	St. Lucia 1970	St. Lucia 1980	St. Lucia 1970-1980	Grenada 1970	Grenada 1980	Grenada 1970-1980	St. Vincent 1970	St. Vincent 1980	St. Vincent 1970-1980	Dominica 1970	Dominica 1980	Dominica 1970-1980
MALES												
14-19	3,339	5,989	2,650	2,699	4,209	1,510	3,034	5,429	2,395	2,218	3,970	1,752
20-24	2,754	5,526	2,772	3,039	6,699	3,660	2,518	5,974	3,456	2,170	4,557	2,387
25-29	2,023	3,084	1,061	1,841	4,091	2,250	1,555	3,307	1,752	1,335	2,615	1,280
30-34	1,584	1,516	- 68	1,518	2,045	527	1,297	1,516	219	1,076	1,596	520
35-39	1,562	1,069	- 493	1,449	969	- 480	1,307	646	- 661	1,094	861	- 233
40-44	1,543	904	- 639	1,543	875	- 668	1,161	617	- 544	1,077	716	- 361
45-49	1,623	1,046	- 577	1,280	945	- 335	1,077	801	- 276	1,007	801	- 206
50-54	1,347	1,134	- 213	1,155	1,124	- 31	998	770	- 228	1,010	832	- 178
55-59	1,131	1,208	77	1,002	962	- 40	880	752	- 128	796	768	- 28
60-64	791	896	105	909	821	- 88	673	654	- 19	657	688	31
65+	955	1,088	- 133	1,047	1,287	240	703	909	206	770	679	109
All Ages	18,652	23,460	4,808	17,482	24,027	6,545	15,203	21,375	6,172	13,210	18,283	5,073
FEMALES												
14-19	2,087	3,396	1,309	1,791	2,620	829	1,788	2,967	1,179	1,592	2,566	974
20-24	1,936	3,011	1,075	2,089	4,222	2,133	1,472	2,816	1,344	1,507	2,582	1,075
25-29	1,129	1,559	430	1,191	2,221	1,030	888	1,581	693	788	1,393	605
30-34	856	1,032	176	970	1,176	206	785	870	85	639	862	223
35-39	844	664	- 180	1,027	666	- 361	813	501	- 312	638	519	- 119
40-44	800	582	- 218	948	608	- 340	696	491	- 205	543	453	- 90
45-49	770	690	- 80	876	759	- 117	624	567	- 57	583	538	- 45
50-54	572	618	46	715	701	- 14	531	480	- 51	559	462	- 97
55-59	507	583	76	568	594	26	378	375	- 3	438	433	- 5
60-64	377	388	11	479	442	- 37	283	316	33	293	350	57
65+	458	452	- 6	546	590	44	270	278	8	381	384	3
All Ages	10,336	12,975	2,639	11,200	14,599	3,399	8,528	11,242	2,714	7,961	10,542	2,581

Table SA1.19. (continued)

Age	St. Kitts			Montserrat			Belize		
	1970	1980	1970-1980	1970	1980	1970-1980	1970	1980	1970-1980
				MALES					
14-19	1,413	2,286	873	419	625	206	4,860	7,890	3,030
20-24	1,019	3,211	2,192	435	643	208	3,889	7,633	3,744
25-29	556	1,831	1,275	260	505	245	2,928	5,474	2,546
30-34	468	500	32	184	427	243	2,779	3,257	478
35-39	590	138	- 452	150	248	98	2,496	2,343	- 153
40-44	610	166	- 444	172	174	2	2,356	2,293	- 63
45-49	743	354	- 389	175	141	- 34	1,931	2,096	165
50-54	738	425	- 313	172	148	- 24	1,565	2,004	439
55-59	751	557	- 194	199	140	- 59	1,438	1,559	121
60-64	623	518	- 105	160	117	- 43	1,123	1,176	53
65+	553	777	224	228	260	32	1,451	1,878	427
All Ages	8,064	10,763	2,699	2,554	3,428	874	26,816	37,603	10,787
				FEMALES					
14-19	907	1,413	506	289	416	127	1,429	2,219	790
20-24	718	2,119	1,401	281	455	174	1,247	2,396	1,149
25-29	427	998	571	133	293	160	639	1,203	564
30-34	349	315	- 34	107	139	32	510	679	169
35-39	406	166	- 240	85	93	8	470	474	4
40-44	436	155	- 281	104	86	- 18	396	411	15
45-49	421	257	- 164	114	84	- 30	327	416	89
50-54	394	304	- 90	90	67	- 23	282	357	75
55-59	365	290	- 75	83	80	- 3	266	277	11
60-64	291	243	- 48	72	57	- 15	177	203	26
65+	275	315	40	76	69	- 7	194	244	50
All Ages	4,989	6,575	1,586	1,434	1,839	405	5,937	8,879	2,942

Table SA1.20. Projected Labor Force by Sex under Three Alternate Assumptions about Migration and Two Alternate Assumptions about Participation Rates, 1980

Country	ASSUMPTION					
	1x4	2x4	3x4	1x5	2x5	3x5
			MALES			
Jamaica	561,977	501,327	477,137	514,843	468,209	437,119
Trinidad and Tobago	303,882	275,901	263,205	294,216	267,961	254,833
Guyana	218,889	218,401	196,584	199,533	187,372	179,201
Barbados	71,575	65,406	59,978	70,385	63,875	58,981
St. Lucia	28,846	23,460	22,752	26,300	22,595	20,744
Grenada	27,237	24,027	22,071	27,020	23,603	21,895
St. Vincent	25,096	21,375	17,631	24,540	20,889	17,241
Dominica	20,165	18,283	16,343	18,885	17,095	15,306
St. Kitts	12,451	10,763	10,762	10,937	9,452	9,453
Montserrat	3,345	3,428	3,345	3,206	3,206	3,206
Belize	40,018	37,603	35,126	39,732	37,303	34,875
All countries	1,313,481	1,199,974	1,124,934	1,229,597	1,121,563	1,052,849
			FEMALES			
Jamaica	281,948	262,957	241,347	228,355	208,624	195,471
Trinidad and Tobago	98,923	93,411	87,646	82,903	76,602	73,453
Guyana	53,086	52,021	49,557	53,086	50,978	49,557
Barbados	45,042	42,222	37,566	44,419	40,206	37,047
St. Lucia	14,429	12,975	12,051	12,542	11,156	10,467
Grenada	15,873	14,599	12,871	16,445	14,372	13,335
St. Vincent	12,477	11,242	9,195	10,936	9,498	8,059
Dominica	11,024	10,542	9,162	8,311	7,609	6,907
St. Kitts	6,994	6,575	6,052	5,889	5,096	5,096
Montserrat	2,053	1,839	1.691	1,280	1,280	1,280
Belize	8,852	8,879	8,134	8,996	8,631	8,266
All countries	550,701	517,262	475,272	473,162	434,053	408,937

1 = Zero migration
2 = Reduced migration compared to 1960-1970
3 = Migration at 1960-1970 level
4 = Participation rates at 1970 level
5 = Participation reduced at the 1960-1970 rate

Table SA1.21. Migration to Canada by Country of Citizenship

	First Quarter		
	1975	1976	% Decline
Barbados	220	167	24.1
Grenada	82	70	14.6
Jamaica	2,062	1,583	23.2
Trinidad & Tobago	1,008	660	34.5
Guyana	1,141	859	24.7
TOTAL	4,513	3,339	26.0

SOURCE: Immigration 77, Quarterly Statistics, Employment and Immigration Canada.

Table SA1.22. Work Rate by Age Groups and Sex in the CARIFTA States, April 1970

(Percent)

	14 Years of Age & Over			14 to 19		20 to 24		25 to 59		60 and over	
	Male & Female	Male	Female	Male	Female	Male	Female	Male	Female	Male	Female
1. Jamaica	45.8	65.5	28.0	24.7	13.0	69.7	39.3	83.0	35.4	56.4	13.1
2. Trinidad and Tobago	39.5	60.8	19.2	17.0	6.8	59.1	26.6	84.5	25.1	41.2	8.2
3. Guyana	39.8	65.6	14.7	23.8	6.3	72.5	19.4	89.2	19.0	40.4	7.1
4. Barbados	53.6	72.5	38.1	35.6	18.9	87.2	57.2	92.6	50.1	51.7	16.7
MDC Mean*	44.7	66.1	25.0	25.3	11.3	72.1	35.6	87.3	32.4	47.4	11.3
MDC Total	43.6	64.8	24.2	23.1	10.3	68.5	33.0	85.1	31.0	50.4	11.7
5. Belize	48.4	79.4	17.7	49.8	15.9	89.2	29.3	93.9	17.8	67.6	9.2
6. St. Lucia	49.5	72.7	31.0	40.4	22.1	85.5	43.5	89.8	35.7	57.0	17.6
7. Grenada	49.8	69.6	33.9	30.0	14.1	83.1	48.2	91.9	45.2	63.9	19.9
8. St. Vincent	46.7	68.8	29.2	34.5	16.6	82.9	38.3	89.4	37.8	56.9	14.0
9. Dominica	52.4	73.9	34.9	37.7	24.3	90.0	51.3	92.6	41.0	59.3	18.8
10. Antigua	-	-	-	-	-	-	-	-	-	-	-
11. St. Kitts - Nevis	50.3	70.8	34.0	38.5	21.3	89.7	55.1	91.0	43.9	60.4	18.5
12. Montserrat	52.1	74.9	33.0	53.1	28.6	91.7	57.5	87.8	40.1	57.2	13.7
LDC Mean*	49.9	72.9	30.5	40.6	20.4	87.4	46.2	91.0	37.4	60.3	16.0
LDC Total	49.4	73.3	29.3	39.3	18.6	86.6	42.5	91.6	35.4	61.2	16.3
CARIFTA Mean*	48.0	70.4	28.5	35.0	17.1	81.9	42.3	89.6	35.6	55.6	13.0
CARIFTA Total	44.3	65.7	24.8	25.8	11.4	70.4	34.1	85.8	31.5	51.7	12.3

* Unweighted.

Source: Commonwealth Caribbean Census, 1970 and 5% sample of Census of Antigua, 1970.

Table SA1.23. Main Activity of Nonworking Population 14 Years and Over

(Thousands)

	Total Not Working	Not Wanting Work					Wanting Work			
		Total	Home Duties	Part Time Students	Retired & Disabled	Others Not Stated	Total	Not Seeking Work	Seeking 1st Job	Other Seeking Work
1. Jamaica	448.1	339.3	231.1	19.7	74.1	14.3	108.8	47.8	31.0	29.9
2. Trinidad & Tobago	287.8	222.2	168.0	10.2	35.0	9.1	65.6	3.0	38.3	24.4
3. Guyana	196.2	167.0	127.4	7.9	22.9	8.9	29.2	6.6	17.5	5.1
4. Barbados	56.7	48.1	30.7	1.1	14.3	2.1	8.6	1.7	5.1	1.8
MDC Mean*										
MDC Total	988.8	776.6	557.2	38.9	146.3	34.4	212.2	59.1	91.9	61.2
5. Belize	27.8	25.9	22.7	0.1	2.5	0.6	1.9	0.4	1.1	0.5
6. St. Lucia	22.7	19.8	14.0	0.5	4.0	1.3	2.9	0.3	1.5	1.0
7. Grenada	18.4	15.5	11.2	0.2	3.7	0.4	2.9	0.2	2.0	0.6
8. St. Vincent	18.8	15.9	11.9	0.2	3.1	0.7	3.0	0.5	1.9	0.6
9. Dominica	14.4	12.6	8.7	0.2	3.2	0.5	1.7	0.3	1.1	0.4
10. Antigua	16.0	13.6	8.7	0.2	2.7	1.8	2.5	0.3	1.6	0.6
11. St. Kitts - Nevis	8.8	8.0	5.2	0.0	2.4	0.3	0.8	0.1	0.5	0.2
12. Montserrat	3.0	2.7	1.7	0.0	0.8	0.1	0.3	0.1	0.1	0.1
LDC Mean*										
LDC Total	129.9	113.9	85.1	1.4	22.4	5.7	16.0	2.2	9.8	4.0
CARIFTA Mean*										
CARIFTA Total	1,118.7	890.5	641.3	40.3	168.7	40.1	228.2	61.3	101.7	65.2

* Unweighted.

Source: Commonwealth Caribbean Census, 1970 and 5% sample of Census of Antigua, 1970

Table SA1.24. Work Seekers by Age Group and Sex in the CARIFTA States, 1970

(Thousands)

	14 Years of Age & Over			14 to 19		20 to 24		25 to 59		60 and over	
	Male & Female	Male	Female	Male	Female	Male	Female	Male	Female	Male	Female
1. Jamaica	60.9	37.0	23.9	17.5	10.9	6.7	5.5	12.0	7.2	0.9	0.2
2. Trinidad and Tobago	62.6	47.3	15.3	20.0	7.8	12.5	4.6	13.9	2.8	0.9	0.1
3. Guyana	22.6	17.0	5.6	10.3	3.3	4.1	1.6	2.4	0.7	0.1	0.0
4. Barbados	6.9	3.2	3.6	2.2	2.4	0.6	0.8	0.4	0.4	0.1	0.0
MDC Mean*											
MDC Total	153.0	104.5	48.4	50.0	24.4	23.9	12.5	28.7	11.1	2.0	0.3
5. Belize	1.5	1.3	0.2	0.9	0.2	0.2	0.0	0.2	0.0	0.0	0.0
6. St. Lucia	2.6	1.5	1.1	0.9	0.7	0.2	0.2	0.3	0.2	0.0	0.0
7. Grenada	2.3	1.3	1.1	0.7	0.8	0.3	0.2	0.2	0.1	0.0	0.0
8. St. Vincent	2.5	1.4	1.1	1.0	0.7	0.3	0.2	0.1	0.1	0.0	0.0
9. Dominica	1.5	0.8	0.6	0.6	0.4	0.1	0.1	0.1	0.1	0.0	0.0
10. Antigua	2.1	1.0	1.1	-	-	-	-	-	-	-	-
11. St. Kitts - Nevis	0.6	0.3	0.3	0.3	0.3	0.0	0.0	0.0	0.0	0.0	0.0
12. Montserrat	0.2	0.1	0.1	0.1	0.1	0.0	0.0	0.0	0.0	0.0	0.0
LDC Mean*											
LDC Total	13.3	7.7	5.6	-	-	-	-	-	-	-	-
CARIFTA Mean*											
CARIFTA Total	166.3	112.3	54.0	-	-	-	-	-	-	-	-

* Unweighted.

Source: Commonwealth Caribbean Census, 1970 and 5% sample of Census of Antigua, 1970.

Table SA1.25. Unemployment Rates by Age Groups and Sex in the CARIFTA States, April 1970[1]

(Percent)

	14 Years of Age & Over			14 to 19		20 to 24		25 to 59		60 and over	
	Male & Female	Male	Female	Male	Female	Male	Female	Male	Female	Male	Female
1. Jamaica	11.3	10.2	13.5	40.9	43.9	13.7	17.0	5.2	6.6	2.3	2.0
2. Trinidad and Tobago	22.0	22.1	21.7	65.2	63.9	34.7	29.3	10.3	7.1	7.1	3.5
3. Guyana	12.8	11.9	16.3	47.2	51.7	16.8	21.7	2.7	3.7	1.7	1.1
4. Barbados	7.7	6.0	10.2	28.2	44.5	6.1	12.9	1.3	2.0	1.3	0.5
MDC Mean*	13.4	12.5	15.4	45.4	51.0	17.8	20.2	4.9	4.9	3.1	1.8
MDC Total	14.0	13.5	15.3	48.5	49.9	20.2	20.3	5.9	5.9	3.0	1.9
5. Belize	4.7	4.8	3.9	18.7	12.9	4.3	1.5	1.3	0.7	1.0	1.3
6. St. Lucia	9.1	8.2	10.9	28.4	33.2	7.5	11.9	3.2	3.6	2.0	1.4
7. Grenada	9.3	7.3	12.4	27.8	46.7	11.2	16.9	1.8	3.1	0.6	0.6
8. St. Vincent	10.7	9.6	12.8	34.2	43.5	12.2	12.5	1.3	2.9	1.2	1.3
9. Dominica	7.0	6.2	8.3	28.7	29.6	4.6	9.2	1.1	1.4	0.2	1.0
10. Antigua	10.0	7.7	14.3	-	-	-	-	-	-	-	-
11. St. Kitts - Nevis	5.1	4.2	6.6	16.3	26.0	5.0	6.8	1.1	1.7	0.7	0.5
12. Montserrat	4.7	3.2	7.3	11.9	26.6	1.4	5.3	2.1	1.9	1.3	2.7
LDC Mean*	7.2	6.2	8.9	23.7	31.2	6.6	9.2	1.7	2.3	1.0	1.3
LDC Total	7.7	6.7	9.8	25.3	33.1	7.5	10.7	1.7	2.5	1.0	1.1
CARIFTA Mean*	10.0	8.3	11.3	31.6	38.4	10.7	13.2	2.9	3.2	1.8	1.4
CARIFTA Total	13.2	12.7	14.5	45.1	47.2	18.7	19.1	5.5	5.5	2.7	1.8

1/ Unemployment Rates ($u_{j,k}$) are defined as the ratio of the number of persons in each group (j,k) who claimed to have been "seeking work" as their main activity during the 12 months preceding April '70 ($U_{j,k}$) To those who claimed "working" as their main activity ... ($E_{j,k}$) plus $U_{j,k}$.

* Unweighted.

Source: Commonwealth Caribbean Census, 1970 and 5% sample of Census of Antigua, 1970.

Table SA1.26. Work, Labor Force Participation, Employment, and Unemployment Rates, CARIFTA Region and Member States, April 1970

(Percent)

		Work (m)	LFP (b)	Employment (e)	Unemployment (u)
0.	Total CARICOM Region	44.3	53.4	83	17
1.	Jamaica	45.8	55.9	82	18
2.	Trinidad and Tobago	39.5	51.0	73	23
3.	Guyana	39.8	47.1	85	15
4.	Barbados	53.6	59.1	91	9
5.	Belize	48.4	51.1	95	5
6.	St. Lucia	49.5	54.7	91	9
7.	Grenada	49.8	55.1	90	10
8.	St. Vincent	46.7	52.9	58	12
9.	Dominica	52.6	56.6	93	7.0
10.	Antigua	47.0	53.0	89	11
11.	St. Kitts	50.3	53.3	94	6
12.	Montserrat	52.1	55.5	93	7
	Average	48.0	53.4	88	12

Table SA1.27. Working-age Population and Employment and Work Rate in the CARIFTA States, Intercensal (1960–70) Percentage Change by Sex

(Percent)

	Population 14 Years And Older			Employment			Work Rate		
	Total	Male	Female	Total	Male	Female	Total	Male	Female
1. Jamaica	7.6	9.7	5.8	- 18.9	- 13.0	- 29.0	- 24.6	- 20.7	- 33.0
2. Trinidad and Tobago	13.9	12.6	15.1	- 12.0	- 10.5	- 16.4	- 22.8	- 20.6	- 27.2
3. Guyana	24.5	24.5	24.6	- 1.4	+ 3.5	- 18.0	- 20.8	- 16.8	- 35.6
4. Barbados	4.0	9.6	- 0.2	- 1.4	+ 1.5	- 5.7	- 5.2	- 7.2	- 5.6
MDC Mean*	12.5	14.1	11.4	- 8.4	- 4.6	- 17.3	- 18.4	- 16.3	- 25.4
MDC Total	11.7	13.0	10.5	- 13.4	- 8.6	- 23.3	- 22.5	- 19.1	- 30.6
5. Belize	22.8	25.6	20.6	+ 20.7	+ 19.2	+ 27.7	- 1.8	- 5.1	+ 5.7
6. St. Lucia	5.8	4.4	6.9	- 7.3	- 5.5	- 5.8	- 12.4	- 9.5	- 16.4
7. Grenada	7.2	12.6	3.2	+ 2.8	+ 5.9	- 2.0	- 4.0	- 5.9	- 5.0
8. St. Vincent	4.9	5.9	4.6	- 10.3	- 4.9	- 18.7	- 14.4	- 10.2	- 22.2
9. Dominica	8.4	9.8	7.3	- 12.1	- 2.4	- 24.7	- 18.8	- 11.1	- 30.0
10. Antigua	21.7	23.8	20.7	+ 17.1	+ 20.2	+ 13.6	- 3.9	- 2.9	- 6.1
11. St. Kitts - Nevis	- 23.4	- 22.1	- 24.4	- 12.7	+ 8.4	- 33.8	+ 14.6	+ 39.3	- 12.4
12. Montserrat	- 1.4	8.8	- 6.8	- 9.8	+ 4.3	- 27.8	- 8.5	- 2.2	- 22.4
LDC Mean*	5.2	8.6	4.0	- 5.7	+ 5.1	- 8.9	- 7.3	- 2.8	- 13.6
LDC Total	7.5	9.8	5.9	- 0.4	+ 5.6	- 10.6	- 7.3	- 3.8	- 15.5
CARIFTA Mean*	7.7	10.4	6.4	- 6.6	- 2.2	- 11.7	- 11.0	- 6.1	- 17.5
CARIFTA Total	11.1	12.6	9.9	- 11.8	- 6.9	- 21.5	- 20.7	- 17.3	- 28.7

* Unweighted.

Table SA1.28a. Workers in Highly Skilled Categories as a Percentage of All Workers in Each CARIFTA State, 1970

	Professional and Technical	Administrative and Managerial
1. Jamaica	6.5	0.7
2. Trinidad & Tobago	9.7	1.2
3. Guyana	9.7	0.8
4. Barbados	9.2	1.4
MDC Mean*	8.8	1.0
MDC Total	8.0	0.9
5. Belize	8.4	0.5
6. St. Lucia	7.5	0.9
7. Grenada	7.6	0.9
8. St. Vincent	8.6	0.7
9. Dominica	6.8	0.7
10. Antigua	8.5	6.3
11. St. Kitts - Nevis	8.7	0.9
12. Montserrat	9.4	1.3
LDC Mean*	8.2	1.5
LDC Total	8.0	1.4
CARIFTA Mean*	8.4	1.3
CARIFTA Total	9.0	1.0

*Unweighted.

Source: Commonwealth Caribbean Census, 1970.

Table SA1.28b. Occupational-Skill Wage Indexes, CARIFTA States, 1973

Wage of General Labourer = 100

	General Labourer	Mechanic	Accountant
1. Jamaica	100	213	328
2. Trinidad and Tobago	100	172	589
3. Guyana	100	227	731
4. Barbados	100	174	577
MDC Mean*	100	196	530
5. Belize	100	158	1,167
6. St. Lucia	100	333	1,250
7. Grenada	100	299	690
8. St. Vincent	100	429	842
9. Dominica	100	259	844
10. Antigua	100	299	690
11. St. Kitts - Nevis	100	239	2,041
12. Montserrat	100	282	658
LDC Mean*	100	273	974
CARIFTA Mean*	100	238	772

* Unweighted.

Source: Mahabir (1973)

Table SA1.29. Number of Work Permits Issued in St. Lucia during the Period April 1971–November 1973, by Industry or Occupation

	Year			
	1971-73	1971 1/	1972	1973 2/
INDUSTRY				
Airlines	28	6	15	7
Banks	57	17	25	15
Construction	252	108	82	62
Hotels	178	49	79	50
OCCUPATION				
Managers	252	77	91	84
Engineers	184	83	59	42
Accountants	98	35	35	28
Electricians	22	10	11	1
Plumbers	16	8	7	1
Surveyors	21	8	8	5
Architects	16	6	4	6
Fishermen	9	4	1	4
Secretaries	15	5	6	4
Teachers	8	3	1	4
Doctors	12	4	5	3
Radio Announcers	12	4	6	2
Merchants	17	10	4	3
Insurance Agents	5	5	0	0
Domestic Staff	8	4	3	1
Hairdresser	1	1	0	0
Total	1,212	447	442	323

Source: Government of St. Lucia; Ministry of Labour.

1/ April to December
2/ January to November

Table SA1.30. Workers Holding Diplomas or Degrees as Percentage of Government Employees, Nongovernment Employees, and Own-account Workers, CARIFTA States, 1970

(Per cent)

	Of Government Employees	Of Non-Government Employees	Of Own Account Workers
1. Jamaica	6.4	1.9	0.6
2. Trinidad & Tobago	5.0	1.9	2.0
3. Guyana	3.7	1.3	0.7
4. Barbados	6.0	1.7	2.5
MDC Mean*	5.3	1.7	1.4
MDC Total			
5. Belize	6.5	1.8	1.2
6. St. Lucia	3.3	1.5	1.3
7. Grenada	5.9	1.1	1.4
8. St. Vincent	4.6	1.1	1.2
9. Dominica	5.8	1.5	0.9
10. Antigua			
11. St. Kitts - Nevis	7.7	1.4	3.8
12. Montserrat	6.8	2.5	3.5
LDC Mean*	5.8	1.6	1.9
LDC Total			
CARIFTA Mean*	5.6	1.6	1.7
CARIFTA Total	5.3	1.7	1.0

* Unweighted.

Source: Roberts (1974), Table 7.

Table SA1.31. Skill or Occupational Composition of Emigration Workers in Jamaica, 1967–70

Category	1967-1970 000s	1967-1970 (%)	1967 000s	1967 (%)	1968 000s	1968 (%)	1969 000s	1969 (%)	1970 000s	1970 (%)
Professional, Technical and Related	7.3	(14.3)	1.8	(17.2)	2.1	(13.4)	2.0	(14.3)	1.4	(12.5)
Administrative, Executive and Managerial	0.8	(1.6)	0.1	(1.4)	0.2	(1.1)	0.2	(1.5)	0.3	(2.5)
Clerical	6.6	(12.9)	1.2	(12.1)	1.8	(11.3)	1.9	(13.4)	1.7	(15.4)
Sales	0.8	(1.6)	.1	(1.3)	.2	(1.2)	.3	(1.9)	0.2	(2.2)
Craftsmen	6.8	(13.3)	.9	(8.6)	1.4	(9.3)	2.1	(14.3)	2.4	(21.6)
Other Skilled	7.9	(15.4)	1.3	(12.7)	2.2	(14.4)	2.2	(15.3)	2.2	(20.2)
Semi-skilled + Unskilled	20.4	(39.8)	4.6	(44.4)	7.5	(48.2)	5.5	(38.3)	2.8	(25.2)
Unclassified	0.6	(1.2)	.2	(2.3)	.2	(1.1)	0.1	(1.0)	0.1	(0.8)
Total Workers	51.2	(100)	10.3	(100)	15.5	(100)	14.4	(100)	11.1	(100)

Source: Government of Jamaica, Central Planning Unit, Economic Survey of Jamaica: 1970; 1972. page 48 and 27 respectively.

Table SA1.32. Some Labor Market-related Ratios for Certain CARIFTA States, 1970 and 1973

	Per Cent		Ratios of
	Paid workers to Total Employment 1/	Trade Union Members to Total Employment 2/	"Factory Operatives" to Agricultural Laborers Wage Rates 3/
1. Jamaica	68.8	30	2.3
2. Trinidad and Tobago	87.5	26	3.7
3. Guyana	80.1	30	1.6
4. Barbados	92.0	50	2.0
MDC Mean*	82.1		2.4
5. Belize	73.3	n.a.	4.8
6. St. Lucia	72.6	10	1.9
7. Grenada	83.0	33	2.2
8. St. Vincent	83.8	n.a.	2.7
9. Dominica	75.5	25	2.1
10. Antigua	84.7	60	2.8
11. St. Kitts - Nevis	87.8	n.a.	1.0
12. Montserrat	81.1	n.a.	n.a.
LDC Mean*	80.2		2.4
CARIFTA Mean*	80.8		2.4

*Unweighted.

Source: 1/ Census 1970; 2/ Caribbean Employers Confederation (1973); 3/ Mahabir (1973)

Table SA1.33. Wage Gap Index, 1973, and per Capita Income and Aggregate Employment Rate, 1970, CARIFTA States

	Wage Gap 1/ Index (x_1)	Per Capita 2/ Income (x_2)	Unempoyment 3/ Rate (y)
1. Jamaica	230	1,265	11.3
2. Trinidad and Tobago	370	1,701	22.0
3. Guyana	160	666	12.8
4. Barbados	200	1,218	7.7
5. Belize	480	1,046	4.7
6. St. Lucia	190	661	9.1
7. Grenada	220	629	9.3
8. St. Vincent	270	415	10.7
9. Dominica	210	534	7.0
10. Antigua	280	774	10.0
11. St. Kitts - Nevis	100	663	5.1
12. Montserrat	n.a.	1,008	4.7

1/ Per cent ratio of "factory operatives" to "agricultural laborers" wage rates (same as column 3, Table 3.2.1)

2/ In EC $ for 1970

3/ Census, 1970

Table SA1.34. Regression Results

ALL CARICOM states except Montserrat and Belize (N = 10)

$$y = -1.26364 + 0.03712\ x_1 + 0.00409\ x_2$$

Std. error coef.	(0.01540)	(0.00277)
Computed t-ratio	(2.40997)*	(1.47389)

Adjusted R^2 = 0.66 $\quad F(2,7) = 8.11$*

* Significant at the 5% level.

Source: S.A. Table 1.33

Table SA1.35a. Poverty Indexes,[1] CARIFTA States, 1970–73

	Degree of Poverty				Extent of Poverty		
	Mortality		Child Malnutrition (c)	"FWI" Index (d)	Proportion in Lowest Paid Group (e)	Proportion of Self-employed (f)	Low Education Attainment (g)
	Infant (a)	Child (b)					
1. Jamaica	39	45	10.4	2.08	54.0	31.2	90.5
2. Trinidad & Tobago	37	19	N.A.	3.09	23.7	12.5	70.0
3. Guyana	40	32	18.4	2.14	38.4	19.9	81.7
4. Barbados	42	22	16.2	2.21	23.0	8.0	83.0
MDC Mean*	39.5	29.5	15.0	2.38	34.7	17.9	81.3
MDC Total							
5. Belize	N.A.	N.A.	N.A.	2.60	44.1	26.7	79.2
6. St. Lucia	42	N.A.	14.0	4.27	44.5	27.4	86.6
7. Grenada	34	32	N.A.	4.28	37.4	17.0	90.6
8. St. Vincent	95	N.A.	26.5	4.89	39.8	16.2	89.4
9. Dominica	56	27	8.4	3.74	48.5	24.5	88.7
10. Antigua	38	N.A.	2.3	2.68	10.2	15.3	N.A.
11. St. Kitts - Nevis	59	12	18.3	7.72	38.7	12.2	83.3
12. Montserrat	38	34	N.A.	3.68	23.6	18.9	81.3
LDC Mean*	51.7	26.2	13.9	4.23	35.8	19.8	85.6
LDC Total							
CARIFTA Mean*	47.3	27.9	14.3	3.61	35.5	19.1	84.0
CARIFTA Total							

* Unweighted

1/ Definitions of indices, years and sources in following page.

S.A. Table 1.35 (continued)

Notes

(a) Number of deaths among infants under one year of age per 1,000 live births during the year 1972; source: Caribbean Food and Nutrition Institute, "Nutrition in the Commonwealth Caribeean - 1973"; mimeo, 1973.

(b) Number of deaths among children 1 to 4 years of age per 10,000 children in that age group during 1972; source: same as (a) above.

(c) Type II plus III of Gomez's index of nutritional status among children under 5 years of age; i.e., percentage of children under 5 years of age weighing less than 75 per cent of the age-specific "standard weight" in each state; the year is not stated in the source (which is the same as for (a) and (b) above), but it is presumed to correspond to 1972 as well.

(d) The "FWD" (Food Working Days) index is the number of days that a person in the occupational category showing the lowest mean wage rate in each territory would have had to work in June-August 1973 to buy the following food basket in that territory:

(1) 4 lbs. of rice
(2) ½ quart of cooking oil
(3) 1 dozen eggs
(4) 2 lbs. of frozen chicken
(5) 3 lbs. of salt cod
(6) 2¼ lbs. of white sugar
(7) 5 lbs. of ripe bananas
(8) 1 lb. of onions
(9) 2 packs of cigarettes.

The number of days of work (D_i) required to buy the specified

Table SA1.35a. (continued)

"food basket" in states = 1, ... 11; is computed as:

$$D_i = \frac{1}{W_i^*} \sum_{j=1}^{9} p_{ij} q_{ij} \quad ; i = 1, \ldots 11 \quad j = 1, \ldots 9$$

where: W_i^* is the daily equivalent mean wage rate for the lowest paid occupational category in state i

p_{ij} is the unit price of food item j in state i

q_{ij} is the number of units of item j included in the food basket (same for all states)

Sources:

W_i's and p_{ij}'s: Mahabir (1973),

(e) Proportion of total working population classified in the occupational groups "farm managers, supervisors and farmers"; "other agricultural workers" and "not elsewhere classified or stated" in 1970; Source: Census, 1970.

(f) Proportion of total working population classified as "self employed" in 1970; Source: Census, 1970.

(g) Proportion of total male working population not having passed any public examinations, including those certifying satisfactory completion of primary education in 1970; Source: Census, 1970.

Table SA1.35b. Standardized Poverty Indexes[1] CARIFTA States, 1970–73

	Degree of Poverty				Extent of Poverty		
	Mortality						
	Infant (a)	Child (b)	Child Malnutrition (c)	"FWD" Index (d)	Proportion in Lowest Paid Group (e)	Proportion of Self-employed (f)	Low Education Attainment (g)
1. Jamaica	82.5	161.3	72.7	57.6	152.1	163.4	107.7
2. Trinidad & Tobago	78.2	68.1	N.A.	85.6	66.8	65.4	83.3
3. Guyana	84.6	114.7	128.7	59.3	108.2	104.2	97.3
4. Barbados	88.8	78.9	113.3	61.2	64.8	41.9	98.8
MDC Mean* MDC Total	83.5	105.7	104.9	65.9	97.7	93.7	96.8
5. Belize	N.A.	N.A.	N.A.	72.0	124.2	139.8	94.3
6. St. Lucia	88.8	N.A.	97.9	118.3	125.4	143.5	103.1
7. Grenada	71.9	114.7	N.A.	118.6	105.4	89.0	107.9
8. St. Vincent	200.8	N.A.	185.3	135.6	112.1	84.8	106.4
9. Dominica	118.4	96.8	58.7	103.6	136.6	128.3	105.6
10. Antigua	80.3	N.A.	16.1	74.2	28.7	80.1	N.A.
11. St. Kitts - Nevis	124.7	43.0	128.0	213.9	109.0	63.9	99.2
12. Montserrat	80.3	121.9	N.A.	101.9	66.5	99.0	96.8
LDC Mean* LDC Total	109.3	93.9	97.2	117.2	100.8	103.7	101.9
CARIFTA Mean* CARIFTA Total	100.0	100.0	100.0	100.0	100.0	100.0	100.0

1/ Definitions of indices, years and sources are at the bottom of Table 1.35.

Table SA1.36. Unemployment Characteristics, CARIFTA Region, 1970a

	Male			Female			Combined			Share in Total
	Labor force	Unemployed (000s)	Unemployment rate [(2) ÷ (1)] %	Labor force	Unemployed (000s)	Unemployment rate [(5) ÷ (4)] %	Labor force	Unemployed (000s)	Unemployment rate [(8) ÷ (9)] %	Unemployment
	(1)	(2)	(3)	(4)	(5)	(6)	(7)	(8)	(9)	(10)
Total Labor force	872.9	111.3	12.75	368.0	53.3	14.48	1240.9	164.6	13.26	164.6=100
By Highest Exam. passed										
None	757.2	101.0	13.33	287.6	45.8	15.92	1044.8	146.8	14.05	89.2
School	33.0	4.5	13.63	22.0	2.7	12.27	55.1	7.2	13.06	4.4
leaving						7.39				
1 to 5 or	41.3	3.9	9.44	31.1	2.3	1.88	72.3	6.2	8.57	3.8
more years						0.0				
Diploma	7.5	0.1	1.33	5.3	0.1	1.88	12.9	0.2	1.55	0.1
Degree	9.1	0.1	1.09	2.7	0.0	0.0	11.8	0.1	.84	...
Others, N/S	24.9	1.8	7.22	19.3	2.3	11.91	44.0	4.1	9.31	2.5

a/ Exclusive of Antigua due to insufficient data.

Source: Caribbean Regional Census Program .

Table SA1.37. Percent Distribution of Total Working Population by Occupational Group, 1970

	Total Working Population	Prof. and Technical	Admin. & Manager-ial	Clerical and Related	Trans. and Comm.	Sales Worker	Service Worker	Farm Managers Supervis-ors & Farmers	Other Agr. Work-ers.	Production and Relat-ed Workers	Not Elsewhere Classified or Stated
1. Jamaica	100	6.5	0.7	6.5	1.0	7.6	14.4	19.8	9.3	24.7	9.5
2. Trinidada & Tobago	100	9.7	1.2	10.6	1.1	8.8	12.2	2.5	12.4	32.6	8.8
3. Guyana	100	9.7	0.8	8.0	0.9	6.8	10.5	11.8	16.4	24.9	10.2
4. Barbados	100	9.2	1.4	8.9	1.4	9.0	19.2	0.8	14.7	27.9	7.5
MDC Total	100	8.0	0.9	7.9	1.1	7.9	13.6	12.7	11.7	26.9	9.2
5. Belize	100	8.4	0.5	5.6	1.0	7.3	9.2	19.2	14.3	23.9	10.6
6. St. Lucia	100	7.5	0.9	5.5	0.6	7.1	9.0	15.8	24.5	24.9	4.2
7. Grenada	100	7.6	0.6	6.1	0.7	6.6	13.0	7.3	25.1	28.0	5.0
8. St. Vincent	100	8.6	0.7	5.0	1.0	6.9	12.0	6.7	19.6	25.8	13.5
9. Dominica	100	6.8	0.7	5.4	1.0	6.6	11.2	14.2	27.3	19.8	7.0
10. Antigua	100	8.5	6.3	12.9	0.8	4.3	24.7	8.1		32.3	2.1
11. St. Kitts - Nevis	100	8.7	0.9	7.0	0.8	8.2	13.3	2.6	30.8	22.2	5.3
12. Montserrat	100	9.4	1.3	7.2	1.0	7.8	17.0	4.3	16.7	32.7	2.6
LDC Total	100	8.0	1.4	6.5	0.9	6.7	12.7	31.2		25.5	7.0

Table SA1.38. Percent Distribution of Male Working Population by Occupational Group, 1970

	Total Working Population	Prof. and Technical	Admin. & Manager-ial	Clerical and Related	Trans. and Comm.	Sales Worker	Service Worker	Farm Managers Supervis-ors & Farmers	Other Agr. Work-ers.	Production and Relat-ed Workers	Not Elsewhere Classified or Stated
1. Jamaica	100	4.5	0.9	3.6	0.6	5.0	5.2	27.2	12.2	29.6	11.3
2. Trinidada & Tobago	100	7.5	1.5	7.5	1.3	8.4	7.3	3.1	13.8	39.0	10,5
3. Guyana	100	7.2	1.0	6.1	1.1	5.6	6.7	13.4	18.3	28.6	12.0
4. Barbados	100	9.2	2.0	6.1	2.2	6.1	11.0	1.3	14.9	38.0	9.2
MDC Total	100	6.1	1.1	5.2	1.0	6.0	6.5	16.6	13.9	32.4	11.1
5. Belize	100	4.8	0.6	3.9	1.1	6.1	4.6	22.5	17.0	26.6	12.8
6. St. Lucia	100	4.9	1.1	3.2	0.7	3.5	4.0	20.1	26.5	31.5	4.4
7. Grenada	100	6.0	0.9	4.7	0.9	5.2	6.5	8.9	24.0	37.3	5.6
8. St. Vincent	100	6.6	1.0	3.3	1.3	5.8	5.5	9.2	20.6	33.1	13.6
9. Dominica	100	4.4	1.0	3.4	1.2	3.1	4.2	19.4	29.0	26.1	8.2
10. Antigua	100										
11. St. Kitts - Nevis	100	5.9	1.3	5.4	1.1	5.6	5.7	3.2	32.6	32.2	7.0
12. Montserrat	100	6.7	1.6	4.2	1.0	5.3	8.8	4.7	17.1	47.5	2.9
LDC Total	100	5.4	0.9	3.9	1.1	5.0	5.1	15.4	23.2	31.2	8.8

Table SA1.39. Percent Distribution of Female Working Population by Occupational Group, 1970

	Total Working Population	Prof. and Technical	Admin. & Managerial	Clerical and Related	Trans. and Comm.	Sales Worker	Service Worker	Farm Managers Supervisors & Farmers	Other Agr. Workers.	Production and Related Workers	Not Elsewhere Classified or Stated
1. Jamaica	100	10.7	0.3	12.4	1.8	13.0	33.4	4.3	3.5	14.7	5.8
2. Trinidada & Tobago	100	16.4	0.4	20.0	0.6	10.2	26.9	0.7	8.1	13.0	3.7
3. Guyana	100	20.6	0.3	16.1	0.0	11.7	26.9	4.8	8.1	8.9	2.6
4. Barbados	100	9.3	0.4	13.4	0.3	13.4	31.8	0.2	14.3	12.5	4.4
MDC Total	100	12.8	0.3	14.5	1.2	12.3	31.2	3.1	6.2	13.5	4.9
5. Belize	100	23.7	0.3	12.6	0.3	12.3	28.8	5.2	2.8	12.4	1.6
6. St. Lucia	100	12.3	0.5	9.8	0.3	13.8	18.4	8.0	20.8	12.5	3.7
7. Grenada	100	10.2	0.3	8.4	0.4	8.9	23.9	4.7	26.8	12.6	3.9
8. St. Vincent	100	12.4	0.2	8.2	0.5	8.9	24.1	2.1	17.8	12.4	13.5
9. Dominica	100	11.0	0.3	8.8	0.5	12.6	22.9	5.3	24.3	9.1	5.2
10. Antigua	-	-	-	-	-	-	-	-	-	-	-
11. St. Kitts - Nevis	100	13.3	0.3	9.6	0.5	12.7	25.9	1.7	27.9	5.7	2.4
12. Montserrat	100	14.3	0.8	12.9	0.8	12.3	32.1	3.7	15.8	5.1	2.2
LDC Total	100	13.3	0.3	9.5	0.4	11.4	23.7	4.8	20.4	11.0	5.1

Table SA1.40. Percent Distribution of Total Working Population by Industrial Group, 1970*

	Total Working Populat-ion	Agric., Forestry, Hunting & Fishing	Mining Refining & Quarry-ing	Manu-factur-ing	Construct-ion & Installat-ion	Elect., Gas, Water & Sanitary Services	Comm-erce	Trans-port Storage Comm-unicat-ions	Servic-es	N.A./N.S. N.E.C. 1/
Jamaica	100	29.4	1.5	14.4	6.9	0.8	8.8	3.9	24.8	9.5
Trinidad	100	15.7	5.2	13.4	9.4	2.6	12.7	7.0	30.0	4.0
Guyana	100	29.0	4.9	15.0	4.5	0.7	10.8	4.9	28.1	2.1
Barbados	100	16.2	0.4	14.6	12.7	1.3	14.4	5.5	30.5	4.4
MDC Total	100	24.9	2.9	14.3	7.6	1.2	10.6	5.0	27.0	6.5
Belize	100	35.6	0.1	14.6	9.3	1.0	8.4	4.6	23.1	3.3
St. Lucia	100	39.3	0.0	8.1	11.8	1.9	11.7	4.0	21.3	1.9
St. Vincent	100	29.0	0.2	7.8	12.1	0.9	12.1	4.5	30.3	3.1
Dominica	100	39.2	0.0	7.8	9.7	1.0	14.1	3.6	23.7	0.9
Antigua	100	10.7	0.2	11.5	13.3	1.7	9.8	11.6	40.1	1.0
St. Kitts-Nevis	100	34.1	0.0	10.4	9.6	1.8	11.4	4.6	25.2	2.9
Montserrat	100	20.1	0.4	5.4	23.1	1.5	11.6	5.4	30.5	2.0
LDC Total	100	31.8	0.1	10.2	11.3	11.3	1.3	11.1	5.3	26.7

* Because the statistical breakdown for Grenada was non-comparable, the working population of 26,000 has been omitted from this table.

1/ Not applicable, Not Stated or Not Elsewhere classified.

Table SA1.41. Percent Distribution of Male Working Population by Industrial Group, 1970

	Total Working Population	Agric., Forestry, Hunting & Fishing	Mining, Refining & Quarrying	Manufacturing	Construction & Installation	Elect., Gas, Water & Sanitary Services	Commerce	Transport, Storage, Communications	Services	N.A./N.S./N.E.C. 1/
Jamaica	100	39.5	2.2	13.7	10.1	1.0	5.6	4.4	13.7	9.8
Trinidad & Tobago	100	17.9	6.7	13.0	12.0	3.2	11.7	8.5	22.7	4.3
Guyana	100	32.8	5.9	15.8	5.5	0.8	9.4	5.7	21.8	2.3
Barbados	100	16.8	0.6	15.3	20.3	2.0	11.8	7.9	20.7	4.6
MDC Total	100	31.1	3.9	14.0	10.5	1.6	8.4	5.9	18.0	6.6
Belize	100	41.9	0.1	14.8	11.4	1.1	6.9	5.5	14.6	3.7
St. Lucia	100	45.7	0.0	6.6	17.4	2.2	7.3	5.8	13.1	1.9
Grenada	100	34.1	0.1	8.7	21.6	1.4	7.9	7.7	13.9	4.6
St. Vincent	100	32.2	0.3	8.1	15.9	1.1	10.4	6.5	22.4	3.0
Dominica	100	46.5	0.0	6.8	14.2	1.2	9.9	5.3	15.2	0.9
Antigua	-	-	-	-	-	-	-	-	-	-
St. Kitts - Nevis	100	36.5	0.0	13.3	15.0	2.4	8.8	6.6	14.5	2.8
Montserrat	100	20.1	0.6	5.9	34.4	2.0	8.8	7.1	19.3	1.8
LDC Total	100	39.5	0.1	9.9	16.1	1.5	8.3	6.2	15.5	2.9

1/ Not applicable, not stated or not elsewhere classified.

Table SA1.42. Percent Distribution of Female Working Population by Industrial Group, 1970

	Total Working Population	Agric., Forestry, Hunting & Fishing	Mining, Mining & Quarrying	Manufacturing	Construction & Installation	Elect., Gas, Water & Sanitary Services	Commerce	Transport, Storage, Communications	Services	N.A./N.S./N.E.C. 1/
Jamaica	100	8.4	0.3	16.1	0.3	0.2	15.4	2.7	47.7	8.9
Trinidad & Tobago	100	9.0	0.7	14.8	1.6	0.5	15.6	2.7	51.7	3.3
Guyana	100	12.8	0.7	11.4	0.2	0.2	16.6	1.4	55.3	1.3
Barbados	100	15.4	0.0	13.5	0.9	0.3	18.4	1.7	45.6	4.1
MDC Total	100	9.8	0.4	15.0	0.7	0.3	15.9	2.5	49.1	6.3
Belize	100	8.9	0.0	13.9	0.3	0.4	14.9	1.0	59.3	1.3
St. Lucia	100	27.4	0.1	11.0	1.2	1.3	19.7	0.9	* 36.4	2.0
Grenada	100	31.6	0.2	6.7	6.9	54.6	54.6	54.6	54.6	54.6
St. Vincent	100	23.1	0.0	7.2	5.1	0.5	15.3	0.8	44.7	3.3
Dominica	100	26.9	0.0	9.6	2.2	0.6	21.1	0.7	38.0	0.9
Antigua	-	-	-	-	-	-	-	-	-	-
St. Kitts - Nevis	100	30.2	0.1	5.6	0.6	0.8	15.7	1.1	42.9	3.0
Montserrat	100	20.2	0.0	4.4	2.1	0.5	17.0	2.3	51.4	2.1
LDC Total 2/	100	25.2	0.1	8.9	3.1	0.8	17.7	0.9	21.7	1.7

* Distribution by sector - IBRD estimate.

1/ Not Applicable, Not Stated or Nor Elsewhere Classified.

2/ Excluding Antigua

Table SA1.43. Percent Change in Total Working Population by Occupational Group, 1960–70

	Total Working Population	Prof. and Technical	Admin. & Managerial	Clerical and Related	Trans. and Comm.	Sales Worker	Service Worker	Farm Managers Supervisors & Farmers	Production and Related Workers	Not Elsewhere Classified or Stated
1. Jamaica	-18.7	+ 2.1	-1.4	+1.0	-1.7	-1.0	-2.9	-14.8	- 6.5	+ 6.4
2. Trinidada & Tobago	-12.2	+ 1.4	-1.5	+1.7	-8.2	+ .2	-5.0	- 7.7	+ 1.7	+ 5.3
3. Guyana	- 1.2	+ 3.3	-2.1	+2.6	-7.8	+ .7	-1.4	- 7.1	+ 3.4	+ 7.3
4. Barbados	- 1.2	+ 4.0	-1.8	+4.4	-7.7	- .9	+0.9	- 9.8	+ 3.3	+ 6.4
MDC Total	-33.3	+10.8	-6.8	+9.7	-25.4	-1.0	-8.4	-39.4	+ 1.9	+25.4
5. Belize	+20.9	+ 8.3	-3.3	+1.8	-2.0	+2.9	-3.8	-11.2	+15.4	+12.9
6. St. Lucia	- 6.9	+ 3.4	-1.3	+2.4	-3.5	+2.4	- .7	-15.1	+ 2.1	+ 3.5
7. Grenada	+ 3.2	+ 2.8	-2.8	+2.8	-4.2	+1.5	+1.0	- 9.6	+ 7.4	+ 4.4
8. St. Vincent	-10.0	+ 2.3	+2.1	+1.5	-6.8	+1.7	+ .5	-18.7	+ .5	+11.1
9. Dominica	-12.5	+ 1.9	+1.9	+2.3	-4.4	+2.1	- -	-14.8	- 3.6	+ 5.9
10. Antigua										
11. St. Kitts - Nevis										
12. Montserrat	-13.0	+ 4.5	-1.1	+3.2	- .6	+2.4	- .1	-26.4	+ 6.9	- 1.8

Table SA1.44. Percent Change in Male Working Population by Occupational Group, 1960–70

	Total Working Population	Prof. and Technical	Admin. & Managerial	Clerical and Related	Trans. and Comm.	Sales Worker	Service Worker	Farm Managers Supervisors & Farmers / Other Agr. Workers	Production and Related Workers	Not Elsewhere Classified or Stated
1. Jamaica	-12.8	+2.1	- 1.8	- .2	-3.0	+ .4	+1.3	- 16.7	- 4.2	+ 9.3
2. Trinidada & Tobago	-10.6	+ .7	- 1.6	+ .4	-10.9	+1.3	-2.8	- 7.2	+ 3.3	+ 6.2
3. Guyana	+ 3.7	+2.6	- 2.2	+1.5	-9.9	+1.4	+ .5	- 4.8	+ 5.6	+ 9.0
4. Barbados	+ 1.8	+5.0	- 1.2	+2.6	-12.7	+1.1	+1.8	- 7.9	+ 5.2	+ 8.0
MDC Total	-17.9	+10.4	- 6.8	+4.3	-36.5	+4.2	+0.8	- 36.6	+ 9.9	+ 32.5
5. Belize	+19.2	+ 5.0	- 3.9	+ .6	- 2.5	+2.4	-1.7	- 12.9	+17.1	+ 15.2
6. St. Lucia	- 4.9	+ 2.3	- .6	+ .7	- 4.6	+2.0	- .2	- 14.5	+ 6.3	+ 3.8
7. Grenada	+ 6.1	+ 2.2	- 2.4	+1.9	- 6.9	+2.3	+ .1	- 11.5	+15.3	+ 5.1
8. St. Vincent	- 4.6	+ 2.0	- 1.9	+ .5	- 9.3	+2.7	- .2	- 15.3	+ 5.5	+ 11.5
9. Dominica	- 3.1	+ 1.3	- .8	+1.1	- 5.8	+1.9	+ .2	- 10.8	+ 2.3	+ 7.6
10. Antigua										
11. St. Kitts - Nevis										
12. Montserrat	+ .7	+ 2.5	- 1.9	+1.1	- 1.4	+2.5	+2.9	- 21.5	+17.0	- .3

Table SA1.45. Percent Change in Female Working Population by Occupational Group, 1960–70

	Total Change	Prof. and Technical	Admin. & Manager-ial	Clerical and Related	Trans. and Comm.	Sales Worker	Service Worker	Farm Managers Supervis-ors & Farmers	Production and Relat-ed Workers	Not Elsewhere Classified or Stated
1. Jamaica	-28.8	+2.2	-.8	+3.2	+ .4	-3.3	-10.1	-11.6	-10.3	+1.6
2. Trinidada & Tobago	-16.7	+3.4	-1.3	+5.2	-.6	-3.0	-11.1	-9.1	-2.9	+2.7
3. Guyana	-17.8	+5.6	-1.8	+6.4	-1.0	-1.7	-8.0	-14.8	-4.3	+1.7
4. Barbados	-5.6	+2.7	-2.6	+7.1	-0.4	-3.9	-0.3	-12.6	+0.7	+3.8
MDC Total	-68.9	+13.9	-6.5	+21.9	-1.6	-11.9	-29.5	-48.1	-16.8	+9.8
5. Belize	+28.5	+23.6	-0.9	+7.3	-0.2	+5.1	-13.4	-3.5	+8.2	+2.2
6. St. Lucia	-10.2	+5.2	-2.5	+5.4	-1.6	+3.1	-1.5	-16.2	-5.2	+3.0
7. Grenada	-1.2	+3.7	-3.5	+4.1	+0.1	+0.3	+2.3	-6.8	-4.7	+3.3
8. St. Vincent	-18.3	+2.8	-2.5	+3.1	-2.8	+0.2	+1.7	-24.0	-7.5	+10.6
9. Dominica	-24.8	+2.7	-3.3	+3.9	-2.6	+2.4	-0.3	-20.0	-11.3	+3.7
10. Antigua										
11. St. Kitts - Nevis										
12. Montserrat	-30.6	+7.0	0	+6.0	+0.5	+2.4	-4.0	-32.7	-6.2	-3.6

Table SA2.1. Gross Domestic Product at Market Prices, 1966–74
(millions of Eastern Caribbean dollars)

	1966	1967	1968	1969	1970	1971	1972	1973	1974	Average Annual Growth Rate 1966-1973 %
Barbados	193.8	217.8	250.8	283.0	333.0	369.2	410.3	488.9	n.a.	14.1
Guyana	388.8	425.3	459.5	498.6	533.0	566.1	546.3	608.7	n.a.	6.6
Jamaica	1797.6	1946.4	2083.2	2325.6	2666.4	2998.1	3514.3	3647.0	4998.7	10.4
Trinidad	1267.5	1361.0	1590.3	1638.1	1717.8	1911.7	2102.1	2423.4	n.a.	9.7
ECCM	258.5	261.4	284.2	317.1	340.0	377.1	417.0 1/	442.8 1/	n.a.	8.0

1/ Preliminary

Source: Economic Surveys of Governments; IBRD reports.

Table SA2.2. Barbados: Gross Domestic Product by Sector of Origin at Current Factor Cost, 1966–72

(millions of current Eastern Caribbean dollars)

	1966	1967	1968	1969	1970	1971	1972/1
Sugar	32.0	35.1	28.6	24.0	27.1	24.0	27.6
Other Agriculture	11.4	12.7	13.1	13.3	13.2	14.0	16.6
Construction	15.3	16.4	20.0	22.3	27.5	28.2	29.0
Manufacturing and Mining /2	19.6	21.1	23.8	27.1	31.4	37.0	43.6
Transport and Public Utilities	10.3	14.6	18.2	18.4	20.9	24.0	27.6
Distribution	37.3	39.2	50.0	59.2	71.2	78.2	84.0
House Ownership	6.8	7.3	8.0	9.0	11.1	12.2	13.4
Services /3	18.0	22.0	32.0	38.9	44.8	56.6	60.0
Government	21.3	25.8	30.0	35.3	42.7	47.3	54.9
GDP at Factor Cost	172.0	194.2	223.7	247.5	289.9	321.5	356.7

/1 Provisional estimates.
/2 Revised up to 1969 on the basis of industrial surveys in 1970 and 1971.
/3 Revised up to 1969 on the basis of new estimates on tourism earnings.

Source: Ministry of Finance and Planning; Barbados Statistical Service; and mission estimates.

Table SA2.3. Guyana: Gross Domestic Product by Sector of Origin at Current Factor Cost, 1960–74

(millions of Eastern Caribbean dollars)

	1960	1961	1962	1963	1964	1965	1966	1967	1968	1969	1970	1971	1972	1973	1974
Agriculture, Forestry & Fishing	68.8	76.0	78.4	73.7	73.3	78.2	74.2	80.1	79.8	89.4	90.1	101.7	95.6	97.9	245.9
Sugar	35.2	36.1	35.3	41.9	32.3	34.9	31.2	38.2	35.4	44.7	42.8	54.3	52.2	45.8	170.4
Rice	11.7	13.0	13.1	9.9	15.5	15.7	14.8	11.9	12.7	10.3	13.2	11.2	8.3	11.8	26.4
Other crops	8.8	9.2	9.7	7.3	8.4	9.4	10.0	10.7	11.5	13.5	13.7	14.5	14.0	16.3	17.5
Livestock	3.4	6.9	9.8	6.9	8.4	8.5	7.5	8.5	9.2	9.9	10.2	11.3	10.9	12.3	13.5
Forestry	6.6	6.9	6.4	4.3	4.9	5.2	6.0	5.4	5.5	5.5	5.1	5.0	5.0	6.3	6.9
Fishing	3.1	3.9	4.1	3.4	3.8	4.5	4.7	5.4	5.5	5.5	5.1	5.4	5.2	5.5	11.1
Mining and Quarrying	29.1	37.3	49.9	35.5	53.5	54.0	58.9	66.5	79.4	86.0	95.5	95.8	89.0	74.2	108.1
Bauxite and Alumina	21.4	28.6	39.5	29.6	45.4	42.7	49.0	56.8	73.4	82.1	91.0	91.1	84.4	70.3	104.4
Other	7.7	8.7	10.4	6.2	8.1	11.3	9.9	9.7	6.0	3.9	4.5	4.7	4.6	3.9	3.7
Manufacturing and Processing	27.2	31.5	35.6	39.7	37.0	42.7	42.5	46.5	49.0	52.5	57.0	61.3	59.1	57.5	109.9
Sugar Milling	11.1	13.9	16.9	20.4	12.1	12.9	11.6	14.1	12.4	15.7	15.0	19.1	18.3	16.1	59.9
Rice Milling	2.2	2.7	2.0	3.2	4.9	4.9	4.7	3.8	4.2	2.7	3.9	3.2	2.2	2.7	5.8
Other	13.9	14.9	16.7	16.1	20.0	24.9	26.2	28.6	32.4	34.1	38.1	39.0	38.6	38.7	43.3
Distribution	37.2	39.2	36.6	33.7	39.1	39.4	42.1	44.7	51.3	52.3	53.5	54.5	52.8	59.3	71.5
Transport and Communications	19.8	21.8	22.1	18.2	19.9	21.3	23.7	24.6	25.9	27.3	27.7	29.8	27.9	34.2	41.5
Construction	25.0	20.8	20.8	13.8	15.1	17.1	21.8	25.3	30.0	35.4	36.8	38.6	39.3	44.1	51.6
Rent of Dwellings	8.2	8.4	8.5	8.7	8.3	8.4	9.0	9.5	9.8	10.3	10.8	11.3	11.0	11.4	12.1
Financial Services	8.5	9.1	9.0	8.7	9.0	9.8	11.2	11.6	12.5	13.4	16.3	18.4	17.6	20.4	24.0
Government	25.6	30.5	30.5	28.1	32.3	40.2	43.7	50.1	51.9	55.2	61.9	70.0	72.9	111.6	118.8
Other	13.0	13.3	13.8	12.7	12.7	14.0	15.0	16.0	15.6	16.1	17.8	19.0	18.2	20.0	23.0
TOTAL	262.4	287.9	305.2	273.1	300.2	325.1	342.1	374.9	405.2	437.9	467.4	500.4	483.4	530.6	806.3

Source: Ministry of Economic Development, Statistical Bureau.

Table SA2.4. Jamaica: Gross Domestic Product by Sector of Origin at Current Factor Cost, 1960–74
(millions of Eastern Caribbean dollars)

	1960	1961	1962	1963	1964	1965	1966	1967	1968	1969	1970	1971	1972	1973	1974
Agriculture, Forestry and Fishing	124.8	133.0	137.8	164.2	164.2	165.6	180.7	187.2	186.0	185.0	189.1	242.2	264.5	275.4	355.4
Mining, Quarrying and Refining	99.6	105.8	110.9	109.2	125.3	138.5	235.7	246.0	240.0	299.3	383.0	378.2	332.2	336.7	723.6
Manufacturing	140.9	157.0	157.7	189.4	202.3	214.3	237.6	248.2	276.2	291.4	318.0	362.9	409.9	419.3	561.9
Construction	122.6	124.3	174.8	125.0	139.4	152.6	166.1	175.0	227.8	252.5	295.2	314.9	349.7	383.6	458.4
Electricity, Gas and Water	10.8	13.0	13.9	15.1	17.0	19.2	21.6	21.8	24.2	31.0	34.8	41.0	40.8	42.1	59.5
Transportation, Storage and Communication	80.4	89.0	91.9	90.2	97.2	105.6	116.4	127.4	139.0	151.9	168.7	195.4	225.1	247.0	306.7
Distribution	186.7	183.4	184.6	184.8	192.5	205.7	218.9	225.8	245.5	262.6	303.4	356.4	568.6	511.5	615.6
Finance	38.9	48.0	52.3	45.4	50.2	63.1	70.8	78.5	84.0	109.0	135.4	161.0	192.7	234.8	303.3
Ownership of Dwellings	32.4	36.0	38.2	41.3	45.4	49.2	52.6	53.8	54.7	59.5	66.2	70.6	76.1	71.2	90.3
Public Administration	63.8	72.0	82.6	89.3	98.6	107.0	120.7	145.4	167.0	195.1	245.5	304.8	383.0	441.8	676.6
Miscellaneous Services	135.1	145.9	158.6	174.0	182.9	205.0	216.2	227.0	238.1	248.2	268.8	297.8	339.4	326.2	392.0
TOTAL	1036.1	1107.4	1153.2	1227.8	1315.0	1425.8	1637.3	1736.2	1883.0	2085.4	2408.2	2725.2	3181.9	3289.5	4543.2

Source: National Income and Product Department of Statistics, Jamaica, IBRD Report.

Table SA2.5. Trinidad and Tobago: Gross Domestic Product by Sector of Origin at Current Factor Cost, 1966–72[1]

(millions of Eastern Caribbean dollars)

	1966	1967	1968	1969	1970	1971	1972/2
Agriculture, Forestry and Fishing	60.5	62.0	73.9	75.7	83.1	89.2	85.3
Sugar cane	(24.3)	(23.5	(26.8)	(26.6)	(31.1)	(31.2)	32.7
Other	(36.2)	(38.5)	(37.1)	(49.1)	(52.0)	(58.0)	51.6
Mining, Quarrying and Refining	267.3	298.6	371.9	308.1	284.0	295.6	264.9
Manufacturing	102.5	123.6	145.5	177.0	187.3	224.2	225.2
Construction	61.3	70.6	72.6	77.4	89.9	149.4	133.8
Electricity and Water	28.6	31.0	32.2	37.0	36.4	40.3	36.7
Transport, Storage and Communication	182.6	193.7	214.7	231.5	249.0	274.0	248.5
Trade (inc. Hotels and Restaurants)	176.5	178.3	217.5	228.2	239.3	287.4	284.8
Banking and Insurance	56.5	56.7	68.7	84.0	85.8	109.2	108.0
Ownership of Dwellings	48.2	52.6	54.8	57.7	59.5	67.8	64.1
Public Administration	137.0	146.4	169.5	176.6	192.0	269.2	267.7
Miscellaneous Services	62.1	68.9	70.3	75.0	94.2	121.6	111.1
TOTAL	1183.1	1282.4	1491.6	1528.2	1600.5	1928.1	1830.1

/1 Because of a change in the method of calculation, the figures have been revised till only 1966 and earlier figures would not be comparable.
/2 The decline in 1972 is because of the depreciation of the TT dollar vis-a-vis the EC dollar.

Source: Ministry of Planning and Development and Mission estimates.

Table SA2.6. Antigua: GDP at Factor Cost, 1960–74
(thousands of Eastern Caribbean dollars)

	1960	1961	1962	1963	1964	1965	1966	1967	1968	1969	1970	1971	1972[P]	1973[P]	1974[P]
Export Agriculture	4100.0	2852.8	2448.8	3382.3	2532.8	n.a.	1090.0	198.5	1525.3	1181.2	1507.9	1789.7	3,000	3,500	4,000
Other Agriculture	1380.0	1265.3	1146.6	1131.4	1164.7	n.a.	926.7	951.6							
Construction	2400.0	3200.0	4545.8	3998.7	4433.6	n.a.	17508.1	13139.5	9521.3	7817.2	7941.9	12354.4	6,000 1/	6,500 1/	7,500 1/
Manufacturing	395.0	440.0	607.4	664.5	683.0	n.a.	980.0	1280.3	3143.0	4317.6	5127.0	1501.0	5,500	7,000	7,000
Distribution	(3500.0	4050.0)	3666.8	3869.0	3870.0	n.a.	5320.4	5440.2	8042.3	7908.1	8746.1	8428.7	20,000	22,000	25,000
Finance	(	)	756.5	1000.0	1045.0	n.a.	1522.0	1652.4	1617.7	1090.8	1357.2	2771.1	5,000	6,200	7,500
Transportation	820.0	790.0	841.2	970.2	1026.0	n.a.	1688.6	1597.8	2542.1	2272.4	2563.5	2309.2	6,500 2/	7,200 2/	8,000 2/
Hotels	(2420.0	2580.0)	1762.7	2259.7	2430.5	n.a.	4099.6	5551.2	9012.9	8589.9	8142.9	12123.5	9,000 3/	9,500 3/	11,500 3/
Services and Professionals	(	)	1043.4	1177.5	1222.5	n.a.	1867.0	2382.5	2218.6	2272.4	2211.7	3694.8	5,000	5,500	7,000
Rent of Dwellings	1400.0	1550.0	1621.0	1650.0	1675.0	n.a.	2021.8	2987.0	2311.0	2636.0	2965.6	3463.9	7,000	7,500	8,000
Government	3950.0	4352.6	4229.1	4744.0	5042.6	n.a.	5224.9	7125.6	6285.9	7362.7	9701.1	9294.7	12,000	12,500	15,500
Utilities	-	-	-	-	-	n.a.	-	-	-	-	-	-	2,200	2,500	3,000
Total GDP	20360.5	21080.7	22669.3	24847.3	25125.7	36270.9	42158.1	42306.0	46220.0	45449.0	50265.0	57731.0	81,200	89,900	104,000

Source: BDD Report; Colonial Office Report; Statistical Abstracts; mission estimates.

P - Provisional
1/ - Includes mining
2/ - Includes communications
3/ - Includes entertainment

Table SA2.7. Dominica: GDP at Factor Cost, 1961–73
(thousands of Eastern Caribbean dollars)

	1961	1962	1963	1964	1965	1966	1967	1968	1969	1970	1971	1972	1973
Export Agriculture	3893.2	3618.3	4691.2	5511.8	4774.4	5117.0	5398.8	5528.1	5558.3	5836.6	6093.2	6900.0	9000.0
Other agriculture	2917.0	2917.5	2998.7	3088.6	3573.6	3830.1	4041.0	4094.9	4071.3	4169.0	4352.3	6100.0	7000.0
Fishing and Livestock	668.0	732.6	791.8	807.5	972.0	1041.8	1099.2	1126.1	1097.5	1137.0	1187.0		
Construction	1814.9	1918.8	1911.8	2529.8	2244.5	2941.5	3103.5	3275.9	3363.3	3638.4	3798.3	7100.0	7300.0
Manufacturing	1486.7	1815.9	1286.5	1563.5	2229.9	2390.0	2521.6	2900.5	2938.4	3069.9	3204.8	3500.0 1/	3600.0 1/
Distribution	2507.5	955.3	1264.1	1618.0	2029.8	2175.5	2295.3	2456.8	2545.0	2728.8	2848.8	3100.0	3200.0
Finance	501.2	550.6	541.7	547.1	714.7	766.0	808.2	819.0	849.7	871.7	910.0	-	-
Transportation	622.6	562.1	652.7	846.1	1086.4	1164.4	1228.5	1296.7	1345.3	1440.2	1503.5	-	-
Services and Professions	1175.4	1192.4	1210.3	1235.0	1629.6	1746.5	1842.7	1979.2	2159.6	2387.7	2492.6	-	-
Rent of Dwellings	2276.9	2729.8	2911.0	2924.0	3602.2	3860.8	4073.3	4163.1	4213.0	4434.3	4629.2	-	-
Government	3266.2	3189.2	3481.3	3408.0	5231.8	5607.3	5916.0	6483.6	7257.6	8186.4	8546.2	8600.0	10900.0
Others	-	-	-	-	-	-	-	-	-	-	-	9900.0	10500.0
Total GDP	21129.6	20182.5	21741.1	24106.4	28589.0	30641.0	32328.0	34124.0	35403.0	37900.0	39566.0	45100.0	51500.0

1/ Includes mining

Source: BDD Report; Colonial Office Report; Statistical Abstracts; mission estimates.

Table SA2.8. Grenada: GDP at Factor Cost, 1960–74
(millions of Eastern Caribbean dollars)

	1960	1961	1962	1963	1964	1965	1966	1967	1968	1969	1970	1971	1972	1973	1974
Export Agriculture	(9450.0)	5501.0	5200.0	6084.0	5400.0	8210.0	8188.2	8926.2	9442.3	10689.5	8437	6329	6210	8407	10440
Other Agriculture	( )	5661.0	5831.0	4176.0	4800.0	5200.0	6089.8	5994.0	6585.4	7334.8	6098	6371	6825	6820	7488
Construction	4340.0	2820.0	2961.0	2082.0	2930.0	3070.0	3291.8	3665.4	4261.1	4321.3	8906	6194	6165	6369	5328
Manufacturing	667.0	620.0	651.0	1454.0	1140.0	1122.0	1316.7	1336.8	1501.1	1762.6	2317	2467	2508	3191	3384
Distribution	7836.0 1/	3950.0	3970.0	4119.0	4280.0	4370.0	5596.0	5907.7	6585.4	7505.4	9998	11112	10041	10723	11592
Finance	-	-	-	1362.0	1416.0	1473.0	1769.3	1811.1	2033.7	2274.4	2112 3/	2321 3/	3013 3/	3143 3/	3888 3/
Transportation	-	800.0	824.0	1063.0	1116.0	1172.0	1399.0	1466.1	1646.3	1876.3	3431 4/	3424 4/	3412 4/	3469 4/	4176 4/
Services and Professions	-	2010.0 2/	2111.0 2/	2347.0 2/	1600.0	1680.0	2016.2	2113.0	2372.7	2729.2	2196	1927	2198	2348	2736
Hotels	-	-	-	-	805.0	1050.0	1645.9	1811.1	2130.6	3070.4	1801	1934	1903	2338	2016
Rent of Dwellings	2130.0	2107.0	2170.0	2355.0	2449.0	2547.0	3086.0	3191.0	3583.2	4150.7	4218	4324	6008	5972	6552
Government	3950.0	5245.0	5450.0	4439.0	4550.0	4650.0	6748.1	6899.5	8280.2	11144.4	11757	12727	12780	11959	14400
Total GDP	28373.0	28714.0	29168.0	29481.0	30486.0	34544.0	41147.0	43122.0	48422.0	56859.0	61271	59160	61063	64739	72000

1/ Includes Services and Transport
2/ Includes Hotels
3/ Includes Insurance
4/ Includes Communication

Source: BDD Reports; Colonial Office Reports; Statistical Abstracts; mission estimates. IBRD Report.

Table SA2.9. Montserrat: GDP at Factor Cost, 1961–73
(thousands of Eastern Caribbean dollars)

	1961	1962	1963	1964	1965	1966	1967	1968	1969	1970	1971	1972	1973
Export Agriculture	n.a.	280.0	170.0	190.0	196.0	271.0	77.0	128.0	110.0	64.0	66.0	30.0	20.0
Other Agriculture	n.a.	1206.0	1200.0	1210.0	1210.0	1193.0	1241.0	1493.0	1639.0	1774.0	1826.0	2100.0	2200.0
Construction	n.a.	430.0	580.0	900.0	1242.0	1335.0	2052.0	1628.0	1468.0	2119.0	2181.0	3900.0	46 00.0
Manufacturing	n.a.	70.0	83.0	85.0	88.0	100.0	129.0	153.0	144.0	190.0	196.0	300.0	300.0
Distribution	n.a.	405.0	420.0	591.0	756.0	1341.0	1481.0	1617.0	1767.0	1838.0	1892.0	2500.0	2500.0
Finance	n.a.	-	-	-	-	322.0	551.0	565.0	624.0	689.0	709.0	-	-
Transportation	n.a.	43.0	40.0	40.0	82.0	97.0	118.0	144.0	152.0	191.0	196.0	-	-
Services and Professions	n.a.	-	-	-	-	-	-	-	-	-	-	-	-
Hotels	n.a.	122.0	135.0	180.0	378.0	347.0	270.0	508.0	567.0	716.0	737.0	-	-
Rent of Dwellings	n.a.	260.0	265.0	270.0	291.0	345.0	589.0	690.0	768.0	860.0	885.0	-	-
Government	n.a.	1010.0	989.0	1000.0	1395.0	1661.0	1837.0	1964.0	2085.0	2456.0	2528.0	3000.0	3600.0
Others	-	-	-	-	-	-	-	-	-	-	-	3700.0	4100.0
Total GDP	3500.0	3826.0	3882.0	4466.0	5858.0	7352.0	8737.0	9356.0	9833.0	10897.0	11790.0	15500.0	17300.0

Source: BDD Reports; Colonial Office Report; Statistical Abstracts;mission estimates.

Table SA2.10. St. Kitts: GDP at Factor Cost, 1961–73
(thousands of Eastern Caribbean dollars)

	1961	1962	1963	1964	1965	1966	1967	1968	1969	1970	1971	1972	1973
Export Agriculture	6858.7	6425.0	6152.8	8023.8	8136.9	6874.7	6895.6	5972.4	5869.4	4570.0	3961.4	5800	5800
Other Agriculture	2200.0	2230.0	2261.4	3005.7	3048.1	4720.8	4735.2	4479.3	4350.9	4478.6	4229.9	4800	4900
Construction	1851.9	1909.2	1968.3	2745.4	2784.1	2532.4	2545.2	2405.6	3387.3	4113.0	4968.5	8700	10400
Manufacturing	150.0	200.0	435.8	567.2	575.2	619.6	621.5	691.2	730.0	822.6	940.0	1100 1/	1200 1/
Distribution	2150.4	2800.2	2283.7	4080.5	4138.0	3334.1	3344.2	3318.0	3620.9	3747.4	3994.9	6000	6800
Finance	-	-	715.0	-	-	1150.7	1154.2	1078.4	1138.8	1188.2	1208.6	-	-
Transportation	256.2	333.0	432.2	379.4	384.7	826.1	828.7	857.2	1080.4	1157.7	1107.8	-	-
Services and Professions	1210.5	1246.8	1324.1	1801.3	1826.7	1770.3	1775.7	1714.3	1752.1	1889.0	1880.0	-	-
Hotels	-	-	-	-	-	442.6	443.9	580.6	730.0	914.0	940.0	-	
Rent of Dwellings	1250.0	1262.5	1275.0	1635.6	1658.7	1475.2	1479.8	1437.8	1460.0	1553.8	1544.3	-	-
Government	3903.4	3499.1	3456.2	4910.6	4979.8	5753.5	5771.0	5115.2	5081.0	6032.5	8795.6	8800	10200
Others	-	-	-	-	-	-	-	-	-	-	-	7800	9000
Total GDP	19831.1	19905.8	20304.5	27150.5	27536.0	29505.0	29595.0	27650.0	29201.0	30467.0	33571.0	43000	48300

1/ Includes mining

Source: BDD Reports; Colonial Office Report; Statistical Abstracts,

Table SA2.11. St. Lucia: GDP at Factor Cost, 1961–73
(thousands of Eastern Caribbean dollars)

	1961	1962	1963	1964	1965	1966	1967	1968	1969	1970	1971	1972	1973
Export Agriculture	n.a.	n.a.	6410.0	7244.0	n.a.	n.a.	n.a.	n.a.	14171.1	10686.7	13145.4	8200	8000
Domestic Agriculture	n.a.	n.a.	3391.0	3400.0	n.a.	n.a.	n.a.	n.a.	4350.2	4007.5	4483.1	4400	5300
Manufacturing	n.a.	n.a.	1549.0	1600.0	n.a.	n.a.	n.a.	n.a.	2504.6	2404.5	2659.5	2600 1/	2900 1/
Construction	n.a.	n.a.	2322.0	2800.0	n.a.	n.a.	n.a.	n.a.	9293.6	12824.1	12689.5	9800	7400
Transportation	n.a.	n.a.	825.0	850.0	n.a.	n.a.	n.a.	n.a.	1977.4	2070.6	2811.4		
Distribution	n.a.	n.a.	5499.0	5400.0	n.a.	n.a.	n.a.	n.a.	10480.0	10953.9	11929.6	16800	17300
Finance	n.a.	n.a.	-	-	n.a.	n.a.	n.a.	n.a.	2438.7	2404.5	2735.5	-	-
Services and Professions	n.a.	n.a.	2135.0	2516.0	n.a.	n.a.	n.a.	n.a.	4547.9	4074.3	4787.0	-	-
Hotels	n.a.	n.a.	-	-	n.a.	n.a.	n.a.	n.a.	1845.5	2204.1	4027.2	-	-
Rent of Dwellings	n.a.	n.a.	2048.0	2100.0	n.a.	n.a.	n.a.	n.a.	3822.9	3206.0	3647.3	-	-
Government	n.a.	n.a.	4721.0	5506.0	n.a.	n.a.	n.a.	n.a.	10480.0	11955.8	13069.4	14600	14600
Others	-	-	-	-	-	-	-	-	-			16900	17300
Total GDP	26500.0	27800.0	28900.0	31416.0	42630.0	49341.0	51267.0	54442.0	65912.0	66792.0	75985.0	73300	72800

1/ Includes mining

Source: BDD Reports; Colonial Office Report; Statistical Abstracts; mission estimates.

Table SA2.12. St. Vincent: GDP at Factor Cost, 1961–73
(thousands of Eastern Caribbean dollars)

	1961	1962	1963	1964	1965	1966	1967	1968	1969	1970	1971	1972	1973
Export Agriculture	4694.0	4500.0	4680.0	4788.0	4940.0	4599.0	4494.0	4571.0	5088.0	4779.0	5124.0	4900	6600
Other Agriculture	5250.0	5310.0	3210.0	3300.0	3420.0	3691.0	3999.0	4250.0	4361.0	4484.0	4693.0	5100	5800
Manufacturing	255.0	260.0	1004.0	1054.0	1106.0	1144.0	1007.0	1313.0	1382.0	1424.0	1457.0	1500 1/	1400 1/
Construction	1076.0	1428.0	1538.0	1800.0	1604.0	1880.0	1752.0	2025.0	2372.0	3782.0	4340.0	4200	4300
Distribution	4750.0	4891.0	3516.0	3783.0	4071.0	4287.0	4179.0	5035.0	5207.0	5950.0	6361.0	10200	11200
Finance	-	-	1040.0	1081.0	1124.0	1169.0	1216.0	1475.0	1552.0	1692.0	1844.0	-	-
Transportation	632.0	648.0	708.0	750.0	795.0	801.0	841.0	926.0	1102.0	1173.0	1234.0	-	-
Services	1951.0	2100.0	1112.0	1167.0	1225.0	1286.0	1350.0	1440.0	1555.0	1602.0	1650.0	-	-
Hotels			269.0	380.0	477.0	567.0	241.0	465.0	987.0	1285.0	1437.0	-	-
Rent	2525.0	2575.0	2572.0	2700.0	2835.0	2931.0	3020.0	3115.0	3227.0	3390.0	3556.0	-	-
Government	3542.0	3964.0	4628.0	4750.0	4973.0	5876.0	6256.0	6742.0	7052.0	7461.0	7893.0	7300	8200
Others	-	-	-	-	-	-	-	-	-	-	-	11700	12300
Total GDP	24676.0	25676.0	24277.0	(25553.0)	26570.0	28231.0	(28355.0)	31361.0	33885.0	37022.0	39589.0	45000	49700

1/ Includes mining.

Source: BDD Reports, Colonial Office Report, Statistical Abstracts, mission estimates.

Table SA2.13. Gross Domestic Product of LDCs, 1965 and 1971[1]

(thousands of Eastern Caribbean dollars)

	Antigua			Dominica			Grenada			Montserrat		
	1965	1971	Average Annual Rate of Growth	1965	1971	Average Annual Rate of Growth	1965	1971	Average Annual Rate of Growth	1965	1971	Average Annual Rate of Growth
Personal Consumption Expenditure	31,739	64,468	11.2	26,894	40,466	7.5	32,139	64,574	12.8	7,632	13,122	9.8
Government Consumption Expenditure	4,623	11,950	17.1	4,484	9,955	13.8	6,224	15,451	14.9	1,405	2,642	11.3
Gross Capital Formation (I)	19,909	12,850	-10.9	7,303	13,831	14.4	7,501	20,327	19.5	2,707	4,034	4.2
Exports of Goods and Services (X)	16,610	28,364	9.2	10,990	16,090	7.0	15,140	22,762	9.0	1,893	2,719	8.6
Imports of Goods and Services (M)	29,312	51,118	7.5	17,337	33,058	13.4	19,449	46,046	16.6	4,833	8,463	9.8
GDP at market prices	43,569	66,534	6.2	32,334	47,304	6.5	41,555	77,100	11.4	8,550	14,054	8.9
C + I + G, or Total Expenditure, (E)	56,271	89,288	6.1	38,681	64,272	9.6	45,864	100,382	14.3	11,744	19,798	8.6

Some Ratios

	Antigua			Dominica			Grenada			Montserrat		
	1965	1971	Average 1965-71	1965	1971	Average 1965-71	1965	1971	Average 1965-71	1965	1971	Average 1965-71
I/GDP	45.7	19.3	32.0	22.6	29.2	22.6	18.0	26.4	23.2	31.7	28.7	35.3
X/GDP	38.1	42.6	40.4	34.0	34.0	36.2	36.4	29.5	33.1	22.1	19.3	19.8
M/GDP	67.3	76.8	77.1	53.6	69.9	58.8	46.8	59.7	53.9	57.1	60.2	62.6
I/E	35.4	14.4	23.4	13.0	21.5	18.5	16.4	20.2	19.2	23.0	20.4	24.6
X/E	29.5	31.8	29.5	19.5	25.0	29.5	33.0	22.7	27.4	16.1	13.7	13.8
M/E	52.1	57.2	56.4	30.8	51.4	47.9	42.4	45.9	44.6	41.6	42.7	43.6

	St. Kitts			St. Sereia			St. Vincent			Belize		
	1965	1971	Average Annual Rate of Growth	1965	1971	Average Annual Rate of Growth	1965	1971	Average Annual Rate of Growth	1968	1970	Average Annual Rate of Growth
Personal Consumption Expenditure	23,075	30,208	4.7	35,832	75,660	12.9	23,277	42,755	11.2	88,080	111,000	12.3
Government Consumption Expenditure	4,382	8,184	7.4	7,070	12,915	9.8	5,048	11,145	13.4	11,550	13,920	8.3
Gross Capital Formation (I)	6,745	17,553	14.0	9,569	42.494	22.7	5,374	17,785	22.7	35,160	41,880	9.2
Exports of Goods and Services (X)	10,316	12,338	2.6	16,823	24,187	5.9	8,018	10,801	8.0	34,680	41,640	9.6
Imports of Goods and Services (M)	14,342	30,544	12.0	22,216	66,968	19.7	14,842	36,712	17.6	53,760	69,480	13.7
GDP at market prices	30,176	38,039	3.0	47,077	88,283	10.4	26,895	45,774	9.8	116,040	138,960	9.4
C + I + G, or Total Expenditure, (E)	34,202	56,245	7.3	52,471	131,069	15.6	33,699	71,685	13.8	135,120	166,880	11.1

Some Ratios

	St. Kitts			St. Sereia			St. Vincent			Belize		
	1965	1971	Average 1965-71	1965	1971	Average 1965-71	1965	1971	Average 1965-71	1968	1970	Average 1968-70
I/GDP	22.4	46.9	28.1	20.3	48.1	33.5	20.0	38.3	28.3	30.3	30.1	29.1
X/GDP	34.2	32.4	33.5	35.7	27.4	30.7	29.8	23.6	27.6	29.9	30.0	30.4
M/GDP	47.5	80.3	58.6	47.2	75.8	59.5	55.2	80.2	64.1	46.3	50.0	48.6
I/E	19.7	31.7	22.4	19.2	32.4	26.0	15.9	24.8	20.7	26.0	25.1	24.7
X/E	30.2	21.9	26.8	32.1	18.4	23.9	23.8	15.1	20.3	25.7	25.0	25.7
M/E	41.9	54.3	46.8	42.3	51.1	46.2	44.0	51.2	47.0	39.8	41.7	41.1

Source: CARICOM Secretariat; IBRD Reports; National Statistical Sources.

1/ For Belize the years shown are 1968 and 1970.

Table SA2.14. CARICOM National Accounts Projections at 1971 Prices, 1970–80

(millions of Eastern Caribbean dollars)

	1970	1971	1972	1973	1974	1975	1976	1977	1978	1979	1980
GDP	6213	6585	6830	6910	7342	7824	8361	8935	9549	10206	10911
Imports GNFS	2883	3198	3327	3320	3703	4226	4544	4926	5344	5803	6302
Exports GNFS	2501	2571	2669	2751	3200	3463	3681	3964	4268	4594	4948
Resource Gap	-382	-627	-658	-569	-503	-763	-863	-962	-1076	-1209	-1354
Consumption	4909	5418	5600	5747	5901	6376	6837	7320	7846	8414	9025
Investment	1686	1794	1888	1732	1944	2211	2387	2577	2779	3001	3240

Source: Mission Estimates

Table SA3.1. Barbados: Trade by SITC Sections
(value in thousands of Eastern Caribbean dollars)

SITC	1960	1961	1962	1963	1964	1965	1966
				Imports			
0	21,908	23,218	24,068	26,908	29,031	31,870	34,088
1	2,194	1,894	1,982	2,026	2,129	2,121	2,384
2.	4,385	3,967	3,578	4,251	3,546	3,877	4,407
3	4,253	4,350	11,179	13,713	11,271	11,796	13,149
4	484	396	246	551	568	808	764
5	5,964	6,441	7,046	6,967	8,576	8,330	9,779
6	18,411	17,417	16,873	18,656	20,948	23,207	27,202
7	15,216	12,176	12,786	13,620	18,069	18,930	22,253
8	7,794	7,654	8,421	8,918	10,976	11,347	13,086
9	2,691	2,749	2,901	3,262	3,760	3,980	3,999
Total	83,299	80,262	89,079	98,871	108,874	116,265	131,111
				Domestic Exports			
0	31,499	33,295	33,692	49,762	41,012	42,622	43,581
1	2,428	2,236	1,915	2,035	2,431	2,934	3,463
2	153	201	139	288	174	236	208
3	28	57	65	68	23	57	648
4	252	357	321	307	335	381	258
5	292	325	287	274	250	217	297
6	146	260	280	322	345	408	518
7	13	106	36	58	31	60	68
8	202	222	333	386	513	693	983
9	3	3	2	5	13	11	33
Total	35,016	37,063	37,070	53,506	45,125	47,617	50,056
				Re-Exports			
0	319	259	299	477	514	1,198	2,260
1	369	250	288	366	452	465	432
2	69	9	36	18	16	17	25
3	917	926	8,312	10,655	9,455	9,918	11,224
4	23	10	7	8	6	5	10
5	651	649	748	775	860	604	1,218
6	1,904	1,793	1,625	1,987	1,928	2,077	2,108
7	1,051	1,580	1,068	1,127	1,032	1,546	1,470
8	322	325	437	509	445	411	562
9	272	390	390	362	465	412	596
Total	5,896	6,190	13,209	16,283	15,171	16,652	19,905

Sources: CARICOM SECRETARIAT
OVERSEAS TRADE REPORT

1967	1968	1969	1970	1971	1972	1973	1974
			Imports				
32,534	38,578	42,427	49,196	53,350	63,002	79,716	94,220
2,346	3,327	3,822	5,224	4,700	6,086	6,992	7,553
4,980	5,947	6,279	6,899	7,313	6,723	9,235	12,016
11,609	16,622	14,796	12,991	15,934	15,823	21,822	66,359
1,115	1,601	2,156	3,102	3,951	3,782	3,865	7,516
10,945	12,263	14,358	16,984	18,444	23,050	27,565	34,790
27,199	31,525	40,080	49,017	48,240	56,039	67,432	79,630
25,675	35,089	40,771	55,972	56,017	54,847	67,008	60,146
13,805	17,469	23,766	28,401	28,972	33,171	34,920	42,472
3,845	5,603	6,097	7,219	6,763	7,914	10,046	13,618
134,053	168,025	194,554	235,005	243,685	270,436	328,602	418,319
			Domestic Exports				
46,767	49,333	40,572	42,221	34,082	35,533	43,220	70,836
3,070	3,061	3,132	3,390	4,225	4,802	5,143	5,822
397	366	264	135	296	209	721	1,473
644	629	773	775	134	378	656	2,081
145	62	9	0	2	1	1	16
504	1,074	1,309	2,096	2,534	3,329	4,300	4,867
602	1,076	1,653	1,826	2,122	6,240	4,323	5,833
172	1,967	5,727	6,538	3,753	4,300	6,690	8,974
1,295	2,075	3,914	5,120	6,026	8,305	18,638	24,291
7	6	4	6	8	6	9	21
53,601	59,646	57,357	62,106	53,180	63,103	83,700	124,215
			Re-Exports				
869	569	627	656	923	1,012	986	n.a.
402	385	400	942	744	1,195	1,016	n.a.
15	22	56	65	73	131	196	n.a.
10,263	12,455	8,356	7,365	14,392	10,971	8,981	n.a.
4	5	12	7	6	6	1	n.a.
1,386	1,414	1,317	1,104	1,469	1,993	2,453	n.a.
1,747	1,383	1,233	1,591	1,280	1,149	1,432	n.a.
1,819	2,641	3,227	2,974	4,449	2,441	2,546	n.a.
874	828	851	1,257	2,088	1,069	1,001	n.a.
642	881	820	1,079	1,742	1,392	1,389	n.a.
18,022	20,583	16,898	17,040	27,164	21,359	19,999	49,394

Table SA3.2. Guyana: Trade by SITC Sections
(value in thousands of Eastern Caribbean dollars)

SITC	1960	1961	1962	1963	1964	1965	1966
			Imports				
0	24,755	25,751	26,956	24,605	28,853	30,869	33,432
1	2,118	2,376	1,620	1,596	1,739	1,898	2,124
2	919	811	608	558	792	1,222	1,184
3	11,183	12,927	13,080	12,038	14,540	16,111	16,489
4	1,802	1,370	570	1,303	1,191	2,611	1,744
5	10,246	13,436	13,021	16,883	16,518	18,345	20,076
6	36,085	33,250	27,778	24,981	33,094	42,722	45,981
7	44,899	41,936	30,390	25,062	38,846	48,236	59,873
8	15,092	14,555	11,633	11,046	14,889	17,528	19,965
9	499	589	621	438	464	590	1,138
Total	147,599	147,001	126,277	118,511	150,925	180,131	202,006
			Domestic Exports				
0	78,261	85,877	87,320	103,928	85,841	76,840	84,303
1	3,133	3,183	3,314	3,194	3,819	4,353	3,513
2	36,268	50,050	64,356	60,056	69,923	76,766	87,371
3	1	0	8	0	2	5	5
4	0	0	0	0	0	0	0
5	1,322	1,254	1,528	1,488	1,524	1,504	1,432
6	4,845	5,265	3,937	3,637	4,743	6,194	5,701
7	595	255	6	9	5	1	2
8	365	399	371	335	269	156	252
9	261	262	240	279	438	16	16
Total	125,051	146,545	161,081	172,926	166,564	165,835	182,595
			Re-Exports				
0	61	53	52	39	n.a.	n.a.	75
1	3	5	2	0	n.a.	n.a.	1
2	0	1	18	2	n.a.	n.a.	61
3	245	556	487	256	n.a.	n.a.	26
4	3	1	1	1	n.a.	n.a.	1
5	47	33	23	28	n.a.	n.a.	69
6	151	183	273	231	n.a.	n.a.	356
7	607	486	980	514	n.a.	n.a.	1,547
8	157	112	145	131	n.a.	n.a.	445
9	987	889	1,124	698	n.a.	n.a.	1,255
Total	2,261	2,318	3,106	1,899	2,315	2,118	3,836

SOURCE: CARICOM SECRETARIAT
OVERSEAS TRADE REPORT

1967	1968	1969	1970	1971	1972	1973	1974
			Imports				
33,556	35,538	37,639	37,295	41,529	38,136	51,469	66,788
2,025	2,034	2,164	2,285	2,617	2,475	3,450	3,020
2,807	1,468	1,608	1,601	1,626	1,489	1,368	5,584
18,106	20,746	18,615	23,043	23,567	25,899	44,618	95,299
1,765	2,087	2,784	2,778	3,794	2,889	3,282	11,485
19,114	21,233	23,298	23,638	30,679	32,915	41,916	61,947
48,375	52,836	61,873	67,861	70,111	70,914	84,666	128,114
77,356	61,589	62,951	84,479	68,224	72,348	84,030	112,576
21,288	20,610	23,538	24,035	24,195	26,448	27,424	35,328
900	1,170	1,361	1,223	1,290	850	871	2,145
225,292	219,311	235,833	268,239	267,632	274,363	343,094	522,285
			Domestic Exports				
92,150	110,047	117,278	110,726	128,660	132,278	109,261	322,879
5,791	4,338	3,204	3,823	7,124	5,855	7,790	14,653
85,680	106,832	105,586	142,757	142,482	126,079	131,873	188,256
20	20	14	13	33	17	6	1
0	1	-	0	-	163	170	0
1,382	1,397	1,443	1,743	2,498	2,817	3,345	3,681
6,503	5,241	4,819	4,496	3,812	3,992	5,354	5,656
2	1	59	1	20	1,017	890	10
413	626	1,238	1,970	3,052	3,926	5,331	6,163
19	22	32	37	79	58	301	1,808
191,960	228,525	233,673	265,566	287, 760	276,203	264,321	543,108
			Re-Exports				
138	349	665	517	663	444	574	n.a.
0	1	0	4	1	1	2	n.a.
326	0	189	30	6	1	6	n.a.
38	40	28	15	44	10	10	n.a.
6	1	1	5	13	2	-	n.a.
77	97	87	60	153	75	51	n.a.
669	696	300	592	821	876	605	n.a.
2,131	4,571	5,100	3,157	4,090	3,282	2,270	n.a.
1,449	1,047	943	729	778	623	1,021	n.a.
725	1,274	1,031	1,254	2,218	806	1,044	n.a.
5,559	8,075	8,344	6,364	8,789	6,117	5,584	6,022

Table SA3.3. Jamaica: Trade by SITC Sections
(value in thousands of Eastern Caribbean dollars)

SITC	1960	1961	1962	1963	1964	1965	1966
				Imports			
0	69,989	69,301	77,736	82,245	99,797	97,862	108,488
1	8,422	7,739	8,435	7,917	8,041	7,678	7,914
2	13,378	10,853	12,213	12,383	16,355	16,299	14,922
3	30,676	36,998	35,337	34,881	55,845	43,213	45,796
4	2,641	2,333	1,829	2,021	2,374	4,013	3,612
5	29,629	29,834	31,240	33,692	43,896	42,753	46,494
6	94,263	92,938	96,501	102,005	125,599	133,296	153,640
7	88,853	78,281	86,795	79,718	103,418	109.636	136,514
8	33,267	32,795	31,217	30,988	39,733	40,225	42,585
9	865	824	780	732	789	496	835
Total	371,985	361,896	382,085	386,582	495,848	495,468	560,800
				Domestic Exports			
0	110,185	118,634	117,512	158,133	152,792	134,500	143,752
1	9,977	9,512	8,770	10,556	12,684	13,683	12,588
2	134,491	145,744	149,156	143,923	164,901	172,503	183,998
3	0	9	0	0	4,869	12,817	15,043
4	7	8	30	26	11	28	20
5	2,975	3,255	3,839	4,703	5,172	5,177	8,556
6	2,794	4,019	5,904	4,390	6,672	7,726	5,191
7	2	239	127	252	262	194	208
8	6,970	9,390	13,280	14,814	15,296	13,011	15,100
9	254	225	109	85	103	58	64
Total	267,655	291,035	298,726	336,883	362,763	359,697	384,521
				Re-Exports			
0	258	325	257	245	213	178	239
1	308	193	153	140	193	93	67
2	24	30	216	1,687	114	992	35
3	438	305	173	386	905	975	63
4	1	1	1	4	0	1	2
5	168	146	207	183	147	167	253
6	598	930	963	1,381	1,290	968	761
7	1,958	2,177	9,897	4,376	3,856	2,893	4,079
8	581	326	636	833	1,216	1,577	853
9	3	7	24	35	1	1	23
Total	4,336	4,439	12,526	9,270	7,936	7,846	6,375

SOURCE CARICOM SECRETARIAT
OVERSEAS TRADE REPORT

1967	1968	1969	1970	1971	1972	1973	1974
				Imports			
116,603	139,135	139,256	165,822	183,855	216,494	247,990	393,354
8,239	11,380	11,998	14,521	17,793	19,622	18,559	14,539
18,475	20,321	24,635	24,594	30,570	35,075	52,573	64,378
48,725	54,991	60,721	67,341	104,698	106,960	140,686	398,763
4,160	4,892	5,195	6,094	5,828	8,533	13,323	25,712
48,906	60,725	69,298	78,834	91,926	114,083	127,745	181,886
159,064	196,738	220,896	274,032	259,657	270,501	301,943	405,385
152,298	216,586	268,086	338,976	321,510	308,137	297,667	318,382
48,583	62,615	70,226	78,835	85,998	100,863	94,733	103,201
1,075	1,335	1,511	1,579	1,575	3,297	2,451	3,691
606,127	768,718	871,822	1,050,629	1,103,410	1,183,565	1,297,669	1,909,291
				Domestic Exports			
135,805	149,803	137,308	140,743	137,754	149,951	155,474	246,147
12,491	11,900	14,848	13,536	18,954	21,699	26,065	39,030
194,177	215,730	285,109	454,650	432,431	458,023	493,808	1,085,987
10,578	12,943	14,285	17,465	18,479	18,909	17,760	21,373
23	236	38	52	76	145	188	451
9,427	10,338	11,908	12,593	13,225	15,446	16,126	21,712
4,687	7,721	8,472	7,772	11,790	11,971	14,433	25,049
349	451	821	2,341	1,793	2,670	3,565	4,039
18,200	21,664	21,826	20,668	25,979	24,540	20,103	21,895
50	1	24	58	6	32	125	3
385,787	430,787	494,640	669,878	660,487	703,385	747,650	1,466,287
				Re-Exports			
145	270	244	n.a.	n.a.	n.a.	515	n.a.
46	75	77	n.a.	n.a.	n.a.	182	n.a.
23	24	67	n.a.	n.a.	n.a.	60	n.a.
17	1	87	n.a.	n.a.	n.a.	633	n.a.
0	0	1	n.a.	n.a.	n.a.	19	n.a.
168	100	133	n.a.	n.a.	n.a.	406	n.a.
591	1,055	865	n.a.	n.a.	n.a.	1,146	n.a.
4,573	6,479	11,168	n.a.	n.a.	n.a.	10,009	n.a.
519	326	559	n.a.	n.a.	n.a.	1,316	n.a.
85	91	431	n.a.	n.a.	n.a.	717	n.a.
6,167	8,419	13,632	13,720	18,003	18,435	15,003	25,380

Table SA3.4. Trinidad and Tobago: Trade by SITC Sections
(value in thousands of Eastern Caribbean dollars)

SITC	1960	1961	1962	1963	1964	1965	1966
				Imports			
0	70,559	73,103	76,410	78,047	84,962	87,588	89,747
1	8,190	7,837	7,086	6,090	5,891	6,366	6,408
2	8,955	8,149	9,524	8,506	10,436	9,778	12,458
3	171,146	271,738	278,570	302,943	371,707	401,051	391,264
4	2,623	2,698	1,896	2,671	2,782	4,069	3,761
5	22,728	22,987	23,766	25,473	29,023	34,557	32,844
6	90,464	86,235	92,475	89,264	90,510	103,508	98,962
7	89,076	73,844	78,478	95,619	95,700	129,137	102,746
8	36,686	34,147	34,894	33,472	36,003	38,299	35,738
9	4,164	3,870	3,273	5,100	4,405	3,478	4,685
Total	504,591	584,608	606,371	647,186	731,418	817,831	778,611
				Domestic Exports			
0	55,854	60,012	53,641	69,634	65,108	58,384	54,943
1	3,485	3,649	3,186	2,828	3,489	3,418	3,421
2	6,189	4,779	4,818	4,213	5,199	4,764	5,366
3	392,910	494,248	494,700	526,179	574,245	563,726	582,050
4	123	251	235	187	216	168	233
5	9,732	10,564	15,054	12,589	27,262	35,991	57,397
6	5,195	3,048	4,394	4,450	5,138	5,804	7,016
7	217	17	29	25	26	143	316
8	2,634	2,879	3,477	4,377	5,334	5,743	6,240
9	97	101	124	235	238	173	188
Total	476,436	579,548	579,658	624,717	686,254	678,314	717,170
				Re-Exports			
0	1,034	1,056	987	1,307	922	916	1,091
1	36	53	30	25	37	32	37
2	259	303	157	66	41	48	77
3	621	239	152	625	148	175	373
4	3	5	4	4	6	3	8
5	759	746	512	919	640	1,274	1,603
6	2,870	2,855	2,949	2,455	2,215	1,843	2,659
7	5,711	5,588	5,532	6,432	4,972	4,714	7,240
8	846	1,265	633	788	830	923	1,001
9	3,263	2,275	2,091	4,133	3,845	3,032	4,748
Total	15,402	14,386	13,047	16,754	13,654	12,961	18,837

SOURCE: CARICOM SECRETARIAT
OVERSEAS TRADE REPORT

1967	1968	1969	1970	1971	1972	1973	1974
				Imports			
86,986	87,577	106,179	103,361	114,541	132,923	161,006	250,267
6,451	5,246	6,392	8,079	10,885	10,564	11,343	12,635
10,729	12,135	12,746	13,032	13,252	16,554	18,821	25,050
355,818	468,556	512,171	578,474	665,521	704,779	793,896	2,716,395
3,542	3,654	5,406	8,972	8,132	8,951	11,059	23,013
35,297	35,807	40,254	47,421	52,089	64,609	75,856	116,486
91,930	99,810	121,519	139,446	196,539	201,820	215,040	312,945
95,685	103,823	112,104	135,490	201,122	256,770	201,116	240,289
34,217	35,143	44,896	46,261	61,375	68,852	70,129	75,554
4,688	4,721	6,811	6,485	5,802	5,277	5,767	5,190
725,342	856,473	968,478	1,087,020	1,329,258	1,471,099	1,564,033	3,777,823
				Domestic Exports			
57,004	75,320	77,174	78,914	77,186	88,970	84,128	153,980
3,876	2,429	2,510	2,818	3,135	3,937	7,711	12,237
4,922	4,963	4,767	6,735	4,991	5,163	6,682	9,183
594,403	738,970	733,179	744,020	805,008	832,894	1,126,393	3,553,392
209	530	1,268	1,003	371	155	349	72
77,490	81,422	88,918	75,612	71,310	76,988	74,668	137,938
7,266	9,030	11,982	16,330	17,063	16,990	21,438	24,780
348	680	858	907	1,008	1,909	2,929	10,087
6,946	10,313	14,818	17,610	21,378	25,062	28,308	32,146
210	210	295	367	571	409	523	336
752,673	923,868	935,767	944,315	1,002,020	1,052,476	1,353,130	3,934,152
				Re-Exports			
978	1,283	1,827	2,609	n.a.	n.a.	3,647	4,812
14	16	23	12	n.a.	n.a.	180	46
44	103	136	147	n.a.	n.a.	77	235
162	141	128	186	n.a.	n.a.	3,633	206,055
11	3	6	4	n.a.	n.a.	25	19
1,038	959	1,236	603	n.a.	n.a.	934	2,990
2,767	2,242	2,392	3,255	n.a.	n.a.	2,468	3,552
4,423	13,140	5,148	8,451	n.a.	n.a.	6,461	9,277
899	1,391	1,115	1,196	n.a.	n.a.	1,240	1,866
2,768	2,516	2,488	2,505	n.a.	n.a.	3,124	3,260
13,104	21,794	14,498	18,969	39,607	19,005	21,789	232,112

Table SA3.5. Antigua: Trade by SITC Sections
(value in thousands of Eastern Caribbean dollars)

SITC	1960	1961	1962	1963	1964	1965	1966
			Imports				
0	3,984	4,704	5,657	5,607	6,266	6,551	7,406
1	487	661	547	746	827	908	1,449
2	653	717	786	803	918	621	915
3	1,050	1,812	1,656	2,615	1,596	2,201	7,941
4	244	249	301	275	252	308	325
5	1,082	1,309	1,541	1,571	1,629	1,593	2,046
6	2,915	4,310	4,389	4,315	4,137	6,830	9,253
7	2,965	2,980	3,745	3,953	4,976	9,790	9,269
8	2,165	2,520	2,714	2,878	2,136	3,323	4,448
9	82	264	298	243	316	296	863
Total	15,627	19,526	21,634	23,005	23,054	32,421	43,914
			Domestic Exports				
0	n.a.	n.a.	3,969	6,012	3,436	2,296	121
1	n.a.	n.a.	5	12	31	37	36
2	n.a.	n.a.	320	235	213	131	298
3	n.a.	n.a.	-	-	-	-	-
4	n.a.	n.a.	-	5	-	-	-
5	n.a.	n.a.	2	2	1	1	29
6	n.a.	n.a.	2	1	2	1	6
7	n.a.	n.a.	-	-	-	-	-
8	n.a.	n.a.	6	3	-	6	3
9	n.a.	n.a.	41	4	-	3	-
Total	3,756	3,882	4,343	6,274	3,684	2,475	493

a/ Refers to domestic exports plus re-exports.

Source: CARICOM Secretariat

1967	1968	1969	1970	1971	1972	1973	1974
			Imports				
6,872	8,516	10,243	13,104	14,646	16,420	14,877	21,853
1,417	1,772	2,755	3,025	2,922	3,289	3,709	3,064
1,011	1,132	1,136	1,511	1,337	1,657	2,103	2,066
6,258	13,590	16,192	19,862	38,395	29,369	35,863	82,206
305	328	342	349	420	396	378	854
3,304	2,283	2,164	2,880	4,229	4,354	4,367	5,931
6,540	5,799	6,619	7,304	8,112	8,467	9,783	10,978
8,995	9,699	9,891	16,377	17,694	17,724	15,468	11,086
3,757	6,091	7,510	7,271	7,690	8,152	7,811	5,463
635	65	731	967	1,323	1,149	144	248
39,094	49,275	57,584	72,649	86,767	90,976	94,504	143,750
			Domestic Exports				
84	146	208	247	414	442	276	
36	76	179	202	260	267	474	
10	114	117	162	201	202	474	
1,655	12,570	10,358	20,656	27,644	30,351	48,130	
-	-	1	-	3	2	-	
36	37	43	160	71	96	41	
2	2	1	4	212	236	-	
-	-	-	-	2,428	1,815	2	
124	209	261	415	785	1,062	984	
3	1	-	-	214	165	2	
1,949	13,154	11,168	21,846	32,230[a/]	34,639[a/]	50,382	

Table SA3.6. Belize: Trade by SITC Sections
(value in thousands of Eastern Caribbean dollars)

SITC	1960	1961	1962	1963	1964	1965	1966
			Imports				
0	6,495	6,269	8,411	8,796	9,767	9,181	10,769
1	854	969	1,697	1,453	1,740	1,852	1,648
2	237	256	127	185	140	146	203
3	1,571	1,366	2,041	1,823	1,953	2,140	2,094
4	16	18	108	47	77	140	89
5	1,906	1,693	2,640	2,684	3,042	3,646	3,076
6	4,691	5,412	6,965	7,143	7,861	9,329	9,368
7	4,152	8,476	10,691	7,081	8,620	10,485	14,272
8	2,319	2,452	4,206	3,306	3,751	4,571	4,543
9	298	340	557	548	595	496	452
Total	22,540	27,250	37,443	33,064	37,546	41,986	46,514
			Domestic Exports				
0	6,692	9,430	6,777	11,488	13,200	11,896	15,089
1	-	-	0	0	-	-	27
2	5,310	3,633	2,803	6,190	6,264	5,405	2,867
3	-	-	-	-	-	-	-
4	-	-	-	-	-	-	1
5	55	34	22	28	59	63	117
6	4	0	4	45	0	0	-
7	27	19	10	14	20	14	47
8	9	193	1	592	834	726	760
9	101	115	285	159	184	156	195
Total	12,198	13,424	9,902	18,516	20,561	18,260	19,102
			Re-Exports				
0	n.a.	n.a.	n.a.	n.a.	n.a.	n.a.	n.a.
1	n.a.	n.a.	n.a.	n.a.	n.a.	n.a.	n.a.
2	n.a.	n.a.	n.a.	n.a.	n.a.	n.a.	n.a.
3	n.a.	n.a.	n.a.	n.a.	n.a.	n.a.	n.a.
4	n.a.	n.a.	n.a.	n.a.	n.a.	n.a.	n.a.
5	n.a.	n.a.	n.a.	n.a.	n.a.	n.a.	n.a.
6	n.a.	n.a.	n.a.	n.a.	n.a.	n.a.	n.a.
7	n.a.	n.a.	n.a.	n.a.	n.a.	n.a.	n.a.
8	n.a.	n.a.	n.a.	n.a.	n.a.	n.a.	n.a.
9	n.a.	n.a.	n.a.	n.a.	n.a.	n.a.	n.a.
Total	1,296	1,459	4,955	3,770	2,470	2,696	3,984

p/ Provisional.

Source: CARICOM Secretariat, Ministry of Finance and Economic Development.

1967	1968	1969	1970	1971	1972	1973	1974p/
11,229	13,819	14,499	17,052	18,224	21,000	26,107	35,516
1,358	2,127	2,446	3,848	3,614	1,728	3,792	5,326
189	349	273	401	349	575	703	1,429
2,749	2,974	3,613	3,309	4,012	4,885	5,951	13,740
97	122	161	116	202	157	167	272
3,577	5,248	5,976	6,952	6,440	7,248	9,852	13,714
8,872	11,894	12,756	14,156	13,378	15,785	19,880	23,227
11,164	10,158	11,872	12,609	16,255	17,897	19,231	24,892
4,611	5,802	6,992	7,621	7,810	10,285	13,440	16,408
497	548	633	671	592	581	628	708
44,342	53,041	59,221	66,733	70,877	80,141	99,751	135,232
			Domestic Exports				
16,260	20,383	20,594	22,932	23,648	29,411	38,108	82,613
29	9	4	0	-	1,082	-	2
1,948	1,903	2,072	2,622	2,119	2,728	4,853	6,709
-	-	-	-	-	-	-	-
-	-	-	-	-	-	-	-
100	133	125	98	136	132	205	655
2	0	4	-	-	2	-	16
16	28	96	24	119	30	88	4
1,043	1,318	1,833	1,870	2,346	4,634	7,482	10,091
225	233	301	340	488	265	113	35
19,622	24,006	25,029	27,886	28,856	38,285	50,849	100,125
			Re-Exports				
n.a.	n.a.	n.a.	n.a.	n.a.	n.a.	n.a.	n.a.
n.a.	n.a.	n.a.	n.a.	n.a.	n.a.	n.a.	n.a.
n.a.	n.a.	n.a.	n.a.	n.a.	n.a.	n.a.	n.a.
n.a.	n.a.	n.a.	n.a.	n.a.	n.a.	n.a.	n.a.
n.a.	n.a.	n.a.	n.a.	n.a.	n.a.	n.a.	n.a.
n.a.	n.a.	n.a.	n.a.	n.a.	n.a.	n.a.	n.a.
n.a.	n.a.	n.a.	n.a.	n.a.	n.a.	n.a.	n.a.
n.a.	n.a.	n.a.	n.a.	n.a.	n.a.	n.a.	n.a.
n.a.	n.a.	n.a.	n.a.	n.a.	n.a.	n.a.	n.a.
n.a.	n.a.	n.a.	n.a.	n.a.	n.a.	n.a.	n.a.
4,942	6,227	8,666	9,715	8,353	10,897	12,619	17,634

Table SA3.7. Dominica: Trade by SITC Sections
(value in thousands at Eastern Caribbean dollars)

SITC	1960	1961	1962	1963	1964	1965	1966
				Imports			
0	n.a.	2,898	3,532	3,790	4,400	4,544	4,826
1	n.a.	488	439	405	518	886	881
2	n.a.	208	392	336	506	428	507
3	n.a.	451	351	368	414	460	429
4	n.a.	242	232	211	231	238	142
5	n.a.	1,073	1,336	1,605	2,259	2,201	2,172
6	n.a.	2,149	2,769	2,286	2,804	3,506	3,215
7	n.a.	1,343	1,905	1,242	1,739	2,683	2,431
8	n.a.	1,707	1,727	1,662	2,090	2,246	2,337
9	n.a.	19	115	86	66	86	115
Total	9,964	10,577	12,798	11,991	15,025	17,278	17,057
				Domestic Exports			
0	5,196	6,039	6,540	6,626	7,673	8,564	8,842
1	-	-	-	-	-	-	-
2	438	501	437	511	362	367	256
3	-	-	-	-	-	-	-
4	9	23	12	6	9	11	151
5	366	615	482	518	393	477	665
6	55	54	46	50	59	60	66
7	2	5	-	3	-	-	-
8	6	3	4	5	6	5	8
9	13	12	50	34	18	5	2
Total	6,084	7,252	7,571	7,753	8,521	9,490	9,991
				Re-Exports			
0	n.a.	n.a.	n.a.	-	-	-	1
1	n.a.	n.a.	n.a.	-	-	-	-
2	n.a.	n.a.	n.a.	-	-	1	1
3	n.a.	n.a.	n.a.	-	2	1	1
4	n.a.	n.a.	n.a.	-	-	-	-
5	n.a.	n.a.	n.a.	19	63	2	2
6	n.a.	n.a.	n.a.	1	5	10	8
7	n.a.	n.a.	n.a.	33	34	9	35
8	n.a.	n.a.	n.a.	1	5	4	15
9	n.a.	n.a.	n.a.	12	13	29	34
Total	97	33	114	69	123	56	96

Source: CARICOM Secretariat

1967	1968	1969	1970	1971	1972	1973	1974
			Imports				
4,958	5,852	6,872	7,158	7,711	9,316	9,434	12,538
717	859	1,050	1,418	1,574	1,333	1,155	1,093
611	592	646	662	682	1,054	1,041	1,224
545	629	669	855	923	1,098	1,383	2,331
45	114	114	129	236	351	90	177
2,421	2,523	3,040	2,964	3,391	3,174	3,024	4,091
3,439	3,846	5,120	6,851	7,239	7,761	7,742	8,747
2,379	3,004	4,100	6,548	6,433	4,322	4,930	5,223
2,125	2,676	3,101	4,503	4,587	3,989	3,484	3,477
76	116	115	171	243	482	9	18
17,315	20,211	24,826	31,258	33,019	32,879	32,292	38,918
			Domestic Exports				
9,498	10,896	12,077	9,394	9,929	10,623	13,710	17,582
-	35	38	11	12	32	52	78
224	291	516	348	252	176	190	21
-	-	-	-	-	-	-	-
306	387	417	522	523	761	635	1,062
405	544	844	1,031	1,148	1,239	1,455	1,170
62	70	82	102	77	94	107	90
-	-	1	9	-	-	-	-
15	13	15	11	24	71	75	126
2	1	-	1	25	-	-	-
10,512	12,237	13,989	11,430	11,990	12,995	16,224	20,130
			Re-Exports				
11	2	15	3	n.a.	n.a.	n.a.	n.a.
-	-	-	1	n.a.	n.a.	n.a.	n.a.
-	-	1	4	n.a.	n.a.	n.a.	n.a.
19	8	-	-	n.a.	n.a.	n.a.	n.a.
-	-	-	-	n.a.	n.a.	n.a.	n.a.
114	6	1	-	n.a.	n.a.	n.a.	n.a.
8	9	4	43	n.a.	n.a.	n.a.	n.a.
97	86	119	240	n.a.	n.a.	n.a.	n.a.
22	18	17	19	n.a.	n.a.	n.a.	n.a.
76	48	53	70	n.a.	n.a.	n.a	n.a.
336	177	211	380	289	506	514	819

Table SA3.8. Grenada: Trade by SITC Sections
(value in thousands of Eastern Caribbean dollars)

SITC	1960	1961	1962	1963	1964	1965	1966
			Imports				
0	4,384	4,293	4,529	4,887	5,126	5,467	6,273
1	651	577	431	520	522	579	675
2	474	641	690	397	737	672	902
3	861	689	739	874	1,464	1,298	805
4	96	84	111	76	81	112	108
5	1,403	1,500	1,440	1,695	1,924	2,179	2,366
6	3,210	3,515	3,322	2,750	3,392	3,718	4,252
7	1,892	2,701	1,842	1,750	1,899	2,675	3,268
8	1,839	2,057	2,191	2,052	2,509	2,426	3,066
9	21	26	24	22	19	16	10
Total	14,832	16,083	15,319	15,024	17,673	19,144	21,724
			Domestic Exports				
0	6,912	5,679	5,810	7,624	6,884	10,510	9,854
1	-	-	-	-	-	-	31
2	48	52	66	64	37	57	38
3	-	-	-	-	-	-	-
4	-	-	-	-	-	-	-
5	26	12	10	32	40	92	63
6	-	-	3	2	2	5	5
7	-	-	-	-	-	-	1
8	-	2	25	58	64	7	6
9	10	25	7	3	-	7	5
Total	6,996	5,771	5,920	7,784	7,027	10,678	10,003
			Re-Exports				
0	n.a.	n.a.	n.a.	n.a.	3	n.a.	4
1	n.a.	n.a.	n.a.	n.a.	1	n.a.	-
2	n.a.	n.a.	n.a.	n.a.	2	n.a.	3
3	n.a.	n.a.	n.a.	n.a.	2	n.a.	15
4	n.a.	n.a.	n.a.	n.a.	-	n.a.	-
5	n.a.	n.a.	n.a.	n.a.	37	n.a.	4
6	n.a.	n.a.	n.a.	n.a.	32	n.a.	18
7	n.a.	n.a.	n.a.	n.a.	100	n.a.	132
8	n.a.	n.a.	n.a.	n.a.	16	n.a.	17
9	n.a.	n.a.	n.a.	n.a.	-	n.a.	-
Total	167	160	147	71	194	202	193

Source: CARICOM Secretariat

1967	1968	1969	1970	1971	1972	1973	1974
				Imports			
6,641	7,469	8,970	10,997	12,986	13,284	14,540	n.a.
791	752	1,015	1,587	1,974	1,356	1,075	n.a.
1,192	1,160	1,968	2,130	1,666	1,703	1,994	n.a.
848	1,066	1,440	2,056	2,230	2,342	2,510	n.a.
46	236	194	91	125	118	142	n.a.
2,662	2,884	3,296	3,588	3,852	3,825	3,610	n.a.
4,760	5,401	7,008	10,282	8,965	7,682	7,837	n.a.
3,753	3,337	4,948	7,077	7,235	6,781	6,067	n.a.
3,379	4,026	5,375	6,807	7,004	5,696	4,699	n.a.
9	16	13	17	15	24	13	n.a.
24,082	26,346	34,227	44,632	46,051	42,812	42,487	38,114
			Domestic Exports				
8,330	9,575	14,601	10,797	9,222	9,809	13,440	n.a.
12	11	27	24	9	4	3	n.a.
34	196	83	38	7	6	19	n.a.
-	-	-	-	-	-	-	n.a.
-	-	-	-	-	-	-	n.a.
43	71	27	39	23	89	47	n.a.
4	7	9	8	5	3	4	n.a.
2	-	-	-	-	-	-	n.a.
5	8	24	38	21	37	123	n.a.
2	2	7	10	3	6	-	n.a.
8,430	9,870	14,778	10,953	9,291	9,954	13,637	17,873
				Re-Exports			
n.a.	57	121	179	301	211	173	n.a.
n.a.	1	-	17	3	4	5	n.a.
n.a.	5	5	5	2	6	12	n.a.
n.a.	4	19	13	6	19	10	n.a.
n.a.	-	-	-	-	-	-	n.a.
n.a.	32	14	75	71	41	102	n.a.
n.a.	60	121	351	66	34	121	n.a.
n.a.	78	182	327	371	191	375	n.a.
n.a.	39	199	154	82	68	77	n.a.
n.a.	8	1	-	-	-	-	n.a.
150	283	662	1,122	902	576	874	1,491

Table SA3.9. Montserrat: Trade by SITC Sections
(value in thousands of Eastern Caribbean dollars)

SITC	1960	1961	1962	1963	1964	1965	1966
			Imports				
0	528	590	668	732	n.a.	n.a.	n.a.
1	69	176	161	191	n.a.	n.a.	n.a.
2	107	119	95	81	n.a.	n.a.	n.a.
3	76	129	160	108	n.a.	n.a.	n.a.
4	11	22	16	5	n.a.	n.a.	n.a.
5	139	137	187	159	n.a.	n.a.	n.a.
6	329	353	415	451	n.a.	n.a.	n.a.
7	398	304	444	483	n.a.	n.a.	n.a.
8	218	293	278	421	n.a.	n.a.	n.a.
9	106	69	126	126	n.a.	n.a.	n.a.
Total	1,979	2,190	2,550	2,757	4,020	4,888	n.a.
			Domestic Exports				
0	53	86	213	66	48	67	n.a.
1	-	-	-	-	197	151	n.a.
2	203	205	163	172	-	-	n.a.
3	-	-	-	-	-	-	n.a.
4	-	-	-	-	-	-	n.a.
5	-	-	-	-	-	-	n.a.
6	-	-	-	-	-	-	n.a.
7	-	-	-	-	-	-	n.a.
8	-	-	-	-	-	-	n.a.
9	-	-	-	5	34	-	n.a.
Total	256	291	377	242	279	218	n.a.

Source: CARICOM Secretariat

1967	1968	1969	1970	1971	1972	1973	1974
				Imports			
1,434	1,634	n.a.	1,948	1,816	2,583	2,861	3,870
447	648	n.a.	719	751	916	963	945
475	340	n.a.	377	318	431	529	707
289	484	n.a.	632	605	686	876	1,720
53	46	n.a.	63	68	90	87	170
383	442	n.a.	482	443	763	714	839
1,464	1,576	n.a.	1,622	1,556	2,624	2,470	3,234
1,251	1,380	n.a.	1,529	1,812	2,207	1,823	2,513
1,019	1,167	n.a.	1,422	1,142	1,715	1,743	1,852
109	14	n.a.	6	47	65	76	108
6,923	7,731	n.a.	8,801	8,558	12,080	12,142	15,959
				Domestic Exports			
50	50	39	70	75	58	90	209
1	-	1	2	1	-	-	-
-	3	74	198	22	26	1	7
-	-	-	-	-	-	-	-
-	-	-	-	-	-	-	-
-	-	1	6	-	-	-	9
2	5	-	-	27	38	40	31
-	-	-	-	-	-	-	-
-	-	-	-	-	-	-	2
-	-	-	-	-	-	-	4
53	58	114	277	125	122	131	261

Table SA3.10. St. Kitts: Trade by SITC Sections
(value in thousands of Eastern Caribbean dollars)

SITC	1960	1961	1962	1963	1964	1965
			Imports			
0	3,589	3,727	n.a.	3,955	4,597	4,565
1	688	732	n.a.	612	595	668
2	603	554	n.a.	446	518	566
3	485	551	n.a.	503	438	531
4	126	38	n.a.	148	154	154
5	1,071	1,152	n.a.	1,269	1,282	1,358
6	2,182	2,737	n.a.	2,163	2,170	2,593
7	1,568	2,186	n.a.	1,690	1,508	2,234
8	1,414	1,627	n.a.	1,401	1,369	1,858
9	375	125	n.a.	89	822	100
Total	12,100	13,429	n.a.	12,278	13,453	14,628
			Domestic Exports			
0	9,536	9,173	n.a.	7,717	9,289	8,016
1	33	49	n.a.	71	82	69
2	67	207	n.a.	192	225	282
3	-	-	n.a.	-	-	-
4	-	12	n.a.	-	-	-
5	-	-	n.a.	-	-	-
6	-	10	n.a.	5	1	12
7	-	-	n.a.	-	11	-
8	-	1	n.a.	2	2	3
9	5	7	n.a.	9	4	1
Total	9,641	9,459	n.a.	7,995	9,615	8,383
			Re-Exports			
0	53	47	n.a.	42	28	27
1	26	21	n.a.	42	-	1
2	35	79	n.a.	35	28	21
3	102	72	n.a.	19	15	3
4	-	-	n.a.	2	-	3
5	9	15	n.a.	9	2	2
6	32	42	n.a.	51	31	15
7	40	32	n.a.	44	42	335
8	59	58	n.a.	56	13	23
9	-	-	n.a.	14	-	-
Total	354	366	n.a.	293	159	429

Source: CARICOM Secretariat

1966	1967	1968	1969	1970	1971	1972	1973
				Imports			
5,170	5,198	5,468	5,708	6,382	6,258	7,532	8,154
779	703	656	704	809	919	1,008	901
635	407	579	826	642	681	674	1,596
554	546	646	706	701	1,393	1,107	1,324
182	186	176	149	219	205	215	263
1,544	1,457	1,659	1,747	1,866	1,961	2,652	3,739
3,034	2,868	2,628	3,469	5,137	6,032	5,997	6,393
2,113	3,099	2,271	2,952	4,421	9,702	8,011	10,522
1,736	1,713	2,799	2,469	3,019	3,086	3,111	3,232
69	64	188	574	231	268	256	2
15,818	16,242	17,072	19,304	23,427	30,505	30,562	36,125
				Domestic Exports			
7,976	8,458	6,111	7,648	6,228	5,410	7,585	6,725
73	88	117	139	186	154	126	148
403	108	56	79	123	66	96	80
-	-	-	-	24	37	43	-
-	-	-	-	-	-	-	-
-	-	-	-	-	-	-	15
22	7	6	-	-	1	1	6
-	-	-	-	1,132	1,897	3,380	7,306
1	6	7	7	16	40	176	37
-	-	2	14	1	3	1	-
8,476	8,667	6,298	7,887	7,710	7,608	11,409	14,317
				Re-Exports			
18	79	48	63	30	33	38	n.a.
4	1	2	-	-	-	-	n.a.
19	27	16	8	17	9	25	n.a.
1	1	1	4	8	2	3	n.a.
-	4	1	-	-	-	1	n.a.
3	10	10	9	9	9	52	n.a.
27	64	182	247	189	187	144	n.a.
46	155	341	174	217	91	289	n.a.
20	38	41	65	49	24	49	n.a.
1	-	13	163	65	95	108	n.a.
139	380	653	734	584	451	709	2,259

Table SA3.11. St. Lucia: Trade by SITC Sections
(thousands of Eastern Caribbean dollars)

SITC	1960	1961	1962	1963	1964	1965	1966	1967	1968	1969	1970	1971	1972	1973	1974
Imports															
0	3,019	3,406	3,904	4,143	5,600	5,990	6,989	7,212	7,961	8,753	10,375	12,148	13,179	17,251	22,265
1	762	758	879	1,004	1,200	1,244	1,542	1,436	1,701	2,141	2,751	3,707	3,904	4,151	4,301
2	160	160	283	375	585	623	957	926	898	1,672	1,554	1,802	1,959	2,474	3,335
3	482	441	548	571	554	662	614	823	932	872	1,903	2,375	2,566	2,948	6,471
4	27	27	39	39	33	64	49	49	63	58	85	110	69	95	102
5	1,500	1,404	2,178	2,108	2,725	2,871	3,119	3,681	3,282	4,188	4,280	4,785	6,030	6,343	8,365
6	2,963	3,283	4,007	3,419	3,931	4,036	6,397	6,297	5,555	9,640	13,039	16,275	16,829	17,246	22,509
7	1,597	1,881	2,428	2,602	2,627	3,415	4,384	4,602	4,471	7,608	12,248	17,946	13,523	13,165	12,023
8	1,651	1,902	2,451	2,350	3,118	3,064	4,285	4,468	4,526	6,501	8,277	9,775	10,548	10,473	10,650
9	21	28	29	51	50	45	50	53	63	67	78	77	84	24	93
Total	12,182	13,289	16,745	16,660	20,421	22,014	28,386	29,545	29,452	41,500	54,585	68,998	68,690	74,170	91,115
Domestic Exports															
0	4,401	6,292	6,578	6,604	8,371	9,399	9,486	9,304	10,020	14,150	5,687	7,346	8,920	10,837	22,570
1	-	34	21	19	8	-	-	-	-	-	-	-	-	-	-
2	258	567	719	557	798	654	1,199	1,075	1,344	1,212	1,148	483	279	62	76
3	-	-	-	-	-	-	-	-	-	-	-	-	-	-	4
4	554	708	139	614	474	671	630	662	571	701	1,218	1,287	2,086	2,993	3,226
5	13	1	10	5	4	9	6	4	2	2	5	4	5	32	287
6	3	-	-	-	-	-	-	-	-	1	3	9	2,253	265	3,778
7	1	-	-	-	-	-	4	-	-	-	-	9	39	318	293
8	2	3	10	18	2	4	3	5	1	3	13	67	90	526	699
9	3	1	7	3	1	2	-	1	-	3	2	1	-	3	-
Total	5,236	7,605	7,484	7,821	9,658	10,738	11,327	11,052	11,939	16,072	8,078	9,207	13,673	15,036	30,934

Source: CARICOM Secretariat

Table SA3.12. St. Vincent: Trade by SITC Sections
(thousands of Eastern Caribbean dollars)

SITC	1960	1961	1962	1963	1964	1965	1966	1967	1968	1969	1970	1971	1972	1973	1974
							Imports								
0	2,881	2,918	3,258	3,700	4,416	4,477	4,799	4,593	5,827	6,731	7,511	9,082	10,210	n.a.	n.a.
1	593	677	533	599	667	611	672	643	823	1,062	1,432	1,766	1,705	n.a.	n.a.
2	444	453	487	507	548	510	514	589	791	888	1,168	1,149	1,315	n.a.	n.a.
3	455	469	416	522	506	473	539	500	611	740	890	1,063	1,339	n.a.	n.a.
4	219	216	258	261	285	260	290	309	148	49	34	41	32	n.a.	n.a.
5	1,376	1,426	1,458	1,636	2,459	1,781	1,849	1,892	2,056	2,641	2,805	3,074	3,058	n.a.	n.a.
6	2,809	3,034	2,945	2,560	2,940	2,859	3,288	3,083	3,820	4,942	6,818	8,334	7,105	n.a.	n.a.
7	1,760	1,644	1,254	1,195	1,922	1,915	1,557	2,057	3,207	3,629	5,319	6,081	5,652	n.a.	n.a.
8	1,802	1,332	1,266	1,281	1,710	1,450	1,575	1,640	2,299	3,049	4,212	5,151	4,600	n.a.	n.a.
9	634	563	603	537	611	472	971	502	518	684	328	275	213	n.a.	n.a.
Total	12,973	12,733	12,477	12,796	16,064	14,809	16,054	15,808	20,098	24,416	30,517	36,016	35,227	38,495	50,873
							Domestic Exports								
0	4,778	4,569	4,812	5,025	5,015	4,940	4,834	4,703	6,037	6,071	5,351	4,256	4,907	n.a.	n.a.
1	8	2	1	-	-	-	-	-	1	-	-	4	-	n.a.	n.a.
2	961	930	849	892	956	993	973	966	641	136	44	34	28	n.a.	n.a.
3	-	-	-	-	-	-	-	-	-	-	-	-	-	n.a.	n.a.
4	1	1	1	1	1	2	2	3	92	791	1,059	1,058	936	n.a.	n.a.
5	23	28	9	13	16	21	19	25	8	34	5	2	8	n.a.	n.a.
6	-	-	-	-	-	-	1	1	-	3	4	5	3	n.a.	n.a.
7	-	-	-	-	-	-	-	-	-	1	-	1	-	n.a.	n.a.
8	3	4	2	2	1	-	1	1	2	15	8	11	18	n.a.	n.a.
9	26	35	40	31	51	65	39	51	54	124	58	20	50	n.a.	n.a.
Total	5,799	5,570	5,714	5,965	6,040	6,022	5,869	5,749	6,835	7,176	6,529	5,391	5,951	8,962	n.a.

Source: CARICOM Secretariat

Table SA3.13. Barbados: Trade, Total and CARIFTA, 1963–74

(thousands of Eastern Caribbean dollars)

SITC	1963 Total	1963 Carifta	1963 %	1967 Total	1967 Carifta	1967 %	1971 Total	1971 Carifta	1971 %
				Domestic Exports					
0	49,762	1816	3.6	46,767	1,741	3.7	34,082	3,719	10.9
1	2,035	831	40.8	3,070	1,645	53.6	4,225	2,472	58.5
2	288	192	66.7	397	271	68.3	296	15	5.1
3	68	36	52.9	644	24	3.7	134	20	14.9
4	307	288	93.8	145	119	82.1	2	0	0
5	274	261	95.3	504	476	94.4	2,534	2,332	92.0
6	322	90	28.0	602	224	37.2	2,122	1,428	67.3
7	58	7	12.1	172	79	45.9	3,753	249	6.6
8	386	318	82.4	1,295	1,010	78.0	6,026	2,832	47.0
9	5	4	80.0	7	5	71.4	8	5	62.5
Total	53,506	3,843	7.2	53,601	5,593	10.4	53,180	13,074	24.6
				Imports					
0	26,908	3,366	12.5	32,534	4,231	13.0	53,350	7,240	13.6
1	2,026	30	1.5	2,346	57	2.4	4,700	406	8.6
2	4,251	1,698	39.9	4,980	1,583	31.8	7,313	1,205	16.5
3	13,713	3,973	29.0	11,609	1,370	11.8	15,934	4,667	29.3
4	551	303	55.0	1,115	350	31.4	3,951	1,556	39.4
5	6,967	1,354	19.4	10,945	2,187	20.0	18,444	3,996	21.7
6	18,656	1,062	5.7	27,199	2,452	9.0	48,240	5,529	11.5
7	13,620	7	0.1	25,675	120	0.5	56,017	754	1.3
8	8,918	513	5.8	13,805	826	6.0	28,972	4,555	15.7
9	3,262	192	5.9	3,845	238	6.2	6,763	96	1.4
Total	98,871	12,499	12.6	134,053	13,414	10.0	243,685	30,004	12.3

SOURCE: CARICOM SECRETARIAT

1972			1973			1974		
Total	Carifta	%	Total	Carifta	%	Total	Carifta	%
				Domestic Exports				
35,533	4,655	13.1	43,220	4,716	10.9	70,836	7,798	11.0
4,802	2,920	60.8	5,143	2,895	56.3	5,822	3,350	57.5
209	17	8.1	721	148	20.5	1,473	274	18.6
378	101	26.7	656	83	12.7	2,081	36	1.7
1	1	100.0	1	1	100.0	16	16	100.0
3,329	2,982	89.6	4,300	3,723	86.6	4,867	4,176	85.8
6,240	2,660	42.6	4,323	3,229	74.7	5,833	4,663	79.9
4,300	170	4.0	6,690	355	5.3	8,974	214	2.4
8,305	4,200	50.6	18,638	6,691	35.9	24,291	9,609	39.6
6	4	66.7	9	6	66.7	21	5	23.8
63,103	17,709	28.1	83,700	21,847	26.1	124,215	30,141	24.3
				Imports				
63,002	8,185	13.0	79,716	8,465	10.6	94,220	13,288	14.1
6,086	759	12.5	6,992	1,735	24.8	7,553	3,201	42.4
6,723	909	13.5	9,235	1,542	16.7	12,016	1,876	15.6
15,823	6,790	42.9	21,822	7,837	35.9	66,359	23,264	35.1
3,782	1,561	41.3	3,865	1,710	44.2	7,516	1,910	25.4
23,050	5,573	24.2	27,565	6,260	22.7	34,790	9,253	26.6
56,039	7,313	13.0	67,432	8,014	11.9	79,630	10,209	12.8
54,847	628	1.1	67,008	827	1.2	60,146	1,114	1.9
33,171	4,703	14.2	34,920	6,385	18.3	42,472	8,140	19.2
7,914	79	1.0	10,046	89	0.9	13,618	38	0.3
270,436	36,501	13.5	328,602	42,863	13.0	418,319	72,292	17.3

Table SA3.14. Guyana: Trade, Total and CARIFTA, 1963–74
(thousands of Eastern Caribbean dollars)

SITC	1963 Total	1963 Carifta	1963 %	1967 Total	1967 Carifta	1967 %	1971 Total	1971 Carifta	1971 %
					Domestic Exports				
0	103,928	12,615	12.1	92,150	17,472	19.0	128,660	20,833	16.2
1	3,194	88	2.8	5,791	86	1.5	7,124	518	7.3
2	60,056	602	1.0	85,680	843	1.0	142,482	4,273	3.0
3	0	0	0	20	6	30.0	33	14	42.4
4		-	0	0	0	0	-		0
5	1,488	1,222	82.1	1,382	978	70.8	2,498	2,211	88.5
6	3,637	139	3.8	6,503	184	2.8	3,812	1,109	29.1
7	9	0	0	2	1	50.0	20	8	40.0
8	335	301	89.9	413	316	76.5	3,052	2,844	93.2
9	279	2	0.7	19	16	84.2	79	8	10.1
Total	172,926	14,970	8.7	191,960	19,903	10.4	287,760	31,818	11.1
					Imports				
0	24,605	523	2.1	33,556	755	2.2	41,529	4,678	11.3
1	1,596	12	0.8	2,025	9	0.4	2,617	180	6.9
2	558	29	5.2	2,807	975	34.7	1,626	120	7.4
3	12,038	10,458	86.6	18,106	16,226	89.6	23,567	21,220	90.0
4	1,303	105	8.1	1,765	300	17.0	3,794	713	18.8
5	16,883	2,497	14.8	19,114	3,490	18.3	30,679	6,237	20.3
6	24,981	1,500	6.0	48,375	2,853	5.9	70,111	3,879	5.5
7	25,062	16	0.1	77,356	110	0.1	68,224	155	0.2
8	11,046	266	2.4	21,288	932	4.4	24,195	3,304	13.7
9	438	35	8.0	900	92	10.2	1,290	50	3.9
Total	118,511	15,442	13.0	225,292	25,741	11.4	267,632	40,536	15.1

Source: CARICOM Secretariat

1972			1973			1974		
Total	Carifta	%	Total	Carifta	%	Total	Carifta	%
				Domestic Exports				
132,278	23,633	17.9	109,261	24,103	22.1	322,879	45,969	14.2
5,855	649	11.1	7,790	1,085	13.9	14,653	1,313	9.0
126,079	1,061	0.8	131,873	1,451	1.1	188,256	756	0.4
17	2	11.8	6	6	100.0	1	-	0
163	163	100.0	170	170	100.0	0	0	0
2,817	2,529	89.8	3,345	3,056	91.4	3,681	3,153	85.7
3,992	2,089	52.3	5,354	3,179	59.4	5,656	3,687	65.2
1,017	823	80.9	890	887	99.7	10	9	90.0
3,926	3,762	95.8	5,331	5,157	96.7	6,163	5,812	94.3
58	10	17.2	301	33	11.0	1,808	210	11.6
276,203	34,722	12.6	264,321	39,128	14.8	543,108	60,909	11.2
				Imports				
38,136	7,121	18.7	51,469	8,324	16.2	66,788	8,998	13.5
2,475	474	19.2	3,450	1,726	50.0	3,020	1,443	47.8
1,489	250	16.8	1,368	56	4.1	5,584	540	9.7
25,899	23,778	91.8	44,618	42,501	95.3	95,299	91,781	96.3
2,889	341	11.8	3,282	547	16.7	11,485	956	64.4
32,915	7,627	23.2	41,916	10,037	23.9	61,947	15,994	25.8
70,914	4,121	5.8	84,666	7,095	8.4	128,114	11,411	8.9
72,348	248	0.3	84,030	608	0.7	112,576	1,227	1.1
26,448	3,356	12.7	27,424	5,042	22.5	35,328	5,597	15.8
850	21	2.5	871	51	5.9	2,145	220	10.3
274,363	47,337	17.3	343,094	75,987	13.5	522,285	138,168	26.5

Table SA3.15. Jamaica: Trade, Total and CARIFTA, 1963–74
(thousands of Eastern Caribbean dollars)

SITC	1963 Total	1963 Carifta	1963 %	1967 Total	1967 Carifta	1967 %	1971 Total	1971 Carifta	1971 %
					Domestic Exports				
0	158,133	197	0.1	135,805	1,013	0.7	137,754	4,667	3.4
1	10,556	59	0.6	12,491	75	0.6	18,954	1,440	7.6
2	143,923	17	0	194,177	27	0	432,431	26	0
3	-	-	0	10,578	1,545	14.6	18,479	3,931	21.3
4	26	21	80.8	23	3	13.0	76	7	9.2
5	4,703	1,973	42.0	9,427	4,810	51.0	13,225	8,482	64.1
6	4,390	1,330	30.3	4,687	2,462	52.5	11,790	5,434	46.1
7	252	30	11.9	349	13	3.7	1,793	1,109	61.9
8	14,814	408	2.8	18,200	632	3.5	25,979	6,012	23.1
9	85	30	35.3	50	18	36.0	6	3	50.0
Total	336,883	4,065	1.2	385,787	10,598	2.7	660,487	31,112	4.7
					Imports				
0	82,245	3,707	4.5	116,603	4,166	3.6	183,855	8,944	4.9
1	7,917	11	0.1	8,239	10	0.1	17,793	167	0.9
2	12,383	1,449	11.7	18,475	1,470	8.0	30,570	1,799	5.9
3	34,881	10,801	31.0	48,725	341	0.7	104,698	1,066	1.0
4	2,021	-	0	4,160	-	0	5,828	240	4.1
5	33,692	2,276	6.8	48,906	2,445	5.0	91,926	2,864	3.1
6	102,005	224	0.2	159,064	170	0.1	259,657	2,967	1.1
7	79,718	32	0	152,298	174	0.1	321,510	247	0.1
8	30,988	130	0.4	48,583	119	0.3	85,998	8,185	9.5
9	732	2	0.3	1,075	0	0	1,575	0	0
Total	386,582	18,632	4.8	606,127	8,895	1.5	1,103,410	26,480	2.4

Source: CARICOM Secretariat

1972			1973			1974		
Total	Carifta	%	Total	Carifta	%	Total	Carifta	%
				Domestic Exports				
149,951	7,030	4.7	155,475	9,473	6.1	246,147	9,692	3.9
21,699	1,690	7.8	26,065	3,250	12.5	39,030	4,374	11.2
458,023	131	0	493,808	104	0	1,085,987	125	0
18,909	5,702	30.2	17,760	4,262	24.0	21,373	6,556	30.7
145	67	46.2	188	103	54.8	451	378	83.8
15,446	11,856	76.8	16,126	11,957	74.1	21,712	16,469	75.9
11,971	6,108	51.0	14,433	7,440	51.5	25,049	13,304	53.1
2,670	1,837	68.8	3,565	2,872	80.6	4,639	4,049	87.3
24,540	6,757	27.5	20,103	7,776	38.7	21,895	9,054	41.4
32	1	3.1	125	6	4.8	3	1	33.3
703,385	41,179	5.9	747,650	47,241	6.3	1,466,287	64,002	4.4
				Imports				
216,494	18,599	8.6	247,990	19,774	8.0	393,354	40,608	10.3
19,622	187	1.0	18,559	669	3.6	14,539	516	3.5
35,075	1,294	3.7	52,573	2,982	5.7	64,378	3,740	5.8
106,960	21,289	19.9	140,686	15,078	10.7	398,763	55,638	14.0
8,533	1,198	14.0	13,323	2,409	18.1	25,712	1,796	7.0
114,083	4,034	3.5	127,745	5,183	4.1	181,886	10,779	5.9
270,501	2,962	1.1	301,943	3,741	1.2	405,385	5,344	1.3
308,137	878	0.3	297,667	5,295	1.8	318,382	9,174	2.9
100,863	13,422	13.3	94,733	13,810	14.6	103,201	18,265	17.7
3,297	0	0	2,451	3	0.1	3,691	1	0
1,183,565	63,864	5.4	1,297,669	68,943	5.3	1,909,291	145,861	7.6

Table SA3.16. Trinidad: Trade, Total and CARIFTA, 1963–74
(thousands of Eastern Caribbean dollars)

SITC	1963 Total	1963 Carifta	1963 %	1967 Total	1967 Carifta	1967 %	1971 Total	1971 Carifta	1971 %
				Domestic Exports					
0	69,634	2,806	4.0	57,004	4,664	8.2	77,186	15,610	20.2
1	2,828	345	12.2	3,876	424	10.9	3,135	596	19.0
2	4,213	80	1.9	4,922	237	4.8	4,991	699	14.0
3	526,179	23,486	4.5	594,403	21,209	3.6	805,008	36,782	4.6
4	187	180	96.3	209	186	89.0	371	361	97.3
5	12,589	5,530	43.9	77,490	7,619	9.8	71,310	12,844	18.0
6	4,450	3,579	80.4	7,266	6,905	95.0	17,063	15,817	92.7
7	25	12	48.0	348	150	43.1	1,008	824	81.7
8	4,377	1,974	45.1	6,946	3,185	45.9	21,378	16,433	76.9
9	235	61	26.0	210	51	24.3	571	233	40.8
Total	624,717	38,051	6.1	752,673	44,631	5.9	1,002,020	100,198	10.0
				Imports					
0	78,047	7,843	10.0	86,986	10,186	11.7	114,541	14,292	12.5
1	6.090	187	3.1	6,451	1,064	16.5	10,885	2,210	20.3
2	8,506	1,104	13.0	10,729	1,523	14.2	13,252	926	7.0
3	302,943	-	0	355,818	163	0	665,521	363	0.1
4	2,671	190	7.1	3,542	348	9.8	8,132	711	8.7
5	25,473	1,494	5.9	35,297	2,100	5.9	52,089	5,119	9.8
6	89,264	209	0.2	91,930	156	0.2	196,539	2,493	1.3
7	95,619	13	0	95,685	11	0	201,122	736	0.4
8	33,472	264	0.8	34,217	242	0.7	61,375	4,953	8.1
9	5,100	261	5.1	4,688	188	4.0	5,802	237	4.1
Total	647,186	11,565	1.8	725,342	15,982	2.2	1,329,258	32,039	2.4

Source: CARICOM Secretariat

1972			1973			1974		
Total	Carifta	%	Total	Carifta	%	Total	Carifta	%
				Domestic Exports				
88,970	17,530	19.7	84,128	19,203	22.8	153,980	26,290	17.1
3,937	826	21.0	7,711	1,440	18.7	12,237	2,300	18.8
5,163	318	6.2	6,682	425	6.4	9,183	927	10.1
832,894	43,450	5.2	1,126,393	57,745	5.1	3,553,392	160,137	4.5
155	142	91.6	349	301	86.2	72	15	20.8
76,988	15,928	20.7	74,668	19,619	26.3	137,938	31,641	22.9
16,990	15,347	90.3	21,438	19,210	89.6	32,146	23,144	72.0
1,909	1,645	86.2	2,929	2,725	93.0	10,087	9,935	98.5
25,062	19,031	75.9	28,308	22,618	79.9	24,780	24,643	99.4
409	141	34.5	523	97	18.5	336	115	34.2
1,052,476	114,356	10.9	1,353,130	143,384	10.6	3,934,152	279,147	7.1
				Imports				
132,923	13,851	10.4	161,006	12,360	7.7	250,267	21,732	8.7
10,564	3,145	29.8	11,343	2,961	26.1	12,635	4,154	32.9
16,554	897	5.4	18,821	745	4.0	25,050	1,202	4.8
704,779	457	0.1	793,896	6	0	2,716,395	25	0
8,951	1,389	15.5	11,059	748	6.8	23,013	632	2.7
64,609	7,536	11.7	75,856	8,069	10.6	116,486	10,024	8.6
201,820	5,076	2.5	215,040	5,293	2.5	312,945	9,411	3.0
256,770	2,216	0.9	201,116	2,136	1.1	240,289	3,346	1.4
68,852	6,307	9.2	70,129	8,505	12.1	75,554	10,941	14.5
5,277	292	5.5	5,767	331	5.7	5,190	294	5.7
1,471,099	41,167	2.8	1,564,033	41,153	2.6	3,777,823	61,761	1.6

Table SA3.17. Barbados: CARIFTA Trade by SITC

(thousands of Eastern Caribbean dollars)

SITC	1960	1961	1962	1963	1964	1965	1966
				Imports			
0	3,172	3,368	3,423	3,366	3,690	3,572	3,983
1	19	39	46	30	31	36	49
2	1,969	1,803	1,611	1,698	1,574	1,554	1,698
3	2,929	2,662	3,581	3,973	3,132	2,699	2,698
4	218	30	52	303	275	245	339
5	1,142	1,127	1,290	1,354	1,549	1,490	1,626
6	988	663	906	1,062	1,396	1,518	1,974
7	12	5	13	7	26	69	81
8	426	388	526	514	629	570	647
9	124	149	164	58	405	226	229
Total CARIFTA	10,999	10,232	11,612	12,365	12,708	11,979	13,324
Total Imports	83,299	80,262	89,079	98,871	108,874	116,265	131,111
				Domestic Exports			
0	1,465	1,547	1,663	1,398	2,035	1,902	1,918
1	1,252	1,226	868	831	1,319	1,457	1,972
2	4	1	14	189	69	89	82
3	-	1	38	36	14	5	59
4	240	324	290	288	311	340	233
5	277	305	264	261	225	191	270
6	144	246	206	89	157	95	95
7	12	52	28	7	24	41	54
8	163	187	300	338	461	594	796
9	2	2	2	4	11	4	16
Total CARIFTA	3,559	3,891	3,672	3,441	4,624	4,718	5,495
Total Exports	35,016	37,063	37,070	53,506	45,125	47,617	50,056

Source: "Overseas Trade" Annual Publication, Government of Barbados; CARICOM Secretariat.

1967	1968	1969	1970	1971	1972	1973	1974
				Imports			
4,231	4,534	5,119	6,703	7,240	8,185	8,465	13,288
57	85	287	603	406	759	1,735	3,201
1,583	1,381	1,080	498	1,205	909	1,542	1,876
1,370	3,002	4,645	4,542	4,667	6,790	7,837	23,264
350	573	898	1,387	1,556	1,561	1,710	1,910
2,187	2,228	2,582	3,430	3,996	5,573	6,260	9,253
2,452	3,310	4,045	4,892	5,529	7,313	8,014	10,209
120	681	739	838	754	628	827	1,114
826	1,139	2,015	3,537	4,555	4,703	6,385	8,140
238	274	108	120	96	79	89	38
13,414	17,207	21,516	26,549	30,004	36,501	42,863	72,292
134,053	168,025	194,554	235,005	243,685	270,436	328,602	418,319
				Domestic Exports			
1,741	1,935	2,458	3,058	3,719	4,655	4,716	7,798
1,645	1,294	1,628	1,828	2,472	2,920	2,895	3,350
270	198	55	42	15	17	148	274
24	52	41	28	20	101	83	36
119	17	-	-	-	1	1	16
476	1,021	1,251	1,995	2,332	2,982	3,723	4,176
224	465	1,081	1,248	1,428	2,660	3,229	4,663
79	93	85	176	249	170	355	214
1,010	1,524	2,313	2,819	2,832	4,200	6,691	9,609
5	5	3	5	5	4	6	5
5,593	6,604	8,917	11,199	13,074	17,709	21,847	30,141
53,601	59,646	57,357	62,106	53,180	63,103	83,700	124,215

Table SA3.18. Guyana: CARIFTA Trade by SITC

(thousands of Eastern Caribbean dollars)

SITC	1960	1961	1962	1963	1964	1965	1966	1967	1968	1969	1970	1971	1972	1973	1974
							Imports								
0	420	583	627	523	534	816	901	755	1,343	2,089	3,168	4,678	7,121	8,324	8,998
1	17	16	6	12	5	4	7	9	6	21	16	180	474	1,726	1,443
2	100	172	47	29	37	217	139	975	209	75	57	120	250	56	540
3	9,368	11,533	11,946	10,458	12,971	14,675	15,449	16,226	18,310	17,447	20,569	21,220	23,778	42,501	91,781
4	173	131	21	105	-	245	111	300	199	1,012	567	713	341	547	956
5	1,701	1,804	1,797	2,497	1,801	3,063	3,503	3,490	3,987	4,405	5,258	6,237	7,627	10,037	15,994
6	2,346	1,402	1,540	1,500	1,546	2,038	2,590	2,853	3,878	4,716	5,265	3,879	4,121	7,095	11,411
7	111	88	17	16	27	43	127	110	77	233	155	155	248	608	1,227
8	425	313	282	266	496	514	819	932	1,420	2,306	2,667	3,304	3,356	5,042	5,597
9	38	69	28	35	37	90	129	92	92	87	54	50	21	51	220
Total CARIFTA	14,700	16,110	16,311	15,442	17,452	21,707	23,775	25,741	29,521	32,290	37,777	40,536	47,337	75,987	138,168
Total Imports	147,599	147,000	126,277	118,511	150,925	180,131	202,006	225,292	219,311	235,833	268,239	267,632	274,363	343,094	522,285
							Domestic Exports								
0	15,518	14,541	14,860	12,615	15,849	15,625	14,917	17,472	18,816	18,048	18,381	20,833	23,633	24,103	45,969
1	113	127	103	88	82	85	106	86	117	284	696	518	649	1,085	1,313
2	745	668	944	602	636	593	583	843	963	1,476	968	4,273	1,061	1,451	756
3	-	-	-	-	-	2	3	6	2	1	4	14	2	6	-
4	-	-	-	-	-	-	-	-	1	-	-	-	163	170	-
5	1,119	1,060	1,278	1,222	1,231	1,267	1,086	978	995	1,153	1,417	2,211	2,529	3,056	3,153
6	94	124	139	139	176	203	202	184	321	699	931	1,109	2,089	3,179	3,687
7	492	35	1	-	2	1	1	1	-	52	1	8	823	887	9
8	323	314	345	301	215	121	203	316	359	885	1,722	2,844	3,762	5,157	5,812
9	14	8	9	2	8	4	2	16	2	4	3	8	10	33	210
Total CARIFTA	18,417	16,878	17,679	14,970	18,200	17,899	17,102	19,903	21,577	22,602	24,123	31,818	34,722	39,128	60,909
Total Exports	125,051	146,545	161,081	172,926	166,564	165,835	182,595	191,960	228,525	233,673	265,566	287,760	276,203	264,321	543,108

Source: CARICOM Secretariat

Table SA3.19. Jamaica: CARIFTA Trade by SITC

(thousands of Eastern Caribbean dollars)

SITC	1960	1961	1962	1963	1964	1965	1966	1967	1968	1969	1970	1971	1972	1973	1974
							Domestic Exports								
0	150	146	218	197	332	931	1,016	1,013	1,242	2,497	3,010	4,667	7,030	9,473	9,692
1	72	69	70	59	117	105	90	75	145	390	613	1,440	1,690	3,250	4,374
2	87	22	11	17	13	12	24	27	17	89	42	26	131	104	125
3	-	-	-	-	196	1,433	2,039	1,545	1,941	2,494	2,868	3,931	5,702	4,262	6,556
4	-	1	17	21	4	3	3	3	2	4	3	7	67	103	378
5	720	1,036	1,728	1,973	1,911	2,160	4,691	4,810	5,768	7,565	7,701	8,482	11,856	11,957	16,469
6	1,870	2,076	4,281	1,330	1,765	1,928	2,475	2,462	4,562	5,629	5,543	5,434	6,108	7,440	13,304
7	-	1	12	30	19	10	18	13	47	471	1,443	1,109	1,837	2,872	4,049
8	751	486	512	408	516	510	664	632	1,329	2,777	3,739	6,012	6,757	7,776	9,054
9	30	55	29	30	34	35	19	18	-	12	31	3	1	6	1
Total Carifta	3,680	3,893	6,879	4,065	4,907	7,126	11,039	10,548	15,054	21,928	24,992	31,112	41,179	47,241	64,002
Total Exports	267,655	291,035	298,726	336,883	362,763	359,697	384,521	385,787	430,787	494,640	669,878	660,487	703,385	747,650	1,466,287
							Imports								
0	5,473	4,216	3,772	3,707	4,354	4,491	3,313	4,166	2,784	4,073	7,263	8,944	18,599	19,774	40,608
1	12	13	9	11	13	12	13	10	7	50	132	167	187	669	516
2	1,645	1,349	1,057	1,449	1,899	2,045	1,355	1,470	1,203	1,539	1,506	1,799	1,294	2,982	3,740
3	7,345	10,005	11,652	10,801	5,230	246	481	341	515	771	1,065	1,066	21,289	15,078	55,638
4	211	37	-	-	-	-	-	-	-	-	1	240	1,198	2,409	1,796
5	1,648	1,841	1,843	2,276	3,114	2,928	1,588	2,445	2,872	2,627	2,696	2,864	4,034	5,183	10,779
6	381	495	250	224	48	86	83	170	444	1,094	2,071	2,967	2,962	3,741	5,344
7	3	7	17	32	15	6	3	174	109	113	125	247	878	5,295	9,174
8	237	207	163	130	180	138	115	119	648	2,620	4,174	8,185	13,422	13,810	18,265
9	7	23	7	2	1	1	-	-	2	2	39	-	-	3	1
Total Carifta	16,961	18,191	18,769	18,632	14,853	9,953	6,952	8,895	8,583	12,888	19,072	26,480	63,864	68,943	145,861
Total Exports	371,985	361,896	382,085	386,582	495,848	495,468	560,800	606,127	768,718	871,822	1,050,629	1,103,410	1,183,565	1,297,669	1,909,291

Source: "External Trade" Annual Publication, Government of Jamaica; CARICOM Secretariat.

Table SA3.20. Trinidad and Tobago: CARIFTA Trade by SITC

(thousands of Eastern Caribbean dollars)

SITC	1960	1961	1962	1963	1964	1965	1966
				Imports			
0	8,514	8,104	8,374	7,843	9,822	10,738	10,069
1	836	668	336	187	376	675	1,027
2	559	1,007	1,528	1,104	1,336	1,449	1,564
3	-	-	-	-	-	85	138
4	1	595	-	190	217	189	320
5	884	983	1,334	1,494	1,531	1,504	1,739
6	1,004	924	2,364	209	147	139	106
7	222	32	52	13	9	36	51
8	569	332	355	264	333	363	250
9	370	366	331	261	239	147	255
Total Carifta	12,959	13,010	14,674	11,565	14,009	15,324	15,520
Total Imports	504,591	584,608	606,371	647,186	731,418	817,831	778,611
				Domestic Exports			
0	2,047	2,638	2,448	2,806	3,765	3,789	4,275
1	508	533	394	345	239	237	294
2	115	96	103	80	122	188	230
3	19,151	23,854	26,642	23,486	18,651	18,447	19,954
4	87	191	228	180	203	158	190
5	5,470	5,353	6,149	5,530	6,238	7,712	6,851
6	4,419	2,462	3,622	3,579	4,251	5,006	6,610
7	64	14	27	12	22	102	102
8	1,281	1,451	1,687	1,974	2,618	2,864	3,224
9	73	65	49	61	58	56	59
Total Carifta	33,215	36,657	41,349	38,051	36,167	38,560	41,789
Total Exports	476,436	579,548	579,658	624,717	686,254	678,314	717,170

Source: CARICOM Secretariat

1967	1968	1969	1970	1971	1972	1973	1974
				Imports			
10,186	9,644	10,433	11,006	14,292	13,851	12,360	21,732
1,064	537	684	1,255	2,210	3,145	2,961	4,154
1,523	1,488	1,813	1,528	926	897	745	1,202
163	280	436	351	363	457	6	25
348	266	1,090	1,755	711	1,389	748	632
2,100	2,410	3,167	4,267	5,119	7,536	8,069	10,024
156	321	1,580	2,197	2,493	5,076	5,293	9,411
11	53	338	822	736	2,216	2,136	3,346
242	714	2,206	3,422	4,953	6,307	8,505	10,941
188	251	273	276	237	292	331	294
15,982	15,965	22,020	26,879	32,039	41,167	41,153	61,761
725,342	856,473	968,478	1,087,020	1,329,258	1,471,099	1,564,033	3,777,823
				Domestic Exports			
4,664	5,881	8,637	12,449	15,610	17,530	19,203	26,290
424	465	578	697	596	826	1,440	2,300
237	126	357	221	699	318	425	927
21,209	25,012	31,327	30,205	36,782	43,450	57,745	160,137
186	286	1,144	993	361	142	301	15
7,619	8,292	10,001	10,787	12,844	15,928	19,619	31,641
6,905	8,496	11,182	15,033	15,817	15,347	19,210	23,144
150	512	658	600	824	1,645	2,725	9,935
3,185	5,847	9,021	12,778	16,433	19,031	22,618	24,643
51	73	126	130	233	141	97	115
44,631	54,991	73,032	83,891	100,198	114,356	143,384	279,147
752,673	923,868	935,767	944,315	1,002,020	1,052,476	1,353,130	3,934,152

Table SA4.1. Barbados: Balance of Payments, 1966–73

(millions of U.S. dollars)

	1966			1967			1968			1969		
	Credit	Debit	Balance	Credit	Debit	Balance	Credit	Debit	Balance	Credit	Debit	Balance
Goods and services	72.5	93.7	-21.2	76.7	97.4	-20.7	81.2	105.0	-23.8	88.4	122.8	-34.4
Merchandise	34.6	76.3	-41.7	35.1	76.9	-41.8	33.3	84.0	-50.7	32.7	96.9	-64.2
Transportation	8.9	2.5	6.4	9.5	3.3	6.2	9.1	3.1	6.0	7.5	5.0	2.5
Travel	17.0	1.5	15.5	20.0	2.2	17.8	26.9	2.3	24.6	32.9	3.2	29.7
Investment income	3.5	3.9	-0.4	3.1	3.9	-0.8	2.4	4.3	-1.9	2.5	5.0	-2.5
Government, n.i.e.	1.2	0.2	1.0	1.3	0.9	0.4	1.7	1.1	0.6	2.2	1.2	1.0
Other services	7.3	9.3	-2.0	7.7	10.2	-2.5	7.8	10.2	-2.4	10.6	11.6	-1.0
Unrequited transfers	5.2	2.4	2.8	5.0	1.6	3.4	4.9	1.7	3.2	6.7	1.7	5.0
Private transfers	3.9	1.6	2.3	4.3	0.7	3.6	4.0	0.6	3.4	4.9	0.8	4.1
Central Government	1.3	0.8	0.5	0.7	0.9	-0.2	0.9	1.1	-0.2	1.8	0.9	0.9
Balance on Current Account			-18.4			-17.3			-20.6			-29.4
Capital (net)	11.4	0.5	10.9	13.7	3.3	10.4	11.9	2.5	9.4	15.5	1.1	14.4
Direct investment	7.5	--	7.5	8.2	1.2	7.0	8.4	0.5	7.9	9.1	--	9.1
Other private long-term	2.1	--	2.1	1.8	1.1	0.7	1.1	1.5	-0.4	2.5	0.6	1.9
Liabilities	(2.1)	(--)	(2.1)	(1.3)	(--)	(1.3)	(0.9)	(0.1)	(0.8)	(2.5)	(--)	(2.5)
Assets	(--)	(--)	(--)	(0.5)	(1.1)	(-0.6)	(0.2)	(1.4)	(-1.2)	(--)	(0.6)	(-0.6)
Other private short-term	1.6	0.4	1.2	1.3	1.0	0.3	1.9	0.3	1.6	3.9	0.4	3.5
Liabilities	(1.6)	(--)	(1.6)	(1.1)	(--)	(1.1)	(1.5)	(--)	(1.5)	(3.9)	(--)	(3.9)
Assets	(--)	(0.4)	(-0.4)	(0.2)	(1.0)	(-0.8)	(0.4)	(0.3)	(0.1)	(--)	(0.4)	(-0.4)
Public Sector	0.2	0.1	0.1	2.4	--	2.4	0.5	0.2	0.3	(--)	0.1	-0.1
Securities issued	(--)	(0.1)	(-0.1)	(1.7)	(--)	(1.7)	(0.5)	(--)	(0.5)	(--)	(0.1)	(-0.1)
Other	(0.2)	(--)	(0.2)	(0.7)	(--)	(0.7)	(--)	(0.2)	(-0.2)	(--)	(--)	(--)
Allocation of SDRs	--	--	--	--	--	--	--	--	--	--	--	--
Net errors and omissions			4.2			8.4			16.1			8.8
Net change in reserves (increase -)			3.3			-1.5			-4.9			6.2
Government			3.6			1.2			-1.2			-3.1
East Caribbean Currency Authority			-0.2			0.7			-1.0			-1.0
Commercial banks			--			-4.3			-2.8			10.3
Barbados Savings Bank			-0.1			-0.9			0.1			--

Table SA4.1. (continued)

(millions of U.S. dollars)

	1970			1971			1972[a/]			1973[b/]		
	Credit	Debit	Balance	Credit	Debit	Balance	Credit	Debit	Balance	Credit	Debit	Balance
Goods and services	101.0	147.8	-46.8	115.8	155.4	-39.6	135.6	177.7	-42.1			
Merchandise	35.3	116.9	-81.6	32.0	121.4	-89.4	37.6	140.3	-102.7	53.1	169.7	115.6
Transportation	7.5	5.7	1.8	12.6	6.8	5.8	13.1	7.9	5.2			
Travel	40.4	3.5	36.9	51.4	4.2	47.2	62.6	5.2	57.4	70.6		
Investment income	3.5	6.6	-3.1	3.1	7.7	-4.6	3.0	8.0	-5.0			-6.3
Government, n.i.e.	3.2	1.7	1.5	4.6	2.3	2.3	5.7	2.8	2.9			
Other services	11.3	13.5	-2.2	12.2	13.1	-0.9	13.5	13.5	--			
Unrequited transfers	7.7	2.6	5.1	7.6	2.8	4.8	8.2	2.9	5.3			5.6
Private transfers	5.3	0.9	4.4	5.3	1.0	4.3	5.7	1.1	4.6			
Central Government	2.4	1.7	0.7	2.3	1.8	0.5	2.5	1.8	0.7			
Balance on Current Account			-41.7			-34.8			-36.8			-49.8
Capital (net)	15.3	2.6	12.7	19.4	1.6	17.8			14.4			30.8
Direct investment	8.9	0.4	8.5	11.6	--	11.6			10.8			12.1
Other private long-term	4.8	1.4	3.4	4.0	1.4	2.6			3.0			4.0
Liabilities	(4.7)	(0.1)	(4.6)	(4.0)	(--)	(4.0)						
Assets	(0.1)	(1.3)	(-1.2)	(--)	(1.4)	(-1.4)						
Other private short-term	1.6	0.5	1.1	3.8	--	3.8						
Liabilities	(0.1)	(0.5)	(-0.4)	(3.7)	(--)	(3.7)						
Assets	(1.5)	(--)	(1.5)	(0.1)	(--)	(0.1)						
Public sector	--	0.3	-0.3	--	0.2	-0.2						
Securities issued	(--)	(0.3)	(-0.3)	(--)	(0.2)	(-0.2)						
Other	(--)	(--)	(--)	(--)	(--)	(--)						
Allocation of SDRs	--	--	--	1.4	--	1.4	1.5	--	1.5			--
Net errors and omissions			28.7			16.2			15.6			8.2
Net change in reserves (increase -)			0.3			-0.6			5.3			10.8
Government			0.7			-2.2						
East Caribbean Currency Authority			0.2			-2.5						
Commercial banks			-0.9			4.7						
Barbados Savings Bank			0.3			-0.7						

a/ Estimates
b/ Preliminary staff estimates

Source: IBRD Country Economic Report

Table SA4.2. Guyana: Balance of Payments, 1960–74

(millions of U.S. dollars)

	1960	1961	1962	1963	1964	1965	1966	1967	1968	1969	1970	1971	1972	1973	1974
Trade Balance	-11.3	1.4	22.0	31.7	10.8	-2.2	-5.9	-3.1	8.8	9.4	-0.2	9.9	7.3	-40.2	16.6
Exports (fob)	75.0	87.1	95.9	100.8	98.8	103.3	112.2	122.0	115.2	126.6	133.2	143.6	148.4	137.1	270.1
Imports (cif)	86.3	85.7	73.9	69.1	88.0	105.5	118.1	125.1	106.4	117.2	133.4	133.7	141.1	177.3	253.5
Non-factor Services (Net)	-3.2	-3.1	1.0	-2.1	-3.8	-3.9	-5.9	-2.6	-1.7	0.1	-0.8	-1.0	0.3	-11.0	-0.2
Freight and Insurance	1.6	1.6	1.5	0.7	0.7	0.5	0.5	0.6	0.6	0.5	0.7	0.7	0.8	1.0	1.6
Travel	-1.4	-1.1	-0.9	-1.0	-2.3	-2.3	-2.2	-3.2	-2.7	-0.6	0.4	0.0	-0.3	-4.7	1.1
Other	-3.4	-3.6	0.4	-1.8	-2.2	-2.1	-4.2	0.0	0.4	0.2	-1.9	-1.7	-0.2	-7.3	-2.9
Investment Income	-14.0	-12.8	-21.0	-16.1	-16.8	-14.6	-19.1	-18.1	-21.0	-20.5	-21.2	-16.7	-12.8	-12.3	-23.4
Direct Investment	-13.1	-12.6	-19.9	-14.4	-14.8	-13.9	-17.0	-16.1	-19.7	-19.9	-19.4	-14.4	-8.6	-5.4	-13.5
Public Debt Interest	-2.0	-2.3	-2.7	-3.4	-6.2	-3.4	-3.8	-3.7	-3.0	-2.2	-2.8	-2.7	-5.1	-6.0	-7.6
Other	1.1	2.1	1.6	2.7	4.2	2.7	1.7	1.5	1.7	1.6	1.0	0.4	0.9	-0.9	-2.1
Current Transfers (net) 1/	-0.7	-0.3	-0.6	-1.1	-0.7	-1.7	-0.0	-2.8	-2.3	0.3	0.2	0.2	-0.1	-0.6	-2.9
Current Account Balance	-29.2	-14.8	1.4	12.4	-10.5	-22.4	-30.9	-26.8	16.2	-10.7	-22.0	-7.6	-5.3	-64.1	-9.9
Medium and Long-term Capital	24.8	13.9	7.6	10.4	9.5	15.9	23.3	28.4	17.5	17.5	12.6	14.7	15.5	23.5	27.5
Public Inflow (net)	7.0	9.2	8.5	6.2	4.3	7.9	7.5	8.0	7.3	9.8	8.3	14.8	10.9	-20.1	24.6
(Grant)	2.8	4.2	4.0	2.9	3.7	6.8	6.2	4.6	2.9	2.1	0.6	1.8	1.2	5.1	(31.2
(Loans) 2/	5.6	4.7	5.5	4.4	2.3	2.6	3.7	7.9	8.7	10.8	11.3	15.3	12.2	18.1	(
Amortization	1.1	0.7	1.0	1.1	1.7	1.5	2.4	4.5	4.3	3.1	3.6	2.3	2.5	3.1	6.1
Other	-0.3	1.2	-	-0.6	-	-1.9	0.5	-	-	0.2	-	-	-	-	-
Private (net)	17.8	4.7	-0.9	4.8	5.2	9.9	15.3	20.4	10.2	7.5	4.3	-0.1	4.6	12.4	11.8
Direct Investment	17.8	5.6	-1.8	4.3	5.6	9.4	15.7	18.4	9.6	9.2	4.3	-4.6	-2.6	3.8	5.2
Other 3/	-	-0.9	0.9	0.5	-0.4	0.5	-0.4	2.0	0.6	-1.7	0.0	4.5	7.2	8.6	6.6
Short-Term Capital (net)	-0.5	-0.3	-1.4	0.5	1.9	1.0	-2.5	1.9	1.4	-4.1	-1.8	-2.4	-0.5	1.1	-0.8
Capital Account Balance	24.3	13.8	6.2	10.9	11.4	16.9	20.8	30.3	18.9	13.4	10.8	12.3	15.0	33.6	36.4
Unidentified Transactions	3.1	1.4	-1.3	-9.3	2.0	-4.8	3.0	1.3	-6.5	-7.4	7.1	-0.9	-6.5	1.7	-0.1
SDR's											2.5	2.1	2.6	-	-
Change in Reserve (increase -)	1.8	-0.4	-6.3	-14.0	-2.9	10.3	7.1	-4.8	3.8	4.7	1.6	-6.6	-5.8	28.8	-26.4

1/ Including non-monetary gold.
2/ Excluding grants.
3/ Including financing of autonomous corporations.

Source: IBRD Country Economic Report

Table SA4.3a. Jamaica: Balance of Payments, 1960–74

(millions of U.S. dollars at current prices)

	1960	1961	1962	1963	1964	1965	1966	1967	1968	1969	1970	1971	1972	1973	1974
A. CURRENT RECEIPTS															
Merchandise Exports	117.6	127.2	131.6	148.8	156.2	154.8	197.5	199.2	209.2	243.2	285.1	296.1	302.0	357.2	632.2
Non Factor Services:															
Freight x Mdse. Insurance	(9.2)	(9.8)	(10.6)	(11.0)	(11.8)	(14.4)	(2.6)	(18.2)	(3.7)	(3.8)	(3.9)	(3.9)	(4.3)	(4.4)	(5.1)
Other Transportation							(13.4)		(19.2)	(18.8)	(19.1)	(20.3)	(20.8)	(28.7)	(38.5)
Travel	(28.8)	(29.2)	(26.2)	(27.0)	(31.2)	(46.2)	(56.4)	(57.8)	(73.2)	(77.9)	(79.6)	(90.8)	(107.7)	(115.8)	(124.9)
Government (n.e.i.)	(5.6)	(6.8)	(6.6)	(6.6)	(6.4)	(7.0)	(8.0)	(9.2)	(9.7)	(10.5)	(10.8)	(11.8)	(11.4)	(12.2)	(15.4)
Non-Mdse. Insurance	(3.8)	(5.0)	(6.2)	(7.2)	(8.4)	(8.6)	(9.4)	(10.4)	(11.6)	(13.2)	(12.8)	(17.8)	(11.0)	(11.6)	(14.5)
Other Services	(15.4)	(16.6)	(19.1)	(19.8)	(20.6)	(21.8)	(18.0)	(17.8)	(18.8)	(20.9)	(23.4)	(26.8)	(28.9)	(44.3)	(45.1)
Sub-Total	62.8	67.4	68.7	71.6	78.6	98.0	107.8	113.4	136.2	145.1	149.6	166.4	184.1	217.0	243.4
Goods and Non Factor Services	180.4	194.6	200.1	220.2	234.6	252.8	305.3	312.6	345.4	388.3	434.7	452.5	486.1	574.2	875.6
Factor Services:															
Direct Investment	...	...	...	(1.6)	...	...	(1.1)	...	(1.1)	(1.0)	(0.9)	(0.3)	(0.2)	(0.9)	(1.0)
Other	...	...	...	(3.0)	...	...	(5.4)	...	(9.5)	(11.3)	(12.7)	(12.1)	(12.5)	(15.7)	(19.0)
Sub-Total	4.6	4.6	4.6	4.6	5.0	6.0	6.5	8.0	10.6	12.4	13.6	12.4	12.7	16.6	20.0
Transfers:															
Private	(13.8)	(14.8)	(16.0)	(17.0)	(15.8)	(15.4)	(14.0)	(13.8)	(14.3)	(17.1)	(27.0)	(34.3)	(38.5)	(54.1)	(52.5)
Public	(2.2)	(0.4)	(1.2)	(1.2)	(1.4)	(1.9)	(1.8)	(1.8)	(1.9)	(2.9)	(2.6)	(2.5)	(2.7)	(6.8)	(8.6)
Sub-Total	16.0	15.2	17.2	18.2	17.2	17.2	15.8	15.6	16.2	20.0	29.6	36.8	41.2	60.9	61.1
B. CURRENT EXPENDITURES															
Merchandise Imports	134.0	136.0	137.8	142.0	182.0	182.0	203.2	217.2	276.9	317.6	374.2	395.1	422.9	518.4	739.4
Non Factor Services:															
Freight x Mdse. Insurance	(21.0)	(14.6)	(19.4)	(18.2)	(24.6)	(24.5)	(30.5)	(35.4)	(43.4)	(45.7)	(61.0)	(63.6)	(70.3)	(85.7)	(111.4)
Other Transportation	(8.8)	(8.2)	(5.0)	(6.0)	(7.1)	(7.8)	(8.0)	(9.2)	(14.3)	(14.1)	(14.3)	(12.0)	(12.7)	(20.0)	(26.3)
Travel	(4.8)	(5.2)	(6.0)	(6.6)	(8.4)	(8.4)	(8.4)	(8.6)	(10.4)	(12.5)	(12.9)	(13.6)	(16.5)	(18.1)	(8.8)
Government (n.e.i.)	(0.2)	(0.4)	(1.0)	(1.4)	(1.8)	(2.0)	(2.2)	(2.0)	(2.0)	(1.9)	(1.3)	(1.3)	(1.0)	(2.2)	(3.2)
Non-Mdse. Insurance	(12.4)	(13.2)	(15.0)	(16.6)	(17.8)	(16.6)	(19.8)	(21.2)	(23.1)	(24.0)	(23.3)	(24.3)	(26.2)	(31.4)	(35.6)
Other Services	(8.4)	(8.8)	(10.2)	(10.4)	(8.4)	(12.7)	(8.9)	(12.4)	(10.5)	(15.0)	(10.4)	(17.4)	(15.2)	(26.6)	(31.5)
Sub-Total	55.6	50.4	55.6	59.2	68.1	74.2	77.8	86.8	103.7	113.2	124.2	132.2	141.9	184.6	227.7
Goods and Non Factor Services	189.6	186.4	194.4	201.2	250.1	256.2	281.0	306.0	380.6	430.8	498.4	527.3	564.8	702.4	967.1
Factor Services:															
Direct Investment	...	...	...	(26.4)	...	...	(67.6)	...	(66.4)	(77.3)	(87.5)	(88.6)	(100.5)	(46.2)[1/]	(53.2)[1/]
Other	...	...	...	(4.6)	...	...	(3.8)	...	(5.5)	(7.6)	(7.9)	(9.5)	(12.7)	(23.2)	(32.0)
Sub-Total	26.4	29.6	29.8	31.0	33.6	36.6	71.4	75.2	71.9	84.9	95.4	98.1	113.2	69.4	85.2
Transfers															
Private	(1.6)	(1.8)	(1.4)	(0.8)	(0.8)	(1.2)	(1.0)	(1.0)	(1.0)	(2.4)	(5.2)	(12.5)	(13.7)	(23.4)	(22.1)
Public	(2.4)	(3.8)	(2.4)	(3.0)	(3.4)	(3.8)	(4.4)	(4.6)	(5.0)	(5.7)	(6.0)	(7.1)	(8.1)	(13.5)	(13.8)
Sub-Total	4.0	5.6	3.8	3.8	4.2	5.0	5.4	5.6	6.0	8.1	11.2	19.6	21.8	36.9	35.9
C. CURRENT BALANCES															
Balance on Goods x NFS	-9.2	8.2	5.7	19.0	-15.5	-3.4	24.3	6.6	-35.2	-42.5	-63.7	-74.8	-78.7	-128.2	-91.5
Balance of Factor Income	-21.8	-25.0	-25.2	-26.4	-28.6	-30.6	-64.9	-67.2	-61.3	-72.5	-81.8	-85.7	-100.5	-52.8	-65.2
Balance of Transfers	12.0	9.6	13.4	14.4	13.0	12.2	10.4	10.0	10.2	11.9	18.4	17.2	19.4	24.0	25.2
Total Current Account Balance	-19.0	-7.2	-6.1	7.0	-31.1	-21.8	-30.2	-50.6	-86.3	-103.1	-127.1	-143.3	-159.8	-157.0	-131.5

1/ Adjusted

2/ Source: IBRD Country Economic Report

Table SA4.3b. Jamaica: Balance of Payments, 1971–74

(millions of U.S. dollars at current prices)

	1971	1972	1973	1974
Exports of Goods and NFS	452.5	486.1	574.2	875.6
Merchandise	286.1	302.0	357.2	632.2
NFS	166.4	184.1	217.0	243.4
Imports of Goods and NFS	-527.3	-564.8	-702.4	-967.1
Merchandise	-395.1	-422.9	-518.4	-739.4
NFS	-132.2	-141.9	-184.0	-227.7
Trade Balance	-109.0	-120.9	-161.2	-107.2
Resource Balance	-74.8	-78.7	-128.2	-91.5
Net Factor Payments	-85.7	-100.5	-52.8 1/	-65.2 1/
Interest 2/ 3/	-8.0	-9.9	-15.8	-30.0
Other	-77.7	-90.6	-37.0	-35.2
Transfer Receipts	17.2	19.4	24.0	25.2
Current Account Balance	-143.3	-159.8	-157.0	-131.5
Grants				
Medium- and Long-term Loans 2/	14.6	26.3	119.5	154.8
Gross Disbursements	23.7	41.1	134.8	183.5
Amortization	9.1	14.8	15.3	28.7
International Agencies	3.0	1.1	2.6	3.0
Gross	3.8	2.2	4.1	4.6
Amortization	0.8	1.1	1.5	1.6
Governments	10.9	3.9	28.4	22.3
Gross	11.9	5.5	30.9	25.3
Amortization	1.0	1.6	2.5	3.0
Suppliers	0.2	1.7	14.4	2.2
Gross	0.2	1.8	14.5	4.3
Amortization	0.0	0.1	0.1	2.1
Private Banks	5.3	15.3	79.5	117.0
Gross	7.3	24.1	84.8	136.5
Amortization	2.0	8.8	5.3	19.5
Other Medium and Long-term	-4.8	4.3	-5.4	10.3
Gross	0.5	7.5	0.5	12.8
Amortization	5.3	3.2	5.9	2.5
Direct Foreign Investment	84.9	14.9	30.6	15.9
SDR Allocation	4.7	4.7	-	-
Short-term Capital (net) 4/	75.8	74.9	-12.3	16.9
Change in Reserves (- = increase)	-36.7	+39.0	+19.2	-56.1

/1 Formerly, only the local expenditures (current and capital) by bauxite/alumina companies operating in Jamaica were deducted from the notional export values for bauxite and alumina. The residual, including depreciation, was classified as investment income. In the adjusted balance of payments, depreciation is not included as a factor payment but is instead charged against direct investment; factor payments consist only of wages and salaries paid overseas. As a result, the current account deficit is substantially lower than that obtained using the previous methodology.

/2 Data provided by IBRD External Debt Division.

/3 Interest on public and publicly guaranteed debt only.

/4 Including errors and omissions.

Table SA4.4. Trinidad and Tobago: Balance of Payments, 1966–72

(millions of TT dollars)

	1966	1967	1968	1969	1970	1971	1972
Exports of goods and non-factor services	500.0	560.5	580.1	680.9	646.5	683.0	745.4
Merchandise f.o.b. /1 (adjusted)	(342.2)	(386.3)	(378.7)	(470.3)	(447.6)	(428.6)	(487.7)
Travel	(29.3)	(40.5)	(52.2)	(63.0)	(47.8)	(70.5)	(80.4)
Petroleum processing fees	(45.8)	(42.2)	(52.7)	(56.5)	(55.3)	(56.4)	(56.8)
Transportation /2	(53.3)	(57.8)	(64.0)	(70.1)	(75.6)	(98.6)	(94.0)
Other non-factor services	(29.4)	(33.7)	(32.5)	(21.0)	(20.2)	(28.9)	(26.5)
Imports of goods and non-factor services	465.8	467.3	502.5	575.3	666.4	827.4	909.8
Merchandise c.i.f. /1 (adjusted)	(393.6)	(378.6)	(396.6)	(469.1)	(552.5)	(702.5)	(787.8)
Travel	(22.0)	(31.5)	(35.6)	(41.8)	(45.8)	(48.6)	(52.1)
Transportation	(33.0)	(38.6)	(48.3)	(46.3)	(44.1)	(60.5)	(60.9)
Other non-factor services	(17.2)	(18.6)	(22.0)	(18.1)	(24.0)	(15.8)	(9.0)
Resource gap	34.2	93.2	77.6	105.6	- 19.9	-144.4	-164.4
Investment income (net)	-107.3	-113.7	-126.7	-133.4	-116.8	-118.8	-128.2
Transfers (net)	8.2	- 2.0	- 1.6	- 2.6	- 4.3	- 8.7	- 7.2
Current account balance	- 64.9	- 22.5	- 50.7	- 30.4	-141.0	-271.9	-299.8
Private capital (net)	42.6	42.7	50.9	127.3	173.0	222.7	168.7
Official capital	10.0	2.7	11.8	4.7	- 7.5	29.1	34.7
Drawings	(17.6)	(13.5)	(27.1)	(20.5)	(9.5)	(38.6)	(46.3)
Amortization	(4.1)	(5.6)	(12.2)	(8.4)	(17.4)	(34.7)	(7.5)
Other	(- 3.5)	(- 5.2)	(- 3.1)	(- 7.4)	(0.4)	(25.2)	(- 4.1)
Net non-monetary	52.6	45.4	62.7	132.0	165.5	251.8	203.4
Allocation of SDR's	-	-	-	-	14.8	13.3	13.3
Errors and omissions	- 3.7	- 18.6	33.5	-107.9	- 54.9	49.7	37.5
International reserves	16.0	- 4.3	- 45.5	6.3	15.6	- 42.9	45.6
Monetary authorities	(- 1.5)	(- 10.2)	(- 65.4)	(9.4)	(21.6)	(- 41.7)	(29.7)
Commercial banks	(13.7)	(2.3)	(20.9)	(- 2.7)	(- 7.6)	(- 4.5)	(20.7)
Government	(3.8)	(3.6)	(- 1.0)	(- 0.4)	(1.6)	(3.3)	(- 4.8)

/1 Excludes trade under petroleum processing agreement.
/2 Excludes stores and bunkers under petroleum processing agreement.

Source: IBRD Country Economic Report

Table SA5.1. Barbados: Central Government Current Expenditures (Functional Classifications), 1966/67–1972/73

(in millions of Eastern Caribbean dollars)

		1966/77	1967/68	1968/69	1969/70	1970/71	1971/72	1972/73
A.	General Services	9.4	10.7	11.3	17.5	17.5	17.6	21.6
	1. Admin. and State Services	5.3	4.9	5.3	9.7	8.7	8.0	11.5
	2. Law, Order and Justice	3.6	3.8	3.8	5.0	5.8	6.2	6.6
	3. External Affairs	0.5	2.0	2.2	2.8	3.0	3.4	3.5
B.	Social Services	20.8	23.8	26.1	34.6	45.4	50.5	56.6
	1. Health	6.7	7.4	7.9	11.9	15.3	16.7	18.7
	2. Education	10.1	10.8	12.1	15.5	18.9	22.2	26.0
	3. Housing	-	0.7	0.6	0.7	0.8	1.0	0.9
	4. Social Security	4.0	4.9	5.5	6.5	10.4	10.6	11.0
	- Welfare	(1.6)	(1.8)	(1.8)	(2.3)	(4.3)	(4.6)	(4.9)
	- National Ins.	(-)	(0.2)	(0.2)	(0.3)	(0.3)	(0.3)	(0.3)
	- Pensions	(2.4)	(2.9)	(3.4)	(3.9)	(5.8)	(5.7)	(5.8)
C.	Community Services	2.2	2.7	2.9	3.4	3.4	4.2	4.3
	1. Waterworks	1.8	2.2	2.4	2.7	2.7	3.5	3.5
	2. Fire Service	0.3	0.4	0.4	0.5	0.5	0.5	0.6
	3. Ecclesiastical	0.1	0.1	0.1	0.2	0.2	0.2	0.2
D.	Economic Services	7.6	7.5	8.2	9.6	12.8	13.8	15.1
	1. Agriculture	1.2	1.3	1.4	1.7	2.1	2.7	2.7
	2. Communications and Works	3.7	4.4	4.8	5.4	7.1	7.3	8.1
	3. Trade	2.0	1.1	1.0	1.3	1.6	1.0	1.1
	4. Tourism	-	-	-	-	0.1	1.5	1.8
	5. Economic Planning	0.4	0.4	0.6	0.7	1.1	0.2	0.2
	6. Civil Aviation	0.3	0.3	0.4	0.5	0.8	1.1	1.2
E.	Interest	2.8	3.2	3.6	4.0	3.2	4.6	5.8
	Total	42.8	47.9	52.1	69.1	82.3	90.7	103.4

SOURCE: IBRD Country Economic Report.

Table SA5.2. Barbados: Central Government Capital Expenditures (Functional Classifications), 1966/67–1972/73

(in millions of Eastern Caribbean dollars)

	1966/67	1967/68	1968/69	1969/70	1970/71	1971/72	1972/73
A. General Services	1.9	3.0 1/	1.7	3.9	4.2	3.5	3.4
B. Community Services	1.4	1.4	1.7	1.4	1.8	3.5	3.1
Roads	0.3	0.4	0.4	0.4	0.6	1.0	0.8
Water & Sanitation	1.1	1.0	1.3	1.0	1.2	2.5	2.3
C. Social Services	1.8	1.4	1.7	3.9	5.8	9.1	8.8
Education	0.7	0.6	0.9	0.9	1.2	2.2	2.9
Health	0.4	0.3	0.2	0.7	0.6	0.5	1.0
Housing & Urban Development	0.7	0.5	0.6	2.3	4.0	6.4	4.9
D. Economic Services	6.3	2.8	3.3	1.8	3.6	5.6	6.3
Agriculture	0.7	0.6	0.9	0.8	1.4	2.5	2.3
Industrial Estates & Hotels	4.7	1.1	1.7	0.8	-	0.9	1.3
Transportation & Communication	0.9	1.1	0.7	0.2	2.2	2.2	2.7
Seawell Airport	(0.9)	(1.1)	(0.3)	(0.1)	(2.1)	(1.1)	(1.8)
Other	(-)	(-)	(0.4)	(0.1)	(0.1)	(1.1)	(0.9)
TOTAL	11.4	8.6	8.4	11.0	15.4	21.7	21.6

Source: IBRD Country Economic Report

1/ Includes the assumption of indebtedness of EC$2.1 million of the Caribbean Broadcasting Corporation by the Central Government.

Table SA5.3. Barbados: Central Government Total Expenditures (Functional Classifications), 1966/67–1972/73)

(in millions of Eastern Caribbean dollars)

	1966/67	1967/68	1968/69	1969/70	1970/71	1971/72	1972/73
A. General Services	11.3	13.7	13.0	21.4	21.7	21.1	25.0
1. Admin. and State Services							
2. Law, Order and Justice							
3. External Affairs							
B. Social Services	22.6	25.2	27.8	38.5	51.2	59.6	65.4
1. Health	7.1	7.7	8.8	12.6	15.9	17.2	19.7
2. Education	10.8	11.4	13.0	16.4	20.1	24.4	28.9
3. Housing	0.7	1.2	1.2	3.0	4.8	7.4	5.8
4. Social Security	4.0	4.9	5.5	6.5	10.4	10.6	11.0
- Welfare	(1.6)	(1.8)	(1.8)	(2.3)	(4.3)	(4.6)	(4.9)
- National Ins.	(-)	(0.2)	(0.2)	(0.3)	(0.3)	(0.3)	(0.3)
- Pensions	(2.4)	(2.9)	(3.4)	(3.9)	(5.8)	(5.7)	(5.8)
C. Community Services	3.6	4.1	4.6	4.8	5.3	7.7	7.4
1. Waterworks	2.9	3.2	3.7	3.7	3.9	6.0	5.8
2. Fire Service	0.3	0.4	0.4	0.5	0.5	0.5	0.6
3. Ecclesiastical	0.1	0.1	0.1	0.2	0.2	0.2	0.2
4. Roads	0.3	0.4	0.4	0.4	0.6	1.0	0.8
D. Economic Services	13:9	10.3	11.5	11.4	16.4	19.4	21.4
1. Agriculture	1.9	1.9	2.3	2.5	3.5	5.2	5.0
2. Communications and Works	3.7	4.4	5.2	5.5	7.2	8.4	9.0
3. Trade	2.0	1.1	1.0	1.3	1.6	1.0	1.1
4. Tourism	-	-	-	-	0.1	1.5	1.8
5. Economic Planning	0.4	0.4	0.6	0.7	1.1	0.2	0.2
6. Civil Aviation	1.2	1.4	0.7	0.6	2.9	2.2	3.0
7. Industrial Estates and Hotels	4.7	1.1	1.7	0.8	-	0.9	1.3
E. Interest	2.8	3.2	3.6	4.0	3.2	4.6	5.8
Total	54.2	56.5	60.5	80.1	97.6	112.4	125.0

SOURCE: S.A. Tables 5.1 and 5.2

Table SA5.4. Guyana: Central Government Current Expenditures, 1968–75

(in millions of Guyanan dollars)

	1968	1969	1970	1971	1972	1973	1974	Estimate 1975
General Administration	28.0	34.1	39.6	41.7	49.1	73.9	79.1	92.2
Central Administration	15.7	19.5	21.3	23.0	28.9	43.2	48.5	55.6
Justice and Police	8.9	10.1	10.9	12.1	13.2	18.3	15.5	19.4
Defense	3.4	4.5	7.4	6.6	7.0	12.4	15.1	17.2
Community Services	12.1	14.1	16.2	20.1	18.9	36.2	43.1	56.6
Roads, irrigation and drainage, sea defenses and buildings	8.5	10.1	12.1	15.9	13.8	31.9	37.6	48.8
Fire protection and water supply	1.4	1.6	1.6	1.4	2.0	1.1	1.3	2.1
Post office	2.2	2.4	2.5	2.8	3.1	3.2	4.2	5.7
Social Services	29.9	30.8	36.0	36.5	42.0	56.3	70.7	77.7
Education	16.1	16.6	19.5	20.5	24.7	33.9	43.2	47.4
Health	9.4	9.9	11.0	11.3	12.6	16.6	22.4	24.6
Social security and special welfare services	4.4	4.3	5.5	4.7	4.7	5.8	5.1	5.7
Economic Services	9.2	8.9	10.3	11.8	12.8	14.1	20.9	26.8
Agriculture and natural resources	5.7	5.5	6.6	7.1	8.5	8.1	13.0	19.7
Transport and communications	2.7	2.1	2.9	3.1	2.7	4.4	6.6	5.4
Other	0.8	1.3	0.8	1.6	1.6	1.6	1.3	1.7
Unallocated	11.7	12.0	16.6	18.6	29.8	31.0	32.0	56.7
TOTAL	90.9	99.9	118.7	128.7	152.6	211.5	245.8	310.0

Source: IBRD Country Economic Report

Table SA5.5. Guyana: Central Government Capital Expenditures, 1968–75
(in millions of Guyanan dollars)

	1968	1969	1970	1971	1972	1973	1974	Estimate 1975
General Administration	2.8	0.9	1.6	1.2	2.0	2.4	5.8	12
Central Administration	1.9	0.5	1.1	0.9	1.7	2.0	3.9	8
Defense	0.7	0.2	0.2	0.1	0.1	0.2	1.0	2
Justice and Police	0.2	0.2	0.3	0.2	0.2	0.2	0.9	2
Community Services	19.5	27.0	30.3	34.7	32.9	43.2	47.3	74
Infrastructure	18.8	25.1	24.2	30.7	29.7	39.3	43.0	67
Roads	(12.9)	(14.1)	(10.6)	(10.4)	(5.2)	(9.9)	(8.7)	(18)
Sea and river defense	(2.9)	(2.9)	(8.0)	(11.7)	(12.0)	(10.3)	(12.3)	(11)
Drainage and irrigation	(0.2)	(0.4)	(0.3)	(-)	(1.3)	(9.0)	(11.3)	(16)
Shipping and harbors	(0.2)	(0.2)	(0.2)	(0.9)	(0.7)	(0.8)	(0.9)	(5)
Water supply	(0.7)	(1.1)	(2.3)	(6.2)	(4.1)	(2.8)	(3.3)	(4)
Other infrastructure	(1.9)	(6.4)	(2.8)	(1.5)	(6.4)	(6.5)	(6.5)	(13)
Other community services	0.7	1.9	6.1	4.0	3.2	3.9	4.3	7
Interior development	(0.2)	(1.4)	(3.2)	(3.0)	(0.8)	-	-	(-)
Cooperative development	-	(0.2)	(1.3)	(0.2)	(0.5)	(1.2)	(1.5)	(2)
Community and youth development	(0.5)	(0.3)	(1.1)	(0.8)	(1.9)	(2.7)	(2.8)	(5)
Social Services	3.5	6.9	5.8	2.4	3.5	6.0	15.0	26
Education	2.8	5.4	4.1	1.9	2.4	4.5	11.8	15
Health	0.2	0.2	0.5	0.2	0.3	1.2	0.3	4
Housing	0.2	0.4	1.1	0.2	0.7	-	1.0	5
Other	0.3	0.9	0.1	0.1	0.1	0.3	1.9	2

Economic Services	12.7	8.9	13.4	16.5	20.0	21.9	29.5	70
Agriculture	0.9	2.6	4.4	10.8	11.5	12.3	14.5	25
Rice production	(-)	(1.[illegible])	(2.0)	(9.6)	(9.8)	(n.a.)	(n.a.)	(n.a.)
Beef production	(0.1)	(0.2)	(0.3)	(0.4)	(0.6)	(n.a.)	(n.a.)	(n.a.)
Other	(0.8)	(0.9)	(2.1)	(0.8)	(1.1)	(n.a.)	(n.a.)	(n.a.)
Land development	0.6	2.7	0.6	1.4	4.1	4.2	2.0	5
Forestry and fishing	0.3	0.4	0.3	-	0.1	0.3	0.2	1
Mineral resources	2.2	0.5	0.6	0.3	0.9	0.7	0.7	3
Transport, storage, and communications	4.7	0.5	4.3	0.3	0.1	0.4	1.5	6
Civil aviation	(3.4)	(0.5)	(4.3)	(0.3)	(0.1)	(0.3)	(0.6)	(4)
Other	(1.3)	(-)	(-)	(-)	(-)	(0.1)	(0.9)	(2)
Electricity development	(-)	(-)	(-)	(-)	0.5	0.8	1.5	13
Industrial, agricultural and forestry development	4.0	2.2	3.2	3.7	2.8	3.2	9.1	17
Industry	(1.5)	(1.0)	(0.6)	(0.7)	(0.6)	(2.0)	(5.4)	(10)
Other	(2.5)	(1.2)	(2.6)	(3.0)	(2.2)	(1.2)	(3.7)	(7)
Unallocated	1.2	4.5	1.0	1.0	2.2	2.8	6.0	4
Feasibility studies	1.0	0.4	0.3	0.8	1.1	2.4	3.9	4
Other	0.2	4.1	0.7	0.2	1.1	0.4	2.1	-
TOTAL CAPITAL EXPENDITURE 2/	39.7	48.2	52.1	55.8	60.6	76.3	103.6	186

1/ Anticipated investment in a textile mill, tannery, solvent extraction plant, etc.
2/ Excluding G$107.6 million for DEMBA nationalization in 1971 and G$22.0 million for Reynolds nationalization in 1975.

Source: IBRD Country Economic Report.

Table SA5.6. Guyana: Central Government Total Expenditures, 1968–75

(in millions of Guyanan dollars)

	1968	1969	1970	1971	1972	1973	1974	Estimate 1975
General Administration	30.8	35.0	41.2	42.9	51.1	76.3	84.9	104.2
Central administration	17.6	20.0	22.4	23.9	30.6	45.2	52.4	63.6
Justice and police	9.1	10.3	11.2	12.3	13.4	18.5	16.4	21.4
Defense	4.1	4.7	7.6	6.7	7.1	12.6	16.1	19.2
Community Services	31.6	41.1	46.5	54.8	51.8	79.4	90.4	130.6
Roads, irrigation and drainage, sea defenses and buildings	24.5	27.5	31.0	38.0	32.3	61.1	69.9	93.8
Fire protection and water supply	2.1	2.7	3.9	7.6	6.1	3.9	4.6	6.1
Post Office	2.2	2.4	2.5	2.8	3.1	3.2	4.2	5.7
Shipping and harbors	0.2	0.2	0.2	0.9	0.7	0.8	0.9	5.0
Other infrastructure	1.9	6.4	2.8	1.5	6.4	6.5	6.5	13.0
Other community services	0.7	1.9	6.1	4.0	3.2	3.9	4.3	7.0
Social Services	33.4	37.7	41.8	38.9	45.5	62.3	85.7	103.7
Education	18.9	22.0	23.6	22.4	27.1	38.4	55.0	62.4
Health	9.6	10.1	11.5	11.5	12.9	17.8	22.7	28.6
Social security and special welfare services	4.4	4.3	5.5	4.7	4.7	5.8	5.1	5.7
Other	0.5	1.3	1.2	0.3	0.8	0.3	2.9	7.0
Economic Services	21.9	17.8	23.7	28.3	32.8	36.0	50.4	96.8
Agriculture and natural resources	12.2	12.9	15.1	22.6	27.3	26.8	34.1	60.7
Transport and communications	7.4	2.6	7.2	3.4	2.8	4.8	8.1	11.4
Other	2.3	2.3	1.4	2.3	2.7	4.4	8.2	24.7
Unallocated	12.9	16.5	17.6	19.6	32.0	33.8	38.0	60.7
TOTAL	130.6	148.1	170.8	184.5	213.2	287.8	349.4	496.0

.. not available at time of publication

Source: S.A. Tables 5.4 and 5.5

Table SA5.7. Jamaica: Central Government Current Expenditures (Economic Classification), 1970/71–1975/76

(in millions of Jamaican dollars)

	1970/71	1971/72	1972/73	1973/74	Revised Estimate 1974/75	Budget 1975/76
General Services	66.9	78.0	76.9	113.1	141.6	185.8
Interest Payments	15.8	18.1	21.7	31.0	47.4	59.5
Other General Administration	31.5	37.5	28.7	46.1	43.1	69.4
Security Services	19.6	22.4	26.5	36.0	51.1	56.9
Social and Community Services	66.1	84.4	103.5	132.4	199.4	241.4
Education	35.5	45.3	54.3	80.3	109.3	139.5
Health	20.8	28.9	34.7	36.9	61.7	62.5
Social Security and General Welfare	2.9	5.3	6.4	7.2	9.2	12.2
Housing	3.2	2.6	2.8	2.8	4.1	4.6
Water Supplies	0.9	0.3	1.4	2.4	4.9	6.2
Other Social and Community Services	2.8	2.0	3.9	2.8	10.2	16.4
Economic Services	36.0	41.2	57.8	59.0	81.3	84.6
Agriculture	10.7	9.8	15.0	15.2	10.0	18.7
Industry and Commerce	2.7	2.6	3.2	5.0	10.8	10.6
Transport and Communications	8.9	11.2	11.6	13.4	18.0	17.8
Roads	2.3	5.9	13.8	9.5	13.9	10.7
Fuel and Power	-	-	0.6	1.3	6.3	1.5
Environment	0.8	0.9	1.0	3.0	5.3	6.4
Other Economic Services	10.6	10.8	12.6	11.6	17.0	18.9
Miscellaneous Services	18.8	21.5	41.2	36.9	66.2	76.8
Misc. grants to Local Government	18.8	21.5	26.9	36.9	66.2	72.3
Other Unallocable Expenditure	-	-	14.3	-	-	4.5
GROSS TOTAL	187.8	225.1	279.4	341.4	488.5	588.6
Less Appropriations-in-Aid	10.6	19.8	24.2	23.8	11.1	6.4
NET TOTAL	177.2	205.3	255.2	317.6	477.4	582.2

Source: IBRD Country Economic Report

Table SA5.8. Jamaica: Central Government Capital Expenditures (Economic Classification), 1970/71–1975/76

(in millions of Jamaican dollars)

	1970/71	1971/72	1972/73	1973/74	REVISED ESTIMATES 1974/75	BUDGET 1975/76
GENERAL SERVICES	4.4	4.9	6.2	6.5	27.5	36.8
Other General Administration	3.9	4.2	5.1	4.0	21.4	26.6
Security Services	0.5	0.7	1.1	2.5	6.1	10.2
SOCIAL AND COMMUNITY SERVICES	28.0	35.6	27.7	32.0	59.4	96.9
Education	9.5	14.2	9.9	12.6	20.4	33.2
Health	3.1	3.9	1.4	4.5	5.0	9.0
Social Security and General Welfare	0.1	0.4	0.5	0.2	0.2	0.6
Housing	2.8	4.4	5.1	7.6	18.4	27.1
Water Supplies	5.0	5.1	4.7	5.3	8.7	15.4
Other Social and Community Services	7.5	7.6	6.1	1.8	6.7	11.6
ECONOMIC SERVICES	36.7	38.7	54.1	72.6	119.7	155.5
Agriculture	16.3	12.8	20.3	13.8	26.4	47.2
Industry and Commerce	7.0	8.8	13.2	20.3	30.4	25.7
Transport and Communications	1.7	3.6	2.8	5.1	10.7	11.7
Roads	10.7	11.7	11.7	12.9	29.7	36.8
Fuel and Power	-	-	-	-	8.6	4.0
Other Economic Services	1.0	1.8	6.1	20.5	13.9	30.1
MISCELLANEOUS SERVICES	4.4	7.2	9.0	5.6	13.1	20.6
General Purpose Loans and Grants to Local Government	2.4	2.7	3.4	3.3	10.7	12.0
Other Expenditure	2.0	4.5	5.6	2.3	2.4	8.6
SUBTOTAL	73.5	86.4	97.0	116.7	219.7	309.8
Adjustment	-2.2	-1.9	-1.8	-1.4	-5.5	-30.0
NET TOTAL	71.3	84.5	95.2	115.3	214.2	279.8

Source: IBRD Country Economic Report

Table SA5.9. Jamaica: Central Government Total Expenditures (Economic Classification), 1970/71–1975/76

(in millions of Jamaican dollars)

	1970/71	1971/72	1972/73	1973/74	Revised Estimates 1974/75	Budget 1975/76
General Services	71.3	82.9	83.1	119.6	169.1	222.6
Interest Payments	15.8	18.1	21.7	31.0	47.4	59.5
Other General Administration	35.4	41.7	33.8	50.1	64.5	96.0
Security Services	20.1	23.1	27.6	38.5	57.2	67.1
Social and Community Services	94.1	120.0	131.2	164.4	258.8	338.3
Education	45.0	59.5	64.2	92.9	129.7	172.7
Health	23.9	32.8	36.1	41.4	66.7	71.5
Social Security and General Welfare	3.0	5.7	6.9	7.4	9.4	12.8
Housing	6.0	7.0	7.9	10.4	22.5	31.7
Water Supplies	5.9	5.4	6.1	7.7	13.6	21.6
Other Social and Community Services	10.3	9.6	10.0	4.6	16.9	28.0
Economic Services	72.7	79.9	111.9	131.6	201.0	240.1
Agriculture	27.0	22.6	35.3	29.0	36.4	65.9
Industry and Commerce	9.7	11.4	16.4	25.3	41.2	36.3
Transport and Communications	10.6	14.8	14.4	18.5	28.7	29.5
Roads	13.0	17.6	25.5	22.4	43.6	47.5
Fuel and Power	-	-	0.6	1.3	14.9	5.5
Other Economic Services	12.4	13.5	19.7	35.1	36.2	55.4
Miscellaneous Services	23.2	28.7	50.2	42.5	79.3	97.4
General Purpose Loans and Grants to Local Government	21.2	24.2	30.3	40.2	76.9	84.3
Other Expenditure	2.0	4.5	19.9	2.3	2.4	13.1
GROSS TOTAL	261.3	311.5	376.4	458.1	708.2	898.4
Adjustment for Capital Expenditures	-2.2	-1.9	-1.8	-1.4	-5.5	-30.0
Appropriations-in-Aid	-10.6	-19.8	-24.2	-23.8	-11.1	-6.4
NET TOTAL	248.5	289.8	350.4	432.9	691.6	862.0

Source: S.A. Tables 5.7 and 5.8

Table SA5.10. Trinidad and Tobago: Central Government Current Expenditure (Functional Classification), 1967–74

(in millions of TT dollars)

	1966	1967	1968	1969	1970	1971	1972	Rev.Est. 1973	Budget 1974 1/
FUNCTIONAL CLASSIFICATION									
Total	203.4	213.5	228.4	249.2	278.6	348.2	416.0 2/	456.2	501.9
Administrative Services	46.8	49.7	63.1	63.2	72.7	98.6	114.5	117.5	124.7
(o/w transfers)	(0.3)	(0.5)	(0.7)	(1.8)	(1.5)	(1.7)	(1.9)	(2.1)	(2.1)
Central administration	20.6	21.7	27.7	29.2	30.7	46.7	51.4	54.6	56.9
Financial administration	7.2	8.0	14.8	10.8	10.8	14.2	16.6	17.3	19.6
Defense, justice and police	19.0	20.0	20.6	23.2	31.2	37.6	46.5	45.6	48.2
Community Services	31.1	32.9	25.1	36.5	38.5	41.5	52.2	56.4	67.5
(o/w transfers)	(15.2)	(5.5)	(2.5)	(16.2)	(15.7)	(16.8)	(22.4)	(24.5)	(32.2)
Roads	8.8	9.7	8.6	9.4	10.1	11.2	13.8	14.9	16.5
Transport, storage and communications	10.9	14.1	6.9	16.4	17.5	19.4	23.8	24.1	30.0
Water and sewerage	7.7	5.5	6.5	10.1	10.4	10.2	13.7	16.5	20.1
Other	3.7	3.6	3.1	0.5	0.6	0.7	0.9	0.9	0.9
Social Services	80.2	83.6	90.8	95.6	107.2	137.3	161.6	182.5	193.1
(o/w transfers)	(28.0)	(38.4)	(39.9)	(28.2)	(29.0)	(37.7)	(50.8)	(56.2)	(59.1)
Education	39.4	41.4	45.1	48.5	50.7	66.4	71.2	82.1	89.9
Health	22.6	22.3	24.2	27.5	30.2	39.0	45.7	48.6	50.0
Housing	0.9	0.2	0.4	0.4	0.8	0.8	1.1	0.9	1.1
Pensions and national insurance contributions	7.6	9.4	10.8	18.5	18.3	21.8	35.5	39.8	40.7
Special program works	-	-	-	-	5.8	6.4	5.0	8.0	8.0
Other	9.7	10.3	10.3	0.6	1.3	3.0	3.1	3.1	3.4
Economic Services	12.3	14.2	13.0	12.5	14.8	19.9	24.8	26.8	28.4
(o/w transfers)	(2.3)	(2.3)	(2.3)	(2.7)	(3.6)	(4.5)	(5.9)	(6.7)	(7.5)
Agriculture	8.4	9.6	9.4	8.5	9.1	12.6	15.7	16.8	17.3
Industry	1.3	1.4	1.3	1.5	2.0	3.1	4.5	4.6	5.4
Tourism	0.9	0.9	0.9	1.0	1.4	1.5	1.7	2.0	2.3
Mining	0.3	0.3	0.3	0.3	0.3	0.5	0.6	0.6	0.7
Other	1.4	2.0	1.1	1.2	2.0	2.2	2.3	2.8	2.7
Other Expenditure	33.0	33.1	36.4	41.4	45.4	50.9	63.0	73.0	88.2
Transfers to local authorities	18.6	17.9	18.1	21.4	23.8	27.1	32.6	35.8	37.3
Interest on public debt	12.0	13.3	16.9	19.6	21.5	23.5	27.5 3/	36.4	49.3
Other	2.4	1.9	1.4	0.4	0.1	0.3	0.4	0.8 5/	1.6 5/
Adjustment	-	-	-	-	-	-	2.5 4/	-	-

1/ Excludes provision for renegotiated salary increases for public employees.
2/ Total relates to actual expenditure; components are based on revised estimates.
3/ Actual payments.
4/ Difference between total actual payments and revised estimates.
5/ Includes discrepancies.

Source: IBRD County Economic Report

Table SA5.11. Trinidad and Tobago: Central Government Capital Expenditure (Functional Classification), 1967–74

(in millions of TT dollars)

	1967	1968	1969	1970	1971	1972	Estimates 1973	Budget 1974
				FUNCTIONAL CLASSIFICATION				
TOTAL	54.9	66.8	60.0	98.2	103.6	123.0	112.5	137.7
General Services	2.5	2.1	3.2	4.9	5.0	5.7	7.7	..
Local authorities	(1.0)	(1.2)	(1.8)	(1.3)	(1.5)	(2.0)	(2.7)	..
Other	(1.5)	(0.9)	(1.4)	(3.6)	(3.5)	(3.7)	(5.0)	..
Community Services	12.7	13.2	21.3	25.9	34.5	35.5	31.6	
Water and sewerage	(5.4)	(5.2)	(5.8)	(4.7)	(5.8)	(8.6)	(10.3)	..
Drainage	(0.7)	(1.0)	(1.3)	(1.0)	(1.3)	(1.4)	(1.3)	..
Highways	(4.3)	(4.0)	(8.9)	(10.2)	(14.0)	(11.7)	(11.2)	..
Other	(2.3)	(3.0)	(5.3)	(10.0)	(13.4)	(13.8)	(8.8)	..
Social Services	6.9	12.6	12.5	21.5	33.5	33.3	39.7	..
Education	(4.9)	(8.9)	(5.1)	(8.0)	(14.2)	(19.0)	(22.0)	..
Health	(0.4)	(0.4)	(0.8)	(1.1)	(0.9)	(3.3)	(3.8)	..
Housing and other	(1.6)	(3.3)	(6.6)	(12.4)	(18.4)	(11.0)	(13.9)	..
Economic Services	32.8	38.8	23.0	28.8	30.5	32.7	33.5	..
Agriculture	(10.4)	(11.6)	(14.4)	(11.2)	(12.2)	(14.8)	(13.2)	..
Industry and tourism	(2.1)	(3.0)	(2.9)	(11.5)	(5.2)	(5.3)	(5.9)	..
Transport and communication	(11.4)	(5.8)	(1.3)	(3.5)	(5.7)	(5.6)	(6.3)	..
Fuel and power	(8.4)	(17.8)	(3.3)	(2.0)	(1.7)	(-)	(-)	..
Research	(0.5)	(0.6)	(1.1)	(0.5)	(3.5)	(4.1)	(4.2)	..
Other	-	-	-	-	2.2	2.9	3.9	..
Acquisition of assets 1/	-	-	-	17.1	-	21.4	-	
Adjustment	-	-	-	-	-	- 5.6	-	

1/ Purchase of equity in private companies

Source: IBRD Country Economic Report

Table SA5.12. Trinidad and Tobago: Central Government Total Expenditure (Functional Classification), 1967–74

(in millions of TT dollars)

	1967	1968	1969	1970	1971	1972	Estimates 1973	Budget 1974 1/
				FUNCTIONAL CLASSIFICATION				
TOTAL	268.4	295.2	309.2	376.8	451.8	539.0 2/	568.7	639.6
General and Administrative Services	52.2	65.2	66.4	77.6	103.6	120.2	125.2	..
Central Administration	(21.7)	(27.7)	(29.2)	(30.7)	(46.7)	(51.4)	(54.6)	..
Financial Administration	(8.0)	(14.8)	(10.8)	(10.8)	(14.2)	(16.6)	(17.3)	..
Defense Justice and Police	(20.0)	(20.6)	(23.2)	(31.2)	(37.6)	(46.5)	(45.6)	..
Local Authorities	(1.0)	(1.2)	(1.8)	(1.3)	(1.5)	(2.0)	(2.7)	..
Other	(1.5)	(0.9)	(1.4)	(3.6)	(3.5)	(3.7)	(5.0)	..
Community Services	45.6	38.3	57.8	4.4	76.0	87.7	88.0	
Water and Sewerage	(10.9)	(11.7)	(15.9)	(15.1)	(16.0)	(22.3)	(26.8)	..
Drainage	(0.7)	(1.0)	(1.3)	(1.0)	(1.3)	(1.4)	(1.3)	..
Highways, Transport, Storage - Communication	(128.1)	(19.5)	(34.7)	(37.8)	44.6)	(49.3)	(50.2)	..
Other	(5.9)	(6.1)	(5.8)	(10.6)	(14.1)	(14.7)	(9.7)	..
Social Services	90.5	103.4	108.1	128.7	170.8	194.9	222.2	..
Education	(46.3)	(54.0)	(53.6)	(58.7)	(80.6)	(90.2)	(104.1)	..
Health	(22.7)	(24.6)	(28.3)	(31.3)	(39.9)	(49.0)	(52.4)	..
Housing and Other	(21.5)	(24.8)	(26.1)	(38.6)	(50.4)	(55.7)	65.7	..

Economic Services	47.0	51.8	35.5	43.6	50.4	57.5	60.3	..
Agriculture	(20.0)	(21.0)	(22.9)	(20.3)	(24.8)	(30.5)	(30.0)	..
Industry and Tourism	(4.4)	(5.2)	(5.4)	(14.9)	(9.8)	(11.5)	(12.5)	..
Transport and Communication	(11.4)	(5.8)	(1.3)	(3.5)	(5.7)	(5.6)	(6.3)	
Fuel and Power	(8.4)	(17.8)	(3.3)	(2.0)	(1.7)	(-)	(-)	..
Mining	(0.3)	(0.3)	(0.3)	(0.3)	(0.5)	(0.6)	(0.6)	..
Research	(0.5)	(0.6)	(1.1)	(0.5)	(3.5)	(4.1)	(4.2)	..
Other	(2.0)	(1.1)	(1.2)	(2.0)	(4.4)	(5.2)	(6.7)	..
Other Expenditure	33.1	36.4	41.4	45.4	50.9	63.0	73.0	..
Transfers to Local Authorities	(17.9)	(18.1)	(21.4)	(23.8)	(27.1)	(32.6)	(35.8)	..
Interest on public debt	(13.3)	(16.9)	(19.6)	(21.5)	(23.5)	(27.5) 3/	(36.4)	..
Other	(1.9)	(1.4)	(0.4)	(0.1)	(0.3)	(0.4)	(0.8) 5/	..
Adjustment	-	-	-	-	-	2.5 4/	-	..
Acquisition of assets 6/	-	-	-	17.1	-	21.4	-	..
Adjustment	-	-	-	-	-	-5.6	-	..

1/ Excludes provision for renegotiated salary increases for public employees.
2/ Total relates to actual expenditure; components are based on revised estimates.
3/ Actual payments.
4/ Difference between total actual payments and revised estimates.
5/ Includes discrepancies
6/ Purchase of equity in private companies.

Source: S.A. Tables 5.10 and 5.11.

Table SA6.1. Jamaica: Commercial Bank Assets and Liabilities, Summary Accounts, 1962–74

(In thousands of Jamaican dollars at end of year)

	1962	1963	1964	1965	1966	1967	1968	1969	1970	1971	1972	1973	1974
1. Net Foreign Assets	-11,968	3,454	-17,942	-24,340	-15,792	-10,690	-12,496	-21,743	-21,775	-5,465	-33,323	-75,218	-55,962
(a) Assets	9,652	15,908	7,490	8,040	8,218	5,868	2,172	7,127	16,111	17,388	21,310	45,012	39,332
(b) Liabilities	-21,620	-12,454	-25,432	-32,380	-24,010	-16,558	-14,668	-28,870	-37,886	-22,853	-54,633	-120,230	-95,294
2. Net Position with Bank of Jamaica	11,400	11,210	15,092	13,238	16,836	18,164	31,740	20,266	22,300	30,529	27,082	27,938	65,031
(a) Cash and Deposits with the BJ	11,400	11,210	15,092	13,238	16,836	18,164	34,190	25,656	28,064	37,672	37,088	57,813	67,472
(b) Credit from the BJ	-	-	-	-	-	-	- 2,450	- 5,390	- 5,764	- 7,143	-10,006	-29,875	- 2,441
3. Net Credit to Government	8,546	13,872	12,960	10,540	10,627	17,987	32,257	28,871	41,498	53,505	54,953	63,895	62,869
(a) Treasury Bills (b) Other Government Securities	10,852	15,562	14,534	12,110									
(a) Treasury Bills					12,720	15,216	23,659	21,663	25,917	33,010	33,072	27,198	33,300
(b) Other Government Securities					532	4,044	9,438	8,447	10,661	15,665	16,758	39,969	35,600
(c) Loans and Advances	-	-	-	-	-	-	-	-	6,000	6,000	6,000	7,000	6,999
(d) Deposits	- 2,306	- 1,690	- 1,574	- 1,570	- 2,625	- 1,273	- 840	- 1,239	- 1,080	- 1,170	- 877	-10,272	-13,030
4. Loans and Advances to Government Services	2,268	1,334	2,500	2,608	3,056	2,072	3,464	4,113	6,447	9,222	14,717	26,183	18,063
5. Loans and Advances to Public Utilities					3,064	4,370	5,358	11,909	22,708	21,581	26,641	22,519	27,584
6. Loans and Advances to the Private Sector					128,989	139,281	164,970	228,400	256,042	299,666	378,745	461,663	535,425
5. and 6. combined	80,708	75,352	101,882	124,426									
7. Unclassified Credit (net)	9,800	11,370	13,736	12,458	12,111	10,574	11,970	15,124	1,496	- 4,068	-18,484	-39,653	-70,223
8. Liabilities to the Private Sector	100,754	116,592	128,228	138,930	158,891	181,758	237,290	286,940	328,716	404,970	450,331	487,327	582,787
(a) Demand Deposits	45,518	45,314	48,020	47,748	50,398	58,958	75,628	89,108	92,717	111,966	112,991	124,896	149,388
(b) Savings Deposits	43,130	52,258	61,444	70,732	80,416	92,391	114,848	135,090	149,550	178,854	198,168	220,474	241,399
(c) Time Deposits	12,106	19,020	18,764	20,450	28,077	30,409	46,814	62,742	86,449	114,150	139,172	141,957	192,000

Source: Department of Statistics, Monetary Statistics, March 1974; Bank of Jamaica, Statistical Digest, November 1973 and Bank of Jamaica.

Table SA6.2. Jamaica: Bank of Jamaica, Assets and Liabilities, 1962–74

(In thousands of Jamaican dollars at end of year)

	1962	1963	1964	1965	1966	1967	1968	1969	1970	1971	1972	1973	1974
1. Net Foreign Assets	27,430	36,158	40,090	40,378	55,842	63,384	96,180	94,374	112,042	130,840	113,698	114,585	171,606
(a) Assets	27,430	36,158	40,090	40,378	55,842	63,384	96,180	94,374	112,042	130,840	113,698	114,585	171,606
(b) Liabilities	-	-	-	-	-	-	-	-	-	-	-	-	-
2. Net Domestic Credit	3,508	- 1,654	-130	-892	-10,350	-10,263	-19,244	-25,297	-21,337	-16,272	20,268	19,347	18,733
(a) Central Government (net)	5,148	562	3,096	3,854	- 4,170	- 3,763	-12,744	-18,797	-14,837	- 9,772	26,770	25,847	26,733
Treasury Bills	2,910	2,818	3,392	3,590	3,022	2,118	64	1,876	4,754	7,142	9,434	18,947	15,442
Government Securities	4,692	3,992	6,308	6,004	4,336	2,834	4,340	2,668	1,620	3,100	22,961	15,740	21,061
Advances	-	-	-	-	-	-	-	-	-	-	-	-	-
Deposits	- 2,454	- 6,248	- 6,604	- 5,740	-11,528	- 8,715	-17,148	-23,341	-21,211	-20,014	- 5,625	- 8,840	- 9,770
(b) Official Capital & Reserves	- 1,640	- 2,216	- 3,226	- 4,746	- 6,180	- 6,500	- 6,500	- 6,500	- 6,500	- 6,500	- 6,502	- 6,500	- 8,000
3. Unclassified Net Credit	- 1,326	- 3,182	- 2,070	- 2,322	- 2,902	8	- 3,948	- 1,270	- 6,143	- 5,570	- 7,653	15,782	17,918
4. Liabilities to Banks (net)	11,400	11,210	15,092	13,238	16,836	18,164	31,740	20,266	22,300	30,529	27,083	27,938	65,031
(a) Currency	4,514	4,644	4,528	4,806	6,472	6,781	9,408	10,525	10,269	9,829	12,684	20,222	21,756
(b) Deposits	6,886	6,566	10,564	8,432	10,364	11,383	24,782	15,131	17,795	27,843	24,405	37,591	45,716
(c) Advances	-	-	-	-	-	-	- 2,450	- 5,390	- 5,764	- 7,143	-10,006	-29,875	- 2,441
5. SDR Allocation	-	-	-	-	-	-	-	-	5,320	10,046	14,727	19,382	19,382
6. Currency in Circulation	18,212	20,112	22,798	23,926	25,754	34,965	41,248	47,541	56,942	68,423	84,503	102,394	123,844

Sources: Department of Statistics, Monetary Statistics, March 1974; Bank of Jamaica, Statistical Digest, November 1974 and Bank of Jamaica.

Table SA6.3. Jamaica: Consolidated Accounts of the Banking System, 1962–74
(In thousands of Jamaican dollars at end of year)

	1962	1963	1964	1965	1966	1967	1968	1969	1970	1971	1972	1973	1974
1. Net Foreign Assets	15,462	39,612	22,148	16,038	40,050	52,694	83,684	72,631	90,267	125,375	80,375	39,367	115,644
(a) Assets	37,082	52,066	47,580	48,418	64,060	69,252	98,352	101,501	128,153	148,228	135,008	159,597	210,938
(b) Liabilities	-21,620	-12,454	-25,432	-32,380	-24,010	-16,558	-14,668	-28,870	-37,886	-22,853	-54,633	-120,230	-95,294
2. Net Domestic Credit	95,030	88,904	117,212	136,682	135,386	153,441	186,805	247,996	305,358	367,702	495,324	593,607	662,674
(a) Central Government (net)	13,694	14,434	16,056	14,394	6,457	14,218	19,513	10,074	26,661	43,733	81,723	89,742	89,602
(b) Rest of Public Sector (net))					6,120	6,442	8,822	16,022	29,155	30,803	41,358	48,702	45,647
(c) Credit to Private Sector (net))	82,976	76,686	104,382	127,034	128,989	139,281	164,970	228,400	256,042	299,666	378,745	461,663	535,425
(d) Official Capital & Reserve	- 1,640	- 2,216	- 3,226	- 4,746	- 6,180	- 6,500	- 6,500	- 6,500	- 6,500	- 6,500	- 6,502	- 6,500	- 8,000
3. Unclassified Net Credit	- 7,124	- 7,650	8,960	10,408	6,559	2,028	8,049	13,854	- 4,647	- 9,638	-26,138	-23,871	-52,305
4. SDR Allocation	-	-	-	-	-	-	-	-	5,320	10,046	14,727	19,382	19,382
5. Liabilities to Private Sector	103,368	120,866	148,320	163,128	181,995	208,163	278,538	334,481	385,658	474,393	534,834	589,721	706,631
(a) Currency in Circulation	18,212	20,112	22,798	23,926	25,754	34,965	41,248	47,541	56,942	68,423	84,503	102,394	123,844
(b) Demand Deposits	38,114	45,518	45,314	48,020	47,748	50,398	75,628	89,108	92,717	111,966	112,991	124,896	149,388
(c) Time and Saving Deposits	47,042	55,236	80,208	91,182	108,493	122,800	161,662	197,832	235,999	293,004	337,340	362,431	433,399

Source: Statistical Annex Tables 6.1 and 6.2.

Table SA6.4. Jamaica: Commercial Bank Loans and Advances Classified by Type, 1962–74

(In thousands of Jamaican dollars at end of year)

	1962	1963	1964	1965	1966	1967	1968	1969	1970	1971	1972	1973	1974
1. Agriculture & Fishing	6,326	4,196	7,304	9,700	7,410	6,252	8,032	9,430	10,093	11,959	12,927	15,916	26,586
2. Mining	8,042	4,040	4,050	4,042	4,040	6,062	6,052	8,000	8,126	8,136	8,105	6,613	6,169
3. Manufacturing	11,438	12,528	21,224	27,970	29,419	31,436	37,444	55,441	61,881	59,427	85,865	107,584	112,819
(i) Sugar, rice, and molasses	(3,014)	(3,280)	(5,402)	(8,682)	(10,612)	(9,900)	(7,632)	(14,961)	(17,805)	(11,526)	(15,342)	(19,681)	(16,329)
(ii) Food, drink, and tobacco	(1,652)	(2,702)	(4,058)	(3,258)	(4,100)	(4,086)	(6,032)	(9,913)	(10,941)	(11,001)	(16,622)	(15,239)	(18,691)
(iii) Textile, leather, footwear	(1,634)	(1,376)	(1,464)	(1,914)	(1,648)	(1,110)	(1,382)	(2,340)	(2,918)	(3,597)	(10,058)	(16,788)	(16,177)
(iv) Other industry	(5,138)	(5,170)	(10,300)	(14,116)	(13,059)	(16,340)	(22,398)	(28,227)	(30,217)	(33,303)	(43,843)	(55,876)	(61,622)
4. Construction and Land Development	6,188	6,986	12,914	16,440	10,148	15,254	18,338	31,343	39,150	48,300	72,271	104,104	125,380
5. Credits and Other Financial Institutions	1,692	1,872	2,810	3,562	4,922	3,438	6,174	6,111	9,992	9,615	12,896	13,761	18,120
6. Government Services	2,268	1,334	2,500	2,608	3,056	2,072	3,464	4,113	6,447	9,222	14,717	26,183	18,063
7. Distribution	24,246	21,296	26,006	33,332	34,792	33,614	36,854	43,929	52,381	60,520	69,788	76,247	85,479
8. Tourism (Hotels)	4,016	4,378	3,412	3,482	3,656	3,324	3,886	7,207	9,633	12,126	12,343	14,860	16,146
9. Entertainment	686	1,280	1,688	1,706	2,244	2,338	1,994	1,156	3,344	3,003	3,745	4,615	4,727
10. Professional & Other Services)	) 11,296	) 10,748	) 14,146	) 18,006	) 25,174	) 32,642	40.092	53,103	61,442	86,580	100,805	117,963	139,999
(a) Personal)							-	-	51,482	73,973	85,299	95,012	106,939
11. Public Utilities)	) 6,778	) 8,028	) 8,328	) 6,186	3,064	4,370	5,358	11,909	22,708	21,581	26,641	22,519	27,584
12. Other)					7,185	4,921	6,104	12,680	-	-	-	-	-
Total	82,976	76,686	104,382	127,034	135,109	145,723	173,792	244,422	285,197	330,469	420,103	510,365	581,072

Sources: 1962-1965: Monetary Statistics, 1967, Department of Statistics, Jamaica;
1966-1972: Statistical Digest, Research Department, Bank of Jamaica, various issues;
1973: Bank of Jamaica;
1974: Monetary Statistics, 1974, Department of Statistics, Jamaica.

Table SA6.5. Jamaica: Distribution of Commercial Bank Assets, 1962–74
(In thousands of Jamaican dollars at end of year)

	1962	1963	1964	1965	1966	1967	1968	1969	1970	1971	1972	1973	1974
1. Net Foreign Assets	-11,968	3,454	-17,942	-24,340	-15,792	-10,690	-12,496	-21,743	-21,775	-5,465	-33,323	-75,218	-55,962
2. Net Position with Bank of Jamaica	11,400	11,210	15,092	13,238	16,836	18,164	31,328	19,922	16,893	20,944	17,444	27,635	66,986
3. Net Credit to Government	8,546	13,872	12,960	10,540	10,627	17,987	32,257	27,902	41,498	53,505	54,953	67,003	60,914
4. Credit to Other Public Bodies	2,268	1,334	2,500	2,608	3,056	2,072	3,464	4,113	6,447	9,222	14,717	26,183	18,063
5. Credit to the Private Sector	80,708	75,352	101,882	124,426	132,053	143,651	170,328	240,309	278,750	321,247	405,386	484,182	563,009
(a) Agriculture and Fishing	6,326	4,196	7,304	9,700	7,410	6,252	8,032	9,430	10,093	11,959	12,927	15,916	26,586
(b) Mining	8,042	4,040	4,050	4,042	4,040	6,062	6,052	8,000	8,126	8,136	8,105	6,613	6,169
(c) Manufacturing	11,438	12,528	21,224	27,970	29,419	31,436	37,444	55,441	61,881	59,427	85,865	107,584	112,819
(i) Sugar, Rum, and Molasses	(3,014)	(3,280)	(5,402)	(8,682)	(10,612)	(9,900)	(7,632)	(14,961)	(17,805)	(11,526)	(15,342)	(19,681)	(16,329)
(ii) Food, Drink, and Tobacco	(1,652)	(2,702)	(4,058)	(3,258)	(4,100)	(4,086)	(6,032)	(9,913)	(10,941)	(11,001)	(16,622)	(15,239)	(18,691)
(iii) Textile, Leather, Footwear	(1,634)	(1,376)	(1,464)	(1,914)	(1,648)	(1,110)	(1,382)	(2,340)	(2,918)	(3,597)	(10,058)	(16,788)	(16,177)
(iv) Other Industry	(5,138)	(5,170)	(10,300)	(14,116)	(13,059)	(16,340)	(22,398)	(28,227)	(30,217)	(33,303)	(43,843)	(55,876)	(61,622)
(d) Construction & Land Development	6,188	6,986	12,914	16,440	10,148	15,254	18,338	31,343	39,150	48,300	72,271	104,104	125,380
(e) Credits & Other Financial Institutions	1,692	1,872	2,810	3,562	4,921	3,438	6,174	6,111	9,992	9,615	12,896	13,761	18,120
(f) Distribution	24,246	21,296	26,006	33,332	34,792	33,614	36,854	43,929	52,381	60,520	69,788	76,247	85,479
(g) Tourism	4,016	4,378	3,412	3,482	3,656	3,324	3,886	7,207	9,633	12,126	12,343	14,860	16,146
(h) Entertainment	686	1,280	1,688	1,706	2,244	2,338	1,994	1,156	3,344	3,003	3,745	4,615	4,727
(i) Personal, Professional & Other Services	) 11,296	)10,748	)14,146	)18,006	25,174	32,642	40,092	53,103	61,442	86,580	100,805	117,963	139,999
(i) Personal	)	)	)	)	-	-	-	-	(51,482)	(73,973)	(85,299)	(95,012)	(106,939)
(j) Public Utilities	) 6,778	) 8,028	) 8,328	) 6,186	3,064	4,370	5,358	11,909	22,708	21,581	26,641	22,519	27,584
(k) Other	)	)	)	)	7,185	4,921	6,104	12,680	-	-	-	-	-
6. Unclassified Credit (Net)	9,800	11,370	13,736	12,458	12,111	10,574	11,970	15,124	1,496	-4,068	-18,484	-39,653	-70,223
Total	100,754	116,592	128,228	138,930	158,891	181,758	237,290	286,940	328,716	404,970	450,331	487,327	582,787

Source: Statistical Annex Tables 6.1 and 6.4.

Table SA6.6. Trinidad and Tobago: Commercial Bank Assets and Liabilities, Summary Accounts, 1964–74

(In millions of TT dollars at end of year)

	1964	1965	1966	1967	1968	1969	1970	1971	1972	1973	1974
Net Foreign Assets	21.4	22.1	8.3	5.2	-15.6	-13.0	-5.3	-0.8	-21.3	-23.3	-31.6
Assets	n.a.	n.a.	n.a.	12.0	-	11.5	10.1	24.3	6.9	9.0	8.2
Liabilities	n.a.	n.a.	n.a.	-6.8	-15.6	-24.5	-15.4	-25.1	-28.3	-32.3	-39.8
Claims on Central Bank	19.0	15.3	22.7	21.4	38.5	31.9	35.1	51.3	48.5	69.1	204.7
Currency	19.0	15.3	10.3	8.4	11.6	9.7	9.9	11.5	15.3	20.0	25.1
Deposits	-	-	12.5	13.3	26.9	22.2	25.2	39.8	34.9	52.1	179.6
Advances (Rediscounts)	-	-	-	-0.3	-	-	-	-	-1.7	-3.0	-
Net Domestic Credit	175.8	192.2	215.6	240.2	284.7	338.0	392.0	480.2	605.0	692.9	765.7
Central Government (net)	32.9	24.5	27.9	38.5	61.5	44.3	56.7	110.8	99.5	71.2	115.7
Treasury Bills	(36.1)	(28.5)	(28.9)	(27.8)	(38.4)	(22.0)	(36.1)	(77.3)	(61.0)	(44.5)	(95.6)
Other Securities				(16.7)	(18.6)	(17.9)	(17.5)	(20.3)	(27.9)	(18.0)	(13.6)
Loans and Advances	n.a.	n.a.	n.a.	(-)	(5.0)	(5.0)	(4.7)	(15.5)	(12.3)	(10.2)	(7.9)
Deposits	(-3.2)	(-4.0)	(-1.0)	(-6.0)	(-0.5)	(-0.6)	(-1.6)	(-2.3)	(-1.7)	(-1.5)	(-1.4)
Rest of Public Sector (net)	6.7	6.8	6.8	4.4	4.9	-2.0	-15.6	-11.0	-1.1	43.2	1.0
Credit	(22.5)	(16.9)	(19.4)	(16.0)	(14.0)	(10.2)	(4.6)	(6.5)	(25.8)	(86.1)	(70.4)
Deposits	(-15.8)	(-10.1)	(-12.6)	(-11.6)	(-9.1)	(-12.2)	(-20.2)	(-17.5)	(-26.9)	(-42.9)	(-69.4)
Private Sector	109.4	139.8	153.4	177.1	194.8	266.1	326.4	358.7	500.4	583.4)	653.6
U.S. Counterpart Funds	-2.7	-6.3	-0.8	-1.7	-2.9	-1.6	-0.6	-0.5	-	-	-
Official Capital	n.a.	n.a.	n.a.	-	-	-	-5.0	-5.0	-5.0	-5.0	-5.0
Unclassified (net)	29.5	27.4	28.3	21.9	26.5	31.1	30.0	37.2	11.2	0.1	0.4
Medium-term Foreign Liabilities	-	-	-	-	-	-	-	-	-	21.0 1/	-
Liabilities to Private Sector	216.2	229.6	246.6	266.9	307.7	356.9	421.9	530.6	632.2 2/	717.7	938.8
Demand Deposits	76.3	76.8	77.5	81.4	84.5	81.6	87.1	103.1	121.8	125.3	161.3
Time Deposits	28.0	34.8	44.0	52.7	74.1	104.3	145.6	191.3	213.5	310.1	442.4
Savings Deposits	111.9	118.0	125.1	132.8	149.1	171.0	189.2	236.2	296.9	282.3	335.1

1/ External liability of BWIA assumed by a local commercial bank in January 1973, and renegotiated as a local loan in January 1974.

2/ Excludes share capital of 21.1 million "localized" in 1972.

Source: 1964-72 Central Bank of Trinidad and Tobago.
1973 and 1974, IMF Consultation Report (SM/75/118) dated May 22, 1975

Table SA6.7. Trinidad and Tobago: Central Bank's Assets and Liabilities, 1964–74
(In millions of TT dollars at end of year)

	1964	1965	1966	1967	1968	1969	1970	1971	1972	1973	1974
1. Net Foreign Assets 1/	51.2	48.9	50.9	59.6	125.8	116.4	94.9	136.6	109.5	102.2	734.2
(a) Assets 1/	51.2	48.9	50.9	59.6	125.8	116.4	94.9	136.6	109.5	102.2	734.2
(b) Liabilities	-	-	-	-	-	-	-	-	-	-	-
2. Medium-term Foreign Claims	-	-	-	-	-	-	-	-	-	-	72.8 2/
3. Net Domestic Credit	4.7	2.5	13.4	-12.9	-43.6	-38.5	2.8	-0.2	48.5	79.6	-452.2
(a) Central Government (net)	4.7	6.7	17.6	- 6.4	-36.6	-31.0	10.6	9.0	55.6	83.5	-445.8
Treasury Bills	)	)	)	2.1	9.2	28.9	30.8 3/	-	37.9	55.5	-
Other Securities	) 5.6	) 7.6	) 17.6	0.5	7.7	9.0	12.3	12.7	2.9	8.7	9.2
Loans, Advances & Other Credit 4/	)	)	)	-	-27.0	-27.0	-10.8	10.4	25.4	27.4	-226.5
Deposits	-0.9	-0.9	-	-9.0	-26.5	-41.9	-21.7	-14.1	-10.6	-8.1	-228.5
(b) Rest of Public Sector (net)	-	-	-	-	-	-0.5	-0.8	-2.2	-0.1	3.1	1.6
(c) Official Capital & Reserves	-	-4.2	-4.2	-6.5	-7.0	-7.0	-7.0	-7.0	-7.0	-7.0	-8.0
4. Unclassified Net Credit	-	-0.1	-1.6	17.0	4.8	4.6	8.7	10.7	17.0	18.1	-0.5
5. Liabilities to Banks (net)	19.0	15.3	22.7	21.4	38.5	31.9	35.1	51.3	48.5	69.1	204.7
(a) Currency	19.0	15.3	10.3	8.4	11.6	9.7	9.9	11.5	15.3	20.0	25.1
(b) Deposits	-	-	12.5	13.3	26.9	22.2	25.2	39.8	34.9	52.1	179.6
(c) Advances	-	-	-	-0.3	-	-	-	-	-1.7	-3.0	-
6. SDR Allocation	-	-	-	-	-	-	14.8	28.3	46.2	52.0	52.0
7. Currency in Circulation	36.9	36.0	40.6	42.3	48.5	50.6	56.5	67.5	80.3	78.8	97.6

1/ Includes assets of the former British Caribbean Currency Board. Also includes U.K. securities held by the Government under a repurchase agreement with the Central Bank of TT$27 million in December 1968 and December 1969 and TT$8.9 million in December 1970.

2/ Claims arising from dishbursement of loans to Jamaica and Guyana.

3/ Includes TT$10.1 million of a special Treasury Bill issue relating to the repurchase agreement mentioned above.

4/ Includes contra-entries related to the repurchase agreement mentioned above.

Source: 1964-72, Central Bank of Trinidad and Tobago.
1973 and 1974, IMF Consultation Report (SM/75/118) dated May 22, 1975.

Table SA6.8. Trinidad and Tobago: Consolidated Accounts of the Banking System, 1964–74

(In millions of TT dollars at end of year)

	1964	1965	1966	1967	1968	1969	1970	1971	1972	1973	1974
1. Net Foreign Assets	72.6	71.0	59.2	64.8	110.2	103.4	89.6	135.2	88.1	78.9	702.6
(a) Assets	-	-	-	71.6	125.8	127.9	105.0	160.9	116.4	111.2	742.4
(b) Liabilities	-	-	-	-6.8	-15.6	-24.5	-15.4	-25.1	-28.3	-32.3	-39.8
2. Medium-term Foreign Claims 1/	-	-	-	-	-	-	-	-	-	-	72.8
3. Net Domestic Credit	153.7	173.6	201.5	207.1	217.6	269.9	365.3	453.3	642.3	772.4	313.1
(a) Central Government (net)	37.6	31.2	45.5	32.1	24.9	13.3	67.3	119.8	155.1	154.7	-330.1
(b) Rest of the Public Sector (net)	6.7	6.8	6.8	4.4	4.9	-2.5	-16.4	-13.2	-1.2	46.3	2.6
(c) Credit to the Private Sector (net)	109.4	139.8	153.4	177.1	194.8	266.1	326.4	358.7	500.4	583.4	653.6
(d) Official Capital & Reserves	-	-4.2	-4.2	-6.5	-7.0	-7.0	-12.0	-12.0	-12.0	-12.0	-13.0
4. Unclassified Net Credit	26.8	21.0	26.5	37.3	28.4	34.2	38.3	37.9	28.3	18.2	-0.1
5. SDR Allocation	-	-	-	-	-	-	14.8	28.3	46.2	52.0	52.0
6. Medium-term Foreign Liabilities 2/	-	-	-	-	-	-	-	-	-	21.0	-
. Liabilities to the Private Sector	253.1	265.6	287.6	309.2	356.2	407.5	478.4	598.1	712.5	796.5	1,036.4
(a) Currency in Circulation	36.9	36.0	40.6	42.3	48.5	50.6	56.5	67.5	80.3	78.8	97.6
(b) Demand Deposits	76.3	76.8	77.5	81.4	84.5	81.6	87.1	103.1	121.8	125.3	161.3
(c) Time and Savings Deposits	139.9	152.8	169.1	185.5	223.2	275.3	334.8	427.5	510.4	592.4	777.5

1/ Claims arising from disbursements of loans to Jamaica and Guyana.

2/ External liability of BWIA assumed by a local commercial bank in January 1973, and renegotiated as a local loan in January 1974.

Source: Statistical Annex Tables, 6.6 and 6.7.

Table SA6.9. Trinidad and Tobago: Distribution of Commercial Bank Advances to the Private Sector, 1964–75

(In millions of TT dollars at end of year)

	1964	1965	1966	1967	1968	1969	1970	1971	1972	1973	1974	1975
						(In TT$ million)						
Total	96.9	129.2	144.6	168.5	184.7	255.1	314.8	344.8	475.9	547.1	602.5	810.2
Manufacturing	14.5	24.0	25.5	25.3	32.3	51.2	71.3	72.5	114.0	120.7	130.9	143.7
Chemicals & Fertilizers	(5.5)	(8.4)	(8.2)	(9.9)	(9.0)	(12.1)	(13.3)	(12.4)	(13.7)	(13.9)	(13.7)	(31.9)
Food, Beverages & Tobacco	(3.6)	(5.0)	(5.3)	(6.0)	(7.9)	(12.0)	(10.5)	(10.8)	(16.3)	(19.2)	(23.2)	(23.1)
Textiles, Footwear	(1.4)	(2.5)	(2.8)	(1.6)	(2.7)	(6.9)	(6.6)	(6.8)	(11.1)	(12.1)	(14.0)	(17.5)
Building Products	(1.7)	(3.1)	(3.8)	(4.4)	(3.3)	(7.1)	(9.4)	(8.1)	(11.6)	(16.7)	(21.1)	(19.6)
Other Industry	(2.3)	(5.0)	(5.4)	(3.4)	(9.4)	(13.1)	(31.6)	(34.5)	(61.2)	(58.8)	(58.2)	(56.6)
Agriculture	3.9	6.0	8.2	5.4	7.2	5.2	7.8	7.5	12.9	16.8	19.3	21.5
Construction	4.8	5.2	6.7	9.8	8.7	11.0	13.7	8.1	10.3	19.1	22.6	32.6
Distributive Trades	34.0	38.9	48.6	58.3	64.1	76.6	83.5	87.1	109.9	111.8	110.5	122.2
Individuals (non-business loans)	22.3	28.9	35.2	48.1	47.6	79.3	91.3	112.7	153.4	195.3	237.4	369.9
Professional Services	5.8	10.3	5.8	5.5	10.7	5.4	11.0	12.8	12.7	15.0	15.9	15.0
Financial Institutions	3.5	5.3	5.3	8.7	2.9	4.3	9.6	10.9	13.7	23.7	19.8	19.2
Mining and Refining	n.a.	n.a.	n.a.	1.3	1.5	8.7	10.5	9.6	18.4	15.9	15.5	33.2
Transportation	8.1	10.6	9.3	5.0	5.6	8.4	7.9	14.1	17.2	12.6	15.0	21.7
Other				1.3	4.1	4.9	8.3	9.4	13.4	16.2	16.3	26.1
						(As Percent of Total)						
Total	100.0	100.0	100.0	100.0	100.0	100.0	100.0	100.0	100.0	100.0	100.0	100.0
Manufacturing	15.0	18.6	17.6	15.0	17.5	20.1	22.6	21.0	23.9	22.1	21.6	18.4
Chemicals & Fertilizers	(5.7)	(6.5)	(5.7)	(5.9)	(4.9)	(4.7)	(4.2)	(3.6)	(2.9)	(2.5)	(2.3)	(3.9)
Food, Beverages & Tobacco	(3.7)	(3.9)	(3.7)	(3.6)	(4.3)	(4.7)	(3.3)	(3.1)	(3.4)	(3.5)	(3.9)	(2.9)
Textiles, Footwear	(1.4)	(1.9)	(1.9)	(0.9)	(1.5)	(2.7)	(2.1)	(2.0)	(2.3)	(2.2)	(2.3)	(2.2)
Building Products	(1.8)	(2.4)	(2.6)	(2.6)	(1.8)	(2.8)	(3.0)	(2.3)	(2.4)	(3.1)	(3.5)	(2.4)
Other Industry	(2.4)	(3.9)	(3.7)	(2.0)	(5.1)	(5.1)	(10.0)	(10.0)	(12.9)	(10.7)	(9.7)	(7.0)
Agriculture	4.0	4.6	5.7	3.2	3.9	2.0	2.5	2.2	2.7	3.1	3.2	2.7
Construction	5.0	4.0	4.6	5.8	4.7	4.3	4.4	2.3	2.2	3.5	3.3	4.0
Distributive Trades	35.1	30.1	33.6	34.6	34.7	30.0	26.5	25.3	23.1	20.4	18.3	15.1
Individuals (non-business loans)	23.0	22.4	24.3	28.5	25.8	31.1	29.0	32.7	32.2	35.7	39.4	45.7
Professional Services	6.0	8.0	4.0	3.3	5.8	2.1	3.5	3.7	2.7	2.7	2.6	1.9
Financial Institutions	3.6	4.1	3.7	5.2	1.6	1.7	3.0	3.2	2.9	4.3	3.3	2.4
Mining and Refining	n.a.	n.a.	n.a.	0.8	0.8	3.4	3.3	2.8	3.9	2.9	2.6	4.1
Transportation	8.4	8.2	6.4	3.0	3.0	3.3	2.5	4.1	3.6	2.3	2.5	2.7
Other				0.8	2.2	1.9	2.6	2.7	2.8	3.0	2.7	3.2

Source: 1964–72, *Statistical Digest*, Central Bank of Trinidad and Tobago, various issues.
1973 and 1974, IMF Consultation Report (SM/75/118) dated May 22, 1975.

Table SA6.10. Trinidad and Tobago: Distribution of Commercial Bank Assets, 1964–74

(In millions of TT dollars at end of year)

	1964	1965	1966	1967	1968	1969	1970	1971	1972	1973	1974
1. Net Foreign Assets	21.4	22.1	8.3	5.2	-15.6	-13.0	-5.3	-0.8	-21.3	-23.3	-31.6
2. Net Claims on Central Bank	19.0	15.3	22.8	21.4	38.5	32.0	35.1	51.3	48.5	69.1	204.7
3. Net Credit to Central Government	32.9	24.5	27.9	38.5	61.5	44.3	56.7	110.8	99.5	71.2	115.7
4. Net Credit to Rest of Public Sector	6.7	6.8	6.8	4.4	4.9	-2.0	-15.6	-11.0	-1.1	43.2	1.0
5. Loans & Advances to the Private Sector	96.9	129.2	144.6	168.5	184.7	255.1	314.8	344.8	475.9	547.1	602.5
(a) Agriculture	3.9	6.0	8.2	5.4	7.2	5.2	7.8	7.5	12.9	16.8	19.3
(b) Mining and Refining	n.a.	n.a.	n.a.	1.3	1.5	8.7	10.5	9.6	18.4	15.9	15.5
(c) Manufacturing	14.5	24.0	55.5	25.3	32.3	51.2	71.3	72.5	114.0	120.7	130.2
(i) Chemical & Fertilizers	(5.5)	(8.4)	(8.2)	(9.9)	(9.0)	(12.1)	(13.3)	(12.4)	(13.7)	(13.9)	(13.7)
(ii) Food, beverages & tobacco	(3.6)	(5.0)	(5.3)	(6.0)	(7.9)	(12.0)	(10.5)	(10.8)	(16.3)	(19.2)	(23.2)
(iii) Textiles, footwear	(1.4)	(2.5)	(2.8)	(1.6)	(2.7)	(6.9)	(6.6)	(6.8)	(11.1)	(12.1)	(14.0)
(iv) Building products	(1.7)	(3.1)	(3.8)	(4.4)	(3.3)	(7.1)	(9.4)	(8.1)	(11.6)	(16.7)	(21.1)
(v) Other industry	(2.3)	(5.0)	(5.4)	(3.4)	(9.4)	(13.1)	(31.5)	(34.5)	(61.2)	(58.8)	(58.2)
(d) Construction	4.8	5.2	6.7	9.8	8.7	11.0	13.7	8.1	10.3	19.1	22.6
(e) Financial institutions	3.5	5.3	5.3	8.7	2.9	4.3	9.6	10.9	13.7	23.7	19.8
(f) Distribution	34.0	38.9	48.6	58.3	64.1	76.6	83.5	87.1	109.9	111.8	110.5
(g) Professional and other services	5.8	10.3	5.8	5.5	10.7	5.4	11.0	12.8	12.7	15.0	15.9
(h) Personal	22.3	28.9	35.2	48.1	47.6	79.3	91.3	112.7	153.4	195.3	237.4
(i) Other	8.1	10.6	9.3	6.3	9.7	13.3	16.2	123.5	30.6	28.8	31.3
6. Unclassified Net Credit	39.3	31.7	36.2	28.9	30.7	40.6	36.2	35.5	30.7	31.4	46.5
7. Total	216.2	229.6	246.6	266.9	304.7	356.9	421.9	530.6	632.2	738.7	938.8

Source: 1964-72 Central Bank of Trinidad and Tobago.
1973 and 1974, IMF Consultation Report (SM/75/118) dated May 22, 1975.

Table SA6.11. Guyana: Assets and Liabilities of Commercial Bank, A Summary Account, 1965–74

(In thousands of Guyanan dollars at end of year)

	1965	1966	1967	1968	1969	1970	1971	1972	1973	1974
1. Net Foreign Assets[1/]	12,400	6,100	11,200	- 100	-3,700	-5,600	-5,700	-6,000	5,000	- 388
(a) Assets[1/]	14,600	8,800	14,300	3,600	4,300	4,200	4,600	2,200	13,400	13,912
(b) Liabilities[1/]	-2,200	-2,700	3,100	-3,700	-8,000	-9,800	-10,300	-8,200	-8,400	-14,300
2. Claims on the Bank of Guyana	9,972	11,529	10,639	12,155	15,381	11,209	13,374	22,893	17,029	18,234
(a) Cash in hand	9,972	6,013	6,244	5,127	5,236	3,592	4,065	5,861	6,913	7,276
(b) Deposits with Bank of Guyana	-	5,516	4,395	7,028	10,145	7,617	9,309	17,032	10,116	10,958
3. Net Credit to Central Government	2,867	5,155	11,434	21,948	19,809	20,797	37,728	59,075	66,445	64,696
(a) Treasury Bills	1,018	2,977	2,872	14,094	12,600	14,361	31,878	52,647	60,943	55,618
(b) Debenture	350	2,350	8,572	7,860	7,209	6,436	5,850	6,428	5,502	9,241
(c) Loans and advances	6,128	-	-	-	-	-	-	-	-	-
(d) Deposits	-4,629	-172	-10	-6	-	-	-	-	-	- 163
4. Net Credit to Local Government	198	445	521	367	296	636	485	720	241	1,088
(a) Loans and advances	560	512	682	668	682	1,046	897	1,084	1,533	1,676
(b) Deposits	-362	-67	-161	-301	-386	-410	-412	-364	-1,292	-588
5. Net Credit to Public Financial Institutions	-404	-51	-70	-569	-836	-1,477	-2,545	-2,975	-5,403	-5,485
(a) Loans and advances	-	1	-	-	-	349	-	51	486	1,029
(b) Deposits	-404	-52	-70	-569	-836	-1,826	-2,545	-3,026	-5,889	-6,514
6. Net Credit to Statutory Boards & Other Public Authorities	10.461	11,037	6,706	6,487	9,293	11,335	10,894	9,617	9,618	42,567
(a) Loans and advances	11,198	11,935	7,613	7,741	10,057	12,436	13,215	12,177	20,308	55,818
(b) Deposits	-737	-898	-907	-1,254	-764	-1,101	-2,321	-2,560	-10,690	-13,251
7. Credit to Private Sector	30,213	41,092	44,187	56,803	67,581	80,189	83,819	83,486	101,467	113,633
(a) Loans & advances (residents)	30,098	40,999	44.147	56,468	67,395	79,983	83,788	83,452	101,377	113,421
(b) Loans & advances (non-residents)	115	93	40	335	186	206	31	34	90	212
8. Unclassified Net Credit	7,219	6,533	7,826	5,627	7,870	7,046	8,042	9,883	5,531	2,993
9. Liabilities to the Private Sector	72,926	81,840	92,443	102,718	115,694	124,135	146,097	176,699	199,928	231,352
(a) Demand deposits	14,958	17,051	18,300	19,189	21,212	19,852	23,350	28,405	28,385	49,312
(b) Time and saving deposits	56,227	62,450	71,537	81,326	91,613	101,056	119,225	142,099	165,848	174,787
(c) Deposits by non-residents	1,741	2,339	2,606	2,203	2,869	3,227	3,522	6,195	5,695	7,253

1/ To the nearest $100 thousand only.

Source: Bank of Guyana, Annual Reports.

Table SA6.12. Guyana: Bank of Guyana, Assets and Liabilities, 1965–74

(In thousands of Guyanan dollars at end of year)

	1965	1966	1967	1968	1969	1970	1971	1972	1973	1974
1. Net Foreign Assets	19,019	27,088	36,913	46,459	40,842	40,220	56,142	72,970	27,398	133,901
(a) Assets	19,019	27,088	36,913	46,459	40,842	40,220	56,142	72,970	27,398	133,901
(b) Liabilities	-	-	-	-	-	-	-	-	-	-
2. Net Domestic Credit	3,114	7,571	1,317	-2,574	10,360	13,868	12,828	15,606	80,728	19,137
(a) Central Government (net)	3,351	12,609	7,043	4,201	17,386	21,160	20,386	23,510	89,258	28,396
Treasury Bills	150	1,234	2,246	1	3,107	7,950	13,248	25,102	65,363	15,571
Government Securities	3,201	3,258	3,273	3,301	3,190	3,200	3,644	3,655	3,422	4,686
Advances	-	8,117	1,524	899	11,089	10,010	3,494	-	20,473	8,139
Deposits	-	-	-	-	-	-	-	-5,247	-	-
(b) Official Capital and Reserve	-237	-5,038	-5,726	-6,775	-7,026	-7,292	-7,558	-7,904	-8,530	-9,259
3. Unclassified Net Credit	-109	-2,495	1,991	1,502	- 840	7,717	-6,557	-3,833	-22,023	-53,922
4. Liabilities to Banks	9,972	11,529	10,639	12,155	15,381	11,209	13,374	22,893	17,029	18,234
(a) Currency	9,972	6,013	6,244	5,127	5,236	3,592	4,065	5,861	6,913	7,276
(b) Deposits (net of advances)	-	5,516	4,395	7,028	10,145	7,617	9,309	17,032	10,116	10,958
5. SDR Allocation	-	-	-	-	-	5,040	9,320	14,722	14,722	18,093
6. Currency in Circulation	12,052	25,625	29,582	33,232	34,981	45,556	39,719	47,128	54,352	62,789

Source: Bank of Guyana, Annual Reports.

Table SA6.13. Guyana: Consolidated Accounts of the Banking System, 1965–74

(In thousands of Guyanan dollars at end of year)

	1965	1966	1967	1968	1969	1970	1971	1972	1973	1974
1. Net Foreign Assets	31,419	33,188	48,113	46,359	37,142	34,620	50,442	66,970	32,398	133,513
(a) Assets	33,619	35,888	51,213	50,059	45,142	44,420	60,742	75,170	40,798	147,813
(b) Liabilities	-2,200	-2,700	-3,100	-3,700	-8,000	-9,800	-10,300	-8,200	-8,400	-14,300
2. Net Domestic Credit	46,721	65,296	65,142	82,533	106,682	125,572	143,209	165,529	251,966	224,055
(a) Central Government (net)	6,218	17,764	18,477	26,149	37,195	41,957	58,114	82,585	155,703	93,092
(b) Rest of Public Sector (net)	10,255	11,431	7,157	6,285	8,753	10,494	8,834	7,362	4,456	38,170
(c) Official Capital & Reserve	237	-5,038	-5,726	-6,775	-7,026	-7,292	-7,558	-7,904	-8,530	-9,259
(d) Credit to Private Sector	30,485	41,139	44,234	56,874	67,760	80,413	83,819	83,486	100,337	102,052
3. Unclassified Net Credit	6,838	8,981	8,770	7,058	6,851	14,539	1,485	6,050	-15,362	-45,334
4. SDR Allocation	-	-	-	-	-	5,040	9,320	14,722	14,722	18,093
5. Liabilities to Private Sector	84,978	107,465	122,025	135,950	150,675	169,691	185,816	223,827	254,280	294,141
(a) Currency in Circulation	12,052	25,625	29,582	33,232	34,981	45,556	39,719	47,128	54,352	62,789
(b) Demand Deposits	14,958	17,051	18,300	19,189	21,212	19,852	23,350	28,405	28,385	49,312
(c) Time and Saving Deposits	56,227	62,450	71,537	81,236	91,613	101,056	119,225	142,099	165,848	174,787
(d) Deposits by Non-Residents	1,741	2,339	2,606	2,203	2,869	3,227	3,522	6,195	5,695	7,253

1/ Includes deposits of nonbank intermediaries

Source: Statistical Annex Tables 6.11 and 6.12.

Table SA6.14. Guyana: Commercial Bank Loans and Advances to the Private Sector, 1965–74

(In thousands of Guyanan dollars at end of year)

	Dec. 31 1965	Dec. 31 1966	Dec. 31 1967	Dec. 31 1968	Dec. 31 1969	Dec. 31 1970	Dec. 31 1971	Dec. 31 1972	Dec. 31 1973	Dec. 31 1974
Private Financial Institutions	1,252	2,140	2,685	3,362	2,606	3,047	2,276	1,393	1,842	1,033
Insurance Companies	40	171	121	55	94	715	112	61	155	105
Building Society	-	4	505	6	-	-	-	-	-	9
Credit Unions	306	344	284	1,499	233	164	119	83	303	175
Brokers & Moneylenders	885	1,522	1,571	1,336	1,534	70	72	95	19	360
Trust Companies	21	99	204	466	92	58	137	18	148	384
Investment Companies					653	2,040	1,836	1,136	1,217	-
Business Enterprise 1/	24,802	32,981	33,968	43,431	51,991	64,094	67,441	65,566	75,906	89,015
Agriculture	2,458	2,391	3,901	3,918	5,090	6,392	7,183	8,490	9,540	9,359
Sugarcane (excluding sugar estates)	13	44	50	32	29	559	729	873	1,036	940
Paddy	1,821	1,629	3,072	1,873	2,734	2,908	3,347	3,257	3,388	3,892
Livestock	186	244	166	265	356	670	852	1,027	1,049	1,476
Forestry	286	306	145	247	410	128	163	248	417	161
Shrimp and other fishing 2/	39	47	294	1,393	1,386	1,737	1,078	1,051	1,236	1,617
Other agriculture	113	121	174	108	175	390	1,014	2,034	2,414	1,273
Manufacture	11,833	17,460	14,289	16,671	21,053	26,559	33,830	29,138	34,624	44,486
Mining and processing of bauxite	11	-	36	67	2	11	4,442	-	-	11,581
Other mining and quarrying	267	656	623	443	1,156	779	685	593	703	507
Timber and sawmilling	557	974	1,402	2,094	1,308	2,109	2,526	3,023	3,272	3,842
Housing construction	}1,056	}1,963	}1,561	}3,574	1,951	2,199	2,429	1,114	1,356	n.a.
Other construction & engineering					3,184	3,338	6,067	8,010	7,057	7,858
Sugar & Molasses (including sugar estates)	4,454	7,013	6,494	2,690	721	4,524	2,844	670	753	119
Rice milling	3,631	4,338	2,381	1,334	1,419	1,400	1,421	1,375	1,617	1,363
Beverages, food, tobacco	722	970	432	3,061	6,977	6,626	7,703	7,952	10,647	8,402
Textiles & clothing 3/					923	1,407	1,617	1,682	2,941	4,324
Other manufacturing 4/	1,135	1,546	1,360	3,408	3,412	4,166	4,096	4,719	6,278	6,490

Services n.e.s.	10,511	13,130	15,778	22,842	25,848	31,143	26,428	27,938	31,740	35,170
Transportation	159	317	714	457	2,146	3,063	1,736	1,705	2,320	2,902
Entertainment & catering					1,210	1,515	1,735	1,871	1,558	3,161
Distribution 5/	9,481	11,422	13,028	19,968	19,797	24,263	19,155	21,207	24,609	25,813
Professional services					1,161	1,453	1,341	1,072	1,105	1,130
Other services	871	1,391	2,036	2,417	1,534	849	2,461	2,083	2,150	2,164
Individual Customers	4,044	5,878	7,494	9,675	12,798	12,842	14,071	16,493	23,629	23,373
For housing 6/	809	976	1,274	1,593	4,665	(5,290)	5,028	6,992	10,084	11,384
For other durable goods					314	390	564	783	2,697	3,064
For travel 7/	102	215	300	233						
For other purposes 8/	3,133	4,687	5,920	7,849	7,819	7,162	8,479	8,718	10,848	8,925
TOTAL a/	30,098	40,999	44,147	56,468	67,395	79,983	83,788	83,452	101,377	113,421

1/ Until December 1968 some of these categories appeared separately as "other customers".

2/ Up to December 31, 1968 this is the sum of two categories "Fishing" and "Shrimp and other fishing".

3/ Probably included in "Other manufacturing" up to December 31, 1968.

4/ Includes "Handicraft and repairshops", up to December 31, 1968.

5/ Up to December 31, 1968 this was for "Distributive trades: (i) oil companies including exploration (ii) others".

6/ Up to December 31, 1968 this was "For purchase of land and real estate".

7/ From December 31, 1969, this item is included in "for other purposes".

8/ Up to December 31, 1968 includes "Non-profit making institutions". From December 31, 1971, includes real estate mortgage loans.

a/ Excluding credit to non-residents.

Source: Bank of Guyana: Consolidated Monthly Statements for Commercial Banks.
Economic Bulletin, No. 9, October 1975.

Table SA6.15. Guyana: Distribution of Commercial Bank Assets, 1965–74

(In thousands of Guyanan dollars at end of year)

	1965	1966	1967	1968	1969	1970	1971	1972	1973	1974
1. Net Foreign Assets /1	12,400	6,100	11,200	-100	-3,700	-5,600	-5,700	-6,000	5,000	-388
2. Net Claims on Bank of Guyana	9,972	11,529	10,639	12,155	15,381	11,209	13,374	22,893	17,029	18,234
3. Net Credit to Central and Local Government	3,065	5,600	11,955	22,315	20,105	21,433	38,213	59,795	66,686	65,784
4. Net Credit to Public Financial Institutions	-404	-51	-70	-569	-836	-1,477	-2,545	-2,975	-5,403	-5,485
5. Net Credit to Statutory Boards and Other Public Institutions	10,461	11,037	6,706	6,487	9,293	11,335	10,894	9,617	9,618	42,567
6. Credit to the Private Sector	30,213	41,092	44,187	56,803	67,581	80,189	83,819	83,486	101,467	113,633
a. Agriculture and Fishing	2,458	2,391	3,901	3,918	5,090	6,392	7,183	8,490	9,540	9,359
(i) Rice Paddy	(1,821)	(1,629)	(3,702)	(1,873)	(2,734)	(2,908)	(3,347)	(3,257)	(3,388)	(3,892)
(ii) Other	(637)	(762)	(829)	(2,045)	(2,356)	(3,484)	(3,836)	(5,233)	(6,152)	(5,467)
b. Mining	278	656	659	510	1,158	790	5,127	593	703	12,088
c. Manufacturing	10,499	14,841	12,069	12,587	14,760	20,232	20,207	19,421	25,508	24,540
(i) Sugar and Molasses	(4,454)	(7,013)	(6,494)	(2,690)	(721)	(4,524)	(2,844)	(670)	(753)	(119)
(ii) Food, Drink and Tobacco	(722)	(970)	(432)	(3,061)	(6,977)	(6,626)	(7,703)	(7,952)	(10,647)	(8,402)
(iii) Timber and Sawmilling	(557)	(974)	(1,402)	(2,094)	(1,308)	(2,109)	(2,526)	(3,023)	(3,272)	(3,842)
(iv) Rice Milling	(3,631)	(4,338)	(2,381)	(1,334)	(1,419)	(1,400)	(1,421)	(1,375)	(1,617)	(1,363)
(v) Other Manufacturing /2	(1,135)	(1,546)	(1,360)	(3,408)	(4,335)	(5,573)	(5,713)	(6,401)	(9,219)	(10,814)
d. Construction and Land Development	1,056	1,963	1,561	3,574	5,135	5,537	8,496	9,124	8,413	7,858
e. Other Financial Institutions	1,252	2,140	2,685	3,362	2,606	3,047	2,276	1,393	1,842	1,033
f. Distribution	9,481	11,422	13,028	19,968	19,797	24,263	19,155	21,207	24,609	25,813
g. Professional and Other Services	1,030	1,708	2,750	2,874	6,051	6,880	7,273	6,731	7,133	9,357
h. Personal /3	4,044	5,878	7,494	9,675	12,798	12,842	14,071	16,493	23,629	23,373
i. Other (Credit to non-residents)	115	93	40	335	186	206	31	34	90	212
7. Unclassified Net Credit	7,219	6,533	7,826	5,627	7,870	7,046	8,042	9,883	5,531	2,993
Total Assets = Liabilities to the Private Sector	72,926	81,840	92,443	102,718	115,694	124,135	146,097	176,699	199,928	231,352

/1 Correct to the nearest $100,000 only.

/2 Includes "Handicraft and repair shops" up to December 31, 1968.

/3 Includes housing, and real estate mortgage loans from December 31, 1971 onwards.

Source: Statistical Annex Tables 6.11 and 6.14.

Table SA6.16. Leeward and Windward Islands: Selected Monetary Statistics, 1966–74

(In thousands of Eastern Caribbean dollars at end of year)

	1966	1967	1968	1969	1970	1971	1972	1973	1974
1. Commercial Bank Deposits	73161	78780	129986	165180	188836	224971	264181	293505	350004
Demand	15209	15374	26008	36382	31954	32419	37457	44294	57882
Time and Saving	57952	63406	103978	128798	156882	192552	226724	249211	292182
2. Net Bank Balances due from abroad	4625	3926	6601	34292	22406	15289	-8228	-14091	+14485
Balances due from abroad (+)	26334	27351	44048	67923	58456	57704	32901	41711	70194
Balances due to abroad (-)	-21709	-23425	-37447	-33631	-36050	-42415	-41129	-55802	-55709
3. Net Bank Balances abroad as Percent of Deposits	6.3	5.0	5.1	20.8	11.9	6.8	-3.1	-4.8	+4.1
4. Money Supply	30070	32977	46454	60469	61200	65468	74036	78550	94748
Demand Deposits	15209	15374	26008	36382	31954	32419	37457	44294	57882
Notes and Coins held by Public	14861	17603	20446	24087	29246	33049	36579	34256	36866

Source: East Caribbean Currency Authority: annual reports.

Table SA6.17. Jamaica: Local Assets of Life Insurance Companies, 1966–74

(In millions of Jamaican dollars at end of period)

	1966	1967	1968	1969	1970	1971	1972	1973	1974
1. Loans	9.5	12.1	10.4	14.6	16.5	17.3	22.6	23.9	24.2
2. Government Securities	11.9	17.0	15.0	22.2	22.7	21.2	26.8	27.6	30.7
(a) Treasury Bills	0.1	0.5	-	0.5	-	0.5	0.5	0.6	0.7
(b) Other	11.8	16.5	15.0	21.7	22.7	20.7	26.3	27.0	30.0
3. Mortgages	15.7	20.4	20.8	26.4	30.6	40.2	48.4	54.2	55.3
4. Other Financial Assets	9.9	11.6	14.4	19.9	23.0	19.9	29.2	33.8	37.5
(a) Non-Government Local Securities	8.8	9.8	10.3	15.9	18.1	16.2	22.4	23.7	27.1
(b) Cash	1.1	1.8	4.1	4.0	4.9	3.7	6.8	10.1	10.4
5. Other Assets	4.9	4.7	5.3	6.2	8.1	13.6	18.4	17.7	20.3
6. Total	51.9	65.8	65.9	89.3	100.9	112.2	145.4	157.2	168.0
Number of companies reporting	16	17	17	18	18	22	n.a.	n.a.	n.a.

Source: 1966-71: Table 30, *Monetary Statistics 1971*, Department of Statistics, Jamaica.
1972-74: Table 13, *Monetary Statistics 1974*, Department of Statistics, Jamaica.

Table SA6.18. Trinidad and Tobago: Local Assets of Life Insurance Companies, 1965–72

(In thousands of TT dollars at end of period)

	1965	1966	1967	1968	1969	1970	1971	1972
1. Policy Loans	14,568	16,832	20,714	22,099	22,438	25,202	26,369	24,414
2. Government Securities	13,559	15,056	24,372	34,068	43,594	49,232	55,617	62,811
(a) Treasury Bills	2,682	2,558	2,416	1,981	2,052	2,233	2,200	681
(b) Other	10,877	12,498	21,956	32,087	41,542	46,999	53,417	62,130
3. Mortgages	30,449	33,780	39,456	43,767	47,821	54,395	56,731	59,969
(a) Loans on Residential Property	29,586	33,213	39,044	43,359	47,250	53,149	55,383	57,620
(b) Loans on Business Property	863	567	412	408	571	1,246	1,348	2,349
4. Other Financial Assets	5,954	5,405	6,599	7,756	12,132	19,433	22,826	18,373
(a) Deposits in Local Banks	3,632	3,102	3,547	4,205	7,739	15,242	17,952	14,130
(b) Shares in Local Business	2,322	2,303	3,052	3,551	4,393	4,191	4,874	4,243
5. Other Assets	6,592	7,182	12,891	8,192	9,063	12,121	17,886	16,092
(a) Fixed Assets	920	1,042	1,062	1,076	1,114	1,207	1,386	502
(b) Real Estate	5,012	5,135	5,856	5,298	5,215	6,018	7,005	7,614
(c) Other	660	1,005	5,973	1,818	2,734	4,896	9,495	7,976
6. Total	71,122	78,252	104,030	115,881	135,037	160,382	179,427	181,658

Source: Financial Statistics, 1972, Trinidad and Tobago Central Statistical Office.

Table SA6.19. Selected Interest Rates, 1967–74
(Percentage per annum at end of period)

	JAMAICA							
	1967	1968	1969	1970	1971	1972	1973	1974
Commercial Banks								
Deposits								
Time (3-6 months)	4.5	3.5	4.0	4.5	3.5-5.0	4.0-8.5	5.0-8.5	8.0-12.5
Time (6-12 months)	4.75-5.0	4.0-4.5	4.5-5.0	6.0-8.0	4.5-7.0	4.5-9.0	7.5-9.0	9.5-12.0
Savings	4.0	3.0	3.5	3.5	3.0	3.5	4.0	6.0
Weighted Average								
Lending								
Prime	8.0	7.0	8.0	8.0	7.0	8.0	9.0	11.0
Weighted Average								
Bank Rate	6.0	5.00	6.00	6.00	5.00	6.0	7.0	9.0
Securities Markets								
Treasury Bills (90 days)	5.35	3.48	3.82	4.38	3.52	4.97	7.18	7.20
Long-Term Government Bonds (yields)	7.25	7.25	7.45	8.55	8.20	8.50		
Government Savings Bank Deposit	2.5	2.5	2.5	2.5	3.0	3.0		

	TRINIDAD AND TOBAGO							
	1967	1968	1969	1970	1971	1972	1973	1974
Commercial Banks								
Deposits								
Time (3-6 months)	4.50	4.25-4.75	4.75-6.00	4.50-8.00	4.00-6.00	3.00-5.00		
Time (6-12 months)	3.50	3.50-4.00	4.00-5.50	3.75-6.00	3.25-6.00	2.50-5.00		
Savings		4.40	4.58	5.04	4.90	3.62		
Weighted Average								
Lending								
Prime	7.75	7.25-7.75	8.00	7.50-8.00	7.00-7.50	6.25-7.50		
Weighted Average		8.25	8.15	8.64	8.59	8.26		
Bank Rate	6.00	6.00	6.00	6.00	5.00	5.00	6.00	6.00
Securities Markets								
Treasury Bills (90 days)	6.10	5.12	5.21	5.32	4.87	3.31	5.79	4.92
Long-Term Government Bonds (yields)	8.00	7.95	7.29	8.33	8.26	7.49		
Government Savings Bank Deposit								

	GUYANA							
	1967	1968	1969	1970	1971	1972	1973	1974
Commercial Banks								
Deposits								
Time (3-6 months)	4.00-4.50	4.00-4.50	4.75-5.50	4.75-5.50	4.75-5.50	4.00-4.50	4.00-4.50	4.00-4.50
Time (6-12 months)	4.50-5.00	4.50-5.00	5.50-6.50	5.50-6.50	5.50-6.50	4.50-5.50	4.50-5.50	4.50-5.50
Savings	3.50	3.50	3.50	3.50	3.50	3.50	3.50	3.50
Weighted Average								
Lending								
Prime	7.50	7.50	7.50	7.50	7.50	7.50	7.50	7.50
Weighted Average				8.41	8.67	8.81	8.83	8.80
Bank Rate	6.50	6.50	6.50	6.50	6.50	6.50	6.50	6.50
Securities Markets								
Treasury Bills (90 days)	6.34	6.01	6.12	6.09	5.88	5.88	5.88	5.88
Long-Term Government Bonds (yields)	7.00	7.00	7.00	7.00	7.00	7.00	7.00	7.00
Government Savings Bank Deposit	3.00	3.50	3.50	3.50	3.50	3.50	3.50	3.50

Comparative International Rates

	1967	1968	1969	1970	1971	1972	1973	1974	1975
Bank Rate									
United Kingdom	8.00	7.00	8.00	7.00	5.00	9.00	13.00	11.50	11.25
United States	4.50	5.50	6.00	5.50	4.50	4.50	7.50	7.75	6.00
Canada	6.00	6.50	8.00	6.00	4.75	4.75	7.25	8.75	9.00
Treasury Bills (90 days)									
United Kingdom	7.48	6.78	7.65	6.82	4.41	8.31	12.14	10.99	
United States	4.99	6.20	8.10	4.83	3.73	5.11	7.35	7.11	
Canada	5.95	6.24	7.81	4.44	3.21	3.65		7.12	8.64

Sources: Bank of Jamaica, Statistical Digest, November 1973; Central Bank of Trinidad & Tobago, Statistical Digest, May 1973; Bank of Guyana, Annual Report, 1971.

Table SA7.1. Total and Agricultural GDP at Factor Cost, 1965–73

(In millions of Eastern Caribbean dollars)

		1965	1966	1967	1968	1969	1970	1971	1972	1973
Barbados	Total	160.4	172.0	194.2	223.7	247.5	289.9	321.5	357.0	425.9
	Agricultural	42.0	43.4	47.8	41.7	37.3	40.3	38.0	44.2	46.1
Guyana	Total	325.1	342.1	374.9	405.2	437.9	467.4	500.4	483.4	530.5
	Agricultural	78.2	74.2	80.1	79.8	89.4	90.1	101.1	95.7	97.6
Jamaica	Total	1426.3	1637.0	1735.4	1883.0	2085.6	2339.5	2624.3	3034.9	3152.7
	Agricultural	165.8	180.3	186.9	186.0	184.9	189.2	242.2	264.6	275.4
Trinidad	Total	1176.0	1183.1	1282.4	1491.6	1528.2	1600.5	1773.8	1944.4	2233.3
	Agricultural	105.5	60.5	62.0	73.9	75.7	83.1	82.1	90.6	103.3
MDCs	Total	3087.8	3334.2	3568.9	4003.5	4299.2	4697.3	5220.0	5819.7	6342.4
	Agricultural	391.5	358.4	376.8	381.4	387.3	402.7	463.4	495.1	522.4
ECCM	Total	207.1	231.6	234.3	253.3	277.6	292.7	324.1	364.1	394.2
	Agricultural	74.1	n.a.	n.a.	68.1	71.9	57.7	69.5	64.3	73.3
Belize	Total	n.a.	n.a.	n.a.	105.5	110.7	126.6	n.a.	n.a.	n.a.
	Agricultural	n.a.	n.a.	n.a.	18.2	18.3	19.2	n.a.	n.a.	n.a.
LDCs	Total	207.1	231.6	234.3	358.8	388.3	419.3	324.1	364.1	394.2
	Agricultural	74.1	n.a.	n.a.	86.3	90.2	76.9	69.5	64.3	73.3
REGION	Total	3294.9	3334.2 1/	3568.9 1/	4362.3	4687.5	5116.6	5544.1	6183.8	6736.6
	Agricultural	465.6	358.4 1/	376.8 1/	467.7	477.5	479.6	532.9	559.4	595.7

1/ MDCs only.

Table SA7.2. Total Population and Labor Force and Employment in Agriculture, 1970

	Total	Labor Force	Employed	Emp. in Agric.
Belize	120,000	33,000	31,000	10,900
Guyana	714,000	184,000	155,000	49,600
Jamaica	1,960,000	587,000	478,000	181,600
TT	1,030,000	288,000	222,000	51,100
B'os	240,000	91,000	82,000	13,100
ECCM	475,000	141,000	127,000	50,800
	4,539,000	1,324,000	1,095,000	357,100

Sources: Mission estimates

Belize: estimated

Guyana: ratio of employment in sugar with respect to total (IBRD)

Jamaica: Green paper, p.7

Trinidad: IBRD report

B'os: Statistical annex, IBRD mission

ECCM: Extrapolated from figures for St. Lucia

Note: These figures do not necessarily tally with those of previous Bank reports since new information has been made available (see Moran's estimates). The ratios of agricultural employment to total employment have been taken from Bank reports, whenever available (see table).

Table SA7.3. Agricultural GDP, Exports, and Imports, 1966–74

		1966	1967	1968	1969	1970	1971	1972	1973	1974
Agricultural GDP	M EC$	358 1/	377 1/	468	478	480	533	559	596	n.a.
Agricultural Exports 2/	M EC$	407	415	472	475	461	475	521	527	911
Agricultural Imports 2/	M EC$	361	356	402	439	498	552	624	722	956
Exports Volume										
Sugar	M L.T.	1.10	1.08	1.13	1.05	.97	1.02	.95	.84	.94
Bananas	000 L.T.	342	338	319	305	253	249	246	200	169

1/ MDCs only

2/ Sections 0, 1 and 4 of SITC

Table SA7.4. Production of Main Agricultural Commodities, 1966–72

	Unit	1966	1967	1968	1969	1970	1971	1972	Average Annual Rate of change over relevant period (percent)
Sugar	million L.T.	1.23	1.30	1.27	1.19	1.14	1.20	1.13	- 1.4
Bananas 1/	000 L.T.	378.8	358.8	336.7	349.8	275.6	252.2	247.2	- 7.4
Cocoa	million lbs.	29.4	26.3	31.4	25.4	32.2	24.8	30.8	.8
Coffee	million lbs.	13.0	14.1	17.3	12.0	11.3	14.7	11.0	- 2.8
Citrus 2/	million lbs.	585.7	517.8	513.6	478.6	464.5	512.5	545.6	- 1.2
Rice	000 L.T.	146.0 3/	186.1	151.0	123.9	132.5	146.3	106.2	-12
Corn	million lbs.	n.a.	n.a.	n.a.	30.9	53.6	55.1	59.4	25
Meats	million lbs.	n.a.	n.a.	131.4	140.2	156.4	163.8	155.7	4.5
Beef 4/	million lbs.	n.a.	n.a.	41.2	43.6	40.2	40.4	36.4	- 3
Poultry 4/	million lbs.	n.a.	n.a.	56.2	60.0	80.8	94.5	87.9	11.3
Milk 4/	million lbs.	n.a.	n.a.	140.4	144.5	159.9	150.4	157.8	3
Vegetables - Root Crops Pulses 4/	million lbs.	n.a.	n.a.	575	604	724	926	969	14

1/ Exports only
2/ Fresh, limes not included
3/ Guyana only
4/ MDC's only

Table SA7.5. Volume of Main Agricultural Exports, 1965–74

	Unit	1965	1966	1967	1968	1969	1970	1971	1972	1973	1974	1965-74 Average
Sugar	million L.T.	1.19	1.10	1.08	1.13	1.05	0.97	1.02	0.95	0.84	0.94	1.03
Bananas	000 L.T.	357.7	342.4	338.4	318.8	304.6	253.3	248.6	246.2	200.4	168.7	277.9
Rice	000 L.T.	93.6	108.1	100.0	94.2	73.3	60.2	72.2	69.0	47.9	39.4	75.8
Citrus	million lbs.	n.a.	142.2	135.1	116.8	116.4	102.5	110.3	99.3	61.7	81.3	107.3 1/
Cocoa	million lbs.	22.5	19.5	17.2	21.0	21.4	23.2	17.1	22.0	16.1	16.7	19.7
Coffee	million lbs.	9.5	7.0	7.4	11.4	7.3	6.5	9.6	6.8	7.0	4.4	7.7

1/ 1966-74 average.

Source: Official Trade Statistics

FAO Trade Yearbook, 1974

Table SA7.6. Exports of Agricultural and Food Products, 1965–72[1]

(In millions of Eastern Caribbean dollars)

	1965	1966	1967	1968	1969	1970	1971	1972
	in million EC dollars							
Barbados	44.1	46.0	50.0	52.4	43.7	44.5	41.7	40.2
Guyana	92.9	97.0	107.3	116.4	119.8	117.2	137.8	142.3
Jamaica	146.2	154.4	149.6	159.8	151.8	150.8	156.6	172.2
Trinidad	61.8	58.4	60.9	78.3	80.9	82.9	87.6	87.5
MDC's	345.0	355.8	367.8	406.9	396.2	395.4	423.7	442.2
ECCM	44.6	42.1	41.6	43.8	56.8	40.7	37.6 2/	35.0 2/
Belize	14.1	17.2	17.6	21.8	22.2	24.6	27.2	29.4
Total	403.7	415.1	427.0	472.5	475.2	460.7	488.5	506.6

1/ Sections 0, 1 and 4 of SITC

2/ Estimated

Source: Official Trade Statistics

Table SA7.7. Imports of Agricultural and Food Products, 1965–72[1]
(In millions of Eastern Caribbean dollars)

	1965	1966	1967	1968	1969	1970	1971	1972
	in millions of EC dollars							
Barbados	34.8	37.2	36.0	43.5	48.4	57.5	62.0	72.9
Guyana	35.2	37.3	37.3	39.7	42.6	42.4	47.9	43.2
Jamaica	109.4	119.7	128.9	155.2	154.4	185.3	209.2	246.8
Trinidad	98.0	100.2	97.0	96.5	117.1	120.5	144.4	138.1
MDC's	277.4	294.4	299.2	334.9	362.5	405.7	463.5	501.0
ECCM 2/	39.0	44.2	44.2	48.0	58.3	66.2	72.8	80.0
Belize 3/	11.2	12.5	12.9	16.3	17.1	22.3	25.5	28.1
Total	327.6	351.1	356.3	399.2	437.9	494.2	561.8	609.1

1/ Sections 0,1 and 4 of SITC.
2/ 1972 estimated from 10% rate of increase over 1971. Values for Antigua.
3/ 1972 estimated with 15% increase over 1971.

Source: Official Trade Statistics

Table SA7.8. Exports of Agricultural Products, Selected Years

(In millions of Eastern Caribbean dollars)

	1965		1968		1971		1972	
	Value	o/o	Value	o/o	Value	o/o	Value	o/o
Sugar	230.5	57.1	267.4	56.6	276.4	56.6	308.1	60.8
Bananas	51.5	12.8	60.0	12.7	47.2	9.7	43.2	8.5
Rice	32.1	5.7	27.6	5.9	21.0	4.3	24.8	4.9
Citrus	28.6	7.1	26.0	5.5	22.8	4.7	21.4	4.2
Cocoa	8.6	2.1	13.4	2.8	10.1	2.0	12.2	2.4
Subtotal	342.3	84.8	394.4	83.5	377.5	77.3	409.7	80.8
Others	61.4	15.2	78.1	16.5	111.0	22.7	96.9	19.2
Total	403.7	100.0	472.5	100.0	488.5	100.0	506.6	100.0

Source: Official Trade Statistics.

Table SA7.9. Food Imports

(In millions of Eastern Caribbean dollars)

	1965		1972	
	Value	o/o	Value	o/o
Meat	47.4	14.5	82.6	13.6
Dairy Products	54.0	16.5	85.2	14.0
Cereals	91.0	27.8	158.6	26.0
Fish	25.7	7.8	36.3	6.0
Animal Feed	16.1	4.9	30.5	5.0
Subtotal	234.2	71.5	393.2	64.6
Fruit and Vegetables	28.9	8.8	56.8	9.3
Oils and Fats	12.8	3.9	24.9	4.1
Others	51.7	15.8	134.2	22.0
Total	327.6	100.0	609.1	100.0

Source: Mission Estimates from Trade Statistics.

Table SA7.10. Data of Employment, Selected Years and Countries

Jamaica (in '000s)	1953	April 1960	April 1969	October 1969	April 1972	October [illegible]
Total population	1420	1610	1850 1/			19[illegible] 2/
Labor force	639	655				712
Total employed	531	570	610	624	609	627
Employed in Agriculture	250	234	238	236	209	211
% of total employed	47.1	41.1	39.0	37.8	34.3	33.7

Guyana	1960	1965	1970
Total population	560,300	647,000	714,000
Labor force	175,000	193,000	210,000
Total employed	161,200	165,900	178,000
Employed in Agriculture	59,790	57,975	57,400
% of total employed	37.1	34.9	32.2

Trinidad (in '000s)	1960	1965	1970	1971
Total population	834.4	973.9	1026.7	1030.0
Labor force	323.4 2/	347.8	363.5	366.8
Total employed	n.a.	n.a.	n.a.	n.a.
Employed in Agriculture	65.5 3/	75.9	82.4	75.1
% of labor force	20.3	21.8	22.7	20.5

1/ 1970 Census

2/ 1973 Figure

3/ 1963 Figure

Source: IBRD reports

Table SA7.11. Comparative Weekly Wages in Agriculture and in the General Economy, 1973

(In Eastern Caribbean dollars)

	Agricultural Worker	General Worker
	----------in EC$--------	
Barbados	27/36	42/48
Guyana	30	32
Jamaica	29/42	25/83
Trinidad & Tobago	15/25	24/45
Antigua	36	40
Dominica	15/20	24/30
Grenada	15/25	15/25
Montserrat	n.a.	35
St. Kitts	40	20/25
St. Lucia	21	16/20
St. Vincent	15/20	15/20
Belize	23	20/28

Source: Mission estimates.

Table SA7.12. Distribution of Land Holdings

MDC's	Number (Including Guyana) '000s	Percent	Acres Less Guyana '000s	Percent
Less than 5 acres	208.8	73.7	- 274.7	13.1
5 to less than 25 acres	65.8	23.2	505.6	24.1
25 to less than 100 acres	6.6	2.3	209.2	10.1
More than 100 acres	2.2	.8	1104.9	52.8
Total	283.4	100.0	2094.4	100.0

ECCM	Number '000s	Percent	Acres '000s	Percent
Landless	4.5	7.4	-	-
Less than 25 acres	55.4	90.8	147.0	42.9
25 to less than 50 acres	.5	.8	18.2	5.3
More than 50 acres	.6	1.0	177.3	51.8
Total	61.0	100.0	342.5	100.0

Belize 1/	Number '000s	Percent	Acres '000s	Percent
Less than 20 acres	5.2	77.6	56.3	2.4
20 to less than 100 acres	1.1	16.4	96.0	4.1
More than 100 acres	.4	6.0	2191.0	93.5
Total	6.7	100.0	2343.3	100.0

1/ Freeholds only

Sources: MDC's: Tables

ECCM: Statistical Annex of ECCM study paper

Belize: Ministry of Agriculture

Table SA7.13. MDCs: Production of Root Crops and Vegetables, 1968–72
(In millions of pounds)

	1968	1969	1970	1971	1972
	----------------	in million lbs	----------------		
Root Crops					
Barbados 1/	58	60	62	63	65
Guyana	91	102	108	113	112
Jamaica	228	238	304	429	452
Trinidad	37	42	43	45	46
MDC's	414	442	517	650	675
Vegetables 2/					
Barbados 3/	12	13	13	14	15
Guyana	4	4	5	7	8
Jamaica	106	105	149	208	218
Trinidad	39	40	40	47	53
MDC's	161	162	207	276	294
Total	575	604	724	926	969

1/ Estimated with 3 o/o annual increase between 1968 and 1972.

2/ Includes pulses.

3/ Estimated with 6 o/o annual increase between 1968 and 1972.

Source: Economic Surveys
Statistical Digests
Mission Estimates

Table SA7.14. MDCs: Imports and Production of Selected Vegetables, 1972

(In millions of pounds)

	Potatoes	Onions	Carrots	Peas-Beans	Tomatoes	Pumpkins	Cabbage
	------------------------------------in million lbs.------------------------------------						
Imports							
Barbados	12.4	2.8	.2	3.4	.2	n.a.	.4
Guyana	18.7	4.9	-	7.9	-	.2	-
Jamaica	6.3	10.7	.2	4.0	-	n.a.	1.3
Trinidad	33.0	8.1	2.0	27.0	-	.1	.8
Total	70.4	26.5	2.4	42.3	.2	n.a.	2.1
Production							
Barbados	-	2.5	1.4	.3	.8	.6	.6
Guyana	-	-	.1	.5	5.6	n.a.	1.7
Jamaica	29.7	.4	20.0	12.0	18.0	40.0	21.0
Trinidad	-	-	-	7.5	14.0	1.2	8.1
Total	29.7	2.9	21.5	20.3	38.4	n.a.	31.4

Table SA7.15. Vegetable Exports, 1968–74
(In thousands of Eastern Caribbean dollars)

	1968	1969	1970	1971	1972	1973	1974
Antigua	n.a.	1.7	n.a.	n.a.	n.a.	7.8	n.a.
Dominica	75.4	44.1	42.2	94.0	200.0	214.5	276.0
Grenada	-	3.0	2.2	1.9	2.0	31.3	n.a.
Montserrat	13.5	28.0	26.1	37.2	40.3	47.2	75.0
St. Kitts	n.a.	9.8	42.0	86.6	10.7	n.a.	n.a.
St. Lucia	6.5	5.7	4.0	8.1	42.0	80.0	278.5
St. Vincent	360.9	476.0	385.0	450.0	572.0	n.a.	n.a.

Source: Statistical Offices
St. Vincent Marketing Board

Table SA7.16. Copra Production, 1965–71

(In long tons)

	1965	1966	1967	1968	1969	1970	1971
Dominica	187	384	1552	1731	1670	1740	1712
Grenada	452	548	463	420	438	575	732
Guyana	4636	5777	4832	7013	7436	5074	6522
Jamaica	17197	16633	18210	16496	15372	15438	18440
St. Kitts	116	n.a.	n.a.	70	102 /1	102 /1	104
St. Lucia	5019	5343	5963	6053	6122	6471	5240
St. Vincent	2436	2306	2425	2519	2165	2931	2570
Trinidad	12053	12158	12370	13469	14098	10755	12253
Total	42096	43149	45873	47821	47403	43086	47523

1/ Exports of copra.

Source: CARIFTA Secretariat.

Table SA7.17. Import Trade of Oils and Fats,[1] 1965–70

(In millions of Eastern Caribbean dollars)

	Intra-regional Imports						Extra-regional Imports					
	1965	1966	1967	1968	1969	1970	1965	1966	1967	1968	1969	1970
Copra	1.2	0.2	2.5	1.7	1.4	0.9	-	-	-	-	-	-
Other oilseed and nuts	-	-	0.2	-	-	-	-	-	0.6	0.4	1.6	-
Unrefined coconut oil	0.6	0.7	0.9	0.3	0.8	1.2	0.3	-	-	-	-	-
Refined coconut oil	0.5	0.2	0.4	0.7	2.2	2.4	-	-	-	-	-	-
Refined soybean oil	-	-	-	-	-	-	2.1	1.3	0.9	1.3	0.6	1.4
Other vegetable oil	-	-	-	-	-	-	2.0	1.4	1.4	2.0	1.4	1.6
Hydrogenated oils and fats	-	-	-	-	-	-	2.8	2.1	1.5	1.8	2.2	3.1
Margarine	1.0	0.9	1.1	1.1	1.4	1.4	0.4	0.5	0.5	0.6	0.5	0.5
Lard	0.1	-	0.1	0.1	0.1	-	1.2	1.3	1.1	1.2	1.7	1.9
Lard substitutes and other shortenings	0.2	0.2	0.2	0.1	0.2	0.4	0.2	0.1	-	-	0.1	0.3
Others	0.9	0.1	-	0.1	-	0.1	0.3	1.2	1.7	2.5	2.0	1.5
Total	4.5	2.3	5.4	4.1	6.1	6.4	9.3	7.9	7.7	9.8	9.9	10.3

\- nil or negligible.

1/ Excluding soaps and oilseed cakes and meals.

2/ Includes: unrefined soybean oil, and other vegetable oil imported for the manufacture of hydrogenated oils.

Source: Adapted from statistical information of CARIFTA Secretariat.

Table SA7.18. Regional Production, Consumption, and Deficits of Oils and Fats in Copra Equivalent, 1965–71

(In thousands of long tons)

Year	Production of Copra	Consumption of Oils and Fats (Copra Equivalent)		Regional Deficit (Copra Equivalent)	
		Exclud. Oil for Hydrogenation	Includ. Oil for Hydrogenation	Exclud. Oil for Hydrogenation	Includ. Oil for Hydrogenation
1965	42.1	53.6	58.8	11.5	16.7
1966	43.1	47.9	54.3	4.8	11.2
1967	45.9	49.7	56.6	3.8	10.7
1968	47.8	54.6	63.2	6,8	15.4
1969	47.4	60.0	67.5	12.6	20.1
1970	43.1	68.5	76.4	25.4	33.3
1971	47.5	63.4	80.5	15.9	33.0
Annual Growth Rate 1965-71	2.0	2.8	5.4	5.6	12.0

Source: CARIFTA Secretariat.

Table SA7.19. Regional and World Prices, Copra and Coconut Oil, 1965–73

(Eastern Caribbean dollars per long ton)

	Regional Price		World Price			
	Copra	Raw Coconut Oil	Copra	Raw Coconut Oil	Refined	Refined Soybean Oil
1965	340	575	391	542	606	466
1966	360	609	320	433	564	452
1967	360	609	349	506	578	439
1968	390	660	472	705	811	362
1969	410	689	410	524	734	402
1970	410	689	460	685	807	587
1971	430	723	381	570	743	624
1972	430	723	264	384	456	483
1973	430	772	275	-	627	-

Source: CARIFTA Secretariat

Table SA7.20. MDCs: Imports of Major Agricultural Commodities, 1972

	Unmilled corn	Unmilled wheat	Flour	Milk[1/]	Butter	Meats	Beef
	million lbs.						
Barbados	9	-	28	47.2	1.6	15.9	5.0
Guyana	10	88	6	41.6	1.0	1.8	1.2
Jamaica	246	162	175	110.0	8.5	54.4	18.3
Trinidad	137	111	43	102.2	4.5	19.0	6.8
MDC's	402	361	252	314.0	15.6	91.1	31.3

	Eggs million	White Potatoes	Onions	Peas Beans	Animal Feeds	Fertilizer 000 L.T.
		million lbs.				
Barbados	2.7	12.4	2.8	3.4	80.1	15.4
Guyana	5.7	18.7	4.9	7.9	12.0	47.5
Jamaica	16.7	6.3	10.7	4.0	54.7	62.1
Trinidad	11.3	33.0	8.1	27.0	73.6	6.8
MDC's	36.4	70.4	26.5	42.3	220.4	131.[illegible]

1/ Fresh equivalent (Dry to fresh ratio assumed to be 1:4)

Table SA7 21. MDCs: Production of Major Commodities Imported, 1972

	Corn	Milk	Meats	Beef	Poultry	Eggs
	million lbs.					million
Barbados	5.0	16.2	7.0	.5	3.2	17.5
Guyana	6.2	38.3	23.9	9.6	10.8	49.5
Jamaica	16.0	84.0	66.7	21.8	34.3	139.2
Trinidad	-	19.3	49.4	4.5	39.6	63.5
MDC's	27.2	157.8	147.0	36.4	87.9	269.7

	White Potatoes	Onions	Animal Feed	Peas and Beans
	million lbs.			
Barbados	-	2.5	45.0 1/	.3
Guyana	-	-	n.a.	.5
Jamaica	29.7	.4	354.2	12.0
Trinidad	-	-	19.5 2/	7.5
MDC's	29.7	2.9	n.a.	20.3

1/ Estimated

2/ Exports only

Table SA7.22. Rice: Production, Imports, and Total Supply, 1971

	Production	Imports (Exports)	Consumption
	------ 000' long tons ------		
Barbados	- -	8.2	8.2
Guyana	120.0	(66.7)	53.3
Jamaica	0.3	36.9	37.2
Trinidad	8.5	33.4	41.9
Belize	3.3	- -	3.3
ECCM	- -	12.1	12.1
Total	132.1	90.6	156.0

Table SA7.23. Rice: Regional Situation, 1971
(In long tons)

Production	132,100
Intra Regional Imports	61,500
Extra Regional Imports	29,100
Total Imports	90,600
Extra Regional Exports	5,200
Regional Consumption	156,000

Source: Mission Estimates
IBRD Reports
Trade Statistics

Table SA7.24. Rice: Guyana Exports

	1968	1969	1970	1971	1972
Volume (thousand long tons)					
to Carifta	61.0	53.9	57.4	61.5	65.7
to others	30.9	7.6	1.2	5.2	3.1
Total exports	91.9	61.5	58.6	66.7	68.8
Unit Export Price (EC$/Metric Ton)					
to Carifta	291	306	303	317	364
to others	303	312	325	292	300
Weighted average	295	307	309	315	361
World Price	403	374	288	258	282
Production (000 L.T.)	142.4	113.8	122.1	134.2	94.0
Value of Exports (million EC$)	27.6	19.2	18.4	21.0	24.8

Table SA7.25. Rice Utilization, Guyana
(Percentage)

Local Consumption	35.0
Retained by producers	(25.0)
Local sales	(10.0)
Animal feed and seeds	15.0
Exports	50.0
Total Production	100.0

Table SA7.26. Rice Production, Excluding Guyana

	1967	1968	1969	1970	1971	1972
	in million lbs					
Belize	2.3	4.1	5.0	5.0	7.4	6.3
Jamaica	2.9	1.4	1.3	0.7	0.6	0.6
Trinidad	10.4	13.7	16.3	17.6	19.0 1/	20.5 1/
Total	15.6	19.2	22.6	23.3	27.0	27.4

1/ Assuming 8 o/o annual increase from 1970 level.

Source: Ministries of Agriculture

IBRD Report on Trinidad

Table SA7.27. Rice Imports, MDCs, 1972

	Quantities		Value (Cif)		Cif Unit Price
	Total	From Guyana	Total	From Guyana	From Guyana
	--- million lbs ---		---- EC$ million---		EC ¢/Pb
Barbados	14.2	14.2	2.2	2.2	15.5
Jamaica	81.5	49.3	21.8	13.1	26.5
Trinidad	66.2	66.2	9.0	9.0	13.6
Total	161.9	129.7	33.0	24.3	18.7
in 000 L.T.	72.3	57.9			

Source: Trade Statistics.

Table SA7.28. Corn Production, 1967–72

	1967	1969	1970	1971	1972
	in million lbs				
Barbados	--	3.9	4.8	3.4	5.0
Guyana	n.a.	3.5	4.1	5.3	6.2
Jamaica	8.0	8.5	9.7	11.4	16.0
Trinidad	--	--	--	--	--
Belize	14.8	15.0	35.0	35.0	32.2
ECCM	--	--	--	--	--
Total	n.a.	30.9	53.6	55.1	59.4

Source: Economic Surveys - Statistical Digests

Table SA7.29. Grain Imports in MDCs, 1972

	Unmilled Corn	Unmilled Wheat	Flour	Others	Total
	------------------- in million lbs -------------------				
Barbados	9	--	28	4	41
Guyana	10	88	6	2	106
Jamaica	246	162	175	18	601
Trinidad	137	111	43	9	300
MDC's	402	361	252	33	1,048

Source: Trade Statistics.

Table SA7.30. Meat Production, 1968–72

	1968	1969	1970	1971	1972
	million lbs				
Barbados	3.6	4.9	6.0	6.9	7.0
Guyana	17.0	18.0	19.1	21.6	23.9
Jamaica	67.3	73.8	75.0	77.1	66.7
Trinidad	35.7	35.5	48.1	49.7	49.4
MDC's	123.6	132.2	148.2	155.3	147.0
ECCM 1/	4.3	4.4	4.5	4.7	4.8
Belize 1/	3.5	3.6	3.7	3.8	3.9
Total	131.4	140.2	156.4	163.8	155.7

1/ 1972 estimated, then 3 o/o annual increase assumed to derive previous years production.

Table SA7.31. Meat Production, Imports, and Supply, 1972

	Production		Imports		Supply	
	All meats	Beef +meat	All meat	Beef +Veal	All meat	Beef +Veal
	million lbs					
Barbados	7.0	0.5	15.9	5.0	22.9	5.5
Guyana	23.9	9.6	1.8	1.2	25.7	10.8
Jamaica	66.7	21.8	54.4	18.3	121.1	40.1
Trinidad	49.4	4.5	19.0	6.8	68.4	11.3
MDC's	147.0	36.4	91.1	31.3	238.1	67.7
ECCM	4.8	2.8	17.0	6.8	21.8	9.6
Belize	3.9	1.7	4.0	--	7.9	1.7
Total	155.7	40.9	112.1	38.1	267.8	79.0

Source: Trade Statistics
Economic Surveys (Jamaica)
IBRD Reports
Mission Estimates

Table SA7.32. Beef and Veal Production, MDCs, 1968–72

	1968	1969	1970	1971	1972
	million lbs				
Barbados[1]	0.7	0.7	0.7	0.7	0.5
Guyana	8.8	9.4	8.8	9.5	9.6
Jamaica	28.6	30.3	27.4	25.8	21.8
Trinidad	3.1	3.2	3.3	4.4	4.5
Total MDC's	41.2	43.5	40.2	40.4	36.4
Percent of all meats - MDC's	33.6	33.6	27.7	26.7	25.5

1/ Purchases by Barbados Marketing Corporation only.

Table SA7.33. Poultry Production, MDCs, 1968–72

	1968	1969	1970	1971	1972
	million lbs				
Barbados	1.2	1.6	2.2	3.0	3.2
Guyana 1/	5.9	6.0	7.5	8.7	10.8
Jamaica	21.9	26.3	31.0	40.2	34.3
Trinidad	27.2	26.1	40.1	42.6	39.6
Total MDC's	56.2	60.0	80.8	94.5	87.9
Percent of all meats - MDC's	45.5	45.4	54.5	60.8	59.8

1/ Commercial sales only.

Source: Economic Surveys - Statistical Digests
Mission estimates.

Table SA7.34. Egg Production and Imports, 1972

	Production	Import	Supply
	-------------	million	-------------
Barbados	14.8	2.7	17.5
Guyana	26.4	23.1	49.5
Jamaica	122.5	16.7	139.2
Trinidad	52.2	11.3	63.5
MDC's	215.9	53.8	269.7
ECCM	17.0 1/	3.2 2/	20.2
Belize	n.a.	n.a.	n.a.
Total 3/	232.9	57.0	289.9

1/ Mission estimate.

2/ Based on imports for 1969, assuming a 2.5 o/o annual increase

3/ Belize excluded.

Source: Trade Statistics.

FAS Reports.

Economic Surveys and Statistical Digest.

Table SA7.35. Dairy Production and Imports, 1972

	Production	Imports	
	Fresh Milk	Milk 1/	Butter
	---------- million lbs ----------		
Barbados	16.2	11.8	1.6
Guyana	38.3	16.0	1.3
Jamaica	84.0	29.0	8.5
Trinidad	19.3	27.3	4.5
MDC's	157.8	84.1	15.9
ECCM	n.a.	10.5 2/	1.2
Belize	n.a.	7.5 3/	--
Total	n.a.	102.1	17.1

1/ Dried, evaporated, condensed, powdered, etc.

2/ Based on 1969 imports, assuming a 2.5 o/o annual increase.

3/ Estimated from value of imports of BH $ 3.3 million in 1972 (includes butter).

Source: Official Trade Statistics.

Economic Surveys and Statistical Digests.

Table SA7.36. Production of Root Crops and Vegetables, MDCs, 1968–72

	1968	1969	1970	1971	1972
	in million lbs				
Root Crops					
Barbados 1/	58	60	62	63	65
Guyana	91	102	108	113	112
Jamaica	228	238	304	429	452
Trinidad	37	42	43	45	46
MDC's	414	442	517	650	675
Vegetables 2/					
Barbados 3/	12	13	13	14	15
Guyana	4	4	5	7	8
Jamaica	106	105	149	208	218
Trinidad	39	40	40	47	53
MDC's	161	162	207	276	294
Total	575	604	724	926	969

1/ Estimated with 3 o/o annual increase between 1968 and 1972.

2/ Includes pulses.

3/ Estimated with 6 o/o annual increase between 1968 and 1972.

Source: Economic Surveys
Statistical Digests
Mission Estimates

Table SA7.37. Animal Feed Imports, 1972

	Volume (million lbs)	Value (million EC ¢)
Barbados	80.1	5.6
Guyana	12.0	0.3
Jamaica	54.7	9.1
Trinidad	73.6	11.2
MDC's	220.4	26.2
ECCM 1/	31.0	3.8
Belize 1/	4.2	0.5
	255.6	30.5

1/ Estimated.

Source: Trade Statistics.

Table SA7.38. Production of Animal Feed, Selected Countries, 1966–72

	1966	1967	1968	1969	1970	1971	1972
	million lbs						
Barbados	34.9	30.4	31.3	32.4	39.6	44.2	n.a.
Jamaica	77.4	99.1	112.2	174.6	203.9	305.1	354.2
Trinidad (exports)	n.a.	n.a.	17.8	12.9	13.1	19.9	19.5
	n.a.	n.a.	161.3	219.9	256.6	369.2	n.a.

Source: Economic Surveys - Statistical Digests.
Trade reports (Trinidad).

Table SA7.39. Fertilizer Imports, 1972

MDC's	N	P	K	Others	Total	Value
	-------- in thousand long tons				---------	EC$ million
Barbados	3.4	--	--	12.0	15.4	7.0
Guyana	36.3	7.8	2.3	1.1	47.5	1.4
Jamaica	30.9	5.3	12.3	13.6	62.1	5.4
Trinidad	0.3	0.7	3.7	2.1	6.8	2.2
Total MDC's	70.9	13.8	18.3	28.8	131.1	16.0
ECCM - 1969	6.1	1.5	2.5	14.9	25.0	n.a.

Source: Trade Statistics.

Table SA7.40. Cane Production, WISA Countries, 1965–72

	Acreage Under Cane Cultivation (000 tons)	Acreage Reaped (000 tons)	Cane Milled (million tons)	Tons Cane Per Acre Reaped
1965	434.4	410.8	12.7	30.9
1966	436.5	411.2	12.4	30.1
1967	438.0	427.2	12.5	29.3
1968	441.6	418.9	12.0	28.7
1969	445.7	424.3	12.2	28.8
1970	457.7	414.9	12.3	29.5
1971	463.2	410.5	12.1	27.4
1972	467.4	425.4	11.5	27.0

SOURCE: WISA

Table SA7.41. Sugar Yields, Selected Years

	1963	1965	1969	1970	1971	1972
	long tons/acre reaped					
Barbados	4.13	3.96	2.76	3.12	2.76	2.52
Guyana	3.26	2.87	2.89	2.90	2.70	2.43
Jamaica	3.28	3.41	2.53	2.36	2.57	2.50
St. Kitts	3.29	3.37	3.34	3.76	2.56	2.46
Trinidad	2.45	2.68	2.51	2.34	2.26	2.43
WISA	3.18	3.17	2.68	2.60	2.57	2.49
Belize	N/A	N/A	N/A	N/A	1.71	

SOURCE: WISA and Belize Sugar Industries.

Table SA7.42. Production, Consumption, and Exports of Sugar, 1969–73

	1969	1970	1971	1972	1973 (est.)
	---------------in thousand long tons---------------				
WISA					
Production	1,136.8	1,077.7	1,131.0	1,060.5	949.4
Local sales	159.2	154.0	182.1	179.8	187.0
Total exports	983.0	920.3	956.8	874.4	762.4
To UK	709.2	698.0	757.0	717.0	n.a.
To US	202.7	190.0	186.9	154.3	n.a.
To Canada	70.0	29.3	11.1	2.9	n.a.
To Other	1.1	2.1	1.8	.2	n.a.
Belize					
Production	52.1	66.8	64.9	70.0	70.2
Local sales	2.8	2.5	3.4	3.4	4.0
Total exports	48.7	58.6	57.3	67.3	74.7
To Uk	20.5	20.5	20.5	25.5	20.5
To US	14.3	13.6	12.8	34.4	42.2
To Canada	13.9	24.5	24.0	7.4	12.0
Total Exports	1,031.7	978.9	1,014.1	941.7	837.1
To UK	729.7	718.5	777.5	742.5	n.a.
To US	217.0	214.5	199.7	188.7	n.a.
To Other	85.0	55.9	36.9	10.5	n.a.

Table SA7.43. World Position of West Indies Sugar

	Exports 1/		Production 2/
	1967	1970	1971
	----in million metric tons-----		
Cuba	5.6	6.9	6.0
EEC	.7	1.6	8.7
Australia	1.7	1.4	2.7
USSR	1.1	1.2	8.4
Philippines	.9	1.2	-
Brazil	1.0	1.1	5.3
West Indies	1.1	1.0	1.2
South Africa	.9	.8	1.7
Dom. Republic	.6	.8	1.1
Total World Exports	20.2	22.2	

1/ Raw and refined sugar, raw equivalent basis.

2/ Major exporting countries only.

SOURCE: FAO Trade Yearbooks
International Sugar Organization

Table SA7.44. Value of Sugar Exports, 1965–72

	1965	1966	1967	1968	1969	1970	1971	1972
	---in thousand EC dollars---							
Barbados	40.0	40.4	43.4	42.6	33.4	36.7	36.9	34.9
Guyana	60.2	61.4	72.5	79.0	89.0	84.6	101.6	103.3
Jamaica	85.0	89.8	84.6	91.0	78.5	80.9	84.4	91.4
St. Kitts	7.9	7.8	8.1	5.6	7.4	5.7	4.9	3.9
Trinidad	42.4	38.0	38.0	48.6	52.4	42.8	52.0	53.6
Belize	6.0	8.0	10.4	13.2	12.1	14.3	16.2	21.0
Total	241.5	245.4	257.0	280.0	272.8	265.0	296.0	308.1

Table SA7.45. Sugar Production, 1965–74

	1965	1966	1967	1968	1969	1970	1971	1972	1973	1974
	in thousand long tons									
Barbados	195.9	172.2	200.8	159.4	139.8	154.5	134.8	111.2	120.1	110.2
Guyana	309.0	289.4	343.5	316.9	364.2	311.0	369.1	315.0	268.7	339.6
Jamaica	489.2	500.0	448.8	444.9	382.9	370.1	378.9	373.0	325.8	380.9
St. Kitts	39.4	38.4	38.4	34.5	35.4	26.6	25.6	25.6	23.6	27.6
Trinidad	252.9	210.6	200.8	243.1	240.2	217.5	217.5	231.3	181.1	189.0
Belize	35.4	43.3	58.1	64.0	52.2	66.9	72.8	70.9	80.7	87.6
Total	1321.8	1253.9	1290.4	1262.8	1214.7	1146.6	1198.7	1127.0	1000.0	1134.9

Source: FAO Production Yearbooks

Table SA7.46. Sugar Exports to the United Kingdom and the United States, 1969–72

	U.K.					U.S.				
	Quota	1969	1970	1971	1972	Quota	1969	1970	1971	1972
	'000 long tons					'000 long tons				
Antigua	10.0 1/	-	4.3	10.5	-	-	-	-	-	-
Barbados	133.8	119.3	133.8	115.4	92.8	5.5	3.2	2.9	1.7	1.9
Guyana	189.5	196.7	160.0	241.0	214.0	91.0	98.0	105.0	90.9	85.9
Jamaica	233.3	221.3	229.8	230.6	234.3	77.0	60.8	63.5	68.1	41.3
St. Kitts	33.8	33.2	24.4	23.5	24.0	1.5	-	-	-	-
Trinidad	134.6	138.7	145.8	136.1	151.9	30.0	40.8	19.2	26.2	25.2
WISA	725.0	709.2	698.1	757.1	717.0	205.0	202.8	190.6	186.9	154.3
Belize	20.5	20.5	20.5	20.5	25.5	45.5	14.3	13.7	12.8	34.4
Total	745.5	727.7	718.6	777.6	742.5	250.5	217.1	204.3	199.7	188.7

1/ Quota to be reallocated among the other WISA countries.

Source: WISA and Belize Sugar Industries

Table SA7.47. Distribution of Sugar Production and Exports, WISA Countries, Selected Years.

	1963	1967	1970	1972
	------------ Percent ----------			
Production				
Barbados	15.2	16.2	14.4	10.5
Guyana	25.3	27.8	28.9	29.7
Jamaica	38.1	36.9	34.2	35.6
St. Kitts	3.2	3.1	2.5	2.4
Trinidad	18.2	16.0	20.0	21.8
WISA	100.0	100.0	100.0	100.0
Exports				
Barbados	16.3	17.7	15.5	11.2
Guyana	25.5	29.9	31.3	34.3
Jamaica	35.7	33.8	31.9	31.5
St. Kitts	3.2	3.3	2.7	2.7
Trinidad	17.1	14.8	18.2	20.3
WISA	97.8 1/	99.5 1/	99.6 1/	100.0

1/ Excludes Antigua

Source: Adapted from WISA information.

Table SA7.48. Comparison of Sugar Yields per Acre, Selected Countries, 1971–72

(In metric tons)

	Crop Yield Per Acre	Sugar Yield	Sugar Yield Per Acre
	(Tons of Cane)	(Ton Cane Per Ton Sugar	(Ton Sugar)
Sugar Cane			
Hawaii	86.7	9.7	8.95
Australia	33.7	6.9	4.86
Taiwan	32.6	9.7	3.38
Costa Rica	33.2	10.4	3.19
Domin. Republic	26.1	8.2	3.18
Guyana	33.1	11.5	2.88
Jamaica	27.5	11.0	2.50
Trinidad	26.7	10.9	2.45
Mexico	25.1	10.3	2.44
Martinque	27.3	19.5	1.40
Sugar Beet	(Ton Beets)	(Ton Beets Per Ton Sugar)	(Ton Sugar)
Belgium	21.2	5.2	4.08
France	17.2	5.6	3.07
W. Germany	18.7	6.2	3.02
U. K.	16.1	6.4	2.52

SOURCE: Calculation based on USDA FAS, Foreign Agricultural Circular, Sugar FS-3-72. December, 1972, Washington, D.C.

Table SA7.49. Pattern of Control in the Caribbean Sugar Industry

	Field				Factory			
		Private					Private	
	Public	Local	Expatriate	Percent of Independent Growers	Number of Factories	Public	Local	Expatriate
Barbados 1/	nominal	yes	no	15	12	no	yes	no
Guyana 2/	no	some	yes	9	11	no	1 fact.	most
Jamaica 3/	yes	yes	some	n.a.	15	no	most	some
St. Kitts 4/	nominal	yes	few	100	1	no	joint	
Trinidad	yes	yes	few	40	6	yes	no	no
Belize	no	yes	1000 acres	96	2	no	no	yes

1/ Barbados: Government owned plantations account for some 5% of the cane grown

2/ Guyana: 1 sugar factory is owned by a local company with predominantly local shareholders. Local shareholders have substantital holdings in several other factories.

3/ Jamaica: Restructuring in progress

4/ St. Kitts: ____________ do ________

Table SA7.50. Labor Productivity, Field Operations[1]

	1965	1967	1969	1970
	--Man-hours per long ton of cane--			
Belize	6.5	6.3	6.5	6.3
Jamaica	7.5	6.5	7.0	N/A
Trinidad 2/	7.2	7.0	5.8	5.7
Louisiana	3.6	2.4	2.6	N/A
	--Man-hours per long ton of sugar--			
Belize	59.5	57.0	61.5	N/A
Jamaica	69.0	62.0	65.0	N/A
Trinidad 2/	70.1	75.4	57.8	65.8
Louisiana	42.7	26.0	27.6	N/A

1/ Planting, Cultivation, Harvesting.

2/ Derived from man-days figures, with assumption of five (5) hours work per day.

SOURCE: Trinidad, IBRD Caroni Project

Others - Sugar Industry Commission of Engrury, British Honduras, 1971.

Table SA7.51. Estimation of Use of Mechanical Harvesting Equipment, 1972
(In percentage of total cane reaped)

	Mechanical Loading	Mechanical Harvesting (Combine)
Barbados	16	E
Guyana	-	E
Jamaica	90 1/	E
St. Kitts	100	E
Trinidad	52	8-9
Belize	N/A	E
Region	34	1

E: Experimental, not yet commercially used (negligible)

1/ Estates only

SOURCE: WISA

IBRD Caroni Project

Table SA7.52. Comparative Costs in the West Indies

	1970	1971	1972	1973	1974
	Percent of Regional Average				
Barbados	92	103	107	92	103
Guyana	84	82	85	90	85
Jamaica	108	105	104	102	106
Trinidad	115	120	110	115	115
Weighted Regional Average	100	100	100	100	100
Weighted Regional Average EC$/Ton	275	273	306	363	396
Wei Weighted Regional Export Price (EC$/Ton)	248	297	303	307	419

Table SA7.53. Index of Prices of Imported Supplies

	1970	1971	1972	1973	1974	1974 % of total	% change 1970-74
Fertilizers	21.1	21.6	23.1	29.3	38.1	19.1	80.6
Field Chemicals	9.2	8.9	10.2	11.0	11.7	5.8	27.2
Petroleum Products	13.4	16.1	18.0	25.8	53.6	26.9	300.0
Factories Supplies + Spares	16.6	18.4	19.8	22.6	28.7	14.4	72.9
Ag. Equipt. Supplies + Spares	20.2	25.5	29.0	29.6	32.5	16.3	60.9
Others 1/	19.5	22.9	25.5	27.1	34.9	17.5	79.0
Total	100.0	113.4	125.6	145.4	199.5	100.0	99.5
Annual % Increase		13.4	10.8	15.8	37.2		18.9

1/ Building materials and general supplies.

Table SA7.54. Comparative Cost Data (Indexes)

	1970	1971	1972	1973	1974
West Indies	100	100	112	133	146
Other Commonwealth Countries 1/	100	105	119	151	173
West Indies as a % of others	154	146	145	136	130

1/ Australia, Fiji, Mauritius.

Table SA7.55. Cane Farmers' Comparative Budgets, Trinidad

(In TT dollars)

	EXAMPLES (TT$) (by farm size)		
	A	B	C
I. Income			
1. Plant cane, at $12/ton 1/			
A. 7.5 tons (1/2 ac at 15 ton/ac)	90.00	-	-
B. 36 tons (2 ac at 18 tons/ac)	-	432.00	-
C. 216 tons (12 ac at 18 tons/ac)	-	-	2,592.00
2. Ratoon cane, at $12/ton			
A. 42 tons (3-1/2 ac at 12 tons/ac)	504.00	-	-
B. 260 tons (13 ac at 20 tons/ac)	-	3,120.00	-
C. 2,024 tons (88 ac at 23 tons/ac)	-	-	24,228.00
3. Total cane income	594.00	3,552.00	26,880.00
4. Fertilizer subsidy, at 40 cents/ton 2/	19.80	118.40	790.40
5. Total income	613.80	3,670.40	26,089.60
II. Expenditure			
1. Plant cane			
A. 1/2 ac, net cash outlay $129.00/ac	64.50	-	-
B. 2 ac, net cash outlay $192.50	-	385.00	-
C. 12 ac, net cash outlay $409.50	-	-	4,914.00
2. Ratoon cane			
A. 3-1/2 ac, net cash outlay $9.50	33.25	-	-
B. 13 ac, net cash outlay $81.00	-	1,053.00	-
C. 88 ac, net cash outlay $207.00	-	-	18,216.00
3. Rent, at $10/ac 3/	40.00	150.00	1,000.00
4. Total expenditure 4/	137.50	1,588.00	24,130.00
III. Balance	476.30	2,082.40	1,959.60
Balance per ton cane produced	9.63	7.04	0.87
Cash expenditure per ton produced	2.78	4.01	10.77
Cash return per ac/cane	119.08	138.83	19.60

NOTE: 1/ Cane price at $12/ton is approximately average price received 1968/71.
2/ Fertilizer subsidy may not always apply, and is not likely in 1972.
3/ Rent is sometimes more than $10/ac.
4/ Finance charges and managerial overheads are not included.

A: Part time farmer, 4 acres of cane, family labor
B: Full time farmer, 15 acres of cane, family labor
C: Full time farmer, 100 acres of cane, hired labor

SOURCE: IBRD Caroni Project, March 1973.

Table SA7.56. Exports of Bananas, 1965–74

	1965	1966	1967	1968	1969	1970	1971	1972	1973	1974
Value (million EC$)										
Dominica	7.0	6.7	7.7	11.2	10.2	7.8	7.7	4.7	9.4	12.5
Grenada	2.3	2.6	3.5	3.9	2.9	2.5	1.8	1.5	2.0	3.3
St. Lucia	9.3	9.1	9.0	9.8	12.9	5.4	7.0	8.3	10.2	21.2
St. Vincent	3.1	3.5	3.1	4.1	4.2	3.3	3.0	3.2	5.0	8.1
Windwards	21.7	21.9	23.3	29.0	30.2	19.0	19.5	17.7	26.6	45.1
Jamaica	29.3	30.2	32.0	33.1	29.9	28.4	28.1	28.4	35.3	25.9
Total	51.0	52.1	55.3	62.1	60.1	47.4	47.6	46.1	61.9	71.0
Volume (000 L.T. tons)										
Dominica	48.4	39.1	42.1	54.9	49.3	35.7	38.3	35.6	27.9	29.5
Grenada	20.7	20.9	25.6	26.8	22.6	18.8	14.0	13.0	10.4	7.9
St. Lucia	80.2	77.3	73.4	71.2	67.3	36.8	41.9	45.4	34.1	35.4
St. Vincent	28.4	25.0	24.1	27.5	29.9	26.6	28.5	24.9	20.1	23.6
Windwards	177.7	162.3	165.2	180.4	169.1	117.9	122.7	118.9	92.5	96.4
Jamaica	180.0	180.1	173.2	138.4	135.5	135.4	125.9	127.3	107.9	72.3
Total	357.7	342.4	338.4	318.8	304.6	253.3	248.6	246.2	200.4	168.7

Sources: WINBAN and Official Trade Statistics

Table SA7.57. Imports of Bananas into the United Kingdom, 1966–72

	1966	1967	1968	1969	1970	1971	1972
	in thousand long tons						
Windwards	162.6	159.1	178.9	196.2	134.9	125.0	111.3
Jamaica	198.2	193.1	153.7	150.2	122.2	124.4	121.9
Others	13.2	10.0	12.3	10.8	46.8	72.6	75.0
Total	374.0	362.2	344.9	357.2	303.9	322.0	308.2
	Percent						
Share of Caribbean countries	96.5	97.2	96.4	97.0	84.6	77.5	75.7
Windwards	43.5	43.9	51.9	54.9	44.4	38.8	36.1
Jamaica	53.0	53.3	44.5	42.1	40.2	38.7	39.6

Source: Economic Aspects of the Banana Industry in St. Lucia, A. Tench, 1973.

Table SA7.58. Yield of Bananas in Selected Countries, 1965/66 and 1969/70

	1965/66	1969/70
	--------Tons per acre----------	
Costa Rica	8.9	20.6
Ecuador	3.9	11.8
Guatemala	7.2	8.3
Honduras	16.0	15.2
Jamaica	3.7	2.9
Paraguay	12.0	13.0
Dominican Republic	-	5.8

Source: Organizacion de los Estados Americanos, America en cifras 1972, Washington, D.C., 1972

Table SA7.59. Per Capita Consumption and Retail Price of Bananas in Selected Countries

	Consumption per Capita (kg)		Retail Price	Main Source
	1965	1970	(1969 index)	of fruit
U.K.	7.3	6.3	100 (base)	West Indies
Belgium	7.7	7.7	120	Ecuador
Italy	5.4	5.9	138	Somalia
Netherlands	6.1	6.9	88	Ecuador
France	8.8	9.0	116	French Antilles
Germany	9.8	9.0	88	Central America
North America	9.4	9.6	95	Central America
Japan	3.7	6.5	162	Taiwan

Source: Economic Aspects of the Banana Industry in St. Lucia, A. Tench, Castries 1973

Table SA7.60. Windward Islands: Schedule of Prices for the Period May–November 1973 (WINBAN/Geest Agreement)

(In Eastern Caribbean dollars per ton)

GMP For Carton Fruit	U.K. Interim Bonus	Geest Contract Costs	Balance Due to Associations
508.8	7.4	202.4	299.0
499.2	7.4	202.4	289.4
489.6	7.4	202.4	279.8
480.0	7.4	202.4	270.2
470.4	7.4	202.4	260.6
460.8	7.4	202.4	251.0
456.0	7.4	202.4	246.2
451.2	7.4	202.4	241.4
441.6	7.4	202.4	231.8
432.0	7.4	202.4	222.2

Source: WINBAN.

Table SA7.61. Formation of Retail Price, 1969

	Windward Islands [1/]	Jamaica
	----------in percent------------	
F.O.B. price	22.8	30.3
Freight, Insurance, Landing	19.5	20.5
Importers margin	1.1	1.4
Ripeners mark up	31.2	24.6
Retail Gross margin	25.4	25.4
Retail Price	100.0	100.0

1/ Before introduction of boxing

Source: Dominica Banana Industry Study, Phase III, Progress Report No. 1, Resources Management Consultants Ltd., March 1973

Table SA7.62. Selected Banana Prices, Jamaica and Windward Islands, 1965–72

	Jamaica			Windward Islands								
	GBP[1/]	F.O.B[2/]	Growers	GMP[3/]	F.O.B[4/]	Dominica Ass'n	Dominica Growers	Grenada Ass'n	Grenada Growers	St. Vincent Ass'n	St. Vincent Growers
	--in EC$ per ton----			in EC$ per ton							
1965	292.4	146.4	63.4	n.a.	123.9	not available					
1966	297.8	151.5	74.0	n.a.	130.5	not available					
1967	338.2	166.1	73.5	288.0	135.7	122.3	96.5	119.2	97.7	124.2	94.8
1968	388.1	216.2	68.4	298.9	146.4	136.0	112.7	134.0	115.4	130.9	100.6
1969	373.7	198.3	72.5	336.8	151.9	135.5	104.6	128.6	127.2	143.7	112.0
1970	390.4	213.4	88.3	322.6	133.5	125.7	94.1	120.7	117.4	139.6	108.1
1971	419.5	225.2	90.0	328.8	151.3	117.5	90.0	113.1	n.a.	148.5	109.3
1972	427.9	225.1	90.0	331.9	125.9	125.3	93.2	n.a.	n.a.	n.a.	n.a.

1/ Green boat price, includes delivery to wholesalers
2/ Value of exports divided by volume exported
3/ Green Market price
4/ Total value of exports of the Windwards divided by total volume exported

Sources: Jamaica Banana Board
WINBAN and Banana Association

Table SA7.63. Windward Islands: Geest Contract Costs, Selected Years

(In pounds sterling)

	1973	1972	1964
Summer bonus	-	0.69	0.64
Cash Transfer Charges	0.18	0.13	0.07
West Indies Expenses[1/]	4.48	8.19	6.61
Insurance	0.08	0.08	0.08
Freight	21.00	20.00	18.25
Dock Charges	6.23	5.77	3.42
Distribution	6.16	6.37	4.40
Cost of Shrinkage	2.13	1.38	1.11
Cost of Wastage	0.04	0.07	0.24
Allowances to Green Handlers	0.17	0.06	0.20
Handling Charges	1.70	1.70	1.59
Others[2/]	-	-	1.48
TOTAL	42.17	44.44	38.42

1/ Part of the W.I. expenses are now included in the basic price paid to associations.

2/ Wrapping materials and unsaleable.

Source: A. Tench (op. cit.) and WINBAN.

Table SA7.64. Seasonality Aspects, St. Lucia

Average exported production by month		1966-1972	(A)
Average grower price (Basic)	"	1966-1972	(B)
Rainfall for Roseau	"	1961-1970	(C)

	A	B	C
	Tons	EC¢	Inches
January	5401	3.50	5.08
February	5419	3.53	4.16
March	6090	3.68	3.08
April	5795	4.25	3.99
May	6251	4.50	6.04
June	5659	4.90	9.12
July	5337	4.90	11.17
August	4777	4.68	9.48
September	4590	4.90	10.80
October	5049	4.86	10.26
November	5009	4.79	7.93
December	5310	4.07	6.20

Source: Economic Aspects of the Banana Industry in St. Lucia. A. Tench, Castries, 1973.

Table SA8.1. Relation between Area, Population, and Length of Roads

	Area Sq. Mi	Population[1] Number	Population Density	Road Miles	Density of Roads mi/sq. mi	Density of Roads mi/000 Inhabitants
Antigua	170	65,000	382.4	605	3.6	9.3
Dominica	304	70,302	231.3	748	2.5	10.6
Grenada	133	93,384	702.1	610	4.6	6.5
Montserrat	39	11,498	294.8	150	3.8	13.0
St. Kitts	136	46,081	338.8	183	1.3	4.0
St. Lucia	238	100,259	421.3	411	1.7	4.1
St. Vincent	150	86,944	579.6	606	4.0	7.0
Belize	8,867	120,000	13.5	1,389	.15	11.6
				4,702		

1/ 1970 Census

January 1974

Table SA8.2. Road Network of LDCs

(In miles)

	Paved Roads	All Weather Roads	Gravel Roads	Dry Weather Roads	Tracks	Total
1. Antigua	150			455		605
2. Dominica	231	166		72	279	748
3. Grenada	375		110	125		610
4. Montserrat	92			58		150
5. St. Kitts	60	23	70	30		183
6. St. Lucia	117	51	209		35	412
7. St. Vincent	57	130	204	—	215	606
Subtotal	982	370	593	740	529	3,314
8. Belize	174	—	816	235	164	1,389
Total	1,156	370	1,409	975	693	4,703

Source: Ministry of Communications and Works.

January 1974

Table SA8.3. Relation between Area, Population, and Number of Vehicles, 1970

	Area Sq. Mi	Population[1] Number	Total Vehicles	Vehicles/ Sq. Mi	Vehicle/ 1000 Inhabitants
Antigua	170	65,000	6,900	40.6	106.2
Dominica	304	70,302	2,382	7.8	33.9
Grenada	133	93,384	5,159	38.8	55.2
Montserrat	39	11,498	1,030	26.4	89.6
St. Kitts	136	46,081	2,801	20.6	60.8
St. Lucia	238	100,259	4,556	19.1	45.4
St. Vincent	150	86,944	3,809	25.4	43.8
Belize	8,867	120,000	6,906	.8	57.6

1/ 1970 census.

January 1974

Table SA8.4. Motor Vehicles Licensed

		1965	1970	1972
Antigua	Cars[1/]	2,263	4,587	-
	All vehicles	4,120	6,900	-
Dominica	Cars[1/]	669	1,342	2,118
	All vehicles	1,546	2,382	3,115
Grenada	Cars[1/]	2,165	3,662	-
	All vehicles	3,310	5,159	-
Montserrat	Cars[1/]	407	803	956
	All vehicles	640	1,030	1,239
St. Kitts	Cars[1/]	1,297	1,733	1,851
	All vehicles	1,971	2,801	3,104
St. Lucia	Cars[1/]	1,544	2,872	3,004
	All vehicles	2,588	4,556	4,730
St. Vincent	Cars[1/]	1,365	2,203	2,670
	All vehicles	2,629	3,809	4,415
Subtotal	Cars[1/]	9,710	17,202	-
	All vehicles	16,804	26,637	-
Belize	Cars[1/]	1,438	4,051	4,491
	All vehicles	3,247	6,906	8,060[2/]
TOTAL	Cars[1/]	11,148	21,253	'
	All vehicles	20,051	33,543	

1/ Include taxi and rental cars.

2/ Estimate.

Source: Abstract of Statistics of the Leeward and Windward Islands, UWI, 1971 - Statistical Digests;
Traffic in St. John's, UNDP, Antigua, January 1973;
Annual Statistical Abstracts;
Feasibility Study, "Report of Roads and Bridges," Crown Agents, Grenada, June 1972;
Police Departments.

January 1974

Table SA8.5. Vehicle Fleet of Barbados

	Total Motor Vehicles	Cars	Population	Vehicles per 1,000 Population	Cars per 1,000 Population
1954	6,794	4,421	215,000	31.6	20.6
1960	11,191	7,480	232,327	48.2	32.2
1965	16,043	11,446	235,234	68.2	48.7
1966	17,524	12,440	235,815	74.3	52.8
1967	18,911	12,899	236,397	80.0	54.6
1968	21,178	14,773	236,978	89.4	62.3
1969	22,699	15,918	237,560	95.6	67.0
1970 1/	24,891	17,970	237,700	104.7	75.6
1971 1/	27,083	20,022	238,247	113.7	84.1
1972	29,275	22,075	238,800	122.6	92.4

1/ Mission estimates.

Source: Bridgetown Transportation Study, Wallace Evans & Partners, Barbados, 1972.
Figures for 1972, Ministry of Communications and Works.

January 1974

Table SA8.6. Road Investment Program in LDCs[1]

(In millions of Eastern Caribbean dollars)

	1974	1975	1976	1977	1978	Total
Antigua						
Roads	.70	1.21	1.55	.67	.56	4.69
Dominica						
Feeder Roads	1.18	1.17	1.12	1.12	1.12	
Major Roads	2.00	2.00	1.50	1.50	1.50	
Bridges	.50	.30	.30	.30	.30	
	3.68	3.47	2.92	2.92	2.92	15.91
Grenada						
Feeder Roads	1.10	1.10	1.00	1.00	1.00	
Major Roads	2.00	2.00	2.00	2.00	2.00	
Bridges	.25	.25	.25	.25	.25	
	3.35	3.35	3.25	3.25	3.25	16.45
Montserrat						
Roads	.62	.64	.60	.30	.30	2.46
St. Kitts						
Roads	2.14	2.95	1.75	.55	.55	7.94
St. Lucia						
Feeder Roads	1.34	1.34	1.33	.50	.50	
Major Roads	4.55	6.39	6.66	.50	.50	
	5.89	7.73	7.99	1.00	1.00	23.61
St. Vincent						
Main Roads	4.22	5.10	2.50	2.50	1.00	
Feeder Roads	1.00	1.00	.90	.50	.50	
	5.22	6.10	3.40	3.00	1.50	19.22
Belize						
Roads	4.50	4.80	3.10	5.50	5.50	23.40
Total	26.10	30.25	24.56	17.19	15.58	113.68

1/ Mission's estimates based on the information provided by the Governments.

January 1974

Table SA8.7. Road Investment Program in Barbados

(In millions of Eastern Caribbean dollars)

Project	1973/74	1974/75	1975/76	1976/77	Total
Main roads	.70	.74	.72	.58	2.74
Feeder, subsidiary & tenantry roads	.70	.63	.66	.68	2.67
Public transport	.58	.46	.46	-	1.50
Car parks	.12	.12	.13	.14	.51
Parking systems	.05	.05	.06	.06	.21
Bus stands	.025	.025	.03	.03	.11
Bridges	.25	-	-		.25
Total	2.425	2.025	2.06	1.49	7.99

Source: Development Plan.

January 1974

Table SA8.8. Current CDB Banana Feeder Road Projects in Grenada, St. Vincent, St. Lucia, and Dominica

	Grenada	St.Vincent	St.Lucia	Dominica	Total
Total cost (million EC$)	2.01	2.00	2.81	2.28	9.10
Miles of roads	30.00	26.25	37.25	35.00	128.50
Construction cost (EC$/mile)	62,000	70,700	70,700	60,700	-
Farm families served by roads	875	2,195	312	1,212	4,594
New roads to be built (miles)	NA	14	29	6	-
Phasing of construction (yrs)	3	3	3	3	-
Annual maintenance cost (EC$/mile)	1,930	1,930	1,930	1,930	-
Land benefited by the roads (acres) 1/	4,170	4,960	9,343	7,762	26,235
Land in cultivation (acres)	2,000	3,300	1,487	3,302	10,089
Land to be brought under cultivation (acres)	2,170	1,660	7,856	4,460	16,146
Net economic benefits to the country per annum (EC$ million) 2/	NA	.86	.98	1.00	-
Additional revenue to the Govt. through taxes per annum (EC$ million)	NA	.17	.20	.20	-
Estimated value of production per annum (EC$ million).					
Present:					
Bananas	.42	.87	.25	.93	3.07
Other crops		.16	.15	.28	

Table SA8.8. (continued)

	Grenada	St. Vincent	St. Lucia	Dominica	Total
Potential:					
Bananas	1.15	1.29	.36	1.37	5.55
Other crops		.34	.36	.66	
Possible new cultivation:					
Bananas	.30-.50	.59	1.38	.95	4.92
Other crops		.54	.53	.53	
Man days work for local labor force					
Construction	195,430 3/	171,000 3/	280,000	228,000	874,430
Maintenance	5,790 3/	5,165 3/	7,200	6,755	24,910

1/ Engineering estimates.
2/ Net benefits from the additional yields after taking into account the cost of imported inputs.
3/ Mission's estimates based on the CDB reports.

NA - not available.

Source: Appraisal Reports, Caribbean Development Bank.

January 1974

Table SA8.9. Maintenance Funds for Roads in LDCs, 1973
(In millions of Eastern Caribbean dollars)

		Allocated	Desired 2/
Antigua		1.02	1.10
Dominica		.70	1.90
Grenada		.83 1/	1.30
Montserrat		.19	.19
St. Kitts		.11	.30
St. Lucia		.93 1/	1.30
St. Vincent		.60	1.80
	Subtotal	4.38	7.89
Belize		1.20	1.65
	Total	5.58	9.54

1/ 1972.

2/ Estimates.

January 1974

Table SA8.10. Ports and Shipping Facilities

Deep Water Ports

Facilities	Kingston Jamaica	Port-of-Spain Trinidad	Bridgetown Barbados	St. John's Antigua	St. Georges Grenada	Castries St. Lucia	Kingstown St. Vincent
No. of berths	9	8	8	2	2	3	2
Wharf length (ft)	4,500	4,400	4,400 1/	1,220	800	1,440	900
Depth of water (ft)	35	30	32	35	30	21-27	30
Special loading and unloading facilities	Containers 2/	Containers 2/	Sugar	Oil	Bananas	Bananas	Bananas
Porth authority	Yes	Yes	No	Yes	No	Yes	Yes

Other Ports

Facilities	Basseterre St. Kitts	Roseau Dominica	Plymouth Montserrat	Belize City Belize	Georgetown Guyana
No. of piers	3	1	1	1	12
Length (ft)	1,100	175	150	1,050	50-750 each
Depth of water (ft)	7-11	12	9	8	16-29 4/
Special loading and unloading facilities	Sugar and oil	3/	Oil	Sugar and oil	Bauxite, sugar, molasses and rice
Port authority	No	Yes	No	No	No

1/ Of this, 2,700 feet is break water.
2/ Other specialized commodities are handled outside the main port.
3/ Bananas, citrus, pumice, and timber are handled outside the main port.
4/ Vessels requiring more than 20 ft draught cannot enter the river.

Source: Information obtained in the mission.

Table SA8.11. General Cargo Traffic

(In thousands of tons)

	Actual					Forecast			
	1968	1969	1970	1971	1972	1973	1975	1980	1985
Kingston, Jamaica									
Imports									
Exports									
Total	984	1,044	1,178	1,213	1,272	1,225	1,426	2,132	
Port-of-Spain, Trinidad									
Imports	461	587	591	606	623	645	699	777	
Exports	202	262	309	316	266	218	232	262	
Total	663	849	900	922 2/	889 2/	863	931	1,039	1,094
Bridgetown, Barbados									
Imports	296	344	389	382	407		463	498	588
Exports	43	45	48	57	61		73	114	157
Total	339	389	437	439	468		546	612	745
St. George's, Grenada									
Imports	79	85	113	114	107				
Exports	35			23	25				
Total	114			137	132				
Castries, St. Lucia									
Imports	76	110	147	143			110	130	152
Exports	74	83	74	47			59	65	72
Total	150	193	221	190			169	195	224
Kingstown, St. Vincent									
Imports	47	56	60	69	67	58			
Exports	45	44	55	31	42	28			
Total	92	100	115	100	109	86			
Basseterre, St. Kitts									
Imports	51	55	67	46	60		52	60	70
Exports	39	41	35	37	35		45	43	41
Total	90	96	102	83	95		97	103	111
Roseau, Dominica									
Imports	63	66	81	80			87	114	151
Exports	65	66	49	46			72	91	113
Total	128	132	130	126			159	205	264
Plymouth, Montserrat									
Imports	22	23	26	23	38	34			
Exports	0.6	0.3	0.7	0.5	0.1	0.3			
Total	22.6	23.3	26.7	23.5	38.1	34.3	28.5		
Belize City, Belize									
Imports	200	110	115	109	93		141	184	246
Exports	100	84	95	82	77		123	155	194
Total	300	194	210	191	170		264	339	440
Regional Total	2,882.6	3,136.3	3,459.7	3,424.5	3,491.1				

1/ Traffic volumes for Antigua and Guyana not included as these are available only in value terms.
2/ Estimates.

Table SA8.12. Volume of Cargo Handled by WISCO, 1971

	Tons Loaded	%	Tons Discharged	%	Total	%
Trinidad	15755	27.7	12949	21.8	28,704	24.7
Grenada	444	0.8	3276	5.5	3,720	3.2
St. Vincent	296	0.5	3184	5.4	3,480	3.0
Barbados	9920	17.5	8887	15.0	18,807	16.2
St. Lucia	583	1.0	4872	8.2	5,455	4.7
Dominica	427	0.8	2602	4.4	3,029	2.6
Montserrat	142	0.2	2355	4.0	2,497	2.2
Antigua	645	1.1	5235	8.9	5,880	5.1
St. Kitts	231	0.4	3421	5.8	3,652	3.1
Jamaica	24407	42.9	10473	17.7	34,880	30.1
Guyana	4011	7.1	1957	3.3	5,968	5.1
Total	56861		59211		116,072	

Source: WISCO Annual Report, 1971.

Table SA8.13. WISCO Interport Cargo Flow, 1971

(In tons)

PORT OF DISCHARGE / PORT OF LOADING	TRINIDAD		GRENADA		ST. VINCENT		BARBADOS		ST. LUCIA		DOMINICA		MONTSERRAT		ANTIGUA		ST. KITTS		JAMAICA		GUYANA		TOTAL	
	R	G	R	G	R	G	R	G	R	G	R	G	R	G	R	G	R	G	R	G	R	G	R	G
TRINIDAD	–	–	89.5	1031.48	53	712.05	25	1431.22	122	873.29	61	867.92	18.5	836.75	99.5	1832.31	22.5	1088.47	1	6446.29	–	143.75	492	15263.54
GRENADA	–	66	–	–	–	9.25	–	216.5	–	48.46	.1	7	–	1.6	–	10.56	1	7.9	–	74.75	–	–	2	442
ST. VINCENT	–	53.89	–	40.37	—	–	–	49.6	–	40.84	–	38.37	–	3.74	–	38.33	–	10.16	–	20.53	—	–	–	295.83
BARBADOS	-	331.11	4.05	1020.56	2.55	731.72	–	–	3.3	1635.5	.38	792.54	–	907.31	–	1294.72	3.8	903.65	–	2288.85	–	–	14.08	9905.96
ST' LUCIA	–	149.58	–	49.31	–	98.12	2	72.09	–	–	–	29.6	–	13.46	–	16.97	–	31.69	–	120.18	–	–	2	581.
DOMINICA	–	2.97	–	7.92	–	21.37	–	160.84	–	52.64	–	–	–	27.65	–	62.45	–	56.18	–	34.55	–	–	–	426.57
MONTSERRAT	–	14.78	–	2.9	–	31.66	–	45.85	–	9.36	–	16.52	–	–	.05	3.25	–	2.8	.05	16.6	–	–	.1	142.51
ANTIGUA	–	80.3	.63	74.67	.62	46.38	–	106.16	–	66.01	1.18	92.92	–	46.59	–	–,	–	72.84	–	56.42	–	–	2.43	641.29
ST.KITTS	–	29.53	–	11.5	–	58.02	–	29.79	–	26.92	–	20.72	–	12.58	–	9.65	–	–	–	32.29	–	–	–	231
JAMAICA	13.13	9114.9	2.1	963.91	2.61	1259.77	19.58	17.32	2.57	2294.46	.25	725.92	.15	239.67	4.33	1138.87	1.48	1229.72	–	–	59.48	1516.36	105.68	24300.9
GUYANA	–	3472.75	–	–	–	–	–	–	–	–	–	–	–	–	–	–	–	–	–	538.56	–	–	–	4011.31
TOTAL	13.13	13315.81	96.28	3202.62	58.78	2968.34	46.58	7928.37	127.87	5047.46	63.81	2591.51	18.65	2089.35	103.88	4407.1	28.78	3403.41	1.05	9629.02	59.48	1660.11	618.29	56,241.91

"R" –Refrigerated
"G" –General

Source: Annual Report & Account's, 1971

Table SA8.14. Annual Cruise Ship Visitor Arrivals

	1968	1969	1970	1971	1972
Antigua	12,788	25,208	18,705	37,658	63,784
Barbados	75,981	80,565	79,635	79,159	100,086
Dominica	3,287	n.a	n.a	n.a	n.a
Grenada	26,500	39,118	41,261	48,652	94,060
Jamaica	94,021	97,377	86,247	66,366	71,450
Montserrat	910	478	1,821	1,803	1,066
St. Kitts	7,187	6,933	5,442	1,722	4,672
St. Lucia	23,261	40,541	40,837	42,859	37,267
St. Vincent	18,823	14,323	16,094	12,327	11,418
Trinidad & Tobago	n.a	n.a	n.a	79,890	66,390

Source: Tourism Supply Study, Caribbean Region, the Shankland Cox Partnership, 1973.

Table SA8.15. Selected Ocean Shipping Rates between Canada and the Caribbean

(U.S. dollars per ton)

Commodity	Guyana	Trinidad	Barbados	Leeward and Windward Islands (except Montserrat)	Montserrat	Jamaica
Asbestos	83	91	85	87	109	51
Cereals in bags	68	76	70	72	90	38
Furniture						
< $300 per ton	50	61	55	56	69	44
> $300 per ton	63	96	90	69	85	44
Canned goods	50	56	50	64	93.50	42
Clothes & dry goods	58	64	58	64	85	55
Coffee (in bags)	58	66	60	67	83	78
Flour	61	69	63	69	85	55

Source: Saguenay Ocean Shipping Line Rates for 1973.

Table SA8.16. Selected Ocean Shipping Rates between the U.S. Atlantic and Gulf Ports and the Caribbean[1]

(U.S. dollars per ton)

Commodity	Guyana	Trinidad Gulf Ports	Trinidad Atlantic Ports	Leeward, Windward Islands and Barbados	Jamaica Gulf Ports	Jamaica Atlantic Ports
Apples	61.50	68.50	70.00	70.00	83.50	83.50
Feed animal or poultry	34.00	41.50	42.50	42.50	open	45.50
Fertilizer in bulk, in bags	30.00	38.50	39.00	39.00	35.00	44.00
Corn	42.50	50.50	51.50	51.50	79.50	79.50
Fish	117.00	123.00	126.00	126.00	57.00	57.00
Meat	114.00	119.50	122.50	122.50	72.50	81.00
Clothing	94.00	100.50	102.50	102.50	60.50	60.50
Coffee in bags	51.50	59.00	60.00	60.00	-	-

1/ The freight rates to Guyana, Trinidad, Leeward and Windward Islands, and Barbados are controlled by the Leeward and Windward Islands and Guianas Conference, while the United States Atlantic and Gulf-Jamaica Conference controls the rates to Jamaica.

Source: Conference Rates, 1973

(Table continues on next page.)

Table SA8.16. (continued)

Commodity	Leeward & Windward Islands, Barbados Trinidad & Guyana	Jamaica
Bauxite in bulk, in bags or drums		
in lots of less than 50 tons	34.00	Open
in lots of more than 50 tons	26.00	Open
Beans, cocoa	51.50	-
Canned goods	50.50	32.00 1/
Clothing, manufactured	48.00	-
Coconuts in bags less than 70 culls	1.55 per bag	28.50
less than 175 culls	2.90 per bag	
Coffee	50.50	42.50
Nutmegs	80.50	-
Sugar raw	44.00	-
refined	46.00	-

1/ Citrus fruit segments

Source: Conference Rates, 1973

Table SA8.17. Airports in the CARICOM Region

Location	Largest Aircraft Regularly Served	Length of Runway (ft)	Remarks
A. Long/Medium Range Jet Airports			
Barbados	DC 8 B 747	11,000	New terminal being built. B 747 charters only.
Guyana	DC 8 B 707	7,400	
Jamaica (Kingston)	DC 8 B 747	7,600	
Jamaica (Montego Bay)	DC 8 B 747	7,100	
Trinidad	DC 8	9,500	New terminal planned.
Antigua	L 1011 DC 8	9,000	New terminal planned.
St. Lucia (Hewanorra)	DC 8 L 1011	9,000	New terminal being built.
St. Kitts	B 727 DC 9	6,000	Plans to extend to 7,600 ft. New terminal being planned.
B. Medium Range Turbo-Prop, Small Jet Airports			
Belize	BAC 111	6,300	
Tobago	BAC 111	6,000	
St. Lucia (Vigie)	HS 748 BAC 111	5,700	New terminal planned. No night jet landings.
Montserrat	HS 748	3,420	No night flying.
St. Vincent	HS 748	4,850	No night flying.
Dominica	HS 748	5,000	No night flying. New site being sought.
Montserrat	HS 748	3,420	No night flying.
C. Feeder Airports			
Anguilla	Islander	3,000	
Barbuda	"	1,500	
Nevis	"	2,000	
Carriacou	"		

Note: There are a number of smaller strips being used or planned in the Grenadines group of small islands between St. Vincent and Grenada .

Table SA8.18. Number of Terminating Passengers[1]

(Thousands)

	Actual	Forecast		
	1970	1975	1980	1985
Barbados	252	458	1,154	1,623
Jamaica	544	1,032	1,078	2,492
Trinidad	114	250	440	710
Antigua	50	100	175	275
St. Lucia	28	117	322	550
St. Kitts	33	78	149	252
Belize	58	55	97	143
Montserrat	15	22	36	57
St. Vincent	30	62	107	171
Grenada	50	113	247	425
Dominica	18	40	80	123
	1,192	2,327	3,885	6,821

1/ Statistics for Guyana are not available.

Source: Eastern Caribbean Aviation Facilities, 1970.
Jamaica Airports, 1970-1990.
Government of Belize Airport Study, 1973.
Proposed Development Program for Seawell, Barbados, 1971.

Table SA8.19. Air Freight Volumes[1]

(In thousands of kilograms)

	Actual	Forecast		
	1970	1975	1980	1985
Barbados	6,008	16,810	51,680	104,000
Jamaica	13,478	19,968	29,952	49,921
Trinidad [2]	2,990	6,161	13,862	22,922
Antigua	3,500	9,200	23,000	46,000
St. Lucia	617	2,320	7,300	22,300
St. Kitts	804	2,190	4,400	8,800
Belize	2,084	5,662	8,788	18,301
Montserrat	98	223	553	1,338
St. Vincent	262	840	2,400	6,300
Grenada	649	1,670	4,430	11,300
Dominica	800	1,900	4,800	11,800
Total	31,290	66,944	151,165	302,982

1/ Statistics for Guyana are not available.
2/ Estimates.

Source: Eastern Caribbean Aviation Facilities, 1970.
Jamaica Airports, 1970-19[illegible].
Government of Belize Airport Study, 197[illegible].
Proposed Development Program for Seawell, Barbados, 1971.
Piarco International Airport Study, 1969.

Table SA8.20. Direct Air Passenger Services in the CARICOM Regions, 1973

To \ From	Belize	Jamaica	Antigua	Barbuda	St. Kitts	Nevis	Anguilla	Montserrat
Belize		2 VIS						
Jamaica	2 VIS		2 B11 1 707 7 DC9					
Antigua		1 707 2 B11		14 BN	21 BN 25 748	21 BN		7 BN 14 748
Barbuda			14 BN					
St. Kitts			21 BN 25 748			49 BN	7 BN	7 BN
Nevis			21 BN		49 BN		7 BN	7 BN
Anguilla					7 BN	7 BN		
Montserrat			14 748 7 BN		7 BN	7 BN		
Dominica			21 748 7 BN		7 748 7 BN	7 BN		7 748
St. Lucia			2 707 13 B11 19 748 7 BN		9 748 7 BN	7 BN		1 748
Barbados		7 707 2 B11	14 707 19 B11 6 DC8 2 V10 14 748		2 748			7 748
St. Vincent			11 748 7 BN		2 748 7 BN	7 BN		7 748
Grenada			6 B11 6 748 7 BN		7 BN	7 BN		6 748
Carriacou			7 BN		7 BN	7 BN		7 BN
Trinidad		4 DC9 7 707 2 B11	11 707 5 DC8 2 V10 15 B11 7 748					7 748
Tobago			4 B11					
Guyana		4 DC9	3 707 2 V10					

EQUIPMENT CODES:

VIS	Viscount	V10	VC10
707	Boeing	DC8	DC8
DC9	DC9	CVL	Caravelle
B11	BAC 111	727	Boeing 727
BN	Islander	CV4	Convair 440
748	Avro 748		

Dominica	St. Lucia	Barbados	St. Vincent	Grenada	Carriacou	Trinidad	Tobago	Guyana
		7 707 2 B11				7 707 2 B11 4 DC9		4 DC9
7 BN 14 748	11 B11 1 707 18 748 7 BN	17 707 5 DC8 17 B11 14 748 2 V10	11 748 7 BN	11 B11 3 748		14 707 19 B11 5 DC8 1 V10	4 B11	2 707 2 V10
7 748		7 748	7 748					
	7 748 7 BN	7 748	7 748 7 BN					
15 748 7 BN		1 707 11 B11 3 DC9 7 748	4 748 14 BN	11 B11 3 748 7 BN	7 BN	3 707 11 B11 3 DC9	4 B11	2 707
10 748	3 707 13 B11 8 748 3 DC9		18 748	11 B11 13 748		7 748 33 707 8 DC8 19 B11 3 V10 7 DC9	4 B11	7 707 3 V10
7 748 7 BN	5 748 14 BN	3 B11 18 748		6 748 14 BN	14 BN	7 748		
6 748 7 BN	6 B11 7 BN	10 B11 10 748	3 B11 6 748 14 BN		28 BN	11 B11 6 748 7 CV4	4 B11	
	7 BN		14 BN	28 BN				
7 748	3 707 13 B11 1 748 3 DC9	34 707 8 DC8 3 V10 19 B11 7 DC8 7 748	7 748	7 B11 6 748 7 CV4			4 B11 53 CV4	12 707 3 V10 2 727 5 DC9 2 CVL
	4 B11					4 B11 53 CV4		
	1 707	5 707 3 V10				12 707 3 V10 2 727 5 DC9 2 CVL		

FREQUENCY PER WEEK AND EQUIPMENT

Source: OAS North American Aug. 1, 1973
International July 1973

Table SA8.21. One-way Economy Air Passenger Fares in the CARICOM Region, 1973

(U.S. dollars)

BETWEEN	Belize	Jamaica	Antigua	Barbuda	St. Kitts	Nevis	Anguilla	Montserrat	Dominica	St. Lucia	Barbados	St. Vincent	Grenada	Carriacou	Trinidad	Tobago	Guyana
Belize		66															
Jamaica			107								144				152		161
Antigua				9	12	12	24	9	20	38	51	56	62		65	65	106
Barbuda					20	20	33	18	24	45	59	65	70		74	74	
St. Kitts						4	17	12	28	46	58	55	67		70	70	
Nevis							20	12	28	46	58	55	67		70	70	
Anguilla								24	44	62	74	82	86		87	87	
Montserrat									29	45	59	65	70		74	74	
Dominica										20	39	40	50		55	55	
St. Lucia											21	12	23		36	36	[illegible]
Barbados												21	21		32	32	65
St. Vincent													17	12	36	36	
Grenada														7	19	19	
Carriacou																	
Trinidad																6	58
Tobago																	
Guyana																	

Source: OAG North American, August 1973
International, July 1973

Table SA8.22. Intraregional Air Freight Rates, 1973

(Cost per kilo in cents)

From \ TO	BELIZE	JAMAICA	ANTIGUA	ST. KITTS	MONTSERRAT	DOMINICA	ST. LUCIA	BARBADOS	ST. VINCENT	GRENADA	TRINIDAD	GUYANA	Currency EC$ except where stated
BELIZE													
JAMAICA			51 22	50			45 25	46 27		46 27	45 24	62 40	B$ J$
ANTIGUA						13		40 32			44 34		
ST. KITTS		1.08	08		17		28						
MONTSERRAT			17										
DOMINICA			13	19			15	26	26	28			
ST. LUCIA		96	23	28		15		24 14		17			
BARBADOS		98 63	40 28	45 30	32	26 24	24 12		24	26 24	26 20	49 40	
ST. VINCENT													
GRENADA			36					26	12		24		
TRINIDAD		96 51	44 28	53 32		34 28	26 24	26 16	26 24	24 10			
GUYANA		1.46 1.12	77 65	84			60 54	54 39	54	54 52	50 35		TT$ G$

Upper Figure - General cargo for 500 kilos minimum
Lower Figure - (Where quoted) cheapest specific cargo rate

Source: Air Cargo Guide, July 1973

Table SA8.23. Extraregional Air Freight Rates, 1973

(Cost per kilo in local currency)

From	To	Exports: London	Exports: Amsterdam	Exports: New York	Exports: Montreal	Imports From: London £	Imports From: Amsterdam F	Imports From: New York US$	Imports From: Montreal C$	To
Belize	B$	2.56	2.59			.70 .57				Belize
Jamaica	J$	1.05 .37	1.08 .86	50 21	.61 .22	.55 .41	4.85 3.97	.25 .12	.30 .11	Jamaica
Antigua	EC$	2.59 .89	2.63	1.06	1.34 .51	.56 .45	4.40	.24 .12	.31 .14	Antigua
St. Kitts	EC$		2.61	.98	1.26	.56		.23	.29	St. Kitts
St. Lucia	EC$	2.59 .76		1.20 .71	1.38	.60		.28 .16	.34	St. Lucia
Barbados	EC$	2.79 .89	2.83 1.00	1.26 .47	1.54 .47	.60 .46	4.72	.29 .16	.36 .15	Barbados
Trinidad	T$	2.83 .89	2.89	1.34 .51	1.62 .55	.61 .38	4.82 4.40	.29 .21	.38 .19	Trinidad
Guyana	G$	3.46 1.27	3.50			.69 .59	5.38	.37	.44 .19	Guyana
						.44		.29 .22		Grenada
						.60				St. Vincent

Highest figure - General Cargo for 500 kilos minimum
Lowest Figure (where quoted) - Cheapest specific cargo rate

Source: Air Cargo Guide, July 1973

Table SA8.24. Basic Characteristics of Aircraft Suitable for Intraregional Operations

Aircraft	HS 748 Turbo Prop	DC 9 Jet	F 27 Turbo Prop	F 28 Jet	DHC 7 Turbo Prop	BAC 111 Jet	B 737 Jet
No. of engines	2	2	2	2	4	2	2
Capital cost new US$ (mil.)	1.6	5.2	1.6	4	n.a.	5.2	6
Seating capacity	48	125	56	79	54	119	130
Runway length Takeoff (ft.)	4050	7500	5470	5490	1800	7470	8800
Runway length Landing (ft.)	3370	4780	3290	3540	1900	4770	4660
Max. takeoff payload (lbs.)	12500	36500	12200	17547	11060	26187	33980
Cruising speed	242	465	256	451	238	457	460

Notes: Seating Capacities are not necessarily the maximum given for some variations.

Runway Takeoff lengths assume full payload and fuel.

Reduced payloads would reduce length closer to landing distance requirements.

Maximum payload assumes maximum range at cruising speed.

Cruising speed assumes most economic performance.

Source: Flight International, and Technical Publications

Table SA9.1. CARICOM: Annual Tourist Arrivals and Rates of Growth, 1968–72

	Antigua[1]	Dominica	Grenada	Montserrat[2]	St.Kitts/ Nevis	St. Lucia	St. Vincent[3]	Total LDC	Barbados	Jamaica	Trinidad Tobago	Total MDCs	CARICOM
Stop-Over Visitor Arrivals: (Number)													
1968	55838	9977	23164	6215	9797	22653	12472	140116	115695	258460	91660	465815	605931
1969	61262	8246	29627	7475	11779	25382	15569	159340	134303	276926	94510	505739	665079
1970	65369	12450	30436	8382	13472	29529	17586	177244	156417	309122	96890	562429	739673
1971	67637	14708	35626	7270	15105	33198	17407	190951	189075	359323	111330	659728	850679
1972	72328	15294	37933	11463	16245	42399	16902	212564	210430	407806	114550	732786	945350
Annual Rates of Growth of Stop-Over Visitor Arrivals, 1968 - 1972 (%):													
1968/69	9.7	neg.	27.9	20.3	20.2	12.0	24.8	13.7	16.1	7.1	4.3	8.6	9.8
1969/70	6.7	51.0	2.7	12.1	14.4	16.3	13.0	11.2	16.5	11.6	neg.	11.2	11.2
1970/71	3.5	18.1	17.0	neg.	12.1	12.4	neg.	7.7	20.9	16.2	28.1	17.3	15.0
1971/72	6.9	4.0	6.5	57.7	7.5	27.7	neg.	11.3	11.3	13.5	2.9	11.1	11.1

Notes: 1/ 1971 data have been used because of non-availability of 1972 data

2/ Includes cruise visitors

3/ Air arrivals only

Source: Multiple, but mainly Tourism Supply Study - Caribbean Region, the Shankland Cox Partnership, 1973

Table SA9.2. CARICOM: Countries of Tourist Origin, Distribution, and Growth Rates, 1968 and 1972

	Antigua[1]	Dominica	Grenada	Montserrat[2]	St.Kitts/ Nevis	St. Lucia	St. Vincent[3]	Total LDC's	Barbados	Jamaica	Trinidad & Tobago	Total MDCs	Total CARICOM
Number of Visitors - 1968:													
USA	30296	2272	9600	3484	3525	6492	2878	58547	41287	201790	33560	276637	335784
Canada	7473	630	2859	985	685	2036	1244	15912	27879	24526	9710	62115	78027
U.K.	4544	690	3610	367	455	2907	1222	13795	11493	9694	7840	29027	42822
Caribbean	11143	5910	5229	2289	4948	9289	3706	50487	26136	6001	17440	49577	148525
R.O.W.	2382	475	1866		184	1927	1137		8902	16449	23110	48461	
Number of Visitors - 1972:													
USA	30552	2719	13157	4200	4151	7756	5786	68321	75525	316191	39810	431526	499847
Canada	6958	776	5431	1279	1022	4406	1122	20994	61918	38331	12620	112869	133863
U.K.	5506	1547	4419	779	807	7158	879	21095	14851	16860	10320	43031	63126
Caribbean	21372	9695	11216	6271	9920	18388	7331	96770	39139	19067	25770	83976	242979
R.O.W.	3249		3710		345	4690	583		18916	17357	25960	62233	
Distribution of Visitor by Country of Origin 1968 (1972) - Percent:													
US	54.3(45.3)	22.8(18.4)	41.4(34.7)	48.9(33.5)	36.7(25.6)	28.7(18.3)	28.2(36.9)	42.2(33.0)	35.7(35.9)	78.1(77.5)	36.6(34.8)	59.4(56.6)	55.4(53.2)
Canada	13.4(10.3)	6.3(5.3)	12.3(14.3)	13.8(10.2)	7.0(6.3)	9.0(10.4)	12.2(7.1)	11.5(10.1)	24.1(29.4)	9.5(9.4)	10.6(11.0)	13.3(14.8)	12.9(14.2)
U.K.	8.1(8.1)	6.9(10.5)	15.6(11.6)	5.2(6.2)	4.6(5.0)	12.8(16.9)	12.0(5.6)	9.9(10.2)	9.9(7.1)	3.8(4.1)	8.6(9.0)	6.2(5.8)	7.1(6.7)
Caribbean	20.0(31.6)	59.2((65.8)	22.6(29.6)	32.1(50.1)	50.5(61.0)	41.0(43.4)	36.4(46.7)	36.4(46.7)	22.6(18.6)	2.3(4.7)	19.0(22.5)	10.6(11.0)	24.6(25.9)
R.O.W[4]	4.3(4.8)	4.8(	8.1(9.8		1.9(2.1)	8.5(11.0)	11.2(3.7		7.7(9.0)	6.3(4.3)	25.2(22.7)	10.4(8.2	
Annual Compound Growth Rates 1968 - 1972 (Percent):													
US	6.3	4.6	8.2	4.8	4.2	4.5	19.1	3.9	16.3	11.9	4.8	11.8	10.5
Canada	neg.	5.4	17.4	6.7	10.5	21.3	neg.	7.2	22.1	11.9	6.8	16.1	14.4
U.K.	6.6	22.4	5.2	20.7	15.4	25.3	neg/	11.2	6.6	14.8	7.1	9.7	10.2
Caribbean	24.2	11.0	21.0	28.7	19.0	18.6	18.6	17.7	10.6	33.5	12.6	14.0	13.1
R.O.W.[4]	11.0		18.7		17.0	24.9	neg.		20.7	1.4	3.0	6.5	
TOTAL	6.7	10.2	13.0	15.2	13.5	17.0	11.4	10.6	16.0	12.1	5.7	12.0	11.6

Notes: 1/ 1971 data have been used because of non-availability of 1972 data.

2/ Includes Cruise visitors.

3/ R.O.W. = Rest of World

Source: Multiple, but mainly Tourism Supply Study - Caribbean Region, the Shankland Cox Partnership, 1973

Table SA9.3. Tourist Arrivals by Season, 1972

	Winter (Dec. - March) Number	Winter (%)	Summer (April - Dec.) Number	Summer (%)
Antigua (1971)		40		60
Dominica	5335	36.2	9402	63.8
Grenada	16123	42.5	21810	57.5
Montserrat				
St. Kitts				
St. Lucia	17035	40.2	25363	59.8
St. Vincent	5662	36.1	10039	63.9
TOTAL LDCs				
Barbados	82805	39.4	127544	60.6
Jamaica	153889	37.7	253917	62.3
Trinidad/Tobago	40850	35.7	73700	64.3
TOTAL MDCs	277544	37.9	455161	62.1
TOTAL CARIFTA				

Source: Multiple, but mainly Tourism Supply Study - Caribbean Region, the Shankland Cox Partnership, 1973

Note: Monthly breakdowns were not available for all islands. Since the islands do not show a seasonal breakdown themselves, the Mission used monthly data for December to March for the winter season and montly data from April to November for the summer season.

Table SA9.4. Distribution of Visitor Arrivals by Quarter, Various Years

		Jan-Mar	April-Jun	July-Sept	Oct - Dec
Antigua	- 1968	33.8	19.8	23.2	23.2
	- 1971	32.2	20.8	24.3	22.7
Barbados	- 1968	27.6	21.1	25.2	26.1
	- 1971	29.8	19.3	24.2	26.7
Jamaica	- 1968	29.7	22.9	25.6	21.8
	- 1971	29.5	23.1	26.5	20.9
St. Vincent	- 1968	20.1	28.1	27.9	23.4
	- 1971	31.0	23.2	26.5	19.3
Dominica (Air)	- 1972	24.9	20.0	28.8	26.3
Grenada	- 1972	32.9	19.9	24.6	22.6
Montserrat	- 1970	32.6	19.9	21.0	26.5
St. Lucia	- 1971	25.1	22.4	25.6	26.9

Source: The Shankland Cox Partnership

Table SA9.5. Tourist Arrivals, Average Length of Stay, Bednights, Implicit Occupancy Rates, 1968 and 1972

	Tourist Arrivals 1968		Avg. Length of Stay 1968	Tourist Bednights 1968		Available Bednights 1968		Implicit Occupancy Rate % 1968	Tourist Arrivals 1972		Avg. Length of Stay 1972	Tourist Bednights 1972		Available Bednights 1972		Implicit Occupancy Rate % 1972
	No.	%		No.	%	No.	%		No.	%		No.	%	No.	%	
Antigua	55838	39.6	4	223352	32.3	696420	40.0	32.0	72328	33.9	2.5	180820	15.3	877825	26.1	20.6
Dominica	9977	7.1	4	39908	5.8	54750	3.1	72.9	14737	6.9	4	58948	5.0	165345	4.9	35.6
Grenada	23164	16.1	7	162148	23.4	273020	15.7	59.4	37933	17.8	12	455196	38.4	632910	18.8	71.9
Montserrat	7125	5.1	10	71250	10.3	123005	7.1	57.9	12529	5.9	10	125290	10.6	181040	5.4	69.2
St.Kitts-Nevis	9797	6.9	5	48985	7.1	208050	12.0	23.5	16245	7.6	5	81225	6.9	339450	10.1	23.9
St. Lucia	22653	16.1	3.5	79286	11.4	208780	12.0	38.0	42399	19.9	3.5	148396	12.5	831470	24.7	17.8
St. Vincent	12472	8.8	5.4	67349	9.7	176295	10.1	38.2	16902	7.9	8	135216	11.4	340545	10.1	39.7
TOTAL LDCs	141026	100	4.9	692278	100	1740320	100	39.8	213073	100	5.6	1185091	100	3368585	100	35.2
Barbados	115695	24.8	6	694170	19.7	1956400	30.5	35.5	210430	28.7	6.5	1367795	26.0	2837145	26.7	48.2
Jamaica	258460	55.5	9	2326140	66.0	3509840	54.7	66.3	407806	55.7	8	3262448	62.0	6524010	61.5	50.0
Trinidad/Tobago	91660	19.7	5.5	504130	14.3	951190	14.8	53.0	114550	15.6	5.5	630025	12.0	1249030	11.8	50.4
TOTAL MDCs	465815	100	7.6	3524440	100	6417430	100	54.9	732786	100	7.2	5260268	100	10610185	100	49.6
TOTAL CARICOM	606841		6.9	4216718		8157750		51.7	945859		6.8	6445359		13978770		46.1

Notes: 1. The number of tourist bednights is derived by multiplying total arrivals by average length of stay.
2. Data for average length of stay have been derived from many sources and for the smaller islands could be subject to wide margins of error.
3. Available bednights = number of beds in tourist accommodation x 365 nights.
4. The occupancy rate = tourist bednights ÷ available bednights.
5. The occupancy rate shown for Montserrat may be too high since some villa accommodation to which long-stay tourists are attracted, may have escaped inclusion in available bednights.

Source: Multiple but mainly Shankland Cox, opus. cit.

Table SA9.6. Hotel Occupancy Rates (Bed/Room Occupancy Rates) by Month, 1972

	Jan.	Feb.	Mar.	April	May	June	July	Aug.	Sept.	Oct.	Nov.	Dec.	Annual Average	Standard Deviation	Comment
Antigua	13.1	27.5	70.5	25.0	21.0	18.8	12.0	12.5	2.4	18.2	12.5	26.5	22.0	± 16.3	All hotels (beds)
Barbados	48.6	75.4	60.0	50.8	32.3	24.3	43.4	48.6	31.1	43.0	58.4	58.4	48.3	± 13.7	Hotels and guest-houses (beds)
Dominica	32.3	46.0	28.7	26.9	17.8	15.8	23.3	28.4	15.6	16.2	20.3	17.5	23.8	± 8.6	Hotels and guest-houses (beds)
Jamaica	57.5 51.1	74.0 66.2	59.7 57.1	54.2 48.5	34.9 32.3	37.1 34.4	55.3 46.1	59.0 53.3	30.2 28.9	27.4 30.9	49.5 46.2	56.3 51.0	49.2 45.3	± 11.1	All hotels (rooms) All hotels (beds)
Montserrat	7.4	24.1	43.9	46.3	25.6	11.0	9.4	30.2	11.5	8.8	6.0	7.3	19.3	± 13.9	All hotels and guest houses (beds)
St. Lucia	27.8	69.6	47.5	31.3	18.3	8.6	23.3	25.4	12.6	18.3	22.7	36.5	28.7	± 15.9	Hotels and guest-houses (beds)
Trinidad & Tobago	60.1	57.2	55.2	48.6	46.5	35.9	44.2	52.2	45.3	44.8	51.6	45.6	47.0	± 6.7	Hotels (rooms)

Source: Shankland Cox opus cit.

Table SA9.7. Comparative Supply of Tourist Accommodation

	CARIBBEAN		LDC's			CARIFTA		
	Beds Number	Growth Rate Percent	Beds Number	Market Share Percent	Growth Rate Percent	Beds Number	Market Share Percent	Growth Rate Percent
I. Hotels								
1968			3330			17179		
1969			4385		14.5	19388		12.9
1970			5512		25.7	22064		13.8
1971			6280		13.9	25047		13.5
1972	96054		7235	7.5	15.2	27691	28.8	10.6
1977 a/	113576	3.4	9543	8.4	5.7	35677	31.4	5.2
II. Guest Houses								
1968			308			1422		
1969			392		27.3	1492		4.9
1970			362		neg.	1269		neg.
1971			501		38.4	1571		23.8
1972	5843		578	9.9	15.4	1895	32.4	20.6
1977 a/	5757	neg.	627	10.9	1.6	1834	31.9	neg.
III. Cottages/ Apartments								
1968			440			3559		
1969			800		81.8	4543		27.6
1970			940		17.5	5133		13.0
1971			1131		20.3	7985		55.6
1972	24839		1416	5.7	25.2	8712	35.1	9.1
1977 a/	26360	1.2	2058	7.8	7.8	9954	37.8	2.7
IV. Total Accommodations								
1968			4578			22160		
1969			5577		21.8	25423		14.7
1970			6814		22.2	28466		12.0
1971			7912		16.1	34603		21.6
1972	126736		9229	7.3	16.6	38298	30.2	10.7
1977 a/	145693	2.8	12228	8.4	5.8	47465	32.6	4.4

Note: a/ Beds available in 1973 (or 1972) plus those under construction. The growth rate shown for 1977 is an annual average compound growth between 1973 and 1977.

Table SA9.8. Supply of Accommodation, 1968–73

(Number of beds)

		Antigua	Dominica	Grenada	Montserrat	St. Kitts	St. Lucia	St. Vincent	Total LDC's	Barbados	Jamaica	Trinidad/ Tobago	Total MDC's
1968	Hotel	1798	100	484	96	370	541	441	3830	3765	7350	(2234)a/	13349
	Guest House	110	50	100	6			42	308	378	364	(372)a/	1114
	Cottage/Apt			164	245		31		440	1217	1902		3119
	Total	1908	150	748	347	370	572	483	4578	5360	9616	(2606)a/	17582
1969	Hotel	1888	165	664	96	440	640	492	4385	4356	8413	2234	15003
	Guest House	124	50	130	14			74	392	354	374	372	1100
	Cottage/Apt			506	262		32		800	1580	2163		3743
	Total	2012	215	1300	372	440	672	566	5577	6290	10950	2606	19846
1970	Hotel	2102	180	970	116	485	1040	619	5512	3430	10760	2362	16552
	Guest House	80	50	130	26			76	362	149	406	352	907
	Cottage/Apt	80		500	280		80		940	1601	2592		4193
	Total	2262	230	1600	422	485	1120	695	6814	5180	13758	2714	21652
1971	Hotel	2062	242	1042	140	533	1620	641	6280	3768	12099	2900	18767
	Guest House	80	65	156	26	101		73	501	189	501	380	1070
	Cottage/Apt	90		550	310	101	80		1131	3485	3369		6854
	Total	2232	307	1748	476	735	1700	714	7912	7442	15969	3280	26691
1972	Hotel	2208	364	1028	140	683	2152	660	7235	4314	13120	3022	20456
	Guest House	86	67	186	26	140		73	578	430	487	400	1317
	Cottage/Apt	111	22	520	330	107	126	200	1416	3029	4267		7296
	Total	2405	453	1734	496	930	2278	933	9229	7773	17874	3422	29069
1973	Hotel	2330	382	1120	140	703	2822	748	8245	4161	13895	(3022)b/	21078
	Guest House	86	78	202	26	140		73	605	320	(487)b/	(400)b/	1207
	Cottage/Apt	111	32	526	342	187	126	(200)b/	1524	(3029)b/	(4267)b/		7296
	Total	2527	492	1848	508	1030	2948	1021	10374	7510	18649	(3422)b/	29581

NOTE: a/ estimated assuming supply is unchanged from 1969.
b/ estimated assuming supply is unchanged from 1972.

Sources: Mainly Shankland Cox opus cit.

Table SA9.9. Growth Rates of Supply by Type of Accommodation

(Percentage)

		Antigua	Dominica	Grenada	Montserrat	St.Kitts	St.Lucia	St.Vincent	Total LDC's	Barbados	Jamaica	Trinidad/ Tobago	Total MDC's
1968-69	Hotel	5.0	65.0	37.2	0	18.9		11.6	14.5	15.7	14.5	0	12.4
	Guest House	12.7	0	30.0	233.3		18.3	76.2	27.3	neg.	2.7	0	neg.
	Cottage/Apt			308.5	6.9		3.2		81.8	29.8	13.7		20.0
	Total	5.4	43.3	73.8	7.2	18.9	17.5	17.2	21.8	17.4	13.9	0	12.5
1969-70	Hotel	11.3	9.1	46.1	20.8	10.2		25.8	25.7	neg.	27.9	5.7	10.3
	Guest House	neg.	0	0	85.7		62.5	2.7	neg.	neg.	8.6	neg.	neg.
	Cottage/Apt			neg.	6.9		250.0		17.5	1.3	19.8		12.0
	Total	12.4	7.0	23.1	13.4	10.2	66.7	22.8	22.2	neg.	25.6	4.1	9.1
1970-71	Hotel	neg.	34.4	7.4	20.7	9.9		3.6	13.9	9.8	12.4	22.8	13.4
	Guest House	0	30.0	20.0	0		55.8	neg.	38.4	26.8	23.4	8.0	18.0
	Cottage/Apt	12.5		10.0	10.7		0		20.3	217.7	30.0		63.5
	Total	neg.	33.5	9.2	12.8	51.5	51.8	2.7	16.1	43.7	16.1	20.8	23.3
1971-72	Hotel	7.1	50.4	neg.	0	28.1		3.0	15.2	14.5	8.4	4.2	9.0
	Guest House	7.5	3.1	19.2	0	38.6	32.8	0	15.4	27.5	neg.	5.3	23.1
	Cottage/Apt	23.3		neg.	6.4	5.9	57.5		25.2	neg.	26.6		6.4
	Total	7.8	47.6	neg.	4.2	26.5	34.0	30.7	16.6	4.4	11.9	4.3	8.9
1972-73	Hotel	5.5	4.9	8.9	0	2.9		13.3	14.0	neg.	5.9	0	3.0
	Guest House	0	16.4	8.6	0	0	31.1	0	4.7	neg.	0	0	neg.
	Cottage/Apt	0	45.4	1.2	3.6	74.8	0	0	7.6	0	0		0
	Total	5.1	8.6	6.6	2.4	10.8	29.4	9.4	12.4	neg.	4.3	0	1.8
1968-73	Hotel	5.3	30.7	18.3	7.8	13.7		11.1	16.6	2.0	13.6	6.2	9.6
	Guest House	neg.	9.3	15.1	34.2		39.1	11.9	14.5	neg.	6.0	1.4	1.6
	Cottage/Apt			26.2	6.9		32.4		28.2	24.4	17.5		18.5
		5.8	26.8	19.8	7.9	22.7	38.8	16.1	17.8	6.7	14.2	5.6	11.0

Note: Growth rates for 1968-73 are average annual compound rates.

ırce: Calculated from Table 8.

Table SA9.10. Standard Return Air Fares and per Diem Expenses, Selected Destinations, 1974

Destination	US $ Return Air Fare from Washington	Per Diem[1/] US $
Bahamas	210	50
Barbados	420	45
Bermuda	190	45
Colombia	480	40
Dominican Republic	270	40
French W.I.	370	35
Haiti	320	35
Hawaii	480	55
Jamaica	320	45
Mexico	310	45
Neth.Antilles	380	45
Trinidad & Tobago	450	45
Venezuela	460	50
Greece	880	55
France	590	65
Italy	700	60
Portugal	560	40
Spain	590	45
Switzerland	620	60
U.K.	560	55
Yugoslavia	760	35
Fiji	1350	35
India	1570	45
Kenya	1350	50
Morocco	600	45

1/ Per diem expenses include hotels (generally first class), meals, gratuities, valet, transportation, baggage handling, airport tax, communications and other miscellaneous costs.

Source: IBRD

Table SA9.11. Comparative Price Levels, Sunflight Tours, 1973–74

Destination from Toronto	No. of Weeks	Type of Accommodation	Type of Rate	Price US$ Dec.16-Apr.14	Price US$ Oct.14-Dec.9
Bahamas					
Freeport	one	Holiday Inn	EP	239	209
	two	"	"	329	269
	two	Studio Apts.	"	249-259-	239-
	one	"	"	199	187
Nassau	one	Holiday Inn	"	269	219
Barbados	two	1-bed.Apts.	"	399	317
	two	Studio Apts.	"	409-419-	3[illegible]9-
	one	Holiday Inn	CP	439	
Curacao & Caracas	one	"	EP	469	
	each	"			
Grenada	one	"	EP	349-379	
Guadeloupe	one	Hotel	"	409-509	
	two	"	"	569-729	
Haiti	one	"	CP	319-339	299-309
	two	"	MAP	519-599	459-519
Honolulu	two	Holiday Inn	EP	499	479
	8 days	Hotel	"	409	399
Jamaica					
Montego Bay	one	Holiday Inn	EP	299	269
	two	"	"	419	339
	two	Apartments	"	399-	299-
Ochos Rios	one	"	"	279	249
	two	"	"	389-	299-
	one	Playboy	"	309	
Martinique	one	Hotel	"	392-489	
Mexico					
Acapulco	one	Holiday Inn	"	320	
Cozumel	one	Hotel	MAP	339	
Miami	one	"	EP	199-259	172-219
	two	"	"	339-369	239-289
St. Lucia	one	Holiday Inn	"	329-349	
	two	Hotel	"	389-449	
San Juan	one	Holiday Inn	"	279-299	
Spain					
Canary Islands	one	1-bed.Apts.	"	367	
	two	Studio Apts.	"	437-	417-
	one	Hotel	CP	407	
	two	"	"	517	477
Costa del Sol	one	Holiday Inn	EP	347	347
	two	"	"	417-437	
	two	Efficiency Apts.	CP	437-457	

Note: In all cases prices are for double occupancy for a twin-bedded room. Surcharges are payable on certain dates in the peak period for some destinations. The prices quoted may be on offer only during part of or on certain dates within the Dec.16-Apr.14 and Oct.14-Dec.9 periods.

Abbreviations: EP = Room only - no meals, CP = Room and breakfast (may be either full or Continental), MAP = Modified American Plan: Hotel room rate includes breakfast and dinner, AP = Room and breakfast, lunch and dinner.

Table SA9.12. Comparative Prices in Tourist Accommodation, 1973

(U.S. dollars)

Country	Season	HOTELS High	HOTELS Low	GUEST HOUSES High	GUEST HOUSES Low	COTTAGES/APTS. High	COTTAGES/APTS. Low
Antigua	S	MAP 43 S 55 D	MAP 12 S 20 D	EP 6 S a) 12 D	EP 6 S a) 10 D	EP 17 S 21 D b)	
	W	MAP 84 S 98 D	MAP 16 S 27 D			EP 28 S 33 D	
Dominica	S	MAP 20 S 30 D	MAP 9 S 18 D	MAP 12 S a) 22 D		EP 80 - 100/WK b) (2-3 R)	
	W	MAP 40 S 60 D	MAP 9 S 18 D	MAP 14 S a) 25 D	MAP 12 S a) 22 D		
Grenada	S	MAP 48 S 60 D	MAP 10.25 S 22 D	MAP 14 S 26 D	MAP 6 S 11 D	n/a	EP 60/WK 2 R
	W	MAP 84 S 94 D	MAP 11 S 22 D	MAP 17.95 S 30.75 D	MAP 6 S 11 D	EP 260/WK 1 R	EP 68/WK 1R 75/WK
Montserrat	S	MAP 20 S 30 D	MAP 12 S 18 D	AP 18 S a) 30 D		EP 60/WK S 75/WK D b)	EP 60/WK S 75/WK D
	W	MAP 38 S 52 D	MAP 16 S 26 D	AP 30 S a) 43 D		EP 100/WK S 125/WK D b)	100/WK S 125/WK D b)
St. Kitts	S	AP 40 S 70 D	AP 11 S 22 D	AP 20.50 S 30.75 D	EP 5 S 10 D	EP 200/WK 3R	EP 60/WK 1R
	W	MAP 54 S AP 80 D	AP 11 S 20 D		EP 5 S 10 D	EP 310/WK 3R	EP 90/WK 1R
St. Lucia	S	MAP 34 S 50 D	MAP 12 S 22 D	MAP 10.25 S 20.50 D	MAP 5.25 S 10.50 D	EP 20 2R b)	EP 12 Studio b)
	W	MAP 60 S 90 D	AP 12 S 24 D	MAP 8 S a) 17 D		EP 44 2R	EP 25 Studio
St. Vincent	S	AP 40 S 65 D	AP 7 S 12.50 D	MAP 14 S c) 26 D	MAP 9 S c) 16 D	EP 75/WK 2P	EP 63/WK 1R
	W	AP 80 S 110 D	AP 8 S 12.50 D			EP 150/WK 2P	EP 105/WK 1R
LDCs	S	MAP 48 S AP 70 D	AP 7 S 12.50 D	AP 20.50 S 30.75 D	MAP 5.25 S 10.50 D		
	W	MAP 84 S 98 D AP110 D	AP 8 S 12.50 D		MAP 6 S 11 D		
Barbados	S	MAP 42 S 61 D	MAP 8.50 S 15 D	MAP 15 S 34 D	MAP 7 S 15 D	EP 165/WK 1R 220/WK 2R	EP 60/WK 1R 100/WK 2R
	W	MAP 90 S 115 D	MAP 18 S 28 D	MAP 31 S 45 D	AP 9 S 18 D	EP 290/WK 1R 595/WK 2R	EP 92/WK 1R 140/WK 2R
Jamaica	S	MAP 69 S 79 D	EP 8 S 13 D	MAP 12.50 S EP 18 D	EP 4.40/P	EP 210/WK 1R 280/WK 2R	EP 100/WK 2R
	W	AP 117 S 150 D	EP 10 S 15.50 D	MAP 25 S 36 D	EP 5.50/P	EP 455/WK 1R 525/WK 2R	EP 175/WK 2R
Trinidad & Tobago	S	MAP 40 S 56 D	MAP 6.50 S 10.50 D	EP 12 S 20 D	EP 2.80 S 4.50 D	EP 200/WK 1R b)	
	W	MAP 60 S 84 D		EP 16 S 30 D			
MDCs	S	MAP 69 S 79 D	MAP 6.50 S 10.50 D	MAP 15 S 34 D	EP 2.80 S 4.50 D		
	W	AP 117 S 150 D		MAP 31 S 45 D			

Source: Official Hotel & Resort Guide (Nov. 1973)

Notes: a) based on 1 guest house
b) " " 1 cottage/apt.complex
c) " " 2 guest houses

Notes: P = Person
R = Room
WK = Week

Table SA9.13. Comparative Hotel Prices, Holiday Inns and Hilton Hotels

Note: These may not be the exact dates for each island & hotel		Holiday Inn a)				Holiday Inn b)				Holiday Inn c)				Hilton Hotel a)				Hilton Hotel b)				Hilton Hotel c)			
		4-15-72- 12-14-72		12-15-72- 4-14-73		4-15-73- 12-14-73		12-15-73- 4-14-73		April 15- Dec. 14		Dec. 15- April 15		4-15-72- 12-14-72		12-15-73- 4-14-73		4-15-73- 12-14-73		12-15-72- 4-14-73		April 15- Dec. 14		Dec. 15- April 14	
		S	D	S	D	S	D	S	D	S	D	S	D	S	D	S	D	S	D	S	D	S	D	S	D
Antigua	MAP	25	40	48	68	29	46	50	64	33	52	54	68												
	EP	15	20	41	51	17	22	38	40	21	28	42	44												
Dominica	MAP																								
	EP																								
Grenada	MAP	25	40	49	66	27	42	48	60	31-37	49-56	50-58	64-72												
	EP	15	20	39	46	17	22	38	40	19-25	25-32	38-46	40-48												
Montserrat	MAP																								
	EP																								
St.Kitts-Nevis	MAP									31	49	54	68												
	EP									19	25	42	44												
St. Lucia	MAP	25	40	49	66	27	42	48	60	30	47	49	62												
	EP	15	20	39	46	17	22	38	40	19	25	38	40												
St. Vincent	MAP																								
	EP																								
Jamaica	MAP	31-41	37-47							32.5-42.5	51-61	54.5-62.5	73-81							55-70	60-80	35-45	48-58	58-78	68-83
	EP	20-30	26-36					34-42	48-56	20-30	26-36	42-50	48-56	30-40	40-50							25-35	28-38	43-68	48-68
Barbados	MAP	27	42	53	71	29	46	55	75	36-41	57-62	60-72	80-92									36-42	57-61	68-78	87-97
	EP	17	22	43	51	17	22	43	51	24-29	33-38	48-60	56-68									23-27	31-35	55-65	61-71
Trinidad/Tobago	MAP													56	88	60-88	92-120					36-46	53-63		
	EP													36	48	40-68	52-80					24-34	29-39		

Sources: a) Caribbean Vacation Planner, 9th edition
b) Caribbean Vacation Planner, 10th edition
c) Official Hotel & Resort Guide, Published Nov. 73

Table SA9.14. Additions to Supply by Category to 1977

Category of Accommodation	Antigua	Dominica	Grenada	Montserrat	St.Kitts/ Nevis	St.Lucia	St.Vincent	Total LDCs	Barbados	Jamaica	Trinidad/ Tobago	Total MDCs	Total CARICOM
Hotel	3182	398	1142	140	723	2822	1136	9543	4361	18175	3598	26134	35677
Guesthouse	86	84	202	26	140		89	627	320	(487)+	(400)+	1207	1834
Cottage/Apt.	199	40	804	342	267	206	(200)+	2058	(3629)+	(4267)+		7896	9954
TOTAL	3467	522	2148	508	1127	3028	1425	12228	8310	22929	3998	35237	47465
Absolute Percent Increases in Accommodation 1972 - 1977													
Hotel	36.6	4.2	2.0	0	2.4	0	51.9	15.7	4.8	30.8	19.1	24.0	21.7
Guesthouse	0	7.7	0	0	0		21.9	3.6	0	0	0	0	0.1
Cottage/Apt.	79.3	25.0	52.8	0	42.8	63.5	0	35.0	19.8	0		8.2	12.9
TOTAL	37.2	6.1	16.2	0	9.4	2.7	39.6	17.8	10.6	23.0	16.8	19.1	18.8

Note: The data refer only to accommodation under construction and not to additional accommodation that might be at the planning stage.

Source: Shankland Cox, opus cit.

Table SA9.15. Projection of Tourist Arrivals, Bednights, and Implicit Occupancy Rate, 1972–77

A. LDC FORECAST

	Arrivals: Compound Growth Rate 1972-1977 Percent	Arrivals: Numbers 1977	Share in Total LDC Arrivals Percent	Average Length of Stay 1972 Nights	Tourist Bednights: Number 1977	Tourist Bednights: Share in Total LDC Bednights 1977 Percent	Available Bednights Number 1977	Share in Total LDC Available Bednights Percent	Implicit Occupancy Rates 1977 Supply Percent
Antigua	6.5	99089	23.3	2.5	247722	11.7	1265455	28.6	19.6
Dominica	10.0	23729	5.6	4.0	94916	4.5	190530	4.3	49.8
Grenada	6.5	51792	12.2	12.0	623664	29.3	784020	17.7	79.5
Montserrat	6.5	17166	4.0	10.0	171660	8.1	185420	4.2	92.6
St. Kitts-Nevis	15.0	32675	7.7	5.0	163375	7.7	375950	8.5	43.4
St.Lucia	32.5	173178	40.7	3.5	606123	28.5	1105220	25.0	54.8
St.Vincent	10.0	27221	6.4	8.0	217765	10.2	520125	11.7	41.9
TOTAL LDCs		425030	100.0		2125225	100.0	4426720	100.0	48.0

B. MDC and CARICOM - LOW FORECAST

	Arrivals: Compound Growth Rate 1972-1977 Percent	Arrivals: Numbers 1977	Share in Total MDC Arrivals Percent	Average Length of Stay Nights	Tourist Bednights: Number 1977	Tourist Bednights: Share in Total MDC Bednights 1977 Percent	Available Bednights Number 1977	Share in Total MDC Available Bednights Percent	Implicit Occupancy Rates 1977 Supply Percent
Barbados	4.0	256020	25.5	6.5	1664130	22.9	3033150	23.6	54.9
Jamaica	8.0	599198	59.6	8.0	4793584	65.8	8369085	65.1	57.3
Trinidad & Tobago	5.5	149711	14.9	5.5	823410	11.3	1459270	11.3	56.4
TOTAL MDCs		1004929	100.0		7281124	100.0	12861505	100.0	56.6
TOTAL CARICOM		1429959			9406349		17288225		54.4

C. MDC and CARICOM - HIGH FORECAST

Barbados	8.5	316413	28.2	6.5	2056685	25.3	3033150	23.6	67.8
Jamaica	10.0	656775	58.5	8.0	5254200	64.6	8369085	65.1	62.8
Trinidad & Tobago	5.5	149711	13.3	5.5	823410	10.1	1459270	11.3	56.4
TOTAL MDCs		1122899	100.0		8134295	100.0	12861505	100.0	63.2
TOTAL CARICOM		1547929			10259520		17288225		59.3

Table SA9.16. Projection of Tourism Revenues, 1977

	Tourist Arrivals in 1972	Avg. length of stay in 1972	Annual compound growth of bednights, 1972-1977	Tourist Bednights in 1977	LOW VALUE: Average Daily Expenditure in 1972	LOW VALUE: Tourism Revenues in 1972 (U.S. $ millions)	LOW VALUE: Tourism Revenues in 1977 (1972 prices) (U.S. $ millions)	HIGH VALUE: Average Daily Expenditure in 1972	HIGH VALUE: Tourism Revenues in 1977 (1972 prices) (U.S. $ millions)
	(number)	(nights)	(%)	(number)	($)			($)	
	(1)	(2)	(3)	(4)	(5)	(6)	(7)	(8)	(9)
Antigua	72328	2.5	6.5	247722	25	4.520	6.193	30	7.432
Dominica	14737	4	10	94916	20	1.179	1.898	25	2.373
Grenada	37933	12	6.5	623664	25	11.380	15.592	30	18.710
Montserrat	12529	10	6.5	171660	25	3.132	4.292	30	5.150
St. Kitts-Nevis	16245	5	15	163375	25	2.031	4.084	30	4.901
St. Lucia	42399	3.5	32.5	606123	30	4.452	18.184	35	21.214
St. Vincent	16902	8	10	217765	30	4.056	6.533	35	7.622
LDC TOTAL	213073			2125225		30.750	56.776		67.402
Barbados	210430	6.5	4	1664130	30	41.034	49.924	35	58.245
			(8.5)	(2056685)			(61.701)		(71.984)
Jamaica	407806	8	8	4793584	30	97.873	143.808	35	167.775
			(10)	(5254200)			(157.626)		(183.897)
Trinidad/Tobago	114550	5.5	5.5	823410	25	15.751	20.585	30	24.702
			(5.5)	(823410)			(20.585)		(24.702)
MDC TOTAL	732786			7281124		154.658	214.317		250.722
				(8134295)			(239.912)		(280.583)
TOTAL CAR/COM	945859			9406349		185.408	271.093		318.124
				(10259520)			(296.688)		(347.985)

Notes:
(1) Source: Shankland/Cox - opus cit. and Island sources.
(2) Source: Shankland/Cox and others.
(3) Source: As analyzed in this report.
(4) Col. (1) x Col. (2) x Col. (3).
(5) Imputed to each island according to known price differentials, supply, misc. etc.
(6) Island calculations where available, otherwise Col.(4) x Col. (5).
(7) Col. (4) x Col. (5).
(8) Imputed to each island according to known price differentials, supply, misc. etc.
(9) Col. (4) x Col. (8).

Table SA9.17a. Projections of Cruise Revenues for LDCs under Various Assumptions, 1977

	Cruise passengers "Mean" 1968-72	Cruise passengers "Actual" 1972	Avg. daily[1/] expenditure 1972 US $	Total cruise revenues '72 "Mean"	Total cruise revenues '72 "Actual"	Annual rate[2/] of growth 1972-77 (A)%	Annual rate of growth 1972-77 (B)%	Total cruise revenues 1977 "Mean" (A)	Total cruise revenues 1977 "Actual" (A)	Total cruise revenues 1977 "Mean" (B)	Total cruise revenues 1977 "Actual" (B)	Annual rate[2/] of growth 1972 - 77 (C)%	Total cruise revenue 1977 "Mean" (C)	Total cruise revenue 1977 "Actual" (C)
St. Lucia	36,953	37,267	10	369,530	372,670	10	12.8	545,132	599,528	674,392	680,123	18	845,396	852,580
Dominica	1,500[1/]	1,500[1/]	10	15,000	15,000	10	12.8	24,158	24,158	27,375	27,375	18	34,316	34,316
Grenada	49,918	94,060	10	499,180	940,060	10	12.8	803,934	1513,976	911,003	1715,610	18	1,142,004	2,150,632
Montserrat	1,215	1,066	10	12,150	10,660	10	12.8	19,568	17,168	22,174	19,454	18	27,796	24,388
St. Vincent	14,597	11,418	10	145,970	114,180	10	12.8	235,086	183,888	266,395	208,378	18	333,944	261,216
St. Kitts	5,191	4,672	10	51,910	46,720	10	12.8	83,602	75,243	94,740	85,264	18	118,758	106,884
Antigua	31,628	63,784	10	316,280	637,840	10	12.8	509,372	1027,247	577,211	1164,058	18	723,573	1,459,225
LDC Total	141,002	213,768		1,410,020	2,137,680			2,270,852	3441,208	2573,290	3900,262		3,225,787	4,889,241
St. Lucia	36,953	37,267	20	739,060	745,340	10	12.8	1190,264	1220,378	1348,784	1360,246	18	1,690,791	1,705,159
Dominica	1,500[1/]	1,500	20	30,000	30,000	10	12.8	48,315	48,315	54,750	54,750	18	68,633	68,633
Grenada	49,918	94,060	20	998,360	1,881,200	10	12.8	1607,869	3029,691	1822,007	3433,190	18	2,284,008	4,303,734
Montserrat	1,215	1,066	20	24,300	21,320	10	12.8	39,135	34,336	44,348	38,909	18	55,593	48,775
St.Vincent	14,597	11,418	20	291,940	228,360	10	12.8	470,172	367,776	532,790	416,757	18	667,889	522,433
St. Kitts	5,191	4,672	20	103,820	93,440	10	12.8	167,203	150,486	189,472	170,528	18	237,515	213,768
Antigua	31,628	63,784	20	632,560	1,275,680	10	12.8	1018,744	2054,495	1154,422	2328,116	18	1,447,145	2,918,427
LDC Total	141,002	213,768		2,820,040	4,275,360			4,541,702	6885,477	5146,573	7802,496		6,451,574	9,780,929

Notes: 1/ Arbitrary estimates - high and low
2/ 10% growth under assumption A is an arbitrary estimate; 12.8% growth under assumption B is the annual rate of growth of cruise passengers for 1968-1972; 18% is assumed to be the maximum feasible growth rate.

Sources: Basic data: Shankland Cox opus cit. and Island sources.

Table SA9.17b. Projections of Cruise Revenues for MDCs under Various Assumptions, 1977

	Cruise Passengers "Mean" 68-72	Cruise Passengers "Actual" 1972	Avg. daily expenditure 1972 US $	Total cruise revenues '72 "Mean"	Total cruise revenues '72 "Actual"	Annual Rate of Growth (compound) 1972 - 1977 (A)	(B)%	(C)%	(A) Total Cruise Revenues 1977 "Mean"	(A) Total Cruise Revenues 1977 "Actual"	(B) Total Cruise Revenues 1977 "Mean"	(B) Total Cruise Revenues 1977 "Actual"	(C) Total Cruise Revenues 1977 "Mean"	(C) Total Cruise Revenues 1977 "Actual"
Barbados	83,085	100,086	10	830,850	1,000,860	No Growth	7.1a/	10	830,850	1,000,860	1,170,759	1,410,322	1,338,092	1,611,895
Jamaica	83,092	71,450	10	830,920	714,500		6.4b/	10	830,920	714,500	1,133,092	974,335	1,338,204	1,150,709
Trinidad/ Tobago	81,444	66,390	10	814,440	663,900		7.8b/	10	814,440	663,900	1,185,637	966,486	1,311,663	1,069,218
MDC Total	247,621	237,926		2,476,210	2,379,260	No Growth			2,476,210	2,379,260	3,489,488	3,351,143	3,987,959	3,831,822
Barbados	83,085	100,086	20	1,661,700	2,001,720		7.1a/	10	1,661,700	2,001,720	2,341,518	2,820,644	2,676,184	3,223,790
Jamaica	83,092	71,450	20	1,661,840	1,429,000		6.4b/	10	1,661,840	1,429,000	2,266,184	1,948,670	2,676,410	2,301,419
Trinidad/ Tobago	81,444	66,390	20	1,628,880	1,327,800		7.8b/	10	1,638,880	1,327,800	2,371,275	1,932,972	2,623,328	2,138,435
MDC Total	247,621	237,926		4,952,420	4,758,520				4,952,420	4,758,520	6,978,977	6,702,286	7,975,922	7,663,644

NOTES: a/ Actual 1968-72 Growth Rate
b/ Implicit growth rates needed to achieve peak 1969 cruise arrivals
c/ Column C is considered to be the maximum feasible growth rate, given the present volume of cruise traffic

Sources: Basic data from Shankland Cox opus cit. and island sources.

Table SA9.18a. Tourism and Cruise Revenues: Projections for LDCs, 1977

(Million US$)	Tourism Revenues HIGH	Tourism Revenues LOW	Cruise Revenues I HIGH	Cruise Revenues I LOW	Total Revenues I HIGH	Total Revenues I LOW	Total Revenues I AVG.	Cruise Revenues II HIGH	Cruise Revenues II LOW	Total Revenues II HIGH	Total Revenues II LOW	Total Revenues II AVG.
A. Assuming 10% growth rate for cruise visitors:												
St. Lucia	21.214	18.184	0.600	0.595	21.814	18.779	20.296	1.200	1.190	22.414	19.374	20.894
Dominica	2.373	1.898	0.024	0.024	2.397	1.922	2.160	0.048	0.0 48	2.421	1.946	2.184
Grenada	18.710	15.592	1.514	0.804	20.224	16.396	18.310	3.030	1.608	21.740	17.200	19.470
Montserrat	5.150	4.292	0.020	0.017	5.170	4.309	4.740	0.039	0.034	5.189	4.326	4.758
St. Vincent	7.622	6.533	0.235	0.184	7.857	6.717	7.287	0.470	0.368	8.092	6.901	7.496
St. Kitts-Nevis	4.901	4.084	0.084	0.075	4.985	4.159	4.572	0.167	0.150	5.068	4.234	4.651
Antigua	7.432	6.193	1.027	0.509	8.459	6.702	7.580	2.054	1.019	9.486	7.212	8.349
TOTAL	67.402	56.776	3.504	2.208	70.906	58.984	64.945	7.008	4.417	74.410	61.193	67.802
B. Assuming 12.8% growth rate for cruise visitors:												
St. Lucia	21.214	18.184	0.680	0.674	21.894	18.858	20.376	1.360	1.349	22.574	19.533	21.054
Dominica	2.373	1.898	0.027	0.027	2.400	1.925	2.162	0.055	0.055	2.428	1.953	2.190
Grenada	18.710	15.592	1.716	0.911	20.426	16.503	18.464	3.433	1.822	22.143	17.414	19.778
Montserrat	5.150	4.292	0.022	0.019	5.172	4.311	4.742	0.044	0.039	5.194	4.331	4.762
St. Vincent	7.622	6.533	0.266	0.208	7.888	6.741	7.314	0.533	0.417	8.155	6.950	7.552
St. Kitts-Nevis	4.901	4.084	0.095	0.085	4.996	4.169	4.582	0.189	0.171	5.090	4.255	4.672
Antigua	7.432	6.193	1.164	0.577	8.596	6.770	7.683	2.328	1.154	9.760	7.347	8.554
TOTAL	67.402	56.776	3.970	2.501	71.372	59.277	65.323	7.942	5.007	75.344	61.783	68.562
C. Assuming 18% growth rate for cruise visitors:												
St. Lucia	21.214	18.184	0.853	0.845	22.067	18.993	20.530	1.705	1.691	22.919	19.875	21.397
Dominica	2.373	1.898	0.034	0.034	2.407	1.932	2.170	0.069	0.069	2.442	1.967	2.204
Grenada	18.710	15.592	2.151	1.142	20.861	16.734	18.798	4.304	2.284	23.014	17.876	20.445
Montserrat	5.150	4.292	0.028	0.024	5.178	4.316	4.747	0.056	0.049	5.206	4.341	4.774
St. Vincent	7.622	6.533	0.334	0.261	7.956	6.794	7.375	0.668	0.522	8.290	7.055	7.672
St. Kitts-Nevis	4.901	4.084	0.118	0.107	5.019	4.191	4.605	0.238	0.214	5.139	4.298	4.718
Antigua	7.432	6.193	1.459	0.724	8.891	6.917	7.904	2.918	1.447	10.350	7.640	8.995
TOTAL	67.402	56.776	4.977	3.137	72.379	59.877	66.129	9.580	6.276	77.360	63.052	70.205

Notes: i) The "HIGH" ("LOW") values are the higher (lower) of the values computed for cruise revenues using the "mean" and "actual" visitors in 1972 as base.
ii) Assumption I is based on an average expenditure of US$10 per cruise visitor.
iii) Assumption II is based on an average expenditure of US$20 per cruise visitor.

Source: Previous tables.

Table SA9.18b. Tourism and Cruise Revenues: Projections for LDCs, MDCs, and CARICOM, 1977

(US $ million)	Tourism Revenues High[b]	Tourism Revenues Low[b]	Cruise Revenues I High[a]	Cruise Revenues I Low[a]	Total Revenues I High	Total Revenues I Low	Total Revenues I Average	Cruise Revenues II High[a]	Cruise Revenues II Low[a]	Total Revenues II High	Total Revenues II Low	Total Revenues II Average
A. Assuming 10% growth in cruise arrivals for LDCs and no growth for MDCs:												
Barbados	71.984	49.924	1.001	0.831	72.985	50.755	61.870	2.002	1.662	73.986	51.586	62.786
Jamaica	183.897	143.808	0.831	0.714	184.728	144.522	164.625	1.662	1.429	185.559	145.237	165.398
Trinidad/ Tobago	24.702	20.585	0.814	0.664	25.516	21.249	23.382	1.629	1.328	26.331	21.913	24.122
TOTAL MDCs	280.583	214.317	2.646	2.209	283.229	216.526	249.877	5.293	4.419	285.876	218.736	252.306
TOTAL LDCs	67.402	56.776	3.504	2.208	70.906	58.984	64.945	7.008	4.417	74.410	61.193	67.802
" CARICOM	347.985	271.093	6.150	4.417	354.135	275.510	314.822	12.301	8.836	360.286	279.929	320.108
B. Assuming 12.8% growth in cruise arrivals for LDCs and "implicit" growth for MDCs:												
Barbados	71.984	49.924	1.410	1.171	73.394	51.095	62.244	2.821	2.342	74.805	52.266	63.535
Jamaica	183.897	143.808	1.133	0.974	185.030	144.782	164.906	2.266	1.949	186.163	145.757	165.960
Trinidad/ Tobago	24.702	20.585	1.186	0.966	25.888	21.551	23.720	2.371	1.933	27.073	22.518	24.796
TOTAL MDCs	280.583	214.317	3.729	3.111	284.312	217.428	250.870	7.458	6.224	288.041	220.541	254.291
TOTAL LDCs	67.402	56.776	3.970	2.501	71.372	59.277	65.324	7.942	5.007	75.344	61.783	68.562
" CARICOM	347.985	271.093	7.699	5.612	355.684	276.705	316.194	15.400	11.231	363.385	282.324	322.854
C Assuming 18% growth in cruise arrivals for LDCs and 10% growth for MDCs:												
Barbados	71.984	49.929	1.612	1.338	73.596	51.267	62.432	3.224	2.676	75.208	52.605	63.906
Jamaica	183.897	143.808	1.338	1.151	185.235	144.959	165.097	2.676	2.301	186.573	146.109	166.341
Trinidad/ Tobago	24.702	20.585	1.312	1.069	26.012	21.654	23.833	2.623	2.138	27.325	22.723	25.024
TOTAL MDCs	280.583	214.317	4.262	3.558	284.843	217.880	251.362	8.523	7.115	289.106	221.437	255.271
TOTAL LDCs	67.402	56.776	4.977	3.137	72.379	59.877	66.129	9.580	6.276	77.360	63.052	70.205
" CARICOM	347.985	271.093	9.239	6.695	357.222	277.757	317.491	18.103	13.391	366.466	284.489	325.477

Notes: i) the High (Low) values are the higher (lower) of the values computed for tourism revenues and for cruise revenues.
ii) Assumption I is based on an average expenditure of US$ 10 per cruise visitor.
iii) Assumption II is based on an average expenditure of US$20 per cruise visitor.

Source: Previous tables

Table SA9.19. Number of Rooms under Construction and Current Investment in Hotels, Guesthouses, and Cottages/Apartments to 1977

(Investment in thousands of U.S. dollars)

	Hotel	Guest House	Cottage/Apt.	Total
Antigua	426 rooms $ 8,520	- rooms $ -	44 rooms $ 440	470 rooms $ 8,960
Dominica	8 rooms $ 160	3 rooms $ 15	4 rooms $ 40	15 rooms $ 215
Grenada	11 rooms $ 220	- rooms $ -	139 rooms $1,390	150 rooms $ 1,610
Montserrat	- rooms $ -	- rooms $ -	- rooms $ -	- rooms $ -
St. Kitts	10 rooms $ 200	- rooms $ -	40 rooms $ 400	50 rooms $ 600
St. Lucia	- rooms $ -	- rooms $ -	40 rooms $ 400	40 rooms $ 400
St. Vincent	194 rooms $ 3,880	8 rooms $ 40	- rooms $ -	202 rooms $ 3,920
Total LDCs	649 rooms $12,780	11 rooms $ 55	267 rooms $2,670	927 rooms $15,505
Barbados	100 rooms $ 2,000	- rooms $ -	300 rooms $3,000	400 rooms $ 5,000
Jamaica	2,140 rooms $42,800	- rooms $ -	- rooms $ -	2,140 rooms $42,800
Trinidad/Tobago	288 rooms $ 5,760	- rooms $ -	- rooms $ -	288 rooms $ 5,760
Total MDCs	2,528 rooms $50,560	- rooms $ -	300 rooms $3,000	2,828 rooms $53,560
Total CARICOM	3,177 rooms $63,340	11 rooms $ 55	567 rooms $5,670	3,755 rooms $69,065

Note: Total investment is estimated by assuming the following average costs per room currently under construction:

Hotel	-	$ 20,000
Guest House	-	$ 5,000
Cottage/Apt.	-	$ 10,000

Source: Rooms - Shankland Cox, opus cit.
Investment - comparative Caribbean experience.

Table SA9.20. Direct Employment from Increases in Tourist Accommodation to 1977

(Number of rooms and of employees)

	Hotel	Guest House	Cottage/Apt.	Total
Antigua	426 rooms 426 empl.	- rooms - empl.	44 rooms 22 empl.	470 rooms 448 empl.
Dominica	8 rooms 8 empl.	3 rooms 2 empl.	4 rooms 2 empl.	15 rooms 12 empl.
Grenada	11 rooms 11 empl.	- rooms - empl.	139 rooms 70 empl.	150 rooms 81 empl.
Montserrat	- rooms - empl.	- rooms - empl.	- rooms - empl.	- rooms - empl.
St. Kitts	10 rooms 10 empl.	- rooms - empl.	40 rooms 20 empl.	50 rooms 30 empl.
St. Lucia	- rooms - empl.	- rooms - empl.	40 rooms 20 empl.	40 rooms 20 empl.
St. Vincent	194 rooms 194 empl.	8 rooms 4 empl.	- rooms - empl.	202 rooms 198 empl.
Total LDCs	649 rooms 649 empl.	11 rooms 6 empl.	267 rooms 134 empl.	927 rooms 789 empl.
Barbados	100 rooms 100 empl.	- rooms - empl.	300 rooms 150 empl.	400 rooms 250 empl.
Jamaica	2,140 rooms 2,140 empl.	- rooms - empl.	- rooms - empl.	2,140 rooms 2,140 empl.
Trinidad/Tobago	288 rooms 288 empl.	- rooms - empl.	- rooms - empl.	288 rooms 288 empl.
Total MDCs	2,528 rooms 2,528 empl.	- rooms - empl.	300 rooms 150 empl.	2,828 rooms 2,678 empl.
Total CARICOM	3,177 rooms 3,177 empl.	11 rooms 6 empl.	567 rooms 284 empl.	3,755 rooms 3,467 empl.

Note: (i) It is assumed that the following employee per room ratio will apply: hotel - 1:1; guest house - 0.5:1; cottage/apt. - 0.5:1.

(ii) Only existing rooms and those under construction in 1973 are included.

Source: Shankland Cox, opus cit., and comparative Caribbean experience.

Table SA9.21. Physical Size of CARICOM Islands

Island	Max.Length miles	Max.Width miles	Area sq.miles
Jamaica	144	49	
Dominica	29	16	290
St.Lucia	27	14	238
Tobago	26	7	
St.Vincent & Grenadines	18	11	150
Barbados			166
Grenada			120
Antigua			108
St. Kitts			65
Nevis			36
Montserrat	11	7	39

Table SA10.1. CARIFTA: Manufacturing Sector. Basic Indicators, 1970

	Total Economy					Manufacturing				
							Trade (SITC 5-8)(EC$ m)			
	Population (000)	GDP (EC$ m)	Imports (EC$ m)	Domestic Exports (EC$ m)	Employment (000)	GDP (EC$ m)	Imports	Exports	Domestic Market for Manufactures (EC$ m)	Employment (000)
	(1)	(2)	(3)	(4)	(5)	(6)	(7)	(8)	(9)	(10)
Dominica	71	37.9	31.5	11.4	19.7	3.1	20.6	1.2	22.5	1.5
Grenada	94	59.1	44.1	11.0	25.9	1.8	27.8	0.1	29.5	2.1
St. Lucia	101	66.8	54.6	8.1	26.5	2.4	27.2	..	29.6	2.2
St. Vincent	87	37.0	23.8/a	7.1/a	21.0	1.4	14.3/a	0.1/a	15.6	1.6
Antigua	65	50.3	49.3/b	13.2/b	18.6	5.1	23.9/b	0.2/b	28.8	1.8
Montserrat	12	11.5	8.8	0.3	3.7	0.2	5.2	..	5.4	0.2
St. Kitts	46	30.5	23.4	7.7	12.4	0.8	14.4	1.1	14.1	1.3
Belize	121	126.6	67.1	28.1	31.5	19.8	41.5	2.0	59.3	4.6
LDC Total	597	419.7	302.6	86.9	159.3	34.6	174.9	4.7	204.8	15.3
Barbados	238	289.9	235.0	61.0	83.9	31.4	150.4	15.6	166.2	12.3
Guyana	702	467.4	268.2	260.5	159.0	57.0	200.0	4.8/d	248.8	23.9
Jamaica	1,849	2,339.3	1,044.5	799.7	492.0	317.7	765.6	31.0	1,052.3	71.3
Trinidad	941	1,600.5	523.6/c	542.5/c	229.7	187.3	368.5	33.3/e	522.5	31.0
MDC Total	3,730	4,697.1	2,071.3	1663.7	924.6	593.4	1,484.5	84.7	1,989.8	138.5
CARIFTA Total	4,327	5,116.8	2,373.9	1750.6	1,123.9	628.0	1,659.4	89.4	2,194.6	153.8

a/ 1969
b/ 1969
c/ Net of petroleum trade under processing agreements
d/ Excludes EC$ 3.4 m. of precious and semi-precious stones and pearls, worked and unworked
e/ Excludes EC$77.2 m. of petroleum-based chemicals.

Source: Population and employment: unpublished census data
Trade: national trade returns
GDP: mission estimates
Domestic market for manufactures = manufacturing GDP + manufactured imports - manufactured exports.

Table SA10.2. CARIFTA: Manufacturing Sector. Basic Ratios, 1970

	GDP/P (EC$)	GDP/EM (EC$)	MGDP/MEM (EC$)	Average Daily Wage in Manufacturing 1972 (EC$)	MGDP/GDP (%)	MEM/EM (%)	MIM/IM (%)	MEX/EX (%)	MGDP / (MGDP + MIM - MEX) (%)	MEX/MGDP (%)
	(1)	(2)	(3)	(4)	(5)	(6)	(7)	(8)	(9)	(10)
Dominica	534	1,924	2,070	4	8.1	7.6	65.4	10.5	13.8	9.7
Grenada	629	2,282	860	4	3.0	8.1	63.0	0.9	6.1	1.4
St. Lucia	661	2,521	1,090	4	3.8	8.3	49.8	..	8.1	...
St. Vincent	425	1,762	880	4	3.8	7.6	60.1	1.4	9.0	1.8
Antigua	774	2,704	2,830	6	10.2	9.7	48.5	1.5	17.7	1.0
Montserrat	958	3,108	1,000	4	1.7	5.4	59.1	..	3.7	...
St. Kitts	663	2,460	620	4	2.7	10.5	61.5	14.3	5.7	34.6
Belize	1,046	4,019	4,300	6	15.6	14.6	61.8	7.1	33.4	2.5
LDC Average	703	2,635	2,260		8.2	9.6	57.8	5.4	16.9	3.4
Barbados	1,218	3,455	2,550	7	10.8	14.7	64.0	25.6	18.9	14.9
Guyana	666	2,940	2,380	5	12.2	15.0	74.6	1.8	22.9	2.5
Jamaica	1,265	4,755	4,460	10	13.6	14.5	73.3	3.9	30.2	2.9
Trinidad	1,701	6,968	6,040	9	11.8	13.5	70.4	6.1	35.8	5.5
MDC Average	1,259	4,869	4,280		12.6	14.4	71.7	5.1	29.8	4.4
CARIFTA Average	1,183	4,553	4,080		12.3	13.7	69.9	5.1	28.6	4.4

GDP = Gross Domestic Product
P = Population
EM = Employment
IM = Imports
EX = Exports
MGDP = Gross Domestic Product in Manufacturing
MEM = Manufacturing Employment
MIM = Manufactured Imports
MEX = Manufactured Exports

Note: Manufactured exports are reduced from a gross-to net-value basis, to facilitate comparison with GDP, on the basis of 1971 net-to-gross value ratios obtained from notes to

Source: Col. 4: Mission data.

Table SA10.3. MDCs: Physical Output of Selected Manufactures, 1971

	Unit	Barbados	Guyana	Jamaica	Trinidad
Condensed milk	(000 lbs)	2,112	-	64,707	n.a.
Evaporated milk	(000 lbs)	225	-	n.a.	n.a.
Flour	(m. tons)	-	75	104	n.a.
Biscuits	(000 lbs)	8,585	4,708	n.a.	n.a.
Refined Sugar.	(000 tons)	135	372	379	213
Confectionery.	(000 lbs)	1,452	924	n.a.	n.a.
Animal Feeds	(m. lbs)	46/a	57	31	n.a.
Margarine..	(000 lbs)	3,799	2,370	7,941	7,618 /d
Lard and Substitutes	(000 lbs)	2,204	n.a.	3,484	3,494
Edible oils	(000 gal)	-	899	2,705	1,392
Rum..	(000 gal)	1,526	3,887	2,677	1,887
Other spirits.	(000 gal)	n.a.	112	42/b	n.a.
Beer and stout	(000 gal)	1,111	1,473	9,461	4,296
Cigarettes.	(000 lbs)	343	955	1,366/c	1,795
Woven cotton fabrics	(000 sq. yds)	-	-	6,360	2,600
Bagasse.	(000 sq. ft)	-	-	5,208	n.a.
Sulphuric acid	(tons)	-	-	10,080	-
Fertilizers	(000 tons)	-	n.a.	57	600 /e
Paints	(000 gal)	n.a.	147	1,192	n.a.
Soap.	(000 lbs)	2,411	4,350	16,044	4,073 /b/f
Detergents.	(000 lbs)	n.a.	1,823	8,462	n.a.
Matches.	(000 gr.box)	-	117	n.a.	406
Tyres	(000 lbs)	-	-	5,784	n.a.
Cement..	(000 tons)	-	-	424	252
Steel	(tons)	-	-	17,879	-
Gas cookers	(000)	-	-	n.a.	20.0 /e
Radios and TVs	(000)	-	-	16.1	17.0 /e
Refrigerators.	(000)	-	-	n.a.	14.0 /e
Motor vehicles assembly	(000)	-	-	-	5.5 /e

a/ Corn meal only
b/ 1970
c/ million cigarettes
d/ gin
e/ Mission estimates
f/ Toilet soap only

Source: Various national publications.

Table SA10.4. CARIFTA: Trade in Manufactures (SITC 5-8 at f.o.b. values), 1971

(In millions of Eastern Caribbean dollars)

Exporters \ Importers	ECCM	Belize	Total LDCs	Barbados	Guyana	Jamaica	Trinidad	Total MDC	Total CARIFTA	Non-CARIFTA	Grand Total
ECCM /a	0.2	-	0.2	0.1	..	-	0.3	0.5	0.7	2.7	8.4
Belize /a	-	-	-	-	-	..	-	-	..	1.6	1.6
Total LDCs	0.2	-	0.2	0.1	..	-	0.3	0.5	0.7	4.3	5.0
Barbados	2.9	-	2.9	-	0.4	0.2	1.3	2.0	4.9	9.3	14.2
Guyana /b	1.5	..	1.5	0.9	-	1.8	2.4	5.2	6.7	0.3	7.0
Jamaica	2.6	..	2.6	3.2	2.9	-	9.8	15.9	18.5	34.5	52.9
Trinidad /c	17.5	0.1	17.6	10.0	9.7	12.5	-	32.2	49.8	16.0	65.9
Total MDCs	24.5	0.1	24.6	14.1	13.0	14.5	13.5	55.3	79.9	60.1	140.0
Total CARIFTA	24.7	0.1	24.8	14.2	13.0	14.5	13.8	55.8	80.6	64.4	145.0
Non-CARIFTA /d	138.1	39.8	177.9	123.6	162.6	680.8	491.3	1458.0	1636.0		
Grand Total /d	162.9	39.9	202.8	137.8	175.6	695.3	505.1	1513.8	1716.6		

a/ Partially estiamted.
b/ Excludes SITC 672-01: Precious and Semi-Precious Stones (including synthetic).
c/ Excluded SITC 51109030: ammonium compounds; SITC 52102000: tar oils, etc.
d/ Total imports were estimated from c.i.f. import figures divided by a factor of 1.1 to reach estimated f.o.b. values; non-CARIFTA f.o.b. import values were derived as the difference between total imports thus estimated and imports from CARIFTA.

SOURCE: National Trade Statistics (domestic exports).

Table SA10.5. Commonwealth Caribbean: Tariffs and Trade Restrictions

BTN	Product Description	CCM	ECCM	Barbados	Guyana	Jamaica	Trinidad and Tobago
Food	(Specific rates: per 100 lb.)						
0201	Fresh, chilled or frozen meat	0	0	$ 0.84 N	P	30 N	N
16011	Canned sausages	15	15	$ 2.00 N	15 P,e	$ 0.83 N	25 N
16021	Canned corned beef	5	5	$ 2.00 N	E	15 N	N
1603	Meat extracts and preparations	25	25	20	P	30½ N	N
0402	Milk and cream, preserved/concentrated	5	5	$ 1.00 n	E	25 N	n
1001	Wheat	0	0	$ 0.12 N	15	0 N	0
1101	Wheat flour	10	10	$ 0.48 N	$1.09 E	$ 1.20 N	$0.50
1903	Macaroni	30	15	20 N		30 N	N
1908	Biscuits	30	15*	$ 0.48	50 P	$ 0.52 N	15
1905	Cereal preparations	30	30	10 N	P	15	n
2106	Baking powder and natural yeast	30	15	10		15	
2301-6	Animal fodder (excl. pet foods)	0	0	20 n		0 N	n
0701	Vegetables, fresh or chilled	UA 0.75	$0.40	0 N	E	30 N	0.90 N
0802	Fresh citrus fruit	40	15	0 n		5 N	N
2002	Canned vegetables	45	20 (*)	$ 0.60 n	P,e	18½ N	N
2006	Canned fruit	45	30 (*)	20	90 P	18½ N	30 N
2007	Canned vegetables & fruit juice	45	30 (*)	20	P,e	30 N	N
1704	Sugar confectionery, not containing cocoa	45	35	40	E	55 N	
18061	Chocolate confectionary	45	35	30 N	70 E	33 N	40
1513	Margarine	30	5	$ 1.80 N	E	$ 3.00 N	N
1507	Vegetable oils	15	30	$ 0.12 N	E	$ 0.42 N	N
1701	Sugar, refined	30	$3.60	$ 4.00 N	P	$ 0.83 N	N
Beverages	(Specific rates: per gallon)						
2202	Soft drinks	30	30	20	45 P	30 N	25
2203	Beer from malt	UA 5.5	30	$ 1.56	P	$ 1.73 N	$3.00
22093	Rum in bottle not exceeding 80% proof	UA 59	$4.35	$12.30	P	$14.38 N	
22095	Whiskey bottle not exceeding 80% proof	UA 55	$5.83	$17.08		$22.49 N	
22097	Gin bottle not exceeding 80% proof	UA 56	$4.40	$14.80	P	$20.46 N	
Tobacco	(Specific rates: per lb.)						
2401	Unmanufactured Tobacco	UA 3.00	$0.70	$ 3.06	$ 6.70 /a	$ 0.53 N	$2.61 N
24022	Cigarettes	UA18.46	$9.00 *	$ 7.24	$14.60	$ 7.69 N	$5.75
Textiles and Garments							
5501	Raw cotton	10	10	0	15	15	0
5601	Discontinuous Man-Made Fibres	10	10	20	15	15	25
55005	Cotton yarn	20	20	20	25	30	30
5605	Spun man-made fiber yarn	20	20	20	25	7½	30
5509	Cotton fabrics (specific rate: per sq.yd.)	45	25	10	25	20 N	50+$0.10 N
56072	Man-made fiber fabrics (specific rate ")	35	25	10	25	30 N	50+$0.10 N
6101-9	Garments	45	30		70		
	of which important items:						
	ex 6101 mens/boys trousers, woven (cotton)	45	30	35		(35)/c	30
	ex 6005 womens dresses, knitted (non-cotton)	45	30	20		(30)/d	
	ex 6103 men's shirts, woven (cotton)	45	30	(60)/a		(40)/a	
	ex 6004 women's underwear, knitted(non-cotton)	45	30	25		(80)/e	
	6003 women's stockings, knitted, synthetic, fabric.	20	20	(60)/b		(90)/b	
Shoes and Leather Products							
4102	Bovine cattle leather	10	10	0	15	15 N	25 N
4202	Travel goods	45	30	30	60	30 N	30
6401	Footwear	25	15	30		30½ N	N
Wood Products	(specific rate: per cub. ft.)						
4403	Logs	10	10	20	40	$0.02 N	25
4415	Plywood, veneer	20	15	10	50	20 N	25 N
4421	Wooden packing cases	25	15	20		10	N
4423	Builders' carpentry and joinery	45	35	20 .		20 N	N
9403	Furniture, other, metal and wood	45	30	20 N	50 P	36⅔ N	35 N
9401	Chairs, metal and wood		30	20 N	P	48⅔ N	N
Paper Products							
4701	Pulp	0	0	20	15	12	25
48011	Newsprint	0	0	0	25	20	0
4804	Paperboard	20	20	20	40	20 N	25
4816	Paper boxes and bags	30	20	0		32 N	25 N
Petroleum Products	(specific rates: per gallon)						
2709	Crude oil	15	0	$1.20 N	15	12	25 N
27102	Motor spirit	UA 0.5	30	$0.40			25

a/ Estimated ad valorem equivalent of combined specific/ad valorem tariff on shirts at EC$ 15.00/dozen cif.

b/ Estimated ad valorem equivalent of combined specific/ad valorem tariff on stockings at EC$0.40/pair cif.

c/ Estimated ad valorem equivalent of combined specific/ad valorem tariff on man's trousers at EC$ 60/dozen cif.

d/ Estimated ad valorem equivalent of combined specific/ad valorem tariff on women's dresses at EC$50/dozen cif.

e/ Estimated ad valorem equivalent of combined specific/ad valorem tariff on women's underwear at EC$ 10/dozen cif.

Table SA10.5. (continued)

BTN	Product Description	CCM	ECCM	Barbados	Guyana	Jamaica	Trinidad and Tobago
Chemicals							
2801	Chemical elements, inorganic compounds	10	10	20		15 N	0
3102	Nitrogenous fertilizers (specific rate:/ton)	UA 15	0	$2.00	5	0	0
3209	Paints and enamels	15	15	26	P	20 N	N
3301	Essential oils	30	30	20	40	10 N	20
33061	Bayrum (specific rate: per gallon)	70	70	$4.20		$2.40 N	
33062	Shampoo, toothpaste	35	20	30	40	30	35
33069	Perfumes, cosmetics	55	45	30	L	45 N	N
3401	Soap (specific rate: per 100 lb.)	30	30	$0.72 N	40 E	$0.73	30 N
3402	Detergents	30	30	$0.72 N	P	30 N	N
36061	Matches in containers with 60 matches or less (specific rate: per gross container)	UA 5	60	30 N	P/L	$0.13 N	$0.20
38111	Desinfectants, for retail sale	10	10	20		0	
38112	Desinfectants, not for retail sale	15	10	20		0	
39021	Polymerization products (plastics), ready for use	30	0	10	40	15 N	
39022	Polymerization products, other	15	0	10	15 P/L	15	
3907	Plastic articles	30	30	10		15 N	N
Non-Metallic Minerals							
2523	Cement (specific rate: per ton)	UA 10	0	$6.05 N	$0.38 E	$3.60 N	$0.70 N
6904	Building bricks (specific rates: per 1,000)	25	15	$2.40	40	30	30
6910	Ceramic sinks, basins, etc.	25	25	18		20	
6911	Ceramic tableware	25	25	16	40	30 N	30
7001	Glass in mass	0	0	16	8	12	25
7004	Glass, unworked, cast or rolled	25	15	16	40	20	25
7010	Bottles	30	0	10	40	20	25
Rubber							
4001-4	Natural, synthetic, reclaimed, waste rubber	0	0	0		7½	
4008	Plates, sheets of unhardened vulcanized rubber	20	10	20		7½	
40111	Tyres and tubes for bicycles and tricycles	15	15	32		40	
40119	Tyres and tubes, other (not solid)	35	25	52		40 N	$0.54 N
Metal and Metal Products							
7307	Iron and steel, blooms, billets, slabs	0	0	20	8	5	35
7313	Iron and steel, plates and sheets	10	22	20	10	5 N	
7318	Iron and steel, tubes and pipes	·10	22	20		0	
7321	Iron and steel, structures and parts	35	22	20	40	5 N	30 N
7323	Iron and steel, casks, drums, cans, boxes	22	22	20	15	20 ·	N
7324	Iron and steel, containers for liquified gas	22	22	20		25 N	
7331	Iron and steel, nails and tacks	15	15	20	P/L	25 N	N
7336	Iron and steel, non-electrical stoves	45	22	20		30	N
7338	Iron and steel, baths basins, etc.	30	22	20		25 N	
7401	Copper, unwrought	0	0	20		15	10
7407	Copper, tubes and pipes	10	22	20		5	
7410	Copper, stranded wire, cables	22	22	20		5	25
7601	Aluminum, unwrought	10	0	20		15	
7604	Aluminum foil	10	22	20		15 N	25
7608	Aluminum structures and parts	45	22	20	P	5 N	N
8313	Crown Corks	25	25	20		25	N
Non-Electrical Machinery							
8401	Steam boilers	7½	0	20	8	5	10
84062	Engines for motor vehicle	35	35	20	60	40	35
8412	Air conditioners	30	22	10	15	10 N	45 N
8415	Refrigerators	35	25	10	45-70	10 N	25 N
8424	Ploughs	7½	0	10	8	5	2½
8437	Textile weaving machines	7½	0	0	8	5	
8451	Typewriters	25	22	20	40	20	30
Transportation Equipment							
87011	Agricultural tractors	0	0	5	8	5	30
8702	Motor vehicles	45	35	28	15	40 N	30 N
87062	Motor vehicle parts	35	35	28	·70	40	35
8709	Motorcycles	35	35	30	60-70	40	25
8710	Cycles	25	15	20	40	20	25
8802	Aircraft	10	10	20	8	0	35
89019	Boats, ships for navigation (excl.warships)	25	0	20	40	0	

Table SA10.5. (continued)

BTN	Product Description	CCM	ECCM	Barbados	Guyana	Jamaica	Trinidad and Tobago
Electrical Machinery							
8501	Generators	7½	25	20	8	5	12½
8503	Batteries	30	30	20	40	25 N	30
85072	Electric stoves	30	30	20	60	20 N	15
8513	Telephones & telephone equipment	30	30	20		23 N	25
85151	Radio and TV	45	30	30	70	48½ N	45 N
8520	Electric lamps	30	30	20	40	25 N	30 N
9211	Gramophones	45	25	30		12	N
9212	Gramophone records	35	25	30		12 N	
8504	Electric accumulators	45	30	20 N	P/L	25 N	N
Miscellaneous							
3406	Candles (specific rate: per 100 lbs.)	25	25	$2.00		20 N	N
7112	Articles of Jewelry	60	30	35		40 N	N
9101	Wrist watches	50	20	30	60	30 N	45
9404	Matresses	45	30	20 N	P	30 N	N
9602-9	Brooms & brushes (excl.besoms, etc.)	30	15	20		20 N	N
4602	Matting of plaiting material	45	25	30		20	
9702	Dolls	25	25	18	40	30 N	30 N
98012	Buttons	25	15	20	40	15 N	30
9805	Pencils	22	22	20	40	15	25
58021	Carpets, not knitted, of veg. material	40	40	30		30	

Explanatory Notes

1. Tariffs listed in the table are Most-Favored-Nation (MFN) rates and are either percent *ad valorem* or specific.[1/] *Ad valorem* rates appear in the table as simple figures. Specific rates are expressed in Units of Account (UA) for CARICOM (UA is equivalent to 0.395833 grams of fine gold or about EC$ 0.90 or G$ 1.00 in 1972 values), and in $ for the other schedules (EC$ for the ECCM and $ in national currencies for the other countries).

2. Quantitative Restrictions: tariff rates are followed by notations indicating the nature of trade restrictions as below:

- N: most or all of the item is on the negative list and requires an import licence;
- n: part of the item is on the negative list and requires an import licence;
- P: most or all of item is completely prohibited (Guyana only);
- p: part of item is completely prohibited (Guyana only);
- E: most or all of the item: import allowed only through External Trade Bureau (or other designated agent) (Guyana only);
- e: part of the item: import allowed only through External Trade Bureau (or other designated agent) (Guyana only);
- *: LDCs allowed until May 1, 1983, to phase out tariffs existing against MDCs /(*) indicates that only part of the item is affected_7.

1/ The BTN number and designation refer to the CARICOM schedule: headings for other schedules are the nearest relevant headings.

Table SA10.5. (continued)

3. Preferential Tariff Rates: the following illustrates the most frequent relationships between general (MFN) and Commonwealth Preference ad valorem rates:

General Rate	Commonwealth Preference Rate				
	CARICOM/ECCM	Barbados	Guyana	Jamaica	Trinidad
5	0		2½	0	
10	5	0/5	5		
15	10		10	10	10
20	15	10/15		10/15	15
25	15	15	15	15	15
30	20	10/20		15/20	20
35	25	25			20/25
40	no rate	20	20	20/30	20
45	35	no rate	25	30/35	30
50	40	no rate	30	45	no rate
60	50	no rate	40	no rate	no rate
70	60	no rate	50	no rate	no rate
90	no rate	no rate	70	no rate	no rate

Table SA10.5. (continued)

4. Ad Valorem Equivalent of Specific Tariffs: the following figures give estimates of the *ad valorem* equivalent of major specific tariffs in the CARICOM and ECCM Schedules (based on St. Kitts 1972 average unit values of imports).

	Unit	Unit Price (EC$)	Specific Tariff (EC$)		Ad Valorem Equivalent (%)	
			CARICOM	ECCM	CARICOM	ECCM
Fresh vegetables	100 lb	45.05	0.68	0.50	1.5	1.1
Beer	gal.	2.54	4.95	/a	195	30 /a
Rum	gal.	7.18	53.10	4.35	740	61
Whiskey	gal.	16.23	49.50	5.83	305	36
Gin	gal.	12.96	50.40	4.40	389	34
Cigarettes	lb.	4.23	16.61	9.00	393	213
Refined petroleum	gal.	23.22	0.45	/a	2.4	30 /a
Nitrogenous fertilizer	ton	178.91	13.50	free	7.5	free
Cement	ton	71.04	9.00	free	13	free
Matches	gross of boxes	2.41	4.50	/a	187	30 /a

a/ ECCM rate is *ad valorem*

Table SA10.5. (continued)

5. Sources: tariff data for the MDCs come from the various national schedules in force up to 1973. The sources for the CARICOM and ECCM tariffs are as follows:

The Caribbean Community Secretariat, The Common External Tariff of the Caribbean Common Market (1973?)

East Caribbean Common Market, Customs Tariff: with List of Conditional Duty Exemptions and Reductions (1972?)

Sources on quantitative restrictions are as follows:

Barbados: The Miscellaneous Controls (General Open Import Licence) Regulations, 1973 (September 4, 1973). (Listed items are those which, coming from non-CARIFTA countries, require import licences. Some of the items, e.g. gasoline, motor vehicles, cement, are not locally produced and the control is therefore presumably for balance-of-payments purposes).

Guyana Order Made under the Trade Ordinance, 1958, Nos. 86 and 87 of 1971. (There is apparently no consolidated list of products subject to control and we cannot, therefore, be sure of the inclusiveness of the information presented).

Jamaica Source: Notice No. 2852: The Trade Law, 1955 (Law 4 of 1955): Open General Licence (Imports), May 10, 1973 (See Barbados notes).

Trinidad and Tobago The Trinidad and Tobago Chamber of Industry and Commerce (Northern Division), Consolidated Negative List up to May 5, 1973 (Notice to Importers) 2 of 1973, July 2, 1973.

Table SA10.6. Guyana, 1971: Cost Structure for a Sample of Industries

(Percentage)

	Biscuits (2)	Oil Mills (2)	Aerated Beverages (3)	Alcoholic Beverages (4)	Cigarettes (2)	Garments (8)	Footwear (2)	Sawmills (13)	Furniture (6)	Printing (7)	Paints (2)	Soap (3)
Inputs												
Local (materials, services, fuels)	2.4	67.4	16.7	(25.1	3.2	2.3	1.2	(49.1	10.0	1.0	0.5	4.7
Imported (" " ")	51.7	16.4	10.7	(	69.2	52.4	66.7	(	51.4	25.2	58.9	45.6
Other (repair and maintenance and indirect taxes)	27.4	5.7	27.2	51.4	6.9	10.2	6.9	10.4	10.6	11.5	10.3	16.3
Total	81.6	89.5	54.5	76.5	79.2	64.9	74.9	59.5	72.0	37.7	69.7	66.6
Value Added												
Wages and salaries	25.2	5.6	28.9	11.3	9.6	16.5	11.7	22.6	18.5	30.5	10.4	9.7
Other labor costs	2.7	0.5	1.1	1.3	1.3	0.6	1.1	1.1	1.1	3.5	0.8	0.6
Depreciation	6.5	1.2	5.9	2.9	1.6	1.0	-	5.5	1.1	2.6	1.9	3.8
Surplus (Includes finance charges, pre-tax profits, building rental)	- 16.0	3.1	10.7	7.9	8.3	17.0	12.2	11.3	7.3	25.7	17.1	19.3
Total	18.4	10.5	45.4	23.5	20.8	35.1	25.1	40.5	28.0	62.3	30.3	33.4
Value of Output	100.0	100.0	100.0	100.0	100.0	100.0	100.0	100.0	100.0	100.0	100.0	100.0

Source: Statistical Office, Ministry of Economic Development.

Table SA10.7. Trinidad and Tobago, 1970: Cost Structure for a Sample of Industries

(Percentage)

	Industries				Industry Groups		
Inputs	Processing of Fruit and Vegetables (except citrus)	Feed Mills	Garment Factories	Tyres and Tubes	Food Processing Beverages and Tobacco	Textiles, Garments, Footwear and Hardwear	Sawmills Furniture Wood & Wood-related Industries
Imported materials	31.2	74.4	55.3	25.3	38.5	51.7	19.8
Imported services	0.1	/a	0.2	1.2	0.8	0.2	0.7
Local materials	20.0	5.7	4.4	14.8			
Local fuel and electricity	2.3	1.0	0.7	3.2	23.7	4.8	22.5
Local services: interest & Bank charges	3.3	0.5	1.9	4.9			3.7
transport	1.0	0.7	0.5	0.4			
communications	0.9	0.5	0.5	0.5			
insurance	0.9	0.3	0.5				
advertising	3.2	0.2	0.7	0.8	8.3	11.1	10.7
professional services	0.9	0.3	0.6	0.9			
commissions	-	3.7	3.9				
rent of land and buildings	1.2	0.2	0.5				
rent of machinery	..	0.2	0.2	0.4			
maintenance	0.8	0.1	0.4	0.6			
other	1.7	0.6	2.0	1.9			
Total	67.4	88.2	72.4	54.8	71.2 /b	67.6 /b	57.4
Payments to Government	0.7	0.1	0.5	3.0	/a	/a	/a
Value Added							
Wages, salaries & other labor costs			16.3	20.0	10.8	19.2	18.8
Travel, directors' fees & welfare	19.9	5.0	1.0	2.7	0.6	0.8	1.8
Management fees & royalties			0.4	-	0.9	0.4	-
Depreciation	6.0	0.9	2.1	7.8	2.1	3.0	2.1
Surplus (pre-tax profit)	6.0	5.8	7.3	11.7	14.3	8.8	19.9
Total	31.9	11.8	27.1	42.2	28.8	32.4	42.6
Value of Output (percent)	100.0	100.0	100.0	100.0	100.0	100.0	100.0
TT$ m.	5.4	23.7	35.6	8.8	185.6	54.6	19.5
Return on Total Capital Investment	7.2	17.0	n.a.	n.a.	22.3	12.8	24.1%

a/ Included under Local services

b/ Individual data on input constituents do not exactly correspond to the difference between gross output and value added and have been adjusted pro rata.

Source: Central Statistical Office.

Table SA10.8. A Comparison of Industrial Incentives in the MDCs

	GUYANA	TRINIDAD	BARBADOS	JAMAICA
Industrial Incentives Law	Pioneer Industries 5 Year Income Tax Holiday.	5 Year Income Tax Holiday - special 10 Year exemption for Cement, Fertilizer, Lubricating Oil and Greases.	10 Year Income Tax Holiday.	7 Years initially; Extended to 10 Years for Developed Areas; 15 years for Rural Areas.
Export Industry Encouragement Law	Nil	Yes: No Export duty paid on certain products.	Yes: Special Rates of Income Tax for Export Industries.	Yes: Exemption from Payment of Income Tax for 7 years.
Investment Allowance	Nil	Nil	Nil	Yes: Combined with accelerated amortization.
The Hotels Aid Law	Exists by Implication.	Comprehensive Law patterned along the Jamaican one exists.	Special Law Exists.	A very comprehensive law exists.
Free Entry - Raw Materials	Special Provisions exist for certain Industries in Ordinance.	Yes: Granted very liberally for 5 years.	Granted to Approved Industries.	Yes: Export and Import substitution Industries.
Free Machinery and Building Materials.	Granted for a period of 5 years. Not for rehabilitation.	Granted liberally for period of 5 years.	Granted liberally	Granted liberally
Industrial Sites	Yes - Rental $1.10 and 1.20 per sq.ft.p/a	Yes - Rental	Yes	Yes
Industrial Buildings	Yes - Very few Rental $1.80 per sq.ft. per annum	Yes	Yes - Rental 50¢ per sq. ft.	Yes - Rental
Accelerated Amortisation	Yes - For Industries in Second Schedule List is being added to.	Similar to Guyana Allowance for workers welfare housing.	Yes - Similar to Guyana.	Yes - Similar to Guyana but combined with investment allowance.
Loss Carry Over	Yes	Yes	Yes	Yes

Source: Guyana Development Corporation

Table SA10.9. Summary of Main Aggregates in Regional Industrial Programming

Activity	Projected Volume and Value of Imports, 1975	Target Volume and Value of Domestic Capacity[1], 1975	Approximate Capital Investment	Direct Employment
Iron and steel base metal	229,000 tons $69.0 m.	300,000 tons[2] $96.0	$ 50.0	2,500
Pulp and paper (excluding newsprint)	100,000 tons $58. m.	100,000 $58 m.	$ 109 m.	4,000
Newsprint	$25,000 tons $ 6 m.	$35,000 $ 8.5	$ 27 m.	300
Cotton	—	20,000 tons[3] $10 m.[3]	n.a.	3,000
Cotton textile	15,000 tons $63 m.	15,000 tons $63 m.	$ 100 m.	7,000
Synthetic staple and textile	13,000 tons $63 m.	6,000 $32 m.	$ 84 m.	3,000
Synthetic rubber, plastic material and products	35,000 tons $64 m.	35,000 tons —	$ 60 m.[4]	7,000
Glass — containers	—	88,000 tons[5] $25.4 m.	$ 27 m.	1,300
Glass — sheet	9,300 tons $ 3.2 m.	6,000 tons $ 2.2 m.	$ 2.6	120
Leather tanning (for footwear)	5.7 m.lbs. $14 m.	5.7 m.lbs. n.a.	$ 6 m.	600
Footwear	—	15 m.pairs[5] $30 m.	$ 33 m.	2,500
Leather tanning and products (other than footwear)[7]	—	7.5 m.lbs. $40 m.	$ 20 m.	3,000
Chlorine (electrolytic)	36,000 tons $24.6 m.	36,000 tons $ 3.6 m.	$ 12 m. (Chlorine and Sodium hydroxide (electrolytic) combined)	200
Sodium hydroxide (electrolytic)		41,000 tons $ 4.3 m.		
Sodium hydroxide (lime-soda)	467,000 tons $30.4 m. (Sodium hydroxide, electrolytic and lime-soda combined)	426,000 $53.1 m.[6]	n.a.	n.a.
Motor cars	25,000 units $63 m.	40,000 units $100 m.	$ 42 m.	6,000

Notes: 1. The unit value of domestic production is based, for estimating purposes, on the unit value of imports (1964).

2. This includes the steel which would be used in motor car production. The value of steel production does not exclude the value of imported pig iron or scrap.

3. This is based on the current export selling price of United States cotton.

4. The investment required for fabricating end-products is not included.

5. An estimate of incremental demand.

6. Does not exclude the value of imports of soda ash.

7. Assuming complete import replacement of beef, veal and pork there could be produced by 1975 about 15 m. lbs. of cow and pig leather. We assume here one-half is used for leather products other than footwear (actually only 5.7 m. lbs. of leather was the projected demand for footwear). The estimates of value of output and capital are merely intended as the crudest possible guides to the magnitudes involved.

Source: Appendix 7A of H. Brewster and C.Y. Thomas, The Dynamics of West Indian Economic Integration, 1967.

Table SA10.10. CARIFTA/CARICOM: Actual and Potential Production and Consumption of Cement

(In thousands of tons)

	Estimated Demand		Production Capacity		1978 Unit Cost (1973 EC$ per ton)	
	1972	1978	1972	1978 Est.	Exfactory	Transport
Windwards	45	60	-	60	50	60
Leewards	25	35	-	35	60	60
Belize	20	30	-	n.a.	n.a.	
Barbados	55	75	-	75	50	60
Guyana	125	170	-	170	40	60
Jamaica	425	570	450	800	32	60
Trinidad	170	230	290	500	40	60
CARIFTA Total	865	1,170	740	1,640		

Note: this table provides (i) broad estimates only of present and future regional cement consumption; (ii) estimates of what future production capacity might look like if presently contemplated projects were to go ahead, and (iii) broad estimates of unit production and transport costs meant to provide some initial feel for the relative merits of national versus regional production. The assumptions behind the estimates are as follows:

(a) Estimated demand: 1972. Production and trade statistics (these are estimates based on complete production and incomplete, and sometimes outdated, trade statistics); 1978: assumed 5% per annum growth over 1972.

(b) Production capacity: 1972: based on maximum observed annual production; 1978: based on national stated intentions as follows:

Jamaica has announced an increase in its existing cement plant to 800,000 tons capacity;

Trinidad is contemplating establishing a new mill: we assume a capacity of some 200,000 tons;

Barbados, Guyana, and Antigua are contemplating mills: we assume a capacity equivalent to our 1978 consumption estimates for the national markets of Barbados and Guyana and for the Leewards in the case of Antigua;

Dominica is contemplating the grinding of clinker (imported from Martinique and Guadaloupe): we assume a capacity equivalent to the 1978 consumption estimates for the Windwards.

(c) Costs: the estimated 1973 Trinidad ex-factory cost is estimated at some EC$ 50 per ton whilst average transport costs (WISCO freight rate plus typical port handling changes) within the region are some $ 60. It is assumed that a situation of newer mills and increased regional competition should substantially lower prices (although increased fuel costs will offset this). The costs are calculated as follows:

Plant capacity	Average Cost Index			Hypothetical CARIFTA Costs
	Germany	U.S.	U.K. new	(EC$ per ton)
33,000	150			60
66,000	121			50
100,000	114	116	118	45
200,000	100	100	100	40
400,000	86	89	n.a.	35
500,000	n.a.	84	91	34
1,000,000		63	81	30 (32 for 800,000 tons)
2,000,000			73	

(Average cost indices are taken from Tables 10.4(i) and 10.5 of C.F. Pratten, Economies of Scale in Manufacturing Industry, 1971)

Table SA10.11. CARIFTA/CARICOM Manufacturing Sector: Production, Trade, and Market for Manufactures, 1963, 1967, 1971, and 1973

(In millions of Eastern Caribbean dollars)

	Manufacturing GDP	Imports of Manufactures: Total Imports: CARIFTA	Imports of Manufactures: Total Imports: Other	Imports of Manufactures: Re-Exports	Imports of Manufactures: Retained Imports (2+3-4)	Domestic Exports of Manufactures: CARIFTA	Domestic Exports of Manufactures: Other	Domestic Exports of Manufactures: Total (6+7)	CARIFTA Trade Balance (6-2)	Domestic Market for Manufactures (1+5-8)
ECCM										
1963	6.5	6.9	45.7	0.7	51.9	0.4	0.3	0.7	- 6.5	57.7
1967	8.9	16.2	71.3	0.9	86.6	0.5	0.3	0.8	-15.7	94.7
1971	15.9	37.0	143.4	1.4	179.0	0.7	2.7	3.4	-36.3	191.5
1973	18.1	30.3	146.8	10.9	166.2	2.0	9.4	11.4	-28.3	172.9
Barbados										
1963	15.9	2.9	45.3	4.4	43.8	0.7	0.4	1.0	- 2.2	58.7
1967	21.1	5.4	72.2	5.8	71.8	1.8	0.7	2.5	- 3.6	90.4
1971	37.0	11.1	140.5	9.5	142.1	4.9	9.3	14.2	- 6.2	164.9
1973	53.7	21.5	175.4	7.4	189.5	14.0	20.0	34.0	-7.5	209.2
Guyana										
1963	19.3	4.3	73.7	0.9	77.1	1.6	0.3	1.9	- 2.7	94.5
1967	32.4	7.5	158.7	4.3	161.9	1.0	1.2	2.2	- 6.5	192.1
1971	42.2	13.6	179.6	8.1	185.1	6.7	0.3	7.0	- 6.9	220.3
1973	60.0	22.8	215.2	3.9	234.1	12.3	2.6	14.9 1/	-10.5	272.2
Jamaica										
1963	148.7	3.1	243.9	5.9	241.1	3.7	20.4	24.2	+ 0.6	365.6
1967	223.0	3.1	405.7	5.1	403.7	7.9	24.7	32.7	+ 4.8	594.0
1971	333.7	15.3	749.5	21.4	743.4	18.5	34.5	52.9	+ 3.2	1024.2
1973	428.9	28.0	794.1	12.9	809.2	20.0	24.2	54.2	+2.0	1183.9
Trinidad										
1963	51.6	2.0	241.8	9.6	234.2	11.1	6.9	18.0	+ 9.1	267.8
1967	92.4	2.5	254.6	9.1	248.0	17.8	12.5	30.3	+15.3	310.1
1971	185.7	14.5	541.1	35.9	519.7	49.9	16.0	65.9	+35.3	639.5
1973	291.0	24.0	538.1	11.1	551.0	64.1	42.6	106.7	+40.1	735.3
CARIFTA (Less Belize)										
1963	242.0	19.2	650.4	-	669.6	17.5	28.3	45.8	-	864.1
1967	377.8	34.7	962.5	-	997.2	29.0	39.4	68.5	-	1300.9
1971	614.5	91.5	1754.1	-	1836.6	80.7	62.8	143.4	-	2305.8
1973	851.7	126.6	1859.6	-	1996.2	122.4	98.8	221.2	-	2580.5

1/ Guyana exports of SITC 67201 were not excluded since data for these items are not available.

Notes to S.A. Table 10.11

1. Manufacturing GDP (at factor cost) excludes sugar milling. For Trinidad petrochemicals are excluded. For the LDCs mining is included.

Sources: Bank Economic Reports and Mission estimates.

2. Trade in Manufactures covers SITC 5-8. For Guyana exports of SITC 67201 (precious and semi-precious stones) and for Trinidad exports of SITC 51109030 (ammonium compounds) and 52102000 (tar oils, etc.) are excluded as major export items not included in the GDP coverage. It should be also noted that the following groups of manufactures are also excluded: processed foods (ex SITC 0) because of non-availability of the data; beverages and tobbaco (SITC 1) because imports are small and exports (dominated by rum) are traditional exports more closely related to sugar than to manufacturing; refined petroleum products (ex SITC 3) because the value of output is largely derived from mining rather than manufacturing; refined edible oils (ex SITC 4) because the product is largely agricultural.

Sources: National Trade Statistics and Mission estimates.

3. The domestic market for manufactures is calculated as the sum of GDP and retained imports (imports less re-exports) less domestic exports. For the CARIFTA total, however, it is calculated as the sum of GDP and gross non-CARIFTA imports less domestic exports outside CARIFTA.

Table SA10.12. CARIFTA Manufacturing Sector: Basic Ratios in Trade and Production, 1963, 1967, 1971, and 1973

	ECCM				Barbados				Guyana				Jamaica				Trinidad				CARIFTA (less Belize)			
	1963	1967	1971	1973	1963	1967	1971	1973	1963	1967	1971	1973	1963	1967	1971	1973	1963	1967	1971	1973	1963	1967	1971	1973
Share in Domestic Market																								
Retained Production	10.9	9.1	7.9	8.8	26.7	22.6	19.9	20.8	19.7	16.5	18.1	19.8	38.7	35.9	31.0	34.8	17.3	26.9	25.8	35.1	27.0	28.1	25.8	32.0
CARIFTA Imports	12.0	17.1	19.3	17.5	4.9	6.0	6.7	10.3	4.6	3.9	6.2	8.2	0.8	0.5	1.5	2.4	0.7	0.8	2.3	3.2	-	-	-	-
Other Imports	77.1	73.8	72.8	73.7	68.4	71.4	73.4	68.9	75.7	79.6	75.7	72.0	60.5	63.6	67.5	62.8	82.0	72.3	71.9	61.7	73.0	71.9	74.2	68.0
Total	100	100	100	100	100	100	100	100	100	100	100	100	100	100	100	100	100	100	100	100	100	100	100	100
Share in G.D.P.																								
Retained Production	96.6	97.3	94.7	84.0	98.3	97.0	88.5	81.0	96.6	97.6	94.7	92.0	95.2	95.6	95.2	96.2	89.9	90.1	89.0	88.6	96.5	96.9	96.9	96.4
Exports to CARIFTA	1.0	1.7	1.1	2.8	1.1	2.1	4.0	7.8	2.9	1.1	5.1	6.7	0.7	1.1	1.7	2.1	6.2	5.8	3.3	6.9	-	-	-	-
Other Exports	1.4	1.0	4.2	13.2	0.6	0.8	7.5	11.2	0.5	1.3	0.2	1.3	4.1	3.3	3.1	1.7	3.9	4.1	2.7	4.5	3.5	3.1	3.1	3.6
Total	100	100	100	100	100	100	100	100	100	100	100	100	100	100	100	100	100	100	100	100	100	100	100	100
CARIFTA Trade Balance as Percentage of Manufacturing	-100	-176	-228	-156	-14	-17	-17	-14	-14	-20	-16	-18	0	+2	+1	0	+18	+17	+19	+14	-	-	-	-
(- : negative trade balance																								
(+ : positive trade balance																								
Ratio of Exports to Imports																								
CARIFTA Trade	.05	.03	.02	.07	.24	.33	.44	.65	.37	.13	.49	.54	1.19	2.55	1.21	1.07	5.55	7.12	3.44	2.67				
Other	.01	..	.02	.06	.01	.01	.07	.11	..	.01	..	.01	.08	.06	.05	.03	.03	.05	.03	.08				
Total	.01	.01	.02	.07	.02	.03	.10	.18	.02	.01	.04	.06	.10	.08	.07	.07	.08	.12	.13	.19	.07	.07	.08	.11

Notes: See following page

Notes to S.A. Table 10.12

In order to reconcile the gross output values of trade statistics with the net (GDP) output values of production statistics, the following procedure was adopted:

1. Typical ratios of net-to-gross value were established for the various years and countries, based on data from manufacturing surveys and estimates as follows:

Typical Ratios of Net to Gross Value in Manufacturing

	LDCs	Barbados	Guyana	Jamaica	Trinidad
1963	.30	.25	.35	.30	.29
1967	.30	.25	.35	.30	.30
1971	.25	.30	.32	.30	.31
1973	.25	.30	.32	.30	.31

2. It was assumed that inputs (i.e. gross less net values) were all imported from non-CARIFTA Sources. (This ignores small amounts of local materials and services). In the calculation of shares in the domestic market the procedure was (i) to leave CARIFTA import figures untouched; (ii) to calculate retained local production (GDP) by subtracting from it the GDP element in total exports (calculated by applying the above net-to-gross value ratios); and (iii) to calculate net retained non-CARIFTA imports by subtracting from non-CARIFTA imports less re-exports the input element of total exports (calculated by applying the reciprocal of the above ratios).

3. In the calculation of shares in manufacturing GDP, the procedure was (i) to calculate retained local production as in 2(i) above, (ii) to calculate the GDP value of CARIFTA and extra-CARIFTA exports by applying the net-to-gross-value ratios).

Table SA10.13. Barbados Trade in Selected Manufactures by Major Product, 1974

(In thousands of Eastern Caribbean dollars)

		IMPORTS							DOMESTIC EXPORTS						
		CARIFTA							CARIFTA						
SITC	Product Group	LDCs	Guyana	Jamaica	Trinidad	Total	Other	GRAND TOTAL	LDCs	Guyana	Jamaica	Trinidad-Tobago	Total	Other	GRAND TOTAL
Ex 013	Processed meat	-	-	34	-	34	7263	7297	-	-	-	-	-	-	-
EX 022	Processed milk	-	-	-	-	-	7246	7246	4	30	-	-	34	-	34
Ex 032	Processed fish	-	-	9	-	9	1758	1767	-	-	-	-	-	-	-
Ex 046	Wheat flour	-	-	2	10	12	9451	9463	-	-	-	-	-	-	-
Ex 048	Cereal preparation	-	41	212	385	638	2278	2916	711	19	375	485	1590	65	1655
Ex 053	Processed fruit	23	31	403	944	1401	1450	2851	68	61	200	127	456	49	505
Ex 055	Processed vegetables	78	2	5	120	205	805	1010	1	-	-	2	3	-	3
EX 062	Sugar preparations	1	19	22	47	89	616	705	253	13	137	17	420	27	447
Ex 08	Animal feeds	227	523	21	846	1617	6091	7708	7	-	-	-	7	-	7
Ex 09	Miscellaneous food preparation	33	15	181	846	1075	4944	6019	2813	186	5	106	3110	67	3177
Ex 11	Beverages	15	378	1251	583	2227	3235	5462	711	1	8	1902	2622	2392	5014
Ex 122	Tobacco manufactures	1	223	596	104	924	426	1350	311	405	11	245	972	-	972
Ex 51	Chemical elements	1	45	30	151	227	1949	2176	94	-	63	45	202	-	202
Ex 52	Mineral tars, etc.	-	-	-	-	-	3	3	-	-	-	-	-	-	-
Ex 53	Dyeing, tanning, coloring material	-	-	465	683	1148	1083	2231	871	-	-	5	876	121	997
Ex 54	Medicinal and pharmaceutical products	-	228	153	259	640	6107	6747	213	4	252	114	583	96	679
Ex 55	Essential oils, perfurmes, cosmetics cleansing materials	343	76	1411	4000	5830	3294	9124	271	60	136	297	764	285	1049
Ex 56	Manufactured fertilizers	-	-	-	683	683	2674	3357	-	-	-	-	-	-	-
Ex 59	Explosives and miscellaneous chemicals	1	4	241	246	492	4836	5328	100	-	100	144	344	2	346
Ex 61	Leather manufactures	-	-	6	1	7	1215	1222	-	-	-	-	-	584	584
Ex 62	Rubber manufactures	-	-	4	52	56	2003	2059	-	-	-	-	-	-	-
Ex 63	Wood and cork	3	39	31	69	142	3678	3820	24	-	-	1	25	11	36
Ex 64	Paper and paper products	15	33	374	2214	2636	11146	13782	350	267	19	126	762	2	764
Ex 65	Textiles	35	7	186	201	429	18796	19225	75	289	674	764	1802	341	2143
Ex 66	Non-metallic minerals	3	-	503	3433	3939	7389	11328	55	30	34	94	213	8	221
Ex 67	Precious metals and jewelry	-	-	5	66	71	9675	9746	2	-	-	-	2	-	2
Ex 68	Basic metals	-	-	506	69	575	3001	3576	-	-	-	-	-	3	3
Ex 69	Metal manufactures	6	162	437	1213	1818	12532	14350	825	256	391	379	1851	219	2070
Ex 71	Machinery, except electrical	-	8	-	23	31	20627	20658	10	-	45	67	122	24	146
Ex 72	Electrical machinery	1	-	389	674	1064	26020	27084	29	-	6	19	54	8723	8777
Ex 73	Transport equipment	1	1	-	18	20	12393	12413	36	-	-	1	37	-	37
Ex 81	Pre-fabricated buildings, sanitary, etc.	-	-	-	3	3	2601	2604	-	-	-	-	-	1	1
Ex 82	Furniture	10	4	360	410	784	1080	1864	183	79	-	104	366	44	410
Ex 83	Travel goods	1	48	30	61	140	397	537	59	44	175	46	324	250	574
Ex 84	Clothing	247	771	365	3111	4494	9386	13880	929	245	2604	2196	5974	12377	18351
Ex 85	Footwear	2	57	43	224	326	4479	4805	1	-	6	7	14	-	14
Ex 86	Professional, scientific instruments, etc.	-	6	3	3	12	3922	3934	-	2	-	-	2	30	32
Ex 89	Miscellaneous	24	140	858	1363	2385	16674	19059	658	415	956	888	2917	1868	4785
	TOTAL	1071	2861	9136	23115	36183	232523	268706	9664	2406	6197	8181	26448	27589	54037

Note: Trade in products following under SITC 5-8 in the above table represents 99% of total SITC 5-8 imports and 96% of total SITC 508 Exports

Source: 1974 Annual Overseas Trade Report

Table SA10.14. Guyana: Trade in Manufactures by Major Product, 1972

(In thousands of Eastern Caribbean dollars)

SITC	Major Products	IMPORTS							DOMESTIC EXPORTS						
			CARIFTA							CARIFTA					
		LDCs	Barbados	Jamaica	Trinidad	Total	Other	Grand Total	LDCs	Barbados	Jamaica	Trinidad	Total	Other	Grand Total
013	Processed Meat	-	-	217	9	227	476	703	n.a.	n.a.	n.a.	n.a.	n.a.	n.a.	n.a.
022	Processed Milk	-	221	-	54	275	7,514	7,789	n.a.	n.a.	n.a.	n.a.	n.a.	n.a.	n.a.
048	Cereal Preparations	-	26	24	216	266	1,087	1,353	n.a.	n.a.	n.a.	n.a.	n.a.	n.a.	n.a.
053	Processed Fruit	58	-	297	131	486	444	930	n.a.	n.a.	n.a.	n.a.	n.a.	n.a.	n.a.
055	Processed Vegetables	-	-	74	378	452	n.a.	n.a.	n.a.	n.a.	n.a.	n.a.	n.a.	n.a.	n.a.
062	Sugar Preparations	-	8	26	214	248	n.a.	n.a.	18	8	9	11	45	n.a.	n.a.
08	Animal Feeds	n.a.	n.a.	n.a.	n.a.	n.a.	n.a.	n.a.	9	127	-	63	199	n.a.	n.a.
09	Miscellaneous Food Preparations	10	216	586	857	1,669	n.a.	n.a.	66	12	..	13	91	n.a.	n.a.
112	Alcholic Beverages	1	3	53	184	241	574	815	235	137	57	276	705	5,651	6,356
122	Tobacco Manufactures	-	22	104	..	126	n.a.	n.a.	n.a.	n.a.	n.a.	n.a.	n.a.	n.a.	n.a.
533	Paints	-	-	56	977	1,033	1,561	2,594	n.a.	n.a.	n.a.	n.a.	n.a.	n.a.	n.a.
541	Medicinal & Pharmaceutical Products	-	60	292	181	533	5,166	5,699	374	182	170	469	1,195	141	1,336
552	Perfume, Cosmetics, Soaps, etc.	14	38	1,122	1,811	2,985	926	3,911	771	149	18	531	1,469	94	1,563
561	Manufactured Fertilizers	-	-	46	2,136	2,182	2,108	4,290	31	31	1	19	82	n.a.	n.a.
599	Miscellaneous chemicals (mostly plastic)	-	75	406	136	617	7,500	8,117	n.a.	n.a.	n.a.	n.a.	n.a.	n.a.	n.a.
629	Rubber Manufactures (mostly tires)	-	-	2	319	321	4,277	4,598	n.a.	n.a.	n.a.	n.a.	n.a.	n.a.	n.a.
632	Wood Manufactures	n.a.	n.a.	n.a.	n.a.	n.a.	n.a.	n.a.	155	35	4	261	455	n.a.	n.a.
641, 642	Paper and Paper Products	-	61	116	1,023	1,200	5,995	7,195	39	8	-	273	320	1	321
ex. 65	Textile Fabrics	-	3	6	64	73	6,770	6,843	2	8	530	107	647	n.a.	n.a.
ex. 66	Non-Metalic Minerals	-	123	121	498	742	6,003	6,745	50	77	138	112	377	n.a.	n.a.
672 & 673	Precious Stones & Jewelry	n.a.	n.a.	n.a.	n.a.	n.a.	n.a.	n.a.	18	367	11	46	442	n.a.	n.a.
684 & 685	Basic Metals (Aluminum & lead)	-	-	60	59	119	n.a.	n.a.	n.a.	n.a.	n.a.	n.a.	n.a.	n.a.	n.a.
699	Metal Manufactures	2	159	533	852	1,546	13,923	15,469	n.a.	n.a.	n.a.	n.a.	n.a.	n.a.	n.a.
721	Electrical Machinery	..	..	69	90	160	13,741	14,060	n.a.	n.a.	n.a.	n.a.	n.a.	n.a.	n.a.
735	Ships and Boats	-	-	-	64	64	1,421	1,485	1	-	-	890	891	n.a.	n.a.
811	Prefabricated Buildings and Parts	n.a.	n.a.	n.a.	n.a.	n.a.	n.a.	n.a.	414	49	-	463	926	n.a.	n.a.
821	Furniture	-	9	113	51	173	487	660	3	4	-	2	9	n.a.	n.a.
831	Travel Goods	-	12	4	14	30	n.a.	n.a.	17	30	32	28	107	n.a.	n.a.
841	Clothing	43	233	75	586	937	1,747	2,684	402	518	814	715	2,449	105	2,554
851	Footwear	2	2	96	104	204	4,770	4,974	139	50	589	75	853	n.a.	n.a.
ex. 89	Miscellaneous	16	234	576	1,112	1,938	8,712	10,650	53	22	7	94	176	n.a.	n.a.
	Other ex. SITC 5-8	15	6	83	209	313	n.a.	n.a.	21	8	1	27	57	n.a.	n.a.
Sub	Total SITC 5-8	92	1,022	3,794	10,332	15,240	185,901	201,141	2,277	1,406	2,117	3,336	9,136	2,530	11,666
	Total of itemized products	161	1,511	5,157	12,329	19,160	n.a.	n.a.	2,818	1,822	2,381	4,475	11,496	n.a.	n.a.

Source: Guyana trade returns.

Table SA10.15. Jamaica Trade in Selected Manufactures by Major Product, 1973

(In thousands of Eastern Caribbean dollars)

IMPORTS

SITC	Product Group	CARIFTA: LDCs	CARIFTA: Barbados	CARIFTA: Guyana	CARIFTA: Trinidad	CARIFTA: Total	Other	GRAND TOTAL
013 1/	Processed meat	-	-	-	-	77	10106	10183
022 1/	Processed milk	-	-	-	-	-	15035	15035
032	Processed fish	-	-	-	-	-	14120	14120
046	Wheat flour	-	-	-	-	-	28356	28356
048	Cereal preparations	1	360	33	524	918	8824	9742
053	Processed fruit	486	117	-	101	704	2915	3619
055	Processed vegetables	-	1	-	925	926	1544	2470
062	Sugar preparation	-	79	16	571	666	243	909
08	Animal feeds	-	-	-	-	-	12067	12067
09	Miscellaneous food preparations	26	1	10	1178	1215	6855	8070
11	Beverages	-	55	88	505	648	10871	11519
122	Tobacco manufactures	-	-	-	20	20	336	356
51	Chemical elements	-	-	-	91	91	50342	50433
52	Mineral tars, etc.	-	-	-	-	-	100	100
53	Dyeing, tanning, coloring materials	-	-	-	726	726	4106	4832
54	Medicinal and pharmaceutical products	-	270	236	61	567	15295	15862
55	Essential oils, perfumes, cosmetics, cleansing material	53	258	25	1429	1765	6152	7917
56	Manufactured fertilizers	-	-	-	1736	1736	6506	8242
59	Explosives and miscellaneous chemicals	-	4	-	223	227	22694	22921
61	Leather manufactures	-	-	-	-	-	7516	7516
62	Rubber manufactures	-	-	-	3	3	13057	13060
63	Wood and cork	-	-	1	13	14	10098	10112
64	Paper and paper products	-	9	-	378	387	49231	49618
65	Textiles	15	196	563	538	1312	67620	68932
66	Non-metallic mineral	3	9	199	3	214	33618	33832
67	Precious metals and jewelry	-	-	-	133	133	52815	52948
68	Basic metals	-	-	-	-	-	21156	21156
69	Metal manufactures	-	143	8	1476	1627	43151	44778
71	Machinery, except electrical	-	97	-	442	539	142543	143082
72	Electrical machinery	-	-	-	4653	4653	74204	78857
73	Transport equipment	97	-	-	3	100	75628	75728
81	Pre-factricated buildings, sanitary, etc.	-	-	-	1	1	9320	9321
82	Furniture	-	11	-	66	77	2484	2561
83	Travel goods	-	30	14	96	140	1765	1905
84	Clothing	352	1438	1294	6946	10030	4725	14755
85	Footwear	3	-	700	1066	1769	4359	6128
86	Professional, scientific instruments, etc.	-	-	1	15	16	19041	19057
89	Miscellaneous	68	325	3	1291	1687	39318	41005
	TOTAL	1104	3403	3191	25213	32988	888116	921104

DOMESTIC EXPORTS

SITC	Product Group	CARIFTA: LDCs	CARIFTA: Barbados	CARIFTA: Guyana	CARIFTA: Trinidad	CARIFTA: Total	Other	GRAND TOTAL
013 1/	Processed meat	-	-	-	-	811	89	900
022 1/	Processed milk	-	-	-	-	-	65	65
032	Processed fish	-	-	7	-	7	2	9
046	Wheat flour	-	1	-	-	1	-	1
048	Cereal preparations	113	254	115	211	693	321	1014
053	Processed fruit	357	316	819	1058	2550	6552	9102
055	Processed vegetables	-	1	58	15	74	420	494
062	Sugar preparation	78	10	24	46	158	52	210
08	Animal feeds	7	221	-	34	262	49	311
09	Miscellaneous food preparations	196	150	537	434	1317	340	1657
11	Beverages	479	688	243	370	1780	15272	17052
122	Tobacco manufactures	14	366	515	144	1039	6877	7916
51	Chemical elements	63	37	107	435	642	770	1412
52	Mineral tars, etc.	-	-	-	-	-	-	-
53	Dyeing, tanning, coloring materials	416	416	5	547	1384	622	2006
54	Medicinal and pharmaceutical products	448	148	251	330	1177	627	1804
55	Essential oils, perfumes, cosmetics, cleansing material	1261	1040	1373	2954	6628	2065	8693
56	Manufactured fertilizers	-	-	-	14	14	22	36
59	Explosives and miscellaneous chemicals	132	136	122	333	723	73	796
61	Leather manufactures	1	2	-	31	34	255	289
62	Rubber manufactures	3	-	17	12	32	127	159
63	Wood and cork	19	6	1	1	27	61	88
64	Paper and paper products	204	238	93	617	1152	432	1584
65	Textiles	7	51	720	322	1100	1277	2377
66	Non-metallic mineral	36	552	212	142	942	2854	3796
67	Precious metals and jewelry	49	4	10	317	330	45	425
68	Basic metals	71	306	57	434	868	1519	2387
69	Metal manufactures	1010	242	535	1119	2906	422	3328
71	Machinery, except electrical	12	4	2	301	319	236	555
72	Electrical machinery	414	255	189	1606	2464	423	2887
73	Transport equipment	94	-	-	3	97	26	123
81	Pre-factricated buildings, sanitary, etc.	-	-	-	-	-	-	-
82	Furniture	146	102	173	580	1001	375	1376
83	Travel goods	5	4	-	-	9	466	475
84	Clothing	189	299	134	1736	2358	7586	9944
85	Footwear	44	21	149	325	539	301	840
86	Professional, scientific instruments, etc.	3	11	18	20	52	119	171
89	Miscellaneous	307	587	807	2084	3785	3511	7296
	TOTAL	6178	6468	7293	16575	37325	54253	91578

1/ Import and export data for 1972

Table SA10.16. Trinidad: Trade in Selected Manufactures by Major Product, 1974

(In thousands of Eastern Caribbean dollars)

		IMPORTS							DOMESTIC EXPORTS						
		CARIFTA							CARIFTA						
SITC	Product Group	LDCs a/	Barbados	Guyana	Jamaica	Total	Other	GRAND TOTAL	LDCs b/	Barbados	Guyana	Jamaica	Total	Other	GRAND TOTAL
013	Processed meat	-	-	-	134	134	5376	5510	-	-	-	-	-	6	6
022	Processed milk	-	-	-	-	-	24512	24512	37	-	140	55	232	498	730
032	Processed fish	-	-	-	-	-	2693	2693	-	-	-	-	-	-	-
046	Wheat flour	-	-	-	-	-	9266	9266	13	-	-	-	13	45	58
048	Cereal preparations	-	517	10	101	628	7848	8476	252	672	1038	1563	3525	2360	5885
053	Processed fruit	224	178	5	330	737	1744	2481	231	932	490	278	1931	2325	4256
055	Processed vegetables	42	-	-	3	45	1809	1854	32	144	381	1295	1852	127	1979
062	Sugar preparation	-	24	16	89	129	1599	1728	62	33	84	639	818	20	838
08	Animal feeds	2	-	42	-	44	16307	16351	-	24	-	-	24	2116	2140
09	Miscellaneous food preparations	54	190	14	523	781	8801	9582	2013	893	1794	1753	6453	867	7320
11	Beverages	6	2007	293	562	2868	5708	8576	676	589	435	235	1935	9890	11825
122	Tobacco manufactures	-	269	-	435	704	79	783	-	105	1	17	123	16	139
51	Chemical elements	-	-	1	443	444	31153	31597	514	222	276	17	1029	24886	25915
52	Mineral tars, etc.	-	-	-	-	-	38	38	-	-	-	2	2	64894	64896
53	Dyeing, tanning, coloring material	-	-	84	920	1004	6253	7257	188	554	560	678	1980	2764	4744
54	Medicinal and pharmaceutical products	-	135	596	653	1384	14544	15928	79	63	37	-	179	82	261
55	Essential oils, perfumes, cosmetics, cleansing material	18	503	950	4060	5531	4220	9751	3104	3190	3230	2103	11627	1111	12738
56	Manufactured fertilizers	-	-	-	-	-	2235	2235	525	636	6113	4768	12042	15456	27498
59	Explosives and Miscellaneous chemicals	15	18	25	409	467	26120	26587	241	250	315	215	1021	458	1479
61	Leather manufactures	-	-	-	5	.5	1323	1328	-	-	-	-	-	2	2
62	Rubber manufactures	1	-	1	98	100	9327	9427	101	57	317	1	476	5	481
63	Wood and cork	-	1	331	52	384	5894	6278	85	39	-	8	132	36	168
64	Paper and paper products	4	179	394	1522	2099	53970	56069	1494	1925	2537	390	6346	939	7285
65	Textiles	1	683	64	789	1537	64920	66457	400	219	1193	1613	3425	467	3892
66	Non-metallic mineral	4	59	342	411	816	17168	17984	2455	2829	1203	6	6493	357	6850
67	Precious metals and jewelry	5	-	158	789	952	101579	102531	90	67	10	24	191	158	349
68	Basic metals	-	-	-	260	260	10487	10747	159	9	34	-	202	4	206
69	Metal manufactures	10	419	891	1934	3254	38868	42122	1633	837	1353	663	4486	1060	5546
71	Machinery, except electrical	27	83	32	522	664	125476	126140	5	-	40	-	45	50	95
72	Electrical machinery	4	3	2	2578	2587	38338	40925	536	582	819	7227	9164	645	9809
73	Transport equipment	85	11	2	-	98	73127	73225	20	49	15	-	84	99	183
81	Pre fabricated building, sanitary, etc.	1	-		-	1	4904	4905	6	29	-	-	35	3	38
82	Furniture	3	199	34	738	974	1330	2304	601	410	132	158	1301	27	1328
83	Travel goods	-	83	73	23	179	1081	1260	48	58	49	210	365	31	396
84	Clothing	985	2153	1588	1212	5938	6834	12772	1926	2950	973	7054	12903	3256	16159
85	Footwear	-	19	197	100	316	9808	10124	487	142	305	1276	2210	876	3086
86	Professiona, scientific instruments	3	1	-	12	16	11053	11069	-	-	-	-	-	20	20
89	Miscellaneous	43	1001	77	2395	3516	29604	33120	1043	1262	1239	1754	5298	5822	11120
	TOTAL	1537	8735	6222	22102	38596	775396	813992	19056	19771	25113	34002	97942	141778	239720

a/ Excludes Montserrat
b/ Includes Montserrat and Grenadines

Source: Overseas Trade 1974

Table SA10.17. MDCs: Indicators of Competitiveness by Major Product in Intra-CARIFTA Trade

	Barbados	Guyana	Jamaica	Trinidad
I. Competing Products				
Canned milk				* /a
Biscuits, macaroni				*
Sugar confectionery			*	*
Animal feeds		* /b		*
Margarine	*			*
Alcoholic Beverages /a	E	*E	E	
Paints	*			*
Medicinal/pharmaceutical products		*	*	
Cosmetics, perfumes, cleansing products.			*	*
Plastic products			*	
Rubber articles				*
Paper articles				*
Finishing of textile fabrics		*		*
Jewelry	E	*		*
Fabricated aluminum products	*			
Electric accumulators				*
Small boats		*		
Furniture				*
Clothing	*E	*	E	*
Footwear		*		*
Records	*		*	
Electronic assembly	E			
II. Monopolistically-Available Products				
Canned meat			*	
Canned fruit			E	*E
Canned vegetables				*
Cocoa powder			*	
Cement				*
Glass bottles			*	*
Cotton weaving			*	*
Razor blades			*	
Gas stoves			*	
Cans				*
Crown corks				*
Electric light bulbs				*
Ratio/TV/gramophones				*
Insulated cable			*	*
Refrigerators				*
III. Resource-Based Products				
Manufactured fertilizer				*E
Wood products		*		
Agricultural lime	*			
Flat glass		*		
Aluminium in primary form			*	

* = Significant positive trade balance in intra-CARIFTA trade (1972).

E = Significant export item to non-CARIFTA countries (1972).

Definitions of product groups:

Competing products: those produced in at least three MDCs and using non-industrial inputs that are available at comparable prices.

Monopolistically-Available products: products which are only produced in Jamaica and/or Trinidad.

Resource-based products: products where local inputs are apparently vital to competitiveness.

a/ partly resource-based.

b/ resource-based.

Table SA11.1. General Consumer Price Indexes, 1962–75
(1964 = 100)

	1962	1963	1964	1965	1966	1967	1968	1969	1970	1971	1972	1973	1974	1975
Barbados	97.1	98.9	100.0	102.5	103.3	116.2	122.3	131.9	141.8	158.6	185.3	257.5	309.8	332.9
Guyana	97.3	99.7	100.0	102.8	104.9	108.0	111.3	112.7	116.6	118.5	124.4	136.6	163.5	172.0
Jamaica	96.4	98.0	100.0	102.8	104.8	107.7	114.1	121.3	133.2	142.1	150.3	180.3	227.8	265.5
Trinidad-Tobago	95.5	99.2	100.0	101.7	106.0	108.2	117.1	120.0	123.0	127.3	139.2	159.8	195.0	228.0
Antigua	94.7	96.2	100.0	99.9	98.8	105.8	114.0	118.8	126.1	137.3	149.2	168.1	204.5	231.1
Dominica	97.0	98.5	100.0	100.0	101.8	107.0	110.8	115.6	130.6	137.8	137.1	149.0	212.6	242.4
Grenada	97.0	98.5	100.0	101.3	105.5	111.7	121.6	129.6	135.8	142.6				
Monteserrat	97.0	98.5	100.0	105.0	110.2	115.8	121.6	129.3	137.1	160.4	163.4	179.4	212.7	
St. Kitts	95.2	97.6	100.0	100.8	101.4	103.8	114.1	117.9	136.5	134.2	142.6	157.4	202.0	
St.Lucia	95.2	97.6	100.0	104.3	106.8	110.2	114.6	117.2	132.9	144.1		176.2	236.6	
St. Vincent	94.3	97.1	100.0	103.8	107.9	111.0	114.0	118.9	123.8	128.7	144.9	168.5	228.9	
Belize	98.1	99.0	100.0	100.9	105.5	107.1								

Source: Official National Reports

Table SA11.2. Exchange Rates, 1965–74

	1965	1966	1967	1968	1969	1970	1971	1972	1973	1974
1US$ = EC$ (Eastern Caribbean)	1.71	1.71	1.75	2.0	2.0	2.0	2.00	1.92	1.91	2.00
1US$ = TT$ (Trinidad and Tobago)	1.71	1.71	1.75	2.0	2.0	2.0	1.84	2.04	1.95	2.00
1US$ = G$ (Guyana)	1.71	1.71	1.75	2.0	2.0	2.0	2.00	2.10	2.10	2.18
1US$ = J$ (Jamaica)	.7143	.7143	.7267	.8333	8333	.8333	.8271	.7936	.8547	.91
1US$ = B$ (Belize)	1.43	1.43	1.43	1.66	1.66	1.66	1.54	1.54	n.a.	2.00
1TT$ = EC$	1.00	1.00	1.00	1.00	1.00	1.00	1.00	1.00	1.00	1.00
1G$ = EC$	1.00	1.00	1.00	1.00	1.00	1.00	1.00	.92105	.92105	.92105
1J$ = EC$	2.40	2.40	2.40	2.40	2.40	2.40	2.40	2.40	2.150	2.245
1B$ = EC$	1.20	1.20	1.20	1.20	1.20	1.20	1.20	1.20	1.20	1.20

Source:

CARICOM Secretariat

Index

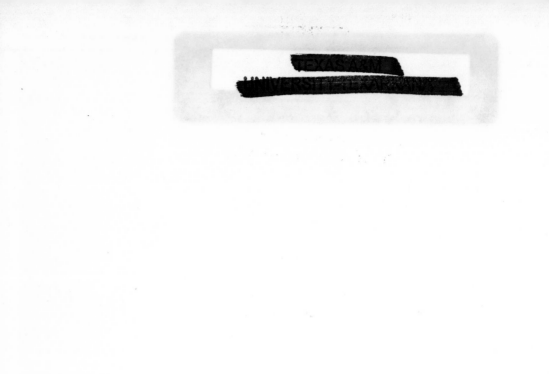